DAVIES

PRINCIPLES
OF
TAX LAW

EIGHTH EDITION

by

David W. Williams, LL.M., Ph.D., C.T.A.,
SOLICITOR
Judge of the Upper Tribunal (retired)

Geoffrey Morse, LL.B., BARRISTER
Professor of Corporate and Tax Law, University of Birmingham

Sandra Eden, B.A., LL.B., C.T.A.
Senior Lecturer, University of Edinburgh

SWEET & MAXWELL

THOMSON REUTERS

First Edition (1980) Introduction to Revenue Law by F.R. Davies
Second Edition (1985) Introduction to Revenue Law by F.R. Davies, David
Williams and Geoffrey Morse
Third Edition (1996) Davies: Principles of Tax Law by Geoffrey Morse, David
Williams and David Salter
Fourth Edition (2000) Davies: Principles of Tax Law by Geoffrey Morse and
David Williams
Fifth Edition (2004) Davies: Principles of Tax Law by Geoffrey Morse and
David Williams
Sixth Edition (2008) Davies: Principles of Tax Law by Geoffrey Morse and
David Williams
Seventh Edition (2012) Davies: Principles of Tax Law by Geoffrey Morse and
David Williams
Eighth Edition (2016) Davies: Principles of Tax Law by Geoffrey Morse, David
Williams and Sandra Eden

Published in 2016 by Thomson Reuters (Professional) UK Limited trading as
Sweet and Maxwell, Friars House, 160 Blackfriars Road, London, SE1 8EZ
part of Thomson Reuters (Professional) UK Limited (Registered in England
& Wales, Company No 1679046). Registered Office and address for service:
2nd floor, 1 Mark Square, Leonard Street, London, EC2A 4EG).

For further information on our products and services,
visit www.sweetandmaxwell.co.uk

Typeset by Servis Filmsetting Ltd, Stockport, Cheshire, SK2 5AJ
Printed and bound by CPI Group (UK) Ltd, Croydon, CR0 4YY

No natural forests were destroyed to make this product; only farmed timber was
used and re-planted.

A CIP catalogue record of this book is available from the British Library.

ISBN: 978-0-414-03748-9

Christine Morse

(1945–2012)

Memory is the treasury and guardian of all things

(Cicero)

David Williams (1946–2016)

It is with much sadness that I have to report the untimely death, on 1 September 2016, of our co-editor of this book, Dr David Williams, after a sudden and short illness. His last academic task was to complete work on the proofs of this edition. It was his idea originally to take over the book when Ron Davies was reluctant to continue into a second edition. David and I worked together on six previous editions and became close and long term family friends. It was his idea to dedicate this book to my late wife as he said that she was integral to his memory of our work together over the years.

David's contribution to tax scholarship took two forms. As an academic he taught both undergraduate and postgraduate students for several years at the universities of Bristol and Manchester, culminating in his appointment to the first chair in tax law at the Centre for Commercial Law at Queen Mary. He was a contributor to the British Tax Review and involved in the Tax Law Rewrite Project of which he was a strong advocate.

David then left full time academic life to take up a judicial role, initially as a social security commissioner and subsequently as a judge of what became the upper tax tribunal until his retirement in 2014. His judgments were often both thought provoking and indicative of his considerable intellect. A particular interest of his was the interaction of the tax and social security systems and he was working on his other co-authored book on the latter this summer.

Coming from a science background and with a deep love of politics David always saw the bigger picture and was fascinated by the devolution of tax initially to Scotland and then to his adopted country of Wales. He taught himself Welsh and was much involved in the life of rural North Wales after his retirement, not least as a volunteer coastguard. He is survived by his wife, Elisabeth, and their three sons and four grandchildren.

Geoffrey Morse

PREFACE

There really has never been a more important or interesting time to study the basics of tax law. It seems recently that nearly every week a new furore arises over taxation, filling newspaper columns, the internet, in all its manifestations, and political debate. The revelations over the "Panama papers", the complex tax arrangements of many well-known companies, the ownership of offshore trusts and the existence of tax havens, many of which are affiliated to the UK in one way or another, have generated a great deal of public disquiet. There is a general feeling that big companies and rich individuals are not paying their share of tax even though they are benefitting from the expenditure from tax receipts. Politicians would do well to heed this public disquiet—perceived tax inequalities on a grand scale have in the past led to the fall of kings, politicians and the loss of colonies amongst other things.

Yet it is important to insert a word of caution here. Tax can only be levied if the law charges it; any other system is unworkable. Exactly how much tax X Plc should pay cannot be decided by you, me, the person next to us or even the tabloid press. Tax evasion (fraud, dishonesty) is illegal but arranging one's affairs so as to minimise tax within the law is not. One person's tax avoidance (morally repugnant) is another's tax planning (acceptable/ prudent). How many of those "appalled" by the current revelations would not structure their wills so as to minimise their liability to inheritance tax (avoidance or planning?) or pay a plumber in cash to evade liability to VAT—what is the difference? One of degree and scale perhaps? Governments make the rules by which tax is levied—if there is unacceptable tax avoidance then the rules must be changed to stop it, there is no other way. It seems, however, that there is only the apparent political will to talk about this if there is a sufficiently large scandal. Effective actions (and increased funding) rarely follow.

So tax law has to be the bedrock of taxation—any unlawfully levied tax must be returned by the authorities. In this eighth edition of this book we have sought once more to follow Ron Davies' original intention as he wrote the first edition back in 1980 when the world was a little less frenetic and the internet in its infancy. Tax law is an enormously complex and lengthy body of law; the legislative basis alone fills many shelves with the case law filling the remainder. We have sought to distil this down into about 500 pages. To do this we have excluded international taxation (much used by the avoiders) as it is a development from the basic tax laws which we do cover. We have also largely ignored the complex and voluminous domestic anti-avoidance legislation as that is very subject specific and again is a spin off from the basic precepts. We have also concentrated on the five major taxes—the three chief money raisers, income tax (to which we must add national insurance, the stealth tax rarely mentioned in budget speeches) and VAT; and the two "lawyers' taxes" on capital—capital gains tax and inheritance tax. In the main we have not referred to decisions of the First-tier Tribunal as they have no precedent effect.

Since the previous edition the prospect of a partial devolution of tax rates and thresholds to Scotland has been crystallised and will come into effect in 2017. Wales and Northern Ireland wait in the wings. The administration of tax assessment and collection has also been radically altered with the demise of tax offices (and personnel) and the rise of on-line accounting. The Tribunal system of tax appeals is also now firmly established with an interesting effect on the question of separating fact and law. All these and more is reflected in a recasting of the first part of the book to more accurately portray the tax system and the origins of tax law as it now stands.

With regard to the substantive law, there have of course been incremental developments in both the legislative and case law applicable to the basics of each tax. Employees' income tax continues to be rigidly applied, with recent changes preventing agency workers from claiming commuting costs and a clear attack on the company car amongst others. The latter is also a good example of the tax authorities losing a case and so changing the rules at the next opportunity. Self-employed allowable expenses continue to concern the courts, although the introduction of simplified accounting for small businesses is to be welcomed.

The major changes to capital taxation concern the reduction of capital gains tax rates (except for the disapproved of second home), the introduction of investment relief and the extension of entrepreneurs' relief. For inheritance tax the introduction of the "residence nil-rate band" is a major development. That will allow a potential extra £350,000 of tax free inheritance for a couple if they have (or had) a house worth that and it is left to their descendants, giving a possible overall tax free total on the death of the second spouse/civil partner of £1 million by 2020.

That does of course mask the fact that the underlying tax free amount is frozen for the next five years. The legislation to achieve all this is long and complex, unnecessarily so, and must be largely impenetrable to non-lawyers.

VAT as the newest tax is still the source of most changes and developments at a basic level. Two major areas await a hoped for clarification by the higher courts—one is the application of the EU "abuse of law" principle to linear VAT mitigation/avoidance schemes, and the other is the conflict between two basic principles, that unlawfully levied tax must be returned and that no one should get an unjustified windfall as a result. VAT is sui generis in tax law, currently being an EU tax and one where the taxable person is not the actual taxpayer, that is the customer. The effects of a probable UK exit from the EU on VAT law must wait for another edition when it becomes a reality.

In the preparation of this edition we have gratefully welcomed a new editor, Sandra Eden from the University of Edinburgh. Not only has she taken primary responsibility for the parts on capital gains tax and inheritance tax, but as the case-note editor of the *British Tax Review* kept a careful note of our errors of style and format. In keeping with the new devolved approach to tax we do now have editors resident in each of England, Wales and Scotland.

We continue as editors, however, to take responsibility collectively for all errors and omissions in this edition and we are grateful to the publishers for their aid and assistance. The law is presented as known to us on 14 April 2016.

Geoffrey Morse

David Williams

Sandra Eden

Worcestershire, Gwynedd and Edinburgh

July 2016

CONTENTS

Preface   ix
Table of Cases   xv
Table of Statutes   xli
Table of Statutory Instruments   li

PART ONE INTRODUCTION

Chapter 1   Understanding Tax   3
Chapter 2   National, International and Local Tax   18
Chapter 3   Handling Tax Laws   35
Chapter 4   Tax Administration   67

PART TWO TAXATION OF INCOME

Chapter 5   Trading Income and Losses   81
Chapter 6   Property Income   111
Chapter 7   Intellectual Property and Other Income   118
Chapter 8   Capital Allowances   133
Chapter 9   Employment Income   144
Chapter 10   Pensions, Social Security and Credits   177
Chapter 11   Savings and Investment Income   189
Chapter 12   The Taxation of Trusts and Estates   199
Chapter 13   Taxation of Individuals   212
Chapter 14   Taxation of Companies   230

PART THREE TAXATION OF CAPITAL GAINS

Chapter 15   Capital Gains Tax   249
Chapter 16   Gains and Losses   287
Chapter 17   Exemptions and Reliefs   302

PART FOUR INHERITANCE TAX

Chapter 18   Evolution of Inheritance Tax   325
Chapter 19   Chargeable Transfers   329
Chapter 20   Exemptions and Reliefs   350
Chapter 21   Computation   376

CONTENTS

Chapter 22   Settled Property   397
Chapter 23   Liability and Incidence   419
Chapter 24   Administration and Collection   425

PART FIVE VALUE ADDED TAX

Chapter 25   The Charge to VAT   433
Chapter 26   VAT Rates and Exemptions   474
Chapter 27   VAT Computation and Accountability   492

Index   515

TABLE OF CASES

Aberdeen Construction Group Ltd v Inland Revenue Commissioners
[1978] A.C. 885; [1978] 2 W.L.R. 648 HL.................................... 16–07, 16–09
Administrators of the Estate of Caton v Couch (Inspector of Taxes);
Caton's Administrators v Couch (Inspector of Taxes) [1997] S.T.C. 970;
70 T.C. 10 CA.. 16–07
Alexander v Inland Revenue Commissioners [1991] S.T.C. 112; (1991) 23
H.L.R. 236 CA.. 21–35
Alloway v Phillips (Inspector of Taxes) [1980] 1 W.L.R. 888; [1980] 3 All
E.R. 138 CA.. 7–35
American Express Services Europe Ltd v Revenue and Customs
Commissioners [2010] EWHC 120 (Ch); [2010] S.T.C. 1023; [2010]
B.V.C. 381; [2010] S.T.I. 374.. 25–55
Amministrazione delle Finanze dello Stato v San Giorgio SpA (199/82)
[1983] E.C.R. 3595; [1985] 2 C.M.L.R. 658.................. 25–09, 27–47
Anglo Persian Oil Co Ltd v Dale (Inspector of Taxes) [1932] 1 K.B. 124
CA.. 5–28
Anson v Revenue and Customs Commissioners [2015] UKSC 44; [2015] 4
All E.R. 288; [2015] S.T.C. 1777; [2015] B.T.C. 21; 17 I.T.L. Rep. 1007;
[2015] S.T.I. 2019.. 3–57
Apple and Pear Development Council v Customs and Excise
Commissioners (102/86) [1988] 2 All E.R. 922; [1988] S.T.C. 221
ECJ.. 25–41
Argos Distributors Ltd v Customs and Excise Commissioners (C–288/94)
[1997] Q.B. 499; [1997] 2 W.L.R. 477 ECJ.................... 27–21, 27–22
Artic Systems Ltd. See Jones v Garnett (Inspector of Taxes)
Attorney General v Seccombe [1911] 2 K.B. 688 KBD.................... 19–17
Auto Lease Holland BV v Bundesamt für Finanzen [2005] S.T.C. 598;
[2003] E.C.R. I-1317 ECJ.. 25–52
Baird v Williams (Inspector of Taxes) [1999] S.T.C. 635; 71 T.C. 390.......... 9–38
Baker (Inspector of Taxes) v Archer Shee [1927] A.C. 844 HL.................. 12–01
Ball v Johnson 47 T.C. 155; (1971) 50 A.T.C. 178.......................... 9–14
Ball v National and Grindlay's Bank [1973] Ch. 127; [1972] 3 W.L.R. 17
CA.. 14–32
Banca Antoniana Popolare Veneta SpA v Ministero dell'Economia e delle
Finanze, Agenzia delle Entrate (C–427/10) [2012] S.T.C. 526; [2012]
S.T.I. 279 ECJ.. 25–11
Barclays Bank Trust Co Ltd v Inland Revenue Commissioners [1998]
S.T.C. (SCD) 125.. 20–38
Barclays Bank Trust Co Ltd v Revenue and Customs Commissioners
[2011] EWCA Civ 810; [2011] B.T.C. 375; [2011] W.T.L.R. 1489.......... 22–12
Barclays Mercantile Business Finance Ltd v Mawson (Inspector of Taxes)
[2004] UKHL 51; [2005] 1 A.C. 684; [2004] 3 W.L.R. 1383.............. 3–46

Barker v Revenue and Customs Commissioners [2011] UKFTT 645 (TC);
   [2012] S.F.T.D. 244 15–23
Barrett v Powell [1998] S.T.C. 283; [1998] 2 E.G.L.R. 117 17–20
Batey v Wakefield [1982] 1 All E.R. 61; [1981] S.T.C. 521CA 17–05
Belgocodex SA v Belgium (C–381/97) [2000] S.T.C. 351; [1998] E.C.R.
   I-8153 ECJ 25–08
Benham's Will Trusts, Re [1995] S.T.C. 210; [1995] S.T.I.186 23–13
Bennett v Inland Revenue Commissioners [1995] S.T.C. 54; [1995] S.T.I. 13 ... 20–06
Bentley v Pike (Inspector of Taxes) [1981] S.T.C. 360; 53 T.C. 590 16–01
Bentleys Stokes & Lewless v Beeson (Inspector of Taxes) [1952] 2 All E.R.
   82; [1952] 1 T.L.R. 1529 CA 5–30, 5–32
Berkshire Golf Club v Revenue and Customs Commissioners [2015]
   UKFTT 627 (TC); [2016] S.F.T.D. 244; [2016] S.T.I. 220 27–48
Berkshire Golf Club, The v Revenue and Customs Commissioners. See
   Berkshire Golf Club v Revenue and Customs Commissioners
Bertelsmann AG v Finanzamt Wiedenbruck (C–380/99) [2001] S.T.C.
   1153; [2001] E.C.R. I-5163 ECJ 25–45
Beynon v Customs and Excise Commissioners [2004] UKHL 53; [2005] 1
   W.L.R. 86; [2004] 4 All E.R. 1091; [2005] S.T.C. 55; [2004] B.T.C. 5794;
   [2005] B.V.C. 3; [2004] S.T.I. 2434; (2004) 148 S.J.L.B. 1404 25–55
Bird v Inland Revenue Commissioners [1989] A.C. 300; [1988] 2 W.L.R.
   1237 3–17
Birkdale School Sheffield v Revenue and Customs Commissioners [2008]
   EWHC 409 (Ch); [2008] S.T.C. 2002; [2008] B.T.C. 5274 26–22
Birmingham Hippodrome Theatre Trust Ltd v Revenue and Customs
   Commissioners [2014] EWCA Civ 684; [2014] 1 W.L.R. 3867; [2014]
   S.T.C. 2222; [2014] B.V.C. 27; [2014] S.T.I. 2223 27–47
Blackwell v Revenue and Customs Commissioners [2015] UKUT 418
   (TCC); [2015] B.T.C. 526 16–07
BLP GROUP PLC v Customs and Excise Commissioners [1996] 1 W.L.R.
   174; [1995] S.T.C. 424 ECJ 27–41, 27–43, 27–44
BMW (GB) Ltd v Customs and Excise Commissioners [1997] S.T.C. 824;
   [1997] B.T.C. 5273 27–36
Bond (Inspector of Taxes) v Pickford [1983] S.T.C. 517 CA 15–66
Booth (EV) (Holdings) Ltd v Buckwell (Inspector of Taxes) [1980] S.T.C.
   578; 53 T.C. 425 16–09
Booth v Ellard [1980] 1 W.L.R. 1443; [1980] 3 All E.R. 569 CA 15–51, 15–52
Boots Co Plc v Customs and Excise Commissioners (C–126/88) [1990]
   S.T.C. 387; [1990] E.C.R. I-1235 ECJ 27–17, 27–20
Bowden (Inspector of Taxes) v Russell and Russell [1965] 1 W.L.R. 711;
   [1965] 2 All E.R. 258 5–30
Bower (Deceased), Re [2008] EWHC 3105 (Ch); [2009] S.T.C. 510; 79 T.C.
   544; [2009] B.T.C. 8106; [2009] W.T.L.R. 619; [2009] S.T.I. 188 21–33
Bower v Revenue and Customs Commissioners; sub nom. Revenue and
   Customs Commissioners v Bower
Brander v Revenue and Customs Commissioners [2010] UKUT 300
   (TCC); [2010] S.T.C. 2666; 80 T.C. 163; [2010] B.T.C. 1656; [2010]
   W.T.L.R. 1545; [2010] S.T.I. 2427 20–37
Bridport and West Dorset Golf Club Ltd v Revenue and Customs
   Commissioners [2011] UKFTT 354 (TC); [2011] S.T.I. 1954 27–48
British American Tobacco International Ltd v Belgium (C–435/03) [2006]
   S.T.C. 158; [2005] E.C.R. I-7077; [2005] 3 C.M.L.R. 33; [2005] B.T.C.
   5724; [2005] B.V.C. 755; [2005] S.T.I. 1256 25–30

British Railways Board v Customs and Excise Commissioners [1977]
S.T.C. 222 CA.. 25.57
British Salmson Aero Engines Ltd v Inland Revenue Commissioners
[1938] 2 K.B. 482 CA 5–28
British Telecommunications Plc v Revenue and Customs Commissioners
[2006] S.T.C. (S.C.D.) 347; [2006] S.T.I. 1494 15–21
Brown v Bullock (Inspector of Taxes) [1961] 1 W.L.R. 1095; [1961] 3 All
E.R. 129 CA.. 9–38
Brown v National Provident Institution [1921] 2 A.C. 222; 8 T.C. 57 HL 3–14
Buccleuch (Duke of) v Inland Revenue Commissioners [1967] 1 A.C. 506;
[1967] 2 W.L.R. 207; [1967] 1 All E.R. 129; [1967] R.V.R. 42; [1967]
R.V.R. 25; (1966) 45 A.T.C. 472; [1966] T.R. 393; (1967) 111 S.J. 18...... 21–41
Bugeja v Customs and Excise Commissioners (No.2). See Lex Services Plc
v Customs and Excise Commissioners
Bullivant Holdings Ltd v Inland Revenue Commissioners [1998] S.T.C.
905; [1998] B.T.C. 234 15–18
BUPA Hospitals Ltd v Customs and Excise Commissioners [2006] Ch.
446; [2006] S.T.C. 967 ECJ.. 27–31
Burca v Parkinson (Inspector of Taxes) [2001] S.T.C. 1298; 74 T.C.
125 .... 15–16, 16–05
Burden v United Kingdom [2008] S.T.C. 1305; [2008] 2 F.L.R. 787
ECHR... 20–02, 21–07
Butler v Evans (Inspector of Taxes) [1980] S.T.C. 613; 53 T.C. 558............. 15–14
Buzzoni v Revenue and Customs Commissioners [2013] EWCA Civ 1684;
[2014] 1 W.L.R. 3040; [2014] 1 E.G.L.R. 181; [2014] B.T.C. 1; [2014]
W.T.L.R. 421... 19–16
Byrom (t/a Salon 24) v Revenue and Customs Commissioners [2006]
EWHC 111 (Ch); [2006] S.T.C. 992; [2006] B.T.C. 5210; [2006] B.V.C.
279; [2006] S.T.I. 378; [2006] N.P.C. 12.. 25–58
Cairns v Revenue and Customs Commissioners [2009] UKFTT 67 (TC);
[2009] S.T.C. (S.C.D.) 479; [2009] W.T.L.R. 793; [2009] S.T.I. 1801 24–03
Calvert v Wainwright [1947] K.B. 526; [1947] 1 All E.R. 282 KBD 9–14
Campbell (Trustees of Davies Education Trust) v Inland Revenue
Commissioners [1970] A.C. 77; [1968] 3 W.L.R. 1025 HL......................... 7–25
Campbell Connelly & Co Ltd v Barnett (Inspector of Taxes) [1994] S.T.C.
50; 66 T.C. 380... 17–28
Capcount Trading v Evans (Inspector of Taxes) [1993] 2 All E.R. 125;
[1993] S.T.C. 11 CA 16–01
Card Protection Plan Ltd v Customs and Excise Commissioners
(C–349/96) [1999] 2 A.C. 601; [1999] 3 W.L.R. 203 ECJ............. 25–54, 25–55,
25–60, 26–16, 26–21
CEC. See Customs and Excise Commissioners
Chaloner (Inspector of Taxes) v Pellipar Investments Ltd [1996] S.T.C.
234; 68 T.C. 238 15–22
Chinn v Collins. See Chinn v Hochstrasser (Inspector of Taxes)
Chinn v Hochstrasser (Inspector of Taxes); sub nom. Chinn v Collins
[1981] A.C. 533; [1981] 2 W.L.R. 14; [1981] 1 All E.R. 189; [1981] S.T.C.
1; 54 T.C. 311; [1980] T.R. 467; (1981) 125 S.J. 49.................................. 12–11
Cirdan Sailing Trust v Customs and Excise Commissioners [2005] EWHC
2999 (Ch); [2006] S.T.C. 185; [2006] B.T.C. 5414 26–15
Clark v Oceanic Contractors [1983] 2 A.C. 130; [1983] 2 W.L.R. 94
Clark v Revenue and Customs Commissioners [2005] S.T.C. (S.C.D.) 823;
[2005] W.T.L.R. 1465; [2005] S.T.I. 1758 20–37

Clarke (Inspector of Taxes) v BT Pension Scheme Trustees [2000] S.T.C.
222; [2000] O.P.L.R. 53 CA
Clore (Deceased) (No.3), Re. *See* Inland Revenue Commissioners v Stype
Trustees (Jersey) Ltd
Colaingrove Ltd v Revenue and Customs Commissioners [2015] UKUT
80 (TCC); [2015] S.T.C. 1725; [2015] B.V.C. 510; [2015] S.T.I. 1530 25–60
College of Estate Management v Customs and Excise Commissioners
[2005] UKHL 62; [2005] 1 W.L.R. 3351; [2005] S.T.C. 1957 25–55
Collins v Revenue and Customs Commissioners (2007) Sp Comm 06661 ... 16–04
Commission of the European Communities v Finland (C–246/08) ECJ
[2009] E.C.R. I-10605; [2010] B.V.C. 1062 25–42
Commission of the European Communities v Germany (C–109/02) [2006]
S.T.C. 1587; [2003] E.C.R. I-12691; [2005] B.T.C. 5511; [2005] B.V.C.
542; [2003] S.T.I. 1850 .... 27–19, 27–20
Commission of the European Communities v Germany (C–287/ 00) [2002]
S.T.C. 982; [2002] E.C.R. I-5811 ECJ 26–22
Commission of the European Communities v Italy (C–104/86) [1988]
E.C.R. 1799; [1989] 3 C.M.L.R. 25 25–09
Commission of the European Communities v United Kingdom (416/85)
[1990] 2 Q.B. 130; [1988] 3 W.L.R. 1261 ECJ 26–09, 26–18
Commission of the European Communities. *See also* European Commission
Commissioner of Stamp Duties (NSW) v Permanent Trustee Co of New
South Wales [1956] A.C. 512; [1956] 3 W.L.R. 152; [1956] 2 All E.R. 512;
49 R. & I.T. 416; [1956] T.R. 209; 91 C.L.R. 1; (1956) 100 S.J. 431 19–17
Conservative Central Office v Burrell [1982] 1 W.L.R. 522; [1982] 2 All
E.R. 1 3–17
Cooke (Inspector of Taxes) v Blacklaws [1985] S.T.C. 1; 58 T.C. 255 9–07
Corbett v Inland Revenue Commissioners [1938] 1 K.B. 567 CA 12–01
Countess Fitzwilliam v Inland Revenue Commissioners [1993] 1 W.L.R.
1189; [1993] 3 All E.R. 184; [1993] S.T.C. 502; 67 T.C. 614; [1993] S.T.I.
1038; (1993) 90(45) L.S.G. 46; (1993) 137 S.J.L.B. 184 3–45
Countrywide Estate Agents FS Ltd v Revenue and Customs Commissioners
[2011] UKUT 470 (TCC); [2012] S.T.C. 511; [2012] B.T.C. 1501; [2012]
S.T.I. 216 5–20
CPG Logistics Ltd v Revenue and Customs Commissioners [2010]
UKFTT 345 (TC) 27–46
Craven (Inspector of Taxes) v White (Stephen) [1989] A.C. 398; [1988] 3
W.L.R. 423 HL 3–45
Crowe v Appleby (Inspector of Taxes) [1975] 1 W.L.R. 1539; [1975] 3 All
E.R. 529 15–53
Curnock v Inland Revenue Commissioners [2003] S.T.C. (S.C.D.) 283;
[2003] W.T.L.R. 955; [2003] S.T.I. 1052 .... 21–22, 21–40
Customs and Excise Commissioners (No.2) v Bugeja. *See* Lex Services Plc
v Customs and Excise Commissioners
Customs and Excise Commissioners v Barclays Bank Plc [2001] EWCA
Civ 1513; [2001] S.T.C. 1558; [2002] 1 C.M.L.R. 3; [2001] B.T.C. 5531;
[2001] B.V.C. 606; [2001] S.T.I. 1359; (2001) 98(44) L.S.G. 36 25–67
Customs and Excise Commissioners v Blackpool Pleasure Beach Co [1974]
1 W.L.R. 540; [1974] 1 All E.R. 1011; [1974] S.T.C. 138; [1974] T.R. 157;
(1974) 118 S.J. 297 26–15
Customs and Excise Commissioners v British Telecommunications Plc
[1999] 1 W.L.R. 1376; [1999] 3 All E.R. 961; [1999] S.T.C. 758; [1999]
B.T.C. 5273; [1999] B.V.C. 306; (1999) 96(28) L.S.G. 27 .... 25–54, 27–04

Customs and Excise Commissioners v Cantor Fitzgerald International
(C–108/99) [2001] S.T.C. 1453; [2001] E.C.R. I-7257; [2001] 3 C.M.L.R.
56; [2002] C.E.C. 119; [2001] B.T.C. 5540; [2002] B.V.C. 9; [2001] 46
E.G. 177 (C.S.); [2001] N.P.C. 144 25–10
Customs and Excise Commissioners v Civil Service Motoring Association
Ltd [1998] S.T.C. 111; [1998] B.T.C. 5003; [1998] B.V.C. 21.................... 26–18
Customs and Excise Commissioners v Colour Offset Ltd [1995] S.T.C. 85;
[1995] C.O.D. 229.. 26–15
Customs and Excise Commissioners v Diners Club Ltd [1989] 1 W.L.R.
1196; [1989] 2 All E.R. 385; [1989] S.T.C. 407; [1989] C.C.L.R. 107........ 25–48
Customs and Excise Commissioners v Electronic Data Systems Ltd [2003]
EWCA Civ 492; [2003] S.T.C. 688; [2003] B.T.C. 5395; [2003] B.V.C.
451; [2003] S.T.I. 883.. 26–19
Customs and Excise Commissioners v Euphony Communications Ltd
[2003] EWHC 3008 (Ch); [2004] S.T.C. 301; [2004] B.T.C. 5413; [2004]
B.V.C. 473; [2003] S.T.I. 2466.................................... 25–45, 27–09, 27–26
Customs and Excise Commissioners v Ferrero UK Ltd [1997] S.T.C. 881;
[1997] B.T.C. 5294; [1997] B.V.C. 408 26–11
Customs and Excise Commissioners v Harpcombe Ltd [1996] S.T.C. 726.. 27–40
Customs and Excise Commissioners v Jamieson [2002] S.T.C. 1418; [2002]
B.T.C. 5275; [2002] B.V.C. 354; [2001] S.T.I. 938..................................... 25–66
Customs and Excise Commissioners v Kilroy Television Co Ltd [1997]
S.T.C. 901; [1997] B.T.C. 5308; [1998] C.O.D. 78..................................... 27–36
Customs and Excise Commissioners v Littlewoods Organisation Plc. *See*
Lex Services Plc v Customs and Excise Commissioners
Customs and Excise Commissioners v Oliver [1980] 1 All E.R. 353; [1980]
S.T.C. 73; [1980] T.R. 423 25–29
Customs and Excise Commissioners v Ping (Europe) Ltd [2002] EWCA
Civ 1115; [2002] S.T.C. 1186; [2002] B.T.C. 5464; [2002] B.V.C. 592;
[2002] S.T.I. 1094 27–13
Customs and Excise Commissioners v Plantiflor Ltd [2002] UKHL 33;
[2002] 1 W.L.R. 2287; [2002] S.T.C. 1132; [2002] 3 C.M.L.R. 5; [2002]
B.T.C. 5413; [2002] B.V.C. 572; [2002] S.T.I. 1093; (2002) 99(36) L.S.G.
39; (2002) 152 N.L.J. 1385.. 25–51, 27–14
Customs and Excise Commissioners v Polak unreported (2002)................. 25–09
Customs and Excise Commissioners v Primback Ltd (C–34/99) [2001]
1 W.L.R. 1693; [2001] S.T.C. 803; [2001] E.C.R. I-3833; [2001] 2
C.M.L.R. 42; [2001] All E.R. (EC) 714; [2001] C.E.C. 132; [2001] B.T.C.
5240; [2001] B.V.C. 315; [2001] S.T.I. 835 .... 27–22, 27–25
Customs and Excise Commissioners v Professional Footballers
Association (Enterprises) Ltd [1993] 1 W.L.R. 153; [1993] S.T.C. 86;
(1993) 137 S.J.L.B. 44 ....
Customs and Excise Commissioners v Redrow Group Plc [1999] 1 W.L.R.
408; [1999] 2 All E.R. 1; [1999] S.T.C. 161; [1999] B.T.C. 5062; [1999]
B.V.C. 96; [1999] E.G. 20 (C.S.); (1999) 96(9) L.S.G. 32; (1999) 143
S.J.L.B. 58; [1999] N.P.C. 18.. 25–52, 27–39
Customs and Excise Commissioners v Richmond Theatre Management
Ltd [1995] S.T.C. 257; [1995] S.T.I. 190.. 27–30
Customs and Excise Commissioners v Robert Gordon's College [1996]
1 W.L.R. 201; [1995] S.T.C. 1093; 1996 S.C. (H.L.) 6; 1996 S.L.T. 98;
[1995] E.G. 179 (C.S.); (1996) 140 S.J.L.B. 20; [1995] N.P.C. 178.............. 3–44
Customs and Excise Commissioners v Royal Exchange Theatre Trust
[1979] 3 All E.R. 797; [1979] S.T.C. 728; [1979] T.R. 281 25–71

Customs and Excise Commissioners v Safeway Stores Plc [1997] S.T.C.
163; [1997] B.T.C. 5003; [1997] B.V.C. 99 .... 26–12, 26–14
Customs and Excise Commissioners v Telemed Ltd [1992] S.T.C. 89 25–61
Customs and Excise Commissioners v University of Leicester Students
Union [2001] EWCA Civ 1972; [2002] S.T.C. 147; [2002] E.L.R. 347;
[2002] B.T.C. 5064; [2002] B.V.C. 269; [2002] S.T.I. 38; (2002) 99(10)
L.S.G. 33 26–22
Customs and Excise Commissioners v Westmorland Motorway Services
Ltd [1998] S.T.C. 431; [1998] R.T.R. 440; [1998] B.T.C. 5136; [1998]
B.V.C. 154 .... 27–10, 27–11
Customs and Excise Commissioners v Zielinski Baker & Partners Ltd
[2004] UKHL 7; [2004] 1 W.L.R. 707; [2004] 2 All E.R. 141; [2004] S.T.C.
456; [2004] B.T.C. 5249; [2004] B.V.C. 309; [2004] S.T.I. 502; [2004] 10
E.G. 185 (C.S.); (2004) 101(12) L.S.G. 37; (2004) 148 S.J.L.B. 268 3–56
Customs and Excise Commissioners v Zoological Society of London
(C–267/00) [2002] Q.B. 1252; [2002] 3 W.L.R. 829; [2002] S.T.C. 521;
[2002] E.C.R. I-3353; [2002] 2 C.M.L.R. 13; [2002] All E.R. (EC) 465;
[2002] C.E.C. 316; [2002] B.T.C. 5224; [2002] B.V.C. 414; [2002] S.T.I.
356; 26–22
Danfoss A/S v Skatterministeriat (C–94/10) October 2011 not yet reported
ECJ 25–11
Daphne v Shaw (1926) 43 T.L.R. 45; 11 T.C. 256 8–10
Davies (t/a Special Occasions/2XL Limos) v Revenue and Customs
Commissioners [2012] UKUT 130 (TCC); [2012] S.T.C. 1978; [2012]
B.V.C. 1699; (2012) 162 N.L.J. 1179 26–15
Davis & Dann Ltd v Revenue and Customs Commissioners [2016] EWCA
Civ 142; [2016] B.V.C. 11; [2016] S.T.I. 1157 25–14
DB Group Services (UK) Ltd v Revenue and Customs Commissioners
[2016]. See UBS AG v Revenue and Customs Commissioners
Debenhams Retail Plc v Customs and Excise Commissioners [2005]
EWCA Civ 892; [2005] S.T.C. 1155; [2005] B.T.C. 5394.... 25–15, 25–50, 27–14
Degorce v Revenue and Customs Commissioners [2015] UKUT 447
(TCC); [2016] S.T.C. 542; [2015] B.T.C. 528 5–06
Dial-a-Phone Ltd v Customs and Excise Commissioners [2004] EWCA
Civ 603; [2004] S.T.C. 987; [2004] B.T.C. 5581 27–41
Dixons Retail Plc v Revenue and Customs Commissioners [2014] 2 W.L.R.
893; [2014] S.T.C. 375; [2014] B.V.C. 2; [2013] S.T.I. 3573 .... 25–29, 25–42
Drummond v Revenue and Customs Commissioners [2009] EWCA Civ
608; [2009] S.T.C. 2206; 79 T.C. 793 16–02
Duple Motor Bodies v Ostime. See Ostime (Inspector of Taxes) v Duple
Motor Bodies Ltd
Dyer v Dorset CC [1989] Q.B. 346; [1988] 3 W.L.R. 213 CA 17–06
E Buyer Ltd v Revenue and Customs Commissioners [2016] UKUT 123
(TCC); [2016] Lloyd's Rep. F.C. 225; [2016] B.V.C. 510 25–14
EC Commission. See Commission of the European Communities;
European Commission
Eclipse Film Partners No.35 LLP v Revenue and Customs Commissioners
[2015] EWCA Civ 95; [2015] S.T.C. 1429; [2015] B.T.C. 10; [2015] S.T.I.
52 .... 3–54, 5–05
Edinbugh Telford College v Revenue and Customs Commissioners [2006]
CSIH 13; [2006] S.T.C. 1291 25–65
Edwards (Inspector of Taxes) v Bairstow and Harrison [1956] A.C. 14;
[1955] 3 W.L.R. 410 HL 5–05

Edwards (Inspector of Taxes) v Clinch [1982] A.C. 845; [1981] 3 W.L.R.
707 HL 9–03

Eilbeck v Rawling (1982). *See* Ramsay (WT) Ltd v Inland Revenue
Commissioners

Elderkin (Inspector of Taxes) v Hindmarsh [1988] S.T.C. 267; 60 T.C. 651;
[1988] B.T.C. 129; (1988) 32 S.J. 935 9–42

Elida Gibbs Ltd v Customs and Excise Commissioners (C–317/94) [1996]
S.T.C. 1387; [1996] E.C.R. I-5339 ECJ 27–21, 27–23, 27–25

Ellesmere (Earl of) v Inland Revenue [1918] 2 K.B. 735 KBD 21–33

Elliniko Dimosio v Karageorgou. *See* Greece v Karageorgou

EMI Goup Electronics Ltd v Coldicott (Inspector of Taxes) [2000] 1
W.L.R. 540; [1999] S.T.C. 803; [1999] I.R.L.R. 630; 71 T.C. 455; [1999]
B.T.C. 294; (1999) 96(32) L.S.G. 34; (1999) 143 S.J.L.B. 220 .... 9–11, 9–45

Emmerson (Inspector of Taxes) v Computer Time International Ltd (In
Liquidation) [1977] 1 W.L.R. 734; [1977] 2 All E.R. 545; [1977] S.T.C.
170; (1977) 242 E.G. 963; 50 T.C. 628; [1977] T.R. 43; (1977) 121 S.J.
224 16–03

Empire Stores Ltd v Customs and Excise Commissioners (C–33/93) [1994]
3 All E.R. 90; [1994] S.T.C. 623 ECJ 27–09

EMS-Bulgaria Transport OOD v Direktor na Direktsia 'Obzhalvane
i upravlenie na izpalnenieto' Plovdiv (C–284/11) [2012] S.T.C. 2229;
[2012] S.T.I. 2461 27–37

Ensign Tankers (Leasing) Ltd v Stokes (Inspector of Taxes) [1992] 1 A.C.
655; [1992] 2 W.L.R. 469; [1992] 2 All E.R. 275; [1992] S.T.C. 226; 64
T.C. 617; [1992] S.T.I. 364; (1992) 89(17) L.S.G. 49; (1992) 136 S.J.L.B.
89 .... 3–41, 3–45, 3–46, 3–54, 3–57, 5–06

Ensign Tankers case. *See* Ensign Tankers (Leasing) Ltd v Stokes
(Inspector of Taxes)

European Commission v France (C–479/13) [2015] S.T.C. 1706; [2015]
B.V.C. 14; [2015] S.T.I. 715 26–16

European Commission v France (C–94/09) [2012] S.T.C. 573; [2010]
E.C.R. I-4261 25–60

European Commission v Luxembourg (C–502/13) [2015] S.T.C. 1714;
[2015] B.V.C. 15 26–16

European Commission v United Kingdom (C–161/14) EU:C:2015:355;
[2015] S.T.C. 1767; [2016] C.E.C. 203; [2015] B.V.C. 50; [2015] S.T.I.
1881 25–06

European Commission. *See also* Commission of the European Communities

Ewart v Taylor (Inspector of Taxes) [1983] S.T.C. 721; 57 T.C. 401 15–66

Executors of Postlethwaite v Revenue and Customs Commissioners (2006)
Sp Comm 00571 19–11

Expert Witness Institute v Customs and Excise Commissioners [2001]
EWCA Civ 1882; [2002] 1 W.L.R. 1674; [2002] S.T.C. 42 .... 26–19, 26–22

Fall (Inspector of Taxes) v Hitchen [1973] 1 W.L.R. 286; [1973] 1 All
E.R. 368; [1973] S.T.C. 66; 49 T.C. 433; [1972] T.R. 285; (1972) 117 S.J.
73 9–06

Farmer v Inland Revenue Commissioners [1999] S.T.C. (S.C.D.) 321 Sp
Comm 20–37

Fazenda Publica v Camara Municipal do Porto (C–446/98) [2001] S.T.C.
560; [2000] E.C.R. I-11435 ECJ 25–04, 25–05

FD Fenton Will Trusts v HMRC. *See* Trustees of FD Fenston Will Trusts
v Revenue and Customs Commissioners

Ferrazzini v Italy [2001] S.T.C. 1314 ECHR; (2002) 34 E.H.R.R. 45 2–30

Fetherstonaugh (formerly Finch) v Inland Revenue Commissioners [1985]
   Ch. 1; [1984] 3 W.L.R. 212 20–36
Fielder (Inspector of Taxes) v Vedlynn Ltd [1992] S.T.C. 553; [1992] S.T.I.
   264 16–04
Figg v Clarke (Inspector of Taxes) [1997] 1 W.L.R. 603; [1997] S.T.C. 247...15–53
Finance and Business Training Ltd v Revenue and Customs Commissioners
   [2016] EWCA Civ 7 26–22
Finanzampt Burgdorf v Manfred Bog [2011] S.T.C. 1223 ECJ 26–14
Finanzamt Bergisch Gladbach v Skripalle (C–63/96) [1997] S.T.C. 1035;
   [1997] E.C.R. I-2847 ECJ 25–08
Finanzamt Goslar v Breitsohl (C–400/98) [2001] S.T.C. 355; [2000] E.C.R.
   I-4321 ECJ 25–64, 27–34
Finanzamt Munchen III v Mohsche (C–193/91) [1997] S.T.C. 195; [1993]
   E.C.R. I-2615 ECJ 25–04
Findel v Revenue and Customs Commissioners [2011] UKFTT 723 (TC);
   [2012] S.T.I. 79 25–50
Fischer v Finanzamt Donaueschingen (C–283/95) [1998] All E.R. (EC)
   567; [1998] S.T.C. 708 ECJ 25–04
Fitzpatrick v Inland Revenue Commissioners (No.2) 1992 S.C. 207; 1993
   S.L.T. 54 IH 9–36
Fleming (t/a Bodycraft) v Customs and Excise Commissioners [2008]
   UKHL 2; [2008] 1 W.L.R. 195; [2008] 1 All E.R. 1061; [2008] S.T.C.
   324; [2008] 1 C.M.L.R. 48; [2008] Eu. L.R. 455; [2008] B.T.C. 5096;
   [2008] B.V.C. 221; [2008] S.T.I. 181; (2008) 158 N.L.J. 182; (2008) 152(5)
   S.J.L.B. 30; [2008] N.P.C. 5 25–04
Fleming and Condé Nast v Customs and Excise Commissioners [2008]
   UKHL 2; [2008] 1 W.L.R. 195 [2008] S.T.C. 324 HL 2–28
Floor v Davis (Inspector of Taxes) [1980] A.C. 695; [1979] 2 W.L.R. 830
   HL 15–43
Fonecomp Ltd v Revenue and Customs Commissioners [2015] EWCA Civ
   39; [2015] S.T.C. 2254; [2015] Lloyd's Rep. F.C. 149; [2015] B.V.C. 9;
   [2015] S.T.I. 355 25–14
Freemans Plc v Customs and Excise Commissioners (C–86/99) [2001]
   1 W.L.R. 1713; [2001] S.T.C. 960; [2001] E.C.R. I-4167; [2001] 2
   C.M.L.R. 46; [2001] C.E.C. 118; [2001] B.T.C. 5307; [2001] B.V.C. 365;
   [2001] S.T.I. 871 27–15
Furniss (Inspector of Taxes) v Dawson [1984] A.C. 474; [1984] 2 W.L.R.
   226 HL 3–45
G v G (1975) 6 Fam. Law 8 20–16
Gallagher v Jones (Inspector of Taxes) [1994] Ch. 107; [1994] 2 W.L.R.
   160 CA 5–16
Garner (Inspector of Taxes) v Pounds Shipowners & Shipbreakers Ltd
   [2000] 1 W.L.R. 1107; [2000] 3 All E.R. 218 HL........................ 16–05, 16–08
Geoffrey E Snushall Ltd v Customs and Excise Commissioners. See
   Snushall (Geoffrey E) Ltd v Customs and Excise Commissioners
Gilbert (Inspector of Taxes) v Hemsley [1981] S.T.C. 703; [1981] I.R.L.R.
   501; 55 T.C. 419; [1981] T.R. 327; (1981) 125 S.J. 567 9–25
Gilbert v Revenue and Customs Commissioners [2011] UKFTT 705 (TC)...17–20
GlaxoSmithKline Services Unlimited v Revenue and Customs
   Commissioners [2011] UKUT 432 (TCC); [2012] S.T.C. 10; [2011]
   B.V.C. 1735... 26–10
Golding (Inspector of Taxes) v Kaufman [1985] S.T.C. 152; 58 T.C. 296 ... 15–41
Goodwin v Curtis (Inspector of Taxes) [1998] S.T.C. 475; 70 T.C. 478 CA...17–04

Gordon v Inland Revenue Commissioners [1991] S.T.C. 174; 1991 S.C. 149 IH 17–26

Gray v Inland Revenue Commissioners [1994] S.T.C. 360; [1994] 38 E.G. 156; [1994] R.V.R. 129; [1994] S.T.I. 208; [1994] E.G. 32 (C.S.); [1994] N.P.C. 15 .... 21–33, 21–41

Grays Timber Products Ltd v Revenue and Customs Commissioners [2010] UKSC 4; [2010] 1 W.L.R. 497; [2010] 2 All E.R. 1; [2010] S.T.C. 782; 2010 S.C. (U.K.S.C.) 1; 2011 S.L.T. 63; 2010 S.C.L.R. 239; 80 T.C. 96; [2010] B.T.C. 112; [2010] S.T.I. 393; (2010) 154(5) S.J.L.B. 30; 2010 G.W.D. 8–145 .... 9–48, 16–12, 21–35

Great Western Railway Co v Bater (Surveyor of Taxes) [1922] 2 A.C. 1 HL 9–03

Greece v Karageorgou (C–78/02) [2006] S.T.C. 1654; [2003] E.C.R. I-13295; [2006] B.T.C. 5732; [2006] B.V.C. 801; [2003] S.T.I. 1937 25–19

Green v Inland Revenue Commissioners [1982] S.T.C. 485; 1982 S.C. 155 IH 17–08

Gregg v Customs and Excise Commissioners (C–216/97) [1999] S.T.C. 934; [1999] E.C.R. I-4947; [1999] 3 C.M.L.R. 343; [1999] All E.R. (EC) 775; [1999] C.E.C. 460; [1999] B.T.C. 5341; [1999] B.V.C. 395 25–09

Grey v Tiley (1932) 16 T.C. 414 7–35

Griffin (Inspector of Taxes) v Craig-Harvey [1994] S.T.C. 54; 66 T.C. 396 ...17–08

Griffiths, Re (2008). See Ogden v Trustees of the RHS Griffiths 2003 Settlement

H & M Hennes Ltd v Customs and Excise Commissioners [2005] EWHC 1383; [2005] S.T.C. 1749; [2005] B.T.C. 5387 26–15

Halifax Plc v Customs and Excise Commissioners [2006] Ch. 387; [2006] 2 W.L.R. 905 ECJ 25–15, 25–16

Hamblett v Godfrey (Inspector of Taxes) [1987] 1 W.L.R. 357; [1987] 1 All E.R. 916 CA 9–11

Hanson v Revenue and Customs Commissioners [2012] UKFTT 95 (TC); [2012] W.T.L.R. 597; [2012] S.T.I. 1388 20–44

Harnas & Helm CV v Staatssecretaris van Financiïn [1997] All E.R. (EC) 267; [1997] S.T.C. 364 ECJ 25–75

Harrier LLC v Revenue and Customs Commissioners [2011] UKFTT 725 (TC); [2012] S.F.T.D. 348; [2012] S.T.I. 80 26–15

Harthan v Mason [1980] S.T.C. 94; 53 T.C. 272 .... 15–51, 15–52

Hartwell Plc v Customs and Excise Commissioners [2003] EWCA Civ 130; [2003] S.T.C. 396; [2003] B.T.C. 5206 .... 25–60, 27–23

Hatt v Newman (Inspector of Taxes) [2000] S.T.C. 113; 72 T.C. 462 15–28

Hawkinson v Revenue and Customs Commissioners unreported 2011 4–16

Hayes Will Trusts, Re [1971] 1 W.L.R. 758; [1971] 2 All E.R. 341 21–33

Healey v Revenue and Customs Commissioners [2014] UKFTT 889 (TC)... 5–33

Heaton (Inspector of Taxes) v Bell [1970] A.C. 728; [1969] 2 W.L.R. 735 HL 9–12, 9–24

Henke v Revenue and Customs Commissioners [2006] S.T.C. (S.C.D.) 561; [2006] S.T.I. 1888; (2006) Sp Comm 550 .... 17–03, 17–07

Highland Council v Revenue and Customs Commissioners [2007] CSIH 36; [2008] S.T.C. 1280; 2007 S.C. 533 25–57

Hillyer v Leeke [1976] S.T.C. 490; [1976] T.R. 215 5–32

HMRC v Bower. See Bower v Revenue and Customs Commissioners

HMRC v Healey. See Healey v Revenue and Customs Commissioners

HMRC v Martin. See Martin v Revenue and Customs Commissioners

HMRC v Mayes. See Mayes v Revenue and Customs Commissioners

HMRC. See Revenue and Customs Commissioners

Hoare Trustees v Gardner (Inspector of Taxes) [1979] Ch. 10; [1978] 2
W.L.R. 839 15–64
Hoechst Finance v Gumbrell (Inspector of Taxes) [1983] S.T.C. 150; 56
T.C. 594 CA 14–33
Honour (Inspector of Taxes) v Norris [1992] S.T.C. 304; 64 T.C. 599 17–06
Honourable Society of Middle Temple, The v Revenue and Customs
Commissioners [2013] UKUT 250 (TCC); [2013] S.T.C. 1998; [2013]
B.V.C. 1690; [2013] S.T.I. 2218; (2013) 163(7567) N.L.J. 21......... 25–55, 25–56
Hood v Revenue and Customs Commissioners [2016] UKFTT 59 (TC);
[2016] S.F.T.D. 351; [2016] W.T.L.R. 835; [2016] S.T.I. 1159.................. 19–16
Hood's Executors. See Hood v Revenue and Customs Commissioners
Horizon College v Staatsssecretariat von Financien (C–434/05) [2008]
S.T.C. 2145; [2007] E.C.R. I-4793 ECJ.. 26–22
Horton v Young (Inspector of Taxes) [1972] Ch. 157; [1971] 3 W.L.R. 348
CA 5–35
Hutchison 3G UK Ltd v Customs and Excise Commissioners (C–369/04)
[2008] S.T.C. 218; [2007] E.C.R. I-5247; [2007] 3 C.M.L.R. 26; [2010]
B.V.C. 55; [2007] S.T.I. 1764 25–73
I/S Fini H v Skatteministeriet [2005] S.T.C. 903; [2005] E.C.R. I- 1599
ECJ 27–35
Ian Flockton Developments Ltd v Customs and Excise Commissioners
[1987] S.T.C. 394 27–38
Ideal Tourisme SA v Belgium (C–36/99) [2001] S.T.C. 1386; [2000] E.C.R.
I-6049 ECJ 25–05
Ingram v Inland Revenue Commissioners [2000] 1 A.C. 293; [1999] 2
W.L.R. 90 HL... 19–19, 19–20, 19–22
Inland Revenue Commissioners v Aken [1990] 1 W.L.R. 1374; [1990]
S.T.C. 497; (1990) 87(36) L.S.G. 44; (1990) 134 S.J. 1042.......................... 5–06
Inland Revenue Commissioners v Barclay Curle & Co Ltd [1969] 1 W.L.R.
675; [1969] 1 All E.R. 732; [1969] 1 Lloyd's Rep. 169; 1969 S.C. (H.L.)
30; 1969 S.L.T. 122; (1969) 48 A.T.C. 17.. 8–08
Inland Revenue Commissioners v Brander & Cruickshank (A Firm) [1971]
1 W.L.R. 212; [1971] 1 All E.R. 36; 1971 S.C. (H.L.) 30; 1971 S.L.T. 53;
46 T.C. 574; (1970) 115 S.J. 79 9–06
Inland Revenue Commissioners v Church Commissioners for England
[1977] A.C. 329; [1971] 1 W.L.R. 1761; [1976] 3 W.L.R. 214; [1976] 2 All
E.R. 1037; [1976] S.T.C. 339; 50 T.C. 516; [1976] T.R. 187; (1976) 120
S.J. 505... 7–27
Inland Revenue Commissioners v Clay [1914] 3 K.B. 466 CA 21–33
Inland Revenue Commissioners v Cock Russell & Co Ltd [1949] 2 All E.R.
889; 65 T.L.R. 725; 29 T.C. 387; [1949] T.R. 367; (1949) 93 S.J. 711 5–23
Inland Revenue Commissioners v Crossman [1937] A.C. 26; [1936] 1 All
E.R. 762 .... 21–33, 21–35
Inland Revenue Commissioners v Duke of Westminster [1936] A.C. 1; 19
T.C. 490 HL...3–45, 7–28
Inland Revenue Commissioners v Eversden [2003] EWCA Civ 668; [2003]
S.T.C. 822; 75 T.C. 340; [2003] B.T.C. 8028; [2003] W.T.L.R. 893; [2003]
S.T.I. 989; (2003) 100(27) L.S.G. 38; (2003) 147 S.J.L.B. 594................. 19–17
Inland Revenue Commissioners v George [2003] EWCA Civ 1763; [2004]
S.T.C. 147; 75 T.C. 735; [2004] B.T.C. 8003; [2004] W.T.L.R. 75; [2003]
S.T.I. 2276; (2004) 101(3) L.S.G. 34 20–37
Inland Revenue Commissioners v Gray (1994). See Gray v Inland Revenue
Commissioners

Inland Revenue Commissioners v Green. *See* Green v Inland Revenue
Commissioners
Inland Revenue Commissioners v Helen Slater Charitable Trust Ltd
[1982] Ch. 49; [1981] 3 W.L.R. 377; [1981] 3 All E.R. 98; [1981] S.T.C.
471; 55 T.C. 230; [1982] T.R. 225; (1981) 125 S.J. 414 15–45
Inland Revenue Commissioners v John Lewis Properties Plc [2002] EWCA
Civ 1869; [2003] Ch. 513; [2003] 2 W.L.R. 1196; [2003] S.T.C. 117; 75
T.C. 131; [2003] B.T.C. 127; [2003] S.T.I. 29; (2003) 147 S.J.L.B. 180;
[2003] N.P.C. 1 5–19
Inland Revenue Commissioners v Land Securities Investment Trust Ltd
[1969] 1 W.L.R. 604; [1969] 2 All E.R. 430; 45 T.C. 495; [1969] T.R. 173;
(1969) 113 S.J. 407 7–27
Inland Revenue Commissioners v Livingston 1927 S.C. 251; 1927 S.L.T.
112 IH 5–11
Inland Revenue Commissioners v Lloyds Private Banking Ltd [1998]
S.T.C. 559; [1999] 1 F.L.R. 147; [1998] 2 F.C.R. 41; [1998] B.T.C. 8020;
[1999] Fam. Law 309; (1998) 95(19) L.S.G. 23; (1998) 142 S.J.L.B. 164....22–16
Inland Revenue Commissioners v Lord Rennell [1964] A.C. 173; [1963] 2
W.L.R. 745; [1963] 1 All E.R. 803; (1963) 42 A.T.C. 55; [1963] T.R. 73;
(1963) 107 S.J. 232 20–07
Inland Revenue Commissioners v Macpherson [1989] A.C. 159; [1988] 2
W.L.R. 1261; [1988] 2 All E.R. 753; [1988] S.T.C. 362; [1988] 2 F.T.L.R.
199; [1988] B.T.C. 8065; (1988) 132 S.J. 821 .... 19–38, 22–24, 22–41
Inland Revenue Commissioners v Maxse [1919] 1 K.B. 647 CA 5–14
Inland Revenue Commissioners v National Book League [1957] Ch. 488;
[1957] 3 W.L.R. 222; [1957] 2 All E.R. 644; 50 R. & I.T. 603; 37 T.C.
455; (1957) 36 A.T.C. 130; [1957] T.R. 141; (1957) 101 S.J. 553 7–25
Inland Revenue Commissioners v Plummer [1980] A.C. 896; [1979] 3
W.L.R. 689 HL 12–11
Inland Revenue Commissioners v Richards Executors [1971] 1 W.L.R.
571; [1971] 1 All E.R. 785; 1971 S.C. (H.L.) 60; 1971 S.L.T. 107; 21 T.C.
626; [1971] T.R. 2; (1971) 115 S.J. 225 16–08
Inland Revenue Commissioners v Scottish & Newcastle Breweries Ltd
[1982] 1 W.L.R. 322; [1982] 2 All E.R. 230; [1982] S.T.C. 296; 1982 S.C.
(H.L.) 133; 1982 S.L.T. 407; 55 T.C. 252; [1980] T.R. 421; (1982) 126
S.J. 189 8–09
Inland Revenue Commissioners v Scottish Provident Institution [2004]
UKHL 52; [2004] 1 W.L.R. 3172; [2005] 1 All E.R. 325; [2005] S.T.C.
15; 2005 1 S.C. (H.L.) 33; 76 T.C. 538; [2004] B.T.C. 426; 7 I.T.L. Rep.
403; [2004] S.T.I. 2433; (2004) 148 S.J.L.B. 1404 3–46
Inland Revenue Commissioners v Spencer-Nairn [1991] S.T.C. 60; 1991
S.L.T. 594 IH 19–09
Inland Revenue Commissioners v Stannard [1984] 1 W.L.R. 1039; [1984]
2 All E.R. 105; [1984] S.T.C. 245; (1984) 81 L.S.G. 1523; (1984) 128 S.J.
400 23–05
Inland Revenue Commissioners v Stype Investments (Jersey) Ltd
[1982] Ch. 456; [1982] 3 W.L.R. 228; [1982] 3 All E.R. 419; [1982] B.T.C.
8039 23–05
Inland Revenue Commissioners v Stype Trustees (Jersey) Ltd [1985] 1
W.L.R. 1290; [1985] 2 All E.R. 819; [1985] S.T.C. 394; (1986) 83 L.S.G.
205 24–02
Inland Revenue Commissioners v Willoughby [1997] 1 W.L.R. 1071;
[1997] 4 All E.R. 65; [1997] S.T.C. 995; 70 T.C. 57; [1997] B.T.C. 393;

(1997) 94(29) L.S.G. 28; (1997) 147 N.L.J. 1062; (1997) 141 S.J.L.B.
176 3–42–3–44
Inland Revenue Commissioners v Wolfson [1949] 1 All E.R. 865; 65
T.L.R. 260; 42 R. & I.T. 196; 31 T.C. 141; [1949] T.R. 121; [1949] W.N.
190; (1949) 93 S.J. 355 12–15
Institute of Chartered Accountants in England and Wales v Customs and
Excise Commissioners [1999] 1 W.L.R. 701; [1999] 2 All E.R. 449; [1999]
S.T.C. 398; [1999] 2 C.M.L.R. 1333; [1999] B.T.C. 5165; [1999] B.V.C.
215; (1999) 96(20) L.S.G. 40; (1999) 149 N.L.J. 559; (1999) 143 S.J.L.B.
131 25–72
International Bingo Technology SA v Tribunal Economico-Administrativo
Regional de Cataluna (TEARC) (C–377/11) [2013] S.T.C. 661; [2012]
S.T.I. 3225 27–02
Investment Trust Companies (in Liquidation) v Revenue and Customs
Commissioners [2015] EWCA Civ 82; [2015] S.T.C. 1280; [2015] B.V.C.
10; [2015] S.T.I. 519 27–49
Investment Trust Companies (In Liquidation) v Revenue and Customs
Commissioners [2012] EWHC 458 (Ch); [2012] S.T.C. 1150; [2012]
B.V.C. 109 25–11
Isle of Wight Council v Revenue and Customs Commissioners [2015]
EWCA Civ 1303; [2016] P.T.S.R. 620; [2016] B.V.C. 3; [2016] S.T.I. 65.. 25–65
Jarmin v Rawling [1994] S.T.C. 1005; 67 T.C. 130 17–20
Jasmine Trustees Ltd v Wells & Hind (A Firm) [2007] EWHC 38 (Ch));
[2008] Ch. 194; [2007] 1 All E.R. 1142 15–54
JD Wetherspoon Ltd v Revenue and Customs Commissioners (C–302/07)
[2009] S.T.C. 1022; [2009] E.C.R. I-1467; [2009] 2 C.M.L.R. 53; [2009]
B.V.C. 821; [2009] S.T.I. 693 25–07
JD Wetherspoon Plc v Revenue and Customs Commissioners [2012]
UKUT 42 (TCC); [2012] S.T.C. 1450; 81 T.C. 588; [2012] B.T.C. 1578;
[2012] L.L.R. 641; [2012] S.T.I. 1382 8–09
Jerome v Kelly (Inspector of Taxes) [2004] UKHL 25; [2004] 1 W.L.R.
1409; [2004] 2 All E.R. 835 15–27
Jones v Garnett (Inspector of Taxes) [2007] UKHL 35; [2007] 1 W.L.R.
2030; [2007] 4 All E.R. 857; [2008] Bus. L.R. 425; [2007] S.T.C. 1536;
[2007] I.C.R. 1259; [2007] 3 F.C.R. 487; 78 T.C. 597; [2007] B.T.C. 476;
[2007] W.T.L.R. 1229; [2007] S.T.I. 1899; (2007) 157 N.L.J. 1118; (2007)
151 S.J.L.B. 1024 .... 12–16, 14–14
Jones v Inland Revenue Commissioners [1997] S.T.C. 358; [1997] B.T.C.
8003; [1997] E.G. 21 (C.S.); [1997] N.P.C. 26 21–42
JP Commodities Ltd v Revenue and Customs Commissioners [2007]
EWHC 2474 (Ch); [2008] S.T.C. 816; [2008] B.T.C. 5563 25–13
JP Morgan Fleming Claverhouse Investment Trust Plc v Revenue and
Customs Commissioners (C–363/05) [2008] S.T.C. 1180; [2007] E.C.R.
I-5517 ECJ 25–11
Julius Fillibeck Sohne GmbH & Co KG v Finanzamt Neustadt (C–258/95)
[1998] 1 W.L.R. 697; [1998] All E.R. (EC) 466 ECJ 25–42
KapHagRenditefonds 35 Spreecenter Berlin-Hellersdorf 3. Tranche GbR v
Finanzamt Charlottenburg [2005] S.T.C. 1500; [2003] E.C.R. I-6851 ECJ.. 25–75
Keeping Newcastle Warm Ltd v Customs and Excise Commissioners
(C–353/00) [2002] All E.R. (EC) 769; [2002] S.T.C. 943 ECJ 27–05
Kellogg Brown & Root Holdings (UK) Ltd v Revenue and Customs
Commissioners [2010] EWCA Civ 118; [2010] Bus. L.R. 957; [2010]
S.T.C. 925; [2010] B.T.C. 250; [2010] S.T.I. 558 .... 15–18, 15–28

Kelsall Parsons & Co v Inland Revenue Commissioners 1938 S.C. 238;
  1938 S.L.T. 239; 21 T.C. 608 IH.. 5–20
Khan (t/a Greyhound Dry Cleaners) v Customs and Excise Commissioners
  [2006] EWCA Civ 89; [2006] S.T.C. 1167; [2006] B.T.C. 5267; [2006]
  B.V.C. 336; [2006] S.T.I. 537 25–19
Kidson v MacDonald [1974] Ch. 339; [1974] 2 W.L.R. 566 .... 2–23, 15–51
Kimberly-Clark Ltd v Customs and Excise Commissioners [2003] EWHC
  1623 (Ch); [2004] S.T.C. 473; [2004] B.T.C. 5567 25–55
King v UK (No.2) [2004] S.T.C. 911; [2007] B.T.C. 74 ECHR 2–30
King v UK (No.3) [2005] S.T.C. 438; (2005) 41 E.H.R.R. 2 ECHR............... 2–30
Kingfisher Plc v Customs and Excise Commissioners [2000] S.T.C. 992;
  [2000] B.T.C. 5420; [2001] B.V.C. 49; [2000] S.T.I. 1610.............. 27–22, 27–25
Kirby (Inspector of Taxes) v Thorn EMI Plc [1988] 1 W.L.R. 445; [1988] 2
  All E.R. 947 CA.. 15–14, 15–21
Kirkham v Williams (Inspector of Taxes) [1991] 1 W.L.R. 863; [1991]
  S.T.C. 342 CA.. 5–13
Kirkwood (Inspector of Taxes) v Evans [2002] EWHC 30 (Ch); [2002] 1
  W.L.R. 1794; [2002] S.T.C. 231; 74 T.C. 481; [2002] B.T.C. 50; [2002]
  S.T.I. 155; (2002) 99(10) L.S.G. 33; (2002) 146 S.J.L.B. 45...................... 9–42
Kittel v Belgium (C–439/04) [2008] S.T.C. 1537; [2006] E.C.R. I-6161
  ECJ... 25–14, 25–15
Kretztechnik AG v Finamzampt Linz [2005] 1 W.L.R. 3755; [2005] S.T.C.
  1118 ECJ.. 27–44
Kuehne & Nagel Drinks Logistics Ltd v Revenue and Customs
  Commissioners [2012] EWCA Civ 34; [2012] S.T.C. 840; [2012] B.T.C. 58...9–11
Kuwait Petroleum (GB) Ltd v Customs and Excise Commissioners
  (C–48/97) [1999] All E.R. (EC) 450; [1999] S.T.C. 488 ECJ.......... 25–61, 27–20
Kuwait Petroleum (GB) Ltd v Customs and Excise Commissioners. See
  Lex Services Plc v Customs and Excise Commissioners
Lake v Lake (1989) [1989] S.T.C. 865 20–30
Landboden-Agrardienste GmbH & Co KG v Finanzamt Calau (C–384/95)
  [1998] S.T.C. 171; [1997] E.C.R. I-7387 ECJ.. 25–42
Lau v Revenue and Customs Commissioners [2009] S.T.C. (S.C.D.) 352;
  [2009] W.T.L.R. 627.. 20–29
Law Shipping Co Ltd v Inland Revenue Commissioners (1923–24) 17 Ll.
  L. Rep. 184; 1924 S.C. 74 IH... 5–38
Lawson (Inspector of Taxes) v Johnson Matthey [1992] 2 A.C. 324; [1992]
  2 W.L.R. 826; [1992] 2 All E.R. 647; [1992] S.T.C. 466; 65 T.C. 39;
  [1992] S.T.I. 529; (1992) 136 S.J.L.B. 164 5–28
Leader v Counsel (Inspector of Taxes) [1942] 1 K.B. 364 KBD 7–35
Lebara Ltd v Revenue and Customs Commissioners (C–520/10) [2012]
  S.T.C. 1536; [2012] B.V.C. 219.. 25–42
Leeds City Council v Revenue and Customs Commissioners [2015] EWCA
  Civ 1293 27–47
Letts v Inland Revenue Commissioners [1957] 1 W.L.R. 201; [1956] 3 All
  E.R. 588 19–17
Levob Verzekeringen BV v Staatssecrataris van Financiīn [2006] S.T.C.
  766; [2005] E.C.R. I-9433 ECJ... 25–58
Lewis (Inspector of Taxes) v Rook [1992] 1 W.L.R. 662; [1992] S.T.C. 171
  CA 17–06
Lex Services Plc v Customs and Excise Commissioners [2003] UKHL 67;
  [2004] 1 W.L.R. 1; [2004] 1 All E.R. 434; [2004] S.T.C. 73; [2004] R.T.R.
  18; [2003] B.T.C. 5658; [2004] B.V.C. 53; [2003] S.T.I. 2274; (2004)

101(3) L.S.G. 34; (2003) 147 S.J.L.B. 1430.......... 25–10, 25–44—25–46, 25–61, 27–03, 27–08, 27–11, 27–12, 27–16, 27–23, 27–24
Lidl & Companhia v Fazenda Publica (C–106/10) [2011] S.T.C. 1979; [2011] S.T.I. 2699 ECJ.. 27–04
Littlewoods Organisation Plc v Customs and Excise Commissioners. *See* Lex Services Plc v Customs and Excise Commissioners
Littlewoods Retail Ltd v Revenue and Customs Commissioners [2015] EWCA Civ 515; [2015] 3 W.L.R. 1748; [2015] S.T.C. 2014; [2015] B.V.C. 26; [2015] S.T.I. 1791.. 25–11, 27–47
Livewire Telecom Ltd v Revenue and Customs Commissioners. *See* Revenue and Customs Commissioners v Livewire Telecom Ltd (2009)
Lloyds TSB Bank Plc (Personal Representative of Antrobus (Deceased)) v Inland Revenue Commissioners [2002] S.T.C. (S.C.D.) 468; [2002] W.T.L.R. 1435 Sp Comm 20–44
Local Authorities Mutual Investment Trust v Customs and Excise Commissioners [2003] EWHC 2766 (Ch); [2004] S.T.C. 246; [2004] Eu. L.R. 320 25–07
London & Thames Haven Oil Wharves Ltd v Attwooll (Inspector of Taxes) [1967] Ch. 772; [1967] 2 W.L.R. 743 CA 5–20
London CC v Attorney General [1901] A.C. 26 HL 1–16
Longson v Baker (Inspector of Taxes) [2001] S.T.C. 6; 73 T.C. 415........... 17–07
Loquitur Ltd, Re [2003] EWHC 999 (Ch); [2003] S.T.C. 1394; [2003] 2 B.C.L.C. 442; 75 T.C. 77; [2003] S.T.I. 1029; [2003] S.T.I. 1873............. 17–29
Lord Fisher DSC v Customs and Excise Commissioners [1981] 2 All E.R. 147; [1981] S.T.C. 238 25–71
Lowe v Ashmore [1971] 1 All E.R. 1057 6–05
Loyalty Management UK Ltd v Revenue and Customs Commissioners. *See* Revenue and Customs Commissioners v Loyalty Management UK Ltd
Lucas v Cattell 48 T.C. 353; [1972] T.R. 83.. 5–31
Lurcott v Wakeley & Wheeler [1911] 1 K.B. 905; [1911–13] All E.R. Rep. 41 CA.. 5–38
Lynall (Deceased), Re [1972] A.C. 680; [1971] 3 W.L.R. 759 HL................ 21–34
Lyon (Inspector of Taxes) v Pettigrew [1985] S.T.C. 369; 58 T.C. 452 15–28
Lyon's Personal Representatives v Revenue and Customs Commissioners [2007] S.T.C. (S.C.D.) 675; [2007] W.T.L.R. 1257; (2007) SpC 00616 19–17
McCall v Revenue and Customs Commissioners [2009] NICA 12; [2009] S.T.C. 990; [2009] N.I. 245 20–37
McClure (Inspector of Taxes) v Petre [1988] 1 W.L.R. 1386; [1988] S.T.C. 749; 61 T.C. 226; (1988) 85(17) L.S.G. 50; (1988) S.J. 1119 6–05
Macfarlane v Inland Revenue Commissioners 1929 S.C. 453; 1929 S.L.T. 395 IH.. 12–07
McGowan (Inspector of Taxes) v Brown & Cousins (t/a Stuart Edwards) [1977] 1 W.L.R. 1403; [1977] 3 All E.R. 844... 5–21
McGregor v Adcock [1977] 1 W.L.R. 864; [1977] S.T.C. 206...................... 17–20
McKnight v Sheppard [1999] 1 W.L.R. 1333; [1999] 3 All E.R. 491 HL 5–32, 5–34
MacNiven (Inspector of Taxes) v Westmoreland Investments Ltd [2001] UKHL 6; [2003] 1 A.C. 311; [2001] 2 W.L.R. 377 3–46
Maco Door and Window Hardware (UK) Ltd v Revenue and Customs Commissioners [2008] UKHL 54; [2008] 1 W.L.R. 1790; [2008] S.T.C. 2934 17–20

Macpherson v Inland Revenue Commissioners. *See* Inland Revenue
Commissioners v Macpherson
Mahageben kft v Nemzeti Ado- es Vamhivatal Del-dunantuli Regionalis
Ado Foigazgatosaga (C–80/11) [2012] S.T.C. 1934; [2013] C.E.C. 306;
[2012] S.T.I. 2733 27–37
Mairs (Inspector of Taxes) v Haughey [1994] 1 A.C. 303; [1993] 3 W.L.R.
393; [1993] 3 All E.R. 801; [1993] S.T.C. 569; [1993] I.R.L.R. 551; 66
T.C. 273; [1993] B.T.C. 339 9–09
Makins v Elson [1977] 1 W.L.R. 221; [1977] 1 All E.R. 572 17–05
Mallalieu v Drummond (Inspector of Taxes) [1983] 2 A.C. 861; [1983] 3
W.L.R. 409 HL .... 5–32—5–35
Mallender v Inland Revenue Commissioners [2001] S.T.C. 514; [2001]
B.T.C. 8013 20–39
Mansworth (Inspector of Taxes) v Jelley [2002] EWCA Civ 1829; [2003]
S.T.C. 53; 75 T.C. 1; [2003] B.T.C. 3; [2002] S.T.I. 1808; (2003) 100(10)
L.S.G. 29 .... 15–18, 15–42
Marcus Webb Golf Professional v Revenue and Customs Commissioners
[2013] EWCA Civ 1225 26–22
Markey (Inspector of Taxes) v Sanders [1987] 1 W.L.R. 864; [1987] S.T.C.
256 17–05
Marks & Spencer Plc v Customs and Excise Commissioners (No.1) [2000]
S.T.C. 16; [2000] 1 C.M.L.R. 256 CA 26–09
Marks & Spencer Plc v Customs and Excise Commissioners [2003] Q.B.
866; [2003] 2 W.L.R. 665 ECJ 2–28, 25–07, 25–11
Marks & Spencer Plc v Revenue and Customs Commissioners [2008]
S.T.C. 1405 ECJ 25–07, 25–09, 26–09
Marks & Spencer Plc v Revenue and Customs Commissioners [2009]
UKHL 8; [2009] 1 All E.R. 939; [2009] S.T.C. 452 25–09
Marks v Revenue and Customs Commissioners [2011] UKFTT 221 (TC);
[2011] S.T.I. 1842 .... 16–12, 21–33
Marquess of Linlithgow v Revenue and Customs Commissioners [2010]
CSIH 19; [2010] S.T.C. 1563; 2010 S.C. 391; 2011 S.L.T. 58; [2010]
B.T.C. 487; [2010] S.T.I. 1278; 2010 G.W.D. 11–206 .... 19–05, 19–06
Marren (Inspector of Taxes) v Ingles [1980] 1 W.L.R. 983; [1980] 3 All
E.R. 95 HL 16–04, 16–26
Marriott v Lane [1996] 1 W.L.R. 1211; [1996] S.T.C. 704 17–20
Marson (Inspector of Taxes) v Morton [1986] 1 W.L.R. 1343; [1986]
S.T.C. 463 5–08
Martin v Inland Revenue Commissioners [1995] S.T.C. (S.C.D.) 5 Sp
Comm 20–37
Martin v Lowry (Inspector of Taxes) [1927] A.C. 312 HL 5–11
Martin v Revenue and Customs Commissioners [2014] UKFTT 1021 (TC) ... 9–13
Matthews v Revenue and Customs Commissioners [2012] UKFTT 658
(TC); [2013] W.T.L.R. 93; [2013] S.T.I. 299 19–05
Mayes v Revenue and Customs Commissioners; sub nom. Revenue and
Customs Commissioners v Mayes [2011] EWCA Civ 407; [2011] S.T.C.
1269; 81 T.C. 247; [2011] B.T.C. 261; [2011] S.T.I. 1444 3–46
Mayflower Theatre Trust Ltd v Customs and Excise Commissioners
[2007] EWCA Civ 116; [2007] S.T.C. 880; [2007] B.T.C. 5221 ..... 27–43, 27–44
Melville v Inland Revenue Commissioners [2001] EWCA Civ 1247; [2002]
1 W.L.R. 407; [2001] S.T.C. 1271; 74 T.C. 372; [2001] B.T.C. 8039;
[2001] W.T.L.R. 887; (2001–02) 4 I.T.E.L.R. 231; [2001] S.T.I. 1106;
(2001) 98(37) L.S.G. 39; [2001] N.P.C. 132 .... 17–23, 19–06, 22–60

Mesto Zamberk v Financni reditelstvi Hradci Kralove (2014). *See* Zamberk v Financni reditelstvi v Hradci Kralove (C–18/12)

Midland Bank Plc v Customs and Excise Commissioners (C–98/98) [2000] 1 W.L.R. 2080; [2000] All E.R. (EC) 673 ECJ 26–27, 27–38, 27–40, 27–41, 27–44

Miller v Inland Revenue Commissioners [1987] S.T.C. 108 CS 22–17

Minden Trust (Cayman) v Inland Revenue Commissioners [1985] S.T.C. 758; (1985) 82 L.S.G. 2824 CA 22–08

Miners v Atkinson (Inspector of Taxes) [1997] S.T.C. 58; 68 T.C. 629; [1997] B.T.C. 32; (1996) 93(3) L.S.G. 29 9–41

Minister Finansow v MDDP sp z oo Akademia Biznesu sp komandytowa (C–319/12) [2014] S.T.C. 699; [2014] B.V.C. 11; [2013] S.T.I. 3775 26–22

Mitchell (Inspector of Taxes) v Ross [1960] Ch. 498; [1960] 2 W.L.R. 766 CA 9–05

Mobilx Ltd (In Administration) v Revenue and Customs Commissioners [2010] EWCA Civ 517; [2010] S.T.C. 1436; [2010] Lloyd's Rep. F.C. 445; [2010] B.V.C. 638; [2010] S.T.I. 1589 25–14

Moodie v Inland Revenue Commissioners [1993] 1 W.L.R. 266; [1993] 2 All E.R. 49 HL 3–45

Moore & Osbourne v Inland Revenue Commissioners. *See* Trafford's Settlement, Re

Moore v Griffiths (Inspector of Taxes) [1972] 1 W.L.R. 1024; [1972] 3 All E.R. 399 9–15

Moore v Thompson (Inspector of Taxes) [1986] S.T.C. 170; 60 T.C. 15 17–05

Moorhouse (Inspector of Taxes) v Dooland [1955] Ch. 284; [1955] 2 W.L.R. 96 CA 9–15

Moorthy v Revenue and Customs Commissioners [2016] UKUT 13 (TCC); [2016] I.R.L.R. 258; [2016] B.T.C. 501; [2016] S.T.I. 310 9–46

Morrison v Revenue and Customs Commissioners [2014] CSIH 113; [2015] S.T.C. 659; 2015 S.C. 392; 2015 S.L.T. 169; [2015] B.T.C. 1; 2015 G.W.D. 2–56 16–06

Munby v Furlong (Inspector of Taxes) [1977] Ch. 359; [1977] 3 W.L.R. 270 CA 8–10

Munro v Commissioner of Stamp Duties [1934] A.C. 61 PC (Aus) 19–19

Murray (Inspector of Taxes) v Goodhews [1978] 1 W.L.R. 499; [1978] 2 All E.R. 40 CA 5–21

Nadin v Inland Revenue Commissioners [1997] S.T.C. (SCD) 107 20–06

National and Provincial Building Society v UK [1997] S.T.C. 1466; (1998) 25 E.H.R.R. 127 ECHR 2–30

Naturally Yours Cosmetics Ltd v Customs and Excise Commissioners (C–230/87) [1988] S.T.C. 879; [1988] E.C.R. 6365 ECJ 25–43

Nelson Dance Family Settlement, Re [2009] EWHC 71 (Ch); [2009] S.T.C. 802; 79 T.C. 605 .... 20–36, 20–41

New Angel Court Ltd v Adam (Inspector of Taxes) [2004] EWCA Civ 242; [2004] 1 W.L.R. 1988; [2004] S.T.C. 779 15–32

Newsom v Robertson (Inspector of Taxes) [1953] Ch. 7; [1952] 2 All E.R. 728 CA 5–35

Nichols v Inland Revenue Commissioners [1975] 1 W.L.R. 534; [1975] 2 All E.R. 120 CA 19–19

Norbury Developments Ltd v Customs and Excise Commissioners (C–136/97) [1999] All E.R. (EC) 436; [1999] S.T.C. 511 ECJ 25–04

Norseman Gold Plc v Revenue and Customs Commissioners [2016] UKUT 69 (TCC) 25–42

O'Brien (Inspector of Taxes) v Benson's Hosiery (Holdings) Ltd [1980]
A.C. 562; [1979] 3 W.L.R. 572 HL 15–15, 15–21, 15–22
O'Grady v Bullcroft Main Colleries Ltd (1932)17 T.C. 93 5–38
O'Rourke v Binks [1992] S.T.C. 703 CA 15–33
Oakes v Commissioner of Stamp Duties of New South Wales [1954] A.C.
57; [1953] 3 W.L.R. 1127 PC (Aus) 19–17
Odeon Associated Theatres Ltd v Jones; sub nom. Odeon Cinemas Ltd v
Jones [1973] Ch. 288; [1972] 2 W.L.R. 331; [1972] 1 All E.R. 681; 48 T.C.
257; [1971] T.R. 373; (1971) 115 S.J. 850 .... 5–38, 16–02
Odeon Cinemas Ltd v Jones (1972). See Odeon Associated Theatres Ltd v
Jones
Odhams Leisure Group Ltd v Customs and Excise Commissioners [1992]
S.T.C. 332 26–15
Office des Produits Wallons ASBL v Belgium (C–184/00) [2003] All E.R.
(EC) 747; [2003] S.T.C. 1100 ECJ 27–05
Ogden v Trustees of the RHS Griffiths 2003 Settlement; sub nom. Griffiths
(Deceased), Re [2008] EWHC 118 (Ch); [2009] Ch. 162; [2009] 2 W.L.R.
394; [2008] 2 All E.R. 655; [2008] S.T.C. 776; [2009] B.T.C. 8027; [2008]
W.T.L.R. 685; [2008] S.T.I. 250 .... 20–35, 24–13
Optigen Ltd v Customs and Excise Commissioners [2006] Ch. 218; [2006]
S.T.C. 419 ECJ 25–14, 25–74
Oram v Johnson [1980] 1 W.L.R. 558; [1980] 2 All E.R. 1 16–10
Ostime (Inspector of Taxes) v Duple Motor Bodies Ltd; sub nom. Duple
Motor Bodies v Ostime [1961] 1 W.L.R. 739; [1961] 2 All E.R. 167; 39
T.C. 537; (1961) 40 A.T.C. 21; [1961] T.R. 29; (1961) 105 S.J. 346 5–24
Owen v Elliott (Inspector of Taxes) [1990] Ch. 786; [1990] 3 W.L.R. 133
CA 17–08
Owen v Pook (Inspector of Taxes) [1970] A.C. 244; [1969] 2 W.L.R. 775 HL .. 9–41
PA Holdings Ltd v Revenue and Customs Commissioners; sub nom.
Revenue and Customs Commissioners v PA Holdings [2011] EWCA
Civ 1414; [2012] S.T.C. 582; 82 T.C. 1; [2011] B.T.C. 705; [2011] S.T.I.
3268 .... 9–08, 11–15
Padmore v Inland Revenue Commissioners [2001] S.T.C. 280; 73 T.C. 470;
[2001] B.T.C. 36; 3 I.T.L. Rep. 315; [2001] S.T.I. 99; (2001) 98(6) L.S.G.
46; (2001) 145 S.J.L.B. 27 12–17
Parker Hale Ltd v Customs and Excise Commissioners [2000] S.T.C. 388;
[2000] B.T.C. 5153 25–35
Parsons [1943] Ch. 12 CA 19–05
Partridge v Mallandaine (1887) L.R. 18 Q.B.D. 276 5–14
Pawson (Deceased) v Revenue and Customs Commissioners [2013] UKUT
50 (TCC); [2013] S.T.C. 976; [2013] B.T.C. 1605; [2013] W.T.L.R. 469;
[2013] S.T.I. 584 20–37
Pearson v Inland Revenue Commissioners [1980] Ch. 1; [1979] 3 W.L.R.
112 CA 22–15
Pendragon Plc v Revenue and Customs Commissioners; sub nom.
Revenue and Customs Commissioners v Pendragon Plc [2015] UKSC
37; [2015] 1 W.L.R. 2838; [2015] 3 All E.R. 919; [2015] S.T.C. 1825;
[2015] B.V.C. 30; [2015] S.T.I. 1921 .... 2–20, 2–22, 25–16
Pepper (Inspector of Taxes) v Hart [1993] A.C. 593; [1992] 3 W.L.R.
1032; [1993] 1 All E.R. 42; [1992] S.T.C. 898; [1993] I.C.R. 291; [1993]
I.R.L.R. 33; [1993] R.V.R. 127; (1993) 143 N.L.J. 17; [1992] N.P.C.
154 .... 3–35, 3–43, 9–28
Pepper v Daffurn [1993] S.T.C. 466 17–20

Peugeot Motor Co Plc v Customs and Excise Commissioners [2003]
EWHC 2304 (Ch); [2003] S.T.C. 1438 .... 25–54, 25–61
Phillips v Revenue and Customs Commissioners [2006] S.T.C. (S.C.D.)
639; [2006] W.T.L.R. 1281 Sp Comm 20–37
Phizackerley v Revenue and Customs Commissioners [2007] S.T.C.
(S.C.D.) 328; [2007] W.T.L.R. 745; (2007) Sp Comm 00591 .... 20–16, 21–23
Pickford v Quirke (1927) 13 T.C. 662 CA 5–10
Pilgrims Language Courses Ltd v Customs and Excise Commissioners
[1999] S.T.C. 874; [2000] E.L.R. 18 CA 25–54
Pimblett (John) and Sons v Customs and Excise Commissioners [1988]
S.T.C. 358 CA 26–13
Pirelli v Revenue and Customs Commissioners (No.2) [2008] EWCA Civ
70; [2008] S.T.C. 508; [2008] 2 C.M.L.R. 19 2–29
Pitt (Inspector of Taxes) v Castle Hill Warehousing Co [1974] 1 W.L.R.
1624; [1974] 3 All E.R. 146; [1974] S.T.C. 420; [1974] T.R. 219; (1974)
118 S.J. 864 5–28
PM v United Kingdom [2005] S.T.C. 1566; [2005] 3 F.C.R. 101
ECHR 2–30
Polysar Investments Netherlands BV v Inspecteur der Invoerrechten en
Accijnzen Arnhem (C–60/90) [1993] S.T.C. 222; [1991] E.C.R. I-3111
ECJ 25–67
POWA (Jersey) Ltd v Revenue and Customs Commissioners [2012]
UKUT 50 (TCC); [2012] S.T.C. 1476; [2012] B.V.C. 1596 25–14
PricewaterhouseCooper v Information Commissioner [2011] UKUT 372
(AAC) 4–20
Proctor & Gamble UK v Revenue and Customs Commissioners [2009]
EWCA Civ 407; [2009] S.T.C. 1990; [2009] B.T.C. 5462 .... 26–10, 26–11
Purple Parking Ltd v Revenue and Customs Commissioners (C–117/11)
[2012] S.T.C. 1680; [2012] B.V.C. 268; [2012] S.T.I. 2546 .... 25–55, 25–56
Purves v Harrison [2001] S.T.C. 267; 73 T.C. 390 17–20
PwC v Information Commissioner v HMRC. See PricewaterhouseCooper
v Information Commissioner
R. (on the application of Cart) v Upper Tribunal [2011] UKSC 28; [2012]
1 A.C. 663; [2011] 3 W.L.R. 107; [2011] 4 All E.R. 127; [2011] P.T.S.R.
1053; [2011] S.T.C. 1659; [2012] 1 F.L.R. 997; [2011] Imm. A.R. 704;
[2011] M.H.L.R. 196; [2012] Fam. Law 398; [2011] S.T.I. 1943; (2011)
161 N.L.J. 916; (2011) 155(25) S.J.L.B. 35 2–22
R. (on the application of Huitson) v Revenue and Customs Commissioners
[2011] EWCA Civ 893; [2012] Q.B. 489; [2012] 2 W.L.R. 490; [2011]
S.T.C. 1860; [2011] B.T.C. 456; 14 I.T.L. Rep. 90; [2011] S.T.I. 2307;
[2011] N.P.C. 91 2–22
R. (on the application of Premier Foods (Holdings) Ltd) v Revenue and
Customs Commissioners [2015] EWHC 1483 (Admin); [2015] S.T.C.
2384; [2015] B.V.C. 29; [2015] S.T.I. 1737 27–49
R. (on the application of Prudential Plc) v Special Commissioner of
Income Tax [2013] UKSC 1; [2013] 2 A.C. 185; [2013] 2 W.L.R. 325;
[2013] 2 All E.R. 247; [2013] S.T.C. 376; [2013] 2 Costs L.R. 275; [2013]
1 F.C.R. 545; 82 T.C. 64; [2013] B.T.C. 45; [2013] C.I.L.L. 3309; [2013]
S.T.I. 264; [2013] 5 E.G. 96 (C.S.); (2013) 163 N.L.J. 109 1–22
R. (on the application of Rowe) v Revenue and Customs Commissioners
[2015] EWHC 2293 (Admin); [2015] B.T.C. 27 2–31
R. (on the application of Wilkinson) v Inland Revenue Commissioners
[2005] UKHL 30; [2005] 1 W.L.R. 1718; [2006] 1 All E.R. 529; [2006]

S.T.C. 270; [2005] U.K.H.R.R. 704; 77 T.C. 78; [2005] S.T.I. 904; (2005)
102(25) L.S.G. 33 3–25
R. v Customs and Excise Commissioners Ex p. Sims [1988] S.T.C. 210;
[1987] B.T.C. 5057 26–12
R. v Customs and Excise Commissioners Ex p. Building Societies
Ombudsman Co Ltd [2000] S.T.C. 892; [2000] B.T.C. 5384 CA 25–07
R. v Hashash [2006] EWCA Crim 2518; [2008] S.T.C. 1158; [2008] B.T.C.
5173 25–74
R. v Inland Revenue Commissioners [2003] S.T.C. 1113 CA 2–30
Raha v Revenue and Customs Commissioners (2010) (52TC281) [2010]
S.T.I. 259 .... 16–02, 16–07
Ramsay (WT) Ltd v Inland Revenue Commissioners [1982] A.C. 300;
[1981] 2 W.L.R. 449; [1981] 1 All E.R. 865; [1981] S.T.C. 174; 54 T.C.
101; [1982] T.R. 123; (1981) 11 A.T.R. 752; (1981) 125 S.J. 220 3–42,
3–45—3–47, 3–50, 16–08, 19–38
Randall v Plumb [1975] 1 W.L.R. 633; [1975] 1 All E.R. 734 .... 16–05, 16–06
Rank Group Ltd v Revenue and Customs Commissioners (C–259/10)
[2012] S.T.C. 23; [2011] B.V.C. 389 ECJ 25–09, 26–23
Ransom (Inspector of Taxes) v Higgs [1974] 1 W.L.R. 1594; [1974] 3 All
E.R. 949 HL 5–06
Ratcliffe v Revenue and Customs Commissioners [2013] UKFTT 420 (TC) ...9–42
Redlihs v Valsts ienemumu dienests (C–263/11) [2013] S.T.C. 144 25–74
Reed Employment Ltd v Revenue and Customs Commissioners [2014]
EWCA Civ 32; [2014] S.T.C. 1026; [2014] B.V.C. 6; [2014] S.T.I. 868 27–48
Reed Employment Plc v Revenue and Customs Commissioners [2015]
EWCA Civ 805; [2015] B.T.C. 24; [2015] S.T.I. 2531 9–12
Reetsma Cigarettenfabriken GmbH v Ministerio delle Finanze (C–35/05)
[2008] S.T.C. 3448; [2007] E.C.R. I-2425 ECJ 25–11, 27–49
Regent Oil Co Ltd v Strick (Inspector of Taxes) [1966] A.C. 295; [1965] 3
W.L.R. 636 HL 5–29
Reisdorf v Finanzamt Koln-West (C–85/95) [1997] S.T.C. 180; [1996]
E.C.R. I-6257 ECJ 27–34
Revenue and Customs Commissioners v Apollo Fuels Ltd [2016] EWCA
Civ 157; [2016] B.T.C. 12; [2016] S.T.I. 1155 9–30
Revenue and Customs Commissioners v Atkinson [2011] UKUT 506
(TCC); [2012] S.T.C. 289; [2011] B.T.C. 1917; [2012] W.T.L.R. 197;
[2012] S.T.I. 277 20–45
Revenue and Customs Commissioners v Banerjee [2010] EWCA Civ 843;
[2011] 1 W.L.R. 702; [2011] 1 All E.R. 985; [2010] S.T.C. 2318; 80 T.C.
205; [2010] B.T.C. 662; [2010] S.T.I. 2347 9–39
Revenue and Customs Commissioners v Bower (Deceased), Re. See
Bower v Revenue and Customs Commissioners
Revenue and Customs Commissioners v Bridport and West Dorset Golf
Club (C–495/12) [2014] S.T.C. 663; [2014] B.V.C. 1; [2014] S.T.I. 257 26–18
Revenue and Customs Commissioners v Brockenhurst College [2015]
EWCA Civ 1196; [2015] B.V.C. 52; [2016] S.T.I. 72 26–22
Revenue and Customs Commissioners v Collins [2009] EWHC 284 (Ch);
[2009] S.T.C. 1077; 79 T.C. 524; [2009] B.T.C. 91; [2009] S.T.I. 552 16–03
Revenue and Customs Commissioners v Compass Contract Services UK
Ltd [2006] EWCA Civ 730; [2006] S.T.C. 19[2006] EWCA Civ 730;
[2006] S.T.C. 1999; [2006] B.T.C. 5499; [2006] B.V.C. 569; [2006] L.L.R.
408; [2006] S.T.I. 162299 .... 26–12—26–14
Revenue and Customs Commissioners v David Baxendale Ltd [2009]

EWCA Civ 831; [2009] S.T.C. 2578; [2009] B.V.C. 663; [2009] S.T.I.
2348 25–55
Revenue and Customs Commissioners v Decadt [2007] EWHC 1659
(Ch); [2008] S.T.C. 1103; 79 T.C. 220; [2007] B.T.C. 586; [2007] S.T.I.
1434 9–39
Revenue and Customs Commissioners v Dempster (t/a Boulevard) [2008]
EWHC 63 (Ch); [2008] S.T.C. 2079; [2008] B.T.C. 5150; [2008] B.V.C.
275; [2008] S.T.I. 185.. 27–37
Revenue and Customs Commissioners v EB Central Services Ltd (for-
merly Excess Baggage Plc) [2008] EWCA Civ 486; [2008] S.T.C. 2209;
[2008] B.T.C. 5423; [2008] B.V.C. 543; [2008] S.T.I. 1361 26–09
Revenue and Customs Commissioners v Empowerment Enterprises Ltd
[2006] CSIH 46; [2008] S.T.C. 1835; 2007 S.C. 12[2006] CSIH 46; [2008]
S.T.C. 1835; 2007 S.C. 123; 2006 S.L.T. 955; [2007] B.T.C. 5931; [2007]
B.V.C. 878; [2006] S.T.I. 2344; 2006 G.W.D. 32–6823 26–19
Revenue and Customs Commissioners v Forde & McHugh Ltd [2014]
UKSC 14; [2014] 1 W.L.R. 810; [2014] 2 All E.R. 356; [2014] S.T.C. 724;
[2014] I.C.R. 403; [2014] Pens. L.R. 203; 82 T.C. 165; [2014] B.T.C. 8;
[2014] S.T.I. 739 3–55
Revenue and Customs Commissioners v Frank A Smart and Sons Ltd
[2016] UKUT 121 (TCC); [2016] B.V.C. 511; [2016] S.T.I. 1339 27–44
Revenue and Customs Commissioners v Gracechurch Management
Services Ltd [2007] EWHC 755 (Ch); [2008] S.T.C. 795; [2007] B.T.C.
5468; [2007] B.V.C. 379; [2007] S.T.I. 1173; (2007) 151 S.J.L.B. 507;
[2007] N.P.C. 39 27–35
Revenue and Customs Commissioners v Greener Solutions Ltd [2012]
UKUT 18 (TCC); [2012] S.T.C. 1056; [2012] Lloyd's Rep. F.C. 235;
[2012] B.V.C. 1551 25–14
Revenue and Customs Commissioners v Jeancharm Ltd (t/a Beaver
International) [2005] EWHC 839 (Ch); [2005] S.T.C. 918; [2005] B.T.C.
5285; [2005] B.V.C. 316; [2005] S.T.I. 907 27–35
Revenue and Customs Commissioners v Littlewoods Trading Ltd. See
Littlewoods Retail Ltd v Revenue and Customs Commissioners
Revenue and Customs Commissioners v Livewire Telecom Ltd [2009]
EWHC 15 (Ch); [2009] S.T.C. 643; [2009] B.T.C. 5173; [2009] B.V.C.
172; [2009] S.T.I. 190.. 25–14
Revenue and Customs Commissioners v London Clubs Management
[2011] EWCA Civ 1323; [2012] S.T.C. 388; [2011] B.V.C. 406; [2011]
S.T.I. 3187.. 27–45
Revenue and Customs Commissioners v Lord Howard of Henderskelfe's
Executors [2014] EWCA Civ 278; [2014] 1 W.L.R. 3902; [2014] 3 All
E.R. 50; [2014] S.T.C. 1100; [2014] B.T.C. 12; [2014] W.T.L.R. 791;
[2014] S.T.I. 1560 17–13
Revenue and Customs Commissioners v Loyalty Management UK Ltd
(C–53/09) [2010] S.T.C. 2651; [2011] B.V.C. 1; [2010] S.T.I. 2706........... 25–52
Revenue and Customs Commissioners v Loyalty Management UK Ltd
[2013] UKSC 15; [2013] 2 All E.R. 719; [2013] S.T.C. 784; [2013] 2
C.M.L.R. 51; [2013] B.V.C. 67; [2013] S.T.I. 591 .... 25–52, 27–20
Revenue and Customs Commissioners v McLaren Racing Ltd [2014]
UKUT 269 (TCC); [2014] S.T.C. 2417; 82 T.C. 345; [2014] B.T.C. 518;
[2014] S.T.I. 2288 5–34
Revenue and Customs Commissioners v Moorbury Ltd [2010] UKUT 360
(TCC); [2010] S.T.C. 2715; [2010] B.V.C. 1553; [2010] S.T.I. 2640 25–15

Revenue and Customs Commissioners v Newey (t/a Ocean Finance) (C–653/11) [2013] S.T.C. 2432; [2013] B.V.C. 259; [2013] S.T.I. 2304 25–16

Revenue and Customs Commissioners v Open University [2016] EWCA Civ 114; [2016] S.T.I. 519 25–65

Revenue and Customs Commissioners v PA Holdings (2011). *See* PA Holdings Ltd v Revenue and Customs Commissioners

Revenue and Customs Commissioners v Pal (t/a Tapas Bar Cerveceria) [2006] EWHC 2016 (Ch); [2008] S.T.C. 2442; [2007] B.T.C. 5967; [2008] B.V.C. 3; [2006] S.T.I. 2074 25–66

Revenue and Customs Commissioners v Pendragon (2015). *See* Pendragon Plc v Revenue and Customs Commissioners

Revenue and Customs Commissioners v Robert Gordon University Governors [2008] CSIH 22; [2008] S.T.C. 1890; 2008 S.C. 419; 2008 S.L.T. 476; 2008 S.C.L.R. 299; [2008] B.T.C. 5348; [2008] B.V.C. 469; [2008] S.T.I. 943; 2008 G.W.D. 13–251 26–22

Revenue and Customs Commissioners v Robertson's Electrical Ltd [2005] CSIH 75; [2007] S.T.C. 612; 2006 S.C. 261; 2005 S.L.T. 1149; 2006 S.C.L.R. 493; [2007] B.T.C. 5763; [2007] B.V.C. 710; [2005] S.T.I. 1813; 2005 G.W.D. 37–699 27–32

Revenue and Customs Commissioners v S&I Electronics Plc [2012] UKUT 87 (TCC); [2012] S.T.C. 1620; [2012] Eu. L.R. 600; [2012] Lloyd's Rep. F.C. 449; [2012] B.V.C. 1629 25–14

Revenue and Customs Commissioners v School of Finance and Management (London) Ltd. *See* School of Finance and Management (London) Ltd v Customs and Excise Commissioners

Revenue and Customs Commissioners v Total Network SL [2008] UKHL 19; [2008] 1 A.C. 1174; [2008] 2 W.L.R. 711; [2008] 2 All E.R. 413; [2008] S.T.C. 644; [2008] Lloyd's Rep. F.C. 275; [2008] B.P.I.R. 699; [2008] B.T.C. 5216; [2008] B.V.C. 340; [2008] S.T.I. 938; (2008) 152(12) S.J.L.B. 29 25–13

Revenue and Customs Commissioners v Total UK Ltd (2008). *See* Total UK Ltd v Revenue and Customs Commissioners

Revenue and Customs Commissioners v UBS (2016). *See* UBS AG v Revenue and Customs Commissioners

Revenue and Customs Commissioners v Weald Leasing Ltd [2011] S.T.C. 596; [2011] C.E.C. 1039; [2011] B.V.C. 118; [2011] S.T.I. 264 .... 25–08, 25–16

Revenue and Customs Commissioners v Weight Watchers UK Ltd [2008]. *See* Weight Watchers (UK) Ltd v Revenue and Customs Commissioners

Revenue and Customs Commissioners v William Grant & Sons Distillers Ltd. *See* Revenue and Customs Commissioners v William Grant & Sons Distillers Ltd

Revenue and Customs Commissioners v William Grant & Sons Distillers Ltd (Scotland) [2007] UKHL 15; [2007] 1 W.L.R. 1448; [2007] 2 All E.R. 440 5–16

Reynaud v Inland Revenue Commissioners [1999] S.T.C. (S.C.D.) 185 Sp Comm 19–38

Rice v Revenue and Customs Commissioners [2014] UKFTT 133 (TC)..... 17–20

Ricketts v Colquhoun (Inspector of Taxes) [1926] A.C. 1; 10 T.C. 118 HL 9–38, 9–41

Robson v Mitchell [2005] EWCA Civ 585; [2005] S.T.C. 893; [2005] B.T.C. 321 15–37

Rolfe (Inspector of Taxes) v Nagel [1982] S.T.C. 53; 55 T.C. 585 CA........... 5–21

Roome v Edwards (Inspector of Taxes) [1982] A.C. 279; [1981] 2 W.L.R.
268 HL.. 15–65
Rosgill Group Ltd v Customs and Excise Commissioners [1997] 3 All E.R.
1012; [1997] S.T.C. 811 CA 25–43, 25–45, 27–06, 27–09, 27–16
Roskams v Bennett 44 R. & I.T. 76; 32 T.C. 129; (1950) 29 A.T.C. 281........ 9–38
Rosser v Inland Revenue Commissioners [2003] S.T.C. (S.C.D.) 311;
[2003] W.T.L.R. 1057; [2003] S.T.I. 1152 ....20–43—20–45
Rowe v HMRC (2015). See R. (on the application of Rowe) v Revenue
and Customs Commissioners
Royal Bank of Scotland Group Plc v Customs and Excise Commissioners
(Reciprocity Fees) [2002] S.T.C. 575; 2002 S.L.T. 664 IH 26–25
Royal Bank of Scotland Group Plc v Revenue and Customs Commissioners
(C–488/07) [2009] S.T.C. 461; [2008] E.C.R. I-10409; [2009] C.E.C. 398;
[2009] B.T.C. 5249; [2009] B.V.C. 248; [2009] S.T.I. 89 27–45
Royscot Leasing Ltd v Customs and Excise Commissioners (C–305/97)
[2000] 1 W.L.R. 1151; [1999] All E.R. (EC) 908 ECJ............................... 27–36
Russell v Inland Revenue Commissioners [1988] 1 W.L.R. 834; [1988] 2
All E.R. 405 .... 20–30, 20–36
Russell v Revenue and Customs Commissioners [2012] UKFTT 623
(TC).. 17–20
Rutledge v Inland Revenue Commissioners 1929 S.C. 379; 1929 S.L.T.
296 5–08
Rysaffe Trustee Co (CI) Ltd v Inland Revenue Commissioners [2003]
EWCA Civ 356; [2003] S.T.C. 536.................................. 19–38, 22–08, 22–36
SA Dangerville v France [2003] S.T.C. 771; (2004) 38 E.H.R.R. 32 ECHR .. 2–30
Salt v Chamberlain [1979] S.T.C. 750; 53 T.C. 143 5–08
Samadian v Revenue and Customs Commissioners [2014] UKUT 13
(TCC); [2014] S.T.C. 763; 82 T.C. 252; [2014] B.T.C. 504; [2014] S.T.I.
586 5–35
Samuel Jones & Co (Devonvale) Ltd v Inland Revenue Commissioners
1952 S.C. 94; 1952 S.L.T. 144 IH 5–38
Sansom v Peay (Inspector of Taxes) [1976] 1 W.L.R. 1073; [1976] 3 All
E.R. 375 17–08
School of Finance and Management (London) Ltd v Customs and Excise
Commissioners [2001] S.T.C. 1690; [2002] B.T.C. 5030; [2002] B.V.C.
158; [2001] S.T.I. 1663.. 26–22
Scott v Ricketts [1967] 1 W.L.R. 828; [1967] 2 All E.R. 1009 CA.................. 7–35
Scottish Football League v Revenue and Customs Commissioners [2013]
UKUT 160 (TCC).. 25–61
Secretan v Hart [1969] 1 W.L.R. 1599; [1969] 3 All E.R. 1196 15–02
Seymour v Reed (Inspector of Taxes) [1927] A.C. 554 HL............................ 9–15
Sharkey (Inspector of Taxes) v Wernher [1956] A.C. 58; [1955] 3 W.L.R.
671; [1955] 3 All E.R. 493; 48 R. & I.T. 739; 36 T.C. 275; (1955) 34
A.T.C. 263; [1955] T.R. 277; (1955) 99 S.J. 793 5–25
Shilton v Wilmshurst (Inspector of Taxes) [1991] 1 A.C. 684; [1991] 2
W.L.R. 530 HL.. 9–09
SHIPS2. See Mayes v Revenue and Customs Commissioners
Sillars v Inland Revenue Commissioners [2004] S.T.C. (S.C.D.) 180; [2004]
W.T.L.R. 591 Sp Comm 19–05, 19–16
Simpson (Inspector of Taxes) v Tate [1925] 2 K.B. 214; 9 T.C. 314 KBD..... 9–39
Simpson v John Reynolds & Co (Insurances) Ltd [1975] 1 W.L.R. 617;
[1975] 2 All E.R. 88 CA.. 5–21
Skerritts of Nottingham Ltd v Secretary of State for the Environment,

Transport and the Regions (No.2) [2000] 2 P.L.R. 102; [2000] J.P.L. 1025 CA 17–06

Smith (Inspector of Taxes) v Abbott [1994] 1 W.L.R. 306; [1994] 1 All E.R. 673 HL 9–39

Smith v Revenue and Customs Commissioners [2007] EWHC 2304 (Ch); [2008] S.T.C. 1649; 78 T.C. 819 19–36

Smith's Potato Estates Ltd v Bolland (Inspector of Taxes) [1948] A.C. 508; [1948] 2 All E.R. 367 HL 5–36

Snell v Revenue and Customs Commissioners [2006] EWHC 3350 (Ch); [2007] S.T.C. 1279 15–35

Snushall (Geoffrey E) Ltd v Customs and Excise Commissioners [1982] S.T.C. 537; [1982] B.T.C. 5028 26–15

Spearmint Rhino Ventures (UK) Ltd v Revenue and Customs Commissioners [2007] EWHC 613 (Ch); [2007] S.T.C. 1252 25–78

Spectros International Plc (In Voluntary Liquidation) v Madden (Inspector of Taxes) [1997] S.T.C. 114; 70 T.C. 349 16–04

Springthorpe v Revenue and Customs Commissioners [2010] UKFTT 582 (TC); [2011] S.T.I. 1220 17–04

St Barbe Green v Inland Revenue Commissioners [2005] EWHC 14 (Ch); [2005] 1 W.L.R. 1772; [2005] S.T.C. 288 19–04

St Helen's School (Northern) Ltd v Revenue and Customs Commissioners [2006] EWHC 3306 (Ch); [2007] S.T.C. 633; [2007] B.T.C. 5059 27–45

Staatssecretaris van Financien v Coffeeshop Siberie vof (C–158/98) [1999] All E.R. (EC) 560; [1999] S.T.C. 742 ECJ 25–09, 25–30

Staatssecretaris van Financien v Heerma (C–23/98) [2001] S.T.C. 1437; [2000] E.C.R. I-419 ECJ 25–66

Staatssecretaris van Financien v Shipping & Forwarding Enterprise Safe BV (C–320/88) [1991] S.T.C. 627; [1990] E.C.R. I- 285 ECJ 25–33

Stamp Duties Commissioner of New South Wales v Permanent Trustee Co (1956). *See* Commissioner of Stamp Duties (NSW) v Permanent Trustee Co of New South Wales

Stanley v Inland Revenue Commissioners [1944] K.B. 255 CA 12–09

Stanton Ltd v Drayton Commercial Investment Co Ltd [1983] 1 A.C. 501; [1982] 3 W.L.R. 214 HL 16–10

Starke v Inland Revenue Commissioners [1995] 1 W.L.R. 1439; [1996] 1 All E.R. 622 CA 20–44

Steibelt (Inspector of Taxes) v Paling [1999] S.T.C. 594; 71 T.C. 376 17–28

Stenhouse's Trustees v Lord Advocate [1984] S.T.C. 195; 1984 S.C. 12 OH... 22–15

Stephenson (Inspector of Taxes) v Barclays Bank Trust Co Ltd [1975] 1 W.L.R. 882; [1975] 1 All E.R. 625 ....15–50—15–52

Stevenson (Inspector of Taxes) v Wishart [1987] 1 W.L.R. 1204; [1987] 2 All E.R. 428 CA 12–08

Stewart (t/a GT Shooting) v Customs and Excise Commissioners [2001] EWCA Civ 1988; [2002] S.T.C. 255; [2002] B.T.C. 5238 .... 25–35, 25–42

Strong & Co of Romsey Ltd v Woodifield (Surveyor of Taxes) [1906] A.C. 448 HL 5–34

Sub One Ltd (t/a Subway) v Revenue and Customs Commissioners [2014] EWCA Civ 773; [2014] S.T.C. 2508; [2014] B.V.C. 29; [2014] S.T.I. 2111 .... 25–07, 25–09, 26–09, 26–13

Sumption v Greenwich LBC [2007] EWHC 2776 (Admin); [2008] 1 P. & C.R. 20; [2008] J.P.L. 783 17–06

Supreme Petfoods Ltd v Revenue and Customs Commissioners [2011] UKFTT 19 (TC) 26–10

Swires (Inspector of Taxes) v Renton [1991] S.T.C. 490; 64 T.C.
315 15–66
T-Mobile Austria GmbH v Republic of Austria (C–284/04)[2008] S.T.C.
184; [2007] E.C.R. I-5189 ECJ.. 25–73
Talacre Beach Caravan Sales Ltd v Customs and Excise Commissioners
[2006] S.T.C. 1671; [2006] E.C.R. I-6269 ECJ 25–60, 26–09
Tarlo Worldwide Ltd v Revenue and Customs Commissioners [2012]
UKFTT 85 (TC) 25–14
Taxation Commissioner of Australia v Squatting Investment Co [1954]
A.C. 182; [1954] 2 W.L.R. 186 PC (Aus)..................................... 5–21
Taylor Clark International Ltd v Lewis (Inspector of Taxes) [1998] S.T.C.
1259; 71 T.C. 226 CA.. 15–38
Taylor v Good (Inspector of Taxes) [1973] 1 W.L.R. 1249; [1973] 2 All
E.R. 785... 5–13
Taylor v Provan (Inspector of Taxes) [1975] A.C. 194; [1974] 2 W.L.R. 394
HL 9–38, 9–41
Teleos Plc v Customs and Excise Commissioners [2007] S.T.I. 2216; [2008]
1 C.M.L.R. 6 ECJ 25–13
Telewest Communications Plc v Customs and Excise Commissioners
[2005] EWCA Civ 102; [2005] S.T.C. 481; [2005] B.T.C. 5125 ...... 25–34, 25–58
Tennant v Smith (Surveyor of Taxes) [1892] A.C. 150 HL........................... 9–31
Tesco Plc v Customs and Excise Commissioners [2003] EWCA Civ 1367;
[2003] S.T.C. 1561 27–17
Thorncroft Ltd v Revenue and Customs Commissioners [2011] UKFTT
694 (TC)... 26–10
Todd (Inspector of Taxes) v Mudd [1987] S.T.C. 141; 60 T.C. 237 17–29
Tolsma v Inspecteur der Omzetbelasting, Leeuwarden (C–16/93) [1994]
S.T.C. 509; [1994] E.C.R. I-743 ECJ 25–42
Tomlinson (Inspector of Taxes) v Glyn's Executor & Trustee Co [1970]
Ch. 112; [1969] 3 W.L.R. 310 CA.. 15–52
Total UK Ltd v Revenue and Customs Commissioners; sub nom. Revenue
and Customs Commissioners v Total UK Ltd [2007] EWCA Civ 987;
[2008] S.T.C. 19; [2007] B.T.C. 5895; [2007] B.V.C. 762; [2007] S.T.I.
2562; (2007) 104(42) L.S.G. 32 .... 27–20, 27–25
Tower MCashback LLP 1 v Revenue and Customs Commissioners [2011]
UKSC 19; [2011] 2 A.C. 457; [2011] 2 W.L.R. 1131 3–46
Tower Radio Ltd v Revenue and Customs Commissioners [2015] UKUT
60 (TCC); [2015] S.T.C. 1257; [2015] B.T.C. 505 9–48
Town & County Factors Ltd v Customs and Excise Commissioners
(C–498/99) [2003] All E.R. (EC) 33; [2002] S.T.C. 1263 ECJ................... 25–42
Town & County Factors Ltd v Customs and Excise Commissioners [1998]
S.T.C. 225; [1998] B.T.C. 5012 25–20
Trafford's Settlement, Re [1985] Ch. 32; [1984] 3 W.L.R. 341; [1984] 1
All E.R. 1108; [1984] S.T.C. 236; (1984) 81 L.S.G. 900; (1984) 128 S.J.
333 22–15
Tremerton Ltd v Customs and Excise Commissioners [1999] S.T.C. 1039;
[1999] B.T.C. 5413.. 27–40
Trinity Mirror Plc (formerly Mirror Group Newspapers Ltd) v Customs
and Excise Commissioners [2003] EWHC 480 (Ch); [2003] S.T.C. 518;
[2003] B.T.C. 5516.. 25–36
Trustees of FD Fenston Will Trusts v Revenue and Customs
Commissioners [2007] S.T.C. (S.C.D.) 316; [2007] S.T.I. 556 16–07
Trustees of the Nell Gwynn House Maintenance Fund v Customs and

Excise Commissioners [1999] 1 W.L.R. 174; [1999] 1 All E.R. 385 HL .. 25–49, 27–06
Tucker v Granada Motorway Services Ltd [1979] 1 W.L.R. 683; [1979] 2 All E.R. 801 HL 5–28
Turner v Follett [1973] S.T.C. 148; 48 T.C. 614 CA 15–17
UBS AG v Revenue and Customs Commissioners; sub nom. DB Group Services (UK) Ltd v Revenue and Customs Commissioners [2016] UKSC 13; [2016] 1 W.L.R. 1005; [2016] S.T.C. 934; [2016] B.T.C. 11; [2016] S.T.I. 513 ....3–47, 3–57, 9–48, 11–15
Underwood v Revenue and Customs Commissioners [2008] EWCA Civ 1483; [2009] S.T.C. 239 15–27
Unilever (UK) Holdings Ltd v Smith (Inspector of Taxes) [2002] EWCA Civ 1787; [2003] S.T.C. 15; 76 T.C. 300 15–34
United Biscuits (UK) Ltd v Revenue and Customs Commissioners [2011] UKFTT 673 (TC) 26–11
University of Huddersfield Higher Education Corp v Revenue and Customs Commissioners [2014] UKUT 438 (TCC); [2015] S.T.C. 307; [2014] B.V.C. 537; [2014] S.T.I. 3076 25–16
University of Southampton v Revenue and Customs Commissioners [2006] EWHC 528 (Ch); [2006] S.T.C. 1389; [2006] B.T.C. 5450 25–72
Vaines v Revenue and Customs Commissioners [2016] UKUT 2 (TCC); [2016] S.T.C. 1201; [2016] B.T.C. 502; [2016] S.T.I. 239 5–32
Value Catering Ltd v Revenue and Customs Commissioners [2011] UKFTT 329 (TC); [2011] S.F.T.D. 868; [2011] S.T.I. 1913 26–14
Van den Berghs Ltd v Clark (Inspector of Taxes) [1935] A.C. 431; 19 T.C. 390 HL 5–19
Van der Steen v Inspecteur van de Belastingdienst (C–355/06) [2008] S.T.C. 2379; [2007] E.C.R. I-8863 ECJ 25–64
Varty (Inspector of Taxes) v Lynes [1976] 1 W.L.R. 1091; [1976] 3 All E.R. 447 17–07
Vaughan-Jones v Vaughan-Jones [2015] EWHC 1086 (Ch); [2015] W.T.L.R. 1287; [2015] S.T.I. 188 20–28
Vehicle Control Services Ltd v Revenue and Customs Commissioners [2013] EWCA Civ 186; [2013] S.T.C. 892; [2013] R.T.R. 24; [2013] B.V.C. 99; [2013] S.T.I. 593 25–48
Vertigan v Brady (Inspector of Taxes) [1988] S.T.C. 91; 60 T.C. 624; (1988) 85(7) L.S.G. 40 9–23
Vestey v Inland Revenue Commissioners [1962] Ch. 861; [1962] 2 W.L.R. 221 7–26
Volkswagen Financial Services (UK) Ltd v Revenue and Customs Commissioners [2015] EWCA Civ 832; [2016] S.T.C. 417; [2015] B.V.C. 32; [2015] S.T.I. 2533 .... 27–44, 27–45
Wakefield College v Revenue and Customs Commissioners [2016] UKUT 19 (TCC); [2016] S.T.C. 1219; [2016] B.V.C. 501; [2016] S.T.I. 247 25–42
Wakeling v Pearce [1995] S.T.C. (SCD) 107 17–07
Walding v Inland Revenue Commissioners [1996] S.T.C. 13 20–36
Walton v Inland Revenue Commissioners [1996] S.T.C. 68; [1996] 1 E.G.L.R. 159 CA 21–35
Wardhaugh (Inspector of Taxes) v Penrith Rugby Union Football Club [2002] EWHC 918 (Ch); [2002] S.T.C. 776; 74 T.C. 499 .... 17–28, 17–29
Wase v Bourke [1996] S.T.C. 18; [1996] 1 E.G.L.R. 164 17–20
Watkins (Inspector of Taxes) v Ashford Sparkes & Harward [1985] 1 W.L.R. 994; [1985] 2 All E.R. 916 5–32

Watton (Inspector of Taxes) v Tippett [1997] S.T.C. 893; 69 T.C. 491;
[1997] B.T.C. 338.. 15–20, 17–28
Webers Wine World Handels-GmbH v Abgabenberufungskommission
Wein (C–147/01) [2005] All ER 224 CJEU 25–09, 27–48
Weight Watchers (UK) Ltd v Revenue and Customs Commissioners; sub
nom. Revenue and Customs Commissioners v Weight Watchers UK
Ltd (2008) [2008] EWCA Civ 715; [2008] S.T.C. 2313; [2009] B.T.C.
5091; [2009] B.V.C. 91; [2008] S.T.I. 1644 25–55
Wellcome Trust Ltd v Customs and Excise Commissioners (C–155/94)
[1996] All E.R. (EC) 589; [1996] S.T.C. 945 ECJ 25–75
West v Phillips (1958) 51 R. & I.T. 560; 38 T.C. 203 5–12
Weston v Garnett [2004] EWHC 1607 (Ch); [2005] S.T.C. 617; [2005]
B.T.C. 113.. 15–38, 17–14
Weston v Inland Revenue Commissioners [2000] S.T.C. 1064; [2000]
B.T.C. 8041 20–37
WHA Ltd v Customs and Excise Commissioners [2004] EWCA Civ 559;
[2004] S.T.C. 1081; [2004] B.T.C. 5425; [2004] B.V.C. 485; [2004] S.T.I.
1202) 27–39
WHA Ltd v Revenue and Customs Commissioners [2013] UKSC 24;
[2013] 2 All E.R. 907; [2013] S.T.C. 943; [2013] B.V.C. 155; [2013] S.T.I.
1769 25–16
Whitechapel Art Gallery v Customs and Excise Commissioners [1986]
S.T.C. 156; [1986] 1 C.M.L.R. 79 VAT Tr (London) 25–71
Whitehouse v Ellam [1995] S.T.C. 503; 68 T.C. 377................................ 15–19
Williams (Inspector of Taxes) v Merrylees [1987] 1 W.L.R. 1511; [1987]
S.T.C. 445 17–05
Williams v Evans (Inspector of Taxes) [1982] 1 W.L.R. 972; [1982] S.T.C.
498 17–28
Wills v Gibbs [2008] S.T.C. 808 20–30
Wimpey International Ltd v Warland (Inspector of Taxes) [1989] S.T.C.
273; 61 T.C. 51 CA.. 8–09
Wisdom v Chamberlain [1969] 1 W.L.R. 275; [1969] 1 All E.R. 332; 45
T.C. 92; [1968] T.R. 345; (1968) 112 S.J. 946....................................... 5–09
Wm Morrison Supermarkets Ltd v Revenue and Customs Commissioners
[2013] UKUT 247 (TCC) 25–60
Woolwich Building Society v Inland Revenue Commissioners [1993] A.C.
70; [1992] 3 W.L.R. 366 HL 3–15
Wright v Boyce (Inspector of Taxes) [1958] 1 W.L.R. 832; [1958] 2 All E.R.
703 CA... 9–14
Yarmouth v France (1887) L.R. 19 Q.B.D. 647 QBD......................... 8–07, 8–10
Yoga for Health Foundation v Customs and Excise Commissioners [1984]
S.T.C. 630; [1985] 1 C.M.L.R. 340 25–08
Yorkshire Cooperatives Ltd v Customs and Excise Commissioners
(C–398/99) [2003] 1 W.L.R. 2821; [2003] S.T.C. 234; [2003] E.C.R.
I-427; [2003] 1 C.M.L.R. 20; [2003] C.E.C. 139; [2003] B.T.C. 5178;
[2003] B.V.C. 234; [2003] S.T.I. 89.............................. 27–18, 27–19, 27–44
Young & Woods v West [1980] I.R.L.R. 201 CA...................................... 9–04
Young v Phillips [1984] STC 520 15–13
Zamberk v Financni reditelstvi v Hradci Kralove (C–18/12) [2014] S.T.C.
1703 26–21
Zim Properties Ltd v Procter (Inspector of Taxes) [1985] S.T.C. 90; 58
T.C. 371 .... 15–15, 15–21

TABLE OF STATUTES

1688	Bill of Rights (c.2)........... 2–02, 3–15, 3–19, 3–42		1975	Inheritance (Provision for Family and Dependants) Act (c.63) 20–25
1773	Tea Act (c 44) 2–02			
1803	Income Tax (c.122) 3–04, 3–44, 7–33		1976	Finance Act (c.40) s.115........................... 19–35
1842	Income Tax Act (c.35) 3–07			
1880	Employers' Liability Act (c.42)................... 8–07		1978	Interpretation Act (c.30).. 2–06
			1979	Customs and Excise Management Act (c.2).......................... 2–15
1890	Partnership Act (c.39).... 13–07			
1894	Finance Act (c.39)............ 3–12			
1911	Parliament Act (c.13)....... 2–03		1980	Housing Act (c.51)......... 17–06
1918	Income Tax Act (c.40) 3–07		1982	Supply of Goods and Services Act (c.29) .. 25–29
1925	Trustee Act (c.19) s.31............................. 12–20			
			1983	Oil Taxation Act (c.56).... 2–05
1925	Law of Property Act (c.20) s.184........................... 19–31		1984	Inheritance Tax Act (c.51) 3–16, 18–04, 19–14, 23–12
1936	Finance Act 3–43			Pt VII......................... 23–02
1949	Parliament Act (c.103) 2–03			Pt VIII 24–01
1952	Income Tax Act (c.10) 3–07, 3–43			s.1.............................. 19–02
				s.2(1) 19–02
1964	Succession (Scotland) Act (c.41) Pt II............................. 20–25			s.3.............................. 21–01
				(1) ... 19–02, 19–03, 19–06
				(2) 19–02
1968	Provisional Collection of Taxes Act (c.2) 2–11			(3) ... 19–05, 19–08, 22–41
				s.3A............................ 19–12
1970	Taxes Management Act (c.9) 2–15, 14–10			s.4........ 19–28, 20–13, 20–26, 21–40, 22–09, 22–21
	s.9.............................. 4–11			(1) 19–28, 19–31
	s.9A............................ 4–15			(2) 19–31
	s.12B 4–13			s.5........ 21–17, 22–20, 22–21
	s.29............................ 4–16			(1) 19–04, 21–40
	s.34............................ 4–19			(b) 20–22
	s.36............................ 4–19			(2) 19–05
	ss.49B—49I 2–16			(5) ... 21–16, 21–22, 21–23
	s.54.................. 2–18, 4–23			s.6.................... 19–02, 20–22
1970	Income and Corporation Taxes Act (c.10).................. 3–43			s.7(4) 21–09
				s.8A............................ 21–06
				s.8B 21–06
1971	Finance Act (c.68).......... 15–46			ss.8E—8M 21–08
1974	Finance Act (c.30)............ 3–12			s.10...... 20–16, 20–17, 22–41, 22–59, 22–61
1975	Finance Act (c.7) 19–32			(1) 19–09
	ss.39—42.................... 19–32			s.11.................. 20–13, 20–16
	s.41............................ 19–35			

(1) 20–13, 20–16
(6) 20–16
s.12............................. 20–17
s.13............................. 20–18
s.13A........................... 20–18
s.14............................. 20–19
s.15.................... 19–08, 20–20
s.16............................. 20–21
s.17............................. 20–27
s.18........ 20–02, 20–16, 20–27
s.19............................. 20–04
s.20............................. 20–05
s.21............................. 20–06
s.22............................. 20–07
s.23.................. 20–08, 21–04
s.24............................. 20–09
s.24A........................... 20–10
s.25............................. 20–11
s.26A........................... 20–11
s.27............................. 20–12
s.29A............... 20–27, 20–33
ss.30—35A 20–11
ss.36—42 23–15
s.41............................. 23–13
s.43........ 21–38, 22–07, 22–08
s.47............................. 22–19
s.47A........................... 22–60
s.48............................. 22–05
(1) 20–23, 22–20
(a) 22–59
s.49............................. 22–21
(1) 22–18
s.49A............... 22–09, 22–11
s.49C........................... 22–13
s.49D........................... 22–13
s.50.................. 22–14, 22–18
(6) 21–38
s.51............................. 22–23
s.52............................. 22–23
(1) 22–22
(2) 22–27
(3) 22–24
(4) 22–26
s.53(2) 22–27
(4) 20–03
s.55A........................... 22–61
s.56(2) 20–03
s.58............................. 22–30
(1) 22–46
ss.58—85 22–30
s.59............................. 22–30
s.60............................. 22–33
s.61............................. 22–33

s.62............................. 22–36
s.62B 22–36
s.63A........................... 22–36
s.63C........................... 22–36
s.64............................. 22–33
s.65(1) 22–41
(2) 22–42
s.66............................. 22–36
(2) 22–39
(6) 22–40
s.67............................. 22–37
s.68............................. 22–44
s.69............................. 22–45
s.70........ 22–46, 22–52, 22–55
s.71............................. 22–47
s.71A.... 20–31, 22–09, 22–48
(3) 22–49
s.71B 22–48
s.71C........................... 22–48
s.71D.............. 20–31, 22–53
s.71E 22–55
s.71F 22–56
s.71G........................... 22–57
s.71H........... 22–48, 22–53
s.76............................. 22–41
s.80............................. 22–33
s.89............................. 22–12
s.89A........................... 22–12
s.89B 22–09, 22–12
s.92................... 19–31, 20–03
s.93............................. 20–27
s.94............................. 19–33
ss.94—98 22–29
s.96............................. 19–33
s.98............................. 19–33
s.101........................... 22–29
ss.103—114 20–36
s.115(2)........................ 20–44
(3) 20–46
ss.115—124C............... 20–41
s.117........................... 20–45
ss.125—130 20–47
s.131........................... 21–09
s.141 .... 20–34, 22–28
s.141A 20–34
s.142.... 19–08, 20–28, 20–30,
24–08
(1) 20–27, 20–29
ss.142—145 20–27
s.143........................... 20–32
s.144........................... 20–31
s.146........................... 20–25
s.150........................... 20–35

s.153A 20–26
s.154 20–26
s.155 20–23
s.155A 20–26
s.160 21–32
s.161 21–37
  (1) 21–37
s.162(5) 21–16
s.163 21–36
s.164 21–16
s.165 21–16
s.167 21–39
s.168 21–34
s.170 21–38
s.171 21–42
  (2) 19–30
ss.171—177 19–30
s.172 .... 19–30, 21–42
s.173 21–42
s.176 21–37
ss.178—189 21–42
ss.190—198 21–42
s.199 23–03
  (3) 23–09
ss.199—214 23–02
s.200 23–04
s.201 23–04
s.203 23–08
s.204 23–10
  (7) 23–06
  (8) 23–06
s.211 23–12
s.215 24–01
ss.215—261 24–01
s.216 24–02
s.218 24–07
ss.221—225 24–10
ss.226—236 24–11
s.230 20–11
s.235 24–13
s.236(3) 24–13
s.237 24–14
s.238 24–14
s.245 24–03
s.245A 24–07
s.262 .... 19–34, 19–37
s.263 19–36
s.264 21–14
s.265 21–12
s.266(1) 21–13
  (2) 21–13
s.268 19–37
  (2) 19–39

  (3) 19–39
s.272 ..... 19–05, 19–06, 22–60
Sch.1 21–02
Sch.1A 21–04
Sch.3 .... 20–11, 20–12
1985 Housing Associations
         Act (c.69) 20–10
1986 Finance Act (c.41)
         s.102 .... 19–14, 19–15, 19–17,
                  19–23, 19–24, 19–33
         (5A) 19–25
         (5B) 19–25
         (5C) 19–25
         s.102A 19–14, 19–20,
                        19–22—19–24
         (2) 19–20
         (3) 19–21
         (4)(b) 19–23
         (5) 19–22, 19–25
         s.102B 19–14, 19–24
         s.102C 19–14
         (6) 19–24
         s.102ZA 19–17
         s.103 .... 21–23, 21–29
         (5) 21–23
         s.104 21–26
         Sch.20 .. 19–14, 19–17, 19–27
         para 6 19–17
1986 Insolvency Act (c.45)
         s.339 20–35
1988 Income and
         Corporation Taxes
         Act (c.1) 3–43, 10–06,
                           14–02
         s.15 (Sch.A) 3–16, 6–02,
                           6–05, 6–07
         s.16 (Sch.B) 6–02
         s.17 (Sch.C) 3–16
         s.18 (Sch.D) 3–16, 7–01,
                     7–23, 7–25, 7–32,
                           7–34, 7–35
         s.19 (Sch.E)..3–16, 9–02, 9–09
         s.20 (Sch.F) 3–16
         s.348 7–29
         s.349 7–29
         s.641 12–22
         s.660A 12–16
         (6) 12–16
1989 Children Act (c.41) 22–48
1992 Social Security
         Contributions and
         Benefits Act (c.4) 3–10,
                           13–24

1992	Taxation of Chargeable	
	Gains Act (c.12) 3–09,	
	15–04, 15–16	
	Pt II................................ 16–01	
	Ch.I................................ 16–01	
	Ch.III............................. 16–01	
	s.1................................... 15–54	
	(1) 15–10	
	s.2...................... 15–13, 16–24	
	(2) 15–11	
	s.3................................... 15–06	
	(1A)........................... 15–13	
	(5A)........................... 16–25	
	(7) 15–08	
	s.4...................... 15–05, 16–17	
	s.10(1) 15–13	
	s.10A............................. 15–13	
	s.12(1) 15–13	
	s.15(2) 15–11	
	ss.15—20 16–01	
	s.16(1) 16–01, 16–23	
	(2) 16–23	
	ss.16ZA—16ZD 15–13	
	s.17...... 15–18, 15–42, 16–03,	
	17–23, 17–25, 17–26	
	(1)(a) 15–17	
	(b) 15–19	
	s.18................................ 16–03	
	(2) 15–18	
	(3) 16–25	
	s.21(1) 15–14	
	(b) 15–17	
	(2) 15–20, 15–22	
	s.22................................ 15–25	
	(1) ... 15–21, 15–22, 15–41	
	(a)—(d) 15–28	
	(2) 15–22, 15–28	
	s.23................................ 15–25	
	s.24.................. 15–25, 15–41	
	(1) 15–23	
	(2) 15–23	
	(b) 15–23	
	s.28....... 15–27, 15–28, 16–04	
	(1) 15–28	
	(2) 15–28	
	s.29................................ 15–43	
	ss.29—34 15–43	
	s.30................................ 15–43	
	s.31................................ 15–43	
	s.35................................ 16–18	
	s.37................................ 16–02	
	(1) 15–20	
	ss.37—52 16–01	
	s.38(1) 16–07	
	(b) 16–07	
	(4) 16–11	
	s.39................................ 16–02	
	s.40................................ 16–10	
	s.42................................ 16–14	
	s.44(1) 16–15	
	s.45................................ 17–13	
	s.48.................. 16–03—16–05	
	s.49.................. 16–05, 16–06	
	s.51................................ 17–15	
	s.58................................ 15–44	
	s.59................................ 15–12	
	s.59A............................. 15–12	
	(5) 17–30	
	s.60................. 15–50, 15–51,	
	15–54, 15–56	
	(1) 15–58	
	(2) 15–50	
	s.62................................ 15–46	
	(1) 15–47	
	(2) ... 15–49, 15–50, 16–26	
	(4) 15–48	
	(6)—(9) 15–48	
	s.64(2) 15–48, 16–26	
	(3) 15–48	
	s.65................................ 15–54	
	s.68................................ 15–50	
	s.69.................. 15–54, 15–64	
	(4) 15–70	
	s.70................................ 15–56	
	s.71................................ 15–66	
	(1) 15–58, 15–62,	
	15–63, 15–64, 15–66	
	(2)—(2D) 15–59	
	s.72................................ 15–63	
	(1) 15–62, 15–63	
	s.73.................. 15–60, 15–62	
	(1)(a) 15–63	
	(b) 15–61	
	s.76(1) 15–67	
	(2) 15–67	
	s.76A............................. 15–68	
	s.104............................. 16–20	
	s.105............................. 16–21	
	s.106A........................... 16–22	
	s.115............................. 17–14	
	s.117................. 15–38, 17–14	
	s.121............................. 17–15	
	s.122............................. 15–33	
	ss.126—140 15–34	
	s.132(3)(b) 15–38	
	s.137............................. 15–35	

ss.144—147 15–41
s.144ZA.................... 15–42
s.152(1)..................... 17–28
s.152—159................. 17–27
s.153.......................... 17–29
s.155.......................... 17–28
s.156A 17–30
s.159.......................... 17–29
s.161.......................... 15–31
　(1) 15–30
　(2) 15–31
　(3) 15–30, 15–32
s.162.......................... 17–26
s.162A 17–26
s.165............... 17–24, 17–25
s.169A 17–30
ss.169B—169G 17–24
ss.169H—169S 17–16
s.169N 15–05
s.171.......................... 15–32
s.210.......................... 17–15
s.222.......................... 17–07
　(6) 17–08
ss.222—226B.............. 17–02
s.223(4)...................... 17–08
s.224.......................... 17–08
s.224(3)...................... 17–02
s.225.......................... 17–08
s.225A 17–08
s.225B 17–08
s.225D 17–08
s.225E 17–03
s.226A 17–09
s.251(1)...................... 15–36
　(3) 15–40
　(4) 15–39
s.252.......................... 17–15
s.253............... 15–37, 15–38
s.256.......................... 17–15
s.257............... 15–45, 17–15
s.260..... 17–09, 17–23, 17–24
s.262.......................... 17–10
　(2) 17–11
　(3) 17–11
　(4) 17–12
s.263.......................... 17–15
s.268.......................... 17–15
s.269.......................... 17–15
s.272............... 15–23, 16–12
s.273............... 15–23, 16–12
s.275.......................... 15–14
s.279A 16–04
ss.279A—279D 16–26

s.286........................... 15–18
　(2) 15–18
　(8) 15–18
s.288(1)...................... 15–13
　(3) 15–07
Sch.1 para 2 15–08
Sch.4A 15–68
Sch.8 16–16
　para 5(1) 15–20
Sch.9 17–14
1994　Value Added Tax Act
　　　(c.23) 25–11, 25–17,
　　　　　　　　25–18, 25–32
　　s.1............................. 3–16
　　s.3(1) 25–25
　　s.4(1) 25–26
　　　(2) 25–26, 25–62
　　s.5............................ 25–37
　　　(2) 25–26, 25–36
　　s.6............................ 27–30
　　s.7A......................... 26–16
　　s.19......................... 27–02
　　ss.24—26B 27–34
　　s.26......................... 27–36
　　s.26A....................... 27–36
　　s.26B....................... 26–29
　　s.36......................... 27–46
　　s.43A....................... 25–67
　　s.80................... 27–47, 27–49
　　　(3) 27–48, 27–49
　　　(7) ... 25–11, 27–47, 27–49
　　s.81......................... 27–47
　　s.94......................... 25–70
　　　(4) 25–77
　　s.96......................... 25–38
　　Sch.4 25–37
　　　para.1.................... 25–37
　　　para.3.................... 25–38
　　　para.5......... 25–61, 27–03
　　Sch.5 para.1 25–38
　　　para.4.................... 27–20
　　Sch.8 .... 26–07, 26–09, 26–18
　　Sch.9 .... 25–62, 26–18
1994　Supply of Goods and
　　　Services Act (c.35) .. 25–29
1995　Finance Act (c.4)
　　　s.154......................... 20–44
1995　Children (Scotland) Act
　　　(c.36) 22–48
1995　Children (Northern
　　　Ireland) Act............. 22–48
1996　Housing Act (c.52)
　　　Pt 1............................. 20–10

1997	Finance Act (c.16).............	2–28
1998	Data Protection Act	
	(c.29)	4–20
1998	Human Rights Act	
	(c.42)	2–10, 2–30
1998	Scotland Act (c.46)	
	Pt 4................................	2–24
	ss.80D—80F	2–24
2000	Freedom of	
	Information Act	
	(c.36)	3–37, 4–20
	s.44................................	4.–20
2001	Capital Allowances Act	
	(c.2) 3–07, 8–02, 8–03,	
	8–07, 8–13, 9–32,	
	14–02, 14–28	
	Pt 2................................	8–03
	Pt 3A..............................	8–03
	Pt 4A..............................	8–03
	Pt 5................................	8–03
	Pt 6................................	8–03
	Pt 7................................	8–03
	Pt 8.......................	7–08, 8–03
	Pt 9................................	8–03
	Pt 10..............................	8–03
	ss.15—20	8–03
	ss.21—23	8–07
	s.39................................	8–16
	ss.44—47	9–32
	s.45A..............................	8–16
	s.51A..............................	8–15
	s.55................................	8–19
	s.71................................	8–10
	s.91................................	8–18
2002	Tax Credits Act (c.21)....	13–32
2003	Income Tax (Earnings	
	and Pensions) Act	
	(c.1) 3–07, 3–16, 5–35,	
	9–02, 9–03, 9–09,	
	9–16, 9–19, 9–24,	
	9–31, 9–36, 9–39,	
	9–43, 9–44, 9–46,	
	9–53, 10–02, 10–06,	
	10–11, 11–01, 11–13,	
	11–15, 14–04	
	Pt 2.......................	7–04, 9–32
	Pt 3.......................	9–17, 9–26
	Ch.1	9–17
	Ch.2	9–17
	Ch.3	9–18
	Ch.4 ......9–19, 9–26, 9–31	
	Ch.5	9–23, 9–31
	Ch.6	9–24

Ch.7	9–17, 9–27	
Ch.8	9–17	
Ch.9	9–17	
Ch.10	9–17, 9–28	
Ch.11	9–17	
Ch.12	9–32, 9–33	
Pt 4................................	9–34	
Ch.2	9–34	
Ch.3	9–34	
Pt 5.......................	9–26, 9–36	
Pt 6................................	9–11	
Pt 7..............	9–11, 9–47, 9–48	
Pt 7A..........3–44, 5–04, 9–15		
Pt 9.........	7–04, 10–09, 10–10	
Pt 10........3–16, 7–04, 10–17,		
10–18, 13–30, 13–31		
Pt 11..............................	9–53	
s.4................................	9–03	
s.5................................	9–03	
s.6(1)	9–09, 9–11	
s.7................................	9–32	
(5)	9–32	
(6)	9–11	
s.11................................	9–13	
ss.48—61	9–07	
s.49(1)	9–07	
s.54................................	9–07	
s.62................................	9–17	
(2)	9–09	
s.63(2)	9–30	
s.64................................	9–17	
s.65................................	9–17	
ss.70—72	9–18	
s.70................................	9–18	
(1)	9–18	
s.71(1)	9–18	
ss.73—96	9–19	
s.75(1)	9–20	
s.84................................	9–21	
s.92................................	9–22	
s.95................................	9–22	
ss.97—113	9–23	
s.99(1)	9–23	
(2)	9–23	
s.100..............................	9–23	
s.114..............................	9–30	
ss.121—148	9–25	
s.147..............................	9–24	
ss.173—191	9–27	
s.188..............................	9–27	
s.201.................	9–28, 9–30	
ss.201—210	9–28	
s.204..............................	9–28	

s.205 9–28
s.206 9–28
ss.216—220 9–30
s.221 9–33
s.222 9–33
s.223 9–33
s.224 9–33
s.225 9–33
s.226 9–33
s.226E 9–15
ss.229—232 9–26
s.231 9–26
s.233 9–26
s.235 9–26
s.236 9–26
ss.237—249 9–26
s.264 9–34
s.288 9–27
s.289 9–27
ss.290—326 9–35
s.317 9–35
ss.318—318D 9–35
s.319 9–35
s.320 9–35
s.323A 9–28
s.328 9–37
s.329 9–37
s.330 9–37
s.333 9–37
s.334 9–37
s.336 .... 9–37, 9–38
s.337 .... 9–40, 9–42
ss.337—342 9–40
s.338 .... 9–40, 9–42
s.339 9–42
s.339A 9–42
ss.343—345 9–43
s.358 9–43
s.401 9–46
ss.401—416 .... 9–10, 9–46
s.403 9–46
s.406 9–46
s.417 9–48
s.420 9–48
s.521(4) 9–47
ss.554A—554Z21 9–15
s.554B 9–15
s.554C 9–15
s.554D 9–15
s.566 10–02
s.570 10–02
s.577 10–07
s.578 10–07

s.579A 10–10
s.656 10–17
Sch.2 9–47
Sch.5 9–47
2003 Finance Act (c.14) 9–47,
                                    15–42
2004 Finance Act (c.12) 10–09,
                         10–12, 11–01
        Pt 4 10–11
        Pt 7 3–51
        ss.57—77 5–03
        s.314 3–51
        Sch.15 19–26
2005 Income Tax (Trading
        and Other Income)
        Act (c.5) 3–07, 3–16,
                    5–02, 5–14, 5–16,
                    5–35, 6–03, 6–11,
                    7–02, 7–06, 7–29,
                    8–13, 11–16, 12–14,
                                    14–04
        Pt 2 .... 5–01, 5–17, 5–18,
                              5–27, 7–04
        Ch 3 5–27
        Ch 4 .... 5–27, 5–39
        Ch 5 .... 5–27, 5–39
        Ch 5A 5–18
        Pt 3 .... 6–08, 7–04
        Ch 4 6–08
        Ch 6 7–04
        Pt 4 .... 7–02, 7–04, 7–20,
                         11–03, 11–04
        Pt 5 .... 3–16, 7–02, 7–04,
                      7–07, 7–10, 7–17
        Ch 2 7–02
        Ch 3 7–02
        Ch 4 7–02
        Ch 5 7–02,
                         12–11—12–13
        Ch 6 7–02
        Ch 7 7–02
        Ch 8 .... 7–02, 7–33
        Pt 6 .... 7–17, 7–18, 7–20,
                         11–03, 11–04
        (3) 7–19
        Pt 7 .... 6–08— 6–10
        Pt 20 Ch 5 12–11
        s.4 3–16
        s.5 5–01
        ss.5—259 5–01
        s.7(1) 5–01
        s.8 5–01
        s.9 5–13

s.12............................. 5–13
s.15............................. 5–04
s.25(1) 5–16
s.26............................. 6–07
s.28.................... 5–27, 8–13
s.29............................. 5–37
s.31............................. 5–27
s.33... 5–27, 6–07, 8–01, 8–13
s.34.................... 5–27, 6–07
(1) 5–30
(2) 5–31
s.35............................. 5–27
s.46............................. 5–30
s.87............................. 5–39
s.88............................. 5–39
ss.172A—172F 5–25
s.202......................... 14–08
ss.241—257 5–48
s.264......................... 6–04
s.266......................... 6–05
s.267......................... 6–05
s.268......................... 6–04
s.270......................... 6–04
s.272.................... 6–07, 8–13
(1) 6–07
s.308......................... 6–07
s.311A 6–07
s.312......................... 6–08
s.369(1)..................... 11–05
s.370......................... 11–05
s.371......................... 11–05
s.372......................... 11–05
s.381......................... 11–05
s.383(1)..................... 11–12
(2) 11–12
(3) 11–12
s.568......................... 12–19
s.574........................... 8–13
s.575........................... 7–04
(1) 7–04
s.583........................... 7–09
s.597........................... 7–08
s.598........................... 7–08
s.620......................... 12–11
s.624......................... 12–18
ss.624—628 12–13
s.625... 12–14—12–16, 12–20
(4) 12–15
s.626..............12–14—12–16
s.627......................... 12–14
s.629.............. 12–18, 12–20
ss.629—632 12–13
s.631................ 12–19, 12–20

s.633......................... 12–21
s.634......................... 12–21
ss.633–637 12–13
s.638.............. 12–21, 12–22
s.646.............. 12–17, 12–20
(2) 12–17
(3) 12–17
s.683...........7–18, 7–30, 7–33
(1) 7–18, 7–22, 7–23,
7–33
(3) 7–24, 7–33
s.687.................... 3–16, 7–33
s.727............................ 7–22
(1) 7–22
s.728............................ 7–22
s.729.................... 7–22, 7–30
Sch.4 .... 11–05, 14–17
2005 Finance Act (c.7) 12–10
2005 Commissioners for
Revenue and
Customs Act (c.11)... 2–12
s.18............................ 4–20
s.23............................ 4–20
2005 Finance (No.2) Act
(c.22) 15–42
2006 Finance Act (c.25).......... 22–06
2007 Income Tax Act (c.3) 3–16,
3–54, 6–11, 7–29,
11–11
Pt 2............................ 13–21
Pt 4............................ 5–40
Pt 8............................ 12–30
Pt 13................... 3–44, 6–11
Ch 3 5–27
Pt 15 Chs 6—8 7–29
s.4............................. 3–14
s.9............................. 12–05
s.11A 13–22
s.11B 13–22
s.15.......................... 12–05
s.24.......................... 13–15
s.24A 13–15
s.58.......................... 13–18
ss.61—66 5–41
s.66........................... 5–41
ss.67—70 5–41
s.72........................... 5–46
s.83.................. 5–42—5–44
s.85........................... 5–43
s.86........................... 5–44
s.89........................... 5–45
s.383......................... 13–11
s.384......................... 13–11

s.386............................ 13–11
ss.388—412 13–11
s.414............................ 12–30
s.418............................ 12–32
s.419............................ 12–32
s.420............................ 12–33
s.479............................ 12–05
s.481............................ 12–05
s.482............................ 12–05
s.484............................ 12–06
s.491............................ 12–04
s.752...........3–44, 6–11, 6–12
s.761(2)........................ 3–44
s.898............................ 7–30
s.899............................ 7–30
    (5) 7–30
s.904................... 7–22, 7–30
s.989.................. 5–05, 14–17
s.992.................. 3–16, 14–05
Sch.24 24–03
2007 Tribunals, Courts and
      Enforcement Act
      (c.15) 2–17, 2–18
2008 Finance Act (c.9) ...2–28, 3–51,
      4–19, 11–06, 24–09,
      25–04
2008 Pension Act (c.30).......... 10–04
2009 Corporation Tax Act
      (c.4) 3–07, 3–16, 3–54,
      8–02, 8–03,
      14–01—14–04, 14–10,
      14–13, 14–24
      Pt 2............................ 14–04
      Pt 3..3–16, 5–27, 7–02, 14–04
      Pt 4............................ 14–04
      Pt 5...... 11–02, 14–04, 14–21,
      14–22
      Pt 6.................. 11–02, 14–04
      Pt 7.................. 11–02, 14–04
      Pt 8..........3–16, 7–02, 14–04,
      14–24
      Pt 9..........3–16, 7–02, 14–04,
      14–24
      Pt 9A.......................... 14–04
      Pt 10.........3–16, 7–02, 14–04
      Pts 11—18.................. 14–04
      Pt 16.................. 11–02, 14–33
      s.2..................... 3–16, 14–13
          (1) 14–03
          (2) 14–03
      s.3................... 14–03, 14–13
      s.4................... 14–03, 14–13
      s.8............................. 14–13

ss.13—18.................... 14–05
s.46............................. 5–16
s.292............................ 14–22
s.295............................ 14–22
s.299............................ 14–22
s.302............................ 14–22
s.313............................ 14–23
    (1) 14–23
ss.464—465 14–21
s.712............... 14–25, 14–26
s.906............................ 14–24
s.933............................ 3–16
s.969............................ 3–16
s.979............................ 3–16
Sch.4 14–13
2009 Finance Act (c.10)........... 4–19
2010 Corporation Tax Act
      (c.4) 3–07,
      14–01—14–03, 14–10,
      14–13, 14–17
      Pt 2............................ 14–04
      Pt 5............................ 14–39
      Pts 8—21C 14–04
      Pt 10.......................... 14–18
      Pt 18.......................... 3–44
      Pt 23.......................... 14–17
      s.5.............................. 14–05
          (3) 14–05
      s.37............................ 14–34
      s.45............................ 14–34
      s.99............................ 14–31
      s.189................ 14–31, 14–32
      s.339.......................... 14–18
      s.439(2)...................... 19–33
      s.671.......................... 14–05
      ss.673—676 14–38
      ss.938—948 14–37
      s.1000 14–17
      s.1001 14–17
      ss.1074—1097 14–20
      s.1127 14–25
      Sch.4 14–13
2010 Income Tax (International
      and Other Provisions)
      Act (c.8).......... 3–07, 3–26,
      14–02, 14–04
      ss.147—217 5–26
2010 Finance Act (c.13)
      s.52............................ 22–09
      s.53............................ 22–09
2011 Budget Responsibility
      and National Audit
      Act (c.4)

	s.1 2–10
	s.2 2–10
2011	Finance Act (c.11) 9–15
	Sch.2 3–44
	Sch.23 4–17
	Sch.25 .... 4–17, 4–18
2012	Scotland Act (c.11) 13–22
2012	Finance Act (c.14) 21–04
	Sch.14 20–11
2013	Finance Act (c.29) .. 3–50, 6–14, 9–47, 9–51
	Pt 5 3–52
	s.176 21–24
	s.207 3–52
	s.222 3–26
	Sch.4 5–17
	Sch.45 para.110 15–13
2014	Pension Act (c.19) 10–02, 10–03
2014	Finance Act (c.26) ... 3–51, 9–47
2014	Wales Act (c.29) 2–25

2014	Taxation of Pensions Act (c.30) 10–11, 10–12
2014	Revenue Scotland and Tax Powers Act (asp 16) 2–24
	Pt 5 2–24
2015	Finance Act (c.11) 9–18
2015	Finance (No.2) Act (c.33) 13–18
	s.1 13–21
2016	Scotland Act (c.11) 13–22
2016	Finance Act 4–12, 6–07, 9–47, 10–12, 11–07, 13–21, 13–22
2016	Succession (Scotland) Act (asp 7)
	s.9 19–31
2016	Tax Collection and Management (Wales) Act (anaw 6) 2–25

TABLE OF STATUTORY INSTRUMENTS

1987 Inheritance Tax
(Double Charges
Relief) Regulations
(SI 1987/1130) 21–26
1995 Value Added Tax
Regulations (SI
1995/2518).... 3–22, 27–40,
27–43
reg.101 .... 27–41, 27–43
reg.102 27–45
2000 Consumer Protection
(Distance Selling)
Regulations (SI
2000/2334) 27–32
2001 Social Security
Contributions
Regulations (SI
2001/1004) 3–10, 3–22,
13–24
2003 Income Tax (Pay
As You Earn)
Regulations (SI
2003/2682) 9–53
2004 Inheritance Tax
(Delivery of
Accounts)
(Excepted Estates)
Regulations (SI
2004/2543) 24–04
2005 Inheritance Tax
(Double Charges
Relief) Regulations
(SI 2005/3441) 21–26
2006 Value Added Tax
(Reduced Rate)
Order (SI 2006/
1472) 26–18
2007 Value Added Tax
(Reduced Rate)
Order (SI 2007/
1601) 26–18

2008 Inheritance Tax
(Delivery of
Accounts)
(Excepted
Transfers
and Excepted
Terminations)
Regulations (SI
2008/605)................ 24–05
2008 Inheritance Tax
(Delivery of
Accounts)
(Excepted
Settlements)
Regulations (SI
2008/606)................ 24–05
2009 Tribunal Procedure
(First-tier
Tribunal) (Tax
Chamber) Rules
(SI 2009/273) ... 2–19, 4–24
2012 Value Added Tax
(Zero-rating and
Exemptions)
Order...................... 26–13
2013 Consumer Contracts
(Information,
Cancellation
and Additional
Charges)
Regulations (SI
2013/3134) 27–32
2015 International Tax
Compliance
Regulations (SI
2015/878).................. 3–48
2015 Income Tax (Approved
Expenses)
Regulations (SI
2015/1948) 9–18

PART ONE

INTRODUCTION

CHAPTER 1

UNDERSTANDING TAX

Introduction

The question "What is a tax?" is surprisingly difficult to **1–01** answer. It is tempting to rely on the well-known reply of the child who was asked to define an elephant. "An elephant is large and grey, and lives in a herd of elephants." Some payments are not clearly one of the herd. This is so, for example, of the profits made on postage stamps or the fees paid to government for the right to operate independent television channels. Clarity is not helped because some politicians find it convenient to say that things are not tax when they certainly seem to look like taxes. An example is national insurance contributions.

Defining taxes

Another way to define taxes is to list those levies that are, **1–02** beyond doubt, UK taxes. (In this book we use standard abbreviations such as UK for United Kingdom throughout to keep things simpler.) Listing all possible charges would be both contentious and boring. So we will stick with the important ones. The top 10 public revenue earners for 2015–16 (with the amounts collected in £ billion) are: income tax (£170 billion), NI (another standard abbreviation in the tax world, for National Insurance) contributions (£115 billion), VAT (even the legislation uses this one: value added tax) less refunds (£103 billion), corporation tax (£43 billion), council tax (£28 billion), business rates (£28 billion), fuel duties (£27 billion), stamp duties (£15 billion), alcoholic drinks (£10 billion), and tobacco taxes (£9 billion). Capital gains tax (CGT) (£6 billion) and inheritance tax (IHT) (£4 billion) do not feature; indeed they collect less than vehicle excise duty (£6 billion). But they rank near the top in terms of complexity and importance to lawyers, so feature strongly in this book. Customs duties do not feature. They are European taxes, not UK taxes at all. The rest of a long list takes us to air passenger duty (£3,100,000,000 paid on our air tickets in a year!), the lottery levy, the sugar tax threatened in 2016, the apprenticeship levy imposed in 2016 . . . (no, stop!).

Why do we tax?

1–03   Before we look in detail at the present UK tax system, it is valuable to spend a little time thinking about tax policy. Why do we tax the way we do? What are the political, economic, social and administrative pressures that have contributed to the shape of our tax system?

The primary purpose of taxation is to raise revenue for government expenditure. The government can raise revenue by borrowing, by "printing" money, and by selling things, but in practice it is unavoidable that taxation should raise most of the government's fiscal requirements. The government spends part of the money on services which private enterprise cannot provide, such as defence and law and order. It also pays for services that it is thought are better provided on a universal basis, such as social security benefits, and education. Attitudes to taxation depend to some extent on the views of taxpayers as to the merits of these items of government expenditure. Do you, for example, think it the job of government to provide a health service, or consumer protection laws, or pensions? If raising money to pay for these things was the only reason for taxes, however, we could have a much simpler system. If we raised the rate of income tax by two per cent, we could abolish inheritance tax and capital gains tax and still make money. Or we could raise the rate of value added tax and abolish most of income tax. Would that be fair? Would it be efficient?

1–04   Another purpose behind taxation is the redistribution of wealth and income. Certain aspects of this idea are generally agreed. It is generally—but not universally—agreed that income tax should be "progressive", and that some government revenue should be spent on welfare services. This was a major reason why the poll tax was so unpopular. People thought it unfair that everyone should pay *the same* tax, whether they were rich or poor, just because they lived in the same town. An unpopular tax is a failure—it loses politicians votes, and it proves too expensive to collect. Of course, for any tax the questions of rate and amount are of immense importance. *How* progressive should income tax be? *How much* should be spent on social services? Once upon a time it was considered right that income tax had a top rate of 98 per cent. Does anyone think that right now? Few do, but "once upon a time" was only 40 years ago. Fashions change in tax as in all else.

Taxes as means of control

1–05   Another purpose behind imposing taxes is control of the economy. Changes in taxation can and do affect the economy, but control is also exercised by adjusting the money supply and credit. A good example of using tax to control behaviour is the use of customs duties. There used to be a very high customs duty on imported leather. The aim was to protect the Scottish leather industry. This tax was successful because it collected no money! This also shows that taxes are not used only to raise money. That is an important point. One main way in which taxes are used to influence people is by what is *not* taxed. For instance, we put value added tax on most things that people buy, but we do not tax medicines.

Taxes may also be used as a kind of social control. We see **1–06** this idea concerning the taxing of alcohol and tobacco. More recently, politicians have decided that cars are less of a good thing, so they have been increasing the cost of taxes on them.

We can also use taxes to make sure people pay the full price for something. This is the idea of a pollution tax. When I buy goods, I pay the price the seller asks. That makes the seller a profit and meets the costs. What if the seller has polluted the local area while making the goods? Perhaps the seller has made something that I am going to dump untidily when I have finished with it (like car tyres or plastic bags)? Taxes can be used to impose the cost of destroying the tyre and collecting up the bags. This is a matter of debate at present. It is not widely used as a form of tax in Britain. There is an informal levy imposed by sellers on the price of every tyre and car battery to pay for its destruction. And in 2011 the Welsh government, which has no taxing powers, imposed a compulsory 5p charge on most single-use bags supplied by a shop to a customer. Is that a tax? Technically not because the Welsh government does not get the revenue, but otherwise it looks much like an elephant. But it worked. So the English copied it—sort of—in 2015, but again the money does not go to the Treasury. What it does is cut down hugely the number of plastic bags people use when shopping.

Principles of taxation

Choosing taxes, and the reasons for taxes, is a fascinating **1–07** topic of academic analysis and discussion. It leads on to an easy question that it is almost impossible to answer: what is the best form of tax? That debate was started in this country by a former customs official, Adam Smith in *The Wealth of Nations* (first published in 1776). Smith set out four "canons" that, in his view, lead to better taxes. In modified form, they still influence official thinking today. The four axioms are:

- people should contribute taxes in proportion to their incomes and wealth;

5

- taxes should be certain, not arbitrary;
- taxes should be levied in the most convenient way;
- the costs of imposing and collecting taxes should be kept minimal.

These are often glossed, as in Budget 2012, where Smith was quoted by the Chancellor as arguing for taxes that are "simple, predictable, support work, and that they are fair". We must add another gloss evidenced in most recent budgets: taxes should be both convenient and competitive internationally. We are a trading nation that competes in a global economy.

Taxation, then, can be used for several purposes other than collecting money. For a more detailed discussion, see the *Mirlees Report, Design of Tax Law*, published in 2011. There is a full discussion of the British tax system conducted by a panel of experts chaired by Sir James Mirlees, a Nobel laureate and published by Oxford University for the Institute for Fiscal Studies.

There is another side to the question of "better" taxes. If a tax operates in a certain way that they can sidestep (such as stamp duty taxing documents, but not oral transactions), people will change the way they do things to pay less tax. That is human nature. A tax that does not alter behaviour is said to be *neutral*. The aim of those designing taxes is to create neutral taxes, unless policy requires a tax to be non-neutral. In practice, taxes often have unintended side effects. The UK suffers, some allege, from this problem of non-neutral taxes.

Is taxation fair?

1–08   Let us look at the tax system from the point of view of justice. The current thinking on this matter concentrates on *equity*, which in this context means fairness. *Horizontal equity* is the idea that people in equal circumstances should pay an equal amount of tax. *Vertical equity* means that people in different circumstances should pay an appropriately different amount of tax.

1–09   Horizontal equity commands strong support. It was the reason that Adam Smith advocated an income tax, and it is a major reason for that form of tax today. Those with similar levels of income should pay similar levels of tax. Why should that be so? There are several ways of justifying the levels of tax paid by individuals. One economic view is the ability-to-pay argument. On that basis, those with equal ability to pay should pay equally. Another economic view is the benefit argument. Those who pay tax should do so according to the benefits they gain. Leaving aside personal circumstances (for example, that A needs more help than B because A is older/younger/less fit than B), again those with similar means should be paying similar taxes. The same result is achieved by taking the lawyer's view of fairness that "we are all equal before the law", or the democratic view that we are all members of the same society, and are equal within it.

Vertical equity is much more controversial. It is generally **1–10** agreed that the richer should pay more tax than the poorer. That was why so many people did not like the poll tax, and found it "unfair". Incidentally, they effectively threw out the benefit argument in so doing, and dismissed the "equal before the law" view as insufficient. But how much more should the richer be paying? Even with a proportional tax the richer do pay more than the poorer. If there were an income tax at a flat rate of 30 per cent, someone with an income of £100,000 would pay £30,000 in tax. This is more than the £300 that someone with an income of £1,000 would pay. Should the person with £100,000 pay more tax than the person with £1,000 not merely absolutely but also proportionally? This is where a progressive tax comes in. Instead of paying at 30 per cent, those on £100,000 income should pay rather more (at least, on part of their income), and those with £1,000 rather less. Again the details become as important as the principle. Precisely what percentage? And on precisely what part of the income? Why?

An important aspect of the justice—or otherwise—of the **1–11** tax system is the *tax base*. The base of a tax means the thing, transaction, or amount on which the tax is raised. All taxes have bases—whether the base is you (in the case of a poll tax), your income, your wealth, the number of shoes you buy, or whatever. This means the precise boundary of what is taxed as distinct from what is not taxed. Let us take an example. Hal has £200,000 in hand. He uses it to buy a house in which he then lives, paying no rent. Cher also has £200,000 in hand. She spends it on buying company shares. She lives in a rented house. Hal pays no tax on the use he has made of his £200,000 (the occupation of his house). Cher does pay tax on the use she has made of her £200,000 (the dividends). Is this fair?

As Adam Smith pointed out, another aspect of justice is certainty. The tax system should be clear, so that a taxpayer can see in advance how much tax must be paid. Secondly, enforcement should be consistent and universal. There is nothing more destructive of taxpayer morality than the suspicion that others are not paying. If you pay only half your income tax because of a trick, why should I pay more than that? Equally, if you get some form of special allowance, why should I not get one too? But if neither of us understands the law, we do not know if we are paying enough. So, certainty also requires rules that can be understood. This thought leads to another of the paradoxes of tax. The simpler the rules are, the less fair they are (because they ignore justified differences). But the fairer they are, the more complex they are. The more complex they are, the harder they are to understand and put into effect. Therefore they are less certain and, arguably, appear less fair. If both simplicity and complexity lead to unfairness, is there a happy medium? Sometimes simple laws are longer than complex laws, as the UK discovered when it emerged from the Tax Law Rewrite with the longest tax code in the world's history. Reacting to this, the government in 2010 set up the Office for Tax Simplification. In its first five years it has triggered major changes: see the OTS website for details.

Is taxation efficient?

1–12   The fourth Smithian canon is cost-effectiveness. The effectiveness of a tax system is partly a matter of success in enforcement, and partly a matter of the total cost of running it and complying with it. Some think that enforcement, in the case of income tax, is not showing a very high success rate. What we call the black economy has grown up, including moonlighting and other forms of tax evasion. Moonlighting is the practice of earning and paying tax on a source of income properly, but then undertaking a second job without declaring the tax. Then there are the ghosts—those who do not appear on any tax department records, and therefore pay no tax. Or do they? In practice, they may pay no direct income tax, but they would be hard put also to avoid all VAT.

Currently, the cost of collecting direct taxes is about one per cent of the total net yield, and the cost of collecting indirect taxes varies from tax to tax. But, of course, this deals only with the direct government costs. There are also hidden *compliance costs*, that is, the costs incurred by taxpayers in paying taxes. Two notable examples of these compliance costs are the costs of an employer for staff hours acting as an unpaid collector of income tax under the PAYE (the Pay as You Earn system) system, and the costs to a trader in complying with the VAT system. Both may also incur substantial costs for professional assistance and advice concerning tax affairs.

There is also an even more deeply hidden cost, a kind of social cost, which the community as a whole pays as part of the price of taxation. What we have in mind is the expenditure (one might almost say waste) of brain power. Some of the best brains in the country are exclusively devoted to tax matters; some on the official side, some on the other side. This brain power could be better employed in increasing the wealth, health or happiness of the community. In the past, this brain drain was closely linked to the immensity of the rates of tax. If someone is asked to pay 98 per cent income tax, or even 75 per cent tax, there is a high premium on good advice to avoid it. If income tax had a maximum rate of, say, 10 per cent, much less time and effort would be devoted to escaping the tax. But what would the state stop doing in return?

As for the effects of taxation, we are afraid that this is a topic where asking questions is easier than answering them. Does a high rate of income tax encourage people to work harder or does it discourage them? Most people would say that it discourages them, that it is a disincentive. But it is quite possible to argue that, on the contrary, it spurs people on to earn more, so that even when the tax is paid they will have enough left to live on. Does a high rate of tax on business raise prices? Does a high rate of tax on individuals raise wages and salaries? No one seems to know the answers. A high *average* rate of tax is probably an incentive to work, whereas high *marginal* rates are disincentives.

Tax evasion, tax avoidance and tax mitigation

Of course, the ideal position for a taxpayer confronted with **1–13** that dilemma in the view of many is to ensure that, whatever others pay, I pay no more tax than I must. And clever planning can result in no tax being paid at all by some taxpayers. This has been most controversial in recent years, but it is a subject that justifies careful thought. In particular, it is most important to emphasise the difference between *tax evasion* and *tax avoidance*. And within those activities regarded as tax avoidance, it is also important to note what may be called *tax mitigation*—ways in which taxpayers are allowed, even encouraged, to cut their tax bills.

Tax evasion means escaping or reducing tax by illegal means. This can range from wrongfully concealing income or assets and failing to declare them through to forging documents. Evasion usually involves dishonesty. In recent years, government has targeted those who seek to evade tax both through the criminal law and by imposing severe tax penalties. We must therefore return to the criminal law of tax in a later chapter.

Tax avoidance takes place when I arrange my affairs and transactions so as to reduce or remove any tax liability on them, but doing so within the letter of the law. This can vary from those who mitigate their liability to tax in a way encouraged by government—for example, putting savings into Premium Bonds where any winnings are tax free—to those who use extremely elaborate schemes designed to turn one form of income or capital into another or to remove it from the UK tax jurisdiction in appearance but not reality. *Tax mitigation*, such as saving in a way encouraged by government, is usually regarded as ordinary behaviour and is often commended. The sometimes brilliant schemes that avoid tax are, however, often subject to strong criticism, particularly where the taxpayer is a major international company or a seriously wealthy individual. Both government and the courts have sought in recent years to reduce the scope of this kind of avoidance, and again we will look at that in more detail below.

Some taxes are more easily avoided than others. For example, income tax is easier to avoid than VAT. You can hide income much more easily than you can hide expenditure. That provides much of the explanation for the growth in importance of VAT. The tax did not exist in 1970. It is now as we saw a major revenue earner in the UK—and everywhere else in Europe. It is also far cheaper to collect than income tax. On the other hand, it contradicts the progressive tax principle. The poor are hit by it relatively hard compared with the rich.

International aspects

1–14   We added a new principle to those of Adam Smith. It is that our tax rules have to work in the context of our international commitments. That has two main aspects: the international agreements that bind the UK and the competitive nature of the UK's world role as a trading nation.

As at the time of writing, the most important of our international commitments is our membership of the EU. It is why the UK has adopted VAT. And it is why we have no separate customs duties in the UK. So we must return to that topic when we examine what we call the geography of tax. Along with that we must also look at the effect of the European Convention of Human Rights on our taxes and tax administration. And we must examine briefly what happens when a taxpayer or source of income is potentially liable to tax in two or more countries.

That last point is also relevant to *tax competition*—the way in which countries seek to use their taxes to assist their international position as traders or countries seeking foreign inward investment. That is also part of the geography of tax.

But we cannot in a book like this do more than outline these issues—international tax is a vast complex of rules and treaties beyond the grasp of most tax practitioners let alone their clients.

It is far beyond the scope of this introduction. We must return home and begin at the beginning.

Britain's entry into the EU limited the powers of the British **1–15** parliament and government in respect of taxation. Certain articles of the EU Treaty prohibit rules of tax that would discriminate against persons in other member states. Another article provides for member states to work towards tax harmonisation, at least on indirect taxes—those on goods. This movement has progressed farthest in the field of VAT. It is partly why VAT is now so important as a British tax, but it is not the only reason. For most of British—and before it, English—history, the extraordinary revenues of the Crown (as taxes were called) came from customs duties on imports, and from excises. Excises have now been replaced by VAT—a European tax. Customs have now been replaced by the Community customs regime.

Our direct taxes have not been affected by the rising tide of EU law. Well, even that is not true, as we shall see. We might avoid the EU tide. We cannot avoid the currents caused by global tax competition. Ours is a world of offshore jurisdictions, tax havens (or tax heavens as French students consistently mistranslate "paradis fiscaux"), customs unions, free-trade zones, enterprise zones, special regimes, jurisdictions, tax holidays, free depreciation regimes . . . in short, a highly competitive marketplace. This is the territory of international tax law, and the many thousands of double tax agreements entered into by states—fascinating, but beyond the scope of an introductory book.

Introducing the taxes

We want to finish this introduction, and start our detailed **1–16** analysis of tax, by introducing the taxes dealt with in this book and then by referring generally to the kinds of taxes that exist, and the issues that each tax must tackle. We want to try to state in a very few words what it is that each tax is taxing.

First, *income tax*. Why? Because it is in government terms the largest revenue raiser, and therefore the most important tax. And because, with corporation tax, it is the most complex tax, and the hardest to understand. And because it involves significant efforts by lawyers and accountants to ensure that their clients comply with the law, and avoid its excesses. What does it tax? In a famous aphorism in *London CC v Attorney General* [1901] A.C. 26 HL, Lord Macnaghten said: "Income tax, if I may be pardoned for saying so, is a tax on income." This is largely, but not absolutely, true. There are some items of income that are not taxed—for example, student grants. So income tax is not a tax on all income. On the other hand, there are some charges to income tax that are imposed on receipts that are not income tax receipts, but rather capital receipts. This is so, for example, of taxing premiums received on leasing land. Anyway, what is income? Such questions are why we wrote much of this book!

Secondly, social security contributions (or *NI contributions* (NICs) as everyone and everything except the law itself terms them), which are the second source of government finance, and, for most people, a second income tax. The law is a little less complex and comprehensive than income tax law but is very similar to parts of income tax law, so it requires less extended treatment.

Thirdly, *VAT* (which is what the Act imposing value added tax calls it, so we shall too). Why? Because it has become the most litigated of the taxes, and is gaining in complexity and practical importance each year.

Fourthly, *corporation tax*. This is simply income tax and capital gains tax imposed on companies. Well, not simply—parts are fiendishly complicated, although we avoid the worst of it!

Fifthly, *capital gains tax* (CGT). Its fiscal significance is trivial compared with the taxes so far listed. Nevertheless, its complexity—and therefore its nuisance value to lawyers—far outweighs its importance in filling a gap in the income tax. What it taxes is the gain represented by the difference between the price at which an item was acquired and the price at which it is sold.

Sixthly, *inheritance tax* (IHT) or, as it used to be called before they thought it fun to change its name, capital transfer tax. It is a tax on capital transfers, and has never been a tax on inheritances, but what does that matter? It is a tax on transfers of property by certain gifts, by transfers into trust, and by operation of law on someone's death from that person's estate. Although whether or not it is accurately named does not matter, accurate advice on where it may affect capital transfers is important. Again we must examine it in detail.

Collecting taxes

1–17   All these taxes, and all other taxes in Britain, can be grouped under three broad heads of taxation in terms of the way they are imposed and collected: withholding taxes, taxation related to particular transactions or their effects (called transactions taxes for short), and taxes based on profits or wealth of any kind (called assessed taxes, but normally now self-assessed). British taxes are of all these kinds, frequently muddled up together.

A withholding tax is a tax imposed on the payer of a sum so that the recipient receives less than would otherwise be received. For example, someone paying patent royalties to another person will be required to deduct from that sum an amount equal to the basic rate of income tax. If this is done, the recipient is treated as having paid tax on those royalties. The tax authorities are always on the lookout for ways of increasing the payment of taxes at source in this way. Most income tax and NICs are collected in this way through the PAYE system. Under most forms of withholding tax, the payer is liable to pay the tax to the tax authorities even though it was the *recipient* who is really paying the tax.

Transactions taxes are those based on particular transactions or their results. VAT is usually imposed on any supply of goods or services made by a business. Stamp duty is imposed whenever a document is used to transfer land. However, as electronic transfers take over, the stamp duty reserve tax and stamp duty land tax have been introduced to cover all transactions. IHT and CGT can be regarded as being transactions taxes.

Assessed taxes are the most important taxes in Britain although most are now self-assessed by taxpayers. Income tax raises most of its money from the income of the employed, the self-employed and those with investment income. So does the National Insurance Fund, save that it does not tax investment income. Then there are the special assessed taxes like petroleum revenue tax.

Anatomy of a tax

Whichever form of tax we adopt, and whatever the fiscal or other reasons for its adoption, the lawyer's task is to identify when it is payable and when not. Tax law, or revenue law as many also call it, is there to define when taxes shall be charged. In respect of each tax this definition will contain the same elements: **1–18**

- the tax base;
- the incidence (including the rate) of the tax; and
- the taxpayer, or person liable to pay.

The rate is often the most important point politically or commercially, but rarely detains the lawyer long. The other issues need further thought.

The tax base, as we have seen already, is the asset, transaction, profit or other thing which is liable to the tax. This may be anything from a television to the net profits of a year's trading.

Each tax will have a limited tax base, the limits being of two kinds: the general limits on that kind of tax, and specific exceptions. Clearly, the wider the tax base of a tax, the more revenue it will collect. The more exceptions that are allowed, the smaller the return from the tax. Over the years, all our main taxes have become subject to important exceptions. This is partly because granting an exception is very easy politically, and votes are not easily won for removing it later. Nonetheless, in the last few years more attention has been turned to both the limits on the tax bases of our taxes and the width of exceptions. It has become common-place to regard exceptions as tax expenditures, that is, subsidies created by the tax not collected. The cost of these tax expenditures is set out in the annual budget statements.

1–19 The second issue is the identity of the taxpayer. Economists talk of this as the incidence of the tax, distinguishing between the *formal incidence* of the tax (who is required by law to pay it) and the *effective incidence* (who ends up paying). Lawyers are concerned only with formal incidence. In most cases under modern laws different people can be made to pay in respect of some taxes, especially when withholding taxes are used to collect the tax. For example, if someone makes a gift of shares to someone else on which IHT ought to be paid, the authorities can try to collect the tax from the donor, the recipient and most subsequent owners of the shares.

The tax professions

Tax expertise

1–20 This chapter is about understanding tax. We therefore end it by considering the professions that help us understand tax— or, more usually, aspects of tax. The sheer volume of tax law is staggering—the standard volumes of the legislation such as the *Yellow* and *Orange Tax Handbooks* and their red and green equivalents published by CCH run to several volumes even though using the smallest print. They include many thousands of pages. This is reflected in the way in which the tax profession has developed to be a free-standing profession with several specialist areas. Yet it remains law that few law firms or accounting firms can ignore because it is relevant to all businesses earning profits, all employers, all employees, all trusts, all those who have investments . . . enough said.

Until relatively recently, it could be assumed that those practicing tax were either lawyers or accountants—and just occasionally both. Historically, this reflected a perceived division of approach behind what lawyers used to call revenue law and what accountants called taxation. Underlying those separate labels were the distinctly separate approaches of those concerned with rules and those concerned with sums. That different labelling has now disappeared, and the separate approaches have blurred. Even the Law Society of England and Wales now refers to the subject as tax law; specialist barristers refer to themselves as the Tax Bar.

As the two approaches coalesced a specialist profession **1–21** emerged. This is now organised separately as the Chartered Institute of Taxation (CIOT). Unlike both the law professions and the accounting professions CIOT is a single UK institute. Its members call themselves chartered tax advisors (CTA). Scotland has both legal professions and a separate Institute of Chartered Accountants from those of England and Wales (ICAS and ICAEW).

In 2012 CIOT absorbed the then separate Institute of Indirect Tax, reflecting the growing importance of indirect taxes to all tax advisers. CIOT now has 17,000 members, with its junior partner the Association of Taxation Technicians having 7,000 members.

The convergence is now recognised for most purposes with lawyers, CTAs and accountants all working within the tax profession. This has led to lawyers working in accounting firms and the reverse, with CTAs working in both. It is perhaps best illustrated by the membership of the government's Tax Professionals' Forum, formed to advise it on technical tax issues. Its membership includes eminent members of each of the professions mentioned above. Further, CIOT and ICAEW now run courses that allow students to qualify for both professions at the same time.

Do differences remain? Yes. In *R. (on the application of* **1–22** *Prudential Plc) v Special Commissioner of Income Tax* [2013] UKSC 1; [2013] 2 A.C. 185, the Supreme Court decided, by five to two, that a company could not claim to withhold documents from HMRC that it was ordered to produce by a tax judge on the grounds of legal advice privilege if the advice was not given by a lawyer. While advice given by a solicitor or a barrister could be the subject of a privilege claim, identical advice given by an accountant or tax professional could not. This was a clear decision given after hearing from the relevant professions and by judges fully aware of the policy effect. Although it is a decision applying to England and Wales, Lord Reed suggested in his judgment that the Scottish courts might take the same approach though that would be a policy decision for them. That may be important as the Scottish courts recently refused to hear an

English Queen's Counsel present a case for HMRC (the standard abbreviation for Her Majesty's Revenue and Customs—itself an abbreviation for the Commissioners for Her Majesty's Revenue and Customs!). A Scottish silk (who was also an English silk) was then appointed, and won the case for HMRC!

The practical effect of the Supreme Court decision is, at least in some cases, less sharp than it might otherwise seem. Barristers may now be instructed directly by accountants, as tax counsel often are. If the relevant advice is run before counsel, legal advice privilege applies even though accountants or other tax professionals have played a major part in formulating it. And at the lower judicial levels of the tribunals any individual may represent another. There is no exclusivity for the legal professions as representatives before the tribunals rather than as advisers. The importance of this becomes clearer when we note in the next chapter that second level appeals from the First-tier Tax Tribunal go to another tribunal and no longer to the Chancery Division of the High Court in England and Wales or the Court of Session in Scotland.

One important aspect of confidential legal advice is tackled in a different way by legislation. Anyone setting up a tax avoidance scheme must now comply with DOTAS—an obligation to ensure compliance with the *Disclosure of Tax Avoidance Schemes* legislation. Behind that, from 2013, is the GAAR, the *General Anti-Abuse Rule*. Both impose burdens on those seeking to avoid tax to do so in a way that complies with disclosure requirements. We must examine these in details when discussing tax avoidance. But it is obvious even from the names of the rules that these cut back heavily on the use of legal privilege to conceal an avoidance scheme.

1–23 Perhaps the most important current aspect of the work of tax professionals is the need to meet the growing requirement that taxpayers self-assess their liabilities to all the main taxes. Increasingly this is an obligation to do so through the internet. In practice, this means that large numbers of taxpayers need professional help with their annual or returns, let alone with any proposed mitigation or avoidance. They can no longer rely on tax officials to do it for them. Failure to comply incurs immediate penalties, which can grow significantly if a taxpayer tries to ignore or sidestep the duties. The result is a significant growth in the number of advisers specialising in different aspects of tax, as much in helping individuals with personal returns and the payroll and VAT responsibilities of small businesses as with dramatic schemes to avoid millions that attract headlines. We return to this in Ch.4.

1–24 Tax laws may be compared more with an iceberg than an elephant. They are certainly vast and often grey to the outsider. But they are also capable of sinking *The Titanic*! In practice, you will find that there is a lot more to the subject when you examine it closely than is seen by those who merely view it from a distance. Let us learn how to negotiate the ice flows.

CHAPTER 2

NATIONAL, INTERNATIONAL AND LOCAL TAX

Introduction

2–01   The powers required to impose, collect and enforce taxes are central to the legal structure of all societies. And the essential nature of a tax is that it can be imposed and collected, where necessary, by compulsion by the authorities of that society. The control over those powers is therefore also a central element of the structure of any state and is therefore usually governed by its constitution.

The constitutional position

2–02   Of course, the UK does not have a constitution—in the sense of a central text defining the fundamental structures of the state and its powers. Nor is there any central text defining the powers to legislate for, administer, or enforce taxes. For that reason, there is also no overall legal definition of a tax in UK law.

Unsurprisingly, there have over the centuries been many disputes about the use of tax powers—from the Peasants' Revolt led by Wat Tyler in 1381 in London when John of Gaunt tried to impose a poll tax to the Poll Tax Riots in London in 1990 when Margaret Thatcher tried the same thing. In between there were other historical incidents with tax at their heart such as the Boston revolt against the collection of taxes under the Tea Act 1773, now commemorated as the Boston Tea Party and recognised as part of the American Revolution or War of Independence (depending on which side of the Atlantic you live).

Historically, the right to tax in the UK, and England before it, is the right of the reigning sovereign using prerogative powers. Those powers are inherent in the status of a sovereign monarch and cannot be controlled by the courts or limited by law save with the consent of the monarch. This proved particularly provocative—not for the first time—under the Stuart kings. The expulsion of James II and the invitation to William to become king in 1688 was used as an opportunity to remove the prerogative power of the monarch to tax in his or her own name without any agreement of others. As the Bill of Rights in 1688 puts it:

"the levy of money for or to the use of the Crown by pretence of Prerogative without grant of Parliament for longer time or in other manner than the same is or shall be given is illegall."

That remains law today. From this follows the assumption that all taxes must be created by Act of the UK parliament. Similarly, any attempt to exceed or modify those powers without going back to parliament was and remains open to challenge in the courts.

Last century, following rows between the House of Lords and the House of Commons, the "grant of Parliament" was restricted to that of the House of Commons alone. Under the Parliament Acts 1911 and 1949 a Bill passed by the House of Commons certified by the Speaker as dealing only with national taxation, public money or loans becomes law one month after a Public Bill is passed by the House of Commons. However, as the government experienced in 2015, when the House of Lords refused to pass amendments to tax credits legislation, that does not apply to other public expenditure nor to statutory instruments.

The position in practice

The idea that the House of Commons alone can impose and ensure the enforcement of all forms of tax in the UK remains central to much political thinking. In practice, things are not that simple. As we have seen, our taxes do not operate in a void, but in a highly competitive international context. As part of that, the UK has been for over 40 years part of the EU, and is also party to many other international agreements that limit or share the right to impose and collect taxes. So we must examine the international aspects of our taxes. And we must look sub-nationally too. Recent years have seen a growing pressure to devolve taxing powers to the nations of Scotland, Wales and Northern Ireland as well as of course England itself. Further, we cannot ignore local taxation imposed and collected by local authorities. A full picture includes consideration of taxes imposed or limited by international agreement, by the EU, by the UK, at the level of Great Britain and separately in the four nations of the kingdom, and at regional and local levels within those nations. The multiple levels at which taxes can in practice be imposed also require appropriate tax authorities and appeal systems.

The main direct taxes in the UK are imposed across the UK as a whole: income tax, CGT, IHT, corporation tax. But we must note that those taxes no longer operate identically across the whole UK if the separate governments and parliaments or assemblies of the four nations decide otherwise. By contrast, the main indirect taxes—VAT and customs duties—operate at a European level, so cannot differ substantially within the UK. A third group of taxes–including stamp duties and local taxes—are now devolved so apply separately in the separate nations. We must now look at each level of taxation in turn.

UK taxation

2–05   Even the identity of the UK itself varies from one tax to another. For direct tax purposes, the UK consists of England, Scotland, Northern Ireland and Wales. In international law the Isle of Man and the Channel Isles are part of the UK, but they are not for direct tax purposes. Each has its own system. The Isle of Man does have essentially the same VAT as the UK, but Jersey and Guernsey do not. Nor are they within our NI and social welfare legislation.

For tax purposes, UK territory extends since 1973 to the territorial sea and continental shelf as well. This provides the authority for the Oil Taxation Act 1983 and subsequent legislation to impose and collect taxes from the North Sea oil and gas fields and other offshore energy installations (and at present the fields offshore from Scotland are treated as being in the UK but not Scotland!). That highly specialist legislation is beyond the scope of this book. Taxing workers on UK offshore oil platforms is not, as we shall see.

More generally, direct taxes are applied by reference both to activities or assets located in the territory of a state and to individuals and companies based in the state. Problems arise where the assets or activities are in one state while the potential taxpayers are in another. So we must also consider when something or someone is regarded for tax purposes as being in the UK or, where it matters, England, Scotland or elsewhere. And it will not surprise you to learn that the rules vary from one tax to another. We look at the important rules about what and who is within the UK direct tax jurisdiction and, separately, the scope of VAT, below.

2–06   All UK taxes are administered by a single national tax authority, the Commissioners of Her Majesty's Revenue and Customs. This body is universally known by the initials HMRC (standing for Her Majesty's Revenue and Customs, the official description now included in the Interpretation Act). We examine the structure and functioning of HMRC later in this chapter. And for simplicity, we use HMRC to describe the predecessors in title that were merged into HMRC: the Commissioners of Inland Revenue and the Commissioners of Customs and Excise.

Enforcement of UK taxes takes place through UK courts

and tribunals. There is a single set of tribunals available to deal with problems involving UK taxes: the First-tier Tribunal Tax Chamber and the Upper Tribunal Tax and Chancery Chamber. Appeals from the tribunals go, however, to different national courts: the Court of Appeal of England and Wales, the Court of Session in Scotland, and the Court of Appeal of Northern Ireland. Again, we must return to these.

In summary, the following remain UK taxes, though with   2–07
some national variations: income tax, corporation tax (but note below), CGT and IHT. NICs are imposed separately in Great Britain and in Northern Ireland, but the laws are for current purposes effectively identical so the reality is a UK levy. These are all important forms of tax and each is examined in this book. The following are levied—or will be under current plans—separately in the four nations or by authorities based in the four nations: some land taxes and stamp duties, council tax, business rates, landfill tax. The detail of these taxes is beyond the scope of this book. The following are imposed or limited at European level, although collected and largely retained by the UK government: VAT, customs duties and some excise duties (tobacco, alcoholic drinks). VAT requires considerable explanation but we do not deal with the other indirect taxes here. Aspects of corporation tax are also subject to EU provisions.

Imposing UK taxes

Legislation is required to impose any UK tax. It is a conven-   2–08
tion that all the main rules of the major direct taxes are imposed by primary legislation. Aside from the codified general tax laws this involves parliament enacting one or two Finance Acts (FA) each year. A limited amount of law is made by subordinate legislation, but in practice this covers details such as interest rates, specialist areas of limited general importance or administrative aspects of the law. The laws imposing NICs are technically not FA measures but are included in Social Security Acts and National Insurance Acts (usually with a British measure paralleled by a Northern Irish measure) enacted by the UK parliament.

Political responsibility for all UK taxation rests with HM   2–09
Treasury and its ministers, in particular the Chancellor of the Exchequer. It is a strong convention, however, that politicians never meddle in the collection of taxes from individual taxpayers. So the Treasury does not get involved directly in the collection and enforcement of taxes. These functions are given to separate government departments that do not have members of

the Houses of Parliament as ministers in charge, but are run by Commissioners or separately appointed officials. The responsibility of the Chancellor and the Treasury is therefore confined to general matters of tax, and in particular tax policies and the task of ensuring that legislation is passed by the Queen in Parliament to authorise any tax.

2–10   Somewhat oddly in a state that prides itself in having no constitution other than its common sense, the coalition government decided in 2011 to ask parliament to enact provisions about tax policy. The result is the Budget Responsibility and National Audit Act 2011. Section 1 of that Act requires the Treasury to prepare a Charter for Budget Responsibility and lay it before the House of Commons for approval. Section 2 requires the Treasury to prepare a Financial Statement and Budget Report for each financial year in conformity with the Charter. The rest of the Act creates an Office for Budget Responsibility with the duty on reporting on the sustainability of public finances.

The Charter is neither a formidable document nor an inflexible one, and it was amended with effect from 2015 in 2014. It states the Treasury's objectives for fiscal policy with commendable brevity. There are two: "to ensure sustainable public finances that support confidence in the economy, promote intergenerational fairness, and ensure the effectiveness of wider government policy" and "to support and improve the effectiveness of monetary policy in stabilising economic fluctuations." The second of those is the province of the Bank of England and beyond the scope of this work. You might like to consider the first of them alongside the Adam Smith principles of tax set out in the previous chapter. The Charter is of course to be read with the rights set out in the Human Rights Act. Hence perhaps the reference to intergenerational fairness rather than other kinds of fairness.

The Office for Budget Responsibility does in practice have a major role at budget time as it casts a cold eye both on the public finances and on government plans to alter them. Its regular reports now set the context for the government's own financial reports. But the result is for the House of Commons to decide in the annual Finance Act.

2–11   There is a final problem to be noted about imposing UK taxes. The financial year is, for most purposes, 1 April in one year to 31 March in the next. For income tax is it 6 April in one year to 5 April in the next. But the Chancellor customarily announces the Budget in the spring. How does the Queen in Parliament get any new law enacted in time for the new financial year? The answer is a glorious fudge known at the Provisional Collection of Taxes Act 1968. At the end of each budget debate a series of budget resolutions are put to the House of Commons. If they are passed then they take effect as law until 5 August, so giving the Commons a chance to consider the Finance Bill in some detail before it is enacted. Political deals ensure that even in election years a Bill is enacted before that date. The kind of legislative paralysis on tax and fiscal measures that hits some states, such as the US, from time to time has not occurred in the UK.

HMRC

Once the laws are enacted, their administration and enforce-   **2–12** ment passes from the politicians to administrators. For centuries there were two teams of administrators dealing with our taxes, both teams being headed by Commissioners: the Inland Revenue and Customs and Excise. The Commissioners for Revenue and Customs Act 2005 merged them into a single body, HMRC. It also created a separate Revenue and Customs Prosecution Office. In 2014 that office was abolished and its functions transferred to the Crown Prosecution Service.

HMRC consists formally of a board of Commissioners for Her Majesty's Revenue and Customs and staff all known by the official description of officers of Revenue and Customs. Since the merger HMRC's personnel has been substantially reduced, with total staff of over 100,000 being reduced to under 60,000 and—more dramatically—staff previously located in several hundred local offices being concentrated into some 12 regional centres with a few support and specialist offices. These changes reflect a major ongoing shift of approach by HMRC in handling tax administration using IT (information technology) and call centres instead of local offices as we shall see below. At the same time the powers available to HMRC officers in handling tax issues have been expanded significantly.

HMRC is the sole tax authority throughout the UK for all   **2–13** non-devolved taxes, including VAT and customs duties, subject to two minor but important exceptions. The Border Force is empowered to enforce customs duties requirements. And the National Crime Agency has specific powers to conduct tax checks in cases such as suspected money laundering. There are separate national authorities for the devolved taxes as we note below. HMRC's responsibilities are not limited to the national taxes. It is also responsible for valuations for the national business rate and for two major welfare benefits: child benefit and tax credits. It is further responsible for administering and enforcing the national minimum wage legislation. Another responsibility is the collection of repayments of student loans. The welfare benefits were transferred to HMRC when tax credits were created. They are now to be abolished and replaced by universal credit. As that happens, responsibility will be transferred back to the Department for Work and Pensions and the Northern Ireland equivalent.

2–14   The key interface between HMRC and taxpayers is now usually by self-assessment of the taxpayer—increasingly made online—and any response by HMRC officials to the information given (and payment made) by the taxpayer. The outcome is usually the amount of tax payable–or said to be payable—to HMRC but may be a repayment claim in respect of reliefs due. Separately HMRC has powers to conduct compliance checks on taxpayers which may involve random choices of taxpayers. This will involve HMRC requiring a taxpayer to produce relevant information. A fourth aspect of the interface is the imposition of a penalty on a taxpayer by HMRC for non-compliance. If there is a dispute between the taxpayer and HMRC the end of the process will either be a settlement of the dispute on agreed terms or a formal decision by HMRC confirming its view of the taxpayer's liability. Both the process and the decision give rise to issues about the liability of a taxpayer to pay (or the right to reclaim) and the way in which HMRC has reached its decision.

Controlling the tax authorities

2–15   It is important to note that the tax authorities are constrained to act only within the legislative powers at their disposal. As we explore in the next chapter, the UK has no constitution. It therefore has no constitutional limits on executive action. History is replete with examples of tax authorities being used to extract taxes for dubious official use. In most advanced states, there are therefore constitutional checks on such action. Lacking such limits in the UK, it has been left to judges to prevent the use of arbitrary power. They have been alert to ensure that a tax authority has clear legal authority both to collect a tax, and to carry out the procedures necessary to do this. Taxpayers have also been alert to ensure that any apparent stepping beyond the limits is challenged. The result is a developed administrative law of taxation. If you look at any book on constitutional and administrative law, you will see a significant number of tax cases cited. It is precisely because it is only through such cases that the balance has been struck between the Executive and the taxpayer.

At the same time, the fair enforcement of a tax such as income tax depends heavily on taxpayers honestly providing information about what they are earning. Authorities need strong powers to obtain information and collect taxes from those who do not comply readily or who are dishonest. A balance has to be struck between giving powers to the tax authorities on the one side and respecting rights of taxpayers on the other. In particular, individual taxpayers do not expect their privacy to be invaded by tax officers, nor do businesses wish to sacrifice commercial confidentiality. Both will want to be inconvenienced to the minimum extent by the process of collecting and paying taxes.

The balance is struck in three ways. First, the powers of the tax authorities are limited by law and often subject to internal safeguards. These are found in the Taxes Management Act 1970 (TMA), the Customs and Excise Management Act and the Acts providing for individual taxes. Secondly, a dispute about either the law or the facts (and often also the procedure) can be referred to independent tribunals and courts. Thirdly, independent reviewers can check the fairness and efficacy of administrative issues.

Reviews

Since 2009 the first step in a dispute between HMRC and a tax- **2–16** payer can be a review of the decision by another HMRC officer. This is a process provided for in TMA, ss.49B–49I. It represents a major shift in the previous "take it or leave it" approach sometimes adopted in tax cases. A review may be started at the request of a taxpayer or at the invitation of HMRC. It is not mandatory. But it has proved an effective method of removing disputes from the system. In the two years 2012–14 reviews of penalty decisions resulted in half of all decisions reviewed being cancelled or amended in the taxpayer's favour. Given that the process also avoids any publicity for the taxpayer, it is certainly a step to be considered in any tax dispute. But a taxpayer does not have to ask for a review. And an unsuccessful review can still be followed by an appeal. An alternative that also avoids publicity is the use of an alternative dispute procedure, such as mediation. This also avoids the formality of an appeal and may be appropriate where the dispute is about complicated fact situations.

Tax appeals

There have also been major changes to the way tax appeals **2–17** are handled. A completely new system for hearing tax appeals replaced a centuries-old system (or lack of it) in 2009. This followed the powers granted to the Ministry of Justice and the judges in the Tribunals, Courts and Enforcement Act 2007. The Act consigned the old appellate bodies, the Special Commissioners, the General Commissioners, and the VAT and Duties Tribunal, to history (though they will long feature in the tax law reports).

2–18   The general approach is that any taxpayer is entitled to appeal to an independent tribunal against any decision affecting her or his tax liability. Although there are limited decisions against which there is no direct appeal, those decisions can in practice be challenged by judicial review. And, under the 2007 Act, judicial review cases can be heard by the same tax judges as those who hear the appeals.

A taxpayer who wishes to appeal usually starts by appealing to HMRC and then notifying the appeal to the tribunal. This may be, but does not have to be, preceded by a review. In addition, in practice many officers will seek to reach a settlement of the appeal at that stage. HMRC has the power, under s.54 of TMA, to settle any outstanding appeal by a formal agreement in writing. Once both sides have signed it, the settlement takes effect as if it were a decision on the appeal. That is therefore the end of the appeal, and it is how most tax appeals end. A similar provision applies where HMRC offer a changed decision (or cancellation of a decision) following a review and the taxpayer accepts the cancellation or change.

The tax tribunals

2–19   If an appeal is confirmed on review and cannot be settled, it is referred to the Tax Chamber of the First-tier Tribunal. This has offices in London, Edinburgh, Manchester and Birmingham, although tribunals meet to hear cases throughout the UK. The hearing will be taken by a tribunal judge (salaried or fee-paid). In more complex cases the judge will sit with a "wing member", or two judges may hear the case together. The formality of the hearing will depend on the complexity and importance of the case. At the simplest end, the hearing will be conducted on papers alone. At the most complex end there will be a formal hearing in a courtroom after careful case management. The tribunal's rules, laid down in the Tribunal Procedure (First-tier Tribunal) (Tax Chamber) Rules 2009, give the judge chairing the hearing considerable discretion in how the case should be handled, although there is always a duty to act fairly. And judges can always be asked to give full reasons for any decision taken.

Decisions of the First-tier Tribunal are often decisions about facts or discretions (whether an excuse for not supplying a return was reasonable). Although the tax professions pay close attention to its decisions, all of which are published—and there is much comment on them in the professional press—they have no precedent status. We do not therefore comment on them in this work.

Appeals from the First-tier Tribunal go to the Tax and **2–20**
Chancery Chamber of the Upper Tribunal. This was a major
change in 2009, as previously appeals all went in England and
Wales to the High Court. However, despite its name, the Upper
Tribunal is a court and this Chamber is staffed (in England and
Wales) both by High Court judges of the Chancery Division
(who previously heard the appeals in the High Court) and by
other expert judges, known as Judges of the Upper Tribunal. Its
decisions are of precedent value and bind the First-tier Tribunal.
It hears both appeals from the First-tier Tribunal Tax Chamber,
and judicial reviews about tax issues. An appellant can only
appeal to the Upper Tribunal with permission of either a First-
tier Tribunal judge or a judge of the Upper Tribunal. Permission
will be granted only if the reasons for the appeal suggest an arguable error of law by the First-tier Tribunal. There is no general
right since 2009 to appeal to the Upper Tribunal, though permission is given fairly readily in major cases.

There is an important procedural difference between the
approach of the Upper Tribunal and its predecessor on an
appeal. While the High Court would only consider the appeal
on the facts found at first instance, and so would refer successful
appeals back to the tribunals, the Upper Tribunal can redeter-
mine the facts if it is established that the First-tier Tribunal has
erred and then make its own decision without a further hearing.
The Upper Tribunal was given strong encouragement to do this
by the Supreme Court in *HMRC v Pendragon* (2015). That was
a tax abuse case in which the First-tier Tribunal found that there
was no abuse. The Upper Tribunal found both that that tribunal had erred in law and that on the facts there was abuse. The
Court of Appeal upheld the appeal against the Upper Tribunal,
commenting that it should not have changed the factual analysis.
A unanimous Supreme Court overturned the Court of Appeal
decision and commended the course of action taken by the Upper
Tribunal.

Appeals from the Upper Tribunal go to the Court of Appeal **2–21**
in England and Wales, the Court of Session in Scotland and the
Northern Ireland Court of Appeal. In practice, an appeal can go
to those courts only if there is an issue of general importance in
the decision.

It is possible to bring a judicial review against a decision of the **2–22**
Upper Tribunal but only in strictly limited cases—see *R (on the
application of Cart) v Upper Tribunal* (2011). Upward appeals
go to the Supreme Court, again with permission. In practice,
any issue important enough to warrant an appeal at that level
is likely to have been dealt with by amendments to the law save

where (as in *Pendragon*) it is European law that is in question. This may happen with decisions at lower levels too—though it is rare for such amendments to have retrospective effect. This is a matter of human rights: see *R. (on the application of Huitson) v HMRC* (2010).

Cases can—and do—go on to the Court of Justice of the European Communities (CJEU) and to the European Court of Human Rights, although neither of those courts can impose individual liability to a tax. Both are discussed below.

2–23   We must next turn to the way devolved taxes are handled. But before we do so there is a further general principle to note about UK taxes. Although the legal system of Scotland (and to a lesser extent Northern Ireland and Wales) deals with issues in different ways to English law (consider, for instance, the Scottish laws of contract, property and trusts), the courts take a firm view that UK tax laws must apply equally throughout the UK. Sometimes the legislation deals with national differences, but often it does not. In such cases, it is left to the judges to sort any problems out. This may mean that the laws are generalised to avoid unfairness, as for example in *Kidson v Macdonald* (1974).

Scottish tax administration and appeals

2–24   The Scottish Parliament used its devolved powers to enact the Revenue Scotland and Tax Powers Act 2014, brought into effect in 2015. This creates Revenue Scotland as a department of the Scottish Government and gives it full collection and management powers over the devolved taxes in Scotland. The Act expressly forbids Scottish Ministers from giving directions to or otherwise seeking to control Revenue Scotland, formally copying the understood arrangements applying to HMRC. Much of the rest of the detail is similar to that applying to HMRC.

Part 4 of the Scotland Act 1998 also gives Scottish ministers powers to impose separate rates of income tax in Scotland and make other changes—but these powers have not yet been used. When they are used, close attention will need to be paid to the rules in ss.80D–80F of that Act about who is or is not a "Scottish taxpayer".

The Act creates a Scottish First-tier Tax Tribunal for Scotland and an Upper Tax Tribunal for Scotland, with a common president for both. These also follow the pattern used in the similar tribunals south of the border.

One departure from the English/UK pattern is Pt 5 of the 2014 Act contains a general anti-avoidance rule (or, rather, a series of rules) applying to any devolved tax. It is framed to apply to any future devolved tax as well as those currently devolved.

Welsh tax administration and appeals

Welsh tax devolution is following that in Scotland. In 2016 **2–25** the Welsh Assembly passed the Tax Collection and Management (Wales) Act 2016, creating the Welsh Revenue Authority (Awdurdod Cyllid Cymru in Welsh - the legislation is fully bilingual). This is a formidable piece of legislation that follows the same approaches as that of HMRC and in Scotland.

The UK parliament in the Wales Act 2014 devolved further tax powers to the Welsh Assembly and the current Wales Bill 2016 is planned to extend these. The Welsh Assembly has published a Land Transactions and Anti-avoidance of Devolved Tax (Wales) Bill anticipating these developments.

International aspects

There are three aspects of our tax law where international **2–26** agreements limit or replace UK or national law: the relevant laws of the EU; international agreements to which the UK is a party and which affect UK taxes; and the effect in the UK of the European Convention on Human Rights.

The European Union

The comments below are subject to as yet unknown develop- **2–27** ments to follow from the decision taken in the UK referendum on 23 June 2016 that the UK is to leave the EU.

Another aspect to the shifts of taxing powers is the unavoidable fact that the UK is part of the EU. As a direct result, some of "our" taxes are European taxes, not British taxes at all. The UK is now part of a single customs union with the other members of the EU and the rather wider European Economic Area, together with Turkey and small states and territories such as Monaco and the Channel Isles. This is a vast single market with a single customs law. There is also a single form of VAT throughout the EU together with a legal prohibition against any member state adopting a second VAT. As you will see in the discussion on VAT, most of the key VAT laws are European laws, and much of the case law is that of the CJEU. For both reasons, a tax expert also has to be a European law expert! Repeatedly, we find that it is the European rule, not the British rule, which is to be followed.

The effect of European law on direct taxes is more sensitive politically and is still subject to national vetoes. But here also European law cannot be ignored, and precedence must be given to rights of free movement and establishment over national discriminatory direct tax laws. Law reports show the extent to which British legislation has been challenged (not always successfully) for its alleged failure to comply with European requirements.

These requirements involve the freedoms of movement that cannot be prevented by any fiscal measure. For VAT they also include the prevailing principles of EU law such as legality and proportionality. For example, while the UK parliament can legislate disproportionately and retrospectively about entirely internal taxation if that is its wish, it cannot do so for EU tax law that is directly enforceable and applicable or in any way that brings UK taxes into conflict with the freedoms of movement protected by EU law.

2–28   Recent examples of the limitations imposed by EU law on UK law are the series of decisions that led to the decision of the House of Lords in *Fleming and Condé Nast v HMRC* (2008). This double appeal brought to an end a lengthy series of disputes about late claims for repayment of overpayments of value added tax. These claims arose when HMRC tried to stop a growing number of back claims by shortening the time limit, and limiting the scope, for back claims by a provision in FA 1997. This was challenged successfully before the European Court of Justice (ECJ) in *Marks and Spencer Plc v Customs and Excise* (2002). Customs then tried imposing a transitional period to replace the one found at fault. This was rejected by the House of Lords in these decisions. The final answer (so far) came with a renewed time limit imposed under FA 2008. A comparison of the 1997 and 2008 legislation (removing any attempt to make the measure retrospective, and delaying the intended final time limit by over 12 years) brings home, in every sense, the curbs that European law now place on national tax authorities for VAT.

2–29   The curbs are also present for direct taxes, although the application can be less obvious. Nonetheless, the courts have also spent considerable time in the last decade dealing with a series of challenges, brought together as a series of group litigation cases, to the way in which groups of companies were treated for corporation tax purposes in the EU. At the heart of the litigation was a contention that UK corporation tax laws discriminated between corporate groups involving subsidiary companies elsewhere in the EU as compared with the subsidiaries that were in the UK. And when the CJEU found the UK law to be inconsistent with the European requirements, group litigation was started to try and obtain compensation. For the latest round of another decade-long series of cases see *Pirelli v HMRC (No.2)* (2008).

The judgment of Moses LJ in *Pirelli* does its best to get at the principles of what was going on. It is an illustration of just how complex the issues get when national law has to be read subject both to double tax agreements and European law. And, frankly, the detail is far beyond this book (though an appreciation of the incisive style of Moses LJ is surely not). Nonetheless, it can be summarised as a cautionary tale about the limits of national sovereignty within the EU on any tax question that has commercial implications.

Human rights

The Human Rights Act 1998 adds another European dimen-   **2–30**
sion to our taxes. That Act introduces the principles of the European Convention of Human Rights internally into all aspects of our laws. It also imposes the duty on judges to ensure that human rights are protected, if necessary, by ruling that Acts of Parliament breach them. An early leading British case in the European Court of Human Rights is *National and Provincial Building Society v United Kingdom* (1997). The recent jurisprudence of the Human Rights Court has divided tax law between substance and procedure. In *Ferrazzini v Italy* (2001) the Grand Chamber of the Court, by a majority, ruled that taxpayers do not have any civil rights in respect of tax law. In other words, most of the protections of the European Convention on Human Rights do not apply to disputes about whether, or how much, tax is payable.

A series of cases including *King v United Kingdom (No.2)* (2004), and *King v United Kingdom (No.3)* (2005) have ruled that the penalty provisions in tax laws are to be treated as criminal cases. This requires the full rigour of the right to a fair hearing under Art.6 para.3 of the Convention to be applied by the tribunals and courts to these cases. Separately, individuals have challenged British tax laws as discriminatory, with mixed results. See *PM v United Kingdom* (2005) (is an unmarried father entitled to the same tax reliefs as a married father?) and in the local courts *R. v IRC* (2003) (is a widower of the same status as a widow?). Less obviously, the Human Rights Court has also ruled that a failure by a national government to implement an EU VAT rule can be a breach of a taxpayer's human rights: *SA Dangeville v France* (2003).

Two recent strands of thought about the interaction of taxa-   **2–31**
tion and human rights law show how wide the potential interaction can be. In *Rowe v HMRC* (2015) the Administrative Court was asked to rule that both the legislation empowering HMRC to collect tax in avoidance cases before appeals were decided and the use by HMRC of those powers were unlawful. Part of the attack was an argument that the legislation offended both art.6 of the Convention (fair hearings) and art.1 of Protocol No.1 to the Convention (property rights). Both failed, as did several other lines of attack. But the case illustrates the attempts by

taxpayers to use human rights legislation to limit the powers of tax authorities. On the other hand, there is growing attention to arguments about the interaction of tax avoidance (in particular by international companies) and fairness and other rights of those who rely on public social assistance. This was considered at length in *Tax Abuses, Poverty and Human Rights*, a report issued in 2015 by the International Bar Association's Human Rights Institute.

International taxation

2–32　　Traditionally in international law each state is sovereign and has no jurisdiction to impose or enforce taxes over taxpayers, assets or events in any other state. Nor, again traditionally, will states enforce each other's tax laws. That tradition has now died in practice even if it is present in form. There are now significant multilateral tax agreements and many thousands of bilateral tax agreements under which states and tax authorities agree both to coordinate their management of taxes with international elements and to work together to ensure taxpayers do not use international locations to avoid national taxes. The agreements also stop or reduce much double taxation of the same income from cross-border activities by the separate states. The latest published list of UK agreements includes agreements with some 150 other states and territories (ranging from the Isle of Man and the Channel Isles to the US, Russia and China).

The subject is of immense complexity and importance in practice, but two principal areas of agreement should be noted here. The two principal areas are: dealing with the applicable tax rules where a taxpayer, asset or activity is potentially liable to two or more national taxes, so as to avoid double taxation; and cooperation and exchange agreements to avoid taxpayers either telling one tax authority one set of facts and the other a different set of facts, or pretending to one tax authority that circumstances do not involve that authority. Where an international agreement involves either of those areas then its provisions will usually prevail over UK national law. In other words, it is the terms of the international agreement that provide the relevant tax laws, not the terms of the UK legislation if they are different.

Once upon a time it may have been easy to avoid taxes in one state by pretending either that there was nothing to be taxed or that alternatively tax had been levied in another state. Those stories now rarely work. The individual who contends that he did not declare his income in the UK although resident here because, say, he has paid tax in Gibraltar when he has not may find he has

an enforced change of address that incurs expenditure by Her
Majesty for not having contributed to Her expenditure in either
state!

Readers will no doubt be relieved to know that, having made
these points, we intend to spend no more time than we have to on
international tax—either direct or indirect—in this work.

Local taxation

The final pieces of the UK's fiscal jigsaw are the sub-national, **2–33**
or local, taxes. There are two local taxes: the national business
rate and council tax. Both are property taxes levied on a rent-
based valuation of commercial properties (the business rate)
and residential properties (the council tax). Partly because local
land taxes are fully devolved to Scotland and partly devolved in
Wales, fundamental changes are planned for both taxes which
will have the effects of making them more genuinely local taxes.

Until recently the national business rate was entirely that,
despite the fact that it was levied and collected by local councils.
Although valuations were local and individual to businesses,
the rate levied was set nationally. Funds were remitted to the
Treasury, which then redistributed the money to local councils
according to a national formula. However, since 2013 councils have been entitled to keep half the net local business rates
proceeds. And in Scotland this is a devolved function. In the
2015 Autumn Statement the Chancellor announced a radical
change to this by 2020, with local councils being empowered
to determine their own business rate and all proceeds from the
rate being retained locally. The importance of that change can
be seen when the proceeds from the business rate are compared
with the proceeds from corporation tax. As one business pressure group noted in 2015, local businesses were currently paying
£2.40 in business rates for every £1 they paid in corporation
tax. Nationally, however, corporation tax is more important
as much of it is paid by the UK's biggest companies. When the
reforms take place, there will be equivalent reductions in national
financial support to local councils. And at the same time the
Chancellor announced in Budget 2016 plans to reduce the burden
of the national business rate on small businesses from 2017.

Council tax is also collected locally but again is subject to a
redistribution at national level. There used to be a welfare benefit
called council tax benefit that reduced or removed the burden of
the tax from poorer households. This has now been replaced by a
system of council tax reductions run by individual local councils.
Because council tax reductions are not welfare benefits, they
can be devolved functions in Scotland and Wales, and indeed

the reduction systems of England, Scotland and Wales are now different. The Scottish government proposes to go further and has established a cross-party Commission on Local Tax Reform to consider the best way forward. This is again of major fiscal importance as council tax currently raises more tax revenue than the business rate. Both are in the "top ten" noted at the beginning of Ch.1.

CHAPTER 3

HANDLING TAX LAWS

Introduction

Tax is often regarded as being about numbers. Tax law is **3–01** about words. It is an odd thing that many lawyers seem worried about studying tax, because they are worried about the numbers, while many others are worried about tax, because they are worried about the words! What needs to be understood by many lawyers is that you can be a completely sound tax lawyer yet leave the numbers for others to work out. That is the approach taken in this book. Any examples will be simple ones! At the same time, it is of the highest importance that a tax lawyer is fully competent at interpreting and applying the laws that impose taxes. This is because, quite simply, every tax case is a case about statutory interpretation and application.

The purpose of this chapter is to make an initial survey of **3–02** the raw material of a tax lawyer's work—the statutes and other materials to be used in finding out what the relevant tax law for a particular matter is, what that law means, and how it is to be applied. To do this we must first reflect on the history of tax law. Despite Mr Ford's views on such things, it is not bunk. We must also examine the territorial extent of the tax laws. Having set the scene, we look at the forms of tax legislation, and current criticisms about those forms. Another point of importance is finding out about the current law. Tax law changes with extreme rapidity, and to be out of date is easy but useless. How are tax questions researched? That we must explore. We then look at how the laws are handled—the methods of interpretation and application, including some thoughts on the use of techniques to avoid the application of tax laws. Some of what we say is relevant to the study of any statute law. That does not make it any less important. On the contrary, the techniques involved are central to a lawyer's skills, and repetition of them is always justified.

History

It is no coincidence that some of the oldest documents in **3–03** existence are tax returns. We hold tax laws from over four millennia ago in the British Museum archives. Wherever there is social organisation there is also tax, unless there is almost total slavery or serfdom. Even in the shorter history of England (and the much shorter history of Great Britain) taxation played a central role. It lay behind several rebellions (including, of course, that of the American colonies) and the failure of governments, both ancient and modern. We will not stray into those areas now, fascinating as they are, just for their own sake. Happily, others have chronicled the subject with care. Pre-eminent among recent historians is Basil Sabine, whose *History of Income Tax* and well-written contributions to the *British Tax Review* are of considerable help. Stephen Dowell's *History of Taxation*, written at the beginning of last century, spans the previous 600 years, but is sadly found in too few libraries. Since 2000, Cambridge University has hosted biennial conferences on the history of taxation, producing a wide range of historical studies.

Is not the history of tax yet more clutter in the study of a complex subject? We think not. We need to examine the backgrounds of our taxes. This is because some of them are old and understandable only in the context of their origins. Others of our taxes may be new but there are lessons to be learnt from previous experiments that are of continuing relevance.

The oldest regular tax in England is the **stamp duty**. This was one of the taxes introduced by William of Orange after 1688 drawing on experience back home. So were the window duty (the tax said to be "daylight robbery") and the salt tax (which did wonders for the smuggling trade). The proceeds were exported, in the shape of the English navy, to fight the French. Stamp duty changed little from 1694 to 2003, when it started to become obsolete because of electronic transactions. This is because the essence of a stamp duty is literally a stamp on a document, without which the document is invalid. Since then it has been modernised, and in Scotland replaced by transfer taxes.

Income tax

3–04   The next tax to be introduced was the **income tax**. Its proceeds were also exported to fight the French although, arguably, the tax was the invention of a Frenchman, Colbert. It was adopted in 1799 as a temporary tax to finance the war against Napoleon. At the time, it replaced, and to some extent copied, what were known as the assessed taxes and land tax that had been used for over a century before. The need for new revenue was desperate. The usual practice until then had to be to tax things. In large part this was done by customs duties, the takings from which were reduced sharply by the war at sea. In Britain itself, the usual practice was to put excise taxes on things—windows, servants, tea, wigs—but these were not enough. Pitt introduced a "contribution on property, profits and income". It was based on a voluntary declaration that the sum of money paid was "not less than ten per centum" of the contributor's income. Not surprisingly, it did not raise much. In 1802, after a lull in the fighting, the tax was repealed. In 1803, it was reintroduced by Addington in a more efficient form. The structure was so efficient indeed that it survived two centuries, finally succumbing only to the 21st Century rewrite. Addington's Act lasted to 1815, when peace finally arrived and the tax expired automatically. For 27 years, land taxes and trade taxes were again used, but they proved too weak a tax base for the emerging industrial economy. In 1842 the income tax, still much in its 1803 form, was reintroduced as a temporary measure. The need for revenues might again have had something to do with ships, as that year we seized Hong Kong. Income tax has been with us ever since, although it is still in form a temporary measure.

During its long history the details of the income tax have been chopped and changed by governments. For example, in 1910 we needed some more ships, so a higher rate of tax (in the guise of supertax) was proposed. That is one reason why the present tax is so difficult to understand. It is not the work of any one committee or team of drafters, but a patchwork of the efforts of innumerable minds with differing and often unstated aims. Every so often, someone has a go at sorting it out, but they have rarely succeeded in changing much.

It was always thus. Back in 1752, Lord Chesterfield and other **3–05** "backbench" reformers wanted to change the calendar to get rid of the extra 11 days that had crept into the measurement of the year under the Julian calendar. In those days the official year started on 25 March (Lady Day). Lord Chesterfield and colleagues got their way and, despite rioting, the middle of September (mid-year) was removed in 1752. The end of the year was left as 24 March 1753—except for the Treasury. Then, as now, to lose 11 days from a financial year was just too expensive. So the tax year continued to 5 April 1753. For income tax, it still does, 250 years later. With the daily revenue from the tax exceeding £3 billion, it is unlikely to change.

There have been some spirited attempts to knock the income **3–06** tax into shape. A Royal Commission on Income Tax had a go in 1920 (Cmd. 615). A few changes followed. More ambitious was a Codification Committee in 1936 (Cmd.5131). This conducted the monumental task of sieving through our then tax laws to find the principles and the problems. It is a fascinating study which still repays the reading, but it was never implemented. There was another Royal Commission in the early 1950s, reporting in 1953 (Cmd.8671), 1954 (Cmd.9105) and 1955 (Cmd.9474). It led to several changes but no substantial restructuring. There was a semi-official attempt by a committee chaired by Sir James Meade, a Nobel laureate, to secure major changes in a report on *The Structure and Reform of Direct Taxation* in the 1970s, but the major debate that occasioned achieved limited reforms. Not least, the committee advocated replacing the income tax with an expenditure tax. It didn't happen. Forty years on, a different kind of expenditure tax—VAT—had completely changed the fiscal scenery. So another distinguished committee chaired by another Nobel laureate—the Mirlees Committee—tried again. If anything about tax beyond black letter law interests you, then you should look at this. (It is published on the web by the Institute for Fiscal Studies.) One fears that this will join the previous list of failed best endeavours.

3–07   None of these initiatives did much to improve the shape of our taxes. There was some tidying up from time to time by consolidation, but nothing more adventurous. There was an 1842 Act re-imposing the income tax in a tidier way than in 1803, and a bit more was done in 1853. This kept going until 1918, when the stresses of yet another war forced a consolidation. The 1918 Act was strengthened on a number of occasions (notably in 1936 and during the next war) but it was kept going—in patched up form—until 1952. The Income Tax Act 1952 reconsolidated the law and gave it a more modern appearance. That lasted until the next consolidation, in 1970, with yet another consolidation in 1988. But all the time our tax laws kept growing in length and complexity. And until the Rewrite Project started in 1995 that is all consolidations did. They rarely simplified anything.

Finally, a more serious attempt to give better shape to our laws started in 1995 when years of grumbling boiled up into a most unusual statutory amendment to the Finance Bill 1995 passed against the wishes of the government. The result was the establishment of a process at first optimistically called the Tax Law Simplification Programme, but more realistically established as the Tax Law Rewrite. Teams of expert drafters and officials, working with independent tax experts and judges, worked to rationalise and codify our income tax laws.

The programme took 15 years. The results are an impressive series of Acts of Parliament drafted into a consistent code setting out the law we shall examine in Pt Two of this book. The individual Acts are:

- the Capital Allowances Act 2001 (CAA);
- the Income Tax (Earnings and Pensions) Act 2003 (ITEPA);
- the Income Tax (Trading and Other Income) Act 2005 (ITTOIA);
- the Income Tax Act 2009 (ITA);
- the Corporation Tax Act 2009 (CTA 2009);
- the Corporation Tax Act 2010 (CTA 2010); and
- the Taxation (International and Other Provisions) Act 2010 (TIOPA).

The downside, as we have already noted, is that this law, when taken together with our other tax laws, constitutes the longest tax code—and perhaps the longest law code on any specific topic—in the world's history.

Later taxes

Compared with these taxes, the other taxes in this book are modern, though one of them, **corporation tax**, was in reality a parasitic tax that was just a name for income tax on companies until recently. Only in 2009 did it become an entirely separate tax from income tax. As just noted, corporation tax law has been rewritten. **3–08**

Capital gains tax appeared in 1965. It was and is a device for plugging obvious gaps in the income tax base. In some countries, it forms part of the income tax, and perhaps it should here too. It does already for companies. Corporation tax taxes both income and capital gains, so CGT only applies to individuals and trusts. The law has not been rewritten and was last consolidated in the Taxation of Chargeable Gains Act 1992 (TCGA). **3–09**

National Insurance (NI) contributions date back to 1911 but came to their present form in 1973. The law is now consolidated in the Social Security Contributions and Benefits Act 1992, but most of the detail is in the Social Security Contributions Regulations 2001. Since 1999, NICs have been collected by HMRC. They are in reality a second income tax and these rules are slowly being integrated with income tax rules. **3–10**

Value added tax also appeared in 1973, but for a very different reason. VAT is a peace tax. Several of our taxes were introduced in order to help us beat our European neighbours. This one was introduced so we could join them. The adoption of VAT was a precondition of our entry into the European Community—now the EU. It is the only permissible form of general indirect tax, or sales tax, in the member states of the **3–11**

EU. This is because it proved to be the only major tax that could offer a neutral way of taxing production and consumption, and also handle international transactions neutrally. It was first introduced in the EC in 1967. A single VAT law was created in 1977. In its current form of the VAT Directive (Directive 2006/112) it applies directly in 29 European states—and in similar form in several others. It is in reality a federal tax, and the UK is part of the federation. Other forms of the tax—often called goods and services tax—now apply throughout most of the world.

3–12   **Inheritance tax** has a shorter but odder (and in one way longer) history. It was introduced in 1974 and 1975 as a tax called capital transfer tax, to replace estate duty (dating from 1894) and to succeed to a tradition of taxing estates on death which predates even William of Orange. It had its name changed in 1984 to the present title, although it was not changed into an inheritance tax. It has been reformed since then, but now looks in some ways rather more like the 1894 Act than the 1974 Act! It has been threatened with abolition, but then so have most of the other taxes in this list. If it is abolished, it will only be the third time in our history that an estate duty has been abolished. Each time it has reappeared in a new guise, and with the same problems.

Old ideas and new forms

3–13   History therefore offers us a range of taxes, some a few years old and some over 300 years old. It confronts us with a range of approaches and a range of reasons for the form of tax used. More important to us as lawyers, it confronts us with a wide variety of language. Some is the product of the word processor, while some is only a little younger than the later plays of Shakespeare. It also confronts us with old ideas in new shapes—but we must remember that they are old ideas if we are to treat them correctly.

An annual tax

3–14   One old idea is that taxes are annual. Parliament still has to re-enact the income tax legislation every year. If it does not, then there would be no income tax next year. Read s.4 of the Income Tax Act 2007 (ITA 2007). You will see that it does not operate unless in any year there is a Finance Act imposing the income tax. Read the preamble to any Finance Act. You will see that taxes are still granted annually to the Crown, not imposed by it. It is, we are supposed to believe, a voluntary offering. This fiction has the consequence that the income tax this year is different to the income tax last year. Further, a judge cannot assume that there will be an income tax next year. So any case about income tax can only look at what happens this year. If, for example, tax is imposed on a form of income, that form of income must exist this year to be taxed. It is not enough that it existed last year, or might exist next year.

The judicial reaction to the annual nature of income tax is called the source doctrine: see *Brown v National Provident Institution* (1921) HL. The doctrine means that if, say, a trader retires in one year, and receives income in the next, that income can be taxed in neither year. It was not received in the first year. There was no trade in the second year. It will not surprise you to learn that there are statutory provisions designed to prevent tax avoidance this way, but the doctrine still remains.

A schedular tax?

For most of its history income tax was a schedular tax. The tax was imposed not on "income" but by a series of self-contained charges in different schedules to the original—and all following—Acts. As we see below, this is still important to students because it dominated income tax case law for over a century. But it also introduces a fundamental principle of income tax law. A form of income is only liable to income tax if it is caught within one (or more) of the charging rules. Contrast VAT, which is a tax on *all* forms of supplies of goods and services. Behind the schedular system, and now hidden behind our rewritten income tax laws, is a more fundamental constitutional principle. Following the minor matter of a civil war, and the even more minor matter of the practice of Stuart kings imposing taxes at whim, the Bill of Rights imposed the rule that there can be no taxation without the assent of parliament. For a tax to be imposed, therefore, it has to be shown that parliament has agreed to it. Without clear authority, a tax cannot be raised. This old idea still receives warm support from the judges. Lord Goff said in *Woolwich Building Society v IRC* (1992):

> "the retention by the state of taxes unlawfully exacted is particularly obnoxious, because it is one of the most fundamental principles of our law . . . that taxes should not be levied without the authority of Parliament."

Although income tax has lost its schedules, it is still a series of charges to tax rather than a single charge. However, as we see in detail below, only one income tax charge can apply to one form of income at any time.

3–15

"A tax shall be charged"

3–16   The key sections in any tax law are the charging sections. These are the sections that actually impose the tax. Take them out, and the rest is mere verbiage. They are often signalled by the draftsman stating unambiguously that "a tax shall be charged". Look for this language in s.1 of the Value Added Tax Act 1994 (the VAT Act), the Inheritance Tax Act 1984 (IHTA) or of ITA 2007. But these are not the only charging sections in the Acts. Others are often found lurking in the more obscure parts of the Acts. The completion of the Tax Law Rewrite has replaced the old schedular structure of the income tax and provided entirely separate legislation for corporation tax. But it did not produce a single charge to income tax or corporation tax. The approach of having different provisions for different kinds of income continues. And it will be necessary for some years to understand the old system in order to understand the cases. We list below the different kinds of income, noting the old schedular identity as well as the new rules.

The current kinds of income taxable to income tax and corporation tax are:

- **Annual profits and gains** has long been the phrase used to catch forms of income not caught by other provisions, including a fall-back rule when other rules did not apply. This "catch-all" role was performed by the old Sch.D Case VI. The rule is now in ITTOIA Pt 5 s.687 where the charge is on income from any source not charged under any other provision. For corporation tax, see CTA 2009 Pt 10 s.979;
- **Annuities** were once of considerable importance as investment income, and they were covered by Sch.D Case III. Their main importance now is linked with pensions and the relevant tax law is in ITEPA Pt 10. Other income from annuities for individuals is caught by ITTOIA Pt 5, and for companies by CTA 2009 Pt 10;
- **Capital gains** are sometimes treated as income for individuals receiving them (for example, some capital payments from companies). But most forms of gain are subject to the separate CGT. However, gains of companies are chargeable as part of the corporation tax: see s.2 of CTA 2009;
- **Dividends and other distributions** from UK companies are taxes under the rules applying to savings and investment income in ITTOIA. They used to be caught by the rules in the old Sch.F. Dividends from foreign companies are also now caught under the same rules as UK company

dividends, though they used to be caught by other income tax rules. UK companies do not pay corporation tax or income tax on dividends received from other UK companies. The treatment of a dividend from a foreign company depends on the relationship between the UK company and the foreign company. In the ordinary case it is treated as taxable income by s.933 of CTA 2009;

- **Employment income** together with the income of office holders (such as directors) is the main charge imposed by ITEPA. This has replaced the old Sch.E. **Earnings from employment** are also subject to charge to the Class 1 NICs on both the earner and the employer. Companies cannot in practice receive earnings;

- Income from **intangible fixed assets** received by companies is subject to a charge to corporation tax under CTA 2009 Pt 8, with special rules for sales of assets under Pt 9. This covers income from all forms of intellectual property. The equivalent provisions for individuals are divided between those payments regarded as trading income (e.g. royalties received by a professional writer) and those regarded as savings and investment income, charged accordingly under the appropriate parts of ITTOIA;

- **Interest** was treated differently for income tax if received from a government source (Sch.C) or on a commercial loan (Sch.D Case III), though it is often tax exempt on small savings. The tax charge and exemptions are in ITTOIA. The charge to corporation tax is under a separate regime known as **loan relationships** in CTA 2009;

- **Pension income** is now charged under separate provisions in ITEPA, although most forms of pension used to be regarded as delayed earnings charged under Sch.E. ITEPA also charges the state retirement pension. Companies cannot receive pensions;

- **Professions and vocations** used to be charged separately under Sch.D Case II (perhaps reflecting old attitudes to "trade") but were largely treated in the same way as trades for income tax purposes. They are now swept completely into the ITTOIA charge on trading income. Class 2 NICs apply to the more neutral description of the self-employed. Companies cannot in practice conduct professions—any similar income is trading income in any event. Income from holding an office is charged by CTA 2009 s.969;

- **Property income**, or rents and receipts from land as it was formerly called, used to be charged under separate income tax provisions, referred to as Sch.A. Income is now charged under provisions similar to those for trading income, set out in ITTOIA (for individuals) and CTA 2009 (for companies);

- **Savings and investment income** used to be charged under a variety of provisions but have now been brought together into Pt 4 of ITTOIA. As noted above, corporation tax has a different regime for interest, and does not impose a charge on dividends from UK companies. There are specific rules for UK investment companies (companies, in this sense, do not have "savings". Those with the need for significant reserves, such as life assurance companies, are subject to special rules);

- **Social security income**, like pension income, used to be caught by Sch.E, unless it was exempt from tax. If taxable, it is now subject to a specific regime in Pt 10 of ITEPA. Those receiving social security benefits usually receive NI credits that replace a liability to pay NICs. This does not apply to companies;

- **Trading income** used to be treated differently if a UK trade (Sch.D Case I) or an overseas trade (Case V). There is now a single charge under ITTOIA on individuals and partnerships. The equivalent rules for companies are in CTA 2009 Pt 3. Individual traders are liable to Class 2 NICs as self-employed;

- **Trust income** and **income from estates in administration**. These forms of income are subject to specific provisions set out in an orderly code in ITTOIA. This is applied to companies by CTA 2009 Pt 10.

As the length of this list and the differences between income tax and corporation tax both emphasise, income comes in many forms and may be treated in more than one way. So the absence of a general definition of "income" is of limited importance. What is important is the scope of the rules that impose tax on each specific kind of income. Studying those rules is the essence of the study of this subject.

The relationship between taxes and charging provisions

3–17 Faced with this battery of separate provisions, important questions arise. Can any form of income be charged under two charging sections, or even two taxes at the same time?

As regards income tax and corporation tax, only one can apply to any one taxpayer on any item of income. Corporation tax applies to companies (defined as bodies corporate by ITA 2007 s.992), and income tax to anyone or anything that is not a body corporate. Income tax therefore covers trusts and partnerships. For a fascinating case that decided that the Conservative Party under Mrs Thatcher was not a body corporate (because it consisted of Mrs Thatcher!) see *Conservative Central Office v Burrell* (1982). History does not record whether the tax inspector in that case was duly promoted.

There is also a clear ranking between income tax and CGT (or the corporate equivalents). In every case, it must first be asked if income tax applies. Only if we conclude that it does not do we ask whether there is a charge to CGT. A charge cannot arise to the two taxes at once. Case law establishes that HMRC may raise alternative assessments under both taxes, but can only collect tax under one of them: *Bird v IRC* (1989).

This rule of mutual exclusivity also applies to the income tax **3–18** charging provisions. Whatever may be the theoretical possibilities, a form of income can be charged to income tax once only. If the legislation does not make clear which provision that should be, it will be for the judges to decide. The reason for this is that income tax is regarded as a single tax, not a series of taxes. It follows that only one set of provisions of that tax can apply to any taxable income at any one time.

These rules are necessary because it is not clear from the words of the legislation alone that there is no overlap between the taxes, or to charging provisions. Any other rule would, in principle, be unfair. Note that the rule does not apply to other kinds of taxes. A relationship between VAT and income tax, for example, does not exist. It is therefore irrelevant in law that something is or is not subject to income tax for VAT purposes. In other words, the mutual exclusion rule only applies to similar taxes.

Tax legislation

As we have seen, one of the few clear principles that can **3–19** be said to be constitutional in the UK is the Bill of Rights of 1688/89 providing that taxes cannot be imposed save by consent of parliament. There is no common law of tax, nor any prerogative or other inherent rights to tax. Nor can taxes be imposed by treaty without parliamentary authority to recognise and collect them.

FINANCE ACTS For this reason, we must locate the express **3–20** authority of parliament to impose a tax on every occasion on which we wish to collect tax. If there is no authority, there is no liability to tax. Applying that approach to our tax laws may once have been a simple operation. Now it is enormously complicated. This is because there have been new tax provisions passed by parliament at least once a year for at least 130 years without any break. Since 1894 there has been at least one omnibus **Finance Act** each year. These have rarely shortened the extant law, even when taxes have been abolished.

The primary legislation imposing our main taxes is therefore of formidable dimensions. As a result, there is likely to be some provision covering most forms of income or transaction, and determining whether or not it comes within the tax. We cannot, however, assume this. Leaving aside, for the moment, the problems of interpreting tax laws, the rule remains that unless there is a provision that covers the income or transaction in point, no tax can be collected. At the heart of this process lies the simple fact that the purpose of a tax law is to impose tax on certain things, and not on other things. There may be a range of reasons why parliament has decided to do that. But, following the traditions of British legislation, the reasons why are normally left unstated. The question is always: "is this activity or thing within the scope of a taxing provision?"

3–21 DEVOLVED LEGISLATION The Scottish parliament and the Welsh and Northern Ireland Assemblies all now have devolved powers to impose or modify taxes within their own jurisdictions. In each case this must be done following the proper legislative forms of that nation. But there will be an additional question to be asked in each case of such legislation. Is it within the devolved powers of that government? The answer will be found in the relevant legislation of the UK parliament, but of course there may be more than one view about those provisions. In such cases the law officers of the UK or the devolved governments may refer the matter of competence to the UK Supreme Court. Anyone assuming that the UK Supreme Court will find this an easy task should study the 3:2 split of the court in *Recovery of Medical Costs for Asbestos Diseases (Wales) Bill* (2015). There is plainly scope for interesting litigation here, as there will be if individual taxpayers choose to challenge the competence in connection with specific tax measures.

3–22 DELEGATED LEGISLATION Traditionally, parliament has added extra levels of complexity to the process of imposing taxes by insisting that all major rules of tax are imposed by primary legislation. **Delegated legislation** is therefore limited. This means that any significant detail must be set out in a section of an Act, not in delegated legislation. This rule was in particular applied to the income tax. There were good democratic reasons for this. Every word of every section of a Finance Act is open for political and technical debate and may be the subject of a separate vote. This is restricted in the case of Schedules to the decision whether a Schedule "stand part". It is even more restricted in the case of statutory instruments to a vote whether the instrument be (or not be) made. Despite, or perhaps because of, these limitations, much greater use is made of Schedules and statutory instruments in the more modern taxes. Much of VAT is, for example, to be found in the VAT Regulations 1995, while many important aspects of NIC law is found in the Social Security (Contributions) Regulations 2001. For the sake of completeness, we must also note a small group of orders and directions issued as Non-Statutory Instrument secondary legislation. These are minor matters of legislative effect but made under legislation that does not require the order or direction to be put before parliament in any form or published officially. But they are listed and set out on *GOV.UK* [Accessed 1 June 2016].

Nonetheless, it is a pretence to claim that there is an open tech- **3–23** nical debate on every tax provision. Time does not allow it. A few selected provisions are subject to a high profile political debate on the floor of the House of Commons. Other selected provisions are subject to more technical debate in the Finance Bill committee. Other provisions pass without comment. All provisions pass without comment in the House of Lords, because they are (since the Parliament Acts were passed) effectively debarred from interfering in tax laws. The fact that this results in what some regard as our most important laws being subject to the least thorough scrutiny by parliament is of course justified by an appeal to history and democracy. Perhaps that is another of the principles of our constitution. If so, perhaps, now that the Queen also pays taxes, we should change it.

EUROPEAN LAW Some of our tax laws receive even less **3–24** parliamentary scrutiny. These are the rules imposed by the **European Union Treaties, Regulations and Directives**. Most important is the Community Customs Code (reg.2913/92). By virtue of the Treaty on the Functioning of the European Union (art.288) it is directly effective in all member states without further enactment. No pretence was made to enact it in the UK. VAT is also based on extensive EU law, although most of this is in the form of Directives. Many of the provisions of these Directives apply directly in the same way as provisions in regulations. This is so, even though a Finance Act provision says otherwise. Why? Because EU laws prevail over UK laws.

3–25   EXTRA-STATUTORY CONCESSIONS Before leaving this account of the UK tax rules, we must note another curiosity. This is an accumulation of **extra-statutory concessions (ESCs)** issued or conceded by HMRC and its predecessors over many years. They are rules with a sort of "Alice in Wonderland" nature (or, rather, a grin like that of the Cheshire cat). They are not law, but in practice they prevail over the law. And if you try to invoke them before the tribunals in place of the law, you will be left with nothing but a grin. Their application can be challenged only through the route of a judicial review (though thankfully the tribunals can now handle this along with appeals). They have been criticised on several occasions by the courts—see for example the comments of the Court of Appeal in *R. v Wilkinson* (2003). Why are they still there? The Tax Law Simplification Committee persuaded parliament to remove some, and the Office of Tax Simplification is working to remove others. What is left is a mix of items, including benevolent interpretations to avoid appeals and corner-cutting to avoid excessive complexity—worthy in practice but wrong in principle. There are two lists. The list of those applying to direct taxes is published as *Extra-statutory concessions* and that for VAT as *VAT Notice 48*. Both are on *GOV.UK*.

3–26   INTERNATIONAL TAX AGREEMENTS The final category of tax rule is that of the UK's international tax agreements with other jurisdictions. In many states an international agreement in proper form automatically becomes law with internal effect under the state's constitution. That cannot happen in the UK, so a different method is used. Once an agreement has been ratified by both (or all) states including the UK, the text of the agreement (often in two languages) is scheduled to an **Order in Council** and brought into effect that way. The powers to make and give effect to these orders are in TIOPA where the agreement is for the avoidance of double taxation. Separately, FA 2013 s.222 empowers the Treasury to make regulations to enforce international tax compliance measures in the UK. Confusingly, there is no one common name for these arrangements. For some purposes HMRC refers to them as "double-taxation agreements" (complete with hyphen in some but not all cases! – DTA for short) while if you want to see the full list on *GOV.UK* [Accessed 1 June 2016] look for "tax treaties" which is technically the American phrase. In Europe-speak they are "double taxation conventions".

Finding the law

The first rule in trying to find the current law imposing a tax 3–27 is not to do so from the Acts of Parliament themselves. Even where there is a recent codification, this would be an excessively time-consuming occupation. It is also pointless, because there are splendid commercial consolidations of the law published annually by several publishers. One or other of these consolidations is indispensable for a proper study of tax law. They are also available on the internet as are official versions.

These commercial consolidations are particularly useful because they give the history of sections in the consolidation measures, and cross-reference texts to other relevant provisions. They also set out the SIs, the EU law, and the ESCs.

Using tax laws

There are traditionally two approaches to deciding how a 3–28 tax law works. One is to try and determine its meaning. The other is to try and determine what the tax authorities think it means. These are often different things and require different techniques. For a professional adviser, which technique is appropriate depends on the client. One approach is to seek to establish with the maximum certainty whether the tax authorities will demand that a tax be levied on a transaction. The other approach is to form an independent view about whether tax applies, and be prepared to argue the point before the tribunals and courts if necessary. But even the most law-abiding taxpayer is unlikely to do this to increase a personal tax bill. The first of these approaches is the process of *tax compliance*, that is, of ensuring that the law is obeyed at minimum cost and risk. The other is the process of *tax planning*, under which a taxpayer seeks to explore the law to mitigate a tax burden, or possibly to remove it altogether, within the terms of the law.

Self-assessment has caused these two traditional approaches to coalesce. The aim of self-assessment is to transfer to the taxpayer any decision about the extent to which something should be taxed. Decisions about the relevance of any tax provision to a set of facts, or of interpretation and application of the law to those facts, is for the taxpayer. Of course, tax officials check on the accuracy of the taxpayer's judgment. Self-assessment has also made it more important for the tax authorities to clarify their own views on what taxpayers should be doing. We will look at how they make their views known first, and then how tax laws are interpreted.

The official view

3–29   The need for HMRC to operate tax laws fairly and openly throughout the UK imposes a heavy duty to ensure that tax laws actually work that way. This requires HMRC to deal with any problem thrown up by the tax affairs of any taxpayer in a consistent way. Much of the initial work by HMRC is done following self-assessment returns by taxpayers, so HMRC must ensure full guidance to those taxpayers. But it must also ensure full guidance to its officers, and full guidance to any computer used as part of the process. Computers may be good at many things, but they only work properly with "yes/no" instructions. There is no scope in such a system for administrative discretion or vagueness.

3–30   For this reason HMRC now publishes full guidance about the relevant law. At the same time, governments have in recent years taken considerable steps to consult with the professions and others directly involved, in particular, with technical aspects of tax. A series of other reforms during the same period have seen a major programme of publication undertaken by HMRC including consultations about suggested changes to tax law, policy proposals when government has decided how to take a change forward, and draft legislation ahead of a Finance Bill. Together these increase considerably the information about tax law changes both before they happen and as they happen. This collection of materials is brought together in the HMRC section of the official *GOV.UK* website [Accessed 1 June 2016]. Nonetheless this is essentially a document-based resource and it is therefore necessary to note the kinds of documents available.

3–31   **Primary and secondary legislation**. The most important material is of course the legislation. All legislation of the UK parliament and national parliaments and assemblies are held on the UK's web archive, part of the National Archives. See *www.nationalarchives.gov.uk* [Accessed 1 June 2016]. There is an extremely powerful search engine for this statutory material at *www.legislation.gov.uk* [Accessed 1 June 2016]. Further, this site carries updated and (where necessary) corrected versions of the legislation as well as the original texts. It is always necessary to ensure that you look at the actual form of legislation operative for a particular tax year, rather than the original version when first enacted, so this can be important.

3–32   **Consultations**. The government now regularly conducts consultations about proposed changes to tax law. Consultation documents are sometimes announced by the Chancellor as part of a Budget package, though the documents themselves may be published by the Treasury or HMRC depending on the scope and nature of the changes suggested. These consultations are useful documents in identifying weakness or problems in existing law. Of equal importance are both the responses to a consultation and the government's published position after receiving responses. Responses are regularly published on the website of the professional bodies (such as the Law Societies, the Institutes of Chartered Accountants and the CIOT) and other concerned bodies.

TIIN. No, not a member of the Jedi Council but a **Tax Information and Impact Note**. These notes are issued by HMRC to set out the policy of a tax change that has been decided (or nearly decided bar some details) by government, together with the necessary assessments of the costs and benefits of the proposed new provision. It is often the best place to examine a new measure proposed in an annual Budget. These are all set out under the above heading on the HMRC part of the *GOV.UK* website [Accessed 1 June 2016].   3–33

Explanatory notes. These are now published with and for all Finance Bills and all delegated legislation produced by HMRC. There are also lengthy explanatory notes for all the provisions in the Tax Acts rewritten as part of the Tax Law Rewrite process. In other countries such notes are often given more prominence in the courts than is usual in this country. But astute counsel and taxpayers sometimes find them useful in argument before the tax tribunals.   3–34

Parliamentary proceedings (or, being constitutionally correct, House of Commons Proceedings, as the Lords does not deal with specific tax issues). Treasury Ministers use the House of Commons both to announce new tax matters (including urgent measures that are subject to later retrospective legislation) and to clarify official policy about current and pending legislation. Although the House of Commons rarely debates the tax affairs of an individual taxpayer, ministers will not be drawn on details, and either promise to look into something or give a general answer. But answers to parliamentary questions sometimes produce little nuggets for the experts. In practice, a more important role is played by the **Parliamentary Ombudsman**, or Parliamentary Commissioner for Administration. The Ombudsman has the power to investigate any complaint made by a Member of Parliament about the way the tax affairs of a constituent have been handled. In recent years, that has included many reports on complaints about tax credits in particular, and   3–35 the House of Commons has debated these reports on several occasions.

Of more general importance is the record of ministerial statements and speeches about Finance Bill provisions. These may be relied on in the tribunals and courts in limited circumstances. See the guidance given by the House of Lords (sitting judicially) in *Pepper v Hart* (1992) discussed below.

All UK Parliamentary material can be found on the official website *www.parliament.uk* [Accessed 8 June 2016]. That site holds major archives of the records of speeches and debates on the floor of the House of Commons and in its committees (and of less importance here those of the House of Lords)—technically issued as *Hansard*. But it now has a powerful search engine that allows rapid access to those resources and in addition to all the various reports produced for and by the two Houses.

3–36   **Statements of practice**. These are published formal guidance about how HMRC will deal with particular issues—often complex tax problems of limited national importance. They are published in booklet form like the booklets about ESCs. Old practices dating from before 1978 are given code numbers such as B5. The process was formalised in 1978 and since then newer statements are given numbers reflecting when they are made, such as SP6/81.

3–37   **Instruction manuals**. HMRC and its predecessors started producing manuals for staff many years ago, but until recently the content was a state secret. Thankfully, this secrecy was ended by the Freedom of Information Act 2000 (FOIA). As a result, most of the manuals have now been published (though there are small parts withheld under FOIA exemptions). They deal with the tax laws and how to apply them in considerable detail. And some are of considerable practical importance. Examples are the *Employment Income Manual* and *Employment Status Manual* that set out the official view on who are employees and how they are to be taxed. A full list of the manuals, and their content, is published in the library on the HMRC website.

3–38   HMRC also publishes several series of other forms of information and guidance. Most important are **notices** concerning VAT, customs duties or the other indirect taxes. These may have the force of law directly in limited circumstances but are usually statements of practice. Linked with these are the series of **briefs** published on an ongoing basis, again about VAT and the indirect taxes. These have labels indicating their publication date, such as 8/12. They deal with HMRC views on specific issues, such as a recent decision of a tax tribunal that has general significance.

3–39   Besides these, there are a large number of **booklets and leaf-**

lets, together with fact sheets, information sheets and even CDs containing explanations from the most general guidance about filling in the main tax forms to specific problems of minimal general interest. As with the Notices, some of these can be of considerable importance, particularly in areas where the legislation is not clear. For example, Booklet IR20 on deciding when someone is resident in the UK for tax purposes is informally called the Revenue Code because of its importance. All these appear on the HMRC website, along with **press releases** that are issued daily to draw attention to any new publication or development.

Indirect guidance. HMRC also has the commendable habit   **3–40** of reaching agreement with taxpayer representatives and professional associations about the operation of the taxes in its charge. Agreements may be by way of a fairly formal statement of agreement with appropriate groups, or by way of a letter sent to a group in response to representations. These sometimes receive restricted publication, but bodies such as the Tax Faculty of the Institute of Chartered Accountants, the CIOT and the Law Society's Tax Law Committee regularly publish their own views, and exchanges with HMRC, on points of law.

Interpreting the law

This should be the easy bit. It is not. Consider the following   **3–41** provisions:

"*Interest* means both annual and yearly interest and interest other than annual or yearly interest."
"*Interest* includes dividends and any other return (however described) except a return consisting of an amount by which the amount payable on a security's redemption exceeds its issuing price."
"*Interest and dividends* do not include any interest or dividend which is a distribution."
"*Distribution* . . . means . . . any dividend payable by a company . . ."
"*Trade* includes any trade, manufacture, adventure or concern in the nature of trade."
"*Trade* includes vocation and also includes an office or employment."
"*Profits* means income and chargeable gains."
"*Profits* or *gains* shall not include references to chargeable gains."
"*Income* includes any amount on which a charge to tax is authorised to be made under any of the provisions of this Act."

Rule number one of interpreting legislation should be to note the meanings given to the language by parliament. In tax law, as the above illustrations (all drawn from the Tax Acts) show, this has to be modified by two reflections. The first is that the definitions may themselves add no extra meaning. The second is that words change their meaning from one part to another of the tax legislation. Or, as T.S. Eliot observed, "words strain, crack and sometimes break, under the burden." The job of the lawyer is to ensure that any words that do suffer in this way are patched back up again.

Words can have two kinds of meaning: a technical meaning given by the judges as a matter of law, or "the ordinary English meaning". Which kind of meaning is given to a word is itself a decision of law, but decisions about the language of the tax laws are not consistent on this point. The *Ensign Tankers* case discussed below (see "Escape to Victory?") illustrates this in the way it seeks to apply the simple word "trade". It also illustrates another dilemma of interpretation. If a word has an ordinary meaning, then it is for the tax authorities and the appeal tribunals to determine its meaning. It cannot be appealed to the higher courts, because it gives rise to no question of law. If, however, the word has a technical meaning, then that is a question of law and can be appealed to the courts. The *Ensign Tankers* case also illustrates this problem.

How do we decide the meaning of a word?

3–42   Decisions on the meanings of words and the phrases in which they appear are guided by the rules of statutory interpretation. For a long time, judicial thinking was that tax laws should be interpreted strictly. Judges justified this by references to analogies with the criminal law and by reference to the Bill of Rights. The result could be an excessively literal reading of the words of a tax provision in isolation from its context. More recently, judges have been seeking to establish the view that interpreting tax statutes is no different from interpreting other legislation, save that the words have to be clear before tax can be imposed. The judgment of Lord Wilberforce in the *Ramsay* case (1981) is formative:

> "A subject is only to be taxed on clear words, not on 'intendment' or on the 'equity' of an Act. Any taxing Act of Parliament is to be construed in accordance with this principle. What are 'clear words' is to be ascertained on normal principles; these do not confine the courts to literal interpretation. There may, indeed should be, considered the context and scheme of the relevant Act as a whole, and its purpose may, indeed should be, regarded . . .".

Unfortunately, this statement cannot be left without further comment. First, we must remind you that the Acts being interpreted are frequently codification or consolidation measures. An attempt to look at the purpose of a consolidation measure means looking at the purpose of the provisions lying behind it. In a real sense, what the drafters have stitched together for presentational purposes has to be unstitched to establish what is meant. For an example of the complexities that result from such unstitching, see the Court of Appeal decision in *IRC v Willoughby* (1995).

Part of the reason for the complexity in unstitching is the decision of the House of Lords in the tax case of *Pepper v Hart* (1992). This decided that in cases of ambiguous language, it was proper to look to the record of the House of Commons for any ministerial statements about the intention of parliament behind a specific provision. In the *Willoughby* case, the logic of this was to look through not only the 1988 Taxes Act then in force, but also the 1970 and 1952 Acts that preceded it, back to original enactment of the provision in question in 1936. While this might help deal with ambiguities, the resulting need effectively to ignore the consolidation measure for interpretation purposes is not conducive to an easy operation of the law. It means that a "proper" consolidation should identify where each part of the consolidated provision comes from. This was also a problem for the Tax Law Rewrite. **3–43**

A second reason for complexity is the constant adjustment in the precise terms of sections to deal with both the need to counter avoidance, and the need to avoid injustice in special cases. Some sections have therefore seen considerable amendment during their working lives, including reshaping during the consolidation process. Take the definition of "trade". In 1803, this was defined as including any trade, manufacture, art or mystery. The word was used in a phrase identical to that now in, but its statutory definition has changed. The words are the same as in 1803, but not the extended meaning. Had the relevant minister made its main meaning clear then, should we return to it now? Here again, we have the problem of some words and phrases being "ordinary" while others are "technical". **3–44**

Drafters have evolved several techniques to counter avoidance tactics. One approach is to make the legislation explicitly anti-avoidance. The sections in the *Willoughby* case are a good example. Another is in s.752 and Ch.3 of Pt 13 of ITA 2007. There is a direct equivalent in CTA 2010 Pt 18: "This chapter has effect for the purpose of preventing the avoidance of income tax by persons concerned with land or the development of land." Does a statement like that make it any easier to interpret: "the occasion when the value of any property or right is enhanced . . . may be an occasion when tax is charged" (s.761(2))? Maybe not.

Another approach is to attempt to tie down the extent of the tax provision in exhaustive detail. This can become self-defeating. Have a look at Pt 7A of ITEPA (introduced by Sch.2 to FA 2011). It deals with a simple avoidance problem: taxing payments made to employees through third parties as earnings. Simple? One witness to the House of Lords committee looking at this legislation in draft described it as "the worst legislation he had ever seen". But it is not unlikely that some expert will have found a way round it, requiring it to be made even more complex.

A further reason for complexity in interpretation is the influence of EU law. Some parts of our law are now subject to reference to the ECJ. It is their interpretation, and therefore their techniques of interpretation, that must prevail in these areas. This may lead to inconsistencies, as the approach taken by the ECJ is different to that in a purely national context. Given that VAT is a mixture of European and UK provisions, the result may be untidy. See, for an example, the House of Lords decision in *CEC v Robert Gordon's College* (1995). See also the full discussion of VAT at para.25–15.

Applying the law

3–45   A reference to the ECJ emphasises another aspect of handling tax cases. The ECJ takes the view that it can interpret EU law, but it cannot apply the law to the facts. In the UK, these two stages in a case are often conflated. Take, for example, the child's definition of an elephant as something large and grey and living in a herd of elephants. The definition is that it is large, grey, and sociable. Whether the group of creatures is a herd of elephants is an application of the law to the facts. Application of law to facts in tax matters can be an issue of considerable complexity. If you wish to see how difficult, take a piece of paper and draw a diagram on it of the transactions described by the House of Lords in *Ramsay v IRC* (1981). Then try the same thing with the *Ensign Tankers* case discussed below.

Until the *Ramsay* case, judges would accept any series of transactions, however complicated, as something to be taken at face value. The underlying approach was one said to have been approved by the House of Lords in *IRC v Duke of Westminster* (1936). It was that the *form* of a transaction should be followed, not its *substance*. That doctrine has been modified by a series of cases including the *Ramsay* and *Ensign Tankers* cases but of which the most important is another House of Lords case, *Furniss v Dawson* (1984).

In *Furniss*, Lord Brightman, on behalf of the House, and

following the lines already set out in *Ramsay*, propounded the rule that the court did not have to look at the form in isolation in certain series of transactions, or complex transactions. A broader view of the whole operation could be taken where the series was preordained, and where one or more steps in the series existed for no other purpose than tax avoidance. This broad view allowed the courts in both *Ramsay* and *Furniss* to look at what happened without getting caught up in the interstices of complex constructions which, in substance, had replaced much more straightforward transactions. A later House of Lords case, *Craven v White* (1988) emphasised that the new approach only applied where the conditions were strictly met. A further decision of the House in *Countess Fitzwilliam v IRC* (1993), stressed that the courts could look through a series of artificial transactions to the real transaction underneath if the conditions were met. However, this had to be done to the transactions as a whole, and the Revenue could not pick and chose parts of the series to look through, while taking other parts at face value. However, in *Moodie v IRC* (1993), the House reaffirmed the underlying principle, and applied it notwithstanding an inconsistent decision of the House of an earlier date dealing with the transactions under question.

But the debate has not stopped there. Most important of **3–46** several further judicial bites at the cherry of tax avoidance is the decision of the House of Lords in *MacNiven v Westmoreland Investments* (2001). The decision concerned now-abolished rules about the tax treatment of interest payments. But the issue could also have been, in the views of some, a straightforward application of the *Ramsay* principle. This approach was rejected unanimously by the House of Lords. The judgment of Lord Hoffmann, in particular, was seen as placing important limits on the doctrine. It applies only if the words of the legislation permit, and it does not override those words. The wider approach only applies to a transaction if the tax legislation has "a commercial meaning capable of transcending the juristic individuality of its component parts". In other words, it is back to the proper interpretation of the legislation. Or perhaps it all depends on how one sees the facts, as in the Court of Appeal's criticisms of those below in *Barclays Mercantile v Mawson* (2004).

That case also went to the House of Lords. On this occasion the House issued a single opinion. It is, and is intended to be, a most important statement of approach, and should therefore be read for itself. It categorised the decision in *Ramsay* as a decision that "liberated the construction of revenue statutes from being both literal and blinkered". This was not a new doctrine, but an attempt to rescue tax law from the excess of literal interpretation and put it back into the mainstream. What was needed was close analysis not sweeping generalisations about disregarding transactions. As a result, the Crown lost the appeal.

The following week the House, in a committee consisting of the same five law lords, heard another avoidance case as *IRC v Scottish Provident* (2005). In a short, almost peremptory, single opinion their lordships found for the Crown. On the facts:

> "it would destroy the value of the *Ramsay* principle . . . as referring to the effect of composite transactions if their composite effect had to be disregarded simply because the parties had deliberately included a commercially irrelevant contingency, creating an acceptable risk that the scheme might not work as planned. We would be back in the realm of artificial schemes, now equipped with anti—*Ramsay* devices."

It was thought that the *Barclays Mercantile* case had closed the judicial development of new approaches to anti-avoidance cases and, further, was the case to which reference should be made rather than to *Ramsay* or any of the other predecessors. And so Mummery LJ stated in the tax avoidance case of *HMRC v Mayes* in the Court of Appeal in 2011 (also known as the SHIPS2 case because that was the name given to the tax avoidance scheme in question). In that case the Court dismissed an appeal by HMRC against a refusal by the Upper Tribunal to apply the *Ramsay* approach to a complex tax avoidance scheme involving life assurance. In his view, the detailed and specialised legislation involved did not lend itself to a purposive commercial interpretation. While the judges made it clear they had little enthusiasm for this kind of avoidance scheme, it was for parliament, not the judges, to deal with this kind of avoidance.

But a few weeks later the Supreme Court opened matters up again in a case called *Tower MCashback LLP1 v HMRC*. This was another complicated avoidance scheme, this time using a complicated finance scheme to secure capital allowances from dealings in software. In this case the Supreme Court overruled the Court of Appeal and found for HMRC. In the decision the Supreme Court judges made it clear that *Ramsay* and the early cases still had to be taken into account, as do any cases of the House of Lords in specific areas. One such case—thought by others no longer to be good law—is the *Ensign Tankers* case discussed below.

The only clear result from this is that judges are showing increased hostility to complex, uncommercial tax avoidance cases, but it remains unclear just how far that hostility can be invoked to stop these forms of tax avoidance. The Supreme Court quietly left it to parliament when permission was refused to have the *SHIPS2* case appealed to it. It has been suggested that this was in part because in the same month the Chancellor indicated that the government was considering introducing a general anti-avoidance provision.

That hostility was seen again in the Supreme Court in the **3–47** linked cases of *UBS AG v HMRC; DB Group Services (UK) Ltd v HMRC* [2016] UKSC 13. The cases concerned complicated schemes designed to use exemptions in the legislation taxing the value of shares given to employees by an employer in a beneficial way. If successful, the schemes would have provided for the payment of bonuses to employees of the banks while avoiding a potential charge to income tax and NICs of about £90 million. Other parallel cases used similar schemes to the same effect. HMRC sought to challenge the schemes both on technical grounds and by reference to the principles behind *Ramsay*. The First-tier Tribunal agreed that at the technical level the schemes appeared to work but then found that they did not fall within the intention of parliament in passing the relevant legislation. This was criticised heavily by the Upper Tribunal (twice throwing the ultimate "with all due respect" sideswipe at the tribunal below). It concluded that the First-tier Tribunal's "conclusion in law was an impossible one". The Court of Appeal agreed with the approach of the Upper Tribunal and in part refused leave to the Supreme Court. Read together, these decisions show the two extremes of outcome to which interpretation techniques can take analysis of complicated tax provisions.

The Supreme Court considered both cases in full. Its conclusion, in a single judgment by Lord Reed on behalf of the Court, was to allow the HMRC appeal against the Court of Appeal decision so restoring, subject to a valuation point, the decision of the First-tier Tribunal. It did so because it adopted a purposive construction of the relevant legislation, rejecting the literal approach of the Court of Appeal. It applied to that approach an analysis of the facts reflecting commercial reality. It did so having reviewed and followed the jurisprudence of the House of Lords and then Supreme Court since *Ramsay*. Lord Reed's judgment [61]–[71] provides a summary of that jurisprudence that should be compulsory reading on this topic.

Tax compliance

Until a few years ago introductory discussions about tax and **3–48** tax law could get by with mentions only of two tax issues: tax avoidance and tax evasion. The topic is now of considerably greater political and practical concern, with one result being a need to clarify the vocabulary. **Tax compliance** is a phrase now found routinely in HMRC and professional publications, though it is an invasive species from the US. It arrived following passage by the US Congress of what is often referred to as FATCA – the Foreign Account Tax Compliance Act. It is not in fact an Act but part of another Act passed in 2010. But it does impose extremely important compliance obligations on both US taxpayers with foreign incomes and assets and their agents and other intermediaries handling their affairs whether US or foreign. It is one of a series of obligations requiring agents and intermediaries to report taxable matters. In the UK that series of obligations has now been imposed by HMRC through the International Tax Compliance Regulations 2015. "Tax compliance" in practice involves meeting the obligations in those regulations. In addition HMRC now uses it to describe all investigative steps to check if tax is being paid properly.

Tax evasion is the process of not paying or underpaying tax that should be due and payable by illegal means. This is sometimes labelled **tax fraud** but that is one form of tax evasion. If the law requires that events be reported so that they be taxed, then not reporting is tax evasion. What is not always clear is the extent to which tax evasion is a breach of the criminal law. Many tax requirements are not enforced by criminal law in the UK but by civil penalties. We discuss this further below.

By contrast **tax avoidance** is action to remove or reduce the tax payable by actions that are within the law. This is also called **tax minimisation** or **tax mitigation**. Traditionally, tax avoidance was regarded as an acceptable response to tax laws.

Tax abuse or **abuse of taxpayers' rights** deals with the unacceptable reduction or avoidance of VAT. Technically the taxpayer in VAT is the customer, not the person who pays the VAT to the tax authorities. So reduction of the VAT that would be payable by the end customer of a good or service is not avoidance by that person. To tackle unacceptable reduction of VAT by intermediaries the courts, including the ECJ, have evolved the concept of **abuse of taxpayers' rights**. This is applied if a transaction (notwithstanding formal application of VAT law) results in the accrual of a tax advantage, the grant of which would be contrary to the purpose of those laws and it is apparent from a number of objective factors that the essential aim of the transactions in question was to obtain a tax advantage.

3–49   The target of anti-evasion, anti-avoidance and anti-abuse measures is a reduction in the **tax gap** – the difference between the amount of tax that should be collected by a series of tax measures and the amount of tax that is collected. This includes both avoidance and evasion plus the effect of any mistakes. The UK government calculates the tax gap in the UK each year. It put the figure for 2015 at 6.4 per cent of the tax that should be collected, or £34 billion.

The government and HMRC have adopted a multi-faceted approach to reducing this tax gap. Part of this is an increased use of the criminal law, to which we return. Part is in a significantly greater number of challenges to tax avoidance schemes in the tribunals and courts. Part is increased publicity about schemes that HMRC does not agree are effective and at times about specific tax defaulters—a sharp contrast with the traditional secrecy accorded by HMRC's predecessors to disputes with taxpayers that did not get into the courts. But perhaps the most significant in terms of principle is the enactment of general anti-avoidance and anti-abuse provisions in legislation.

General anti abuse rules

In many countries there are general statutory provisions **3–50** dealing with avoidance either under general law or specifically for tax law. The French approach is the doctrine of *abus de droit*; in the Netherlands there is a principle of *fraus legis*. Put at its broadest, they require that any interpretation and application of the tax laws must be consistent with the purposes of those laws. In the US, the judiciary have introduced rules of substance over form, while in other common law states such as Canada, Australia and Ireland, there are general anti-avoidance provisions in tax legislation.

In recent years in the UK the previously somewhat relaxed view to tax avoidance (and the shadowy area between avoidance and evasion) has been replaced by a more aggressive approach. This has been evidenced in several ways. First, as we have seen above, HMRC has challenged avoidance schemes in the tribunals and courts using *Ramsay*-based arguments, and has been encouraged by successes in pursuing those appeals to the higher courts. Secondly, there is an increasing readiness to include anti-avoidance provisions in individual aspects of tax legislation. Thirdly, a scheme requiring tax avoidance schemes to be registered (DOTAS) was introduced in 2004 and since strengthened. Fourthly, a general anti-abuse rule (GAAR) was introduced in FA 2013. A further aspect is the increased use of the criminal law and courts where the abuse is considered to be evasion and therefore illegal under general law.

DOTAS

3–51 In 2004 parliament adopted a new approach for direct taxes, copying one used for the US federal income tax. Anyone marketing a tax avoidance scheme is to be required to register it with the tax authorities, who will issue the plan with a registration number. Similarly, anyone adopting an in-house scheme must also register it. When the scheme is used, the taxpayer must notify the tax authorities of its use by number. This not only allows tax officials to keep fully abreast of the latest approaches of practitioners (and to block the ones they don't like) but also gives them a chance to rule that a scheme does not work before it is used. See FA 2004 Pt 7.

Initially HMRC saw this as a great success. But before long the number of tax avoidance schemes being registered tailed off. At first it was thought that this was because promoters had been warned off promoting such schemes. Far from it. Instead, they had learnt how to avoid the anti-avoidance rule. An opinion from a QC that the particular scheme did not need to be registered gave the promoters the cover they needed not to tell HMRC, or at least not to tell HMRC until a very late stage. (Section 314 FA 2004 protected, and protects, documents covered by legal professional privilege from disclosure.) Attempts at tightening the scheme had limited success until stronger measures were put in place first in FA 2008 (which required all schemes to have a registration number) and then again in particular in FA 2014. HMRC now has extensive powers to enquire into what are thought to be notifiable schemes. Further, since 2014 it has been able to require those involved in a tax avoidance scheme to pay the tax in full despite or ahead of any rights to appeal. An attempt to block this by judicial review failed, and HMRC commented in 2015 that this had brought in £1 billion in early tax payments in the first year of operation. This removes another previous advantage of a tax avoidance scheme, namely that even if tax was payable there was often a considerable delay in the liability being confirmed and the duty to pay arising.

HMRC has three other points it makes in warning people about the use of registered schemes: those involved may be regarded as risky taxpayers so open to enquiry more generally by HMRC; they do not gain any advantage from using a registered scheme as registration does not constitute any form of approval by HMRC; and HMRC has shown that it is ready to take such schemes to the courts and tribunals. Failure to register now puts a promoter at risk of a fine of up to £1 million. And HMRC has statutory authority to give publicity to failed schemes and those involved in them, and has used it.

GAAR

Impatience at both the increasing complexity of avoidance   **3–52**
schemes despite—and at times even successfully exploiting—anti-
avoidance legislation led the government in 2010 to ask Graham
Aaronson QC, a leading commercial tax expert, to investigate the
introduction of a general anti-avoidance provision. This kind of
measure, though widely used in other countries, had been fought
off on a number of occasions in the UK. His report, *GAAR Study*,
recommended in 2011 a careful set of measures to stop abusive
tax avoidance while protecting ordinary commercial avoidance
schemes. Parliament adopted this suggestion in a general anti-
abuse rule provided for in Pt 5 of FA 2013. "Abusive" is defined
by s.207 as meaning action that cannot reasonably regarded as a
reasonable course of action in relation to the relevant tax provisions. The provisions apply to any arrangements (defined very
widely) where it would be reasonable to conclude that obtaining a tax advantage was the main purpose or one of the main
purposes of the arrangements. The operation of the provisions
is subject to oversight by an advisory committee and HMRC
publish detailed guidance on the operation of the rule in terms
approved by that committee.

Escape to Victory: case studies

The outturn of this legislative and official activism is a possible   **3–53**
range of approaches to ever more complex legislation that have
at times left not only taxpayers but judges struggling to keep up.
Perhaps interpreting and applying tax laws against this background should be straightforward, but it is not. This can be seen
by watching the progress through various appeal stages of arguable cases. But, at first glance, some of these cases seem to be on
the most fundamental issues of tax legislation and yet leave the
courts and tribunals seemingly unable to come to clear conclusions. A few examples illustrate this.

We start with one of the most famous examples of the seem-   **3–54**
ingly simplest of tax principles leaving the courts all over the
place. It is a case called *Ensign Tankers (Leasing) Ltd v Stokes*. It
was finally decided in the House of Lords and reported at [1992]
STC 226. Despite the name of the case, it actually concerned
making a film, released as *Escape to Victory*, that involved in
its cast the unlikely team of Sylvester Stallone, Michael Caine
and Bobby Moore. (The story was about a football match at
the end of the Second War that was used as cover for prisoners
of war to escape – a sort of sporting equivalent to *The Sound of
Music*.) Why was a tanker leasing company involved? That is

the real story. It was because at the time the tax authorities were encouraging potential investors in the film industry by allowing tax benefits for any losses incurred. But to obtain those losses the businesses claiming the relief had to show that they were involved in a trade when investing in a film.

For current purposes we can skip most of the details. It is enough to note that a limited partnership was established to raise money for this film. The scheme was devised so that, it seemed, the investors could not lose. In particular, the scheme involved financial gearing such that the sums put forward as invested were considerably larger than the sums actually risked by the investors. If the film made a profit, fine. If it did not, the investors could claim tax relief for the losses on the engineered basis. Bearing in mind that at that time corporation tax as still 52 per cent, that was a considerable benefit were there losses. There were losses, and under the scheme those losses were magnified. But the inspector of taxes refused the claim for tax relief (for some £5 million). Why? Because the partnership was not carrying on a trade.

This then wandered up through the courts. It started in 1986 with 18 days before the Special Commissioners, where the appeal was rejected. In those days such cases were not reported, and the decision can only be seen as the case stated before the next appeal, to the Chancery Division. See [1989] STC 705. After a further hearing for six days, Millett J (later Lord Millett) upheld the taxpayer's appeal, finding that no reasonable tribunal could have reached the decision reached by the Special Commissioners on the evidence. Two years later a further appeal was heard in the Court of Appeal ([1991] STC 136). After four days, the Court of Appeal unanimously upheld the appeal against the Chancery Division decision, but also held that the Special Commissioners had erred in law, and so the case should be heard again.

Rather than enter this game of snakes and ladders, the case was appealed further to the House of Lords. After a further six days' hearings, the House unanimously upheld the appeal by HMRC. This time the case was remitted to the Special Commissioners with a direction to allow a claim for precise sums incurred by the appellant, and not the inflated sums that had been claimed as a result of the way the partnership was engineered. So the appellant was trading, but what Lord Templeman described in the House of Lords as "play acting" was completely to be ignored.

This was at the time a lead decision about dealing with tax avoidance generally. But the core issue—funding films—came to be dealt with by express legislation. There are now both anti-avoidance provisions in ITA 2007 and allowances for companies in CTA 2009. But these have not stopped avoidance activities. Indeed, there were a considerable number of attempts to step round the "problems" caused by the *Ensign* case. These came to a head when the Court of Appeal heard *Eclipse Film Partners No.35 LLP v HMRC* [2015] EWCA Civ 95. In this case the Court of Appeal endorsed the decisions below, on most points, of both the First-tier Tribunal and the Upper Tribunal in finding—again—that the taxpayers making the claims were not trading. This decision attracted major publicity, not least because according to considerable press publicity at the time the list of investors in the partnerships included the then managers of both Manchester United and Leicester City football clubs and the husband of the then chief of the CPS. The case, and the reaction to it both in the courts and in the media, is a clear example both of the heightened public and political sensitivity to complex tax avoidance and the official and judicial reactions to it. It has not stopped there, nor has action by the authorities. On 1 July 2016, HMRC issued a press release detailing how the criminal courts had convicted a group of film producers, accountants, financial advisers and investment bankers and sentenced them to a total of 36 years' imprisonment for tax cheating and related offences relating to the alleged production costs of films including *Starsuckers* and *Mercedes the Movie.*

Another example of the most fundamental terms causing prob- **3–55** lems in the courts is *HMRC v Forde & McHugh Ltd* reported in the Supreme Court at [2014] UKSC 14. The issue here was the meaning of the term "earnings" for the purposes of Class 1 NICs. In particular, was it coterminous with the term "emoluments" in income tax law. Despite the fact that the term had been used for several decades, an appeal against a decision was sent straight to the Upper Tribunal for first decision. This was early recognition that what seemed an easy question was not. Again, we can ignore most of the facts for current purposes. At heart, the question was whether funds put by the employer into a trust on which the employee could draw on retirement counted as "earnings". The Tribunal decided to allow the appeal by the taxpayer. The Court of Appeal by a majority disagreed (see [2012] EWCA Civ 692). The Supreme Court, again giving a single unanimous judgment, upheld the decision of the Upper Tribunal. In doing so it gave a definitive discussion of the meaning of "earnings" for NI purposes.

A sharp example of the shifts that can occur in tax litiga- **3–56** tion, again on the seemingly simplest of issues, was *Customs and Excise Commissioners v Zielinski* [2004]. The underlying question was whether, for a VAT zero-rating claim, a proposed development was part of one building or two. The taxpayers wanted to convert an old outbuilding in the curtilage of their home, which was a listed building, into a games room. Was VAT due on the work done for this, or not. To obtain the relief at that time, it has to be shown that the claim was made for a "protected building". Was the claim for the outbuilding made as a claim for a protected building? The local tax official said no. The VAT Tribunal said yes. (At that time VAT Tribunal decisions were not fully reported.) This then went to the Chancery Division where Etherton J said no. He did so because the Tribunal had failed to take account of arguments based on EU law. The Court of Appeal was of two minds and decided by a majority that the Chancery Division was wrong. Not to be outdone, the House of Lords was also unable to reach a unanimous view, deciding by a majority (and for a range of reasons) that the Court of Appeal was wrong. The final answer was given by parliament as the relief was abolished in a Finance Act, with even transitional claims being blocked since 2015.

3–57   Behind this is undoubtedly the need to pay close attention to the Supreme Court whenever it decides to hear a tax case. Twice recently it has upheld a decision of the First-tier Tribunal (Tax) and in doing so has overturned decisions of the Upper Tribunal endorsed by the Court of Appeal. The cases of *UBS* and *DB* were noted at para.3–47 above. Another example (where HMRC lost) is *Anson v HMRC* [2015] UKSC 44. This case concerned interpretation of a provision in the double tax agreement between the UK and the US, so its content is beyond the scope of this book. But the decision is to be noted because it is another case where the initial reaction to the decision of the First-tier Tribunal was that it was plain wrong. And so the Upper Tribunal and Court of Appeal decided. But the Supreme Court in a single judgment restored the decision of the First-tier Tribunal and in doing so set aside a previously understood approach to the relevant treaty provision. In doing so it gave a magisterial lecture about how to interpret treaty provisions. Nonetheless, HMRC announced (in Revenue and Customs Briefing 15 (2015) that it was not changing its longstanding practice generally as it regarded this as a decision on its facts. Was it? No doubt a later appeal will help us with that, as with the *Ensign* case.

CHAPTER 4

TAX ADMINISTRATION

Introduction

The administration of UK taxes—their assessment, collection **4–01** and enforcement—has changed profoundly during the last few years and those changes continue as this edition is written. For centuries customs and excise duties were collected by local Collectors of Customs. In the busy ports they were often based in what became magnificent Custom Houses, but most have now gone either to other uses (in Cardiff a restaurant, in Bristol flats) or altogether (Liverpool's was bombed). From the 1800s income tax and related taxes were collected by local officers known for a long time as surveyors of income tax and then as Her Majesty's Inspectors of Tax based with their staffs in cities and towns throughout the land. They are all going. The two old departments were merged into one, as we saw above, and their officers into one large team of officers of revenue and customs. Much more profoundly, the networks of local offices are disappearing, and are being replaced by a few centralised administrative offices. Why?

Three changes have influenced fundamentally the way **4–02** UK taxes are administered. First, any residual local discretions have been removed. All tax matters are now centrally run. Secondly, much of the work in calculating any tax liability has been shifted from officials to taxpayers (and advisers). Thirdly, remote communications (by telephone as well as by email and websites) are replacing the local office. To buttress this, there has been a shift towards forms of tax that are easier to collect remotely (or should be).

Traditionally, taxes were labelled as either direct taxes or **4–03** indirect taxes. Direct taxes were those directly imposed on taxpayers: traditionally including income tax, corporation tax, CGT and (less obviously) IHT. Indirect taxes are those imposed on an intermediary: VAT (where those who pay the tax are called taxable persons because the actual taxpayers are the end customers of any supply); excise duties (usually imposed on manufacturers); customs duties (imposed on importers or exporters). Those differences used to explain why historically there were two government departments collecting taxes: the Inland Revenue dealt directly with taxpayers while Customs and Excise dealt indirectly, with traders.

4–04   Shifts in the nature of our taxes and the ways they are assessed and collected have rendered this old distinction obsolete. Another set of labels, noted in Ch.1, is a more accurate guide to what happens now. Some taxes are transaction taxes, imposed usually on those conducting a business or taxable activity. Some taxes previously referred to as direct taxes are now in reality often in this group: stamp taxes and duties and in part CGT. Other taxes are collected as withholding taxes by the payers not the recipients. Finally, some taxes are collected directly from the tax-payers themselves. These are often called assessed taxes because traditionally they were assessed by HMRC staff and a formal assessment was then sent to the taxpayer for payment. Most of those taxes are now self-assessment taxes, with the taxpayer required or expected to prepare the assessments. But so are some of the transaction taxes such as VAT. In those cases the task of those within the system (taxable persons in VAT speak) is to act both as tax assessor and tax collector.

E-tax

4–05   The common element behind all these reforms is a fundamental shift in the process of tax administration to systems based on information and communications technology. This change has, in historical terms, been as rapid as it is profound. When the first edition of this book was published, the idea that taxation would be imposed by electronic communications was still in the realms of science fiction. It was about the time of the second edition that one of us witnessed in Manchester a demonstration of what may have been the first software programme written about UK tax. The author was (with hindsight, typically) the teenage child of a local partner of a major accounting firm. If that was the first programme, it was entirely appropriate that it was written in Manchester, the birthplace of the programmable computer just four decades before. Just four decades later, tax administration is dominated by the use of computers.

4–06   One of the most important aspects of modern tax administration is the timely collection of information about taxable activities. That used to be done by filling in long paper documents called tax returns, often some time after the end of a tax year. That information can now be collected electronically, often on a real time basis. For example, in 2015 HMRC introduced Real Time Information (RTI), under which employers are obliged to make returns to HMRC promptly after any payment to an employee that carries income tax or NIC liability. And payment must follow after that. If not, the employer is liable to fines. No longer is PAYE collection of income tax and NICs left to follow a paper return completed at the end of the tax year with a check on the employee also by a paper return. Further, those returns are usually now made electronically.

Similarly, many kinds of payment liable to income tax are **4–07** now subject to the imposition of a withholding tax on the payer. But even this is being simplified. This is because the payer (for example, banks and building societies paying interest) is obliged to report to HMRC all payments such as interest. Further, they do this whether income tax has been deducted or not, so HMRC (and through HMRC other government and local authority departments) have, again in real time, information about income received by individuals. Sometimes HMRC also receives the tax. In other cases, it can demand it from the taxpayer without the taxpayer notifying it first.

Making a return

Nonetheless, the key problem remains that the taxpayer knows **4–08** what it, she or he has received and spent during a year and HMRC does not. So it must ensure that taxpayers or others give it the necessary information. Not all taxpayers are required to do this because in practice the effect of exemptions from tax and the payment of tax by employers and intermediaries is that most taxpayers will have paid all the income tax and NICs to which they are liable without any action on their part.

The following groups of taxpayers are required to make **4–09** returns to HMRC:

- most company directors;
- most self-employed or those with property income;
- those receiving capital gains;
- those receiving incomes over £100,000;
- those receiving incomes over £50,000 and child benefit;
- higher rate taxpayers receiving dividends;
- those receiving taxable savings and investment income over £10,000; and
- those receiving untaxed income over £2,500.

A seemingly small change announced in 2016 eases this a little. From 2017 the first £1,000 of trading income and the first £1,000 of property or similar income will not be liable to income tax. This means that someone earning a small amount, say, on Ebay or by letting someone stay in the house for a few nights, is not required to pay tax, and therefore—the main point—is not required to make a return just because of that income.

4–10 The process is started by a requirement to register with HMRC if a tax return should be made. HMRC issues the taxpayer with a unique taxpayer number and notifies the taxpayer in any year when a return is required.

4–11 A taxpayer required to make a return must do so by the required final date. There is a standard form of self-assessment which deals with all usual aspects of income tax, NICs and CGT, with related reliefs. All the relevant parts of this must be completed, along with a calculation of the tax considered to be payable. Increasingly, this is done by using an online form. The form is now a sophisticated document that checks the taxpayer's entries as the form is filled in and calculating the tax payable at each stage. The online forms are available to all taxpayers through the *GOV.UK* [Accessed 8 June 2016] website by using two access codes unique to the taxpayer. The form must be completed, if the electronic route is used, by 31 January in the year following the tax year. For those that use it, this is an effective solution to the problem imposed (by s.9 of TMA) that the taxpayer is required not only to make a full return but to calculate the tax due on the income or gains in the return. It also deals with both the right of a taxpayer to amend a return and the power of HMRC to correct any obvious errors and omissions, as the software checks the information returned in the form and invites corrections. Any tax to be paid (the amount will have been calculated as the form is submitted) is due to be paid the same day, and can again be done electronically by the same route. If the taxpayer wants to use a paper return, that must be done by the previous 31 October. There are penalties for those failing to make returns or pay tax on time, as we see below. HMRC has the power to ask any potential taxpayer to make a return whether registered or not. If such a request is made, the taxpayer has three months from the request to make the return and then pay any tax due.

4–12 The current plans are, however, to phase out all paper returns, or at least as many as can be managed. Two approaches are being taken to that. First, taxpayers are increasingly being required to make any returns on line. A programme entitled Making Tax Digital is being started in 2017 aimed at making aspects of returning information and paying tax entirely electronic. The second approach, for which there are measures in FA 2016, is to introduce what are termed Simplified Assessments. These remove the need for those with straightforward or lower incomes to make any return at all, at least initially, as HMRC will assess any income tax liability by reference to information held from others (for example employers, banks, pension companies) notifying a taxpayer when this is done. HMRC will be able to do this entirely electronically in many cases as all the relevant data will be held on HMRC servers.

Keeping records

Section 12B of TMA requires any person who may be required **4–13** to make a self-assessment return to keep all such records as may be necessary to deliver a "correct and complete" return. The self-employed must keep those records for a total period of six years (technically five years from 31 January in the year following the relevant tax year). Others, such as those paying tax under PAYE, need keep them only for two years. The records must be adequate but can be kept in any way the taxpayer chooses—from card-board boxes to memory sticks. HMRC can give notice to require records to be preserved for longer than this where, for example, there is an ongoing enquiry or appeal. Failure to comply incurs a penalty of £3,000 and may mean that the taxpayer is unable to resist an increased tax assessment. This is because, as we see below, the burden of proof in any dispute is on the taxpayer not on HMRC.

Civil enforcement

The approach taken to enforcing tax obligations was strength- **4–14** ened considerably when the two old departments of state were merged to form HMRC, and have been further strengthened since. We have seen above both the duty to register as a potential taxpayer and the duty to notify any tax avoidance scheme. These reflect the first of the key aspects of tax enforcement: obtaining the relevant information. HMRC then has extensive powers to investigate both returns and other information provided. These include powers to investigate old matters. Both are supported by a strong civil penalties regime with, as a fall back, the criminal law.

Correcting returns and making enquiries

HMRC may correct any obvious error in a return within nine **4–15** months of receiving it. This is done to correct arithmetical errors or accidental mistakes. Aside from that HMRC may only inves-tigate a return if the taxpayer is given notice in writing under s.9A of TMA. This is called a notice of enquiry. It can be issued in most cases at any time within a year of the date by which the return had to be made. It may be a general enquiry into the taxpayer's affairs, or a specific enquiry about an aspect of the taxpayer's affairs. The notice will indicate the intended scope of the enquiry and will usually require the production of relevant documents and information.

There is no fixed time limit in which HMRC may conduct the resulting enquiry. And HMRC may find it appropriate to issue a series of notices of enquiry for several tax years if there is an ongoing enquiry when later tax returns become due. At the end of the enquiry HMRC will issue a notice of closure. This may indicate a formal correction to the self-assessment return perhaps by adding additional taxable income. A taxpayer can only get a continuing enquiry stopped in one of two ways. The first is to reach a settlement with HMRC. The other is to ask the First-tier Tribunal to order the enquiry to be closed. In that case the outcome may be a refusal by the tribunal to issue such a notice (reminding the taxpayer that the application can be renewed) or an order giving HMRC a limited time to complete the enquiry. Part of the closure notice may be a determination not only of tax due but also penalties and interest.

4–16   What happens if HMRC gets to learn of a failure fully to declare income for tax years after it should have been declared? In this case, HMRC may "discover" it. If an officer of HMRC discovers that income which ought to have been assessed to tax has not been assessed or inadequately assessed, or reliefs are excessive, then the officer may make an assessment to tax of the amount which, in the officer's opinion, makes good the loss to the Crown. See s.29 of TMA. This is a wide power allowing an officer to act on best judgment even if there is hardly any evidence, with the burden firmly on the taxpayer to show that the officer is wrong if a discovery assessment is challenged. For a discussion see *Hawkinson v HMRC* (2011). Any such assessment will be accompanied or followed by penalty and interest assessments. However, HMRC run amnesties from time to time to allow taxpayers to make late declarations with an indication of low or minimal penalties.

HMRC's information powers

4–17   There are a number of conflicting principles in play with regard to the exchange of information between a taxpayer and HMRC. The most important arises from the simple but obvious fact that the taxpayer knows the facts and HMRC does not. That is why the burden of proof is placed on a taxpayer in a tax appeal. And it also explains why the First-tier Tribunal has formidable powers requiring disclosure as part of a tax appeal. As a number of recent decisions of that tribunal show, this may involve disclosing all emails sent between parties to an avoidance scheme, subject only to legal professional privilege.

Separately, HMRC has a battery of legal powers to demand information from taxpayers and third parties (or has the right to ask the First-tier Tribunal to order disclosure as part of an investigation). See the extension in FA 2011 Sch.23, allowing HMRC (or a tribunal) to serve a data-holder notice on any data holder. This may require disclosure of information both about individuals and for risk assessment purposes. Further, any information HMRC receives in relation to any aspect of its work can be used for all aspects of its work. And it can exchange information freely with the Department for Work and Pensions and other government departments and public authorities. That has brought a halt to the past practice of someone having one set of accounts for income tax and another for VAT and another again for benefit claims. It is quite common for dishonest individuals to find their benefit claims halted and a repayment demanded because of information HMRC has obtained from banks and passed on to local councils. This follows the standard requirement that banks and similar institutions deduct income tax from taxable savings and pay it, with supporting details, to HMRC. But it may result from notices requiring general disclosure of all customers with relevant forms of income.

The acquisition of information has also been strengthened recently by a series of international agreements under which governments exchange information about taxpayers. This happens as part of EU law within the EU but requires specific international agreements elsewhere. The European measures are in Directive 2010/24 on the Mutual Assistance for Recovery of Taxes. These are given effect in the UK by Sch.25 to FA 2011. For a recent example outside the EU see the UK-Swiss Taxation Cooperation Agreement which came into effect in 2013. Under this agreement, a British taxpayer with investments in Switzerland must either disclose this to HMRC or pay the Swiss authorities' levy of a heavy withholding tax on any income, which tax is passed to HMRC.

Civil penalties

This is another area that has seen a major overhaul in the last few years. It started with the publication from 2006 of a series of consultation papers under the general title of *Modernising Powers, Deterrents and Safeguards.* This resulted in legislation in several of the following Finance Acts to rationalise the penalty regime applying to all taxes and the safeguards applying to those subject to potential enforcement activities.

4-18

The key new penalty is a "Failure to Notify" penalty where someone has failed to inform HMRC in a timely way of something on which there was a duty to inform or make a return (for example someone required to make a return of a capital gain or to act as an employer and collect PAYE from an employee). In such cases there is a liability to a penalty unless there is a reasonable excuse for the delay (such as illness). If a penalty is incurred then its level depends partly on the kind of failure and then on the culpability of those involved in respect of the failure.

In general if a failure was not deliberate and is unprompted (that is, the taxpayer or agent told HMRC before they had any reason to believe that HMRC had started to make enquiries) then the maximum penalty is 30 per cent of any liability to tax that would have occurred with a timely disclosure. The minimum is nil, if the disclosure was made within 12 months of the time when it should have been made, or 10 per cent after that. There is a discretion given to HMRC (or on appeal to the tribunals) to set the level between those limits. This will depend on the timing, nature and quality of the disclosure and the level of cooperation then given to HMRC in determining the tax due.

If the failure to notify is deliberate, then the range of penalties increases to between 20 per cent and 70 per cent for unprompted disclosure, with the minimum at 35 per cent for prompted disclosure. If the disclosure is both deliberate and concealed, then the maximum penalty is increased to 100 per cent and the minima to 30 per cent or 50 per cent. A failure to disclose is concealed if arrangements have been made to conceal the fact that information is withheld. That might mean pretending that income belonged to someone else or deliberately withholding information in such a way that it has led to an assumption that the income did not exist.

Schedule 55 ends with a double-jeopardy rule that states that someone is not liable for these penalties if convicted of a criminal offence involving the failure or action for which a penalty would be levied. That suggests that someone found not guilty, or charged but not prosecuted, will be liable to the civil penalties.

Time limits

4–19   The other important issue in connection with late assessments (such as discovery assessments) and penalties is how far back HMRC can go. This issue has also been the subject of recent rationalisation and reform. The results, brought in with or since FA 2008, are a general series of rules for all taxes. The ordinary time limit for assessments (and corrections of errors or mistakes in assessments) is now four years from the end of the relevant tax year (see the amended form of s.34 of TMA). Section 36 (as amended) extends this time limit to six years where an assessment is made to deal with a loss of tax brought about by the carelessness of the taxpayer or agent. But where the loss results from deliberate action of a person or a failure to notify HMRC of tax liability more generally (for example, when setting up a profitable new business) or failure to comply with DOTAS obligations, then the time limit is 20 years.

This is a particularly serious provision when taken with the other powers we have noted above. If we have deliberately concealed from HMRC and its predecessors our profitable business of, say, buying and selling on the internet, then HMRC can demand all our records, including all our personal bank statements, credit card bills and the like (demanded not from us but from our banks), "discover" that we have been making significant undisclosed and concealed profits, and then impose a discovery assessment on a "best of judgment" basis back to when it considers the business started—perhaps over 10 years ago. It can then levy the "deliberate and concealed" penalty at 100 per cent of the tax it decides is due for each year, and add compound interest (on both the tax due and the penalties). But it will do that without telling anyone (save by implication the banks) that it is doing so. Until recently HMRC was obliged to keep all this information confidential. FA 2009 s.94 gives HMRC power to publish a list of taxpayers who have deliberately evaded paying tax of £25,000 or more and have been penalised as a result. This will link in with the more open approach now to be adopted about tax evasion and criminal prosecutions noted below.

Freedom of information

Another aspect of the more open approach is the extent to which HMRC can be required to disclose information under FOIA. A taxpayer who requires HMRC to produce details of the information held about him or her can do so under the provisions of the Data Protection Act 1998 in accordance with the usual principles of that Act (which are beyond the scope of this work). The more serious issue is to what extent a third party can demand disclosure under the FOIA regime from HMRC about someone else. In practice this breaks into two issues: disclosure of general internal information and disclosure about the tax affairs of a named taxpayer or potential taxpayer. The position about general information is relatively clear. Subject to specific exemptions provided for in FOIA, then HMRC must publish this information. This is a major factor behind the open approach now taken by HMRC to its internal pub-

4–20

lications. It is not so long ago that the then tax departments regarded internal guidance as official secrets. They are now all published (with limited exclusions) in the library on the HMRC website.

The position with regard to individual taxpayers' affairs was less clear. The underlying principle followed by HMRC and its predecessors is that the affairs of any taxpayer are confidential. Even government ministers are not allowed to have access to them. The tradition of secrecy applies to all involved in tax administration, with strong sanctions against anyone unofficially leaking information. (This is an interesting contrast with the much more open approach in some other states. In some Scandinavian states, for example, lists of the amount of tax paid by individuals are published annually.) So HMRC regarded the proper approach to any application to it to disclose information under FOIA about any third party was to block it. The official way of doing that is to neither confirm nor deny that any information is held. This was confirmed by a three judge panel of the Upper Tribunal in *PwC v Information Commissioner and HMRC* (2011). The tribunal held that PwC was not entitled to information from HMRC about one of its clients, even with the consent of that client, under FOIA. This was because HMRC was entitled to refuse the information under the FOIA provision (s.44) allowing it to rely on a prohibition against publication in another Act. That other Act is the Commissioners for Revenue and Customs Act 2005 ss.18 and 23. The tribunal confirmed the view of HMRC that this imposed an absolute ban, unless HMRC itself decided otherwise, notwithstanding the consent of the taxpayer. That has been confirmed by a strengthening of the terms of the legislation.

4–21   Both aspects of this freedom of information are reflected in the huge content of the internet related to taxation. It is a veritable forest for the uninitiated, not least because any unguided web search will probably dig up information about the tax laws of many different countries. Indeed, an unguided general search is likely to produce several million potential entries. The key UK government information, including all the internal guides and public leaflets and forms published by HMRC, is now on the *GOV.UK* website [Accessed 1 June 2016] and you can search it there. Many law and accounting firms and other advisers also publish commentaries and summaries aimed at a wide range of audiences. But beware that some websites include vitriolic attacks on the very idea of tax or tales designed to persuade you that tax is just too complicated to deal with and that you need very expensive advisers. So be careful where you tread!

Rights of appeal

We examined the tribunals and courts that deal with appeals **4–22** above when noting the differences between the four nations of the UK. What is common to all four is a wide right to challenge by review and appeal any potentially final decision taken by HMRC or the national tax authorities. That includes appeals against the automatic £100 penalties for making tax returns late—a major source of appeals—and challenges to HMRC notices requiring disclosure of information.

The first step in many cases is a review of the decision by a **4–23** different officer of revenue and customs to the original decision maker. When a taxpayer issues an appeal the taxpayer can ask for a review. If the taxpayer does not ask, HMRC will often offer a review, particularly in smaller cases such as fixed penalties. If the taxpayer either asks for or accepts a review, then the decision will be looked at again, taking into account any new information offered by the taxpayer (for example, medical evidence explaining a delay in making a return). In practice this results in many decisions being changed in a taxpayer's favour. This may also lead to a settlement agreement between the two parties. HMRC has wide powers to agree settlements under s.54 of TMA. If an agreement is reached, then it has the same effect as a decision on appeal and brings any appeal to an end.

If the taxpayer does not request a review or is not offered one, **4–24** then the case goes direct to a First-tier Tribunal. Here there is close case management of all appeals. In particular, appeals will be listed in one of four separate categories ranging from basic to complex. Basic cases are normally dealt with on the papers and without a hearing. At the other extreme the complex cases will be heard at multi-day hearing before a tribunal judge sitting, usually, with an expert member. Procedure for these different levels of appeal all give considerable discretion to the judge controlling the appeal. The rules are contained in the Tribunal Procedure (First-tier Tribunal) (Tax Chamber) Rules 2008. The tribunal is empowered to take any decision of fact or law that HMRC could take, so may increase the tax payable under a decision as well as confirm, reduce or cancel it.

Traditionally, the appeal system put great weight on the fact- **4–25** finding of the initial tribunal with rights to appeal to the courts only on questions of law. At the same time there was a strong tradition of appealing issues of law "all the way up" to the then House of Lords. Two important changes to this have followed the court and tribunal reforms since 2008. The first is that the Upper Tribunal has the power not only to set aside a decision of the First-tier Tribunal because it is wrong in law, but also to replace it with the decision that the tribunal should have made. Further, the courts have actively encouraged the Upper Tribunal to do this. So it is rare for an appeal to go back to the First-tier Tribunal to be reheard. Linked with this is the guidance thereby given to the lower tribunals on how to handle evidence. As a result, the weighty jurisprudence about what is a question of fact and what is a question of law is now of limited importance. The other important change is a restriction in the right of appeal from the Upper Tribunal to the Court of Appeal in England and Wales, and further on to the Supreme Court. The result is a reduced number of higher-level appeals compared with some past periods. But in addition there is a further right of appeal to the CJEU where that is relevant to deciding the true meaning of a tax law.

Criminal enforcement

4–26   One of the traditional longstanding differences between the Inland Revenue and the Customs authorities was that while customs law was enforced against smugglers and others with the full force of the state, inspectors of tax were usually able to reach secret financial deals with errant taxpayers of which the general public heard nothing. Further, both were in charge of their own criminal prosecution policy and practice. Since 2010 the separate pursuit of tax crime was abandoned and all prosecutions were handed over to the CPS. Although there are a series of specific offences for not complying with tax law, as well as a common law offence of cheating the public revenue, the detail of this law is beyond the scope of this work. But it may be noted that there is now an aggressive use of the criminal law to deal both with those who fail to disclose and pay taxes of all kinds and those who seek to defraud the system by false claims.

PART TWO

TAXATION OF INCOME

CHAPTER 5

TRADING INCOME AND LOSSES

Introduction

We now begin a study of each particular kind of income. It is **5–01** convenient to begin with trading income.

The rules about trading income were codified by the Tax Law Rewrite in ITTOIA Pt 2 (ss.5–259). The basic provision is in s.5 which states simply that: "Income tax is charged on the profits of a trade, profession or vocation." With equal simplicity, s.7(1) imposes the charge on the full amounts of the profits of the tax year. And s.8 provides that the person liable for any tax charged under these provisions is the person receiving or entitled to the profits. In Budget 2016 it was announced that the first £1,000 of trading income would be tax free from 2017/18 onwards.

We must first define "trade" and "profession or vocation". **5–02** Each of these definitions presents in practice a major problem requiring considerable thought in drawing the lines around activities caught within the words. But the operation of the tax rules on trades and on professions is broadly the same, although we will note a few differences. We will therefore follow ITTOIA in assuming trading income includes professional income unless stated otherwise.

The key "trade" problem is this: Is a given sum a trading profit or a capital gain? In the good old days a capital gain was entirely free of tax; since 1965 it has been subject to CGT. CGT is distinct from income tax (this is unaffected by the rates of CGT and income tax). Each tax has its own regime for the computation of gains/losses, and the characterisation of a particular gain/loss can have important repercussions for a taxpayer.

The key "profession" problem is this: Is a given person's exercise of a profession (or vocation) carried on within an office or employment, in which case he is to be taxed on employment income or is it carried on outside any office or employment, in which case he is to be taxed as trading? The issue is between trading and employment income. It is nowadays accepted that the distinction falls to be made on the same principles as in the law of tort, and also employment law. In tort the distinction is important in connection with vicarious liability, and it is generally described as the distinction between an employee and an independent contractor.

Employed or self-employed

5–03   In employment law the same distinction has led to considerable case law, especially on the questions of unfair dismissal and redundancy payments. In tax law it is described as the distinction between employees and the self-employed. In all contexts it is the distinction between a contract of service and a contract for services. For example, a solicitor in private practice, whether as sole principal or as a partner in a partnership or as a member of an LLP, is self-employed and is taxed as if trading. A solicitor engaged in local government or in a public company is employed and has employment income. So does an employed solicitor in private practice; that is, a person qualified as a solicitor who works otherwise than as a partner in a firm of solicitors. Sometimes this distinction can be blurred as in the case of what are known as salaried or fixed share partners or members of an LLP. Many LLPs and partnerships seek to ensure that these probable employees are in fact taxed as self-employed and HMRC have taken measures to counter that for reasons we explain below. Of course in other contexts a person can be both employed and self-employed, e.g. a medical consultant employed by the NHS who also has a private practice.

Is there any importance in this distinction? Yes, there is. The tax rules are different as between trading income and employment income. In particular, an employment income earner is subject to PAYE and the rules governing expenses are far less generous.

Although the advantages are not all one way, most people would rather be taxed on trading income than on employment income, not just because the first £1,000 will be tax free from 2017/18. It is not surprising therefore to find that parliament has intervened to determine whether liability to tax should be trading income or employment income. One such instance concerns what is called "The Lump". The Lump means those in the construction industry who, though performing the functions of employed persons, claim the status of self-employed persons by means of "labour only" sub-contracting. Several attempts at dealing with this situation have been made, and currently the position is governed by ss.57–77 of FA 2004. Except where a sub-contractor holds an "exemption certificate," the contractor must deduct from each payment that it makes to the sub-contractor a sum equal to the basic rate of tax, after allowing for the sub-contractor's expenditure on materials. So a sub-contractor, though nominally remaining self-employed, is to suffer deductions as though employment income. That is the theory of the thing: in practice it does not always work very well.

Attention has also been directed towards "workers supplied **5–04** by agencies." They are taxed as employees of their agencies. Examples of workers caught by this provision are teachers, secretaries, and nurses. This is now subject to the widened catch of the regime under Pt 7A of ITEPA, dealt with as employment income.

A third group of workers have been dealt with differently. These are "divers" and "diving supervisors". Section 15 of ITTOIA provides that the Income Tax Acts shall have effect as if the performance by a diver or a diving supervisor of his duties constituted the carrying on by him of a trade. This is the reverse of the treatment meted out to "The Lump" and to agency workers; it is a case of treating employed persons as self-employed. One gathers that the reason for this generous treatment is the political or economic reason that if it were not done these divers and diving supervisors would leave the North Sea for sunnier places; sunnier fiscally speaking as well as climatically.

ITEPA contains general powers to treat those trying to reduce tax by working through a partnership or "pocket book company" or by other means trying to avoid being an employee, as caught by the employment income charge in any event. We shall return to these new rules and the distinction between "employed" and "self-employed" when we come to deal with employment income.

We want to now discuss more fully the problem: Is a given sum a trading profit or a capital gain? Another way of putting the same question is: What is trading?

What is trading?

There is a kind of definition of "trade" in s.989 of ITA 2007. **5–05** We say a "kind of definition" because it is one of those so-called definitions, common in tax legislation, which merely expand a word without defining it. "Trade", we are told, "includes every trade, manufacture, adventure or concern in the nature of trade". Notice that the last few words are "nature of trade", not "nature of *a* trade". Even so, this is little better than defining an elephant as being either an elephant or something which looks and behaves like an elephant.

Judges have also resisted giving an exhaustive definition to "trade" as widened by s.832. The modern cases revolve around attempts by taxpayers to obtain a tax advantage (e.g. tax relief on interest borrowed) which will only be available if they are trading for tax purposes. The most recent discussion was by the Court of Appeal in *Eclipse Film Partners No.35 LLP v HMRC* (2015). That Court reaffirmed that it is a matter of law whether a particular fact is capable of being an indication of trading and also as to whether a particular activity is capable of being a trade. But whether it is actually a trade is decided by evaluating the facts against the legal background. It follows that the fact finding tribunal's decision can only be challenged if there was an error of principle or if the only reasonable conclusion on the facts is inconsistent with the tribunal's decision (see, e.g. *Edwards v Bairstow* (1956)).

5–06   There was a discussion as to the basics of trading by the House of Lords in *Ransom v Higgs* (1974). There would generally have to be operations of a commercial character providing some kinds of goods or services for reward. That of course requires some form of counter party whether or not that could be described as a customer. In *Ensign Tankers (Leasing) Ltd v Stokes* (1992) the House of Lords decided that if there was a trading activity (financing the production of a film) the presence of a tax saving motive would not alter that fact. In the *Eclipse* case (above), the taxpayers merely organised the licensing and distribution of films which was not enough. It is also true that the profits of an illegal trade can be taxed (see, e.g. *IRC v Aken* (1990)).

Traditionally the courts have applied what are known as the "badges of trade" which are discussed in the next paragraph. But recent cases tend to take a broader view. For example, the Upper Tribunal in *Degorce v HMRC* (2015) said that trade is a concept which anyone can recognise without too close an analysis of its detail. The various badges of trade are therefore helpful but neither exhaustive nor conclusive.

The badges of trade

5–07   The factors which bear on the question "Trade or No Trade" were graphically described by the 1954 Royal Commission on Taxation as "badges of trade". The Commission listed six badges of trade and though subsequent cases have indicated others those six are still the dominant factors. Quite a useful approach to the problem is to ask oneself, when considering a transaction or series of transactions, if it is not trading, what is it? The rival candidate is usually, though not always, investment or income from land. To purchase and then sell an investment is not in itself trading. Another candidate is a hobby, or private and non-commercial activities.

The first point to consider is **what is sold**. Generally, if the subject-matter is such that the purchaser cannot either use it personally or derive an income from it or derive pleasure from it that points towards trading. Thus in *Rutledge v IRC* (1929) the taxpayer, while in Berlin in connection with a cinema business, bought a million rolls of toilet paper for £1,000. Shortly after his return to England, he sold the whole lot to one purchaser at a profit of over £10,000. It was held that this was an adventure in the nature of trade. Notice that in this case, as in many others, the fact that there was only one transaction (a one-off as the saying is) did not prevent its being held to be trading.[1] Contrast the case of *Salt v Chamberlain* (1979). Mr Salt was smitten by computers. He thought he had hit the jackpot by inventing a fool-proof method of investing in shares. He didn't and it wasn't. He lost a lot of money and tried to claim it as a trading loss. The court held that the shares were bought as investments. One test was whether the subject-matter itself produces income. Subsequently, however, in *Marson v Morton* (1986) it was suggested that land could constitute an investment even though it was not income producing.

5–08

The second point is **length of ownership**. This is not a compelling consideration, but there is something in it. Thus a short term purchase of silver as a hedge against inflation was held to be trading in *Wisdom v Chamberlain* (1969). A quick re-sale points towards trading but see also the fifth point, below.

5–09

The third point is **repetition**. Although, as we have seen, a single transaction can amount to trading, there are situations where a single transaction would not be trading but that kind of transaction repeated several times would be trading. In *Pickford v Quirke* (1927) a director of a spinning company formed a syndicate which bought the shares of a mill-owning company and then sold the assets of that company at a profit. He then took part in three similar transactions, although the members of the syndicate were not always the same people. The Court of Appeal held that he was carrying on a trade, even though each transaction considered by itself was not an adventure in the nature of trade.

5–10

The fourth point is **supplementary work** in connection with the

5–11

---

[1] There was a rumour that this case should really be called the case of the *imaginary* toilet rolls. It is said that the taxpayer invented the story of the toilet rolls to explain an increase in wealth, in the same way as many taxpayers claim that their wealth has arisen from betting-winnings (which are not taxable). It is said that this taxpayer thought that the toilet roll story would not be taxable. It is the tax law equivalent of the alleged non-existent snail in the ginger beer bottle.

realised property. In *Martin v Lowry* (1927) HL, the taxpayer (who had had nothing to do with the linen trade) purchased from the government its entire surplus stock of aeroplane linen, about 44 million yards. He found difficulty in selling it, and so he had to advertise extensively, rent offices and engage a manager and staff. He sold the linen to more than a thousand purchasers over a period of about 12 months and made a profit of nearly £2 million. It was held that the operations constituted trading. In *Martin v Lowry* there was a definite sales organisation, but there are cases where simple supplementary work has been held to make the transaction of buying and selling into trading. Thus in *IRC v Livingston* (1927) three individuals, a ship-repairer, a blacksmith and a fish salesman's employee, who had not previously been connected with each other in business, bought a cargo steamer, converted it (partly by their own labour) into a steam drifter, and sold it at a profit. The Court of Session overruled a finding of no trade, and held that this was a trade.

5–12   The fifth point is **why the sale took place**. There may be some explanation why something is sold which negatives the idea of trading. In *West v Phillips* (1958) a builder built some houses to hold as an investment and some for resale. Later on he decided to sell the investment houses, and he did so through the same organisation that sold his trading houses. The Special Commissioners held that there was trading, but the Court of Appeal reversed them, holding that the taxpayer decided to sell his investment houses because of rent control and the rising cost of repairs and higher taxation, and that in respect of the investment houses he was not trading.

5–13   The sixth point is **motive**. Although a trade may be held to exist even where there is no intention to make a profit, the absence of such an intention points against trading, whereas where there is such an intention that points towards trading. It is an important factor in a borderline case. Just such a case was *Taylor v Good* (1973) where the taxpayer bought a house at an auction without really intending to, in the hope that he might live there. He later sold it, making a profit, but the Court of Appeal held he did not intend to trade when he bought it, and had not traded with it (see also *Kirkham v Williams* (1991)).

So much for the case law on trading. Some activities have been declared by statute to be trading. The most important are farming and market gardening. Section 9 of ITTOIA states that "All farming and market gardening in the United Kingdom shall be treated as the carrying on of a trade . . .". There are also "statutory trades" listed in s.12. Finally, other provisions give priority to trading income over other charges where, for example, interest is earned on balances outstanding from customer or on current trading accounts, where a dividend is received as trading income, or where certain property income is received as trading income.

What is a profession?

We must now turn to, professions and vocations. Neither term is defined by the statutes, so the judges have done the job instead. In *IRC v Maxse* it was said that the hallmark of a profession is the use of intellectual skill, with or without manual skills.   **5–14**

"Vocation" is a calling, the way in which someone spends his life. In ordinary speech it carries a rather starry-eyed idea of nurses or others dedicated to their work. This seems to mean that they carry on their work without worrying about mundane things like pay. It is somewhat ironic therefore to find that the leading case on vocations is a case about a bookmaker. The case is *Partridge v Mallandane* (1886). But, although the work of a bookmaker, a jockey and a racing tipster have all been held to be vocations, a full-time gambler is not! This was decided in *Graham v Green* (1925), for the sensible reason (if illogical) that the Revenue would stand to lose far more than it gained from such people, because of loss claims! Anyway, betting and gaming taxes ensure such people contribute their share to the Exchequer. Having noted this, ITTOIA has now removed almost all the differences in treatment between traders and professionals. So these are usually distinctions without a difference.

The computation of profits

The importance of accounts
What we have said so far may suggest that the charge to tax is concerned with individual items of income. This is true of value added tax, and in individual tricky cases for income tax, but not in the vast majority of income tax cases. Remember that there is a charge not on receipts, but on annual profits.   **5–15**

The fundamental point about an assessment on this basis is that taxpayers need to produce accounts to find out for themselves if they have made a profit and for self-assessment purposes.

It is the professional task of accountants to produce accounts of profits and losses, or income and expenditures, over a set period, usually a year. Professional accountants do this in accordance with generally accepted accounting practice.

Companies' accounts are limited by guidelines. Most companies and LLPs must produce and publish annual accounts which follow the forms and formats laid down in the Companies Acts.

Furthermore, the accounts must be independently audited by professional auditors who must certify that the accounts comply with legal requirements, and also reflect a "true and fair view" of the company's profits for the period.

As the prestige of the accounting professions and their role in tax matters grew so the question of relationship between tax law and accounting practices and principles became sharper. The underlying question of the relationship is whether evidence that proper principles of accounting practice requires that an item be dealt with in a certain way should be decisive of its treatment in tax law. For example, if accountancy principles treat an item as revenue expenditure, to be included in the profit and loss accounts, can the item be treated as a capital expense for tax purposes?

Generally accepted accounting practice

5–16   Courts will now readily accept more than in the past that accounts prepared in accordance with accepted principles of commercial accountancy are adequate for tax purposes as a true statement of the taxpayer's profits, etc. However, such accounts will not be acceptable for tax purposes to the extent that they or particular items contained within them conflict with any express or implied statutory rule or are contrary to principles established by case law. It is noteworthy in the latter respect that Sir Thomas Bingham MR in *Gallagher v Jones* (1993) CA said:

> "I find it hard to understand how any judge-made rule could override the application of a generally accepted rule of commercial accountancy which (a) applied to the situation in question, (b) was not one of two or more rules applicable to the situation in question and (c) was not shown to be inconsistent with the true facts or otherwise inapt to determine the true profits or losses of the business."

For many years the view was taken that "profits" for income tax purposes were not the same as commercial profits. One major difference is in the treatment of capital investment and the depreciation of capital assets. That difference led to the creation of the capital allowances system dealt with in Ch.8.

That difference remains, although not for small businesses, but there has been a fundamental shift in thinking about business accounts more generally in recent years. It is increasingly the case that the profits of a business should also be its trading profits for tax purposes. This does not include, as noted, the treatment of capital investment. Nor does it include the rules about which expenses can be deducted from income to find the net profits. We must also examine those rules in more detail.

Aside from these specific, if important, rules the general approach has become one that professionally prepared accounts produced for a business or company will provide the basis for the income on which tax is due. See the decision of the House of Lords in *HMRC v William Grant & Sons Distillers Ltd* (2007).

The underlying principle behind this is that professionally prepared accounts, particularly for larger incorporated taxpayers, must comply with international and national accounting standards and with the requirements of the financial regulators. There is now a detailed series of requirements that must be met by the published accounts of a bigger business. This is now codified into ITTOIA (and for companies into s.46 of CTA 2009). The general approach, in s.25(1) of the Act is that:

> "The profits of a trade must be calculated in accordance with generally accepted accounting practice, subject to any adjustment required or authorised by law, in calculating profits for income tax purposes."

One adjustment authorised by law (that is, in this case, by the tribunals and courts) is where two principles of commercial accountancy can be applied to one issue. In such a case the question may be one for expert accountancy evidence or one where an expert accountant member of the First-tier Tribunal can ensure an expert decision on the point. In such a case it will be the tribunal judges that decide the issue. See the authoritative guidance of the House of Lords in *HMRC v William Grant & Sons Distillers Ltd* (2007). This case (a Scottish case decided deliberately alongside an English case involving Mars Ltd) took a look at the accounting practices dealing with stock in the food and drinks trades. Their Lordships decided that depreciation of stock being carried was a permissible deduction in accordance with general accounting principles even if this involved carrying a deduction forward from one year to the next, as this produced a true and fair view of the profits. It is interesting that this involved overturning decisions of the appellate courts in both England and Scotland to give this wider approach to determining profits.

The outcome of this was to set a higher standard for all businesses in computing trading profits. The government heeded complaints about the effect of this on small businesses and set up an enquiry about it in 2010. In 2012, the Chancellor accepted advice from that enquiry that the resulting standards were too burdensome on small businesses.

Cash basis for small businesses

5–17   As a result, Sch.4 to FA 2013 by amending Pt 2 of ITTOIA introduced an alternative to generally accepted accounting standards for small businesses. This is known as the cash basis. A small business for this purpose is one run by an individual whose receipts for all trades in the tax year do not exceed the VAT registration threshold at the end of that year. Currently (2016/17) that figure is £83,000. Certain specialised businesses are excluded and there are additional rules for businesses run as partnerships. If a person chooses the cash basis for one trade it must be used for any other trades run by that person.

The main point in using the cash basis is that profits are calculated on the simpler basis of trading receipts actually received in the tax year less the allowable expenditure actually spent in that year without necessarily linking the two. Equally importantly if the cash basis is used is that all trading receipts are to be included whether they are income or capital receipts (normally the latter are not included, income tax being a tax on income) and all trading expenditure may be deducted, whether or not it is income or capital expenditure. If capital expenditure is thus allowed (e.g. on a business vehicle) any subsequent receipt from the sale of the asset acquired is therefore a taxable receipt. The effect of this is that small businesses need not necessarily concern themselves with the complex system of capital allowances (see Ch.8) whereby certain types of capital expenditure only, e.g. on machinery and plant, are allowed in a separate system from trading profits. The only exception to that is expenditure on cars where the capital allowances regime applies unless the business mileage rate has been claimed (see the next paragraph). There are, however, drawbacks to the cash basis: sideways loss relief is not allowed (see later in this chapter, but basically if you make a loss in a tax year you cannot set that off against other income), nor is carry back relief for losses in the first three years of trading, and interest payment deductions are limited to £500.

Once the total annual receipts of all a person's trades exceed twice the permitted maximum the trader must leave the cash basis the following year, although there is an exception where that is just one exceptional year and the following year's figure is once again below the maximum

Fixed deductions

5–18   Another consequence of the simplification process was to provide a simplified deduction regime for two common small business expenses, the use of a home for business purposes and motor vehicles.

Chapter 5A of Pt 2 of ITTOIA (added again in 2013) provides first for a flat rate deduction for specified household running costs when a home is used partly for business purposes. The deduction only applies if the business use exceeds 25 hours per month. Business use for this purpose means providing goods or services, maintaining business records and marketing and obtaining new business. Use of the fixed deduction system is optional and does not depend upon the cash basis being in operation. The actual identifiable business portion of other non-listed fixed costs such as insurance and telephone/internet charges may be claimed in addition to the fixed allowance.

Under Ch.5A business vehicle expenses can also now be claimed as an expense on a simplified fixed rate per business mile. This is an alternative to capital allowances, both are not available. The simplified scheme is optional whether or not the cash basis is being used. The fixed rate covers all expenditure relating to the acquisition and running of a vehicle (including depreciation) used for the purposes of the trade (or of course profession). Once claimed it must apply for the duration of the vehicle's use in the business. The mileage rate only applies to journeys which are wholly and exclusively for business purposes (we shall come across those words later on). Any parking, congestion fees or tolls, however, may be claimed in addition.

For other businesses, however, (including all companies) generally accepted accounting practice must be applied. So we must now follow through the details of that approach to calculating trading profits.

Trading receipts

The first question to be asked about any receipt, whether in cash or in kind, is, is it a trading receipt or is it a capital receipt? **5–19**

In some circumstances the answer to the question is perfectly plain. Thus, if a manufacturer sells a factory because a more up-to-date one was built it is clear that the proceeds of the sale constitute a capital receipt, which consequently does not enter into the computation of profits for income tax purposes. It is equally plain that if the same manufacturer sells a widget which has been made in the factory the proceeds of that sale constitute an income receipt which becomes an item in the income tax computation.

In other circumstances, the question "trading receipt or capital receipt?" is quite difficult to answer and can lead to judicial disagreement. See the discussion by the members of the Court of Appeal in *IRC v John Lewis Properties Plc* (2003). This difficulty is particularly so where compensation is paid to a trader, and in cases of voluntary payments to traders.

Compensation

5–20   There is a mass of decided cases on this matter. We will look at three. In *Van den Berghs Ltd v Clark* (1935) HL, the appellant English company entered into agreements with a competing Dutch company under which each company agreed to conduct its business on certain lines. After a dispute it was settled that the agreements should be terminated on condition that the Dutch company paid £450,000 to the English company. It was held that this was a capital receipt, and thus was not taxable. Lord Macmillan said that ". . . the cancelled agreements related to the whole structure of the appellant's profit-making apparatus."

In *Kelsall Parsons & Co v IRC* (1938) the appellants were manufacturers' agents; they held contracts with several manufacturers under which they sold their products for a commission. One of these manufacturers wished to terminate its agency contract and it did so about 16 months before it was due to expire, paying Kelsall Parsons & Co £1,500 as compensation. This sum was held to be an income receipt, and hence taxable. The loss of this one agency clearly did not relate to the whole structure of the appellants' profit-making apparatus. Lord Normand said (in the Court of Session): "The agency agreements, so far from being a fixed framework, are rather to be regarded as temporary and variable elements of the profit-making enterprise."

In *London and Thames Haven Oil Wharves Ltd v Attwooll* (1967) CA the taxpayer company owned a jetty which was seriously damaged by a tanker when it was coming alongside. The owners of the tanker paid a sum of money to the taxpayer of which part was apportioned to physical damage to the jetty and part to consequential damage, namely loss of use of the jetty during the 380 days taken up in repairing it. The Revenue did not seek to tax that part of the payment which was apportioned to physical damage, but it did seek to tax the part apportioned to consequential damage. The assessment was upheld by the Court of Appeal. Diplock LJ gave a limpidly clear judgment. He said:

> "Where, pursuant to a legal right, a trader receives from another person compensation for the trader's failure to receive a sum of money which, if it had been received, would have been credited to the amount of profits (if any) arising in any year from the trade carried on by him at the time when the compensation is so received, the compensation is to be treated for income tax purposes in the same way as that sum of money would have been treated if it had been received instead of the compensation."

The Lord Justice went on to say that two questions have to be asked. First, was the compensation paid for the failure of the trader to receive a sum of money? If the answer to that is yes, there arises a second question: If that sum of money had been received by the trader would it have been credited to the amount of profits of the trader? The same question can be put more shortly, namely, would it have been an income receipt of the trade (and not a capital receipt)? If the answer to that question is yes, the compensation is taxable; if the answer is no, the compensation is not assessable to income tax. In the instant case that part of the compensation which had been apportioned to loss of use of the jetty: (1) was paid for the failure of the trader to receive a sum of money; and (2) represented the profit (surplus of receipts over expenses) which would have followed from the use of the jetty during 380 days. So the assessment was correct.

In essence the issue is often one of fact, i.e. to determine what the payment was received for. Once that is identified the issue of capital or income is usually straightforward. To take just one modern example, in *Countrywide Estate Agents FS Ltd v HMRC* (2011), the taxpayer estate agents entered into an agreement with an insurance company to use only that company's products with the taxpayer's customers. Once it was established that this was not a sale of the agents' goodwill (a capital asset) but the exploitation of that goodwill in return for an upfront payment and commission, the income nature of those receipts became obvious.

Voluntary payments

A problem which has vexed the courts considerably is the   **5–21**
status of a payment made to a trader voluntarily, without a contractual requirement that it be paid. When should such receipts be treated as trading receipts?

It was established by the Privy Council in *Taxation Commissioner of Australia v Squatting Investment Co Ltd* (1954), an Australian case, that the mere fact that a payment was voluntary did not prevent it being a trading receipt. Equally the Court of Appeal in *Simpson v John Reynolds & Co (Insurances) Ltd* (1975) confirmed that not all voluntary payments were taxable. That case concerned a payment of £5,000 by clients of the insurance brokers following the discontinuance of use by the clients of the broker's services following a change in control of the clients, a company. Important factors in the decision were that the payment was unsolicited and of an amount not tied to possible future sales, and that the trading relationship between broker and client had ceased. The payment could not relate to future performance. A different Court of Appeal working on different facts, reached a similar conclusion in *Murray v Goodhews* (1978).

The *Simpson* case was, however, distinguished by another

Court of Appeal in *Rolfe v Nagel* (1982), a case concerning voluntary payments to a diamond broker. It was held that here the sums were compensation for otherwise unremunerated work and were not unsolicited, and thus were trading receipts. Similar thoughts lay behind *McGowan v Brown and Cousins* (1977).

Trading stock

5–22   It is important to grasp that trading stock (stock-in-trade) is an essential item in a trader's account—for tax purposes no less than for commercial purposes. Let us take a simple trading account as it is usually presented.

	£	£
Sales for the year		85,000
Opening stock	3,000	
Purchases	40,000	
	43,000	
Less Closing stock	5,000	
Cost of goods sold		38,000
Trading profit		47,000

Notice that in the account we have used the phrase "trading profit". This account does not deal with expenses such as wages, rent, rates, heating, lighting, telephone, postage. Those matters would be dealt with in a further account, so reducing the trading profit to a taxable profit.

Trading profit is the amount by which the proceeds of the goods sold (£85,000) exceed the cost of those goods (£43,000).

If one omitted stock—both opening and closing—from the trading account one would get a different result. One would get sales £85,000, less purchases £40,000 = profit £45,000. But that would be unreal. This trader has not only made a profit of £45,000 on sales during the year compared with purchases during the year; he has also improved his position by having increased his stock during the year from £3,000 at the beginning of the year to £5,000 at the end of the year, an increase of £2,000.

The closing stock figure for one year becomes the opening stock figure for the next year.

As closing stock represents expenditure on goods not yet sold, that expenditure is credited to the current year and carried forward to be charged in the subsequent year—as opening stock—in which the stock is to be sold.

5–23   In *IRC v Cock, Russell & Co Ltd* (1949) the court gave its approval to the accountancy practice of permitting a trader to value stock at its cost price or its market price, whichever is the lower, and to treat each item of stock separately. So, when any item of stock is expected to fetch less than its cost, its market value (or "net realisable value") (instead of its cost) is included in the total of closing stock. The effect is to charge immediately in the current year that part of its cost which is considered to be irrecoverable. This is now a question of whether the business has accounted for its stock values in a generally accepted way, as judged by accounting standards and not the courts.

Work in progress

"Work in progress" is the phrase used to cover such things **5–24** as goods in the process of manufacture. A manufacturer, at the end of a particular accounting period, will have some items in his factory which are partially but not wholly constructed. Such items are brought into account in the same way (broadly) as is closing stock, although this may not be a simple exercise (see *Duple Motor Bodies v Ostime* (1961) HL). And the same principle applies to many other things besides partially manufactured goods; it applies for example to partially performed contracts of a professional person.

Transfers of stock

One problem confronted by the courts in the case of *Sharkey* **5–25** *v Wernher* (1955), but now solved by specific legislation is that of the private use of business assets. Where a trader transfers business assets (in that case, racehorses) from the business to his or her private ownership, then there must be a charge in the accounts at the market value of the assets transferred. (The same thing must also happen for VAT.) The reverse applies where non-trading stock becomes trading stock. And there are parallel rules about sales and acquisitions by an individual outside the business. See ITTOIA ss.172A–172F. These rules are subject to rules of great importance to those trading internationally, the transfer pricing rules.

Transfer pricing

Whenever a buyer and seller are associated in some way, **5–26** there is always scope for the parties to agree to buy and sell at an artificial price. That may become attractive if it leads to a tax advantage (for example because one of the parties is paying tax on profits at a lower rate than the other party). This had led tax authorities to pay close attention to what is known as transfer pricing and to any price for a deal that may not be the open market arms-length price. There is major scope for this in international trades where a transfer of profits from one jurisdiction to another not only leads to a reduction of tax paid by the associated traders but a complete loss of tax by one state to the other. So there is much concern about this in international tax, but that is beyond the scope of this book. What does need mentioning here is that there are rules to counteract any form of transfer pricing between associated persons within the UK. See ss.147– 217 of TIOPA. They apply whenever a sale and purchase takes place between two persons who are associated—perhaps because one owns the other or there are close corporate or family links. The general rule will be that the sale and purchase will be treated as taking place at the relevant market value.

Trading expenses

5–27   The rules about deduction of trading expenses used to be a legislative mess for all taxpayers big and small, individual and corporate. They have now been rewritten into ITTOIA Pt 2 (with a parallel set of rules for companies in CTA 2009 Pt 3). Simplified expenses rules, as we have seen, can apply to vehicles and homes used for small businesses. Another approach used in checking tax accounts is to accept a set percentage of total expenses for specific kinds of business, so allowing the trader to treat only the balance of receipts as profits unless it is shown that a higher figure is justified on the facts. HMRC can currently check on businesses with excessive expenses by comparing all similar businesses in a particular area. Take for example take away food shops. They will probably have similar levels of business overheads aside from rent. So if one claims to be making a loss when the others are all making profits, then a check on the business (and its VAT returns) may be in order.

  We have already seen the core basic rules for calculating trading income. These are set out in Ch.3 of Pt 2 of ITTOIA, under the title "trade profits: basic rules". And we have noted the key basic rules. We now need to note one more. Section 31 provides that if one provision in this Part of ITTOIA provides for a deduction from profits for tax purposes, and another prohibits it, then the permissive rule has priority over the prohibitive rule.

  That introduces us to Ch.4 of the Part (rules restricting deductions) and Ch.5 (rules allowing deductions).

  Chapter 4 starts with three key rules. First, no deduction is allowed for items of a capital nature (s.33). Read this with s.28 which directs that we read this with the provisions of the Capital Allowances Act which treat allowances and charges made under that Act as receipts or expenses of a trade. It must also now be read with the option for small businesses to use the cash basis, when capital expenditure is then allowable. The second rule is that no deduction is allowed for expenses not incurred wholly and exclusively for the purposes of the trade or for losses not connected with or arising out of the trade. See s.34. The third rule is that no debts may be deducted as expenses unless the debts are either bad or are estimated to be bad. See s.35.

There are then a series of rules of much narrower importance. But we must first look at the first two rules in greater detail.

Revenue, not capital, expenditure

The same distinction falls to be made in regard to expenditure **5–28** as in regard to receipts. It is not an easy distinction to make. In one case Lord Greene MR remarked: ". . . in many cases it is almost true to say that the spin of a coin would decide the matter almost as satisfactorily as an attempt to find reasons". (*British Salmson Aero Engines Ltd v IRC* (1938) CA). But judges do not toss coins, at least not visibly. So we must look at some reasoning.

The first point to be clear about is that a payment which is a revenue receipt in the hands of the payee is not necessarily an item of revenue expenditure by the payer. Equally a payment which in the hands of the recipient is a capital item may be a revenue expenditure on the part of the payer. The two things have to be looked at separately. The principles, however, are the same whether one is considering receipts or expenses.

In some cases of expenditure the matter is perfectly clear. If a manufacturer expends money on a new factory, that is capital expenditure; if he spends money on raw materials, that is revenue expenditure. Adam Smith's distinction between fixed capital and circulating capital is of some help here.

However, in cases where the matter has been less clear–cut reliance has been placed often on the classic statement to be found in the speech of Lord Cave in *British Insulated and Helsby Cables Ltd v Atherton* (1926) HL:

> "When an expenditure is made, not only once and for all, but with a view to bringing into existence an asset or an advantage for the enduring benefit of a trade. I think that there is very good reason . . . for treating such an expenditure as properly attributable not to revenue but to capital."

There is no doubt that this is a helpful general statement, but some qualification is needed. First, it is clear from later cases that "enduring benefit of a trade" must be taken as meaning "a thing which endures in the same way that fixed capital endures": see per Rowlatt J in *Anglo-Persian Oil Co Ltd v Dale*

(1931), approved and adopted by Lord Wilberforce in *Tucker v Granada Motorway Services Ltd* (1979) HL. Secondly, there may be expenditure which has an enduring effect, but which, nevertheless, is not deemed to be capital in nature. Thirdly, the identification of an "asset or advantage for the enduring benefit of a trade" may not be easy. For example, if a taxpayer borrows money for a term, is he to be treated as only receiving cash to be used in his business or is he effectively securing a continuance of his trade [and hence an advantage for his trade] for the duration of the loan?

These difficulties were encapsulated by Megarry J in *Pitt v Castle Hill Warehousing Ltd* (1974), when he added a third limb to Lord Cave's test: In what manner is what is obtained to be used, relied on or enjoyed? Does it have the quality of recurrence, i.e. an active function, e.g. by providing a flow of orders, or a static aspect of something which underpins the trade? For an example of this distinction see *Lawson v Johnson Matthey Plc* (1992) where the House of Lords took the opposite view to the Court of Appeal. As with receipts, the real issue is to identify what has been acquired in return for the expense.

5–29   Probably four main factors emerge from the welter of decided cases on the point: the nature of the benefit acquired in exchange for the payment; the manner in which that benefit is to be used; the means by which it is obtained (periodical payments or lump-sum payment); and, more recently, how the expenditure is treated in standard accounting practice. Different weights are to be attached to these four factors in different circumstances. In *Regent Oil Co Ltd v Strick* (1966) HL Lord Reid said:

> "Whether a particular outlay by a trader can be set against income, or must be regarded as a capital outlay, has proved to be a difficult question. It may be possible to reconcile all the decisions, but it is certainly not possible to reconcile all the reasons given for them ... The question is ultimately a question of law for the Court, but it is a question which must be answered in light of all the circumstances which it is reasonable to take into account, and the weight which must be given to a particular circumstance in a particular case must depend rather on commonsense than on a strict application of any single legal principle."

Wholly and exclusively for the purposes of the trade

5–30   The rule about expenses in s.34(1) is a rule of primary importance, and overrides any rule of accounting practice. It imposes a prohibition on expenses of any kind unless those expenses are shown to meet all three of the tests laid down in the subsection:

1) the expenses must be wholly incurred in the trade; and
2) they must be incurred exclusively in the trade; and
3) they must be incurred for the purposes of the trade.

Although this rule is newly drafted, these tests are of long standing, and there has been much case law about them. And those cases have perhaps added a test that is not in the statute.

"WHOLLY" It seems that the word "wholly" relates to quantum. The whole amount of the expenditure must be laid out for the purposes of the trade, or rather the expense is only allowable up to the amount of it which is laid out for the purposes of the trade.

"EXCLUSIVELY" The word "exclusively" has proved difficult to apply. The classic statement of the law is in the judgment of Romer LJ in *Bentleys Stokes & Lewless v Beeson* (1952) CA. This case was concerned with business entertainment expenditure. At the time of the case there was no special rule relating to such expenditure; there is such a rule now (in s.46 of ITTOIA) disallowing it save in the case of a very limited number of exceptions. Romer LJ said:

"It is . . . a question of fact. And it is quite clear that the purpose must be the sole purpose. The paragraph says so in clear terms. If the activity be undertaken with the object both of promoting business and also with some other purpose, for example, with the object of indulging an independent wish of entertaining a friend or stranger or of supporting a charitable or benevolent object, then the paragraph is not satisfied though in the mind of the actor the business motive may predominate. For the statute so prescribes. *Per contra*, if in truth the sole object is business promotion, the expenditure is not disqualified because the nature of the activity necessarily involves some other result, or the attainment or furtherance of some other objective, since the latter result or objective is necessarily inherent in the act."

And so the Court of Appeal allowed the expenditure which had been incurred in entertaining clients.

Romer LJ made it all sound very easy, but in practice it has not proved easy to separate sole purpose cases from dual purpose cases, and one is sometimes left with the feeling that honesty is not the best policy. In *Bowden v Russell & Russell* (1965) the sole principal of a firm of solicitors visited America and Canada with his wife to attend the annual meeting of the American Bar Association in Washington and the Commonwealth and Empire Law Conference in Ottawa. It was his intention to have also a

TRADING INCOME AND LOSSES

holiday with his wife. The court held that the expenses incurred in connection with the conferences were not deductible, because they were incurred for a dual purpose, the advancement of his profession and the enjoyment of a holiday.

Can there be apportionment?

5–31   These rules and the doctrine of "dual purpose" have been applied somewhat unhappily for many years. Unhappily because of the point already made and because they do not allow sums incurred for two purposes (such as telephone rentals and car expenses) to be apportioned. But in practice every accountant knows that they can be apportioned, as long as one is not too greedy, whatever the strict provisions of the law. Take, for example, *Lucas v Cattell* (1972). This was actually an employment income case but, as we shall see, these parts of the deductions rules are the same for traders. Lucas was required by his employers to have a telephone at home, but they refused to meet the expense of the telephone rental. For several years the Revenue allowed Lucas to deduct a small part of the rental. One year he demanded more! One is reminded of Lionel Bart's famous song from *Oliver*. The result was predictable. Lucas ended up with nothing. His payment was not wholly and exclusively for his employment; and the rental payment could not be severed so that part could be said to be deductible. Section 34(2) now allows an identifiable part or proportion of an expense to be deducted where only that part or proportion is incurred for the trade.

The "object" test

5–32   Then Ann (now Lady) Mallalieu, a barrister, gave the courts a chance to make some sense of the rules. They tried, but they found it difficult to resolve the issues and by a four-to-one majority the House of Lords overruled the Court of Appeal and Chancery Division: *Mallalieu v Drummond* (1983) HL.

The facts could not be simpler. Mallalieu claimed £500 for replacement items of court dress, their laundering and cleaning. This was revenue expenditure which she incurred to comply with the official guidance to barristers on dress in court. It was undisputed evidence that, at the time she bought the clothes, her only conscious motive was to comply with these professional requirements.

The judgment of Lord Brightman (for the majority) made clear that there was another source of unease about the rules in his mind. It is often felt that the expenses rules are over-generous to the self-employed as compared with employees. So his Lordship observed, the case was really about "the right of any self-employed person to maintain . . . partly at the expense of the general body of taxpayers, a wardrobe of everyday clothes which are reserved for work".

After reciting the dual purpose rule, Lord Brightman reminded himself that the "object" of the expenditure was the decisive factor in applying the dual purpose rule. But, he said, the object of expenditure must be distinguished from its effect. Further, the conscious motive of the taxpayer in making the expenditure was not the deciding factor in establishing the "object". "It is inescapable that one object, though not a conscious motive, was the provision of the clothing that she needed as a human being." He adopted the judgment of Goulding J in *Hillyer v Leeke* (1976), which, in effect, rested its conclusion on the "self-evident truth" approach to the question.

Implicitly, this seems to overrule the test laid down in the *Bentleys* case (and cited by Lord Elwyn-Jones in his short, powerful dissent) without mentioning it. So we must now judge the object of an expense objectively, distinguishing its effect. But how do you judge the object of a British medical consultant's flight to the South of France to see a patient (or was it partly to have a holiday?) Objectively? Further, for an example of the anomalies to which the application of this test may give rise, see *Watkins v Ashford Sparkes and Harward* (1985). In *McKnight v Sheppard* (1999) the House of Lords returned to the subject.

The taxpayer had been fined for a breach of the financial conduct rules. He claimed the expenses of defending himself and the amount of the fine against his professional income. The House of Lords this time held that both satisfied the wholly and exclusively test. The possible other purpose, preserving his reputation, etc. was merely incidental to the expenditure. They did, however, disallow the fine on policy grounds. The tax system should not be subsidising penalties. But where a solicitor paid a sum due under an issue unrelated to his practice both to avoid personal bankruptcy and to preserve his position in the firm, the Upper Tribunal had no difficulty in divining a dual purpose.[2]

5–33 The real difficulties in applying *Mallalieu v Drummond*, however, occur with what might be described as everyday living expenses such as eating, clothing, housing etc. The most recent example occurred in *HMRC v Healey* (2014) when a Manchester based actor took the lease of a flat in London whilst he was acting in a musical there. He now claimed the costs of that temporary living accommodation. The Upper Tribunal drew a distinction between business expenses and living expenses. Some of the latter

---

[2] *Vaines v HMRC* (2016).

would never be allowed as being the former (everyday clothing, furnishing a house, etc.) but others could be if there was a business context, even if outside that context they would simply be ordinary expenses (e.g. hotel costs on a business trip). In this particular case the question was whether the sole purpose of taking the flat was to carry out his profession. Were the consequences of taking the flat (e.g. warmth, shelter and comfort) merely incidental to that purpose or a shared purpose? The lower tribunal then answered that question on the facts. Since he had taken a three bed roomed flat (for visitors, etc.) that was an independent purpose from his profession and the dual purpose was fatal to the claim.

5-34 "FOR THE PURPOSE OF" Returning to the words of the section, note that it says that the expenditure must be "for the purposes of the trade". Initially this was given a restricted meaning by Lord Davey in *Strong & Co Ltd v Woodifield* (1906), as being an expense incurred in earning the profits and not an application of the profits once earned. This therefore excluded damages paid to a customer of a licensed house when a chimney fell on him. This test was approved by the majority in the *Mallalieu* case, but impliedly rejected by the House of Lords in *McKnight v Sheppard* (1999) where the costs of defending a misconduct hearing were allowed. They were, said the court, clearly incurred for the purposes of the trade. On the other hand a penalty imposed on a Formula 1 racing team for a breach of the Formula 1 regulations was not allowed: *HMRC v McLaren Racing Ltd* (2014). The money was paid as the result of the team acting contrary to its contractual obligations and was not an unavoidable consequence of carrying out that trade. This could well perhaps have been said of the trader in *McKnight* or a newspaper paying libel damages. But, even if it had been allowed as being for the purposes of the trade, it would still have been disallowed on policy grounds as a penalty which should not be subsidised by the tax system, so that non punitive awards might still be allowable. The position, however, is still far from being clear.

Specific expenses

5-35 We want now to make special mention of certain types of expenditure.

TRAVEL TO WORK AND AT WORK There are no special rules in the Act governing the deduction of travel expenses by traders, so the general rules apply. However, there seems to be a lot of misunderstanding about expenditure on travel from home to work and from work to home. Some people think that home to work (and return) travel is not allowable for employment income taxpayers but is allowable for traders. This is not correct. In practice the courts have reached, albeit by different routes, similar conclusions about the allowability or otherwise of travel expenses under both provisions. This is because the phrases in ITEPA, "travelling in the performance of the duties" and "ordinary commuting", more or less balance the phrase in ITTOIA, "wholly and exclusively for the purposes of the trade" (as applied to travel).

In *Newsom v Robertson* (1953) CA a barrister who had chambers in Lincoln's Inn and lived at Whipsnade was held not entitled to deduct the expenses of travelling between the two places. This was so even though he had at his home a library of law books, and worked at home in the evenings and at weekends. On the other hand, in *Horton v Young* (1972) CA a self-employed bricklayer was held entitled to deduct the expenses of travelling from his home to the various sites on which he worked. At first glance this may seem to be inconsistent with *Newsom*'s case. But this is not so. Mr Horton kept at his home his tools and account books and made his contracts there. It was held that his home was his base, whereas in Mr Newsom's case it was held that his chambers were his base. If your home is your base, travel to work and back home is wholly and exclusively for the purposes of your trade or profession. If your home is not your base then such travel is not wholly and exclusively for the purposes of your trade or profession; it is partly because you choose to live at, e.g. Whipsnade.

In addition, just because you do some work at home does not necessarily make it your base. The issue was clarified by the Upper Tribunal in *Samadian v HMRC* (2014). Dr Samadian, a medical consultant, kept his private patient records at home, and sought to deduct his travelling from there to his consulting rooms in private hospitals. The distinction was made between a situation such as in *Horton* where the taxpayer has only one place of business, his home, and travels to other places on a purely temporary basis as work demands, and cases such as this where the hospitals were also regular places of business. The former are defined as itinerant traders and can include plumbers, electricians, etc. working from home. In all other cases the duality rule in *Mallalieu* will apply. Dr Samadian was travelling to those places of business from his home partly because of where he chose to live. Travelling from the hospital to see a patient in her home was allowable; however, that was travel from a place of business with no dual element.

5–36   Legal and Accountancy Charges   The professional costs incurred in a tax appeal are not allowable. This is because the tax is not an expense in earning a profit—it is the way the profits are spent: *Smith's Potato Estates Ltd v Bolland* (1948) HL. But as a matter of practice the fees paid to an accountant for preparing self-assessment returns are allowed, and so are fees paid for advice on tax liability.

5–37   Interest   Section 29 of ITTOIA provides that interest is always income not capital. Interest is quite capable of being wholly and exclusively laid out for the purposes of the trade and, if it is, it is a deductible expense. This is immensely important in practice. But dividends are never deductible expenses for companies, and nor are the profit shares paid to partners of a partnership.

5–38   Repairs and Improvements   Expenditure on repairs is allowable, whereas expenditure on improvements is not. In a famous passage Buckley LJ (in *Lurcott v Wakely & Wheeler* (1911) CA said:

> "Repair is restoration by renewal or replacement of subsidiary parts of a whole. Renewal, as distinguished from repair, is reconstruction of the entirety, meaning by the entirety not necessarily the whole but substantially the whole subject-matter under discussion."

In subsequent cases the distinction made by Lord Justice Buckley between repair and renewal has been taken to be the same as the statutory distinction between repair and improvements. His idea of "the entirety" seems attractive, but of course it means that everything depends on what the court regards, in any particular case, as the entirety. In *O'Grady v Bullcroft Main Collieries Ltd* (1932) the expense of replacing a chimney by another on a different site was held to be not deductible. But in *Samuel Jones & Co (Devondale) Ltd v IRC* (1951) the expense of replacing a factory chimney was held to be deductible. In the first case the court regarded the chimney itself as the entirety; in the second case the court regarded the chimney as part of a larger entirety, namely the factory.

The distinction between repair and improvements runs into (in some circumstances it is virtually the same as) the distinction between revenue and capital expenditure. In *Law Shipping Co Ltd v IRC* (1924) a trader bought a ship in a state of disrepair. The periodical survey of the ship was overdue, but she was ready to sail, with freight booked, and she did sail. When that voyage was over, the ship underwent survey, and the owners had to spend some £50,000 on repairs, of which some four-fifths was attributable to the disrepair of the ship at the time of purchase. It was held by the Court of Session that that latter expenditure was in the nature of capital expenditure and was therefore not deductible. In *Odeon Associated Theatres Ltd v Jones* (1973) CA, the appellant company bought a large number of cinemas which had not been kept in repair. Some years later they carried out repairs which had been outstanding at the time of purchase. The cinemas were usable in their unrepaired state, but they were not up to the standard set by the new owners. The Special Commissioners made a finding of fact that on the principles of sound commercial accountancy these deferred repairs would be dealt with as a charge to revenue in the accounts of the company. The Court of Appeal held that the cost of the repairs was deductible as revenue expenditure. The *Law Shipping* case (above) was distinguished on three grounds: (1) in that case, but not in this case, the purchase price was less by reason of the disrepair; (2) in that case but not in this case the asset could not (except temporarily) earn profits until it had been repaired; and (3) in that case there was no evidence of accountancy practice, whereas in this case there was such evidence and it pointed towards deductibility.

Rules allowing deductions

Part 2 Ch.5 of ITTOIA sets out the rules that expressly allow   **5–39**
deductions against profits that would fail under the rules prohibiting deductions. There are nearly 40 of these specific rules. Most are focussed on specific trades or activities, but a few are of general importance. There are also a few further rules allowing deductions as exceptions to the rules prohibiting deductions in Ch.4. Several of the items allow expenditure on employees and ex-employees that would not otherwise be allowed. Another item of general importance is in s.87. This allows a trader to deduct expenses of research and development if it is "related to" a trade—a wider test than expenses for the purposes of a trade. And s.88 allows a deduction for payments made to others, such as a university, for research—but in the fields of natural or applied science only.

The treatment of losses

What happens with losses arising in a trade or profession?   **5–40**
These losses can be set off against taxable income from other sources, although not all are available if the option to use the cash basis has been exercised. The tax position of a trade or

profession is calculated by subtracting from the income the relevant expenses. If that calculation leaves a credit balance there is a taxable profit. But if it leaves a minus quantity there is a loss. Thus far, a loss is calculated in just the same way as a profit is calculated. In particular a trader cannot claim for tax purposes to have made a loss merely because a loss is made on one transaction. For example, if a builder undertakes to build a house extension for £75,000 and in the event it costs him £80,000 to build it, he cannot claim to have made a loss of £5,000. What matters is the overall relationship of trading income and expenses throughout a whole year's operation of the trade.

There are four main ways in which relief for losses may be given: set-off against general income and capital gains; carry-forward against subsequent profits; carry-back of terminal losses; and a special mode of relief for losses in the early years of a trade. These rules have now been re-written as Pt 4 of ITA 2007. We will look at these in turn.

Set-off against general income and capital gains

5–41   By ss.61–66 of ITA 2007 a person who sustains a loss in any trade or profession carried on by him either solely or in partnership may make a claim for relief. The relief works by way of setting off the loss in the trade, etc. against profits in some other trade or indeed against any income of the claimant in the same year. If the claimant's income of that same year is not sufficient to absorb the whole of the loss then the balance may be set off against the claimant's income of the preceding year. This relief is not available if the cash basis option has been exercised.

The amount of the loss for the purposes of these sections generally includes capital allowances which are *treated* as trading expenses.

By s.66 a loss is not available for relief unless it is shown that the trade was being carried on on a commercial basis and with a view to the realisation of profits. And by ss.67–70 an even more stringent rule applies to farming and market gardening, namely that a loss cannot be relieved if in each of the prior five years a loss was incurred. The point of these sections is to exclude from loss relief against other income "hobby-trading" and particularly "hobby-farming". Hobby-farming is a pretty popular activity. It arises in this way: a person with a substantial income buys a farm and spends a great deal of money on building it up as a capital asset. If he or she could contrive to have no farming profits because of capital expenditure and set the farming losses against his or her stockbroking profits he or she could lay a gigantic nest-egg largely at the expense of HMRC. HMRC has disobliged.

A claim for relief under these sections against general income may be extended to the claimant's capital gains of the same year. However, the loss must be set off against the general income before relief can be given against capital gains. If the claimant's capital gains of that year are not sufficient to absorb the whole of the loss then the balance may be set off against the claimant's capital gains of the preceding year (this also applies to existing businesses during the transitional year).

Carry-forward against subsequent profits

Section 83 provides for the carrying forward of a loss in one **5–42** year against the profits in a subsequent year of the same trade or profession. Notice that it must be the *same* trade, etc. so that this relief is available to cash basis traders. In that respect this relief is totally different from immediate relief. A loss can be carried forward under s.83 indefinitely, but it must be set off against the first subsequent assessment and then, so far as it remains not fully relieved, against the next assessment, and so on. If a loss has been partially relieved under some other provision, the unrelieved amount may be carried forward. Or a trader can ignore immediate relief and go straight for s.83 relief.

It may happen that the profits of a particular year are not big **5–43** enough to absorb a loss which is being carried forward into that year. In that case, interest or dividends (if there are any) arising to the trader will be treated as though they were trading profits. This point needs a bit of explanation. If interest or dividends which have borne tax by deduction are received by a trader they are not included in the computation of his trading profits. The present point is that those receipts can nevertheless be *treated as* profits, and a carried-forward loss can be relieved against them by means of a repayment of tax.

Another point on s.83 concerns interest, meaning payments of interest outwards. If a trader makes a payment of interest that will, prima facie, be an expense of his trading. But if he has an overall loss the interest will not get relieved. But the amount of the interest payment may be carried forward under s.85 "as if it were a loss."

The general rules for s.83 relief are that not only must the prior **5–44** loss and the subsequent profit be incurred in the same trade, but also the claimant must be the person who incurred the loss. However, there is an important exception to these general rules in s.86 which provides that where a business carried on by an individual (or individuals) is transferred to a company, the individual may claim to set off any losses which he incurred before the transfer against income derived by him from the company after the transfer. The consideration for the transfer of the business must consist solely or mainly of the allotment of shares in the company. The income from the company may take the form of director's remuneration or salary or dividends. Further, a partner does not usually lose the relief available when there is a change in the membership of a partnership, e.g. when a partner joins or leaves the partnership. This is so because a partner is deemed to be a sole trader/professional in respect of his share of the partnership profit or loss. Therefore, his ability to carry forward his share of any such loss against his share of the partnership profits from the same trade or profession in subsequent years is normally unaffected by a change within the partnership (save where the actual trade/profession is subsequently carried on by him alone, see below).

Carry-back of terminal losses

5–45   By s.89 terminal losses (meaning losses outstanding at the termination of a business) may be set off against the profits of a trade or profession in the year of cessation and for the three years of assessment preceding the year in which the cessation or discontinuance occurs. This relief is also available to cash basis traders.

If the business is carried on by a partnership the position is as follows. A partner may claim relief for terminal losses when his deemed sole and separate trade, etc. is discontinued. Broadly, this occurs when he ceases to be a partner, where the actual trade or profession is subsequently carried on by him alone, or when the actual trade or profession ceases. Also on what one might call a statutory discontinuance caused by a change of partners. In the latter case the retiring partner can have relief but the continuing partners cannot. This is fair, because (as we have just seen) they can, despite the discontinuance, have relief against subsequent profits.

Losses in the early years

5–46   The three heads we have so far looked at provide for relief for losses by set-off against any income or capital gains of the same or the preceding year; against profits of the same trade, etc. in any following year; and (for terminal losses) against profits of the same trade in the year of cessation and for three previous years. This relief, which is provided for in s.72, works by way of a set-off of losses in the year of commencement of a trade or profession and/or in the next three years of assessment against any income of the taxpayer for the three years of assessment preceding that in which the loss is sustained. The relief applies to sole traders and to partners and members of an LLP. It does not apply to companies. Of course, a new company would not have any previous income, so the possibility of this relief could not arise. But an existing company sometimes sets up a new trade; it will not qualify for this relief. There is a provision to exclude hobby-trading from the relief. This seems a wise precaution on the part of HMRC. In genuine cases, however, s.72, in effect, provides a subsidy to a loss-making new business. It is not, however, available to cash basis traders.

The basis of assessment

The standard rule for taxing trading profits is to apply the current year basis. The tax payable this year is to be based on this year's profits. As most businesses calculate their profits by reference to a trading year, the rule of convenience that is followed for income tax purposes is that the tax for this tax year is based on the trading year that ends in this tax year. For example, Cas Trader keeps accounts based on the calendar year. In this case the profits for the tax year 2016/2017 (that is from 6 April 2016 to 5 April 2017) will be the profits of the calendar year ending in that year, namely the calendar year 2016. Pru Trader, noticing these rules, may decide to arrange his accounts to end each April. In that case the tax for 2016/2017 is based on the profits for the year ending in April 2016, so leaving an 11-month gap. Provided that is applied consistently by the trader, HMRC will accept this.

Special rules apply both to the opening years of a new business and to the closing year. This is to avoid both double taxation and tax avoidance. There are also rules to avoid distortions when a trader changes the trading year (producing a longer one or a shorter one) and to deal with sums received after a business ends.

Post-cessation receipts

A post-cessation receipt is a sum received after the end of a trade, for example for items sold or services rendered before the trade ended. Most trades are now taxed on what is called the earnings basis as part of generally accepted accounting practice. This means that income is taken into the accounts when it accrues to the trade, not when it is (later) received. So the accounts will usually include all sums earned by the trader even though they are received after the end of the final accounts period.

Small traders can be taxed on a cash basis. In such cases a post cessation receipt is one which would have been taxed had it been received during the trade. There are anti-avoidance provisions,

5–47

5–48

now to be found in ss.241–257 of ITTOIA that catch all such sums and ensure they are added back into a year during which the trade was still continuing. Post cessation expenses may, however, be deductible, if they would have been available during trading.

CHAPTER 6

PROPERTY INCOME

Introduction

"Land" observed Anthony Trollope "is about the only thing   **6–01**
that can't fly away." That is a thought that has long occurred
to HMRC and its predecessors. But alongside that must be
noted the statement of principle that Sir Edward Coke put in
his *Institutes of the Laws of England* in 1628: a man's home is his
castle. The clash between these two approaches to land has given
property taxation (or the taxation of land as it used to be known)
a long and tangled history. Thankfully, for income tax purposes
this has now been much simplified, but a brief note of the history
is still relevant when looking at some of the cases.

History

When income tax was first introduced it was called a tax on   **6–02**
property, profits and income. This was because the original rules
did not tax income from property (or land) but imposed annual
charges based on the value of the land. The first charge, called
Schedule A, was a tax on the ownership of land by reference
to what was termed an annual value. The second charge, called
Schedule B, was on the occupation of land, again by reference to
an annual value. Political considerations, particularly ahead of
elections, stopped sensible regular revaluations of these charges
and they became absurdly low. They were then replaced by a
charge on rents received by landlords, and further changes were
made on several occasions. In the meantime other taxes, not least
capital gains tax and stamp duties at national level and council
tax and the business rate at local level, crept in to tax property—
again by reference to value not income.

Thankfully, the complexities of Schs A and B are now firmly
part of history along with other attempts to tax property income
indirectly. A further level of complexity, also now part of tax
history, was a different approach to taxing income from what
were termed overseas possessions—now gently concealing the
extent to which overseas possessions in those days included
slaves.

Instead the tax charges have evolved through a process completed as part of the Tax Law Rewrite, into a tax charge on income from a property business regardless of where the property is located.

The charge on property business income

6–03   The rules that now apply to taxing income from a property business (not, note, from land or property as such) are in ITTOIA where they are set out, appropriately, immediately following the rules on trading income. We say "appropriately" because most of the rules about trading income now apply also to property business income, as noted below. One point to be emphasised is that these rules apply in principle wherever the property is located. So if I have a holiday property in southern France, and I let it out, then I am for income tax purposes potentially to be treated in the same way as if I let out a holiday property in Cornwall. The key provisions in ITTOIA are noted below. There are equivalent provisions in the Corporation Tax Acts taking the same approach.

6–04   Section 268 charges income tax on "the profits of a property business". And s.270 imposes the tax on the full amount of the profits arising in the tax year. But this wording is somewhat deceptive. This is because the "business" need not be a business. Section 264 states that a UK property business consists of:

"(a) every business which the person carries on for generating income from land in the UK, and
(b) every transaction which the person enters into for that purpose otherwise than in the course of such a business."

6–05   "Generating income from land" is then defined by s.266 to meant exploiting an estate, interest or right in or over land as a source of rents or other receipts. This is further elaborated by s.267. That removes the charge on income from farming and market gardening, and also from most other forms of exploitation of the natural resources found in the soil or land covered in water such as mines, quarries and canals to the charge to trading income.

Hidden behind this is a distinction between what lawyers refer to as land and what the general public calls land. Hence the label "property income" rather than income from land. What these provisions tax is the benefit that arises from exploiting a legal interest in land, not the land itself. The distinction was discussed, by reference to the former income tax rules, in *Lowe v Ashmore*

(1971) and *McClure v Petre* (1988). These cases also make the point that the income tax charge is on income and not capital receipts. Capital receipts are caught by CGT.

In the latter, the taxpayer received a payment in return for the grant of a licence to dump waste on his land. It was held that the payment was a capital receipt and, therefore, not taxable under Sch.A. By granting the licence, the taxpayer deprived himself of a right, namely, the right to dump, which he could otherwise have enjoyed over his land. The payment was the consideration for the disposal of that right. The taxpayer had realised part of the value of his freehold.

Under these rules, each source of income, e.g. each letting **6–06** where the individual has granted a number of leases is treated as part of a single business, and the taxation of the individual in respect of that business is determined by taking into account the income generated and pertinent expenses incurred by such sources as a whole.

Calculating the profits

The rewrite of the new basis of taxing income from interests **6–07** in law was also used to rebase the way in which the profits were to be calculated for income tax purposes. The old Sch.A had its own rules for the income and expenses that could be allowed. The new, and much simpler, approach is to start with the assumption that the rules for calculating trading income also apply to property income. Section 272(1) provides that "the profits of a property business are calculated in the same way as the profits of a trade". Section 272 then specified which of the rules about trading income are to be applied. However, these include the most important provisions such as that applying generally accepted accounting principles (s.26) and excluding expenses not wholly and exclusively for the purposes of the trade (s.34) and capital expenditure (s.33). Some capital allowances can be claimed for capital expenditure on land and buildings.

Another simplification added from 2016 by FA 2016 is a limited exception to the rules that capital expenditure cannot be set off against income for income tax purposes. A practical problem arises with minor capital expenditure by the landlord of furnished residential accommodation. For example, where the landlord has to replace a bed or a washing machine the expense is technically capital. Until 2016 this was dealt with informally by a wear and tear allowance. This is now replaced by what is in effect a "like for like" rule. If the landlord buys a new washing machine to replace a previous one, then the cost of that new machine is deductible as if it were a revenue expense. There are of course limits to deal with avoidance, and to stop double claims both for this and for a capital allowance, but the basic rule is straightforward. See s.311A ITTOIA. The rule is needed because s.308 (furnished lettings) requires that any sum received for the use of furniture is to be included as a receipt in the property business income.

Specific rules about taxing land

6–08   The significant simplification achieved by these rules has removed much of the need for a lengthy discussion about the way profits from land are taxed to income tax. But we must take note of several special sets of rules that apply to particular kinds of income from land. These include special tax exemptions that apply to some forms of such income and also rules that treat capital receipts from land as being income.

As might be expected, there are several additional special rules dealing with different specialised forms of property business and income or expenditure such as the commercial letting of furnished holiday accommodation (Ch.6 of Pt 3), rent from wayleaves for electric lines and similar, some complicated anti-avoidance provisions dealing with lease premiums and similar payments designed to deal with situations that step between income tax and CGT (Ch.4), deductions for expenditure on energy-saving items (s.312). Two special rules deserve further comment: rent-a-room and qualifying care relief, both in Pt 7 of ITTOIA.

Rent-a-room

6–09   The increasing problems of finding residential accommodation, especially in the cities, has led to a growing practice of owner-occupiers having lodgers or guests to stay in their houses on a commercial basis. From an official point of view that is to be encouraged as it eases the accommodation crisis suffered in some places. Two reliefs will help that happen.

The main one is the rent-a-room relief in Pt 7 of ITTOIA. This applies where someone lets out the use of furnished accommodation that is part of the individuals' only or main residence at that time. Unless the individual elects otherwise (because of the expense rules perhaps) the first £7,500 (from 2016) of the income is ignored for tax purposes. If income exceeds that figure, rules catch it as trading income or property income, with allowances for expenses. If income stays below that sum, then there are no tax consequences.

It is proposed from 2017 to deal with small sums obtained from what would otherwise be a property business even more robustly. Such income will simply be ignored up to £1,000 a year. So the person who lets accommodation, say, during a local festival but not on a regular basis will not be expected to declare it or pay tax on it at all.

Qualifying care relief

Alongside that relief in Pt 7 of ITTOIA is a qualifying care **6–10** relief. It is a relief from income tax for those receiving income (often from a local authority or charity) for providing accommodation and maintenance for adults or children needing care. In broad terms the relief is a fixed amount of £10,000 for a year plus up to £250 a week for each week in which care is provided. Alternatively, if the activity is regarded as a trade, then the profits or losses are regarded as nil. However, there are strict rules to prevent this being claimed excessively or used for avoidance purposes.

These reliefs have further value to many taxpayers because the exclusion of these sums from income tax also applies for tax credits purposes. And, at least under the present schemes, some are also ignored for housing benefit and council tax benefit purposes.

Artificial transactions in land

We must finally turn to some anti-avoidance provisions in **6–11** ITA 2007 and not in ITTOIA. Part 13 of ITA 2007 is devoted to tax avoidance or, rather, stopping tax avoidance. And Ch.3 is entitled "transactions in land" (not, notice, transactions in interests in land). Section 752 heads the chapter with a bold set of statements:

> "(1) This Chapter has effect for the purpose of preventing the avoidance of income tax by persons concerned with land or the development of land.
> (2) This Chapter imposes a charge to income tax in some circumstances where gains of a capital nature are obtained from disposing of land."

This is achieved by treating certain capital gains from dealings in land with a charge to income tax. The measures were first included in the income tax legislation before CGT was in place, and when corporation tax had a very different shape and effect to the current form. This was of course long before the anti-avoidance and anti-abuse measures were incorporated into these taxes. At that time if a dealer in land sold the land for a capital sum the proceeds ran free of tax. So it was plainly sensible to catch those receipts which were avoiding income tax and incorporate them by special provision back into the tax base. The provisions proved very successful when HMRC pursued various dealers through the courts with regard to payments felt—by the dealers—not to be within the sections. This may be why they are still in place, though the fiscal context of the provisions has changed so sharply since their introduction that they may not now be needed. This is not least because such transactions are now undertaken by companies, not individuals.

Some tailpieces

CGT

6–12   In considering the taxation of receipts from land, one should bear in mind that as well as income tax (in connection with rents and premiums and s.752 gains) a transaction in land may attract CGT. Aside from the important exemption for principal private residences, this is of importance to individuals as well as companies. This, of course, applies when land is sold.

Stamp duties and land transfer taxes

6–13   For centuries duties were collected on transfers of land in a simple but effective way. Transfers of land require formal documentation. The stamp duty laws required a duty to be paid on any transfer, and for that duty to be evidenced by stamps on the formal documentation. And if the stamps were not on the documents, then the courts refused to recognise them, so they were unenforceable. The same approach was taken to other documents, including cheques, insurance policies and similar formal documents. All have now gone save for the taxes still charged on land transfers. These have however changed in two ways: devolution has led to Scotland having its own land transfer taxes; and electronic operation have required the taxes to be collected in other ways. At the same time politicians have found collecting taxes from this source to be very tempting, particularly given the high values and seemingly ever-increasing prices of much land. Nonetheless, these taxes are the territory of conveyancers and are beyond the scope of this work.

ATED

6–14   FA 2013 introduced a new tax that is conceptually part way between income tax and land transfer taxes. The tax authorities had been facing a growing problem with what are termed enveloped dwellings—residential properties located in the UK but owned by foreign companies. These were in practical terms beyond the reach of taxes such as land transfer taxes in part because the property could change hands effectively through transfers of the company shares without the land being transferred at all. The new tax is an annual charge on such properties, the **Annual Tax on Enveloped Dwellings.** The annual charge applies, from 2016, to properties with a value of over £500,000. There is a set annual charge on such properties. This is put at £3,500 annually for properties worth £500,000 or over, rising to over £200,000 annually on properties worth over £20 million. There are also CGT measures that link in with such properties to deal with any avoidance of that tax.

A final note

And before we depart from the subject, we must mention again the two major local taxes levied on property: the business rate levied by local authorities on commercial premises and the council tax levied on all residential properties. Both rely on the advantage of being able to say precisely where a property is for tax purposes. And they are difficult to avoid for the same reason. This is no doubt why the effective rates of these taxes have been rising steadily in recent years. **6–15**

117

CHAPTER 7

INTELLECTUAL PROPERTY AND OTHER INCOME

Introduction

7–01   This is the area of tax law that has benefitted most in recent years from a combination of specific reform and the attentions of the Tax Law Rewrite. What we are concerned with here are the untidy bits of tax law that seek to tax individuals on income that was not earnings, nor trading income, nor property income, nor savings and investment income. The topic is untidy because there is no one definition of "income" on which tax is imposed, nor has there ever been. If the government wishes to impose tax on a form of income, then it must ask parliament to pass laws to catch that form of income. If we had a single definition of income, as for example is found in the US federal and other income tax laws, then it tends to be left to the judges to draw the line. But in the UK the absence of any general provision available to tax the miscellaneous kinds of income that fall outside the main charging provisions means that those forms of income do not get taxed save by specific additional provisions.

So we need a "sweeper" provision (or series of provisions) to catch and impose tax on these various other forms of income. Under the pre-Rewrite tax law this was Case VI of Sch.D. And there was a long list of individual sections added over many years that treated various forms of income (or sometimes capital, or even deemed income) to be taxable under that case.

7–02   The rewritten laws, as they apply to individuals, must therefore contain a code dealing with these forms of income. And somewhere in that code, or at least in the laws generally, there must be a fall-back provision. Because the line must be drawn somewhere whether or not we have a general definition of income. You will find most of these provisions in the "other income" parts of ITTOIA. Part 5 of ITTOIA is headed "Miscellaneous Income". It is unfortunate that it could not be given a more pleasing title, but it is accurate. Part 5 deals with:

- receipts from intellectual property (Ch.2);
- non-trade receipts from films and sound recordings (Ch.3);
- non-trading income from communications rights (Ch.4);
- settlements (Ch.5);
- income from estates in administration (Ch.6);
- annual payments (Ch.7); and
- income not otherwise charged (Ch.8).

The approach taken for companies differs in several respects. This is in part because the scope of the trading income provisions in Pt 3 of CTA 2009 is wider than the equivalent for income tax. There are also two separate sets of provisions dealing with IP. Part 8 deals with income and gains from intangible fixed assets, including goodwill. Part 9 deals separately with know-how and patents. Part 10 covers miscellaneous income such as income of a company as a beneficiary of a trust or estate, income from holding an office (which cannot be employment income) and annual payments and income not otherwise charged.

We do not agree, however, that it is right to deal with settle-   **7–03** ments and estates in administration as "miscellaneous income" in this work. Those topics raise important issues for lawyers about the structures through which income is received, and are not simply a matter of deciding what is to be taxed. We need to consider how and when income tax is applied to these important legal structures and situations. So we deal with them in a separate chapter. But we do not need to spend time on some of the more specific forms of miscellaneous income. So in this chapter we will look at the increasingly important issue of taxing IP income, and then at annual payments and other income.

Receipts from intellectual property

Before we get into the details of the specific provisions about   **7–04** IP, we must note s.575 of ITTOIA. This sets out the rules giving priority between different sets of charging provisions where one of them is to be found in Part 5. Section 575(1) gives priority as between Pt 2 and Pt 5 to Pt 2. In other words, if the income can be treated both as IP income and as trading income (including income from a profession) then it is to be treated as trading income. So an author who receives royalty payments for her work will be taxed on the payments as trading income and not as royalties. If she gives the rights to her mother, then her mother receives the payments as IP income. But if she sells them to someone who

119

trades in such rights, then again it is trading income. Note that it is therefore the reason why the individual has the rights that dictates how it is taxed.

Section 575 also gives priority where appropriate over the rules in Part 5 to Parts 3 (property income) and 4 (savings income), and also to ITEPA Pts 2 (employment income), 9 (pension income) and 10 (social security income). So for example someone may receive income from rights as part of his employment, in which case the rules about employment income apply.

In all these cases, there is a need to examine any link between the income and any of the prioritised activities of a taxpayer. These rules are also important when we look at the "other income" provisions. The important point to remember is that the rules about IP income and other kinds of "other income" only apply if the main rules about earned income and savings and property income do not apply. So we are concerned in this chapter about income received from these sources, for example, by people who have purchased or been given intellectual property rights, not by the original inventors, creators or authors.

7–05 The concept of IP as a general category of property rights is of course relatively new. It is therefore no surprise to find that the Income Tax Acts had no simple answer to the problem of taxing receipts from this kind of property. The problems were solved (if at all) by an accretion of separate answers produced by parliament and the courts as separate kinds of IP gave rise to a scope for taxation and a need for tax relief. Even HMRC described the eventual result as "complex, inconsistent and out of date" with "no overarching rationale". This was in a technical note produced in 2000, *"Reform of the Taxation of Intellectual Property, goodwill and other intangible assets"*. That description was more than justified. Income from varying forms of intangibles was taxable under several different income tax provisions and under CGT (and its corporate equivalent) with some forms of capital receipt being deemed to be income, and some forms of income being subjected to deduction of income tax at source.

7–06 The result has been tidied by the Tax Law Rewrite. This brings together in a short code within ITTOIA a series of provisions dealing with "intellectual property". The concept of IP is defined widely as including "any patent, trade mark, registered design, copyright, design right, performer's right or plant breeder's right"; any foreign equivalent of any of these; and "any information or technique not protected by" any of those rights.

While that sounds like an all-embracing title, what follows

still reflects the patchwork of provisions on which it is based historically. Provisions still discriminate between royalties (chargeable as annual payments); income other than annual payments; profits arising from the disclosure of know-how; and profits from the sale or licensing of patent rights. The consequence is that an agreement that encompasses several forms of IP and goodwill in a single transaction has to be broken up for tax purposes into its constituent parts. Each element of the capital and income changing hands then has to be assessed separately.

The following is a brief guide to the rules in Pt 5 dealing with   **7–07**
IP income of non-trading individuals. As noted, the rules for companies differ save that, as with individuals, the specific rules apply only when income is not regarded as trading income or otherwise subject to a different regime.

Patents

Perhaps most important of these rules are those applying to   **7–08**
patents. The receipt of a royalty payment for a patent is taxable income. Sums paid as royalties will usually fall within ss.597 and 598 of ITTOIA. This applies to patents, but not to sums not paid as royalties, in the sense that they are not annual payments. Where someone in the UK sells a patent right otherwise than in the course of a trade, the net profit received is treated as income received in instalments over the year of receipt and the next five years. A patent licence is treated as a sale and purchase of those rights. There are also special rules allowing inventors to deduct the expenses of devising a patented invention although the inventor is not a trader. Those rules are important because the individual who thinks up a new invention in his or her spare time may not be trading while doing so. Because of that, under the usual rules for non-trading income, no expenses would be allowed. Yet both the invention itself and the cost of patenting may cost considerable sums. The special rules prevent those costs being ignored as pre-trading expenses. The rules for deduction of the expenses of buying patent rights are treated as capital and are dealt with by capital allowances under the CAA Pt 8. A different approach was adopted for companies from 2013, though it is being modified from 2016 for new entrants. It is termed a "patent box". It allows a company to package its patent rights together and claim a reduced rate of corporation tax of 10 per cent on profits from the commercial exploitation of them, or a proportion of them. This has proved very popular with international companies operating within the UK but for that reason has been criticised elsewhere as too generous. For

this reason a more limited scheme runs from 2016. It does not apply to individuals.

Know-how

7–09   By contrast, profits from the disclosure of know-how are normally charged to income tax as profits when the sums are received otherwise than as part of a trade or the receipts are treated as royalties. This is charged by specific provisions in ITTOIA (see s.583), for otherwise the receipts might fall outside the scope of income tax. This reflects the fact that much "know-how" is in every sense intangible and cannot even be a form of property. This rule applies even though the disclosure is part of a non-enforceable agreement (that is, there is no contract). Receipts will usually be regarded as capital only if the sale is part of the sale of the business to which the knowhow is linked. Expenditure on knowhow acquisition, whether by purchase or internally to the business, is normally revenue expenditure.

Copyright

7–10   Leaving aside for the moment computer software, any income generated from copyrights (payments usually being in the form of royalties or sums paid in advance of or in lieu of royalties) is taxable as trading income, of a copyright held as an investment under Pt 5. Lump sums are accordingly usually regarded as income, not capital. There will only be a capital receipt where the full copyright interest is sold as an investment, in which case CGT will apply. There are no capital allowances for acquiring copyright. Special rules apply to software, and capital allowance may be available.

Trade marks

7–11   Royalties from a trade mark will be taxed as trading income, while lump sums received will normally be treated as capital receipts. The costs of buying a trade mark will be regarded as capital, but no specific capital allowance is available. The costs of creating a trade mark will usually be revenue costs deductible against profits. Much the same rules apply to design rights, and other similar rights.

Goodwill

7–12   This is not a form of property, and has long presented both lawyers and accountants—and therefore tax authorities—with problems. "Goodwill" is often the description given to the unidentifiable extra part of a sale or purchase beyond the identified assets. As such any payment for it is capital. There are no specific capital allowances for acquiring goodwill, but CGT will apply to sale proceeds attributable to it.

Other income

Anything left over, such as a one-off receipt for the provision **7–13** of intangibles that is not capital and not trading income, will in principle be caught as "other income" not IP income. This will apply, for example, to a fee for the use of a single article written for a journal or newspaper. This reflects the rule we have seen that single payments received from an activity of a trading nature will be trading income, while single payments for the disposal of something are usually capital. If the payment is not capital and not from a trading activity, then it is either caught in this way or falls outside the scope of the direct taxes. It is for this reason that there are special rules bringing into charge to income tax the receipt of sums for the provision of know-how or other information. Other relevant items of expenditure can be deducted under the "R and D tax credit" provisions of capital allowances, noted in Ch.8.

This complex of rules means that licensing agreements involv- **7–14** ing a number of different kinds of IP rights may need unpicking to identify: (a) what is capital and what is income; (b) when that capital or income is received or treated as being received; (c) when income tax has to be deducted at source on any payments made; and (d) what deductions for expenses or capital allowances are available. And there may be plenty of scope for argument if the buyer, the seller and HMRC all conclude that their optimal approaches to the agreement are different. This can also give rise to arguments between tax experts and intellectual property experts. One particular reason is the application of the rules about deduction of tax at source to some forms of royalty, rules to which we now turn.

Annual payments

Why do we talk about income tax on "annual payments"? **7–15** Surely, we are not concerned with the nature of a payment, but the nature of income as received by a taxpayer? Yes, we are. But "annual payments" is a phrase from the old tax law of the nineteenth century that has defeated the attempts of drafters to modernise it effectively. We can reduce the difficulty only by referring to the history of the words.

While we cannot change the name, the nature and importance for income tax purposes of annual payments have decreased hugely in recent years. When the income tax was first introduced, an annual payment was regarded as a way that income was transferred from one taxpayer to another. For example, I must pay you an annual payment under a covenant, or a sum by way of annual interest on a loan by you to me. In the original pattern of the income tax that was regarded as transferring or alienating that income from me to you. So you were taxable on that income and not me. But that raised other issues. How did I get tax relief because I reduced my income in that way? And how did the tax authorities find out that I had done this so they could collect the tax from you?

How was this done? Conceptually the answer was ingenious, and the approach was disarmingly simple. I deducted income from the payment when I made it, and paid you only what was left. This was because I was transferring the income to you after tax. I was entitled to keep the income tax I had paid in receiving it, so only paid you what was left. For instance, I have to pay you £100 as income when the tax rate is 20 per cent. I pay you £80 and give you a piece of paper saying that I have deducted £20 from the original £100. That gives me tax relief on the £100 reduction in my income resulting from the payment of it to you, but without me having to claim it from the HMRC. You have in effect paid tax at 20 per cent on the £100 income you have received so you do not have to declare it. This approach was called "charges on income". That is, the £100 was a charge on my income, reducing my income by £100. In effect, this is still what happens when a payment is made to a charity under the gift-aid scheme.

7–16   The effect of this is more dramatic when higher rates of income tax are applied. If I have to pay income tax at 50 per cent, then full relief from income tax can still be claimed. What happens is that, as before, I hand over £80 if I want the charity to receive £100? But I can also claim the balance of the tax relief due when I make my tax return at the end of the year. At that stage I claim the £100 while accepting that £20 relief has already been given. So I receive the other £30 as relief against tax otherwise due at that time. So the £100 gift to the charity has cost me £50 (and, it is worth remembering, it has also cost you and other taxpayers the other £50). There are a few other cases where this approach also applies, as where a covenant is given under a partnership agreement to a former partner. But most forms of this relief have now been stopped.

The charge to tax
7–17   Despite the best efforts of the drafters of the Tax Law Rewrite, the law on this question remains both conceptually unsatisfactory and untidy in detail. It is conceptually untidy because, try

as the drafters and others would, no one could come up with a satisfactory form of wording which removed "payment" from this phrase to replace it with "income" or "receipt" or some other form of wording that reflected the fact that income tax taxes income not payments. This is in part because of the difficulty of turning the case law about annual payments into sensible statutory provisions. And the detailed untidiness is because the lack of any coherent pattern to taxing annual payments leaves the code provisions about annual payments stranded across Pts 5 and 6 of ITTOIA.

The drafters were left recommending the following sweep-up **7–18** provision, to be found in s.683 of ITTOIA:

"(1) Income tax is charged under this Chapter on annual payments that are not charged to income tax under or as a result of any other provision of this Act or any other Act.

(2) Subsection (1) does not apply to annual payments that would be charged to income tax under or as a result of another provision but for an exemption."

The section then signposts nine forms of exempt annual payment, all to be found detailed in Pt 6.

This curious wording hints at, but hides, a significant amount **7–19** of legislative and judicial history. You will notice that the section carefully avoids any attempt at defining what is meant by an annual payment. Well, not quite. Subsection (3) gives some help:

"(3) The frequency with which payments are made is ignored in determining whether they are annual payments for the purposes of this Act."

Well, not quite to that too. If there is only one payment, then it is probably not an annual payment. And there may be questions over totally irregular payments where there is no pattern to the payments. These may be capital payments, not income payments. If so, they will be received as capital receipts and not income.

A clearer picture starts to emerge if we turn at the same time to **7–20** Pt 6, and we also think about what other provisions in the Taxes Acts can catch annual payments of one kind or another.

Historically, the most important kind of annual payment for many people was a payment of annual interest. A typical example used to be the interest paid on a mortgage on a house. That was a long term loan in almost all cases. So the interest paid to the mortgagee was annual interest, and therefore an annual payment. It is for this reason that for many years the income tax system had provisions in it allowing mortgage interest relief. But that is now entirely history. And we have seen that interest is charged to income tax under Pt 4 of ITTOIA as savings or investment income. So it is not charged any longer as an annual payment even if that is what it also is.

7–21　　Once interest was removed from the scope of annual payments, the approach taken was to deal with the problem by generally exempting other forms of annual payment from income tax while making specific kinds of annual payment liable to tax. That sounds more generous than it is. The main use of annual payments, aside from interest payments, was in transferring income from someone liable to pay a higher rate of tax to someone liable to pay a lower rate of tax. In the long distant past when the authors were students, this allowed wealthy parents to transfer income to their broke student children. The students paid no tax, but the parents were no longer liable to pay income tax on the income transferred so might save, say, 50 per cent of the cost. Wealthy ex-husbands could support their ex-wives and children in this way with a generous subsidy from the Treasury thrown in.

7–22　　The direct effect of exempting the receipt of an annual payment is the removal of any reason for that payment to be deductible when paid by the payer. That is confirmed by s.727 of ITTOIA. Subject to two major exceptions only, s.727(1) exempts from income tax any annual payment made by an individual (as against a trust or company) if the payment arises in the UK. The two exceptions follow.

Section 728 removes from exemption any payment made by an individual for commercial reasons in connection with the individual's trade, profession or vocation. An example of this is a payment by a continuing partner in a partnership of an annual payment to a retired or former partner as part of the arrangement under which the partnership interest was passed to the new partner. These payments may not, as receipts, be income from a trade or be a pension, so they will fall within s.683(1).

Section 729 removes from exemption payments for non-taxable consideration. This is an anti-avoidance provision. You will find the other half of the provision in s.904 of ITA 2007. Subject to limited exceptions, the sections catch any arrangement under which the annual payment is made under a liability incurred for consideration. The mischief occurs where all or some of that consideration is non-taxable for some reason (for example, it is itself exempt). This stops a clever device where exempt transfers can take place both ways by stopping the exemption. It is one of the better anti-avoidance provisions in that it is effective, so is rarely called into question. Again, these payments, as received, would not readily fall under another charging provision, so also fall into s.683(1).

The nature of annual payments

We have seen from this that annual payments still have an   **7–23**
important role to play in the income tax system. And we have seen that unusually this part is defined by the nature of the payment, not the nature of the receipt. We must now turn to the lawyer's question: what is an annual payment? As parliament has never defined the term, it has been left to the courts and tribunals to do it. They have done so by identifying a series of characteristics. If all of them are present, then the sum received is received from an annual payment.

The starting point relies on basic English law principles (applied to Scotland also for these purposes). Income tax does not, in the absence of express statutory provision, apply to gifts or other voluntary payments. So for an annual payment to be taxable it must be made under a **binding legal obligation**. That means it must be made either as a result of a contract or as a result of a deed. However, contractual payments will be caught under other charges to income tax because there must be consideration for a contract. So in practice an annual payment will be a payment made under a deed—usually called a deed of covenant. That is a promise for which no consideration is given.

The next test applied in the old decisions was the rule that used to be known as the *eiusdem generis* rule—the word must be taken to have a meaning like the other words in the same context. Under the old income tax law, this was useful because the charge to tax on an annual payment was under the former Sch.D Case III. This applied to "interest, annuities and other annual payments". So an annual payment had to be something like interest or annuities. That no longer works directly, as the charge is now under s.683(1) of ITTOIA. This taxes: "annual payments that are not charged to income tax under or as a result of any other provision . . .". This leaves us with a "what's left" rule, rather than a lookalike rule. So we must continue to rely on the cases, such as those below.

The third rule is easier to state, and has been codified in s.683(3):   **7–24**
"the frequency with which payments are made is ignored in determining whether they are annual payments . . .". This implies that there must be more than one payment, as the law requires for a payment to be "annual". But it also makes it clear that "annual" is not to be taken too literally. In practice it means that the legal

obligation must involve at least two payments and extend into at least two tax years.

7–25   Fourthly, the payment must be, in the hands of the recipient, **pure profit income** and not a receipt which enters into the computation of profit. In *IRC v National Book League* (1957) CA, the League (a charity) decided to raise the membership subscription except that those members who entered into seven-year covenants could continue to pay their subscriptions at the existing rate. Over 2,000 members executed deeds of covenant, and deducted tax in making the covenanted payments. The League claimed repayment of the tax from the Revenue, arguing that the payments were annual payments within Case III. The argument was not upheld. The subscriptions were not pure profit income of the League, because the League had to provide benefits, such as the amenities of a club, in return for the subscriptions. The *National Book League* case left a few questions unresolved because the judges propounded alternative tests for deciding what was pure profit income. However, in *Campbell v IRC* (1970) HL, the House of Lords (although obiter) had another look at the question. They adopted the phrase "pure profit income" to describe Case III, but were at pains to emphasise that non-commercial benefits resulting from a payment, such as having one's name printed in an advertisement or receiving a copy of an annual report, did not count.

7–26   Fifthly, the payment must be of the nature of **income, and not capital**, in the hands of the recipient. The point arises when A sells property to B in return for instalment payments. Are the instalments income or capital? A payment may be of a revenue nature from the point of view of the payer and yet may be of a capital nature in the hands of the payee. If it is of a capital nature in the hands of the payee it cannot be an "annual payment" even from the point of view of the payer. If it is of an income nature in the hands of the payee it may or may not be of a revenue nature from the point of view of the payer. In *Vestey v IRC* (1962) Lord Vestey sold a block of shares valued at £2 million for the sum of £5.5 million payable without interest by 125 yearly instalments of £44,000. It was held that the instalments should be dissected into capital and interest, and that the interest element was taxable income of the payee.

7–27   In *IRC v Church Commissioners for England* (1977) HL the Church Commissioners sold to their tenant the reversion on a lease in consideration of rent charges payable annually for 10 years and totalling £96,000 a year. The tenant was not willing to buy for a single lump sum. The House of Lords held that these payments were pure income in the hands of the payee and were not to be dissected into capital and interest elements. The Church Commissioners, being a charity, were entitled to repayment of the tax which had been deducted by the payer from each payment. (The same rent charges had previously been held—also by the House of Lords—to be capital payments from the point of view of the payer: *IRC v Land Securities Investment Trust Ltd* (1969) HL.)

Why worry about annual payments?

We have spent a considerable time on the complexities of **7–28** annual payments and collection of tax at source for several reasons. It illustrates some fundamental issues about levying income tax in Britain. First, the system must deal fairly with transfers of income under trusts and covenants but must also seek for that reason to curb avoidance. Secondly, the aim is to collect tax at source where possible, but that is not always easy given the flexibility of British trust laws. Thirdly, even with the anti-avoidance and anti-abuse rules now in place, the case of *IRC v Duke of Westminster* (1936) still stands as general authority that in the absence of specific legislation a valid covenant can transfer income from anyone to anyone else for income tax purposes.

Deducting income tax from annual payments

As we have already seen, the old way of dealing with annual **7–29** payments was to exempt the payer from tax and tax the recipient. But the tax was collected by the payer and taken in place of the relief to which the payer was entitled from making the payment. This avoided the need to allow the payer to have a reclaim against income tax paid for the payment.

The provisions dealing with deduction of tax used to be a pair of provisions in the Taxes Act. One allowed deduction of tax and permitted the payer to keep the tax. That happened when the payer had paid the annual payment from his or her own taxes income. The other required the payer to deduct tax and pay it to the tax authorities. That happened when the annual payment was not made out of taxable income. The process of rewriting these provisions has now split what were two sections sitting beside each other in the Taxes Act (the former ss.348 and 349) into a series of separate provisions in ITTOIA to be read alongside several provisions in ITA 2007, and in particular Chs 6–8 of Pt 15 of ITA 2007. That might sound like making things complicated, but you need only look at the lengthy commentary to those former sections in any of the standard works to realise that splitting the provisions into many constituent parts is in practical terms a great simplification. It only looks complicated when, as here, we try and take an overview of the system.

7–30   The starting point is now in ss.898 and 899 of ITA 2007. This is the signposting provision to the sections requiring deduction of income tax from annual payments, and with them patent royalties (which are a specific form of annual payment). It also signposts the main exceptions.

Section 899 defines "qualifying annual payments". These are various kinds of annual payments including those caught under s.683 of ITTOIA. They are caught if they arise in the UK. Different lists of payments apply to companies and to other taxpayers (including individuals). Just as important are the payments that are not qualifying annual payments under s.899(5). This cuts out payments of interest, payments that qualify for other tax relief as payments to charities, and also the payments caught by the anti-avoidance provisions in s.904 of ITA 2007 and s.729 of ITTOIA.

7–31   If an individual makes a qualifying annual payment, and the payment is made for genuine commercial reasons, then the payer *must* deduct tax from the payment when making it at the basic rate in force for that tax year. We emphasise the *must*. There is no option about this. If the payer does not deduct the tax, then it merely means that the payer has to pay HMRC as well as having paid the recipient. So ignoring the provision is not a good idea. Similar duties are imposed separately on companies and other entities making payments (for example, a local council). There are also provisions requiring deduction of tax when patent royalties are paid.

The most common way in which individuals come across these provisions under the new rules is when UK banks or building societies deduct income tax at the basic rate from payments of interest made to individuals.

As a result, the recipient of several forms of annual payment will receive the payments net of tax. If that happens, then the payments are not subject to any further income tax in the hands of the recipient. And the series of provisions noted above prevent the recipient demanding the income tax payment from the payer. There may however be further adjustments at the end of the year if the payer or recipient are subject to higher rate tax, or the recipient is not liable to tax.

Other income

Somewhere in every legislative code that purports to be **7–32** comprehensive there must be final fallback provision to be deployed when all else fails. All taxes imposed under the rule of law must, like history after 1066, at some point come to a.

For the UK income tax this is it. The UK income tax has never attempted to include all income either as an underlying principle or by way of an all inclusive definition. So at some point a line must be drawn between kinds of income that are subject to income tax and kinds of income that are not subject to income tax. In the form of income tax that applied for its first two centuries the answer lay in the schedular system. There was a final fallback provision in the former Sch.D Case VI.

That has now gone, but one of the conceptually difficult deci- **7–33** sions taken in the rewrite exercise was how to replace it. The answer retains some of the air of mystery found in the original 1803 Act. The end is right in the middle. The answer is in Ch.8 of Pt 5 of ITTOIA—at the end of Pt 5 of a 10-part Act which is the fourth of the seven rewrite Acts. Where else would you expect to find it—surely not at the end?

The key provision is s.687 of ITTOIA: the charge to tax on income not otherwise charged to tax. Section 687 carefully ensures that the section does not apply to annual payments (caught under s.683 discussed above). With that exception subs. (1) provides:

"Income tax is charged under this Chapter on income from any source that is not charged to income tax under or as a result of any other provision of this Act or any other Act."

And just to be careful, subs.(3) adds:

"Subsection (1) does not apply to income that would be charged to income tax under or as a result of another provision but for an exemption."

That wording deliberately echoes s.683. What emerges from this is that there are in effect two parallel provisions of last resort in the rewritten income tax code. One applies to annual payments, and the other to any other form of income. The only trouble with this is that in addition to the absence of any definition of annual payment we also find no clue in this section of its real scope. "Income" is not defined.

In the pre-rewrite language of the old Case VI, the central **7–34** wording of the sweeper provision was "annual profits and gains". It was generally agreed that this did not help much, as no one really knew what that meant, and the term "income" has replaced it.

The scope of income

7–35   So what *was* caught by the general aspect of Case VI? In *Scott v Ricketts* (1967) CA, Lord Denning said that what is caught includes "remuneration for work done, services rendered, or facilities provided". A good example of a Case VI profit was in *Leader v Counsel* (1942). A group of racehorse owners purchased a stallion. If any member of the group did not have a mare which required the services of the stallion he could sell his nomination to anyone else. It was held that there was not a trade, but that these receipts from the user of property were income receipts and were taxable under Case VI.

Similarly, income from activities which do not form part of a profession or vocation, but would do so if repeated, may be charged to tax under Case VI. For example, writing one newspaper article does not make someone into a writer. Case VI also catches income made by selling one's story to the newspapers. The wife of one of the Great Train Robbers sold her story to the *News of the World*. In *Alloway v Phillips* (1980) CA, the court held that the £39,000 she received derived from her contract with the newspaper, and that her rights under that contract were "property", so that she was liable under Case VI.

Gifts, betting winnings and "winnings" by finding are not assessable under here any more than they are as trading income.

There are three final points to be made about assessment under these provisions.

First, assessment is on a current year basis, and income tax is computed on the full amount of the profits or gains arising in the year of assessment. Secondly, "arising" has been held to mean "received": *Grey v Tiley* (1932) CA. So assessment is on the cash basis rather than the earnings basis. Thirdly, losses are not so favourably treated as losses of trading income, because a loss of this kind can only be set off against similar profits, not against other kinds of income.

CHAPTER 8

CAPITAL ALLOWANCES

Introduction

The major difference between the taxable profits of most **8–01** trades for income tax purposes and the net profit for commercial purposes is that capital depreciation cannot be deducted for income tax purposes, but must be taken into account if a true and fair view of profits is taken for commercial purposes. For example if the business buys a trade van during the year it will have paid a capital sum for it. But at the end of the year it will be worth less than the price paid because it will have depreciated. That depreciation (perhaps writing the value of the van out of the accounts over five years, say) will be a necessary deduction from commercial profits. But the capital cost of the van is not an allowable expense for income tax purposes: ITTOIA s.33. And depreciation is not an actual expense—it is a notional figure. So that is not deductible either. Equally, any profit or loss selling the van would not be included if it was bought as a trade asset—that would be a capital gain or loss. However, it has long been accepted that a fair tax system must take some account of the capital cost of business assets, particularly those that will waste away over a short period. So a system of capital allowances and charges was introduced many years ago.

The main practical problem with this area of tax law is that **8–02** politicians have been unable to leave it alone. The result is complex law. Capital allowances (the charges bit is forgotten in the usual headings) were consolidated and codified into the first of the rewrite Acts, the CAA.

But that did not end the changes. There was a major rewrite of a central part of the rewrite in 2008. And the Chancellor announced in Budget 2012 another major shift. As part of the simplification of taxing the trading income of small businesses we described at para.5–17, the Treasury promised that there would be "no need to understand capital allowances" for small businesses. Businesses opting for the cash basis of assessment can therefore now claim capital expenditure against their profits. This means that depreciation is irrelevant and they are outside the system of capital allowances. Cars, however, will still be subject to capital allowances unless the business mileage rate has been claimed.

At the other end of the system, capital allowances and charges apply to business profits for corporation tax purposes in exactly the same general way as they apply for income tax. The main relevant rules are in CTA 2009. These parallel the income tax rules so are not mentioned separately in this chapter.

8–03   Capital allowances are available as follows:

- plant and machinery allowances (in Pt 2);
- business premises renovation allowances (Pt 3A);
- flat conversion allowances (Pt 4A);
- mineral extraction allowances (Pt 5);
- research and development allowances (Pt 6);
- know-how allowances (Pt 7);
- patent allowances (Pt 8);
- dredging allowances (Pt 9); and
- assured tenancy allowances (Pt 10).

It can be seen from this list that major items of capital expenditure are not included. The most obvious omissions are industrial buildings and agricultural buildings. Capital allowances could be claimed for both for many years, but no new claims have been allowed since 2012. Buying land as a capital investment for a business was never included. That is dealt with only through taxation of gains and losses. The focus here was restricted to specific expenditure on certain kinds of building, and in particular the renovation of old buildings.

CAA and CTA 2009 are written to apply to individuals and companies conducting trades. Plant and machinery allowances can also be claimed by those subject to taxation on other forms of income: CAA ss.15–20. The list includes property businesses and furnished holiday lettings (Ch.6 above), employees and office holders (Ch.9 below), and companies managing investment businesses.

Why capital allowances?

8–04   As we mentioned above, the system of capital allowances and charges has for many years been a tempting area of law for politicians wishing to chivvy up or clamp down on business activity—and more recently to encourage businesses to stay in the UK rather than go abroad. For many years governments have seen adjustments to the system as a way to encourage businesses to invest in particular activities or areas of the country or to speed up or slow down investment decisions. From the standpoint of the business, there was always the temptation to use an allowance to cut this year's taxable profits. When the rates of income tax and corporation tax applying to the profits of the business were 50 per cent or more that could be particularly tempting.

The result is that the system of allowances and charges got ever more complex and shifted from one year to the next. And it could get very generous. For example, back in 1984 a company could set the full cost of buying most forms of equipment and much of the capital costs of any industrial building directly against profits otherwise taxable at over 50 per cent—a huge subsidy to the business from other taxpayers. Such practices, which were intended to exploit the generosity of the system, brought forth the following lament by Chancellor Nigel Lawson in his Budget Speech in 1984. He said:

". . . Over virtually the whole of the post-war period there have been incentives for investment in both plant and machinery and industrial, although not commercial, buildings. But there is little evidence that these incentives have strengthened the economy or improved the quality of investment. Indeed, quite the contrary . . . too much of British investment has been made because the tax allowances make it look profitable rather than because it would be truly productive. We need investment decisions based on future market assessments not future tax assessments."

This lament served as a prelude to a major clearing-out of old **8–05** rules. But it did not last long. By 2008, many of the old practices had been brought back in by later Chancellors. This led Chancellor Alastair Darling to conduct another major clear-out that year. But you could see the changes starting all over again after the following election, particularly because of the need to respond to a major recession. However, there are now two factors that make the whole system much less complicated. The first is the removal of small businesses run by individuals from the system altogether. The other is that the main rate of corporation tax, once over 50 per cent, has fallen to 20 per cent. That will distort capital investment much less.

We will now look at allowances on plant and machinery, and **8–06** then (much more briefly) at some other allowances.

Plant and machinery allowances

What is plant and machinery?

8–07   Neither machinery nor plant are defined in the tax legislation, and it is often a matter of some difficulty to decide whether a particular item is entitled to an allowance. The meaning to be given to the word plant has been particularly problematic and no attempt was made to codify it in CAA. This is typified by parliament's enactment in 1994 of a rule that buildings and structures *cannot* qualify as plant (subject to the proviso that buildings and structures already so qualifying would continue to do so). CAA ss.21–23 sets out those individual items or assets which fall within these expressions and which *cannot* qualify as plant. But, interestingly, it also lists items or assets which although within the definition of these words may nevertheless qualify as plant. In respect of an item in the latter category, it is open to the taxpayer to establish in the light of the meaning given to plant by the courts that it does in fact qualify. It is to the approach of the courts that we now look.

It is an interesting fact that the case most often cited as a starting point for judicial statements about the meaning of plant is not a tax case at all, but a tort case. The case is *Yarmouth v France* (1887) DC. A workman brought a claim under the Employers' Liability Act 1880 for damages for injuries caused by a defect in his employer's "plant", namely a vicious horse. Lindley LJ (in holding that the horse was plant) said:

". . . in its ordinary sense [plant] includes whatever apparatus is used by a business man for carrying on his business—not his stock-in-trade, which he buys or makes for sale; but all goods and chattels, fixed or movable, live or dead, which he keeps for permanent employment in his business."

8–08   From that beginning a huge structure of case law has been built up as to what may constitute plant. The item must be a good or chattel; it must have some degree of durability; it must be an item *with* which a trade is carried on as distinct from an item which comprises part of the premises or setting *in* which it is carried on.

It is this latter distinction which has often been difficult to draw, although it is established that an item which becomes part of the premises in which the trade is carried on cannot be plant (except in those cases where the premises are themselves plant; for example, *IRC v Barclay Curle & Co Ltd* (1969) HL), and that this will be so even if the item also has a distinct business purpose, e.g. to embellish the premises with a view to pleasing

136

and attracting customers. The determination of whether an item has become part of the premises depends on whether it is more appropriate to describe the item as having become part of the premises as opposed to having retained a separate identity. This is a matter of fact and degree, and a court may take into account whether the item retains visually a separate identity, the degree of permanence with which it is affixed, the incompleteness of the premises without it and the extent to which it was intended to be permanent.

Several cases have involved the refurbishment of restaurants, **8–09** bars, etc. In *Wimpey v Warland* (1989) CA, the court was concerned with whether various improvements including tiling on floors and walls, glass shop fronts, raised and mezzanine floors, staircases and false ceilings which were undertaken at the taxpayer's fast food restaurants were plant. It was conceded that the improvements were designed to attract potential customers and to provide a particular atmosphere which the taxpayer considered conducive to the meals served. Nevertheless, the Court of Appeal decided that the improvements were not plant as they had become part of the premises. In circumstances where items have not become part of the premises, it has been accepted by the courts that they may be plant if the taxpayer's business includes the provision of atmosphere and the items are designed to create that atmosphere (see *IRC v Scottish and Newcastle Breweries* (1982) HL). But in *JD Wetherspoon Ltd v HMRC* (2016), the installation of decorative panelling as part of the refurbishment of a public house was considered to be ordinary panelling which simply turned an unpanelled room into a panelled one. The panelling had lost its separate identity and had become part of the premises. The effect of the installation was therefore on the premises. In the Scottish and Newcastle case the murals, etc. had retained their identity apart from the premises.

It is obviously easier to apply the ideas inherent in Lindley LJ's **8–10** statement in *Yarmouth v France* to a trade than to a profession, and in *Daphne v Shaw* (1926) it was held that law books bought by a solicitor and used in his practice were not plant. However, 50 years later, in *Munby v Furlong* (1977) CA, *Daphne v Shaw* was overruled by the Court of Appeal. Mr Munby, a barrister, won his claim for capital allowances in respect of law reports and textbooks bought in his first year of practice. Lord Denning said:

"Counsel for the Crown ... would confine a professional man's 'plant' to things used physically like a dentist's chair or an architect's table or, I suppose, the typewriter in a barrister's chambers; but, for myself, I do not think 'plant' should be confined to things which are used physically. It seems to me that on principle it extends to the intellectual storehouse which a barrister or a solicitor or any other professional man has in the course of carrying on his profession."

Lord Denning divided what he called "a lawyer's library" into three parts: first, a set of law reports; secondly, textbooks; thirdly, periodicals, including current issues of law reports. Expenditure on this last group was, said Lord Denning, revenue expenditure; expenditure on the first two groups was capital expenditure, and qualified for capital allowances. And another 30 years later, the list would have to include IT equipment and software. Section 71 of CAA makes provision for capital expenditure on this.

Claiming allowances

8–11   If an item constitutes either machinery or plant, capital allowances may be available to a trader, other than a cash basis trader, who has incurred capital expenditure on acquiring that item wholly and exclusively for the purposes of his trade and where as a result of that expenditure the item belongs to the trader. The meaning of the phrase "wholly and exclusively" was considered in Ch.4, although it might be useful to add that where capital expenditure is incurred for the acquisition of plant or machinery to be used partly for trade and partly for other purposes a system of apportionment may be applied.

The word "belongs" has an extended meaning for these purposes. Thus, an item of machinery or plant may be deemed to belong to a person even though technically it belongs to another. This is best explained by the following example. Where a lessee of a building incurs capital expenditure on the provision of machinery or plant, which is required to be provided under the terms of the lease, for the purposes of a trade (in circumstances where that machinery or plant is not installed or fixed so as to become part of the building or land) then the machinery or plant will be deemed to belong to the trader by whom capital allowances may be claimed.

Where one business makes capital contributions to another business's capital expenditure on plant and machinery only the contributor and not the recipient can claim the capital allowances. There are also anti-avoidance provisions aimed at preventing various devices, such as a sale and leaseback, whereby allowances could be claimed without any actual expenditure being incurred.

Using allowances

Finally, before we look at how allowances for expenditure on **8–12** machinery or plant work, we must mention the methods of using the allowances.

When income tax was first introduced, no thought was given to capital expenditure. And in the nineteenth century the courts ruled that no deductions could be made against income tax for capital costs. This meant that the standard deductions from profits of a business for depreciation were not allowed to be set off against taxable profits. But both fairness and expediency prompted the introduction of specific allowances for some kinds of capital expenditure, while continuing to disallow deductions for depreciation. The reason for that was that at that time the way in which depreciation was set against profits was largely a matter of individual choice. There were no equivalents to the standard accounting practices that now exist.

The approach taken was therefore to create allowances that could be set off against taxable profits. They were deductions after profits had been calculated, rather than deductions to be made when calculating profits.

As commercial profits became steadily more standardised, and income tax profits became steadily more aligned with them, this approach gave way to the more realistic approach of treating capital allowances as deductions from gross profits to be made when calculating taxable profits. But the perceived need to retain objectivity and so prevent those deductions being left to individual businesses meant that the refusal to accept traders' own views of their capital depreciation were still not accepted.

The current scheme therefore requires all non-cash basis **8–13** trading and property business accounts to be adjusted with respect to capital expenditure. Any provision in the accounts for depreciation of capital expenditure must be removed. In its place the trader may claim up to the maximum of any capital allowances allowable in respect of capital expenditure of that or past trading years.

The key provisions giving effect to this are not in CAA but in ITTOIA. Section 28 of ITTOIA provides the link:

"The rules for calculating the profits of a trade need to be read with—
  (a)   the provisions of CAA 2001 which treat charges as receipts of a trade, and
  (b)   the provisions of CAA 2001 which treat allowances as expenses of a trade."

This must be read with s.33 of ITTOIA:

"In calculating the profits of a trade, no deduction is allowed for items of a capital nature."

We discussed the nature of those items also in Ch.5. Section 272 of ITTOIA also applies these rules to property businesses, covered by Ch.6. And s.574 of ITTOIA ensures that these rules also apply in respect of IP and similar expenditure incurred as part of a trade or property business, rather than the special rules in Ch.7.

8–14   The capital allowance system has operated with a number of different kinds of allowance and an offsetting balancing charge. The kinds of allowance are:

- **initial allowance**—none are currently in use. However there is an annual investment allowance for small businesses, not using the cash basis, to the same effect;
- **first-year allowance**—this was an allowance for the first year of claim at a greater rate than in later years. These are now only of limited kinds but there are a few enhanced capital allowances which give 100% in the first year;
- **writing-down allowance**—the standard form of allowance for the second and subsequent years over which allowances are granted; and
- **balancing allowance**—this is the final award of allowance when an item is sold or goes out of business use but the business has not had a full allowance.

Annual investment allowance

8–15   This applies to both individuals and companies. Under s. 51A of CAA, an allowance of up to £25,000 could be claimed by a business for expenditure on plant and machinery each year, from 2012. This was intended to allow small businesses to claim an allowance for capital expenditure on allowable forms of equipment without the need to enter the full capital allowance system. The annual figures have varied since 2012, rising to £50,000 in 2015. From January 2016, however, the amount has been fixed at £20,000 with a promise that that is to be a permanent amount. This therefore gives immediate relief up to that amount for expenditure on plant and machinery. Above that amount the trader has to rely on writing down allowances unless it is one of the types of expenditure which qualify for enhanced capital allowances.

First-year allowances/enhanced capital allowances

8–16   Throughout the twentieth century encouragement to businesses to invest was provided by allowing deductions of varying degrees of generosity against the profits of the year in which the expenditure was incurred. From 2008, only the most limited forms of such allowances remain.

Section 39 of CAA limits the allowances to qualifying expenditure. And from 2008 few kinds of expenditure qualify. The list runs from s.45A. It covers only certain kinds of environmentally positive expenditure. Most of those forms of expenditure now entitle the taxpayer to a 100 per cent allowance in the year in which the expenditure in incurred. These are known as *enhanced capital allowances* and apply to expenditure on cars with low carbon dioxide emissions, zero emissions goods vehicles, plant and machinery for gas refuelling stations, plant and machinery for use in designated areas (e.g. enterprise zones) and environmentally beneficial plant and machinery (as listed). These schemes have all been extended beyond their original time span.

Writing-down allowances

Where a person carrying on a trade incurs capital expenditure **8–17** on the provision of an item of machinery or plant wholly and exclusively for the purposes of the trade and in consequence of that expenditure the item belongs to him a writing-down allowance may be available on a 18 per cent per annum reducing balance basis. The special rate (applying for example to long-life assets) is 8 per cent annually. A writing-down allowance may also be claimed by a person who is exercising a profession and by the holder of an office or employment who purchases an item of machinery or plant "necessarily provided for use in the performance of his duties".

EXAMPLE. Suppose trader T, having exhausted his initial investment allowance, buys equipment costing £100,000 in year one.There is no first year allowance or enhanced capital allowance on the equipment. T cannot include anything for this expenditure in the business accounts other than the standard writing-down allowance. This is allowed at 18 per cent annually on a reducing balance basis, in this way. In year one T claims 18 per cent of £100,000 or £18,000. In year two T has £82,000 unallowed expenditure and can claim 18 per cent of that, or £14,760. So in year three T has £67,240 so far unallowed. The maximum for that year is 18 per cent of that total, or £12,103. That leaves £55,137 to be carried forward to year five, and so on.

Pooling of assets

The example in the previous paragraph shows how the allow- **8–18** ance works for one asset. In practice, however, a business will have a number of assets for which claims are made in any year, some purchased more recently than others. The system deals with this by allocating expenditure to pools. Most expenditure on plant and machinery is allocated to a general pool. The unallowed amounts of expenditure for any asset carried forward from the previous tax year is added to the pool. The writing-down allowance is then calculated at the relevant percentage of the total amount in the pool.

A separate pool is operated for all long-life assets. These are assets with likely useful economic lives exceeding 25 years. See CAA s.91. As noted above, this pool is given a reduced rate of allowance. A separate pool may also be operated for short life assets. These are assets with a short predicted life, as the pool can last for only four years. The assumption is that the assets will no longer exist or be in use at the end of the four years. Unlike the pool for long life assets, this pool is created only if the taxpayer elects for it. Separate pools are however required for some kinds of asset, such as expensive cars. Some of these assets are subject to caps and other limits.

Balancing allowances and charges

8–19   As each new item of equipment is purchased, the allowances for it are added to the pool of that kind of expenditure. And the unallowed amounts of each item of expenditure are carried forward from one year to another. So the previous expenditure in the pool steadily gets worth less, while being topped up by new expenditure in any year.

The pools will need other kinds of adjustment during the life of a business in addition to reductions for the annual setting off of writing down allowances against profits and increases for new expenditure.

First, capital items may be sold off at a profit. If this happens, then the amount by which the price received for the asset exceeds the value of the allowance for the equipment in the pool must be deducted from the pool. If the amount received exceeds the amount in the pool then this must be corrected by what is called a balancing charge. This is a direct offset to reflect the fact that the trader has received more for the equipment than the unallowed capital expenditure, so is making a profit against the capital allowances received. The idea is that after the balancing charge is made, the trader will have received a capital allowance equal to, but no more than, the actual cost to the business of the equipment. Section 55 of CAA provides for this. It does so by reference to the formula that the charge is TDR – AQE. In words, that means that the total disposal receipts from items in the pool exceed the available qualifying expenditure in the pool. But if AQE exceeds TDR, then the difference is available for a writing down allowance.

The reverse applies if equipment is written off or scrapped. For example, machinery becomes obsolete or breaks down and is not worth repairing. When this happens, the value of the equipment will be next to nothing. But there may still be a significant unallowed capital expenditure in the pool for it. In that case, the trader can claim a balancing allowance to ensure that the full capital cost is available for allowances. This has the reverse effect to a balancing charge.

If a business comes to an end, then there will probably be a series of both balancing charges and balancing allowances that need to be made to close the pools at the correct values.

EXAMPLE   In year seven T has pooled expenditure of £200,000   **8–20** carried forward from year six. T will receive an allowance of 18 per cent, or £36,000 on this. But T sells an item of specialist equipment for £60,000. So AQE in year seven is £200,000, while TDR is £60,000. So the amount available for allowances is £140,000. The allowance of 18 per cent of that, or £25,200, is deductible against the profits for that year. The AQE for year eight then starts at £114,800. If T in that year sells an asset that has gone up in value for £120,000, the TDR will be £120,000 and the AQE £114,800. So there will be a balancing charge of the difference, £5,200, added as additional income to the trading profits. The initial AQE for year 9 will be zero.

Other capital expenditure

The other kinds of capital allowance listed at the beginning of   **8–21** this chapter are merely noted here. But it is, perhaps, apposite to add in passing that, notwithstanding the generally diminished importance of first year allowances since the middle of the 1980s, it is still possible, in some instances, to enjoy capital allowances which write off capital expenditure in one year (see, for example, the 100 per cent capital allowance available for research and development and business property development).

CHAPTER 9

EMPLOYMENT INCOME

Introduction

9–01   The most important kinds of tax collected by HMRC are those collected, mainly by deduction at source, from employment earnings. Most of us earn most of our money as employees, directors or office holders. HMRC collects two taxes on these earnings: income tax and NICs. And the amount collected add up to over half of all UK taxation collected.

This is partly because the marginal rates at which we pay those taxes are rather higher than most of us imagine. There is much discussion about the "top rate" of tax at 45 per cent. That is the highest marginal rate of income tax in 2016, that is, the rate imposed on the top £1 of earnings. But the true top marginal rate must also include a 12 per cent NICs rate. Median (and average) gross full time earnings are about £27,456 a year (2015). What is the marginal rate on the top £1 of those earnings? The answer is 32 per cent: 20 per cent income tax and 12 per cent NICs, with the employer paying another 13.8 per cent. So, what's the marginal rate? That depends how these things are defined, but the fact that the earner and employer together must pay 45.8p to HMRC for that £1 suggests that we need to pay close attention to this topic. And since 2003, there is a further twist. If the £25,000 is family income, the family may also be receiving tax credits. If so, they lose 41p for each additional £1 (after taking account of tax and NI, or £1.47 gross). That means an effective rate against net pay of (by coincidence?) 32 per cent, or a total deduction from £1 of 64p. So the extra £1 here results in not 45.8p but 77.8p finding its way back to government. What is our top tax rate?

9–02   The importance of this law ensured that it was the first part of our tax laws to be rewritten. Generations of practitioners were brought up to deal with something called Sch.E. And you will find it in many of the old tax cases. But, that part of the tax law was codified into ITEPA. We can now talk about the tax on employment income or, even more simply, earnings. The law then requires specific answers to two central questions: What is employment? What are earnings?

Employment

"Employment" is not defined in ITEPA beyond a few point-   **9–03**
ers. Section 4 tells us that it includes any employment under a
contract of service, a contract of apprenticeship, or in the service
of the Crown. Section 5 adds that the employment income rules
apply equally to office holders. "Office" is defined as including
any position that has an existence independent of the person who
holds it and may be filled by successive holders. Section 5 is a rare
modern example of codification. It enacts the conclusions of the
courts in *GWR v Bater* (1920) and *Edwards v Clinch*, a House of
Lords decision in 1982. Office holders include company directors,
trustees, elected officers such as MPs and independent officials
such as judges. But an office holder such as a director can also be
an employee if there is a contract of service.

"Employment" is a far more difficult word to define, and
attempts to define it for ITEPA were abandoned at an early
stage. The difficulties arise both in law and in fact. This is
in part because of the importance of the distinction between
someone being employed and being self-employed. The question
of drawing that line was considered as part of our discussion of
trading income. It is worth noting how important it is. It is not
only important in deciding if the trading income charge applies to
the income instead of the charge to tax on employment income. It
is also directly relevant to whether the income should be subject
to VAT as income from supplies of goods or services. And it
must be decided if Class 1 NICs are payable both by the earner
and the employer, or whether only the lower Class 2 and Class
4 NICs are payable by the self-employed earner. Then further
differences follow for tax credits, statutory pay and other social
security benefits.

Much of the relevant case law comes from the employment tri-   **9–04**
bunals and onward appeals. An important marker about this was
laid down in *Young and Woods Ltd v West* (1980). In that case the
Court of Appeal emphasised the need to keep the income tax and
contributions rules in line with the rules that entitle employees to
challenge dismissals and claim redundancy payments and gain
other benefits for employees. Similarly, the standard HMRC
manual of guidance for staff on taxing earnings, the *Employment
Income Manual* (available at the HMRC site on the web) draws
attention to this case law.

One important recent reform is a centralisation of the official   **9–05**
decision-making about whether someone is employed or not.
Previously, separate decisions were made for income tax, NICs,
social security benefits and VAT. All decisions are now taken by

145

HMRC Status Teams—backed up by a web-based Employment Status Indicator (again on the HMRC website). All appeals, including those about social security benefits, go to the tax tribunals.

A borderline also occurs between employees and office holders on the one hand and professionals on the other. And do not be misled by names. A "director" may be an employee, as may a "partner". And many professional workers are both employed and self-employed at the same time—for example doctors working both in the NHS and in private practice.

In *Mitchell and Edon v Ross* (1960) CA, the Court confirmed that in such cases the employment income and professional income should be taxed separately. The case went on to the House of Lords on the related point that employment expenses of a doctor not allowed as deductions from employment income could not be set off against the doctor's professional income.

9–06   Someone cannot hold an office or employment as part of a profession. This is because the charge to tax on professions is mutually exclusive to that on employment income. This was made clear in the House of Lords decision in *IRC v Brander and Cruickshank* (1971). It was much criticised, and is not always strictly observed in practice, but remains another part of the borderline.

This clear distinction between a profession and an employment is particularly relevant where the taxpayer enters into a series of engagements. Are those collectively part of exercising a profession (such as acting) or is one or more of them in fact a contract of employment. If there is a clear contract of service then it will be an employment even if it was entered into in the course of the profession: *Fall v Hitchen* (1973).

Personal service companies

9–07   A common borderline problem is that of the one-man or one-woman company. E sets up a small company, Ecoltd, of which she owns all the shares and is the director. Ecoltd contracts with various customers to supply E's services to them. The customers pay Ecoltd. Ecoltd then pays, or does not pay, E. That payment could come as employment income for a contract of employment between Ecoltd and E, or as fees to E as director, or as dividends on E's share, or by way of loans or benefits. That kind of arrangement was queried in the courts in *Cooke v Blacklaws* (1984) but held valid for tax purposes.

A determined effort to squeeze out these personal service or "pocket book" companies was launched in 2000. They became known as IR35 companies as that was the number of the HMRC leaflet about the new rules. Attempts, by reply, to squeeze out the IR35 rules by political means and by challenges on human rights grounds both failed. The rules are now in ss.48–61 of ITEPA under the heading "Application of Provisions to Workers under Arrangements Made by Intermediaries".

The rules apply where someone (the worker) personally performs or is under an obligation personally to perform services for someone else, but where the services are provided under a contract between that person and an intermediary rather than directly with the worker, and the circumstances are such that if the services were provided under a contract directly with the worker the worker would be regarded for income tax purposes as an employee of that person (s.49(1)). The intermediary is often a company but can be a partnership, LLP or a third party individual.

If a worker falls within these rules, then the intermediary is treated as paying a sum known as the "deemed employment payment" to the worker as earnings. That sum is based on 95 per cent of the sums received by the intermediary together with any sums received by the worker from the customers but not charged to tax as employment income less expenses and taxed employment income (s.54). The deemed employment payment is then caught—subject to some limits—by the PAYE rules (below) and fully taxed as employment income, with Class 1 NICs also due.

One of the attractions of personal service companies (PSCs) **9–08** was the low rate of taxation on small companies, when combined with the lower rate of income tax on dividends and the ability to move income to others through the transfer of shares. The quick advantage to most income tax payers has gone now the rate of corporation tax on small companies is the same as the main rate of income tax: 20 per cent. From 2016 the tax on dividends has been increased, and a NI employment allowance removed. This will further dampen the advantages of PSCs. On the other hand the rate of corporation tax will fall to 18 per cent by 2020. Some tax avoidance schemes use less direct routes in attempts to turn earnings into dividends. But the Court of Appeal has taken a robust approach. If money is in fact earnings then it remains earnings even if dressed up as dividends. It is a question of fact. See *HMRC v PA Holdings* (2011).

The legislation has, however, been heavily criticised and HMRC have insufficient resources to investigate such companies on any effective scale. Accordingly HMRC is consulting on a number of intended reform proposals, the main one of which will be to put the onus on the client/engager rather than the PSC to determine whether the worker is subject to IR35. Accordingly if that proves to be the case, the engager will become liable for the employment income tax and NI which should have been deducted at source (under PAYE). Such clients will inevitably be very cautious as a result.

Earnings

9–09   The charge to tax on employment income is a charge to tax on general earnings and specific employment income (s.6(1)). "General earnings" comprise both "earnings" and "any amount treated as earnings" (we shall return to these). "Earnings" are defined by s.62(2) as meaning:

(a) any salary, wage or fee;
(b) any gratuity or other profit or incidental benefit of any kind obtained by the employee if it is money or money's worth; or
(c) anything else that constitutes an emolument of an employment.

This odd definition is where the tax law rewrite procedure broke down on rewriting the old (1803) rules into modern English. It did so because there are conflicting political imperatives on any rewrite measure neither to expand nor to contract the tax base. So ITEPA had to catch everything within the old Sch.E. That Schedule was defined in grand terms as charging tax "in respect of any office or employment on emoluments therefrom". These grand terms, it has to be said, informed few and helped even fewer in recent years. At least the rewriters have put the easy bits at the beginning!

9–10   The reference to "emoluments" keeps in being the decisions of the judges that stressed how wide the catch of employment income was and is. The test set out by Lord Templeman in *Shilton v Wilmshurst* (1991) HL, is therefore still relevant. He said that the phrase "on emoluments therefrom":

". . . is not confined to 'emoluments from the employer' but embraces all 'emoluments from employment'; the section must therefore comprehend an emolument provided by a third party, a person who is not the employer. [The charge] is not limited to emoluments provided in the course of employment; the section must therefore apply first to an emolument that is paid as a reward for past services and as an inducement to continue to perform services and, second, to an emolument that is paid as an inducement to enter into a contract of employment and to perform services in the future. The result is that an emolument 'from employment' means an emolument 'from being or becoming an employee'."

In that case Peter Shilton (then England goalkeeper) was paid what would now seem the trifling sum of £75,000 for a transfer to Southampton from Nottingham Forest. The sum was paid by the team he was leaving, but was held by the House of Lords to be an inducement for signing for the new team, Southampton. It was therefore an emolument for working for Southampton and taxable accordingly. At the same time Lord Templeman interpreted the wording as covering past services, so emphasising that the maxim "past consideration is no consideration" does not apply to emoluments.

Lord Templeman also indicated that a payment would not be caught as an emolument under this general rule if it were paid for something other than being or becoming an employee, for example if it were paid to relieve distress. This view was endorsed in *Mairs v Haughey* (1993) HL in which it was held that a payment to employees to relinquish contingent rights under a non-statutory redundancy scheme was not taxable. Payments such as these take their character from the payments they replace, which in this case would be a redundancy payment that was not taxable if made. However, most redundancy payments are now taxed, save for a £30,000 threshold, by ss.401–416 of ITEPA.

Wide as the test is, it must be shown that the payment is a **9–11** "reward for services". Of course, this can be widened further by statute, and many ITEPA provisions do this. Section 6(1) of ITEPA applies the term "employment income" both to earnings and to "specific employment income". Section 7(6) defines this as bringing into charge both the various forms of income that are neither earnings nor share-related but are set out in Pt 6 of the Act, and sums caught by Pt 7, which applies to income and exemptions relating to securities. Part 6 includes the redundancy payment provisions just mentioned along with provisions dealing with non-approved pension schemes (see pension income).

Even then, payments can still be caught under the general rules beyond the reach of those special provisions. An example is *Hamblett v Godfrey* (1987) CA. In that case the Court decided that sums of £1,000 paid to employees of GCHQ Cheltenham who agreed to give up their rights to belong to trade unions was taxable. There is a good review of the case laws in *EMI*

Group Electronics v Coldicott (1999) CA. Sometimes the argument is put another way. The payment, it is said, is not "from" the employment, so cannot be earnings. The Court of Appeal had little sympathy with an attempt to avoid PAYE deductions and NICs in this way in *Kuehne v HMRC* (2012), where the case law is reviewed. "From" is an ordinary English word, and whether a payment is from employment is a question of fact.

9–12   Where the employer makes a deduction from an employee's salary in return for some benefit, the tax consequences will depend on whether as a matter of contract there is an agreement to accept a lower wage in return for the benefit or there is simply a deduction from the gross wage. In the first case, which is known as a "salary sacrifice", only the lower wage is taxable plus whatever tax and NI consequences attach to the benefit. In the second case the whole cash sum is taxable: see *Heaton v Bell* (1970). In *Reed Employment Plc v HMRC* (2015), an attempt to separate sums paid in respect of travelling expenses to their employees from the rest of the salary (to obtain a tax benefit) failed—the whole amount was subject to PAYE and NI.

9–13   NEGATIVE EARNINGS   If in any tax year an employee makes a repayment to the employer, that can be deducted from the earnings for that year if they are what are known as negative earnings. The position was discussed at length by the Upper Tribunal in *HMRC v Martin* (2014). Mr Martin received a signing on bonus on the basis that he would repay part of it if he left the employment within five years. He left after two years and became liable to repay £162,000. He paid that amount back in year three. Warren J held that negative earnings were the mirror image of earnings (i.e. if they would have been earnings if paid by the employer to the employee then they will be negative earnings if paid by the employee to the employer). He also held that the rewrite into ITEPA (see s.11) had not changed the law. If there are more negative earnings than earnings in a year, then loss relief may be available.

Gifts

9–14   The most difficult area in which to draw the line between emoluments and non-emoluments is in the field of gifts. There is a mass of decided cases on this matter, and it is not easy to discern in them any clear-cut principle. It is tempting to say that if a payment is made by an employer it must be an emolument and if it is made by other persons it is not an emolument. But the cases do not bear that out; the most one can say is that a payment made by an employer is *likely* to be held to be assessable. In *Ball v Johnson* (1971) a bank clerk who was paid £130 by the bank which employed him for having passed the examinations of the Institute of Bankers was held not to be assessable on that amount. In *Calvert v Wainwright* (1947) a taxi-driver was assessed on the tips paid to him by his "fares", who could not be considered to be his employers. Again, it is tempting to say that if a payment is made in pursuance of a term of the contract of employment it must be assessable and if it is made without legal obligation it cannot be assessable. But that again is not borne out by the cases.

In *Ball v Johnson* (above) the £130 was almost paid under a contractual obligation; a term of his employment required him to sit for the examinations, and it was stated in the bank's handbook that it was the usual practice to make such a payment. But perhaps *Ball v Johnson* is rather an exceptional case. We think one can assert that a payment made in pursuance of the contract of employment is almost, but not quite, bound to be assessable. After all, because it is obligatory it is not a gift, so what is it? But the converse is definitely not true; it is not true to say that if a payment is not in pursuance of a contractual obligation it cannot be assessable. In *Wright v Boyce* (1958) CA, a huntsman was held to be rightly assessed on Christmas presents of cash received from followers of the hunt even though his contract of service conferred no right to the gifts. The payments were made in pursuance of a custom. Custom seems to be a very important factor in this area of the law.

The world of sport has produced some interesting cases in this **9–15** field. In *Seymour v Reed* (1927) HL, where a (non-contractual) benefit match was held for a professional cricketer on his retirement, the gate money was held not to be assessable. But in *Moorhouse v Dooland* (1955) CA, money collected (under a contractual right) from the crowd for a professional cricketer for outstanding performances was held to be taxable.

The case of *Moore v Griffiths* (1972) arose out of England's winning the World Cup in 1966. The Football Association paid £1,000 to each member of the squad. These payments were held not to be taxable. Brightman J held that the payments had the quality of a testimonial or accolade rather than the quality of remuneration for services rendered, and he set out a number of factors which pointed to that conclusion. One factor was that "the payment had no foreseeable element of recurrence" (on which one might comment "You can say that again"). Another factor was that "each member of the team, regardless of the number of times that he played or whether he was a player or reserve, received precisely the same sum of £1,000. The sum therefore was not in any way linked with the quantum of any services rendered."

As a result of those decisions tax was payable only on sporting testimonial income received under a contractual right (as in *Moorhouse*) or a custom was established. But in Budget 2016 it was announced that the law would be "clarified" with effect from 2017/18 so that tax would then be charged on income arising from a non-contractual or non-customary sporting testimonial or benefit (new s.226E of ITEPA). This will apply only if the purpose was to raise funds for the employee in recognition of services provided by the employee. There will be a one-off exemption of £100,000 for income arising from relevant events held in a maximum period of 12 months only, beginning with the date of the first event in a "testimonial year", even if that year straddles more than one tax year. That is the common situation still with county cricketers who are sometimes awarded a non-contractual benefit year by their county. This new provision does not apply, however, to the *Bobby Moore* case of a one off payment by the employer (the money was not "raised") or to any of the cases outside the sporting context.

Attempts to avoid tax by disguising earnings as gifts or routing payments through others are now caught by Pt 7A of ITEPA (ss.554A–554Z21) introduced by FA 2011. Known as the disguised remuneration legislation, this has been called "one of the most complicated pieces of tax legislation ever produced". The aim is to block attempts to avoid PAYE and NICs by routing payments through third parties in various ways. The primary targets are: earmarked money or other assets from an employer whereby value later arrives with the employee (or someone else) (s.554B); transfers of sums of money or assets from an employer to an employee or someone identified by the employee by any route (s.554C); and similarly where the use of assets is made available (s.554D). There are important exemptions for SIPs and the like (see Ch.11). The inevitable challenge to ingenious tax avoiders was taken up and Budget 2016 contained new proposals to counter the use of complex structures and specified avoidance schemes (which had been registered with HRMC).

Non-cash payments

9–16   So far we have looked at the rules applying to payments made to an employee in cash. But it was long ago ruled that payments "in kind"—or non-cash form—were also within the scope of emoluments. The old language used the word "perquisites", long ago shortened to "perks" but only removed from the statute in 2003. The most obvious example of a perk until recently was "the company car", but there are many ways in which it was sought to reduce the income tax liability of an employee (and the NICs of the employer too) by converting cash into non-cash forms. We must therefore study the many provisions that bring these non-cash payments within the tax charge.

To do this, legislation must provide two rules for each kind of payment: a rule that makes the payment taxable, and another rule that gives the payment a value. The second rule is normally necessary because a little ingenuity can reduce or even remove value from a benefit. The House of Lords blocked early attempts to avoid employment income by providing, in the words of Lord Halsbury, that a benefit was taxable if it was "capable of being turned into money". Or, in the words of Lord Watson, the Revenue could tax "that which can be turned into pecuniary account." That is relatively easy to apply, say, to a payment in the form of the ownership of a car. You can resell it. But how do you value the non-assignable exclusive right to *use* the car subject to certain further conditions? It cannot legally be turned into pecuniary account. In some cases a third rule is also necessary. That provides when the value is to be applied to the benefit. For example, the long term loan of a car would be expected to, and does, give rise to a charge each year.

These special rules accumulated over many years. ITEPA gave all concerned the opportunity to tidy the rules up into a convenient form. It was used, and the result is:

The benefits code

The benefits code is set out in Pt 3 of ITEPA, after Ch.1   **9–17** (which comprises only s.62 noted above). Chapter 2 defines the code as being the provisions in Chs 2–7, 10 and 11 of that Part. Chapters 8 and 9 list some exemptions. The benefits code applies to anyone liable to be taxed on employment income. Until 2015, those in very lower-paid employments were left outside the scope of parts of the code. Now only low-paid ministers of religion are excluded from most of the code. There are two more general exclusions from the code. Section 64 excludes from the code anything already caught under the general rules. This stops double taxation of benefits. Section 65 authorises dispensations from the code. If HMRC list particular payments, benefits or facilities in an appropriate notice, then no additional tax is imposed under the code. This allows employers to deal with some of the benefits directly with HMRC rather than each employee having to sort the matter out. It makes the job of a payroll department a lot easier. We now outline each part of the code.

Expense payments

9–18   Chapter 3 (ss.70–72) includes extremely wide rules that catch any sums paid to an employee in respect of expenses where the payment is "by reason of" the employment (s.70(1)). But every payment to an employee is assumed to be by way of the employment unless the employer is an individual and the payment is in the normal course of domestic, family or personal relationships (s.71(1)). Payments put at an employee's disposal are also caught. The nature of the expense payment is not relevant to the scope of the sections. The principle is that they should be included in the charge to tax, with the employee being left to claim a deduction if he or she can.

In practice this two-way process was ameliorated by what was known as the dispensation regime, e.g. for the refund of approved travelling expenses, where section 70 was in effect disapplied. FA 2015 abolished that dispensation regime with effect from the 2016/17 tax year and replaced it with a new statutory exemption for amounts which would otherwise be deductible. Thus there will no longer be any reporting requirements and employees will automatically receive the tax relief they are entitled to. This new exemption covers not only deductible expenses such as allowable travelling expenses (see para.9–40 below) but also what are known as approved or flat rate payments for certain deductible expenses. The employer must apply for approval to pay a flat rate. An example of a flat rate expense is a meal allowance in the course of qualifying travel. Under the Income Tax (Approved Expenses) Regulations 2015, the meal allowance is £5 if the travel exceeds 5 hours, £10 where it exceeds 10 hours and £25 where it is more than 15 hours and lasts beyond 20.00.

Vouchers and credit-tokens

9–19   The scope of Ch.4 (ss.73–96) requires a little more explanation—not to mention the translation into understandable English of "credit-token".

The chapter brings together three parallel sets of provisions designed to impose tax on what might be called indirect cash payments. Together they form a mini-code in their own right. The opportunity to rewrite the provisions into ITEPA also allowed a number of minor problems to be ironed out. Nonetheless, to understand the scope of the provisions it is necessary to see just how wide are the definitions of the three key terms: cash voucher, non-cash voucher and credit-token.

A **cash voucher** means a voucher, stamp or similar document **9–20** capable of being exchanged for a sum of money that is at least not substantially less than the expense incurred by the person at whose cost the voucher is provided (s.75(1)). For example, an employer might provide employees with weekly "holiday stamps" that allow the employees to cash them in from time to time to receive sums from the employer towards the cost of a holiday. There are also special rules for "sickness benefits-related vouchers", which bring within these rules what would otherwise be cash vouchers save for the fact that a particular employee avoids sickness or personal injury, so is not claiming much in return for the vouchers.

A **non-cash voucher** means a voucher, stamp or similar docu- **9–21** ment, or token capable of being exchanged for money, goods or services. It includes "transport vouchers" and "cheque vouchers". But something that is a cash voucher cannot also be a non-cash voucher. A "transport voucher" is what most of us would call a ticket, and catches employer-provided season tickets. It also includes any form of pass or other document or token that can be used to obtain transport services. The wide wording has to cover the tokens used in some places to feed into machines, as well as for example Transport for London's Oyster cards. (s.84). A "cheque voucher" is a cheque given by an employer to an employee for the employee to buy particular kinds of goods and services. In practical terms, that means that the cheque is made payable not to the employee but, for instance, to the local travel agents.

And what is a **credit-token**? You probably have some in your **9–22** purse or wallet. They are credit cards, debit cards, or other cards, tokens, documents or other objects given by one person to another where the giver undertakes to provide money, goods or services on its production or to pay any third person for the supply of money goods or services on its production—unless the card or object is a cash voucher or non-cash voucher (s.92).

The mini-code provides that if any of these "documents" or "objects" are provided to an employee then income tax will be imposed on the "cash equivalent" of it or its use as if that were earnings. It defines the cash equivalent in each case and provides rules for the timing of such charges. The converse is that the goods, services or cash received are disregarded for tax purposes (s.95), in order to stop a potential double charge.

Living accommodation

9-23   Providing free or subsidised living accommodation to an employee is a long-standing method of attracting and keeping employees—and is a necessary aspect of some jobs. Chapter 5 (ss.97–113) lays down a series of rules to tax those who gain through employer-assisted accommodation. But it includes important exemptions for those who must live "on the job". There is no tax charge if it is necessary that the employee lives in the accommodation for the proper performance of the employer's duties (s.99(1)). The classic example used to be a lighthouse keeper, but it still applies to many security and care posts. There is also no tax charge if the accommodation is provided for the better performance of the duties of the employment and it is customary to provide accommodation for employees in that kind of employment (s.99(2)). This would apply to many rural economy jobs. Necessity is to be judged objectively rather than by the personal circumstances of the employee. "Customary" is based on statistics and whether it was generally accepted by relevant employers: *Vertigan v Brady* (1988). There is a further narrower exemption if the accommodation is provided as a result of a security threat (s.100).

The general rules catch accommodation provided not only for an employee but also for members of the employee's family. There are then two sets of rules to provide the cash equivalent of the use of the accommodation in any year. If the cost to the employer is over £75,000 then a stricter set of rules apply. That sum is calculated by reference to any purchase and improvement costs borne by the employer. Where the stricter rules apply the employee is charged tax not only on a notional rent but also on notional interest payable to fund the purchase or improvement costs. This method of calculating the taxable amount applies in all cases and is not subject to the "fair bargain" concept (see para.9–30 below).

Cars, vans and related benefits

9-24   Once upon a time (not that long ago) most cars on British roads belonged not to their drivers or families but to an employer. Of course, there are employees who are necessary car users, but not that many. The case of *Heaton v Bell* (1970) HL established that a well-designed car scheme (though not the one in the case) would take the value of an employer-provided car outside the then tax rules. Given the popular status then attaching to big, new cars and the cost to an employee of buying them, the fact that your glossy new car was also indirectly subsidised by your neighbours through their taxes made "company cars" an almost irresistible perk to most. And, as governments were acutely aware, most fleet cars were then "built in Britain". Better still if it was full of extras that were also tax-free, and it was serviced and filled with petrol paid for by the employer but also free of income tax.

For those on the public payroll without access to these perks, it was necessary to pay employees for using their own cars and in some cases to help them buy them. A generous "mileage allowance" could still be quite a help tax free.

The problem with all such schemes is that they are essentially unfair in tax terms. Company car users are subsidised by non-car users or those who have to buy their own cars without tax help. Those with big cars were more subsidised. Even given the political "clout" of car users—and car manufacturers—it was inevitable as car use grew that the tax shelter for company cars would be eliminated. But the ITEPA code rules for cars do more than that. As a result of recent changes, the code positively discourages some aspects of company car use. For example, having a second company car can now prove expensive in post-tax terms, while even the first car may not now be worth it to an employee. It is often now cheaper for an employee to buy a car and claim mileage allowances. Further, the rules have been designed to encourage the use of non-polluting vehicles. The only lobby that did prove successful in limiting the new rules was the classic cars lobby. Rules limit the tax charge on cars over 15 years old, but not old "bangers"—the car must be worth £15,000 to qualify (s.147).

Chapter 6 sets out rules to catch and tax the value of cars and vans provided by employers for the private use of employees or their families. It does not need to deal with the case where the employer gives the employee the car, because the ordinary rules tax the cost of doing so.

Taxing the use of cars

The current rules for taxing the benefit to an employee of the **9–25** provision by the employer of the use of a car are now quite elaborate as the amount to be paid depends of the value of the car, the "carbon footprint" of the car and the extent of any use of that car for work reasons. The picture is complicated because the rules tend to change every year. However, government announces the intended rates two years ahead to provide some certainty. Budget 2012 went further, and announced the intended rates up to 2017. The rates have now been set up to 2018. Here we use the rates announced for 2015 and 2016 for an illustration of the detail. The charge only applies if the car is provided by the employer and is available for private use although it is deemed to be available for private use unless the terms of use prohibit such use and it is not so used (see, e.g. *Gilbert v Hemsley* (1981)). There is a reduction for any payments made by the employee for such use. Tax payments must be made in the year in which there is private use. To counter a successful avoidance scheme it is now provided that this legislation takes precedence over any other charge on the use of the car.

The relevant law is in ss.121–148 of ITEPA. These provide for a cash equivalent of the benefit of a company car which is made available for private use. In broad terms, this is calculated from the list price of the car adjusted by a multiplier called the appropriate percentage. This is a percentage that is set to reflect the volume of carbon dioxide emissions the car produces.

The starting point is the value of the car taken from its list price. This is defined carefully to be the list price of the car published by the manufacturer or distributor for a car sold singly with all relevant charges for delivery up to the day before the day of first registration. This must then be adjusted to include the list price of all accessories added to the car, but is to be reduced to reflect any capital contribution made by the employee/employer to the cost of the car. The only exception to this is for a car for a disabled person. The effect of these rules means that the employee does not gain at all from any discount won by the employer in buying the car. Nor can any advantage be gained by adding accessories to the car. Both were standard practices until the law on these points was made clear.

The next step is to establish the "appropriate percentage" for the car. This depends on the car's fuel, and there are special rules for diesel cars. All cars first registered in this century should have a published CO_2 (carbon dioxide) emission figure. The figure is the amount of the gas emitted measured in grams per kilometre under standard conditions. A full list of all the figures is available on many websites and they do vary from year to year. Currently a standard petrol car has an appropriate percentage of 15 per cent, rising as the CO_2 emissions rise in 1 per cent bands up to a maximum of 37 per cent. There is an additional 3 per cent surcharge on diesel cars whereas electric cars are fixed at 7 per cent for 2016 but rising thereafter. Hybrid cars have their own figures. In Budget 2016 it was announced that as from 2019/20 the appropriate percentage for all cars registered after 1 January 1998 would start at 16 per cent, increasing by 3 per cent bands as CO_2 emissions increase. To reach that figure, purely electric cars will have a 9 per cent figure in 2017/18, rising to 13 per cent in 2018/19 and then 16 per cent from 2019/20. These specific methods of calculating the taxable benefits are paramount and apply in all cases. They are not subject to the "fair bargain" concept (see para.9–30 below).

Mileage allowances and tax exemptions

While the code in Pt 3 of ITEPA brings car benefits into tax, that is not the whole story for the working motorist. We must also note the tax treatment of expenses given for the use by an employee of a privately owned vehicle, and related provisions. The important issue here is when a payment of expenses is exempted from tax. A driver is exempt from tax on the receipt of any approved mileage allowance payments given for the use of the driver's car for business travel. Business travel means travel such that if the employee paid the expenses direct, they would be deductible against income tax under the standard deduction rules (see below). But if the payment is not a refund or payment towards motoring expenses actually incurred, and is not within the exemption, then the sum will be taxable as earnings. **9–26**

The rules (see ITEPA ss.229–232 and 235–236) allow an exemption of 45p for the first 10,000 miles and 25p after that. (Cyclists should note that the mileage rate for using a pedal cycle is 20p—a deliberate encouragement to "get on yer bike".) So an employer paying an employee that rate of allowance (or less) will not deduct tax. It may be taxable above that level, and the employer may be liable to Class 1A NICs.

These rules are separate from the rules (in Pt 5 of ITEPA) for deducting travel expenses. They must also be taken into account here to get the full picture. But there is an overlap because a relief (called mileage allowance relief) is given by s.231 in Pt 4. If a motorist incurs expenses for business travel and the mileage allowances paid by the employer are less than the approved amount, then the employee can claim the difference as a deduction against earnings. This is an important rule in cases where the employer pays a lower rate than the 45p rate. To take a simple example: my employers give me 20p a mile for using my car to drive 5,000 miles in the year for work purposes. But I can claim 45p a mile. The 20p a mile will be paid to me free of income tax (and NICs). I can then claim the additional 25p as an expense against my income tax liability. As that adds up to £1,250, it is not to be ignored. In summary, there are therefore three groups of employees to be considered: those paid the official rate; those paid below the official rate; and those paid above the official rate.

There are separate rules where the employer pays a driver an allowance for taking a passenger in the car for work reasons (see s.233). The approved amount for a passenger payment is 5p a mile for each passenger. In other words, if the employee receives that sum or less from the employer it will be free of tax (and NICs).

Sections 237–249 list other important practical exemptions. There is no liability to tax on the provision of a parking place at or near work. There are exemptions for overnight charges and allowances (for example, for HGV drivers). There is no tax liability on free works transport (including transport for the children of employees) and there are tax exemptions for disabled drivers.

Finally we must note the potential tax charge where an employee is supplied with a company car and is then either given the fuel to run it or is given a fuel allowance. This in practice adds a fourth group to the three we have already noted. HMRC publishes figures that are regularly updated about the amounts allowable a appropriate expenditure under this head. These figures take into account actual car use (by reference to engine size and other factors). HMRC's figures are in practice based on those produced by the AA. You can find the figures on the AA's website under running costs for cars. So long as the amounts paid are within those levels, they will not be taxed.

Loans

9–27   Chapter 7 of the code (ss.173–191) is targeted on cheap loans that are employment-related—that is, loans provided by reason of employment either interest-free or at a low rate of interest as compared with a commercial rate. The rules do not apply to loans totalling under £10,000, to bridging loans connected with employment moves (ss.288–289), to loans where tax relief can be claimed on the interest (for example, as a business expense), or to loans for necessary expenses. All other loans are assessed against "the official rate of interest". This is set from time to time by the Treasury (with different rates for sterling and foreign currency loans). If the interest rate is less than the official rate, and the loan is not an ordinary commercial loan by the employer available generally, then there is a tax charge on the interest that would be payable at the official rate less the actual interest paid.

A separate charge catches and taxes the amount of any loan written off (s.188).

These specific methods of calculating the taxable benefits are paramount and apply in all cases. They are not subject to the "fair bargain" concept (see para.9–30 below).

Residual liability to charge

Sections 201–210, forming Ch.10, provide a "sweeper-up" **9–28** provision aimed generally at any other "employment-related benefit". It catches "a benefit or facility of any kind" provided for an employee (including past and future employees) or a member of the employee's family or household if "provided by reason of the employment". But everything provided by an employer is so regarded unless the employer and employee are members of the same family or household, or it is a normal personal benefit (such as a birthday present) (s.201). In other words, if it wasn't caught by the other parts of the code, it probably will be here. But if it is caught by other parts of the code, then those chapters apply and not this one.

The main issue with such benefits has been the value of the resulting taxable cash equivalent. Under s.204 this is the cost to the provider (which changed the old rule that it was the value to the employee). In the famous case of *Pepper v Hart* (1990), the House of Lords, after referring to the relevant parliamentary debate (which made the case famous) decided that in the case of "in house" or "surplus capacity" benefits only the marginal cost and not the average cost was chargeable. Thus a schoolmaster whose son was educated at the school on a reduced fee basis (an in house benefit) was only taxed on the marginal cost of an additional pupil, i.e. what it cost the school to take on one more pupil, and not the average cost of each pupil at the school, i.e. total cost divided by the number of pupils. As a result some in-house benefits such as sports grounds are excluded from the code altogether. An example of a surplus capacity benefit would be where an employee of an airline is entitled to fly free if there is a spare seat in the plane.

Under ss.205 and 206 if the benefit involves placing an asset at the disposal of the employee or is used for the purposes of the employee, without transferring ownership, the cash equivalent is its annual value (20 per cent of market value) each year unless the cost to the provider is higher. If the asset is actually given to the employee then the market value of the asset at that time becomes the cash equivalent. In the case of an asset with high depreciation, such as a computer, if the asset is made available in year 1 and then transferred in year 2 when its value has dropped sharply, the market value on the transfer is taken to be its original one in year 1.

There is no charge, however, if the benefit was not given for a work-related reason (e.g. for a social reason) and the cost to the employer (or the average cost) does not exceed £50 (s.323A).

What's left

9–29 What's left that is not taxed, other than specifically exempted benefits? We must deal with the extremely important topic of pensions in the next chapter. Apart from what might be termed deferred earnings, the answer is not very much. Perhaps the other main two ways in which an employer can give a benefit to an employee without either incurring tax charges or having to establish some indirect (perhaps foreign) yet legal form of transferring value are the provision of free services (such as additional occupational health services or investment advice) and additional holidays.

"Fair bargain"

9–30 For the purposes of the residual charge something which is a "fair bargain" between the employer and employee is not regarded as a benefit for the purposes s.201. This is where the employee has received goods and services from the employer at exactly the same cost, terms and conditions as any independent person dealing with the employer at arm's length. In *HMRC v Apollo Fuels Ltd* (2016), the Court of Appeal applied that concept to the provision of a company car, although the specific method of calculating the benefit under s.114 (based on CO_2 emissions) would have been greater than the fair bargain cost (see para.9–25 above). That decision was reversed for 2016/17 onwards so that the "fair bargain" concept has been excluded from those benefits which have a specific method of calculating the benefit. Those excluded benefits are living accommodation (see para.9–23 above), cars, vans, etc. and loans (see para.9–27 above).

The code and lower-paid ministers of religion

9–31 Until 2015, ss.216–220 read with s.63(2) prevented the full rigours of the benefit code applying to the low paid. The cash ceiling for "lower-paid employment" was £8,500 (including any benefits, payments treated as earnings, and sums deemed to be earnings from PSCs). That level had not been changed for many years. It meant in practice that the non-benefits code rules only applied to those working part-time. But in 2014, almost 8 million UK workers were working part time, so there was still an important set of rules. And someone working only part-time in each of two or more unconnected employments had each employment considered separately. From 2015, however, all employees are now within the benefits code. The only exception being a person directly employed as a minister of a religious denomination earning less than £8,500 a year.

For those ministers of religion within the lower-paid category, only the following parts of the benefits code apply: Ch.4 (vouchers and credit-tokens) and Ch.5 (living accommodation). The lower-paid are therefore not subject to the code provisions on expenses payments, cars and vans, loans, and the residual charge. Remember, however, that the code provisions do apply to see if the £8,500 limit is exceeded.

Where the code provisions do not apply, the pre-code general income tax rules continue to apply. Those rules do not expressly appear in ITEPA because most of them still rely on the judge-made rules to work the old charge on "emoluments". The primary rule applying to benefits given to lower-paid employees is that in *Tennant v Smith* (1892) HL. Employees are taxed on the resale or second hand value—if there is one—of the benefit.

Amounts treated as earnings

We noted at the start of this discussion that what s.7 of ITEPA   **9–32**
calls "general earnings" are comprised of "earnings" and "any amount treated as earnings". We have now examined fully the meaning of earnings, and must turn to those other amounts. Section 7(5) lists them as being:

- the provisions for agency workers and arrangements made by intermediaries in Pt 2;
- the benefits code provisions;
- payments treated as earnings under Ch.12 of Pt 3; and
- certain balancing charges under CAA.

The provisions dealing with the benefits code and payments through intermediaries have already been discussed.

The agency provisions in ss.44–47, briefly, deal with the treatment of workers who are supplied to employers by agencies. The legal problem is that the "employer" who pays the wages is the agency, not the person from whom the "employee" takes instructions. The result may be much like an ordinary employment contract, but it is not one, and so the income is not employment income. The solution adopted many years ago, and now universally applied, is to treat the agency as the employer and the sums paid as earnings for employment income purposes.

Chapter 12 brings together a small group of specific provisions   **9–33**
catching sums and treating them as earnings. They are: payments to employees absent from work because of sickness or disability (s.221); cases where the employer pays the employee's income

tax (and so increases the employee's income by the amount of the tax paid (ss.222–223); certain payments to pension funds (s.224); and payments or consideration for restrictive undertakings (ss.225– 226). Section 225 deals with a form of payment that cannot possibly be a payment for employment. If you offer to pay me a sum for not working at all, or for not working—say—within 10 miles of my office, that cannot be employment income. But it is income and parliament decided some time ago that it should be taxed and that it is best treated as income from employment.

Exempt income

9–34   Part 4 of ITEPA lists kinds of payments and benefits that are exempt from being taxed as earnings or as employment income. The list is a very long one, and it would be tedious indeed to plough through it. Nor is there any particular set of principles to emerge from it. The provisions are the accumulated wisdom (and lack of it) of many, many Finance Acts. So we will look only at the main structure, and leave the rest until any of you become tax practitioners (when you will need to know the lot). We have already seen the provisions on mileage allowances and transport payments that form Chs 2 and 3 of the Part. Chapter 4 brings together exemptions for education and training, including the failed individual learning accounts schemes. There are then exemptions for recreational benefits including the exemption (in s.264) for an annual "blow out" or staff party—provided the total cost does not exceed a generous £150 a head. (But is that kind of party really recreational?). This is followed by exemptions from the non-cash vouchers and credit-tokens legislation. For example, provisions protect transport company staff from being taxed on their free journeys to work. Removal benefits and expenses for employees moving for work reasons are also exempted, subject to some detailed revenue protection measures.

9–35   There are then measures for "special kinds of employees". However, when you look through the list (ss.290–326) you may wonder what is special about some of them. Three of these, however, are of wide importance. First, there is exemption for subsidised meals at the workplace (s.317). Then provision is made to exempt employer-provided childcare facilities from tax (ss.318–318D). Finally, there is no income tax to pay on the advantage of an employer-provided computer or mobile telephone. (Does anyone other than a parliamentary drafter still call these omnipresent devices telephones?). See ss.319. These provisions show how fast technology dates tax laws, as you cannot use your computer as a mobile phone within the terms of exemptions under s.320 (so they had to repeal it in 2006!), but may be able to use your mobile phone as a computer within the terms of exemption under s.319.

Deductions allowed from earnings

The rules allowing deduction of expenses from earnings were, until reorganisation took place under ITEPA, both overcompacted and dotted about in various parts of the Tax Acts. They are now found together in a properly codified form in Pt 5 of ITEPA. This codification has also allowed the principles limiting deductions to emerge and in some cases to be made clear in the legislation for the first time.   9–36

The rules for deductions
The main rules for deductions are: 9–37

1) no deduction is allowed unless it is subject to express provision in the legislation. This is a general rule of income tax law;
2) a deduction may only be made from the earnings of the employment in question (s.328);
3) the amount of a deduction must not exceed the earnings from which it is deductible (s.329);
4) a deduction from earnings is only allowed once in respect of the same cost (s.330);
5) a deduction is only allowed if the amount is paid by the employee (or by someone else but included in the earnings) (s.333). Where the employee is reimbursed for expenditure, the employee may only deduct the amount reimbursed if the reimbursement is taxed as earnings (s.334); and
6) subject to special provisions, a deduction is allowed only if—
   (a) the employee is obliged to incur and pay it as holder of the employment, and
   (b) the amount is incurred wholly, exclusively and necessarily in the performance of the duties of the employment (s.336).

"Wholly, exclusively and necessarily in the performance of"
Despite all the rewriting, the general rule for deduction is still to be found in one short phrase. It may be called the "general rule", but it is in fact several interactive rules. The words, now in s.336, have not been changed because the meanings of these   9–38

important few words have been exhaustively examined by the judges and because even the smallest change could prove very expensive.

The words "wholly" and "exclusively" are the same as those in the equivalent rule for trading income, and bear the same meaning. But there are two additional tests not required for claims for trading expenses, and which have proved to be exacting tests: the expenses must be necessary to the job, and must be incurred in the performance of the job. Travel expenses are dealt with separately, but they also require the "necessarily" test to be satisfied.

The word "necessarily" has caused many a claim to founder. Stemming from *Ricketts v Colquhoun* (1926) HL, the test is, as Donovan LJ put it in *Brown v Bullock* (1961) CA: ". . . not whether the employer imposes the expense . . . but whether the duties do." A bank manager was required by his employers (it was "virtually a condition of his employment") to be a member of a London club. It was held that the subscription fee was not a deductible expense. This is a harsh doctrine, and it may in time come to be softened if some of the ideas in *Taylor v Provan* begin to percolate through. But it will still be the case that the expense must not be necessitated merely by the personal circumstances of the taxpayer as distinct from the necessities of the job. Thus in *Roskams v Bennett* (1950) Mr Bennett was the district manager of an insurance company. Because of bad eyesight he could not drive a car, and so he found it necessary to maintain an office at home. It was held that the expense occasioned thereby was not deductible. In *Baird v Williams* (1999) the attempt of a Clerk to General Commissioners to deduct the interest on a loan to buy an office for hearing tax appeals similarly failed.

9–39   The phrase "in the performance of the duties" has had similar effects on non-travel expenses as on travel expenses. In *Simpson v Tate* (1925) a county medical officer of health joined certain medical and scientific societies so as to keep himself up-to-date on matters affecting public health. His claim to deduct these subscriptions was rejected, the court holding that the expense was incurred, not in the performance of the duties, but so that the taxpayer might keep himself fit to perform them. This seems a very restrictive doctrine, and indeed this particular point has been altered by statute. ITEPA now permits deduction of (we quote the title to the section) "fees and subscriptions to professional bodies, learned societies, etc." But the doctrine still stands where it has not been changed by statute. In *Fitzpatrick v IRC (No.2)*; *Smith v Abbott* (1994) HL, journalists incurred expenditure in purchasing newspapers and journals. They claimed to deduct this expenditure. The House of Lords by a majority (4–1) rejected this claim. Lord Templeman said "a journalist does not purchase and read newspapers in the performance of his duties but for the purpose of ensuring that he will carry out his duties efficiently".

The issue therefore is whether the expense is incurred in performing the duties of the job or whether it is spent to enable the employee to do the job. Only the former is allowable, even if the contract of employment requires the latter. Two contrasting decisions may illustrate this. In *HMRC v Decadt* (2008), a medical registrar was required as part of his contract to pay for and attend training courses in order to qualify as a consultant. These expenses were disallowed since he was not being a registrar when on the courses—they were to enable him to become a consultant. But in *HMRC v Banerjee* (2010), the Court of Appeal found on virtually identical facts that the expenses were allowable. If the registrar did not attend the courses she would not be allowed to continue as a registrar and so the expense was incurred as part of the duties of a registrar. That decision seems to be at odds with the previous case law.

Travel expenses

Most employees' travel expenses are either travel to work **9–40** or travel in employer-provided cars or other transport. We have already dealt with the rules that tax the provision of cars for private use, with some exemptions, and provide mileage allowances tax-free up to set limits. The final aspect of the taxation treatment of work travel is to note the rule for deducting employee-incurred travel costs. The practical importance of these rules is that they apply to long-distance travel for work reasons by air or train. But the political decision was taken some time ago (after it had first been taken by the judges interpreting the then law) that the cost of travelling *at* work should be deductible, but the cost of travelling *to* work was not to be deductible. At the same time, it is unreasonable to exclude deduction of the costs of travelling to take up overseas jobs, and for similar major journeys, so the rules need exceptions.

The results are in ss.337–342. The original rule in now s.337 is that to claim a deduction for travel (besides meeting rr.1–5 of the main rules) the travel must be necessary for the employment and must be for travelling in the performance of the duties. In 1998 a second, alternative, rule was introduced, which is now found in s.338 onwards. That rule focuses on whether the employee is necessarily travelling to a workplace (excluding most commuting). In practice, however, there are very few cases where the rules actually produce different results. The words of s.337 have been subject to close judicial attention and we must note the main cases. The cases on the second rule are far fewer but again they provide an insight as to the operation of that rule.

9–41   TRAVELLING IN THE PERFORMANCE OF THE DUTIES   The expense of travel from one's home to one's work is not deductible. This basic rule is established by *Ricketts v Colquhoun* (1926) HL. Mr Ricketts was a barrister residing and practising in London. He was also the Recorder of Portsmouth (a part-time office). He claimed to deduct from the emoluments of his Recordership the expenses of travelling between London and Portsmouth and also his hotel expenses in Portsmouth. It was held by the House of Lords that neither the travelling expenses nor the hotel expenses were incurred in the performance of his duties, but rather before and after, and moreover, the expenses were attributable to the Recorder's own choice of residence and were not necessary to the office as such. This latter, very objective, point was rather softened by a later decision of the House of Lords, *Taylor v Provan* (1975), but on narrow facts. In that case the employee's choice of working in two places was held to be genuine and the only way *he* would do the job, which was very specialised.

The cost of travel from one place of work in an employment to another place of work in the same employment is deductible. In *Owen v Pook* (1970) HL, Dr Owen was a GP at his residence in Fishguard, and he also held a part-time appointment at a hospital in Haverfordwest, 15 miles away. Under his appointment Dr Owen was on stand-by duty to deal with emergency cases and he was required to be available by telephone. His responsibility for a patient began the moment he received a telephone call at home. It was held by a majority of the House of Lords that the duties of Dr Owen's employment were performed in two places (where he received the telephone calls and the hospital) and that he could deduct the expenses of travel between those places. This is akin to the trader cases where a taxpayer is held to have his base at his home. But it is not identical, it is wider; sometimes Dr Owen received telephone calls when he was not at home. It seems to have been regarded as more important when he received the calls than where. But undoubtedly the case does establish that if his home is one of the places at which a taxpayer works (and rightly works) under his contract of employment, then the cost of travel from home to another place of work under the contract is deductible. But if there is no necessity for two places of work, then the expenses are not allowable: *Miners v Atkinson* (1997).

TRAVELLING TO A WORKPLACE Because the test in s.337 **9–42** penalised site-based employees, who were always travelling to work (see, e.g. *Elderkin v Hindmarsh* (1988)), a second alternative set of rules was introduced in 1998. Travelling expenses are allowable under ss.338 and 339 for travelling to a place where it is necessary for the employee to attend in the performance of the duties of the employment (known as a workplace). But what is known as *ordinary commuting* is disallowed—that is travelling from home or a non-workplace to a permanent workplace. The key item there is clearly what amounts to a *permanent workplace*. It is defined as a place where the employee regularly attends in the performance of the duties and which is not a *temporary workplace*. The rule also applies to what amounts to substantially ordinary commuting so that, e.g. arranging a business meeting on the way to work will not allow a claim to be made.

So what is a temporary workplace? It is a workplace where the employee's attendance there is to perform a task of limited duration or for some other temporary purpose. Even then, it is not a temporary workplace if the employee spends a period of continuous work at that place (HMRC say 40 per cent of his time) for more than 24 months (or less if the employment is shorter, which cuts out short term temporary employees). It is also not a temporary workplace if the tasks to be carried out are allocated there; as a result, most travel to work will be to a permanent workplace and so still not allowable. This was strengthened by the decision in *Kirkwood v Evans* (2002) that an employee who worked at home four days a week and then travelled to the head office every Friday could not claim his expenses. Although he was in one sense travelling from one permanent workplace to another (which is not ordinary commuting) he was also travelling from home to a permanent workplace (which is), and the latter prevailed.

Otherwise the important thing is to sort out what is a temporary workplace and what is a permanent workplace. One example is *Ratcliffe v HMRC* (2013), where the employee was employed from time to time either on a six-month retainer contract which required him to work at various sites as directed or on a short term contract at a specific site. The former involved travelling from home to temporary workplaces (allowable), but each of the latter involved travelling to a separate permanent workplace for each contract (not allowable). So in every case it is important to define where the employee is travelling from and where he is travelling to.

Where an employee operates from a base or depot that is not a temporary workplace and so travelling to it is not allowed. Area based employees (e.g. sales representatives) cannot claim travelling to the area but can do for travelling within it if none of the workplaces are permanent ones.

Agency workers Where an employee works for an agency and is temporarily assigned on a series of based work contracts to various engagers, each will be regarded as a separate employment contract for tax purposes and so travel to work will be to a permanent workplace. But if the employment contract is so structured that the worker works under one contract (known as an overarching contract), although in many different locations, then those each become temporary workplaces (so long as they are for less than 24 months) and so travelling to them would be allowable. The use of a personal service company as an intermediary between the worker and the engager may also have the same effect. After consultation, new measures were introduced in 2016 to prevent this and to treat such workers in the same way as directly employed workers.

The new provisions (s.339A) provide that in certain circumstances each engagement is to be regarded as a separate employment and so at a permanent workplace. Tax relief is not now available therefore for travel from home, or a non-workplace, to the engager's workplace for workers who are: (i) supplying personal services; (ii) are engaged through an intermediary (as defined); and (iii) are subject to the supervision, direction or control of any person. An employment intermediary is defined as an entity, including a company, a partnership, or an individual, which interposes itself between a worker and the engager, as part of an arrangement for the worker to provide their personal services to the engager. If the intermediary is a personal service company, then condition (iii) does not apply.

Other expenses

9-43   ITEPA also contains many other special rules for deduction, particularly for groups of employees with an international element to their jobs, such as seafarers and non-domiciled employees. Two specific rules are of internal importance.

Sections 343–345 allow employees to deduct various compulsory fees for being members of professions, and the annual fees for joining professional organisations. The scope of both sections is defined by a list: one in the statute and one prepared by HMRC. An example of the former is the fee and compensation fund payment payable by a solicitor for a practising certificate. An example of the latter is the annual subscription to the CIOT. The test for claiming deduction of an annual subscription is that the activities of the body concerned are of direct benefit to, or concern the profession practised in, the performance of the duties of the employment.

By contrast s.358 put a bar on deducting most kinds of business entertainment or gift expenditure. These reflect rules mainly aimed at preventing employers from deducting business entertainment costs as business expenses. It is necessary therefore to control a deduction routed through an employee. The limit on business gifts is put at £50. The bar on deductions for any other form of hospitality expenditure is subject to a strictly limited exception.

Terminal payments

No, this is not something paid for using an airport, though it is about leaving. You may call them "golden handshakes", "golden parachutes", "golden handcuffs", "garden leave payments" or "payments and benefits on termination of employment, etc". They sound much more interesting if the officialese is avoided. But even ITEPA would look gimmicky if it dropped the formal language to adopt the headline texts. So we must use the "termination" language. Behind it are some important rules about payments made when people leave or change their work.

The problem is how to tax a payment made to get someone to leave his or her job. It is not employment income, because the payment is essentially to get someone to end the employment contract. Further, the employee may have enforceable rights to keep that contract. At the same time, many payments to leave are PILONs (payments in lieu of notice) or are earnings by another name. When the employer wants someone to leave, it does not usually want to have the person around during a notice period. Indeed, it may be a security risk to the business for this to happen. So a payment is made and the work is ended. But if there is no continuing contract of employment, and no right to the payment because it is made (at least in form) as an ex gratia payment, is it not a gift?

Whether or not the payment is one within the general scope of the charge on earnings may depend on the precise terms of the employment. In *EMI Group Electronics v Coldicott* (1999) CA, the Court were faced with PILON payments made to employees entitled to six months' notice. The payments equalled six months' pay. The Inland Revenue argued that this was earnings, while the employees argued that these were terminal payments. The reason, as we learn below, is that if the employees were right then the first £30,000 of their PILONs were free of tax, while if they were earnings they would be taxed in the normal way. The

9–44

9–45

Court emphasised that payments in lieu of notice were separate from, and in addition to, any payments because the employment ended. Here there was contractual entitlement as an employee to the sum. It was therefore part of the earnings from that employment.

Had the Court found the sum not to arise from the employment, it would have had to apply the statutory provisions catching terminal payments, or the sums would have escaped tax entirely. In the past that approach was also used for tax planning by extending it to changes in an employment. I pay you a large sum to change the terms of your employment. I could probably, in practical terms, make you do that anyway but I have no legal right to do so. The sum you get is again not earnings—but in substance why not? The judicial answer was because it was not within the then charging provisions. The legislative answer to that was enacted in a series of provisions spread over time.

9–46   As elsewhere, ITEPA now presents us with a code. It is in ss.401–416. Section 401 covers forms of payment for ending or changing the terms of an employment, unless the payment is taxable under some other provision. It applies whether the change is a change in the duties of the employment or the earnings from it. It excludes any pension provision or payments for the death or disability of an employee. There are also limited exceptions that allow an ex-employee to keep only the car, the mobile phone and any computer equipment. Where the employee continues to work for the employer any removal expenses are ignored. Otherwise it applies and s.403 charges such payments only if and to the extent that the payment exceeds a threshold of £30,000.

The rules are drawn widely to link a series of payments, and to catch payments made indirectly to an employee's family or (if deceased) survivors. There are also rules to ensure that the payment falls into tax and does not get missed because it is paid in a tax year after the employment ended or the employee died. The payment is brought into tax in the year in which it is received. If the payment is spread over a number of years, then it will be taxed in those years, but only the first £30,000 received will be exempt, not that sum each year.

The Upper Tribunal in *Moorthy v HMRC* (2016) regarded the ambit of s.401 as being very wide. The wording covered anything directly or indirectly arising from the termination, etc. of a person's employment and it could therefore include payments for compensation for injury to feelings. It also applied to both pecuniary and non-pecuniary loss. The Tribunal also limited the exception in s.406 for death, disability or injury to compensation for an injury which led to the cessation or alteration of the employment and not for other injuries, e.g. to feelings.

Income relating to securities

The simple fact that companies are owned by their sharehold- **9–47**
ers has been seen as one solution to the friction that can occur between employers and their corporate employees. It has also been seen as a way to offer incentives to employees, particularly senior employees, by linking them to the success of the employer. For 40 years various governments have pursued variants of the idea of making all employees, those employees that chose, or selected senior executives into owners of their employers.

At the same time, a straightforward gift of shares in the employer to the employee presented the employee with either an immediate windfall (if the shares were sold immediately) or the possibility of a much larger windfall if they were kept. If this was allowed to happen without a tax charge, then consider-able sums could be lost to the exchequer. So it was necessary to impose conditions on employee shareholding schemes to prevent abuse.

These rules were rewritten for the Tax Law Rewrite into Pt 7 of ITEPA, and then rewritten again by FA 2003 into a replacement Pt 7 which now applies. That Part has since been "simplified" by amendments in the Finance Acts of 2013, 2014 and 2016.

An understanding of these provisions demands a sound knowl-edge of corporate structure and finance laws, as well as of several new terms. For example, a SIP is not how you take your gin and tonic but a share incentive plan (ITEPA Sch.2). It tells you that in the Act. But it does not tell you what a CSOP is in Sch.5. You find it hidden in s.521(4) (company share option plan). And as far as we can see they do not bother to tell you what SAYE means anywhere in the Act (it stands for Save As You Earn).

The Pt 7 rules

Part 7 of ITEPA was, as noted, substantially rewritten and **9–48**
therefore already has some untidy numbering. But its content is usefully summarised in the signposting section, s.417. This tells us that Pt 7 "contains rules about cases where securities, interests in securities or securities options are acquired in connection with an employment". This can take many forms, as the following 13 chapters of the part show.

The key word is "securities" and it is given a wide meaning by s.420. All the following are "securities":

(a) shares in any body corporate (wherever incorporated) or any non-UK unincorporated body;

(b) debentures, debenture stock, loan stock, bonds, certificates of deposit or indebtedness;

(c) warrants or instruments entitling holders to subscribe to present or future securities;

(d) certificates or documents conferring rights in securities held by third parties;

(e) units in collective investment schemes investing in any kind of property and allowing people to participate directly or indirectly from profits or income from the investments;

(f) futures, that is, rights under contracts for future delivery of any property;

(g) rights under contracts for differences or similar to them (that is, designed to secure a profit or prevent a loss against fluctuating prices).

But bills of exchange, money, bank balances, leases or dispositions of property or rights under insurance contracts are not. And if the drafters got that list wrong, then the Treasury can amend it by order.

This section is then followed by similar sections creating potentially sweeping provisions to catch profits or gains from dealing with any security, interest in a security or option to purchase one. The aim is to identify any profit or gain (whether as a single sum or an ongoing benefit of holding a security on advantageous terms) and capture the tax value. But it is difficult to summarise usefully the complex provisions used to do this.

Lord Walker in *Gray's Timber Products Ltd v HMRC* (2010) identified three "conflicting purposes" behind Pt 7. The first was to encourage employee share ownership in their employers; the second, however, was to tie this in with a return for satisfactory performance, so any charge is delayed until there is a chargeable event; but this led to the third, preventing such schemes being used for tax avoidance. To that end the Supreme Court in *UBS AG v HMRC* (2016) applied a purposive construction to exclude shares with a nominal restriction from the definition of restricted securities in the Act so as to prevent an avoidance scheme on bankers' bonuses. See also *Tower Radio Ltd v HMRC* (2015).

Share Incentive Plans

9–49   Alongside these provisions are others to maintain approved schemes for employees to hold securities. These include SIPs, under which employees can be given share incentives, including for example free shares. Under a SIP, any advantage on acquiring a share will be exempt from tax. If a dividend is paid on the share, but reinvested in the plan, then again it will be tax free. And if the employee holds the shares long enough (five years for a free share) then there will be no tax charge on disposal. There are maximum annual amounts.

SAYE

SAYE Option schemes allow employees to use savings built **9–50** up through a contractual savings scheme to hold and then use share options on advantageous terms again without a tax charge. Company Share Option Plans provide a parallel scheme without the external savings contract. Then there is an EMI (Enterprise Management Incentive) scheme and code (allowing a full tax advantage if the incentives are held in the company for 10 years), and provisions dealing with priority share allocations to employees on a public offer of shares.

Employee shareholder status

FA 2013 introduced the concept of an employee shareholder. **9–51** An employee who opts for this status benefits from a number of tax breaks—there is no charge to income tax or NI on the first £2,000 of share value received by the employee and no CGT up to £100,000 of gains over the employee's lifetime. On the other hand they must give up certain employment rights such as redundancy and unfair dismissal.

The only safe conclusion in an introduction is to note that this **9–52** is now the territory of specialists of the same kind as those that can guide you safely across Morecambe Bay sands. They need to know exactly how the tide is flowing that day and where the shifting sands are safe to walk on. Easy when you know how. But those who venture in on their own are not likely to survive if the mists come down. You might like to reflect on how that fits in with the central aims of taxation we discussed in the first chapters.

PAYE

One of the real strengths of the income tax systems applied to **9–53** employees in the UK is the PAYE system. This collects income tax and NICs from employees as they receive their earnings. This has the obvious advantage to the government that it not only knows that it is receiving the tax but that it receives it in a steady flow throughout the year and without delay. It has the second advantage—to the government—that it shifts the burden of collecting tax from most personal taxpayers from its own officials to employers.

The PAYE system is empowered by Pt 11 of ITEPA, and the details are in the Income Tax (Pay As You Earn) Regulations 2003 (SI 2003/2682), rewritten at the same time as ITEPA. These Regulations have been amended on several occasions since.

Tax codes

9–54   Under the PAYE system each employee is issued with a tax code for a tax year by the local tax office. The employer is issued with the same code. Typically it will appear something like 496L. That means that the taxpayer is entitled to the personal allowance but that adjustments have been made to reduce it to leave the individual entitled to £4,960 income free of tax in the year. The employer is then provided by HMRC with tables so that the employer spreads this amount over the year and collects tax and NICs at the correct level each pay day. By the end of the year, the employee should have paid income tax and NICs that are, within a few pounds, the correct amount for the year.

The tax code takes account of personal allowances, other deductions and reliefs, and in some cases also smaller amounts of tax due on other incomes (for example smaller untaxed earnings from another source). It therefore does far more in reality than merely collecting the tax on the earnings paid by the employer.

The power of the PAYE system has not only been built on to collect NICs at the same time as income tax. It is also now used to collect refundable student grants from graduates and to ensure payment of the four forms of statutory pay for sickness, maternity, paternity and adoption.

As a result of all these adjustments, what someone receives in his or her pay packet may be significantly different from the earnings that first go into it.

CHAPTER 10

PENSIONS AND SOCIAL SECURITY INCOME

Introduction

Huge changes have taken place in our social security systems **10–01** and their interactions with personal taxation since the first edition of this book. These changes reflect major demographic shifts in the British population. Put at its simplest, many more of us are living much longer, so there are many more pensioners. At the same time, the number of children joining us is dropping (from an average of 2.4 children a family to about 1.7). Each year there are fewer new members of our society and more old ones. That means that each year there are fewer people of working age to pay for the growing number of pensioners. That also means that it is increasingly important to get as many people of working age as reasonably possible to work. And we need more children to pay our pensions in the future. So it is regarded as responsible government for measures to be taken both to cut the public cost of pensions and to encourage us all to work. Those social imperatives lie behind the tax and credit measures in this chapter.

The most important of these is that of pensions, which is where the biggest changes are continuing to occur. The ages at which both state and private pensions can be claimed have risen and are to rise further, as all undergraduate readers of this book should be aware. At the same time the real values of individual payments of both state and occupational pensions are dropping, in part because the traditional state support for pension schemes given through the tax system is being reduced.

Pension income

"Pension income" is defined in ITEPA s.566 as pensions, **10–02** annuities and income of other types listed in the section. There are 13 in the list, including voluntary annual payments. But the Act carefully avoids defining "pension" beyond saying that it includes pensions paid voluntarily or capable of being discontinued (s.570). The key for income tax purposes is that a pension is normally payable to those who have stopped work either permanently or on a long-term basis because of age, illness, disability or following the death of a partner. In such cases it is a form of deferred earnings from work, or work-linked insurance against loss of earnings.

In this definition there is an obvious overlap between pensions, social security and other payments to those who are out of work but normally work. The approach of ITEPA is to treat as pension income those payments made to the retired (or widows and other survivors of deceased earners) and to treat as social security income those payments made to those whom it is assumed will return to work. So the state pension—which is a social security pension—is treated as pension income and not as social security income. The main practical application of that divide is to treat as pensions those payments to claimants over the state pensionable age for women. Until 2010, that was 60, the retirement age for a woman aged 21 in 1971. It is now rising year by year to catch up with the state pensionable age for men, now 65. Under the Pensions Act (PA) 2014, the state pensionable age for women rises until it reaches 65 in 2018. Then the state pensionable age for both women and men rises to 66 and then 67. Legislation requires that to be reviewed every five years, and the machinery exists to provide that it rises again after that. Someone aged 21 in 2017 is therefore unlikely to reach retirement age much before the age of 70, if then.

The three pillars

10–03   The pension provision in a major economy is often described as a three pillar system consisting of the state pension, work-based pensions and private pensions. There have been major changes to all three of those systems in the UK in recent years, most significantly with the introduction of the measures in the PA 2014 in April 2016.

For all those reaching state pensionable age on or after 6 April 2016 there is an entitlement to claim a state pension. It is a flat-rate weekly pension of £155.65 in 2016. Note that that is £8093 a year, so is less than the personal allowance for income tax. So it is not taxable unless the pensioner has other income as well, in which case it will be added in with the other income (and will usually be taxed indirectly by PAYE with any other pension or pay). Nor does a pensioner have any liability to NICs. (Incidentally, the earnings threshold for paying contributions in 2016 is about the same as the state pension, so there would be no liability anyway.) There are significant differences in this to the entitlements of those who reached state pensionable age before that date, but for simplicity we look only at the new provision here. That is the first pillar of the UK system. Note that the state pension is no longer called (as it was for a century) a retirement income. It is age-related and often enables someone to retire, but there is no requirement that someone claiming this pension has to have stopped work.

The state pension is a "pay as you go" system and is not supported by investments or funds. It is funded on a year by year basis from the national insurance contributions paid in that year. The pension credit is a state welfare payment and is funded out of general taxation. There are therefore no other relevant tax rules about the financing of these provisions.

The second pillar consists of the occupational pension schemes **10–04** run by employers. Under the PA 2008 all employers are required to establish workplace pensions for their employees and to auto-enrol the employees in a pension scheme. This duty is currently being rolled out to cover all employers and their employees by 2018. From then, with some exceptions, any employee aged 22 or more who is earning £10,000 or more must be enrolled in a workplace pension. Both the employer and employee will pay contributions towards that pension. Note that this is neither a tax charge on the employer nor National Insurance. It is a third, separate liability but to all intents and purposes it is the same as a tax or NI charge. Employers that wish to run better schemes than the required scheme may of course do so and meet their obligations in that way. Previously there was a state second pension, but this is now closed.

Workplace or occupational pensions are funded pensions. They must be funded by the contributions made by employers and employees paid into a pension scheme from which the individual pensions can be drawn down later. There were until recently two kinds of pension scheme. The first was a defined benefit scheme—that is, a scheme where the pensioner was entitled to a specific level of pension on retirement. This was often based on the employee's final earnings level, but might be based on average earnings through the period of work. In other words the pension was based not on the contributions paid in but on the earnings of the employee. If the fund could not meet that cost then the employer was required to make it good. Increasingly as pensioners live longer these schemes have become hugely expensive. Most have now been closed to any new employee, and some to all employees. In their place are schemes such as the workplace pension which are defined contribution pensions. Here the amount of pension that an employee receives depends on the total value of contributions paid in by or for her or him.

This will also depend on the market value of the fund at the time of retirement. In other words, the risk of a deficit is taken away from the employer (and the state) and placed on the pensioner.

10–05   The third pillar is that of private provision by individuals for themselves. This is particularly important for the self-employed as they cannot be in workplace pensions (though they can arrange to work for their own company and set up a scheme that way). But this form of retirement provision does not produce pension income. It consists of personal savings and investments and is taxed accordingly (see the next chapter). But it cannot be ignored in considering the overall tax treatment of the incomes of pensioners.

10–06   All forms of pension funds raise important tax questions. A complete account must look at each stage of the funding operation. What is the tax treatment of contributions made by contributors and their employers? What tax is payable by the funds on income and capital gains? How are pensions and lump sums from the funds paid to pensioners treated? Taxation of pensioners is dealt with in ITEPA, though it has been subject to several major amendments even since the rewrite. Other aspects are distributed through the income tax legislation from continuing parts of the Income and Corporation Taxes Act 1988 to several recent Finance Acts.

State pensions

10–07   UK state pensions, including pensions payable to widows, widowers or surviving partners, are taxable along with any death benefit on the full amount accruing to the pensioner in the tax year regardless of when the pension is actually paid. See ITEPA ss.577–578. War pensions are also taxable as are industrial injuries pensions. Only pensions paid to surviving partners of those who died in active service are tax free.

In practice, however, as we have noted, the decision to increase the value of the income tax personal allowance significantly in recent years has the result that those receiving a state pension or similar levels of pension income will not be liable to income tax. And liability of an employee (but not the employer, or anyone self-employed) to pay NICs stops when the employee reaches state pensionable age.

Workplace or occupational pensions

10–08   The tax treatment of funded pension schemes is important because a failure to make proper provision for pension funds may result in excessive taxation. That in turn may result in people failing to build up pension entitlement. And the reverse can be true. If the tax treatment is too generous, then people may save more than they need to.

Tax theorists approach this by looking for the "triple E" scheme. There are three separate stages to any funded occupational pension scheme. First, earners and employers must make contributions from their earnings and profits. Second, the fund itself must ensure it produces adequate returns on the funds to maintain and enhance the value of the fund. Finally, the funds are paid out as pensions and/or lump sums.

If there is no fund, how will the individual be taxed? He or she will have to save from taxed income. The savings will themselves be subject to tax on income and gains. But when the individual cashes the savings and accumulated income, there will be no further tax. This is what the theorists call a "TTE" system. The first two stages are taxed and the third is exempt. That is normally regarded as fair taxation.

If we apply the pension income rules to the pension paid out of a fund without either helping the contributor or the fund, we will have a "TTT" system. It will be taxed at each stage. That is over-taxation and unfair as compared with non-pension savings.

So if we intend to tax the pension, then we must provide tax exemption or relief (an "E") to the contributors and/or the funds.

On this analysis, the standard British approach to funds is **10–09** to give them an "EET" treatment, that is, to exempt both the contributions and the fund income, and collect the tax only on the pension. In substance this is to treat the pension as deferred earnings, and not to collect tax until the deferment ends. That is, of course, to give pension funds a tax preferred status compared with ordinary savings. But there is inevitably a condition attached. Or, to be more accurate, there are a very considerable number of conditions attached.

This is another area where income tax law has been rewritten —though on this occasion not by the Tax Law Rewrite. Indeed, to the annoyance of some, the rewritten provisions about pension income in ITEPA Pt 9 were replaced by new law from FA 2004 within days of enactment. The new rules took effect in 2006. The good news is that the new rules bring a much-needed common approach to the many different approaches to pension income taxation that previously applied. The bad news, as with all forms of pension law, is that the experts cannot forget the law applying in any year from the start of an individual's pension contributions. That requires keeping in existence the relevant rules and records for anything from

40 to 50 years for each individual who makes contributions. Therefore, typically, a properly-run fund has to look 60 years ahead from the entry of a new contributor to the point where most contributors have died. So even phasing a pension scheme out may take a long time. As a result, the tax and pension scheme rules have to deal not only with new schemes but also with older and closed schemes (ones that can receive no new members).

And inevitably as the rules about schemes became more complicated so did the scope for unauthorised schemes, or unauthorised payments under authorised schemes. The tax rules—as that list shows—must deal with each of these.

The Pt 9 rules

10–10 The codified approach now in ITEPA Pt 9 sets out general rules about pension income and then follows this with specific rules about the kinds of pension included under the charge to tax on pension income. A glance at the contents of the Part shows how the reforms from 2006 have changed things. Section 579A now applies the provisions of the Act to a registered pension scheme. That replaces the former provisions for approved retirement benefit schemes (the previous form of occupational pension for most), approved superannuation funds, approved personal pension schemes, and retirement annuity contracts. Then follow the provisions dealing with foreign pensions and with pensions or pension schemes that are not registered or have broken the registration conditions.

Scheme rules

10–11 ITEPA contains the main rules about the tax position of the individual contributors and pensions. The tax treatment of the registered schemes themselves and of employers are in FA 2004 Pt 4 and have not been taken into the main rewrite Acts. This itself has been heavily amended since enactment, not least by the unusual Taxation of Pensions Act 2014. This was unusual because it is purely a tax act and its contents would normally be contained in the appropriate annual Finance Act. It reflects a change in government approach to the release of money from pension funds, allowing much greater flexibility than previously was the case. The 2004 rules, with those amendments, define pension schemes and set the conditions under which they can be registered.

The main limits on schemes from a tax perspective deal with the sums that can be paid into the schemes, and can be paid out, and how the schemes are to be treated for tax purposes. Full tax advantages only apply where the limits both on payments in and payments out are met. The government has been steadily reducing the limits on both in recent years. This reflects concern that the preferential tax treatment of pension funds provided excessive benefits to high earners as compared with others. But a proposal to give tax benefits only at the level of the basic rate of income tax, so excluding any additional advantage to the higher paid, have not been taken forward.

The annual and lifetime limits

Two important limits now apply to the contributions that can   **10–12** be paid into a registered pension scheme without penalty. The first is an annual limit on the amounts a taxpayer can pay into pension schemes. This is a single total that applies regardless of the number of schemes to which a taxpayer contributes. That total has been steadily reduced in recent years, and now stands at £40,000 (in 2016). But it reduced further from that to as low as £10,000 in two situations. First, if the taxpayer uses the new flexibility to draw down funds from a pension scheme during a year, then this directly affects the amount of contributions that can be paid in for that same year. Second, there is a taper to the annual amount applying to the higher paid. If the taxpayer has income over £150,000 in a year, then the amount of the annual allowance drops by £1 for every £2 excess until at £210,000 the lower limit of £10,000 only is allowable. These limits are important because there is liability to a tax charge if they are exceeded. However, any unused annual limit in one year can be carried forward for a further three years to smooth out the situation where there is a short but sharp rise in the taxpayer's income. The (inevitably complex) details are in FA 2004 with the 2014 Act amendment.

The other important limit is a lifetime limit. A taxpayer cannot, over his or her lifetime, hold more than a set limit in registered schemes without incurring tax penalties. Like the annual limit, this lifetime limit has been steadily reduced since its introduction. FA 2016 sets it at £1 million, though there are detailed provisions allowing past savers to protect sums in excess of that amount paid in before the new limit came into effect. But moving forward this means that a taxpayer cannot retain full tax advantages once his or her "pension pot" as the publicity calls the schemes, are in this sense full. Further, this requires higher contributors to keep an eye on the amount they have in each of their pension schemes if (as is often the case) they have more than one. So each pension fund is required to inform its members of the value of their individual share of the funds to alert them to any excess. The value will depend on the kind of fund held. But for defined benefit funds (typically final salary schemes) the lifetime value is based on 20 times the pension.

If there is an excess, then a penalty rate of tax may be applied. If funds are taken out of an "overfull" pension pot, then a rate of 55 per cent applies. This is designed to recoup fully the advantage of having the money held in the scheme. The rate is 25 per cent if the funds are drawn down as income. This applies both when an individual seeks to access the funds and if on the death of the individual it is found that total remaining funds exceed the limit.

Pensions and drawdowns

10–13   A second group of limits apply to obtaining access to the pension pots. Until recently, there were strict limits on the access to funds held in registered schemes, originally designed to ensure that the money was spent on pensions. So funds could only be drawn out under certain conditions. In particular, the funds often could not be taken out as cash but had to be used to reinvest in annuities.

A series of recent reforms have removed much of these restrictions. They were first removed from smaller funds but now apply to all defined contribution funds. The extent to which they apply to defined benefit schemes depends on the scheme. The general position is that a pensioner can receive a pension commencement lump sum from the scheme of a quarter of the pensioner's entitlement free of tax. Sums taken over this amount are taxable at the taxpayer's marginal rate as income. The risk to taxpayers here is that if they choose to take out significant sums from a pension pot in one year, then this will often mean that the taxpayer becomes liable to higher rate income tax on the sum. So the usual approach is to draw down smaller sums so that this does not happen.

Protecting pensioners

10–14   There are further conditions both in tax law and more generally to ensure that pension schemes are properly run. They are beyond the scope of this book. Despite—indeed, because of— the changes and simplifications of this area of tax law in recent years, pensions law and taxation will always remain difficult. This is because pension rights may be acquired by an individual over a period of up to 50 years before he or she claims a pension or dies leaving family to do that. Legislators have always been careful to ensure that previous rights are not lost as new rights come in. So it will be many years before the restrictions now in place, for example, on lifetime limits apply without exception. To protect pensioners and to offer them advice, the government has established both a Pensions Regulator and a Pensions Advisory Service. Their websites contain much valuable detailed information.

A question for discussion has emerged from this: do we need to have all this pensions tax law? Should we not just ensure that people can save effectively, and leave the tax treatment of savings and investments to deal with this? The government took a step in this direction in Budget 2016 as we see in the next chapter. But before we turn to that we must recap on the tax benefits of the existing system. **10–15**

Tax benefits

If a scheme meets all the conditions, then there are significant tax benefits. These generally follow the pattern of "EET". That is, the contributions receive tax preferred status as allowances, and the funds are tax exempt. Tax only applies when the payments out are made—or the rules are broken. **10–16**

Contributions by an employee to a registered scheme can be set off in full against the earned income from which it is paid. Where the contributions are collected by the employer along with PAYE tax, the tax allowance will be set off directly against the tax payable that month by the employee. And employers can claim all their ordinary contributions to pension schemes as deductible expenses in calculating profits. That means they must meet the usual "wholly and exclusively" rule but no other. Compare this with NICs and the state pension. Employers can deduct the cost of their NICs. But employees get no deduction against income tax for the NICs paid.

There is a third tax exemption hidden behind those two. The employee is not regarded as earning the employer contribution. That is true of both NICs and contributions to registered schemes. This can be a valuable addition to total earnings. Say that an employee makes a 5 per cent contribution on gross pay to the fund, and the employer pays a further 10 per cent (plus of course the employer's NIC). In such a case the employee pays income tax on 95 per cent of gross earnings, while another 20 per cent or more of gross earnings goes out untaxed as employer's contributions and the employee's contribution to the registered scheme. And that means that considerably more gets paid to the fund than would be the case if these were taxed.

The second "E" is exemption from both income and corporation tax and any CGT of all profits and gains of the pension fund.

Instead, income tax applies to the receipt of the pension by the pensioner. And, within limits, the "triple E" may still apply to lump sums payable to pensioners upon their retirement. But the general effect is to defer the taxation of pensions until the pensions themselves are payable. As compared with some other forms of tax-privileged savings, this has the advantage that the pension savings are therefore made from untaxed income rather than taxed income.

Social security income

10–17   Part 10 of ITEPA imposes an income tax charge on social security income. "Social security income" is defined by s.656 as including all UK social security benefits in lists in Pt 10 together with equivalent foreign benefits. There are then separate lists of exempt benefits. The lists do not include state pensions or other benefits payable only to those of pensionable age as these are received as pension income.

Well, not quite. Attendance allowances are payable only to the disabled over pensionable age with different benefits payable to those of working age. These allowances are exempt under these provisions rather than under the pension income provisions, following a general approach to exempt from tax those benefits payable to the disabled because of their disabilities rather than as replacement incomes. (The exemption under this provision of pensioners' £100 Christmas bonuses is more pragmatic. It would cost too much to try and tax those that would otherwise be taxable, as most pensioners do not have enough income to bring the bonuses into tax.) Similarly state pension credit is exempted from tax here though it is by definition only payable to pensioners as a supplementary pension.

Another group of benefits that are not usually taxed are those benefits payable to families for children, including (save as below) child benefit and tax credits (with the replacement universal credit). The final exempt benefit worth noting, because of its importance, is housing benefit.

This leaves income-replacement benefits as taxable. In practice that means that someone who, say, receives jobseeker's allowance while not working, but who then gets a job will have the JSA added in when PAYE is later applied to the resulting pay.

High income child benefit charge

The final provisions in Pt 10, added from 2012, impose an **10–18** interesting compromise between taxing and exempting benefits. Child benefit was for decades regarded as a payment by the state to those looking after children. That is usually the mother but could be the father or anyone else with responsibility for the child. Payment is largely free of conditions including any tax liability. A "child" is anyone under 16 and anyone under 19 receiving full-time education other than higher education. The benefit can be claimed by anyone with whom the child is living, or who is paying for the cost of providing for the child (but only one claim is allowed). In 2016 it is worth about £1,000 annually for the first child, with more for each other child.

It was decided that those with higher incomes should not receive this state help. This decision imposed a number of practical problems, not least for HMRC who were no longer concerned with family incomes once separate taxation of all taxpayer had replaced the old rules for adding the income of couples together. The first problem was to set an income level at which to start taxing. It was decided not to use the figure at which higher rate income tax liability started but some other figure. £50,000 was chosen. This is, in general terms, based on the taxable income of the individual before personal allowances. The next problem is how to deal with couples. Child benefit is payable to individuals, not couples. Further, one member of a couple has no right in law to know what the other member of the couple earns, or indeed whether child benefit has been claimed. So machinery had to be put in place to allow one of a couple to find out from HMRC about this, i.e. to find out what the other is earning and claiming. Who knows what that might reveal in some cases! Behind this of course is the perennial problem of whether two people are a couple at any particular time to which there is often no easy answer.

The third problem was how to impose the tax. The answer chosen was to impose a gradual reduction in benefit. The charge is 1 per cent of the child benefit for each £1 over £50,000. In practice this means that those with incomes over £60,000 are faced with a charge equal to the benefit. To try and avoid some of the bureaucracy that involves, taxpayers in this group are allowed to opt out of child benefit. But even that is not so simple. They are officially advised nonetheless to claim the child benefit because if they do not it may affect other benefits, such as home responsibility protection that protects an individual's right in later years to a state pension (for which the partner's income is now irrelevant). And those a little above the £50,000 ceiling in effect face an increased marginal rate of income tax.

Taxing child benefit should have been straightforward as the amount of child benefit received does not directly affect the amount of other benefits (though whether it is received can affect housing benefit). But as this shows, little in tax comes easy.

CHAPTER 11

SAVINGS AND INVESTMENT INCOME

Introduction

This chapter deals with what is for most individuals an untidy **11–01** and complex area of their tax affairs—the taxation of non-earned, non-business income. This is both untidy and complex for a series of reasons. Traditionally, different kinds of savings and investments have different tax treatments. Interest from certain kinds of savings were treated one way while other kinds of savings were treated in others. Then there was a different treatment again for dividends from shares in British companies and another for dividends from shares in foreign companies. Yet other rules applied to income in the form of annuities from capital invested in other ways.

Things are complicated further because of conflicting political and economic aims behind the tax laws. We are encouraged to save. So the income from some forms of savings are tax exempt. But we are only encouraged to save in certain ways, so other kinds of savings income have been subjected to higher taxes rather than lower taxes. At one time, for example, there was a rate of income tax called an investment income surcharge.

There is also the complication that people can gain from their savings by receiving capital gains instead of income. That is a considerable additional complication and we look at it in some detail later in the book.

We can quickly remove another complication. Pensions are not regarded as income from savings or investments even if that is what they actually are. The tax treatment of all forms of pension, including those purchased with capital sums, is now regulated by ITEPA and FA 2004. We discussed this in Ch.10.

To get the full picture, it is therefore necessary to look at the way in which savings income is taxed, then at the rates at which it is taxed, then at the rules of CGT. In this chapter we look at the way the income is taxed, and at some of the main exemptions from tax. We set out the special rates in Ch.13.

There are separate rules for companies. Any company whose **11–02** business is wholly or partly that of making investments is a company with investment business. General corporation tax rules for such companies are set out in CTA 2009 Pt 16.

All companies are subject to different rules to individuals with regard to income and gains from loans and derivate contracts. These are in CTA 2009 Pts 5, 6 and 7. See Ch.14.

11–03   The tax laws setting out the income tax treatment of income from savings and investments were rewritten completely for all individuals by ITTOIA Pt 4 (Savings and Investment Income) and Pt 6 (Exempt Income). The Act dealt with each kind of income and exemption in order of practical importance. It is useful to look at each chapter of Pt 4 and then Pt 6 to see what is covered. We must then look at some of the most important parts in more detail.

Part 4 covers:

- interest;
- dividends and other kinds of distribution from UK companies;
- dividends and similar payments from non-UK resident companies;
- stock dividends from UK companies—that is, the issue of new shares instead of dividends or as an addition to a shareholding;
- sums released from loans made to individuals participating in a close company—this is to stop avoidance by schemes where money is loaned by small closely controlled companies to one of the owners and then the debt owed to the company is released or reduced;
- purchased life annuity payments—part of these payments are a return of the capital sum used to purchase the annuity while other part is income, so special rules are needed to separate the parts; and
- income or capital sums generated from other specialised forms of savings instrument also require special rules, including in particular gains from life insurance.

11–04   Part 6 sets out the main general exemptions from income tax applying to this kind of income. This is one of the areas of law where people try to impress others by giving things long complicated sounding names and then shortening them to a series of initials that only the initiate understand.

Part 6 contains special rules about:

- NS&I (National Savings and Investments) income exemptions;

- income from individual investment plans (better known as ISAs or individual savings accounts, and previously TESSAs);
- SAYE interest (interest from Save As You Earn savings plans);
- dividends from VCTs, or venture capital trusts—a relief for shareholders who invest in smaller companies that are set up to undertake a new business;
- FOTRAs—should be FOTTTNRITUKs, but that doesn't look as good—these cover income from securities that are Free Of Tax to Residents Abroad (or, rather, To Those Not Resident In The UK);
- purchased life annuities (again—these add to the rules in Pt 4);
- other annual payments; and
- other income—and, yes, there is a difference between these last two.

Interest

Section 369(1) of ITTOIA has almost a beauty in its simplicity: **11–05**

"Income tax is charged on interest".

Sections 370 and 371 have a similar starkness. The tax is charged on the full amount of interest arising in the tax year. And the person liable is the person receiving or entitled to the interest.

The beauty starts to disappear swiftly when we turn to s.372. This tells us that "any dividend paid by a building society is treated as interest for the purposes of this Act." And it adds, spoiling the magic totally, that "dividend includes any distribution whether or not described as a dividend".

There follow a series of similar provisions ending with s.381. That informs us that "all discounts, other than discounts in deeply discounted securities, are treated as interest for the purposes of this Act."

Then we notice something missing. There is no definition of "interest". And don't go looking in the impressive Sch.4 list of defined expressions. The only definition of "interest" there is one that applies only to SAYE schemes—for which interest includes any bonus—and, anyway, does not define the term. Interest can be defined as the payment made by a borrower or debtor of money to the lender or creditor for the use of the money by reference to time. For most forms of saving that approach causes no problems. Both short-term loans such as those for the use of funds on a credit card or long term loans such as mortgages are expressly charged at a rate of interest.

In the straightforward case, I borrow £1,000 and pay, say, 10 per cent interest per annum on it. In commercial situations there may be fees, discounts and other variants. So, for example, I pay a facility fee of £100 to the lender for the loan or I receive the loan under a discount, so that I only get £900 of the £1,000 but have to pay the full £1,000 back. There are often good tax reasons (but VAT and corporation tax, not income tax reasons) for these arrangements. In practice they need not trouble us because the rules governing financial services largely prevent individuals lending money in such a way as to run into these problems. With that realisation, we can return to admire the simplicity of provisions that cause few practical problems.

11–06   We must add one important rider to this discussion. FA 2008 now recognises the problems involved in Islamic finance. Under some forms of religious belief it is wrong to earn interest on money. But it is not wrong to make arrangements so that the benefit of credit is recognised in other ways. This causes another problem. It is a major aim of taxation that it applies neutrally to all forms of income. So income tax must apply to any kind of income reward in a similar way.

Non-taxed interest
11–07   Government policy is currently to encourage smaller savers by removing many kinds of interest from liability to income tax. From 2016 this is done in two ways. The first, introduced by FA 2016, is a savings allowance linked to a savings nil rate. The second is an important range of individual forms of savings the income from which is tax free.

The savings allowance is, for 2016, £1,000 savings income. This applies to all basic rate taxpayers and means that in practice most smaller savers will not be liable to tax on their earnings as even at an interest rate of 2 per cent there would have to be an investment of over £50,000 for that limit to be exceeded. So it will only be higher rate or additional rate taxpayers who will be concerned with tax on smaller amounts of interest.

Separately from that, there are a range of tax-exempt savings. You can find out all the details from the advertisements of those who wish you to invest with them. Here is a brief summary of the main forms.

11–08   NATIONAL SAVINGS AND INVESTMENTS The Treasury has power to exempt income or similar payments received from investments in government savings. A popular version of these schemes is the Premium Bond. Some bright person spotted that if you paid all the interest on a government bond issue into a prize fund rather than to the investors, and then gave some of the savers prizes instead of interest, you were giving them gambling winnings and not interest. That is not subject to income tax. Further, if you gave one or two of them large prizes, then you will attract wide interest (in another sense of the word). Then invent ERNIE (the electronic random number indicator equipment) to decide who gets the prizes and you have a winner—for the Treasury, that is. It is also in practice regarded as a winner by the many investors who put up to the maximum £50,000 into the fund. They pay no income tax on their winnings. (They don't count for tax credits either, making families with savings even bigger winners.) The first £70 of income from National Savings Bank accounts are also free of income tax. And special tax exempt terms also apply to investments in National Savings Certificates. Together these schemes attract substantial levels of savings lent direct by individuals to the government (and therefore even safer than houses, as the saying goes). It is therefore not surprising that over £50 billion had been invested in Bonds by 2016.

ISAs   Any individual can also put savings of up to £15,240 **11–09** into an Individual Savings Accounts with a bank, building society or similar body each year and receive the interest from it free of income tax. ISAs are designed to encourage people to save generally, and not just with the Treasury. They are heavily advertised, as are the limits and conditions that apply to an ISA, so we need not set out more details here. In the past there were other forms of this scheme. Lovers of initials may like to note the immediate predecessor was TESSA (Tax Exempt Special Savings Account). But she has now morphed into ISA.

In 2015 the Chancellor added LISA to ISA. LISA is a lifetime ISA, designed to encourage younger savers to save in the long term. As such, it makes an appearance as pension funds are freed up and may be regarded as a competitor for the funds that might otherwise go into pension funds. In outline this allows those under 40 to make regular savings in a scheme that is both tax free (in the same way as established forms of ISA) but also with a bonus at the end of each year. Provided that an individual opens an account before he or she reaches 40 it can be kept open until he or she reaches 50. A contributor can pay in up to £4,000 a year either in regular instalments or as lump sums. Once the sums are in, the government will have them topped up at the end of the year by a 25 per cent bonus. Interest will also be payable and that will be tax free.

However, this is a limited purpose scheme. The money paid in (and the bonuses) can only be used for two purposes: to help buy a new house or as help with pension funding once the individual reaches 60. Nonetheless it has been described as a "no-brainer" for those who can fit within the limits and wish to save. Full details—and of course the inevitable safeguards—are available from providers.

11–10   SAYE Save As You Earn schemes are arrangements allowing employees to buy shares in the employer company. The individual agrees to buy shares in the company under a share option scheme. This will usually allow the individual to buy the shares at some date in the future at a set or reduced price as compared with the market price. For example, the individual agrees to buy the shares in five years time at the current market price. The individual then enters a savings scheme to make regular contributions to save up the sum needed to exercise the option and buy the shares. This can give the individual a double advantage. The shares can be purchased at a discount if the shares gain in value during the period while the individual is saving, and the interest paid while he or she is saving is tax exempt.

Paying tax on interest

11–11   Until 2016/17 all building societies, banks and other financial institutions paying interest on deposits and similar accounts were required to deduct income tax at the basic rate from any payment of interest to an individual and pay it directly to HMRC. As a result the investor received only the interest net of that deduction. This is what made some of the savings schemes noted above attractive, as sums were received without deduction. The deduction system, which had been in place for decades, was stripped away in 2016 and the duty to deduct tax (in ITA 2007) was repealed and replaced by a personal savings allowance. Until then if someone was not a taxpayer he or she had to apply to HMRC to have the interest paid gross or else reclaim it later. From 2016–17 all those who pay only basic rate tax receive a £1,000 annual personal savings allowance under which they can earn up to £1,000 interest or other returns from savings without incurring any tax liability or any need to make a tax return. In practice this not only means that non-taxpayers do not need to get in touch with HMRC at all if they have small amounts of interest but that this is true of most basic rate taxpayers as well. Both those groups of savers will often now get better returns from other forms of savings than the tax exempt savings set out above. However, tax exempt savings remain important to higher rate taxpayers. The tax free amount for those paying tax at 40 per cent is limited to £500, and is nil for those paying additional tax.

HMRC will continue to be informed when interest is payable and intend to collect any tax due in most cases by an adjustment to the tax code of the individual so that it is collected with PAYE tax.

Dividends and distributions

Section 383(1) of ITTOIA charges income tax on dividends and other distributions received by an individual from a UK resident company. Subsection (2) provides that dividends and distributions are to be treated as income for these purposes. Subsection 383(3) adds an important rider. Quoting it, "it does not matter" for the purpose of the section that a distribution is capital, save for subsection (2). In other words, requirements of company law that certain payments may only be made as capital do not apply for income tax purposes. The income tax definition of "distribution" is the same as that in corporation tax law. This is discussed in Ch.13 below. **11–12**

This section alerts us to the need to keep the law about the taxation of dividends separate from the company law provisions about dividends. In practice, to be a dividend or distribution, the payment must be made in accordance with company law provisions. So, for example, a payment out of a one-share company to the company's single shareholder/director/employee is technically only a dividend if the relevant formalities have been met. If they are not met, it may be open for argument that the payment that is said to be a dividend is in fact a payment of earnings (and so subject both to taxation under ITEPA and PAYE, and also NICs), or a loan. **11–13**

Double taxation of dividends

There is also a theoretical problem of fairness involved in the taxation of dividends. Company law requires that the company paying the dividend must pay it from its profits. But corporation tax must be paid on those profits. So the dividend will normally be paid by the company from taxed income. And the company cannot deduct corporation tax as an expense when paying the dividend. Nor, the other way round, can it deduct the dividend when paying corporation tax on its profits. So to tax the dividend in the hands of the shareholder is to tax it a second time. **11–14**

Is that fair? As always, that depends on what is meant by fairness. If that means equal treatment of the payments by the company to the recipient, then it can be argued to be unfair.

Compare what happens when the same company pays interest to a stockholder and a dividend to a shareholder. The company can deduct the cost of the interest from its profits, and therefore pays the interest as a deductible expense. So when it pays the stockholder it is paying out of income that has not been subject to tax. If the stockholder is the same individual as the shareholder, then he or she will receive one form of income from the company subject to tax only once and the other subject to double tax.

In past times, this double taxation was ignored by the income tax system. Then it was taken into account by a system known as advance corporation tax or ACT. Thankfully for the student (but not the taxpayer) the complications of ACT have now been repealed and we need not waste time on them. What came into replace ACT was a special reduced rate of tax on dividends. It is a partial recognition of the double taxation that comes about when an individual receives a taxable dividend.

Tax exempt dividends

11–15   Individuals can avoid all taxation on dividends in the same way as with savings if they hold them through tax savings schemes. The main general provision is by using an ISA in the same way as for investing money in tax-free interest bearing accounts. Again, details are widely available from those who run the schemes and we need not repeat details here. As those details show, they allow investors to invest up to a set amount each year in stocks and shares without having to pay income tax on the dividends. But in practice the reduced income tax rates on dividends have meant that there is no real advantage for many taxpayers in doing this.

There are other schemes to exempt taxation where the shares are held by an employee in an employer share scheme. If the shares are held in an approved share incentive plan (or SIP for short) then dividends can, subject to limits, avoid tax both as earnings (under ITEPA) and under these provisions. However, there will be a charge to income tax under these provisions if any dividend is paid over as a cash dividend rather than held in the scheme. An attempt to turn earnings into dividends by a complicated tax avoidance scheme recently received short shrift from the Court of Appeal in *PA Holdings v HMRC* (2011). This held that if payments were earnings then they could not also be dividends. HMRC has indicated that it will apply this to any tax avoidance scheme using dividends. The potential effect of this decision may mean that any attempt to avoid paying employment income tax (and NICs) through any form of tax exempt dividend is open to attack as a form of ineffective tax avoidance.

That approach will have been buttressed by the approach taken by the courts in other cases using similar approaches such as the decision of the Supreme Court in *HMRC v UBS* (2016) noted above.

Dividends and other payments from foreign companies

These are also subject to income tax, but they present different **11–16** practical and theoretical problems to dividends paid from UK companies. This is because any tax payable by the company on its profits will be paid to a foreign tax authority. In addition, the foreign tax authority many have imposed a withholding tax on the payment of the dividend. So the UK resident shareholder will not be able to argue that tax has already been paid on the profits to the Treasury. And the individual may have suffered foreign tax on the dividend itself.

You will not find the solution to these problems in ITTOIA. They are to be found in the individual provisions of the bilateral double tax agreements that the UK government has concluded with over 100 other countries. The details vary from agreement to agreement and are beyond the scope of this introduction. You need note only that the terms of those agreements, when concluded in proper form, override the terms of ITTOIA, and so may stop the double taxation in the sense of tax by two different national tax authorities.

The same point—the application of double tax agreements overriding ITTOIA—also applies to interest and all other forms of savings income.

Annuities

Many annuities arise under a will or similar instrument of **11–17** gift. These are taxed as "pure profit income". But it is perfectly possible to buy an annuity "in the market". These purchased life annuities, or some of them, have a special rule applying to them. The capital content of each periodic payment to the annuitant is exempt from income tax. The capital is found (putting it broadly) by dividing the purchase price of the annuity by the normal expectation of life of the annuitant, calculated at the date when the annuity begins. Once the calculation has been made the figure remains constant for every year. Income tax is charged each year on the amount by which the annuity payment exceeds this capital content, whether or not the annuitant survives for the period of normal expectation.

Other forms of non-earned income

11–18   This is a big heading, but it is a short reminder of a few short sections dealt with in Ch.7, and what they do not include. That is where we discussed the sections that tax annual payments and also any other kind of income that is not charged anywhere else in the tax legislation. But we see there that they also have limits.

There is no general definition of income tax. We have said it before, and we do not apologise for repeating it. So there may be forms of income that are not caught by those sections and are therefore not subject to income tax.

The provisions about employment income are broad enough to catch anything received by an individual because of his or her employment (whether or not he or she receives it as capital in finance terms). The provisions about trading income catch anything arising from a trade if it is income, not capital. And the same rules apply to any property business if again it is earned income. So no residual provision is needed for any form of earned income.

As this and other chapters show, the approach to non-earned income is not covered by similar broad provisions linking the receipt to a source in such a way as to make anything from that source subject to income tax. So we need to remind ourselves that there may be forms of unearned income that are not subject to income tax. Further, as the history of anti-avoidance provisions in our tax laws show, if there are gaps, people will find them and use them. Then, if the gaps are too big, parliament will block them. But the hunt still goes on, and it can still be successful. It just gets harder each year now that you are required to share your clever ideas with HMRC under the disclosure regime so that they can (and will) bring forward blocking measures under a convenient Finance Act.

CHAPTER 12

TAXATION OF TRUSTS AND ESTATES

Introduction

We need to look now at the way in which the income tax **12–01** system works in relation to trusts and to the estates of deceased individuals.

In the general law—quite apart from tax law—there is a fundamental difference between the position of a person entitled to income of a residuary estate and a person entitled to income arising under a trust. The former is not entitled to anything until it is paid to him or at least appropriated to him: see *Corbett v IRC* (1938) CA. The latter is entitled to his share of the income of the trust from its inception, or, more strictly, to his share of the income of the investments which constitute the trust fund: see *Baker v Archer-Shee* (1927) HL.

We will look at the two situations in turn and then at charities.

Trust income

The existence of trusts causes great difficulties for tax legisla- **12–02** tors and for everyone else connected with tax, including students of tax law. Tax law would be very much simpler if there were no trusts. Lest that statement sound naive it may be pointed out that trusts fulfil a prominent role in tax planning. Nevertheless, many civil law countries do not recognise the concept of trusts. The subject is additionally complicated in Britain because Scottish trusts law is as developed as, but is markedly different from, English trusts law. Scottish lawyers rightly resent the fact that the (English-drafted) provisions in tax statutes are often passed in ignorance of Scottish law, although the provisions are supposed to work evenly on both sides of the border. But even confining ourselves to English law, the difficulties in squaring our trusts laws and our tax laws are considerable: for IHT they have proved fiendish.

For income tax there is a kind of two-tier system: to some extent income tax is charged on the trustees; to some extent it is charged on the beneficiary.

Tax payable by trustees

12–03 Trustees are not companies, so not liable to corporation tax. But they are also not "individuals" for the purposes of income tax. Consequently, they are in principle liable only to the basic rate of income tax on, for example, trading profits they receive, or income from investments. On the other hand, they are not entitled to personal allowances and reliefs. Generally, they are not liable to the higher rate of income tax, or the starting rate. But recently, with one eye on simplicity and the other on avoidance, trusts have been made subject to their own set of tax rates.

Exemption of first slice of income

12–04 Section 491 of ITA exempts from income tax the first £1,000 of trust income in any year. This is a simplification measure. Calculating income tax on trusts is not easy for the trustees, and chasing small trusts is a waste of time for HMRC officials. The apparent generosity of this exemption removes all small trusts from income tax altogether, so reducing the caseload for HMRC by about one third. Little local charities benefitting from what is left of the savings of a long dead benefactor no longer need to fill in endless forms to avoid tax.

The trust rate and dividend trust rate

12–05 Section 9 of ITA sets two special rates of tax for trusts. The trust rate is 45 per cent and the dividend trust rate is 37.5 per cent. Section 15 directs us to s.479 and following for the details of when these apply. Section 479 applies the trust and dividend trust rates to non-charitable accumulation or discretionary trusts. Sections 481 and 482 set out a list of other situations when income received by trustees of non-charitable trusts is taxable at these higher rates.

The application of these rates is intended to prevent income being accumulated in a trust, or distributed by a trust, so as to avoid the individual's higher rate (or dividend upper rate) by deflecting the income elsewhere. It also prevents trusts postponing payment of tax by investing sums tax-free. It means that income can only be accumulated after the appropriate higher rate of income tax has been paid.

Note that these rates apply to the whole of the trust income after expenses and the first slice. So trustees of these trusts may end up paying more income tax on the trust income than a beneficiary would have done if the trust had not been interposed.

Trust expenses

The imposition of higher rates of tax directly on trusts high- **12–06**
lighted the potential unfairness of the previous rule that trustees
could not deduct trust expenses when paying income tax. There
was an implicit trade-off between the lower rate of tax and the
absence of allowable expenses for larger trusts. Removing one
side of that trade-off meant that it was appropriate also to allow
some expenses. Section 484 now allows trustees to deduct their
expenses provided that they are not otherwise allowable (for
example because they are trading expenses of a trade carried on
by the trustees) and that they are properly chargeable to income.
These expenses can be deducted both in calculating the taxable
income of small trusts for the purposes of the exemption of the
first slice, and also when calculating how much tax is payable at
the trust rate or trust dividend rate.

Tax on beneficiaries

A beneficiary's income from a trust forms part of total income **12–07**
for determining reliefs and the rate of tax. It would be nice and
neat if one could say that one works out the beneficiary's tax
bill and then gives a straight credit for the tax already paid by
the trustees. Unfortunately this is not precisely so. There is a
case called *Macfarlane v IRC* (1929) Ct Sess, which held that
although trust expenses are not deductible in computing the trustees' income, they are deductible in computing the beneficiary's
income. That position now, with the advent of the trust rate,
is more complicated, because although trust expenses are not
deductible in computing the trust's liability to basic rate tax,
they are deductible in computing the trust's liability to tax which
arises from the difference between the rate applicable to trusts
and the lower or basic rate. Indeed, to further compound this
complication, such expenses must normally be set off, in the first
instance, against savings income. However, one can say this: the
tax charge on the beneficiary *takes into account* (to some extent)
the tax already charged on the trustees!

Income to which a beneficiary is *entitled* forms part of total **12–08**
income whether or not it is received. This follows from the
general principle stated above, namely that a beneficiary who is
entitled at all is entitled from the very inception of the trust. Of
course this principle does not apply to a discretionary trust; if
there is a discretion whether to pay any particular beneficiary,
there is no entitlement until the discretion is exercised. When a
sum is actually paid to such a beneficiary that sum forms part
of his total income and is taxed, unless it is an annuity, in the

same way as savings income. Whether one is talking of a fixed trust or a discretionary trust, payments in kind may, just as much as money payments, constitute income. This would be so, for example of a right to occupy a house rent free.

A payment may perfectly well be income in the hands of a beneficiary, even although it is made out of the capital (and not the income) of the trust. However, a payment out of capital does not become income in the hands of a beneficiary simply because it is to be used for an income purpose by that beneficiary (see *Stevenson v Wishart* (1987) CA).

12–09 An important tax point arises in connection with income which is accumulated by a trust. One has to make a distinction here between a vested interest and a contingent interest. This is a matter of general law rather than tax law and it involves some fairly complicated points. But broadly the distinction is that a vested interest is one which (generally) cannot be upset, whereas a contingent interest is one which is dependent on some contingency happening. The clearest example is where a trust provides that X is to have a certain interest under the trust when he attains a certain age. As X may never attain that age the interest is until then contingent. When X has attained that age the interest becomes vested. (A person may attain a vested interest in income before attaining, or without ever attaining, a vested interest in the capital of the fund.) For a person who has a vested interest in the income of a trust, that income (as has been said above) forms part of total income, and that is so even if it is not in fact received. But for a person who has only a contingent interest, until that contingency occurs, the income of the trust is not income. It follows that if the trust's income is accumulated it is not his income and it does not become so even if the contingency occurs (e.g. attaining the age of 18) and the accumulations are paid. The payments reach the beneficiary as capital. The leading authority on this point is *Stanley v IRC* (1944) CA.

12–10 FA 2005 introduced legislation to protect disadvantaged individuals being prejudiced by these rules. Where a beneficiary of a trust is a vulnerable person or a child (under 18) who has lost a parent because the parent died, then any trust income received by the beneficiary is to be taxed no more heavily than had the individual received the money directly rather than from a trust.

Tax on settlors

12–11 We must now consider the detailed rules relating to settlements which are intended to curb the use of settlements for tax avoidance.

Section 620 of ITTOIA provides that for the purposes of Ch.5 of Pt 20 a settlement includes "any disposition, trust, covenant, agreement, arrangement or transfer of assets". Broadly speaking, this encompasses two types of settlement, namely, income settlements and capital settlements. An income settlement is a settlement which involves the transfer of income only, e.g. a covenant. A capital settlement is a settlement which involves the transfer of income-producing property, e.g. a trust. An income settlement is the handing-over of fruits; a capital settlement is the handing-over of a fruit tree. An income settlement may provide for payment to trustees or for payment direct to the beneficiary; a capital settlement necessarily involves trustees. In neither instance, however, can a transaction constitute a settlement unless there is an element of bounty; a bona fide commercial transaction is not a settlement for the purposes of Pt XV (see *IRC v Plummer* (1979) HL and *Chinn v Collins* (1981) HL). Special rules are applied to both forms of settlement by Ch.5 of Pt 5 of ITTOIA.

The background to that chapter is that settlements, histori- **12–12** cally, have been a favourite means of tax avoidance, particularly when individuals faced high marginal rates of tax. Indeed, in the absence of statutory intervention, the potential for tax-saving through settlements is self-evident—any settlement would enable an individual with a high rate of tax to unload income on to a comparatively poor member of the family to the advantage of the family viewed as a whole, because the poor member has a lower rate of tax or may not be liable to tax at all. Not surprisingly, therefore, governments have over the years sought to counteract the fiscal efficacy of settlements.

The rules in Ch.5 are the most recent attempt. Where applicable, the rules deem income arising under a settlement during the life of the settlor to be the income of the settlor for *all* income tax purposes. In such instances, the income is treated as arising first in the settlement and then as being transferred to or reverting to the settlor.

The important phrase, however, is "where applicable" for many income settlements (annual payments) made by individuals are denied any effect for income tax purposes. Therefore, in respect of such settlements, the rules in Ch.5 are redundant.

The rules in Ch.5 fall into three categories: **12–13**

1) rules which apply where the settlor (or spouse or civil partner) retains an interest in the settled property (ss. 624–28);
2) rules which apply where a benefit is received by unmarried minor children from a parental settlement (ss.629–32); and

3) rules which apply where the settlor (or his spouse or civil partner) has received a capital sum from the settlement (ss.633–37).

We deal first with the strict provisions dealing with settlements of income (which normally take the form of a covenant or will trust), and then the more usual settlements of capital.

Income settlements

12–14   The ITTOIA provisions about annual payments stop most forms of income settlements (chiefly covenants) being effective to avoid income tax. The income of the payer is computed for income tax purposes without any deduction for the payments. Where they do not apply to an annual payment, the income will be treated as the income of the settlor (payer) under s.625, unless he can show that the income arises from property in which he has no interest or that the income is expressly excluded from the operation of s.625. In the latter respect, s.625 does not apply to income paid under a settlement by one party to a marriage to provide for the other after divorce, annulment or separation to the extent that the income is payable for the benefit of that other (s.626). This applies in a similar way to civil partners. In addition, s.627 provides that income which consists of annual payments made by an individual for bona fide commercial reasons in connection with his trade, profession or vocation or qualifying charitable donations falls outside s.625.

Capital settlements

Settlements where the settlor retains an interest
12–15   Broadly, s.625 of ITTOIA deems all income arising under a settlement during the life of the settlor to be the *income of the settlor* for all income tax purposes unless the income arises from property in which the settlor has no interest.

The settlor is treated as having an interest where that property or any derived property (see s.626) is, or will or may become, payable to or for the benefit of the settlor or spouse or partner in any circumstances whatsoever. Section 625(4) provides that a spouse or partner of the settlor does *not* include a prospective or separated spouse or a widow or widower. Thus, it is the existence of the interest which attracts the charge to tax under s.625 and, perhaps, the most compelling example of where such an interest exists is where a settlement can be revoked and, on revocation, property reverts to the settlor or spouse (but note *IRC v Wolfson* (1949) HL).

The full scope of the section was tested before the House of **12–16** Lords in *Jones v Garnett* (2007), known as the *Arctic Systems* case. Mr Jones set up a small company called Arctic Systems Ltd. He used it as a legal basis for his business as an IT consultant. There were two ordinary shares in the company. He held one and his wife held the other. In 1999–2000 the company earned nearly £80,000. It paid Mr Jones a salary of £6,000, and Mrs Jones a salary of £4,000, and made a profit of £26,000. After paying corporation tax of about £5,000, it paid a dividend that was said to be £25,000 to each shareholder for the year. It was accepted that this was to avoid NICs and higher rate tax on Mr Jones.

HMRC assessed Mr Jones on Mrs Jones' dividend under s.660A of the 1988 Act (now s.625). In HMRC's view, on the grounds that this was a settlement of the one share by Mr Jones on Mrs Jones under that section. The House of Lords unanimously agreed that this was a settlement within the scope of the section. Mr Jones had given his wife the share in a situation that only made sense as a non-commercial transaction. But the Jones' plans were rescued by what was s.660A(6) (and is now s.626). This provides an exception to the charge under the section for outright gifts between husband and wife unless what is given is wholly or substantially a right to income. The House of Lords held this applied, as an ordinary share is not just a right to income. And it noted that this exception came in at the same time as separate taxation of husband and wife was introduced. That may explain why some call this the "husband and wife tax".

This case proved controversial, not least because of the way in which views changed as the case rose through the appeal system. The House of Lords conducted a full study of the case law, and it is a good place to start any study of these difficult provisions. The case also brings home just how wide the sections are. The government announced that it intended to reverse the decision by legislation, and issued a consultation about it. However, this met heavy criticism and the proposal to legislate was postponed then quietly dropped. HMRC, nonetheless, continues to challenge income shifting, though with mixed success. Another case of husband-wife income shifts was challenged before the First-tier Tribunal in *Padmore v HMRC* (2001). HMRC again lost, in part because the judge invoked the principle of reversionary trusts.

The operation of this is limited by subss.(2) and (3) by virtue of **12–17** which the settlor is not to be regarded as having an interest if his or her interest can only take effect on the occurrence of certain specified events, e.g. the bankruptcy of a person who is or may become entitled to the property or any derived property or on the death at any age of a child of the settlor who had become beneficially entitled to the property or any derived property at an age not exceeding 25. In addition, the section does not apply to the income arising under a settlement by one party to a marriage to provide for the other after divorce, annulment or separation to the extent that the income is payable for the benefit of that other (and likewise for civil partners).

If the section applies, the settlor is charged to tax, and the income is treated as the highest part of income. However, the settlor may recover any tax so paid from the trustees or any other person to whom the income is payable under the settlement (s.646).

Benefits received by unmarried minor children from parental settlements

12–18   Generally, any income arising under a settlement which is paid during the life of the settlor to or for the benefit of an unmarried minor (including a stepchild or illegitimate child) of the settlor is treated by s.629 of ITTOIA for all income tax purposes as the income of the settlor. However, this will not apply where the income is treated as the income of the settlor under s.624, nor will it apply where the income paid to a child under such a parental settlement does not exceed, in total, £100 in any tax year.

12–19   In addition, if income arising under a capital settlement in favour of the settlor's unmarried minor children is retained or accumulated by the trustees such income is not treated by reason of s.631 as income of the settlor. In certain circumstances, such a capital accumulation settlement can be used to secure tax savings for the family when it is viewed as a whole. For example, if the accumulated income belongs to the beneficiary because she has a vested interest, e.g. when capital is settled for a minor absolutely, there may be liability to basic rate tax, but this will, broadly speaking, have been borne by the trustees. Section 568 of ITTOIA (imposing the trust rates of tax) does not apply because the income belongs to the beneficiary. Moreover, depending on her other income and allowances, the beneficiary may be able to recover tax paid by the trustees so that the income as long as it remains within the settlement (or is distributed after the beneficiary has reached 18 or married under 18) will in some instances be free of income tax. However, if the beneficiary's interest is contingent, the accumulated income does *not* belong to him.

12–20   Income which is not accumulated but distributed is caught by s.629. This will be so, for example, where income is applied for the child's maintenance, education or benefit under s.31 of the

Trustee Act 1925. And it is no good the trustees thinking that they can avoid s.629 by accumulating income and using capital for maintenance, etc. of the unmarried minor beneficiary. This device is stopped by s.631 which provides that any sum whatsoever paid out for the benefit of an unmarried minor child of the settlor shall be deemed to be income (and not capital) to the extent that there is "available retained or accumulated income". "Available retained or accumulated income" is the aggregate amount of income which has arisen under the settlement since its inception *less* income already treated as income of the settlor or a beneficiary, income paid to or for the benefit of a beneficiary other than an unmarried minor child of the settlor and income properly spent on trust expenses.

If s.629 applies, the settlor is charged to tax, and the income is treated as the highest part of his income. However, as with s.625, the settlor may recover any tax so paid from the trustees or any other person to whom the income is payable under the settlement (s.646).

Capital sums paid to the settlor

Section 633 attacks capital sums paid *to* the settlor (or spouse **12–21** or civil partner) out of the settlement. "Capital sum" is defined to include "any sum paid by way of loan or repayment of a loan" (s.634). This is the key to the understanding of what the section is primarily aimed at. It is designed to stop a settlor (who is a higher-rate taxpayer) making a settlement, causing the trustees to accumulate rather than distribute the income, and causing them to let him (or his spouse) have the income in the form of a loan. For "other" capital sums which fall within this section, see s.634.

Where a capital sum is paid by the trustees to the settlor (or his spouse) such sum (grossed up at the rate applicable to trusts) is to be treated for all income tax purposes as the income of the settlor to the extent that such sum falls within the amount of "income available". "Income available" means, broadly speaking, the aggregate of all income arising to the settlement since its inception which has not been distributed and is not deemed to be income of the settlor under some other provision. The point of this is that what the section is attacking is the payment out as capital of money which came into the settlement as income.

If in the year in which the capital sum is paid such sum exceeds the income available, the excess is carried forward and charged to the settlor in the following year (in so far as there is income available up to the end of that year) and thereafter, if necessary, subject to a maximum of 11 years. However, if the capital sum is paid by way of loan no charge can be raised in any year after that in which the loan is wholly repaid (s.638).

12–22 Section 641 of ITTOIA stops the dodge of ensuring that the payment of a capital sum was made not by the trustees to the settlor but by an associated company which was in some way put in funds by the trustees. The section deems such sums to be paid by the trustees to the settlor and thus to be within the scope of s.638.

The settlor receives a tax credit for tax paid by the trustees, but cannot recover from the trustees any tax for which he may be responsible as a result of the operation of these provisions.

Estate income

12–23 What we are considering here is income arising during the period of administration of the estate of a deceased individual. When an individual dies the estate is administered by executors or administrators. The generic name for these is personal representatives; for tax purposes there is no need to distinguish between the two species.

Tax on administrators

12–24 As with trusts, so with estates, there is a kind of two-tier system of income tax. Personal representatives are like trustees in that they are chargeable to basic rate tax, are not chargeable to the higher rate of tax, and do not qualify for personal reliefs. In another respect, however, personal representatives differ from trustees; they are not chargeable to tax under the trust rates.

Tax on beneficiaries

12–25 How is the beneficiary taxed? That depends on the nature of the benefit. If the will gives an annuity, the annuity payments are part of total income from the date of death. So far as legatees are concerned it is perhaps worth stating the fairly elementary point that a legacy as such is not subject to income tax because it is not income; it is capital. But a legatee may be entitled to interest or (in the case of a specific legacy) to income from the date of death. In those cases the legatee is chargeable to income tax on the interest or income.

Residuary beneficiaries

12–26 What we have to look at in more detail is the position of a residuary beneficiary. One has to distinguish between a beneficiary who has a limited interest in the residue of the estate and a beneficiary who has an absolute interest in the residue. A person has an absolute interest if he has an interest in the capital, and a person has a limited interest if he does not have an absolute interest.

An example of a person with a limited interest is a person who gets a life tenancy. Everything that is paid to him by the personal representatives must be income for the simple reason that he is not entitled to any capital. Therefore very little complication arises in his case. Each sum that is paid to him during the administration counts (grossed-up) as part of his total income for the year of assessment when it is paid. At the end of the administration period any final payment is regarded as the income of the beneficiary in the year of assessment in which the administration ends.

Beneficiaries with entitlements

A beneficiary who has an absolute interest has, by definition, an entitlement to capital. Therefore it is by no means certain that everything paid to him during the administration of the estate is income. To get at his tax liability the income element must be sorted out from the capital element. The first step is to calculate the "residuary income" of the estate for each year of assessment during the administration period. To arrive at residuary income the personal representatives are permitted to deduct certain management expenses. The residuary income of the estate is divided into a residuary income for each beneficiary according to his share. For example, if there are three absolute beneficiaries each with an equal share the residuary income of each is one-third of the residuary income of the estate. Then any sums which are paid to a beneficiary are treated as income for the year of assessment in which they are actually paid in so far as (grossed-up) they do not exceed his residuary income. In so far as they do exceed it they are treated as capital. Finally, if at the end of the administration the beneficiary has not received all the residuary income which is his due, the outstanding amount is regarded as having been paid immediately before the end of the administration period.

12–27

Charitable income

Charities (or, more formally, trusts and similar bodies such as companies limited by guarantee that are established solely for charitable purposes) are exempt from income tax and CGT. That is an extremely valuable tax exemption. It has led to some interesting case law about what is a charity. That is not a question of tax law, and is beyond the scope of this book.

12–28

The most valuable tax exemption enjoyed by charities is that those giving money or assets to charities can also claim tax exemption. What is more, in many cases it is the charity that gets the advantage of the tax exemption, not the donor.

Gift aid

12–29   The modern system of tax help to charities has at its centre a scheme known universally as gift aid. But before we deal with that we should mention that charitable covenants, that is annual payments payable to charities unconditionally for at least four years, or for an uncertain period that may exceed four years, still work as charges on income. So the payer deducts income tax at the basic rate when paying them, and can offset the sum paid against total taxable income. This can also be done by most forms of trust, if the objectives are charitable, without the settlor being caught by the anti-avoidance provisions set out earlier in this chapter. And it can sometimes be linked into the administration of estates, as gifts to charities on death do not suffer IHT. Such generosity is further encouraged by the provision of a lower overall rate of IHT where a significant part of the estate is given to charitable causes. And traders could justify some donations to charities as trading expenses.

12–30   HOW GIFT AID WORKS   Most people do not get involved in these complexities any longer. They can now make one-off payments and have them brought within the gift aid scheme. The rules are in Part 8 of ITA 2007. If an individual makes a qualifying donation to a charity, then he or she is treated as making a donation after basic rate income tax has been deducted. At the same time, his or her basic rate limit is increased by the grossed up amount of the gift. See s.414.

12–31   How does that work? Mel decides to give a £20 note to a charity. Assuming she is an income tax payer, and fills in the right form, she is treated as giving the charity the sum which, after deduction of income tax at 20 per cent, leaves £20—that is, £25. The charity then claims the "missing" 20 per cent from HMRC, so receiving the full £25.

If Mel earns enough to be paying, say, 40 per cent income tax then she can set the full £25 against the total income tax bill at the end of the year to reduce her income so as to give her a full 40 per cent tax relief on the £25. This creates a deduction of a further £5 (as the charity has already had the first £5). The result is that in the outturn it costs Mel £15 to hand her £20 note to the charity, while it gets £25.

QUALIFYING DONATIONS   The most important practical side **12–32** of making a qualifying donation is that the taxpayer must at some point fill in a gift aid declaration. This is the little form that any charity will give you to say that you are a taxpayer and are paying the amount from taxable income.

You must also give the money with no strings attached. Conditional gifts do not count. That presents some charities with a problem. If you pay the charity, for example, for copies of its magazine, then you are not making an unconditional gift. But if you decide to join the charity as an annual member, and annual membership allows you free copies of the magazine, the problem is solved. The annual membership is not a conditional gift, at least it is not if the benefits fall within the allowed benefits under ss.418 and 419 of ITA 2007. These impose limits on the amount of benefit that someone may be given in acknowledgement of a gift. The rules apply fully only if the benefit linked with the gift applies for a full year. If so, then a benefit worth 25 per cent of the amount of a gift of less than £100 can be ignored. If in addition to the magazine and the small piece of paper, you get a membership form telling you that you have joined the charity for a year, that's why.

Section 420 also allows charities to ignore rights of admission **12–33** as benefits. These sections were brought in to help charities such as the National Trust and Royal Society for Protection of Birds. These charities are hugely influential not least because of their size. With several million members each they are the largest such organisations in the world. Both run huge estates and were giving free admission to those properties to members. But until this provision was introduced, there was a danger that the membership fees would be regarded as trading income and not charitable income. Again, there are conditions to the relief. Any benefit given for a gift must be for at least a year's admission. And the gift must be at least 10 per cent more than the individual entry fee to enter the property. And the property must also be open to the public.

So let's say Mel, instead of buying the magazine, wants to go into the museum run by her charity. It is open to the public at a fee of £15, but the public are invited to join the charity. Joining costs £20. On joining, Mel gets free admission for the year— and the bit of paper. She fills it in, hands over the £20, and—as before—her charity gets £25 and it costs her £15. And, as Mel pays higher rate tax, it costs her no more to join than she would have paid only for admission (provided she keeps the receipt).

CHAPTER 13

TAXATION OF INDIVIDUALS

Introduction

13–01   This chapter is entitled "taxation of individuals" for two reasons. The first is that, as we have seen, companies are now subject to an entirely separate tax code. And although trustees, personal representatives, and beneficiaries are also subject to income tax, but not always as individuals, we have covered those issues in the previous chapter. The other reason is that since 1990 income tax is charged on individuals, not on couples. So marriages and civil partnerships are ignored in the income tax code (save for a very few exceptions in the rules).

In addition, to obtain a full picture of the tax rates people actually pay we must examine NICs and then, more briefly as the law is part tax and part social welfare, tax credits and related social welfare benefits. We conclude by bringing them together to look at the overall picture.

Income tax

13–02   We have now examined how each kind of income is identified and worked out for income tax purposes. But we have only one income tax on individuals. So we must now see how all the different kinds of income are added together and taxed each year as one total amount of income. This has to be done as part of each year's self-assessment either by the taxpayer (or his or her accountant) or on the HMRC automatic calculator on the Self-Assessment Website. Either way, this is done as a series of steps:

Step 1
"Income" is income under any charging provision. The first step is to aggregate all the separate amounts of income under these provisions from all sources on which the individual is liable to income tax for the tax year.
Step 2
Deduct from Step 1 income any deductions to which the individual is entitled for the tax year. This will include losses,

charges on income, and any other deductions that are not limited to being offset against a single source. This is known as "total income".

Step 3

Deduct from the Step 2 income the total of any personal allowances to which the individual is entitled for the tax year. This produces the "taxable income" for the year.

Step 4

Calculate the total income tax payable on the Step 3 (taxable) income.

Step 5

Deduct from the Step 4 tax calculation any tax reductions to which the individual is entitled for the tax year. This produces the individual's income tax liability for the year.

The individual is then liable to pay to HMRC the difference between the amount of tax for which he or she is liable and the amount of tax already paid by deduction at source, through the PAYE system, or in any other way.

Before we move on to the details of these steps, we should remember that for most people there is also a liability to NICs to be paid, and that for many families and lower-paid employees or the self-employed there is an entitlement to tax credits.

Step 1: Income from all sources

The first step is to identify and add together the separate calculations of income from each of the charging provisions in the Tax Acts. We must check for each source that we include only the income from that source that is taxable in the tax year with which we are concerned. We have seen that most of these provisions have their own rules for identifying in which year income is to be regarded as taxable, allowing in some cases averaging and instalments. The separate provisions also provide for the expenses that are allowed against the gross income received in computing the amount of income for income tax purposes.

13–03

What must also be emphasised here is that this is not a total of all income of any kind. It is a total of those kinds of income that are taxable. Non-taxable income is not included. This applies, for example, to some kinds of social welfare payments, to most student grants and scholarships, to most betting winnings and to cash gifts between individuals (including sums received on someone's death). Capital gains are not included here, but taxed separately. Income tax only applies to those forms of income specifically charged to the tax under the tax provisions we have discussed above.

Kinds of income

13–04   An individual's income may include items of the following kinds:

1)   Income not taxed by deduction before receipt

The most important kind of income that cannot be subject to income tax at source is trading income. Property income can be taxed at source in special cases but is normally also paid gross. This will apply to both tenants and lodgers.

2)   Income taxed by deduction before receipt

This is where we take account, as we must, of all receipts which were subject to withholding taxes. The point we want to make here is that income taxed by deduction of tax before receipt has to be grossed-up, that is, converted into a gross sum, for the purpose of computing total income. We will explain grossing-up in a moment. The most important example of income taxed by deduction before receipt is salary or wage income. Tax is charged as employment income and is deducted by the employer under the PAYE system. The gross amount, which includes the tax calculated according to the various tax bands, is included in total income, but of course the employee is credited with the tax deducted by his employer. The same is true of pensions taxed at source.

Grossing-up

13–05   Grossing-up is the name given to the process of converting a net sum (the sum left after something has been deducted from the original sum) back to the original, or gross, amount. Employees usually know what their gross pay and net pay are because their pay slips state both amounts, so grossing is no problem for that kind of earned income. It is in practice more important for tax purposes for some kinds of investment income and some kinds of deduction. For example, some kinds of interest paid by commercial concerns to individuals are paid to the individuals net, that is, after the deduction of income tax at a set rate—usually the basic rate of 20 per cent. If the lender receives £80 net interest, then grossing up requires us to find the sum from which a deduction of 20 per cent income tax leaves £80. The sum is £100. But to find it we have to gross up the net sum not at 20 per cent but at 25 per cent (20/80, i.e. the deduction rate divided by the net sum). Grossing-up also applies for claims to the tax back on Gift

Aid. Here a taxpayer is treated as making a Gift Aid donation as a net sum—net of 20 per cent tax. So a gift of £80 becomes a gift of £100 to the charity after grossing up and a tax reclaim by the charity, while the taxpayer pays what is in effect the net sum of £80.

Trust income

A beneficiary under a trust has to include in the total income **13–06** an amount equal to his or her share of the trust income, grossed-up. He or she will have received the share after deduction of tax, and will be credited (depending on the circumstances) with all or some of the tax paid by the trustees. The taxation of trust income is dealt with in Ch.11.

Partnership income

A partnership is defined in the Partnership Act 1890 as the **13–07** relation which subsists between persons carrying on business in common with a view of profit. There is no definition of partnership in the tax legislation, but the existence of partnerships is, as might be expected, acknowledged.

Four non-tax points we wish to make are extremely elementary, but we have found that they come as a surprise to some students. First, a partnership is quite different from a company registered under the Companies Acts, of which the main species is a limited company, e.g. BP. Thus a partnership, unlike a registered company, is not, in English law, a legal entity separate from its members (although, as we shall see, under the old regime it is for purposes of assessment and collection treated as though it were a separate legal entity). Nevertheless, the name of a partnership may contain the word "Company", or "Co", e.g. Price & Co. This does not make it a company in law; it is a partnership. The word "firm" is equivalent to the word "partnership", and should not be used in reference to a company. Secondly, there is no requirement of law or practice that the shares of each partner in the profits (or losses) of the partnership should be equal. Thirdly, a company can be a partner in a partnership. The fourth point is that these rules only apply to individuals who are actually partners. A "salaried partner" who is not sharing in the profits but receives an agreed amount of pay is an employed earner not a partner.

Broadly speaking, the responsibility for the tax payable on the profits of a trade or profession carried on in partnership lies not with the partnership but with the individual partners. Assessments are made on the individual partners, not on the partnership. Each partner is treated as if his share of the partnership profits is derived from a separate trade or profession carried on by him alone, i.e. as a sole trader or professional. This notional sole trade or profession is deemed to begin when he becomes a partner. It comes to an end when he ceases to be a partner or where the actual trade or profession is subsequently carried on by him alone or when it is actually discontinued. The partners are individually liable for tax in accordance with their respective shares in the partnership profits during the period in which the profits accrued.

Classifications of income

13–08   As we have seen, the system requires us to add together all forms of income. But they are not all then treated exactly the same for income tax purposes. At one time, earned income was taxed less heavily than income from property or savings. In broad terms, the opposite is now true, though a full picture demands that we look at all the taxes and not just income tax.

For income tax purposes, income from self-employment and from a property business are now treated in the same way as employment income. The amounts are added together in the calculations and subject to income tax at the same rates. Any income from pensions or social security income will also be added in. But they will be treated differently for NIC purposes, as we see below.

Income from savings is treated more lightly. For a start, most individuals are entitled to at least some of their savings in a form that makes the income tax exempt. So, income from an ISA account, for example, is ignored entirely at this stage. There is also now the personal savings allowance exempting smaller amounts. The dividend rates reflect the fact that the company has already paid corporation tax on the profits used to pay the dividends. None of these forms of income are subject to NICs.

Step 2: Total income

13–09   It is necessary to find a taxpayer's total income for two purposes: first, to determine whether it is enough (or too much) to entitle him or her to personal reliefs; secondly, to determine liability (if any) to the higher rate of tax.

To arrive at total income one deducts what are called "charges on income", certain payments (outward) of interest and any other non-source-specific deductions.

Charges on income

Most payments that used to be deductible at this stage are now **13–10** dealt with in other ways. But a deduction may still apply at this stage for a covenant of income by partners to a retired partner. The new rules applying to most payments to charities are at the end of Ch.12. Those paying higher rate tax will also be entitled to a deduction for that purpose.

Deductible interest payments

We are not speaking here of interest paid out as one of the **13–11** expenses of a business; that is deductible *in computing* the income of that business. We are speaking of payments of interest in respect of which an individual can secure relief from income tax by deducting them *from* income. Relief of this sort was at one time widely available. It has been progressively restricted over recent years. In particular, what used to be called "mortgage interest relief", a deduction for interest paid when buying a home, was abolished in 2000.

Perhaps not surprisingly, these exceptional cases do not include many of the payments of interest most people make, e.g. on a bank overdraft or under a credit card arrangement or hire purchase contract. This is so regardless of the purpose of that kind of loan. Rather they relate to instances where the loan for which the interest is being paid is for one of a number of specified purposes. However, even if the loan is for one of these purposes there are two general restrictions which come into play: first, relief is only given up to the amount of reasonable commercial rate of interest, see s.384 of ITA 2007, and secondly (following amendments to ITA in 2010). no relief at all is given if the sole or main benefit that might be expected to accrue to the claimant from the transaction under which the interest is paid was the obtaining of a reduction in tax liability by means of such relief.

There is a full list of the purposes for which loans may be taken out so that individuals can claim tax relief on the interest paid in s.383 of ITA 2007. The details of each kind of purpose, and the conditions attached to loans for that purpose, follow in code form from s.388 to s.412. Section 386 provides a general rule that where a loan is partly for one of the purposes in the list and partly for some other purpose, then the qualifying part of the mixed loan must be identified for any claim to be made.

LOANS TO INVEST IN A BUSINESS STRUCTURE A series of **13–12** provisions allow a deduction to be claimed on interest paid on loans taken out to invest in close companies, employee-controlled companies, trading partnerships or co-operative enterprises. Together they reflect part of the policy of encouraging individuals to become entrepreneurs by allowing the cost of borrowing stake money to invest in any of these forms of enterprise.

13–13   LOANS TO BUY PLANT AND MACHINERY This fills a gap between the provisions under which a company can borrow to buy plant and machinery on which it can claim a capital allowance and the provisions allowing an individual trader to do that. The rule here allows a partnership to borrow for the same purpose and to offset the interest cost of the loan against the partnership profits. The rule is focussed by requiring that the expenditure be on plant and machinery subject to a capital allowance claim.

13–14   LOANS TO PAY IHT This is a narrow but pragmatic relief. It is available only to the personal representatives responsible for settling an estate. With any larger estate the personal representatives will need to settle the IHT bill with HMRC when they submit their account of the estate to HMRC. So they may have to borrow to pay the tax. But even then, they can only claim relief on a loan for one year.

A limit on deductible expenses

13–15   Those deductions and some other deductions of more limited significance are listed in ITA 2007 s.24. Since 2013 a new s.24A has capped the total allowance in connection with all these expenses. The total allowed may not exceed whichever is the higher of 25 per cent of the total income or £50,000. There are complex rules giving priorities where the result is that not all allowances can be deducted.

Step 3: Taxable income

13–16   Step 2 gave us the total amount of income for any tax year after taking account of all taxable sources of income and all the allowances and deductions to which an individual is entitled by reason of the nature of her or his income and expenditure. We must now take account of other provisions, known as personal reliefs, which depend on personal characteristics of the taxpayer. This step used to be far more important than it is now. The former child allowances and child tax reliefs are now all dealt with separately by the child tax credit. With one exception (blind people), help for disabilities is now given only by social security benefits. And the rules dealing with married couples have largely gone with the introduction of separate taxation. There are two sorts of personal relief left:

- **personal allowances.** These are sums deducted from total income to produce taxable income; and
- **tax reductions.** These sums are set off against the income tax liability to produce the amount of tax payable.

Personal allowances are taken into account at this step. Tax reductions are taken into account at step 5.

Personal allowances

Every individual who claims and meets, or is otherwise exempt **13–17** from, a requirement that she or he is resident in the UK is entitled to claim tax allowances for each tax year. In past years these allowances reflected aspects of the individual's personal position such as age and marriage or other status and—some time ago—gender. From 2016/17 much of this no longer matters save for a specific allowance for the blind. This is worth an additional £2,290 for 2016/17. And again from that year individuals can claim a personal savings allowance in addition to a personal allowance. But at the same time the allowances have become increasingly income-related.

Nonetheless, the main personal allowance is of major significance when looking at the income tax system as a whole as it is in effect a zero-rate provision and removes millions of those with low incomes (including those living on basic state pensions) from any charge to income tax.

The rates are now set for some years ahead. For 2016/17 the personal allowance is £11,000 for every individual, regardless of age or status. For 2017/18 it is £11,500.

From 2016/17 there is also a personal savings allowance, set at £1,000 for that year for those who are or would be basic rate taxpayers, and reduced to £500 for those liable to higher rate tax. (It is nil for those liable to tax at above the higher rate.)

One minor additional detail of the law—but of considerable practical significance to some couples, is the right of one of a couple to transfer up to £1,100 of a personal allowance (the 2016/17 allowance—it is set at 10 per cent of that year's personal allowance) if it is unused and both members of the couple are basic rate taxpayers. There is also still a married couples allowance provided in law (and now available to all couples) but it is only available to those aged over 81 in 2016 and is of limited value—none to higher rate taxpayers—so there are not likely to be many new claimants.

Of more significance to those with high earnings is a restriction **13–18** on the value of the personal allowance to those with higher incomes. This applies if an individual's "adjusted net income" for a year is over £100,000. "Adjusted net income" (s.58 ITA 2007) is taxable income less certain deductions, the most important of which are Gift Aid and pension contributions). An individual whose adjusted net income is more than £100,000 loses £1 for every £2 excess. So at the margin taxable income increases by £1 in addition to each £2 actual income, to be taxed at the 40 per cent rate, or a marginal rate of 60 per cent.

The effect of this cap is increased by a separate series of measures capping the amount of private pension contributions a higher paid individual can deduct from income for tax purposes. There has for some years been a cap on total deductible pension contributions which was steadily reduced until it reached £40,000 annually in 2014. It remains at that total. In addition the Finance (No.2) Act 2015 introduced a tapered reduction in the allowance for high-income individuals. From 2016/17 where the individual's adjusted annual income is over £150,000 the £40,000 cap is steadily reduced until reaching a minimum of £10,000 when income exceeds £210,000.

These measures amount to a "double whammy" on high earners in generous pension schemes as they lose both the zero-tax slice of £11,000 or more before their incomes become taxable and up to £30,000 entitlement to deductible pension contributions. These are of even greater significance in years where the top tax rate is over 40 per cent. And both complicate the issue of marginal rates of tax, to which we must now turn.

Step 4: The rates of income tax

13–19   Having deducted from total income certain of a taxpayer's personal reliefs, we have arrived at taxable income. We must now proceed to establish what amount of tax is payable. This is primarily determined by the rate or rates of tax applicable to an individual's taxable income.

The rates of tax

13–20   If you look for a simple explanation for our tax rates, you will not find it. Throughout the history of income tax the effective level of income tax has gone up and down not only with the state of the economy or, in days gone by, the state of the navy—don't forget that's why the tax was invented—but also differing views about who should pay how much.[1]

---

[1]   A further variant may follow the introduction of the Scottish income tax rate. See para.2–34.

A major problem is the effect of the burden of tax on the lowest paid. If too much income tax, NICs and other taxes are imposed on the lowest paid, then they may find themselves caught in a situation where it is better not to work. This is because the take-home pay of a low paid worker can end up being less than the social security benefits the worker and family get without earning anything. This is called the poverty trap. In recent years much time has been spent in easing the poverty trap. As part of this, income tax personal allowances for families and children were changed into tax credits. And both the exemptions and rates of income tax and NICs have been increased in recent years to remove lower paid workers from both.

At the same time, when things get tough economically there is often a feeling that "the rich should pay". That in the past has led to a top income tax rate of 98 per cent—or, believe it or not, even higher. Those rates of tax no longer work—such money just doesn't get paid or received in ways that could be subject to UK tax (for example, by being routed to other jurisdictions.) Not that the current answer is low. Currently the top main rate is 45–50 per cent (differing from year to year) together with, as we see below, a 2 per cent NIC rate. (The Scottish government has most recently stated that it will not change the rates.) Take that alongside the measures reducing allowances to the high paid that we have just noted, and other measures such as the employer's NICs and the bank payroll tax (a 50 per cent tax imposed for a short period on bankers' pay but paid by the banks: see FA 2010) and it is clear that the rich do pay "more", though it is often far from clear what they do pay. The full picture must also take into account the increasingly aggressive approach of both parliament and the courts to schemes designed either to hide "executive remuneration" or dress it up as something else. And those with families and high incomes will need to take account of the taxability of child benefit where the claimant or partner earns over £50,000.

The following rates of income tax apply from 2016/17. Each **13–21** is expressed as the rate applying to £1 of income. The legislation is in ITA 2007 Pt 2. This was amended by FA 2016 to introduce several categories of rates: savings rates; dividend rates; main rates; Scottish rates; Welsh rates and default rates. The savings and dividend rates apply to all taxpayers liable to income tax. The main rates apply to all resident individuals who are not subject to the Scottish or Welsh rates. The default rates apply to non-resident individuals and to taxpayers that are not individuals (unincorporated organisations with separate identity).

Nil rate or zero rate

There is no general nil or zero rate. But do not forget that this is the effect of the personal allowance and personal savings allowance. However, there is a savings starting rate from 2016–17 which is a zero or nil rate band for those that qualify. The zero rate can be claimed by those whose savings income does not exceed the individual's personal allowances plus the starting rate band of £5,000. (The rate was previously set at 10 per cent.) Where an individual's non-savings income exceeds the starting rate for savings limit, the starting rate for savings is not available. This protects the savings income of smaller earners (or pensioners) from any income tax, but is abated as non-savings income rises. It is not available if the non-savings income exceeds the starting rate band. In those cases there remains the £1,000 exemption (available in addition to the starting rate) introduced in 2016. The importance of the tax treatment being a zero rate rather than an exemption is that the amount of income is added to other income for other purposes, for example to see if the individual reaches the higher rate of tax.

A further change in 2016 is a dividend tax allowance. This applies a nil rate of tax to the first £5,000 dividend income of an individual. It then applies specific dividend rates to dividend income of basic and other rate taxpayers. This follows reform of the taxation of dividends taking effect that year under FA 2016.

Basic rate

This is the rate around which so much political discussion focuses because it appears to be the rate at which most people pay tax. The rate is currently 20 per cent, a rate that has been applied for some years. It applies to the band of income of individuals above the personal allowances (and other zero-rated amounts) up to an annual total that is £32,000 for 2016/17. In other words, taken with the personal allowance of £11,000 for that year, the basic rate applies to income up to a total of £43,000. This is anticipated to increase through both the increased personal allowance and an additional amount in 2017/18 to £45,000.

Income tax lock

The Finance (No.2) Act 2015 s.1 introduced an unprecedented measure locking the basic rate, higher rate and additional rate of income tax at maximum levels set for 2016/17 for the rest of the current parliament. This carries out a political manifesto promise from the 2015 general election, but it does so on a narrow basis. It does not apply to Scotland (see below) and it does not apply to other rates of income tax or to any of the bands or allowances.

Dividend rates

Separate rates apply to dividend income, as noted above. Aside from the £5,000 zero rate, the following rates apply. Basic rate taxpayers pay 7.5 per cent. Higher rate taxpayers pay 32.5 per cent. Additional rate taxpayers pay 38.1 per cent. The reason for these special rates is that companies will have paid (or have been liable to) corporation tax on any income used to fund dividends to shareholders. As noted in our discussion of corporation tax, there are a number of ways in which the UK system has reflected the double taxation that therefore occurs when companies pay dividends out of taxed income to shareholders who are then liable to be taxes on what they receive. The solution since 2016/17, reflecting the steady reductions up to that year in the rates of corporation tax paid by most companies to rates coming down to the 20 per cent rate of income tax, is to charge lower rates than apply to other forms of income.

Higher rate

Income in excess of the higher rate threshold (the sum equal to the main personal allowance and the basic rate band for the year—£43,000 in 2016/17, rising to £45,000 for 2017/18) is taxed at a higher rate which is currently 40 per cent. However, as we have seen, individuals with income in the higher rate bands start to lose deductions and allowances such as the personal allowance and the tax free status of child benefit. When those deductions fall away, the true marginal rate rises from 40 per cent as an allowance is discounted (50 per cent for the personal allowance). The higher rate also currently has an upper level. In 2016/17 it applies to income up to £150,000 a year.

Additional rate

A higher, higher rate was introduced in 2010 "as a temporary measure". But income tax was described that way when introduced in 1803! It was termed the "additional" rate perhaps to give some idea that it would go away again, but it hasn't yet. It was introduced at 50 per cent and remains at 45 per cent for 2016/17 forward. There is continuing argument about what is the appropriate top rate of income tax with strongly conflicting views about the wisdom of high marginal rates of tax. On the one side are those who say that if you tax too highly, then people lose the incentive to work, preferring perhaps to sit on a beach than aid the government's need for finance. On the other side are those who argue that a cut in pay (which is what results from a higher rate of tax) encourages people to work harder. But such debates, it is suggested, should be looking at tax systems as a whole, as we shall discuss below.

Scottish and other rates

13–22   The Scotland Act 2012 inserted s.11A in ITA 2007 to devolve to the Scottish parliament the task of setting Scottish basic and any higher rates of income tax. From 2016/17 the UK rates of tax applying in Scotland are 10 per cent lower than the rate in England, with the Scottish government and parliament having the power to set their own rates above or below the English level. Announcements for 2016/17 are that the rates will be the same as in England for that year. From 2017 setting the rates for Scotland is fully devolved to the Scottish parliament under the Scotland Act 2016.

An equivalent s.11B makes similar provision to devolve powers to set rates in Wales, but these have not yet been activated.

Elsewhere in the tax legislation are other rates. For example there are trust rates, which we note in the relevant chapter. And there are specific income tax charges at other rates. For example someone who has pensions savings totalling over the lifetime maximum is subject to a 55 per cent income tax charge if money is withdrawn from those savings in the form of cash rather than a pension or annuity.

FA 2016 introduced a further category termed the default rates. These apply particularly to non-resident taxpayers, who therefore may be subject to higher or lower rates than resident taxpayers.

... and more

13–23   That is not where the story ends for an individual tax-payer because in practice there are two parts to the tale for most people: NICs and tax credits and related social welfare benefits.

National insurance contributions

13–24   NICs have been part of the UK fiscal system for over a century, but during that time they have been changed completely in their nature. Originally a NIC was a fixed amount a week for each employee within the scope of the system paid by buying a stamp to stick on a NI card each week. If enough were purchased the card holder was entitled to claim certain social security benefits.

Several legislative changes later NICs are levied on all office holders and employees (and their employers) as a second income tax, with a parallel set of provisions dealing with the self-employed. Further contributions can be paid on a voluntary basis by those wishing to claim certain state benefits (mainly the basic state pension). Further, the contributions paid by and for employees are now collected alongside income tax as part of the PAYE system by HMRC, while the self-employed pay their contributions along with their income tax. But both kinds of contribution are significant revenue raisers so form an important part of the overall pattern of tax rates.

The relevant legislation is in the Social Security (Contributions and Benefits) Act 1992 and considerable amending legislation together with a long series of regulations starting with the Social Security Contributions Regulations 2001 (SI 2001/1004), the more recent regulations sometimes being called National Insurance Regulations. They apply throughout England, Scotland and Wales (with no current plans for devolution) with separate parallel laws for Northern Ireland where there is a separate welfare system. Recent amendments to the law have applied the anti-avoidance provisions of income tax to NICs following a series of elaborate avoidance schemes.

Changes taking effect in 2016/17 have simplified the system following changes to the state pension rules taking place at the same time. Further changes were announced in Budget 2016, as noted below.

Pensioners

NICs are only payable by individuals of working age (from 16 up to pensionable age). So pensioners do not pay contributions. But employers are liable to pay secondary contributions on all staff over 16.

Class 1 contributions

These are payable by any employee or office holder with earnings within the relevant bands (primary contributions) and their employers (secondary contributions). There are some technical differences between "earnings" for these purposes and "emoluments" for income tax purposes, but in practice these are of limited importance. So most individuals and their employers pay NICs on the same amounts that the employees pay income tax.

13–25

For 2016/17 primary contributions are payable by earners whose earnings exceed a primary threshold of £155 a week (£8060 a year). The rate is 12 per cent of the amount by which earnings exceed that limit up to a limit of £827 a week (£43,000 a year—the same level as the upper limit for basic rate tax). Those earning over that amount pay 2 per cent on the amount over that limit. Employers pay 13.8 per cent on all earnings over the primary threshold without upper limit.

Class 2 and Class 4 contributions

13–26   Those who are ordinarily self-employed are liable to pay two classes of NICs, Class 2 and Class 4. Class 2 is a small flat-rate weekly contribution of £2.80 a week for 2016/17. It is a compulsory payment if annual earnings are over £5,965 a year. Class 4 contributions are a second levy on the profits calculated for income tax. They are levied for 2016/17 at 9 per cent of the amount earnings exceed a floor of £8060 a year up to an upper limit of £43,000 a year (the same as Class 1 contributions and basic rate income tax).

In Budget 2016 the Chancellor announced that Class 2 contributions are to be abolished in 2018 so that only Class 4 contributions are collected from the self-employed. This will further align NICs to income tax. Until then, Class 2 contributions entitle the self-employed to claim some welfare benefits while Class 4 contributions are purely a tax levy.

Class 3 and other contributions

13–27   There are also Class 3 and Class 3A contributions. These are purely voluntary. And there are Class 1A and Class 1B contributions. These are technical measures designed to plug gaps in the of Class 1 contributions for items such as expenses paid to employees. They are payable by employers only.

13–28   A final point to note is the interaction between income tax and NICs or, rather, the lack of it. Both levies are imposed in parallel. Income tax is not deductible in calculating NIC liability, and similarly NICs paid by individuals are not deductible in computing income tax liability. An employer can however deduct the employer's contribution as an expense from profits.

Tax credits and welfare benefits

13–29   Aside from NICs, the income tax system interacts with the social security and welfare system in a number of ways. Much of the detail is beyond the scope of this book, but the existence of the overlap should be noted if we want a proper picture of how taxes affect individuals.

13–30   One issue is whether welfare benefits are or are not taxable to income tax. Most benefits are taxable but there are exceptions. The state pension is taxable in full, though an individual who receives the basic state pension will not be liable to income tax because the personal allowance has now been raised to a level that exceeds the level of the basic state pension. Tax credits, housing benefit and most forms of benefit payable to the disabled are exempt from income tax. The full details are in ITEPA Pt 10. Nor do NICs apply.

Aside from the above, there are special provisions inserted **13–31** in ITEPA Pt 10 imposing a high income child benefit charge from 2012. If someone claiming child benefit has income of over £50,000 a year (or that person's partner does) then the child benefit is subject to a 100 per cent tax rate. In other words, an income tax charge is imposed which recoups the benefit paid. This is currently the highest rate of income tax imposed. Taxpayers may choose instead not to claim the child benefit to keep matters simple. But not always—as where one partner does not know that the other is claiming the benefit or a couple split up in an untidy manner. Nothing in either tax law or benefit law is ever simple. Allow them to interact, and difficulties multiply.

If proof were needed of that last statement, then the evidence **13–32** is to be found in the tax credits system. The current form of tax credits in 2016 is the successor to forms of welfare benefit dating back to 1973, all of which have hit practical and political problems. The current system was introduced by the Tax Credits Act 2002, and was to be phased in over a few years. But the government decided to start phasing it out before important parts of it had even commenced. This is happening as tax credits are replaced by the universal credit. Universal credit is also being phased in but has hit major difficulties in implementation, with the result that universal credit, as we write, applies to some individuals in some parts of Britain but not to others in other parts of Britain. Original plans were to have most of the new benefit in place, and tax credits phased out, by 2015. As we write the date is put at somewhere in 2021.

There are two forms of tax credit: child tax credit and working tax credit. The former was designed to help take families with children out of poverty. The latter was designed to help those with low incomes stay in work. Linked to both aims, one of the main design aspects of tax credits proved to be a complete failure and had to be withdrawn some years ago. The intention was to align the payments of tax credits as a cash payment to lower paid workers and in particular to the earners in lower income families with their receipt of earnings. The credit was intended to be paid as a form of reverse income tax by employers, linking into the PAYE system and paid in pay packets. That failed. All tax credits have been paid, and paid only, by HMRC direct to claimants—in the case of child tax credits usually to the mother whether or not she is an earner. And part of the original scope of working tax credits—supporting low paid workers—has been repealed while other parts have been cut back sharply.

The potential overlap between taxpayers and tax credit recipients has been substantially reduced both by these changes and by the relatively sharp increases in the income tax personal allowance taken together with increases in the national minimum wage and its redesign as the national living wage. The main continuing area of overlap is the help given to those working with children who can claim both a weekly credit for themselves and their children together with a childcare credit if the children are in paid childcare. The importance to a comparison with income tax is that where the total income of the claimants (calculated in much the same way as income tax) is above a threshold then the tax credits are reduced at a rate of 41 per cent. The threshold for child tax credit is £16,105 for 2016/17, so many lower paid families paying basic rate tax will also be subject to this rate. The threshold for working tax credit is £6,420 so is now substantially below the personal allowance and therefore the start of income tax liability.

"The rate of tax"

13–33   What then is "the rate of tax". As this chapter shows, there is no such thing. And individual rates of tax vary from 0 per cent to 100 per cent depending on who is paying and on what the tax rate is levied. These rates are the marginal rates, that is the rate paid on the highest £1 of the form of income being considered. Politically, the question of the marginal rates set at different levels of income is very sensitive. In practice, "the" marginal rate of tax varies from one individual to another depending on what is to be taken into account.

Take for example an employee earning £20,000 a year and another earning £60,000 a year. The marginal rate is the rate paid on the last £1 by each of them. Take first the lower paid employee. She will be paying 20 per cent income tax on that last £1, together with 12 per cent NICs. If she is receiving child tax credit then she is probably losing the credit at 41 per cent for each £1 extra she earns (as her income exceeds the upper limit for child tax credits). If so, she is paying a marginal rate of 20 per cent plus 12 per cent plus 41 per cent on her top £1. Put another way she will see just 27p of it.

Then take the employee earning £60,000. She will be paying income tax on the top £1 of 40 per cent, together with an NIC of

2 per cent. If she also has children, she may be paying 100% on any child benefit she claims, or she may already have lost it. She will not be entitled to tax credit. As child benefit is not taxable at the main rates or for NICs, there is no overlap. So she could be getting an extra 58p for the top £1 or she could be losing the whole £1.

The story complicates further if we then look at others with incomes at similar figures as self-employed individuals, or as single individuals without children, or as pensioners living on pensions and savings.

But what counts for most people, even if they do not see it that way, is the burden of tax—the total tax paid as a percentage of the total income received. Government statistics examine this together with all the main cash and non-cash benefits received. The figures are published for each year in detail in the Office of National Statistics report *The effects of taxes and benefits on household income* available on *GOV.UK* [Accessed 1 June 2016]. The examples show some stark differences in the end results. Overall, for example, a working household on average has an income before all taxes and benefits of £40,962 for 2012/13, while the end result after all adjustments is a net income of £36,614. At the same time the unadjusted income of the average pensioner household was £11,700 while the net income was £21,900. Any discussion of that gets us deep into pension policy as well as tax policy and benefit policy. Our direct taxes are just part of the story.

CHAPTER 14

TAXATION OF COMPANIES

Introduction

14–01   Income tax was invented some time before joint stock companies. While that was a long time ago, its significance is only now leaving our direct tax laws. UK companies do not pay income tax. Nor do they pay CGT. Instead, they pay a tax called corporation tax on both income and capital gains. However, until very recently they did so on the basis of the same laws as those imposing income tax and capital gains tax. We must now look at CTA 2009, which came into effect on 1 April 2009, and CTA 2010 on 1 April 2011. They come into effect for companies whose accounting periods end on or after those dates. We therefore look only at the new law here.

14–02   The new law is, however, much the same in substance as the old law save that it has been entirely re-enacted as a code as part of the Tax Law Rewrite. The general tax law for companies is now to be found in:

- the Capital Allowances Act 2001 (CAA);
- the Corporation Tax Act 2009 (CTA 2009): this sets out the charge to corporation tax and the general rules applying to the taxation of profits and other income of companies generally;
- the Corporation Tax Act 2010 (CTA 2010): this deals with the rates of corporation tax, relief for losses and within groups of companies and special provisions such as leasing; and
- the Taxation (International and Other Provisions) Act 2010 (TIOPA): this deals with the treatment in the UK of taxable profits that may also be liable to tax in another jurisdiction. These provisions are of considerable importance to any British company trading internationally, but are mainly beyond the scope of this book.

Some of the specialist material still lurks in ICTA and subsequent Finance Acts.

Despite the fact that together CTA 2009 and CTA 2010 had 2,515 sections and eight (large) schedules, there was still not enough time (or enthusiasm) to rewrite all the specialist rules, for example about some kinds of insurance companies. What follows is therefore but the bare skeleton of an enormous beast of a tax.

Taxing companies

The charge to tax is now technically to be found in each year's **14–03** Finance Act. If there is such a charge, then the machinery of CTA 2009 and CTA 21010 swing into effect for the year. The charge is led by s.2(1) of CTA 2009:

> "Corporation tax is charged on profits of companies for any financial year for which an Act so provides."

"Profits" are defined as meaning income and chargeable gains (s.2(2)). Section 3 excludes a charge to income tax if a company is UK resident. Non-resident companies may, however, be liable to income tax rather than corporation tax. Section 4 excludes a charge to CGT on any company.

CTA 2009 provides detailed charging provisions for most **14–04** kinds of company profits. It does so in parallel to ITTOIA. As companies cannot be employees (though they can be office holders) the provisions of ITEPA are mostly irrelevant. The charging provisions in CTA 2009 deal with:

- trading income (Pt 3);
- property income (Pt 4);
- loan relationship profits (Pts 5 and 6);
- profits from derivative contracts (Pt 7);
- gains from intangible fixed assets (Pt 8);
- profits from know-how and patents (Pt 9);
- company distributions (Pt 9A); and
- miscellaneous income (Pt 10).

The other general key parts of these Acts are the charging provisions in Pt 2 of CTA 2009, the provisions on tax rates and calculation of profits in Pt 2 of CTA 2010, together with the closing Parts of both Acts.

Parts 11–18 of CTA 2009 and Pts 8–21C of CTA 2010 contain special rules for special forms of activity together with tax avoidance provisions, and must in practice be read with TIOPA whenever there is an international element involved (as there usually is with any big company).

231

What is a company?

14–05　　The definition of "company" is of importance for both income tax and corporation tax. It is therefore to be found in ITA 2007 s.992: "company" means any body, corporate or unincorporated association, but does not include a partnership, local authority or local authority association. A unit trust is deemed to be a company by CTA 2010 s.671, but special rules apply.

However, in practice it is only companies based (to use the technical term, "resident") in the UK that are subject to the full charge to corporation tax. A resident company is subject to corporation tax on all its profits wherever arising (CTA 2009 s.5). In practice, this will be subject to double tax relief if the profits are also subject to tax elsewhere. But a non-resident company is only liable to corporation tax if it carries on a trade in the UK through a permanent establishment (s.5(3)). In addition, from 2016, a company is taxable in the UK if it carries out a trade of dealing in or developing land (including buildings) in the UK. A company is resident in the UK if it incorporated in the UK or its central management and control is in the UK (CTA 2009 ss.13–18 deal with this).

"Permanent establishment" is a complex concept that may broadly be summarised as some continuing base in the UK— though that base may be little more than a computer server.

Why tax companies?

14–06　　It may be asked, why have a tax on company profits at all? Why not simply tax, in the hands of the shareholders, what emerges from the company in the form of distributions? The answer originally was because of the different rates of tax between income tax and CGT. Taxing only distributions would have meant that that would enable a company to be used as a kind of receptacle in which profits could be stored up tax-free; distribution (and hence income taxation) could be avoided by storing up the profits for years on end and then eventually selling the shares (causing only liability to CGT at a flat rate). This "receptacle problem" (a problem for HMRC) is particularly acute in the case of narrowly-owned companies, such as one-member companies and family companies. Special rules were devised to deal with such companies, called "close" companies and, although the harmonisation of income tax and CGT rates has solved *most* of the "receptacle" problems, other possible tax advantages remain. These include the use of investment companies to avoid higher rate tax on "hidden" distributions.

To incorporate or not?

14–07　　The question whether a particular individual or partnership would gain (tax-wise) by forming a company is not easy to answer except in very general terms, or alternatively in minutely particular terms with a full knowledge of all the circumstances of a particular case. In general, a major pointer is the comparison between the individual's marginal rate of income tax and the relevant rate of corporation tax. This has changed very sharply recently. For example, back in 1979 when the first edition of this book was written the top rate of income tax had just fallen from 98 per cent to 75 per cent. The main rate of corporation tax was then 52 per cent. But by 2003 the starter rate for companies had dropped to zero. That was almost too good to be true. Many self-employed individuals turned their businesses into "pocket-book" companies, and turned themselves into directors and shareholders. They paid themselves next to nothing, but took dividends or loans instead. The result? A corporation tax rate of 0 per cent, lower income tax bills, and no NICs to pay. Rules were quickly introduced to stop this in 2004 because of the loss of corporation tax. Those rules are in addition to the provisions that we saw in the chapter on employment income that treat some earnings of the self-employed as being employment income.

Fifteen years later, the rate of corporation tax is dropping to 17, while separate income tax rates apply without offset to those receiving dividends. At the same time both parliament and the courts have taken stringent steps to stop individuals avoiding income tax (and in some cases NICs too) by agreeing to accept dividends rather than earnings.

If a trader or professional does form a company, he or she ceases to be self-employed and is taxable on any earnings from the company (including director's fees) as employment income. If the money is taken out as dividends, then the dividend rates apply.

The change from income tax to corporation tax is done by a discontinuance of the trade (ITTOIA s.202); loss relief (income tax) can be carried forward; and hold-over relief (CGT) is available.   **14–08**

The decision whether to trade individually or by means of a   **14–09** company is not wholly, perhaps not even primarily, a tax decision. There is one great advantage of incorporation, namely limited liability even for a single member company, although for small companies that may be largely illusory in practice. Also, it is easier for a company to arrange finance (either from inside or outside the business) for expansion, particularly by the use of a floating charge. The disadvantage of more (and expensive) paperwork arising from the requirements of the Companies Acts has to some extent been reduced for small companies in recent years. And, of course, it must be borne in mind that some professions do not permit their practitioners to become incorporated.

The tax laws that apply

14–10   The corporation tax, along with income tax and CGT, is under the care and management of HMRC, and the detailed provisions for administration set out in TMA apply to corporation tax. It is important to appreciate, at the outset, that corporation tax *is* the income tax and capital gains tax on companies. Its administration is closely tied in with that of income tax and CGT.

As we have seen, a major achievement of the Tax Law Rewrite was to separate out the corporation tax code from the income tax code and, in so doing, to bring to an end a continual battle to try and pretend that the rules for individuals and companies could be the same. The relevant substantive law is now in CTA 2009 and CTA 2010.

Taxable periods

14–11   Corporation tax is levied by reference, not to "years of assessment", but to "financial years". A financial year begins on 1 April and ends on 31 March. And each financial year is named by reference to only one calendar year and that is the year in which it begins, not the year in which it ends. So the Financial Year 2010 is the year from 1 April 2010, to 31 March 2011. Assessment is on a current year basis; the tax assessment for 2010 being based on the profits of 2010. But where a company's accounting period does not correspond to the financial year, the profits of the accounting period are apportioned into the appropriate financial years. This is important in that the rate of tax may differ in the two financial years.

Companies are subject to self-assessment. Large companies pay the tax due in quarterly instalments during the year, with rather more generous treatment for smaller companies—but then the many small companies pay hardly any serious amounts of tax.

The rate of corporation tax

14–12   The rate at which corporation tax is to be levied in any year is normally set some time ahead. At the time of the first edition of this book the main rate stood at 52 per cent, as a result of which small profits rates and other adjustments and offsets had to be built into the tax system to prevent excessive taxation. The effect of both international competition and the ability of multinational companies to move both their profits and themselves around and out of the UK's open economy has resulted in a completely different approach being taken to corporation tax rates. In 2016 the rate is set at 20 per cent, reducing to 19 per cent for the following years and then 17 per cent in 2020.

As a result the various offsets and in particular a complicated set of provisions about a small profits rate have all been repealed.

Computing profits

Corporation tax is a charge on profits of companies. "Profits" **14–13** means income and chargeable gains (CTA 2009 s.2). The charge is on the profits arising in the financial year (s.8). Where a company is chargeable to corporation tax, it cannot be charged also to income tax or CGT (ss.3 and 4).

The way in which the profits of a company are calculated parallels in a broad way the way in which income and chargeable gains are taxed on individuals. Different kinds of income are chargeable under different charging sections, with exemptions and other special provisions then applying. Quite how extensive those special rules are for companies is much more obvious now that there are specific Acts imposing the corporation tax. CTA 2009 and CTA 2010 between them, in enacted form, ran to 2,515 sections and six schedules. (If you assume that the schedules don't matter, check Sch.4 to CTA 2010. It lists over 400 defined terms in that Act alone. There is a similar number in the same Schedule in CTA 2009).

The key common feature of both sets of tax provisions is that **14–14** there is no comprehensive definition of "profits" or "income". The government consulted while the rewrite exercise was being undertaken on whether to change the basis of the charge to tax on companies, for example by introducing a comprehensive charge. But it decided against such an approach. As a result, the Tax Law Rewrite undertook the redrafting on the basis that tax can only be levied if the particular kind of receipt is within one of the charges to tax in the Acts. In Ch.2 we surveyed the various kinds of income caught by the income tax legislation and noted while doing so whether the same rules applied in general terms to corporation tax. Some do. Some don't. To save us repeating that here, you should turn back to that account.

There are, of course, many small companies set up to act as a go-between for an individual (or family) to deflect income from being received directly by the individual. We saw in Ch.8 (on employment income) the measures taken by parliament, and the views of the courts, attempting to stop earners turning earnings into something else. And we saw in Ch.11 how HMRC is conducting ongoing litigation attempting to invoke settlement anti-avoidance provisions against individuals using companies to deflect income to someone else (for example from Mr Jones to Mrs Jones in *Jones v Garnett*). Although measures were taken in 2012 to encourage disincorporation the practice of running small businesses and employments through pocket book companies has become endemic in some industries and has even invaded the public sector. Further measures have been announced to damp this down, and some measures, such as tax and NI subsidies to those employing apprentices will help this. The position remains fluid and a full analysis of the position of each individual is the only way of securing an optimal answer.

14–15   We need in this chapter to examine some of the provisions that apply to companies and do not apply to individuals (or apply to them in markedly different ways). We attempt to do so without getting too tied up in the details of company law. But it is worth briefly noting aspects of corporate structure that cannot apply to individuals. The first is that the company belongs to its shareholders. So, for example, the trading income of a company is the company's income and cannot be the trading income of the shareholders. The shareholders only get income (or gains) if the company pays the income out to its shareholders by the correct procedure. They receive the income as a company distribution.

Linked with that, it is of course standard for companies to own shares in other companies. For tax purposes, such ownership comes in two categories. The first is where one company controls the other company, or in usual terms the parent company controls one or more subsidiary companies. Where that happens, tax laws need to take account of the activities of the group of companies as a whole, as assets, profits and debts can be passed from one company to another in the group. That is also referred to as direct investment. At the same time, companies may invest in other companies, or use a small shareholding to create or strengthen links between the two companies without one controlling the other. That is referred to as portfolio investment, and requires a different tax treatment.

We turn first to the tax treatment of payments made by one company to another where the other is a shareholder in the distributing company.

Distributions

14–16   Companies raise their working capital in two ways that might seem similar but are fundamentally different for tax purposes. They can borrow money in various ways from lenders, or they can issue shares and capitalise the sums received for the shares.

The fundamental difference is that the payments made to the lenders, whether or not in the form of interest, are in principle deductible costs in earnings the company's profits. So the company does not get taxed on the money it spends paying that interest. By contrast, the sums paid out by a company to its shareholders must come out of taxed profits. So there is a danger of double taxation. The company pays tax on its profits before it distributes them to its shareholders. And its shareholders pay tax on receiving the distributions. That raises an issue of fairness about the taxation of the receipt of dividends, as we discussed in Ch.10. To deal with this, corporation tax and income tax have special rules for dealing with the taxation of distributions. Corporation tax also has special rules for dealing with sums paid and received as part of a loan relationship. We will examine those after noting how distributions are treated.

Loan relationships

What is a distribution?

"Distribution" is defined by Pt 23 of CTA 2010. (The income tax definition is the same: s.989 ITA 2007 and ITTOIA Sch.4.) As that Part is over 100 sections long, those sections being purely about what is and what is not a distribution and how distributions are charged to tax, it is obvious that the term has no simple definition. The key list of matters included is in s.1000. It includes:

14–17

- any dividend, including any capital dividend;
- any other distribution out of corporate assets save for a repayment of capital on shares;
- any redeemable share capital;
- any security issued in respect of shares but not for new consideration; and
- any interest or other distribution in respect of non-commercial securities.

Then there are anti-avoidance and deeming provisions of such a length that the drafters of CTA 2010 put in a section just to explain how they link to s.1000. See s.1001. Put broadly, this is like the duck rule: if it quacks, it's a duck. If a company pays it out in respect of its share structure, it's a distribution; and the fact it is called interest or some other name does not stop it being a distribution if that is so. And again we emphasise that there is no distinction between capital and income distributions. For income tax purposes in particular if it is a distribution it is income.

Close companies

14–18   The scope of the charge on distributions is made even wider if a company is a close company. A company is a close company if it is closely controlled. The relevant rules are in Pt 10 of CTA 2010. The rules defining when a company is a close company are in s.339. Put broadly, a company is a close company if five or fewer people (referred to as participators) control it or it is controlled by participators who are directors; and the participators stand to receive most of the assets of the company if it is wound up. The definition of who is counted is very wide, so that all family members and associates of an individual are counted as the same person as that individual. If a close company makes a loan to a participator, then it is treated as a distribution. If so, then there is a 25 per cent tax charge on the amount of the loan. The law on this issue may bring to mind the words "sledgehammer" and "mouse". That may be so now, but it is because these provisions were once a powerful set of anti-avoidance provisions preventing companies being used to sidestep the high rates of corporation tax that used to apply in the UK.

What is not a distribution?

14–19   The Companies Act gives companies power to repurchase their own shares and to issue redeemable ordinary shares without requiring a court order. The avowed intention of these provisions was to provide small companies with shares which would be attractive to an outside investor in that he could resell to the company and not be "locked-in" with no opportunity to sell the shares. (Private companies in general have no open market for their shares.) But such a repurchase or redemption will be a distribution for tax purposes in so far as it amounts to more than the original investment. The government therefore introduced an exemption from the distribution rules for certain repurchases and redemptions. We may say, however, that the exemption is extremely limited and in some cases will frustrate the intentions of the companies' legislation.

14–20   There is one other exemption from the distribution rules allowed for by ss.1074–1097 of CTA 2010. This will be on a "demerger", i.e. splitting up one company into two or more. In certain circumstances an issue of shares by the original company to the members of the new companies will not invoke the distribution rules. As with purchases and redemptions this relief only applies to trading companies when the de-merger is wholly or mainly for the benefit of the trade. Advance clearance is possible and desirable.

Loan relationships

It is clear from the definitions above that the concept of "distri-   **14–21**
bution" does not follow the simple divide between dividends on
share capital and interest on loans. So before we turn to look at
loan relationships we need to establish the priority rules between
the treatment of distributions and the treatment of loan relationships. This is set out in ss.464–465 of CTA 2009. Save for certain
tax avoidance provisions, if a credit or debit relates to a sum that,
when paid, is treated as a distribution then it must not be treated
as part of a loan relationship. Subject to that, the only amounts
that can be treated as within the scope of the loan relationship
provisions are those in Pt 5 of CTA 2009.

Part 5 of CTA 2009 brings into one set of rules all aspects of   **14–22**
the taxation treatment of profits and losses, both of an income
nature and of a capital nature, that arise from a loan given or
taken out by a company. This is dealt with by s.295 which sets
out the general rule that all profits arising to a company from its
loan relationships are chargeable to tax as income. Any deficit
arising in the same way is to be taken into account at the same
time: s.292. Further, the rules apply whether or not these arise
from a trade: s.299. For these purposes a company has a loan
relationship if it stands in the position of creditor or debtor as
respects any money debt (whether or not this involves a security)
and the debt arises from a transaction involving the lending
of money: s.302. So all forms of corporate bonds and interest-
bearing debt are covered.

The purpose of the loan relationship regime is to provide an   **14–23**
accounts-related treatment to any credits or debits from a loan
relationship. Section 313 of CTA 2009, which allows for this,
shows just how far corporation tax has moved since the disputes
about the interaction between tax law and company accounts.
Section 313(1) provides that:

> "The general rule is that the amounts to be brought into account by
> a company as credits and debits for any period of account . . . may
> be determined on any basis of accounting that is in accordance with
> generally accepted accounting practice . . .".

This has the effect of turning the question of law about what
should be included into a question of expert evidence about
accounting practice. It also takes the matter beyond the scope of
this book, so at that point we leave it.

Intangibles

14–24   The other topic for which the rules about income for corporation tax vary significantly from those applying for income tax is the main topic we looked at in Ch.6, that of intangibles. The relevant rules are set out in Pt 8 (intangible fixed assets) and Pt 9 (intellectual property: know how and patents) of CTA 2009. Here again we see that for corporation tax purposes the underlying approach is often to rely on accounting concepts and to put aside the traditional legal dichotomy with which the separate issues of income and capital were approached. Indeed, this avoids technical problems about the borderline in areas such as software development. And behind that we see another area where EU law can replace the obligations imposed by UK law. We also need to note that, following from this, s.906 of CTA 2009 ensures that any amount brought into account under these rules cannot be brought into account under any other corporation tax charge. In other words, neither HMRC nor a company can claim that the amounts should be treated differently as trading income.

14–25   Section 712 defines "intangible asset" but it does so purely in referential terms: "intangible asset" has the meaning it has for accounting purposes. That and the following sections must be read with the definition of "generally accepted accounting practice" in s.1127 of CTA 2010. Read together these mean that a UK company that makes up its accounts purely under UK practice must follow relevant financial reporting standards (FRS) or similar standards and rules adopted by the professions for the UK. In this case that means adopting the practices set out in FRS 10 (goodwill and intangibles). If the accounts are within IAS rules (international accounting standards) then they may be applied. But if that is so then the company must follow any relevant rules adopted by regulations by the EU. That means any standard adopted under or in accordance with EU Regulation 1602/2002.

14–26   Section 712 makes it plain that intangible assets include intellectual property such as patents, trade marks, registered designs copyright or plant-breeders' rights or any equivalent of those rights in other countries. It also covers any other information or technique not protected by specific rights but of economic value, or any licence to use someone else's rights, information or technique.

14–27   The central approach of the provisions is that any receipt or gain made in respect of any intangible assets is to be taken into account for corporation tax purposes when it is recognised in the company's accounts. Equally, any expenditure on intangibles (including any wasted expenditure because, for example, a development fails) is taken into account for tax purposes when it is taken into the accounts. However, this is subject to a general rule that capital expenditure on assets can be recognised only through the capital allowance system, not by a deduction under these rules.

While the rules in CAA deal with capital expenditure on new assets, and allow such expenditure to be taken into account over a period of years, those rules do not deal with assets created or developed by a company (for example software or website development). Problems can also arise where a chargeable gain is realised from such an asset as it may be that no capital expenditure was incurred in the creation of the asset. So the role of the capital allowance system is of limited importance. **14–28**

Since those reforms the government has introduced further measures both to assist those engaged in aspects of the information technology business and to deter and counteract those using intangibles to shift profits out of the UK. So for example there is special relief for those engaged in the highly successful UK business of generating video and computer games while there are steps introduced in 2016 to impose withholding taxes on royalties being paid by a UK company to an associated company outside the UK but in a lower tax jurisdiction. **14–29**

Deductions from total profits

Having arrived at the total profits of the company the next thing to do is to consider what items are permitted to be deducted in order to determine the amount on which corporation tax is to be charged. There are four kinds of permitted deductions: (1) charges on income; (2) management expenses; (3) minor capital allowances; and (4) losses. We will deal with these in turn. **14–30**

Charges on income
It will be remembered from Ch.13 (Taxation of Individuals) that, for income tax, certain payments out are called "charges on income" and are deductible in computing "total income". Those deductions are separate from the deductions which are expenses in earning the income under any particular schedule or case. The position is similar for corporation tax. Payments out which are expenses in earning the income under a particular schedule or case are deductible in computing the income of a company under that schedule or case. That still leaves some payments out which, although not deductible in computing income, are deductible **14–31**

from (or "against") the total profits of the company. Many payments are not deductible in either way. Those which are deductible against total profits are called "charges on income": CTA 2010 s.189. Or, where a company is a member of a group of companies, it may in certain circumstances "surrender" its excess of charges on income to another company in the group: CTA 2010 s.99.

14–32   There are various conditions with which a payment must comply if it is to count as a charge on income. The conditions are set out in s.189. In summary, a payment is not to be treated as a charge on income in any of the following circumstances: if the payment is charged to capital; if the payment is not ultimately borne by the company; if the payment is not made under a liability incurred for a valuable and sufficient consideration (subject to the rules for charitable donation, below); if (in the case of a non-resident company) the payment is incurred for the purposes of its overseas operations, if it would be deductible in computing the company's taxable profits. It must be made in return for consideration and not just in the hope of receiving consideration. Thus in *Ball v National & Grindlay's Bank* (1973), money paid under a covenant for the education of overseas employees' children in order to retain their services was held not to be a charge on income. It was a hope of a business advantage only. It is an open question whether payment by the company for the benefit of A with consideration supplied by B will be a charge on income.

Investment management expenses

14–33   Part 16 of CTA 2009 allows deduction of management expenses to any company, whether or not resident in the UK, with investment business here. The rules are broadly compatible with accounting practice. The point of this provision is to make up for the fact that a company, unless trading, has no opportunity of deducting expenses of management in the actual computation of profits. "Management expenses" are given a wide meaning by the courts, but they must relate to some act of management and not be part of the cost of acquiring an asset, e.g. a commission paid by one investment company to another company in return for that company's guarantee of a loan raised by the first, was held by the Court of Appeal to be an acquisition and not a management expense. It was part of the price of raising the loan. See *Hoechst Finance Ltd v Gumbrell* (1983). Individuals cannot claim these expenses.

Losses

Losses of companies under corporation tax are dealt with in **14–34** ways similar to losses of individuals under income tax. Let us first make the general point that a loss in a trade is computed in the same way as trading income is computed. In other words, the computation process may lead to a plus answer or a minus answer.

There are two main ways in which a trading loss of a company may be relieved: CTA 20102 ss.37 and 45.

Set-off against current and previous profits

The company may claim to set off a trading loss in any par- **14–35** ticular accounting period against profits of whatever description (including chargeable gains) of that accounting period. If the loss is not in this way completely absorbed, it can be set against the profits of preceding accounting periods, subject to the limitation that the loss can only be carried back for accounting periods falling within the previous three years. Such a claim must be made within two years and relief is given against a later accounting period before an earlier period. The company must have been carrying on the same trade in the carry-back period. Set-off against general profits, but not carry forward relief, is not allowed unless either: (a) the trade is being carried on in the exercise of functions conferred by an Act of Parliament; or (b) the trade is being carried-on on a commercial basis. It will be noticed that (b) above is parallel to a requirement for income tax designed to exclude hobby-trading from the relief. And the special rules for hobby-farming apply to corporation tax as well as to income tax.

Carry-forward

The company may claim to set off a trading loss of one **14–36** accounting period against trading income from the same trade in succeeding accounting periods. Relief is given against the first available year and then each successive year as appropriate.

Company reconstructions

Where a company ceases to carry on a trade and another **14–37** company begins to carry it on, the change of company is ignored if the fundamental ownership (e.g. by shareholding) is (to the extent of three-quarters or more) the same before and after the change of companies. So if Company A has accumulated losses, and its trade is transferred to Company B (and the common ownership test is satisfied) Company B can use the carry-forward provisions and set off the accumulated losses against profits of the transferred trade (but not against other profits): CTA 2010 ss.938–948. There are restrictions if Company A is insolvent at the time of transfer.

Change of ownership

14–38   Sometimes the converse case arises; that is, the company carrying on the trade remains the same but the underlying ownership changes. There used to be a brisk business in the sale of companies which were bulging with unrelieved tax losses. This commerce was largely struck down by a section which is now CTA 2010 ss.673–676. If in any period of three years there is both a substantial change in the ownership of a company and a "major change in the nature or conduct of a trade carried on by the company" past trading losses will not be available for carry-forward relief. A substantial change in ownership is basically a change in the ownership of more than 50 per cent of the voting share capital. Nor is the relief available if "at any time after the scale of the activities in a trade carried on by a company has become small or negligible, and before any considerable revival of the trade, there is a change in the ownership of the company". The point of this latter provision is to strike at what was once a common practice—keeping a company in existence simply because it was big with losses. Similar rules apply to prevent losses incurred after the change of ownership from being carried back against profits incurred before the change under the three year carry-back reliefs.

Group relief

14–39   A company which is a member of a group of companies may "surrender" a loss to another company which is a member of the same group. This enables the transferee company to claim loss relief: CTA 2010 Pt 5. The claimant company must use the relief in the year it was surrendered. A group for this purpose is where 75 per cent of the ordinary shares of one company is owned by the other. The availability of this relief has, however, led to the creation of strange "groups" of companies the object of which is to allow a profitable company to take the benefit of a loss of a company with insufficient profits. This has led in turn to complex anti-avoidance legislation and many complex cases as to what constitutes a group for this purpose. A similar relief is available within a consortium of companies which together own trading companies.

Restrictions on loss relief

14–40   The Chancellor announced in 2016 that two sets of steps would be taken from 2017 to change loss relief. Smaller companies would be given more flexibility in how they used losses from past years to obtain tax relief. But larger companies face having a ceiling put on the maximum amount of loss relief that can be claimed in any year. This is intended to deal with the practice of some international companies of incurring large losses in the UK because of measures to remove what would otherwise have been profits taxable in the UK out of the tax jurisdiction by way of deductions for interest payable on loans from associated companies in other tax jurisdictions or other similar measures.

TAXATION OF CAPITAL GAINS

CHAPTER 15

CAPITAL GAINS TAX

Introduction

CGT is, not surprisingly, a tax on capital gains. It is not a tax **15–01** on income and is generally free from any overlap with income tax. Nor is it a tax on simple ownership of capital (as a wealth tax would be) but only on gains when an asset is disposed of. Both IHT and CGT are concerned, broadly speaking, with the movement of capital from one person to another, but whereas on such a movement IHT charges tax on the whole amount of capital which moves, CGT charges tax only on the gain as between the value it has at the time of this movement (e.g. sale by A) compared with the value it had on the occasion of its last previous movement (e.g. purchase by A). There are a few occasions when there will be a charge to both taxes where some limited relief is available but, on the whole, they are complementary. In general, IHT was designed to tax voluntary transfers whereas CGT was designed to tax commercial transfers. But changes made to both taxes have led to the paradoxical position that lifetime gifts are now subject to CGT and only occasionally to IHT.

Effect of inflation

The policy thinking behind CGT is that it is arbitrary and **15–02** unfair to tax a person on his income (e.g. dividends) and not to tax a person on his capital gains (e.g. buying shares on the stock exchange and selling them at a higher price). The latter is thought of as being as much a taxable resource as the former, although the UK's method of taxing capital gains is, on the whole, more favourable than the taxation of income.[1]

But the theory was initially spoiled by high rates of inflation. If you bought something in 1978 for £400 and sold it in 1982 the probability is that you would have got around £600 for it. On paper you would have made a gain of £200; in real terms, taking into account the fall in the value of £1 due to inflation, you would

---

[1] IFS Tax By Design The Mirrlees Review 325–326.

not have made any gain at all. Until 1982, however, the legislation made no allowance for such a paper gain. In fact the point was tested in court, and in *Secretan v Hart* (1969) it was held that no adjustment for inflation was allowable.

Development of the tax

15–03   The tax was originally introduced in 1965 and taxed all gains accruing after March 1965. Conservative governments between 1979 and 1997 sought to reduce the impact of the tax (by introducing extensive reliefs) and to remedy the perceived injustice of taxing inflated gains. In 1982 a form of index-linking was introduced, which was refined in 1985 so that some relief was available for the effects of inflation from March 1982. Thus if a person bought an asset in 1972 for £1,000 and sold it in 1992 for £11,000 he would have been able to discount from the total gain of £10,000 a sum for inflation from 1982 to 1992. But he was still liable in full for all gains incurred before 1982. In 1988, therefore, it was decided to take out of the charge all gains, paper or real, incurred before 1982 by "rebasing" the acquisition cost of an asset acquired prior to 1982 to the market value as at March 1982. Thus in our example the gain would be calculated by treating the market value of the asset at March 1982, say £7,000, as the cost of acquiring the asset and deducting that from the sale price of £11,000. That gain of £4,000 would then also have attracted relief for inflation between 1982 and 1992.

In 1998 the Labour government decided that, for individuals, there should be no more relief for the effects of inflation but that instead relief should be given according to the length of time that the asset has been held by the taxpayer. The avowed intention was to discourage short-term gains. This taper relief, as it was known, reduced the chargeable gain by a percentage which increased the longer the asset was held, to a maximum achieved after two years for a business asset and 10 years for other assets. This favourable treatment of business assets was balanced by the phased withdrawal of a relief on the transfer of such assets, known as retirement relief. Indexation relief was still available, however, for inflation between 1982 and 1998 and there was still no charge for any gains accruing before 1982. This complex structure whereby the chargeable gain depended upon whether the asset was acquired before 1982, before 1998 or after that date, was abolished as from the 2008/09 tax year. There is no longer any relief either for the effects of inflation or length of ownership. Rebasing to the market value of a pre-1982 asset as at March 1982, however, still remains. At the same time, by way of compensation, the rate of tax was changed from the taxpayer's marginal rate of income tax (e.g. 40 per cent for a higher rate taxpayer) to a flat rate of 18 per cent.

The immediate combined effect of losing the reliefs and changing the rate was that those owning unquoted shares or interests in a business (supposedly tax favoured as wealth-creating) had their effective rate raised from 10 per cent to 18 per cent, whereas the owners of a second home (regarded as luxury assets) had their rate cut from a minimum of 24 per cent to 18 per cent. Further, for all, relief for inflation up to 1998 was lost. As a result of sustained pressure from industrialists after these changes were announced a new form of relief, entrepreneurs' relief, was introduced for 2008/09. In effect that relief reduced the effective rate on certain business disposals to 10 per cent, but initially only on the first £1 million of such disposals during a taxpayer's lifetime. In 2010, the coalition government changed the rates of tax again so that an individual was charged at 18 per cent up to any unused amount of his income tax basic rate band. For gains above that amount, the rate was 28 per cent. The rate for entrepreneurs' relief was held at 10 per cent but the lifetime limit for that relief was raised to £5 million in 2010 and then to £10 million in 2011. Most recently, the standard rates of tax were cut again from 28 per cent and 18 per cent to 20 per cent and 10 per cent for the year 2016/17. These matters are considered more fully at paras 15–05 and 17–16 below.

Companies and individuals

For administrative and assessment purposes CGT, which **15–04** applies only to individuals and not companies, is similar to income tax and is thus subsumed into the system of self-assessment and payment already explained. It is assessed and charged annually and payment is due by 31 January of the year following the year of assessment. For companies, chargeable gains, although computed in general in the same way as for individuals, are then liable to corporation tax and not CGT.

The law relating to CGT was consolidated in the Taxation of Chargeable Gains Act 1992 (TCGA 1992). **Unless otherwise stated all references in this part of the book are to that Act.** Most amendments made since then have been incorporated into that Act. It is, as we shall see, quite a technical tax and there have been many cases for the courts to decide. Those which relate to the principles of the tax are included below.

Rate of tax

15–05   Until 1988 the tax was charged at a flat rate of 30 per cent. Since then, apart from a brief period in 2008/09, the rates have been linked to the thresholds of the basic and higher rates of income tax. Thus, if an individual's taxable income in any year is less than the basic rate band, gains up to that unused portion are taxed at 10 per cent. Gains above that limit are charged at 20 per cent. These rates do not apply to "upper rate gains" which are broadly gains on the disposal of residential property and "carried interest", which are instead chargeable at 18 per cent and 28 per cent. Gains accruing to trustees or personal representatives are charged at 20 per cent, unless they are upper rate gains which are charged at 28 per cent. Gains eligible for entrepreneurs' relief (see para.17–16 below) and investors' relief are charged at a flat rate of 10 per cent. Such gains are set off against any unused amount of the basic rate band before other gains: ss.4, 169N.

To take an example, suppose the basic rate band for income tax in a given year ends at £38,000. X has taxable income for that year of £28,000. Thus X has £10,000 unused basic rate band. Suppose that X also has taxable gains of £30,000 in that year, of which £5,000 are eligible for entrepreneurs' relief. Those £5,000 gains will be taxed at 10 per cent. Of the other £25,000 gains, only £5,000 will be taxed at 10 per cent, as the entrepreneurial gains will be taken to have exhausted half of X's unused basic rate band. The remaining £20,000 gains will be taxed at 20 per cent.

Exempt amount

15–06   An individual subject to CGT can take advantage of the "exempt amount" for each year. This amount is usually automatically increased by reference to any increase in the consumer prices index (CPI), for the 12 months prior to the September in the previous tax year, rounded up to the nearest £100. The amount is specified by a statutory instrument issued in advance by the Treasury for each tax year provided there is an increase in the CPI. Otherwise, it stays the same: s.3. But any increase is subject to an override in the Finance Act. The exempt amount in 2016/17 is £11,100. Tax is therefore only payable in so far as an individual has taxable gains (chargeable gains less allowable losses) in excess of that amount in the year. The exempt amount is in effect the tax threshold for the year in question and so fulfils the same role for CGT as the personal allowances do for income tax. As with the income tax personal allowance (although unlike the IHT annual exempt amount), it cannot be rolled forward or back if unused. Because CGT is charged by reference to a transaction it is therefore possible to allocate such transactions between years so as to maximise the use of this exemption.

Spouses and civil partners

Spouses and civil partners are taxable as separate individu- **15–07** als for CGT as they are for income tax. Thus, for example, they both have an exempt amount. However, there are two consequences for CGT if the spouses or civil partners are living together. For this purpose an individual is deemed to be living with his or her spouse or civil partner unless they are legally separated or the circumstances are such that the separation is likely to be permanent: s.288(3). The first consequence is that a transfer of assets between the parties is treated as if neither a gain nor a loss has occurred (so that the transferee is deemed to have acquired the asset at the price paid by the transferor) (see below) and the second is that they can only have one main residence to qualify for exemption from the tax (see para.16–16). Thus a cohabiting couple can each have a house which they can sell free of the tax, but not so married couples or civil partners.

Trustees and personal representatives

Trustees, who may be liable to pay the tax in relation to **15–08** changes in the beneficial ownership of the trust property, are only entitled to half the annual exempt amount (Sch.1 para.2). Personal representatives, however, are entitled to the full amount for the year of the death and the two following years. After that they cease to have any exempt amount (s.3(7)). Both trustees and personal representatives are taxed at 20 per cent, or 28 per cent on "upper rate gains" (para.15–05).

Residential property

Gains on a property which is the principal residence **15–09** of the person making the disposal are exempt from tax (see para.17–02). Apart from this important exemption, gains on residential property are subject to a variety of CGT "penalties" in comparison to other property. This is an attempt by the government to discourage investment in buy to lets and to encourage investment in companies.

First, gains accruing after 6 April 2016 on the disposal by individuals of residential property in the UK or elsewhere are "upper rate gains" and do not benefit from the reduction in general CGT rates effected in 2016. This means that they are subject to tax rates of 18 per cent (if the gain falls within the basic rate band of income tax) or 28 per cent rather than the rates of 10 per cent and 20 per cent.

Secondly, whilst property situated in the UK owned by a person resident outside the UK is not generally subject to UK CGT, this is no longer true in relation to gains on the disposals of UK residential property. Again, this charge is limited to gains accruing after the date of the introduction of the change, 6 April 2015. The non-resident charge on such gains for individuals is 28 per cent, or 18 per cent where the gains would sit within the basic rate band of income tax (subject to any annual exemption where available). It is also 28 per cent for non-resident trusts, but is charged at normal corporation tax rates when held by a non-resident company. Again, in relation to individuals, the principal residence exemption is available, although this is unlikely for most non-residents.

Thirdly, gains on residential properties in the UK owned through a company are subject to the ATED rules (see para.6–14). The ATED charge only applies to more valuable properties—originally properties valued at over £2 million but extended gradually to properties valued at over £500,000 from 1 April 2016. When a residential property is subject to the ATED charge, it is also subject to capital gains tax at the ATED rate of 28 per cent when it is disposed of by the company. The ATED rate applies to gains which accrue from 6 April 2013 and applies to companies whether or not they are UK resident.

The charge to tax

15–10   Section 1(1) declares:

> "Tax shall be charged in accordance with this Act in respect of capital gains, that is to say chargeable gains computed in accordance with this Act and accruing to a person on the disposal of assets."

This subsection contains in summary form the whole of the law relating to CGT. We shall know that law when we know what a chargeable gain is, how the Act requires computation to be made, what a person is, what an asset is, and, above all, what a disposal is. It is the disposal which triggers the change. This chapter tells us what a chargeable gain is and what amounts to a person, an asset and a disposal; i.e. the basic charge, including the complications caused by settled property. The next chapter concerns itself with the computation of the gain and the final chapter with the various exemptions and reliefs from the tax.

Chargeable gains

All gains, other than exempted gains, are chargeable gains **15–11** (s.15(2)). The chargeable gain is, broadly speaking, the difference between the cost of the asset and the consideration received on its disposal. The cost is usually referred to as the "base cost". It is important to realise that the consideration received by A on a disposal to B will be B's base cost on a subsequent disposal to C. CGT operates thus by charging the gains on an asset by reference to specific events, known as disposals. As we have seen, where an asset was acquired before 31 March 1982, the base cost will be its market value at that date.

Although each asset disposed of in a year of assessment has to be considered separately, the tax is charged on the total amount of chargeable gains in the year after deducting allowable losses (s.2(2)).

The key requirements for a charge are the disposal of an asset by a chargeable person. Let us now examine each of these in turn (in reverse order).

Persons

"Person" has the same meaning as in income tax law. So not **15–12** only individuals are persons but so also are companies and trustees and personal representatives. As we have seen, however, companies are liable to corporation tax and not CGT on their gains. For CGT purposes in all parts of the UK partners in a general or limited partnership are treated separately as individuals for their share of the gains or losses arising from the disposal of partnership assets or other partnership dealings: s.59. The same principle also applies to members of an LLP by virtue of s.59A, even though it is a body corporate. That tax transparency (as it is called) will cease, however, if the LLP goes into liquidation, when the LLP is deemed to have always owned the relevant assets and the members will instead be assessed on the disposal of their interests in the LLP.

Residence, etc.

A person is chargeable to CGT in respect of chargeable gains **15–13** accruing to him in a year of assessment during any part of which he is resident in the UK (s.2). The meaning of "resident" is the same as for income tax (s.288(1)).

On the other hand, the disposal of an asset which is situated in the UK only has tax implications tax for a person who is not resident here in two situations. First, where a person carrying on a trade through a branch or agency in the UK and disposes of an asset connected with the trade (s.10(1)). Secondly, a disposal of residential property situated in the UK by non-resident person under either the ATED rules or the CGT charge on disposals of UK residential property, discussed at paras 6–14 and 15–09.

To prevent an individual from acquiring a temporary residence outside the UK and then disposing of a UK asset free of tax, s.10A provides a charge on such gains realised during a period of "temporary non-residence" (FA 2013 Sch.45 para.110) which is triggered by the individual's return to the UK. The section applies if the individual was resident in the UK for some part of four of the seven tax years prior to departure from the UK, and the period of non-residence is five years or less. In general, the gains or losses will be computed as if the individual had been resident in the year in question but will be charged at the rate applicable in the year of return.

An individual who is resident but not domiciled in the UK is taxed only if the proceeds are remitted to the UK on gains from the disposal of assets outside the UK (s.12(1)), but there are restrictions on the use of losses on the disposal of such assets (s.16ZA–16ZD) and there is no exempt amount (s.3(1A)). In *Young v Phillips* (1984), the disposal of letters of allotment to shares in a UK company, although taking place in Sark, was held not to fall within s.12(1). The letters carried rights enforceable in the UK and so were not assets situated outside the UK.

Assets

15–14 Section 21(1) provides that all forms of property are assets, and this is so whether they are situated in the UK or not. Thus a UK resident is liable for disposal of non-UK assets. (Section 275 et seq. contains rules for determining where certain kinds of assets are situated.) Section 21(1) then declares that assets include: (a) options, debts and incorporeal property generally; (b) any currency other than sterling; and (c) any form of property created by the person disposing of it, or otherwise coming to be owned without being acquired. Notice that head (b) excludes sterling, so that, e.g. a gift of cash is not subject to CGT. On the other hand, head (c) brings into charge things which were never acquired but were on the contrary created by the taxpayer, such as a building, the copyright of a book, and (very importantly) the goodwill of a business[2] which of course may have been built

---

[2] See, e.g. *Butler v Evans* (1980). In *Kirby v Thorn EMI Plc* (1987), the Court of

up from nothing. Some items, as we shall see later, are expressly stated not to be chargeable assets.

Personal and other rights

Since assets are defined by reference to all forms of property it **15–15** is important to note that this will include all interests in property; for example a lease of land is itself an asset as well as the reversion. There was originally some doubt as to whether purely personal rights could be assets for this purpose; these would include assets such as the right of a protected tenant or a right to damages for an action in tort or delict. The problem is that such rights cannot be assigned or sold, but they can, for example, be surrendered. The point was resolved in *O'Brien v Benson's Hosiery Ltd* (1980) where B was appointed a director of the company in 1968 on a seven-year contract. In 1970 the company released him from this contract in return for a payment of £50,000. HMRC sought to assess the company on this receipt on the basis that it had disposed of an asset, viz. its rights against B under the contract. The House of Lords, reversing the Court of Appeal, held that these rights were assets. The fact that the company could not assign their rights did not matter. The important point was that they could be turned to account, as in fact they had been in this case. As we shall see even the fact that an asset has no obvious market value does not prevent it being an asset—one can always calculate a hypothetical market value.

Non-assignable rights under a contract are therefore assets. Can the same be said of a disputed or moral claim? Some assistance may be derived from the decision in *Zim Properties Ltd v Procter* (1985) that a right to sue for damages in the tort of negligence was an asset on the basis that it could be turned to account (e.g. by a compromise settlement). The judge, applying the *O'Brien* test, thought that all such actions would be assets unless clearly frivolous or vexatious. "Assets" is a wider concept than "property". Since in practice the question will only arise if the "assets" are turned into account (e.g. there is a disposal), the *O'Brien* test suggests that all such rights and claims will be assets if the point arises. Put another way, we can almost say that if you can dispose of something in any of the ways possible under the Act, it is an asset.

The determination that a right to sue can be an asset in *Zim*

Appeal held that where a company, having sold three subsidiaries, agreed not to compete with their businesses it had disposed of its goodwill in those businesses. That was an asset. They overruled the judge's opinion that the company was merely fettering its freedom of commercial activity.

Properties caused concern for the legal profession as it extended the scope of CGT to areas which had hitherto not been thought to be affected. For example, a divorce action is defended on the basis of the split of assets and is settled upon agreement to up the payment by one party to the other. According to the *Zim* analysis, the person receiving the capital sum has disposed of his or her right to sue in return for a capital sum, and is subject to CGT on the receipt. Consequently, after discussions between the Law Societies and HMRC, an extra statutory concession was agreed: ESC D33. This is a practical solution. The concession provides that where there is no relevant asset underlying the right to sue, for example in a divorce action, payment is not to be subject to CGT. This was originally unrestricted but now this applies to the first £500,000 of such a payment. If there IS an underlying asset, the payment is related to the underlying asset. In other words, the "right to sue" element is bypassed.

Disposals

15–16   The basic event on which CGT depends, therefore, is the disposal of an asset. It has been judicially pointed out that, subject to certain exceptions such as options, there can be no disposal of an asset unless the asset existed and was owned by the taxpayer prior to the disposal. Thus creating a contractual right to a payment of money is not a disposal: *Burca v Parkinson* (2001). Whenever a disposal does take place, however, a calculation must be made to see whether there has been a gain or a loss or neither.

The word "disposal" has first of all to be given its ordinary meaning before going on to consider the extended meaning given to it by TCGA 1992. In its ordinary meaning a disposal occurs whenever the owner of an asset (which, remember, may be an abstract entity such as a right) divests himself of his entitlement to the asset. Thus the ordinary meaning includes sale, exchange and gift.

Gifts and disposals not at arm's length

15–17   It is very important to grasp that the making of a gift is a chargeable event. At first sight this may seem very odd. Clearly the giver of a gift has made a disposal, but how on earth can he be said to have made a gain? The point was challenged in court in *Turner v Follett* (1973) CA. It was held that a gift is a chargeable event. In s.17(1)(a) it is now enacted that where a person acquires an asset by way of gift, the disposal of it to him (as well as the acquisition of it by him) shall be deemed to be for a consideration equal to its market value. So if a father gives to his son an asset which he bought for £10,000 and at the time of the gift its market value is £14,000, father has made a chargeable (albeit notional or unrealised) gain of £4,000. But remember that if the gift is a gift of sterling there is no charge to *this* tax (though there may possibly be to IHT) because sterling is not an asset; s.21(1)(b). Otherwise, there would be no yardstick against which to measure gains.

Before IHT was introduced in 1986, a gift of an asset potentially attracted both a charge to capital transfer tax (IHT's predecessor) which charged lifetime gifts, and CGT. Since 1986, most lifetime gifts do not suffer an immediate charge to IHT. There is however still the possibility of a charge to both taxes, most commonly where the gift was made within seven years of the donor's death.

ARM'S LENGTH The market value rule for gifts stated **15–18** in s.17 applies not only to a disposal by way of gift but also to a disposal "otherwise than by way of a bargain made at arm's length". The idea is that if two people are closer than arm's length away from each other their dealings may be not wholly governed by commercial considerations, with the result that a deal may be done at less than market value. This might be so, for example, where a person sells a sailing dinghy to a friend. In such a case, if the section applies, the disposal is deemed for the purpose of CGT to be at market value. So if Fred bought a boat for £60,000 and later sold it to Greg for £70,000 when its value was really £100,000, Fred has a chargeable gain of £40,000 and Greg gets a base cost of £100,000.

Where the parties to a transaction are "connected persons" the transaction is automatically treated as a transaction otherwise than by way of a bargain at arm's length; s.18(2). Whether they are connected persons must be judged at the time of the disposal (see, e.g. *Kellogg Brown & Root Holdings (UK) Ltd v HMRC* (2010)). "Connected person" is defined in s.286(2) as follows: "A person is connected with an individual if that person is the individual's spouse or civil partner, or is a relative, or spouse or civil partner of a relative, of the individual or of the individual's husband or wife." And by s.286(8) "relative" means "brother, sister, ancestor or lineal descendant". There are also definitions in s.286 of "connected person" in relation to trusts, partnerships and companies.

Where the parties are not connected persons, as with Fred and

Greg above, the question as to whether they are at arm's length or not is a question of fact, which amounts in effect to deciding whether there was an element of gift involved. In *Bullivant Holdings Ltd v IRC* (1998), it was held that where X purchased a 25 per cent shareholding in a company from Y for £12,500, they were at arm's length and so that was X's base cost, even though X had acquired a 50 per cent holding in the same company on the same day from Z, which had had its market value of £350,000 attributed to it as X's base cost since X and Z were connected persons. In *Mansworth v Jelley* (2002), Lightman J said that a bargain at arm's length meant a transaction between two parties with separate and distinct interests who have each agreed terms (actually or by inference) with a mind solely to his or her own interests.

Where there is a gift or a sale at an undervalue by persons not at arm's length, the donor or vendor is primarily liable for the tax but if he does not pay it, the donee or purchaser can in certain circumstances be required to pay it.

Other market value cases

15–19   Section 17(1)(b) also applies the market value rule to cases where the consideration cannot be valued, or is connected with the loss of employment, reduction of emoluments or is in respect of the provision or services. In *Whitehouse v Ellam* (1995) it was said that there must be a direct link at the time of the disposal between the disposal and the loss of emoluments.

Part disposals

15–20   A "disposal" includes a part disposal (s.21(2)). Thus where a person disposes of less than the whole of an asset (for example a few hectares of a bigger farm) or disposes of less than his whole interest in an asset (for example grants an easement or servitude over his property) that counts as a part disposal of the whole asset and not a disposal of part of the asset (see *Watton v Tippett* (1996)). Generally speaking, the gain accruing on the disposal is calculated by reference to a proportion of the cost of the entire asset. A part disposal, as illustrated by the easement example above, also includes the disposal of an interest in an asset, which interest is created by the disposal and did not exist before the disposal. The grant of a lease (for a premium) by the owner of freehold land is also a part disposal as the freeholder has disposed of part of his interest in the land.

While we are talking of leases let us point out that a premium for a lease is only chargeable to CGT in so far as it is not chargeable to income tax as income from land (Sch.8 para.5(1)). This is part of a wider principle, namely that any sum charged to income tax is not to count as part of the consideration for a disposal for the purposes of CGT (see s.37(1) at para.16–03 below).

Deriving capital sums from assets

There is an extended meaning of "disposal" in s.22(1) where a **15–21** capital sum is derived from assets by their owner, notwithstanding that no asset is acquired by the person paying the capital sum. One example of this is where a shareholder receives a capital distribution in respect of his shares. Another is where an asset is damaged or destroyed and an insurance payment is received. This section also applies to fix the charge on those personal, non-assignable rights and claims, discussed above, which are assets if they can be turned into account. The "turning to account" is the derivation of a capital sum from the asset, hence the disposal and the charge: *O'Brien v Benson Hosiery (Holdings) Ltd* (1979) HL; *Zim Properties Ltd v Procter* (1985). In the latter case it was stated to be a matter for the exercise of common sense as to the asset from which the sum is derived. It might be the right to payment itself or the property giving rise to that demand (e.g. by a vendor of a house). The section was also applied in *Kirby v Thorn EMI Plc* (1987) to a company entering into a restrictive covenant not to compete with the business it had just sold. It had derived a capital sum from an asset (its goodwill). In *British Telecommunications Plc v HMRC* (2006), however, it was held that if the payment is not for giving up rights under an agreement but rather to give effect to the agreement, it has not been derived from an asset.

SPECIFIC CASES Section 22(1) then goes on to say that the **15–22** principle applies "in particular" (i.e. is not limited to) to four defined circumstances: (a) capital sums received by way of compensation for any kind of damage or injury to assets or for the loss, destruction or dissipation of assets or for any depreciation or risk of depreciation of an asset. An example would be compensation for infringement of copyright; another example would be damages paid by a person who negligently caused physical damage to the asset of another; (b) capital sums received under a policy of insurance covering the risk of any kind of damage, etc. to assets; (c) capital sums received in return for forfeiture or surrender of rights, or for refraining from exercising rights. An example would be a payment received by A for releasing B from his obligation under a contract[3]; (d) capital

---

[3] For example, the disposal of the company's rights in *O'Brien v Bensons' Hosiery (Holdings) Ltd* (1979), see para.15–15 above.

sums received as consideration for use or exploitation of assets. This seems to point towards such transactions as the grant of a right to use a copyright. In *Chaloner v Pellipar Investments Ltd* (1996) it was said that this head could not apply where the owner granted a lease over his property. That would be a part disposal under s.21(2). The head might, however, apply where the owner retained full title to the property, e.g. on the grant of a licence.

The question might be asked as to why a taxpayer should argue for a disposal under head (d) rather than for a part disposal. The answer is that a disposal under heads (a)–(d) takes place when the capital sum is received (s.22(2)), whereas a part disposal takes place on the disposal and, as in the case itself, that can affect the computation of the gain. Curiously, s.22(2) does not apply to other disposals caught by the general wording of s.22(1); it only applies to the specific examples in heads (a)–(d).

Loss, destruction and negligible value

15–23   Another extended meaning of "disposal" is set out in s.24(1):

> ". . . the occasion of the entire loss, destruction, dissipation or extinction of an asset shall . . . constitute a disposal of the asset whether or not any capital sum by way of compensation or otherwise is received in respect of the destruction, dissipation or extinction of the asset."

The *entire* loss, destruction, etc. of an asset would normally mean that it had become valueless, so the deemed disposal is a disposal for a nil consideration. The next subsection—s.24(2)—deals with a situation where there has not been entire loss, destruction, etc. but where the value of an asset has become "negligible", interpreted by HMRC as "worth next to nothing". The effect here is that the owner is deemed to have sold and immediately re-acquired the asset at its then market value. It has been held by the First-tier Tribunal in *Barker v HMRC* (2011) that an asset (shares in that case) cannot be of negligible value for this purpose if it has a market value for CGT purposes as calculated under ss.272 and 273 (see para.16–12 below). However, in this case, the shares were accepted as being of negligible value because, taking into account the information that would have been available to a prospective purchaser, the shares would have been unsaleable and therefore had no market value.

The deemed disposal, being at a negligible value, may well give the owner a loss (compared with the price for which he had acquired the asset); the point of the deemed re-acquisition is that if the value of the asset picks up so that there is a gain on its subsequent disposal, that gain is calculated by reference to this new, low, acquisition value. This subsection only applies if the taxpayer makes a claim to that effect.[4]

Buildings In deciding whether an asset becomes entirely **15–24** lost, destroyed, etc. or whether it merely becomes of negligible value, if the asset in question is a building it is treated as an asset separate from the land on which it stands. But the owner is deemed to have disposed of the land (as well as of the building) and also to have immediately re-acquired the land at its then market value. The effect of this is that any loss relief that the owner gets in respect of the building will be reduced by the amount of any appreciation in the value of the land itself since he acquired it.

Effect of insurance and other compensation payments **15–25** Clearly there can be an overlap between s. 24 (the loss of an asset) and s.22 (capital sums derived from an asset). Suppose A bought an asset for £6,000. Subsequently it was totally destroyed. A is deemed to have disposed of the asset for nothing. That produces a loss of £6,000. A few weeks later an insurance company pays A £6,000. That produces a gain of £6,000. The one balances the other, so all in all there is no loss or gain. Of course, the insurance company may pay A less than £6,000, say £5,500, in which case there is an overall loss of £500. Or the insurance company may pay A more than £6,000, say £7,000, in which case there is an overall gain of £1,000.

There are provisions in s.23 whereby in some situations tax on such a gain may be deferred until there is a disposal in the future. This is a kind of "hold-over" relief. ("Hold-over" relief is another splendid piece of tax jargon, to be found nowhere in the dictionary, but everywhere in the Acts. There are several kinds of hold-over relief in CGT, all amounting only to postponements of tax, rather than complete exemptions.) For example, if our friend A spends the insurance money within one year of receipt on buying a replacement asset for £7,000 the £1,000 gain is dealt with by deducting £1,000 from the acquisition cost of the replacement asset. This will have the effect of increasing by £1,000 the gain to A when he comes to dispose of the replacement asset in the future. So A will be in exactly the same position as he would have been in if the asset had never been destroyed. Suppose A sells the

---

[4] The disposal (loss) is deemed either to have taken place at the date of the claim or at any specified earlier time within two years prior to the tax year at the claim, provided the asset was of negligible value at that earlier time (s.24(2)(b)).

asset (the replacement asset) eventually for £9,000. When he sells the asset, he deducts £1,000 from the replacement cost (which was £7,000) so his gain is £9,000 minus £6,000 = £3,000. If the original asset (which cost £6,000) had never been destroyed his gain would equally have been £3,000.

15–26   A somewhat similar system operates where an asset is not destroyed but only damaged.

Timing of a disposal by contract

15–27   Section 28 provides that where an asset is disposed of and acquired under a contract, then, unless the contract is conditional, the time at which the disposal and acquisition takes place is the time when the contract was made and not the time when the asset is subsequently transferred or conveyed. This is of course particularly relevant to a disposal of land by the traditional method of an exchange of contracts which transfers the equitable title or, in Scotland, conclusion of missives, followed by the conveyance or transfer of the legal title.

But there must be a disposal by the contract, even one of land, for s.28 to operate. In *Underwood v HMRC* (2010), the taxpayer agreed to sell some land to B Ltd on a set date but at the same time exercised an option to repurchase it and sold the land to a third party. There was no transfer of the beneficial interest from the taxpayer to B Ltd. The only result was that he paid £20,000 (the difference between the sale and repurchase prices) to the other party. He was in fact simply treated as a debtor of B Ltd after the set off. It followed that s.28 did not apply (the taxpayer was seeking to create a loss in that year).

It is clear that s.28 fixes the date of the disposal, for timing purposes, as being the date of the exchange of contracts but it does not have the additional effect of fixing the parties to the disposal and acquisition (and their interests) as being the parties to that contract, as distinct from those at the date of completion, where they are different.

This was the decision of the House of Lords in *Jerome v Kelley* (2004), reversing the Court of Appeal. In 1987, A, B and C agreed to sell some land to X. In 1989, A and B each assigned half their interest in the land to D. The transfer of the land to X was completed in 1992. The disposal was held not to have been made by A, B and C only, as to their shares in the land in 1987 but by A, B, C and D as to their shares in 1992. (D was a non-resident trust.) The 1989 assignments were part disposals, by A and B to D. That was the straightforward analysis. Section 28 only fixed the date of the disposal as 1987. Their Lordships were, however, concerned with the potential difficulty with this solution if D had not been in existence in 1987. Although a person could dispose of an asset which he did not own at the time, could he dispose of an asset at a time when it, e.g. a trust, did not exist? The point was left open.

Conditional contracts

Where there is a conditional contract, however, the date of the disposal/acquisition is the date when the condition is fulfilled. This condition must be genuine to invoke this delay (see *Kellogg Brown & Root Holdings (UK) Ltd v HMRC* (2010)). In *Lyon v Pettigrew* (1985), it was noted that there are only really two types of cases which are conditional contracts. "One is a 'subject to contract' contract, where there is clearly no contract at all ... and the other is where all the liabilities under the contract are conditional upon a certain event." In that case, which concerned a hire contract agreement, there was no condition precedent: title in part of the property was only to pass on payment of all instalments. The condition must be a condition precedent to the incurring of a binding contractual obligation. In *Hatt v Newman* (2000), contracts for the sale of a property were exchanged in February 1995, with a completion date of 20 March 1995. This was conditional, however, on planning permission for conversion of the building being granted. Planning permission was granted on 29 March 1995 and legal completion took place on 6 April 1995. The taxpayer's argument (made in person) that the disposal had taken place on 6 April (and so in the next tax year) failed. If this was a conditional contract within s.28(2), the date when the condition was satisfied was 29 March. Alternatively, if the condition was merely a condition subsequent to the incurring of binding contractual obligations, then s.28(1) would fix the date of disposal as being in February 1995. (HMRC actually calculated that the taxpayer's liability would have been greater if he had succeeded in his argument.)

Section 28 does not apply to disposals by derivation of a capital sum from an asset under s.22(1)(a)–(d) where, as we have seen (para.15–22), s.22(2) defers the disposal to the time when the capital sum is actually received.

15–28

Appropriations to and from stock in trade

It will be remembered that in income tax where a trader disposes of part of his stock in trade not by sale but for his own use or for some other non-commercial purpose, he must, for the purposes of income tax, bring into his accounts as a receipt the market value of the asset at that time. And of course the converse

15–29

applies—where a trader transfers an item from his own recreational enjoyment into his trade he can show in his accounts the market value of that item as an expense of the trade.

Transfer to stock

15–30   Now, how does CGT bear on these events? Where a person who is a trader transfers a personal asset to his trade that appropriation is treated as a disposal, thus involving a gain or a loss compared with its earlier acquisition cost: s.161(1). But he can, if he wishes, avoid payment of CGT by electing to bring the asset into trading stock—but not at its then market value, but at its market value reduced by the amount of the chargeable gain or increased by the amount of the allowable loss (s.161(3)). (A partner can only make this election if the other partners concur.) Effectively, the trade is treated as acquiring the asset at the price at which the individual acquired it.

Transfer from stock

15–31   In the converse case, where a trader transfers an item of trading stock to himself in a personal capacity he is treated as having acquired it for a consideration equal to the amount then brought into the accounts of the trade in respect of that item for income tax purposes. Thus the closing figure for the item for income tax purposes is taken as the base cost for CGT purposes: s.161(2). For income tax purposes no doubt the trader would like to put a low figure on the item, thus reducing his trade receipts and so his profits. But a low figure for income tax means a low base cost, which will in the end involve him in more capital gains tax.

To some extent, the practical importance of s.161 is reduced by the presence of an exemption from CGT in the case of a disposal of an asset which is tangible movable property and which is a wasting asset: see below at para.17–13. But of course not all stock in trade is tangible movable property. It may be tangible without being movable (e.g. land) or movable without being tangible (e.g. stocks and shares).

Groups

15–32   The benefits of s.161(3) are available to a group of companies if they can ensure that one company transfers a non-trading stock asset to another member of the group in such a way that the asset is acquired by the second company as trading stock (s.171). In this way, e.g. an allowable capital loss may be converted into a trading loss by electing to use s.161(3). The only requirement is that the acquisition must be by a trading company as trading stock. In *New Angel Court Ltd v Adam* (2003), the judge, after considering a number of cases, said that to qualify the transfer must have some commercial justification or conceivable reason, be normal and the asset must not only be of a kind which is sold in the ordinary course of the second company's trade but must also be acquired for the purpose of that trade with a view to a resale at a genuine profit.

Capital distributions by companies

Where a person receives a capital distribution (other than a new holding, on which see the next heading) in respect of shares in a company, he is treated as if in consideration of that distribution he had disposed of an interest in the shares (s.122). This applies for example when a company makes a "rights" issue of shares[5] and a shareholder sells his rights to a third party. Another example of its application is when a liquidator makes a repayment of capital to shareholders in the course of a winding-up. If, however, the amount of any capital distribution is "small"[6] as compared with the value of the shares the occurrence is not treated as a disposal, but instead the amount of the distribution is deducted from the expenditure allowable as a deduction in computing a gain when the shareholder comes to dispose of the shares in the future. This of course has the effect of increasing the gain and hence the tax. It is a kind of hold-over relief.

15–33

Company adjustments

There are detailed provisions (in ss.126–140) as to the bearing of CGT on the re-organisation of a company's share capital, the conversion of securities and the amalgamation of companies.

15–34

These provisions are very detailed but the general principle with regard to reorganisations is that where a shareholder's former interest in the company (the original holding) now involves different shares which represent the original shares (the new holding), the reorganisation is not to be regarded either as a disposal of the original holding or as an acquisition of the new holding. Instead the two holdings are to be regarded as a single asset acquired by the shareholder at the cost of the original

---

[5] This is an issue of shares which are offered first to existing shareholders.
[6] HMRC take the general view that "small" means less than £3,000 or 5% of the value of the shares, if greater. But it is a question of fact and degree: see *O'Rourke v Binks* (1992).

holding. In *Unilever (UK) Holdings Ltd v Smith* (2003), the Court of Appeal held that this principle did not apply where the shareholder held all the shares of one class in the company and the other class was cancelled on a scheme of arrangement. There was no such disposal or acquisition in that case because: (a) cancelling shares is not a disposal; and (b) the rights attaching to the retained shares had not been altered. Thus the retained shares could not be regarded as a new holding as, although they formed a more significant proportion of the shares of the company, the rights attached to the shares were unaltered. An example where this continuity principle will operate is where a company makes a "bonus" issue or a "rights" issue of shares and a shareholder takes up the shares (a "new holding"). The new shares are treated as acquired when the original shares were acquired, and the acquisition cost of the total holding is the cost of the original shares plus the sum (if any) which the shareholder pays for the new holding. In the case of a company amalgamation (or take-over) then, subject to certain conditions, the exchange of shares in one company for shares in another company does not count as a disposal.

Avoidance conditions

15–35   This rule led to a great deal of tax avoidance and the relief has been subjected to two conditions, namely that the change must be effected for bona fide commercial reasons and it must not form part of a scheme or arrangements of which the main purpose or one of the main purposes is avoidance of tax liability: (s.137).

In *Snell v HMRC* (2007), these two conditions were discussed. It was held that provided there was evidence of bona fide commercial reasons for the deal, the fact that the transaction might have been structured differently did not matter. But that in assessing the avoidance test, the tax liability being avoided could be one which was prospective, contingent or simply deferred. In *Coll v HMRC* (2010), it was held that the section applied to all the shareholders involved and not to each one separately.

Debts

15–36   A debt is an asset for CGT purposes. It is intangible property in the hands of the creditor—a right to receive a payment of money. Importantly however, so far as concerns the *original* creditor, no chargeable gain accrues on the disposal (s.251(1)). And the same is true of the original creditor's personal representative or legatee. At first sight this seems very good of HMRC, but the point is really directed against losses. It is a general principle of CGT law that a loss cannot be claimed from a transaction upon which, if there had been a gain, it would not have been a chargeable gain. In other situations, where the debt has been assigned to another by the original creditor, when the debt is paid off, written off, or is assigned to another assignee, on general principles this is a disposal of the debt by the assignee.

Claiming an allowable loss—loans to traders

This principle that the original creditor cannot claim a loss on a debt is modified for debts which prove to be bad debts by s.253, first introduced in 1978. That section was enacted because huge losses had been incurred during the slump of the mid-1970s. It applies where a loan or part of a loan *to a trader* which has been used wholly for the purposes of the trade becomes irrecoverable. In that case, the original creditor or a guarantor can claim the loss as an allowable loss. In *Robson v Mitchell* (2005) CA, it was held that where a trader borrowed money to refinance an existing debt, the purpose of the original debt was the relevant purpose for s.253. Whether it was actually wholly for the purposes of the trade was a question of fact. The court did not express an opinion on whether, since the section did not include the word "exclusively" as in the trading income expenses provisions, if *part* of the borrowed money was *wholly* expended for the purposes of the trade that would suffice.

15–37

Debt on security

The rule that no chargeable gain (and hence—subject to s.253—no allowable loss) can arise to the original creditor (or his personal representative or legatee) does not apply to a "debt on a security." The courts have struggled to decide what exactly amounts to a debt on a security. The most recent decision is that of the Court of Appeal in *Taylor Clark International Ltd v Lewis* (1998). It does not mean the same as a secured debt, e.g. a debt secured by a mortgage or charge. Instead it is said to encompass debts which are really held as investments, and so can lead to a gain or loss, whether protected by a security or not. One important factor seems to be whether the debt is held in a marketable form. The obvious example is loan stock of a company or local authority (see s.132(3)(b)). However, gains on what are known as "qualifying corporate bonds" (company debentures) are exempt from the charge to CGT for individuals and so cannot give rise to any allowable losses (s.117).[7]

15–38

---

[7] Companies may still get relief on such losses under corporation tax rules. As

Assignees

15–39   As noted above, the assignee of a debt (as distinct from the original creditor) does make a chargeable gain (or an allowable loss) when the debt is satisfied, whether it be a debt on a security or not. This rule (if it stood alone) would open the way to a great deal of tax avoidance, because it is very easy to contrive a loss on a debt. So there are provisions to stop up these possibilities. A loss made by a person on the disposal of a debt is disallowed if he acquired the debt from a "connected person": s.251(4). So if A sells a debt to B for £1,200 and later X (the debtor) pays up £1,000 to B, B cannot claim a loss of £200 if A and B are connected persons. If this were not so, and B *could* claim a loss, it would be a way of B making a gift of £200 to A, to which gift HMRC would be contributing.

Property in satisfaction of a debt

15–40   Sometimes a creditor takes property instead of money in satisfaction of a debt. In that case the base cost of the property is its then market value and no more. This looks as though it is going to prejudice the creditor when he comes to sell the property. And so it does in the case of a creditor who is not the original creditor, but is a person who has acquired the debt by assignment. So if A assigns to B a debt of £5,000 for £5,000 and then X (the debtor) hands over to B property worth £4,500 in satisfaction of the debt, the base cost of the property is £4,500. So if, later, B sells the property for £5,200 he has made a gain of £700. But if the *original* creditor (A) (not having assigned the debt) accepts from the debtor in satisfaction of the debt property worth £4,500 the chargeable gain to A, when he comes to sell the property, is not to exceed the chargeable gain which would have accrued to him if he had acquired the property for a consideration equal to the amount of the debt. So if the debt was £5,000, the property was worth £4,500 and A later sells it for £5,200, A's acquisition cost is £5,000 and his chargeable gain is £200 (not £700). These matters are dealt with in s.251(3).

Options

15–41   An option can be defined as "a right, binding in law, to accept or reject a present offer within a specified time in the future" (HMRC CG12300). The grant can be of a right to the grantee to buy assets at a particular price (a put option) or of a right to

to the need for the bonds to be normal commercial loans see *Weston v Garnett* (2005).

sell assets at a particular price (a sell option). It is an asset for CGT purposes, independent of the asset over which the option is granted, not a part disposal of that asset, although where an option is granted and subsequently exercised, the grant and the exercise are treated as part of the same transaction, and any tax paid on the original grant repaid.

For example A grants to B an option to buy certain property (a put option)[8] for £10,000. This is treated as a disposal by A, but if B subsequently exercises the option and buys the property, the sum paid for the option and the sum paid for the property are added together to ascertain the disposal cost (for A) and the acquisition cost (for B). Supposing, on the other hand, that an option is granted but not exercised within its time limit, so expires: A is left with the gain on the grant of the option; for B the expiry of the option does not count as a disposal for the purposes of s.24 (total loss, asset becoming of negligible value, etc.)—with the result that, although he has lost money, he does not get any loss relief. On the other hand if the option is abandoned by agreement for a consideration, i.e. A pays B to release the option, that will be a disposal by B under s.22(1) (derivation of a capital sum from an asset). Thus if the option is released for a nominal amount, loss relief will be available. These and other rules are set out in ss.144–147, as interpreted by Vinelott J in *Golding v Kaufman* (1985).

Options not at arm's length

Where both the grant and exercise of the option take place in circumstances where s.17 would apply (e.g. because they are not transactions at arm's length), the perceived position was that when the option was exercised, the disposal proceeds/acquisition costs were to be calculated by reference to the sum of the market value of the option when it was granted and the amount actually paid under the terms of the option when it was exercised. In *Mansworth v Jelley* (2003), however, the Court of Appeal decided that this was wrong and that the true interpretation of the sections was that the disposal proceeds/acquisition costs should be simply the market value of the asset at the time of the exercise of the option, thus ignoring the cost or value of the option when granted. As a result, s.144ZA was introduced by FA 2003 to restore the position to that which had been applied prior to the decision, i.e. the market value of the option when granted plus the actual sum paid for the exercise of the option.

15–42

---

[8] A put option is where the seller must sell on request. A call option is one where the buyer must buy on request.

Further amendments were made by the Finance (No.2) Act 2005. Principally these are where the exercise price of the option (now generally used in such cases) is such that it would not normally be exercised in a commercial situation (e.g. if in the case of a call option it is greater than the value of exercise price). In such cases the market value of the asset will be substituted.

Value shifting

15–43   This is the dramatic and cryptic heading given to ss.29–34. Section 29 begins with a general introduction, and it then proceeds to deal with four specific situations.

First, if a person having control of a company exercises his control so that value passes out of his shares (or other rights) or out of the shares (or rights) of a person with whom he is connected into other shares (or rights) that is a disposal of the shares (or rights). An example would be if A, who holds the only shares which carry voting rights in a company, were to pass a resolution to transfer the voting rights to the shares held by other shareholders. It is, after all, a kind of gift. For a more sophisticated example, see *Floor v Davis* (1980) HL.

Secondly, if there has been a shift of value as above, and subsequently the transferor disposes at a loss of some other asset which has depreciated in value by reason of the shift, that loss is not an allowable loss.

Thirdly, if there is a sale and lease back of land or other property and then subsequently there is an adjustment of the rights and liabilities under the lease which is favourable to the lessor, that counts as a disposal by the lessee of an interest in the property. The idea behind this rule is that the seller has really sold the property for less than its true value. Suppose A, the owner of a factory, sells the freehold of it to B for £100,000 and B immediately leases it back to A at a rent of £5,000 a year. Later an adjustment is made in the terms of the lease in favour of B, so that in effect B is to get £6,000 a year from the property. On this footing the price that A received for the freehold turns out be less than what he could have got for it, with the result that A paid less capital gains tax on the disposal of the freehold than he "should" have done. This present provision, by treating the adjustment in the lease as a disposal by A, enables HMRC to pick up the lost tax.

Fourthly, if an asset is subject to some right or restriction and then the person entitled to enforce the right or restriction abrogates it, that abrogation counts as a disposal by that person of the right or restriction. An example of this would be if A, who had chartered a ship from B, were to release B from his obligations under the charterparty. That would be a disposal by A of his rights under the charterparty.

Section 30 was enacted (originally in 1977) to strike at some tax avoidance schemes which were based on transferring some of the value of a chargeable asset into a non-chargeable asset. The section is in very wide terms and has the potential to become a general anti-avoidance weapon. It will not apply if the taxpayer can show that tax avoidance was not the main purpose of the scheme.

Sections 31 (enacted in 1989 and amended in each of 1999, 2002 and 2011) is aimed at preventing a group of companies from selling a subsidiary company with a reduced value, having shifted that value into other companies within the group prior to the sale.

Spouses and civil partners

As we have seen, disposals *between* spouses or civil partners **15–44** who are living together at some point in the tax year in which the disposal takes place are treated (by s.58) "as if the asset was acquired from the one making the disposal for a consideration of such amount as would secure that on the disposal neither again nor a loss would accrue to the one making the disposal."[9] Broadly the effect of this is that the transferee takes the asset at the original or base cost which it had in the hands of the transferor. But it is a little better than that, because the words of the section seem to imply that if there are some incidental costs of such a transfer the base cost for the transferee is to include those costs. Thus if H bought an item for £100 and subsequently transferred it to W and the costs of the transfer were £5, the base cost for W (looking to a future disposal by her) would be £105.

Charities

A disposal to a charity by way of gift is also given no gain/no **15–45** loss treatment under s.257. If the charity subsequently disposes of the property which was given to it, and disposes of it at a gain, the gain will not be a chargeable gain if the gain is applicable and applied for charitable purposes.[10]

---

[9] This rule does not apply if (a) the asset is trading stock of the transferor or is acquired as trading stock of the transferee, or (b) the disposal is by way of *donatio mortis causa*.

[10] An outright transfer by a charitable company to another charity is deemed to be applied for charitable purposes: *IRC v Helen Slater Charitable Trust* (1980).

Death

15–46   Until 1971 death was in itself a chargeable event (i.e. as a disposal by the deceased) for CGT thus providing a double charge with estate duty (the predecessor of IHT). FA 1971 abolished the CGT charge and in most cases, any gains to the date of death are simply cancelled. But a person's death still has important consequences—for his or her survivors. Assets held on death are dealt with in s.62 which provides:

> ". . . the assets of which a deceased person was competent to dispose—
>
> (a) shall be deemed to be acquired on his death by the personal representatives or other person on whom they devolve for a consideration equal to their market value at the date of death; but
>
> (b) shall not be deemed to be disposed of by him on his death . . .".

The main point of the phrase "assets of which a deceased person was competent to dispose" is to exclude settled property in which the deceased had an interest. Settled property is governed by different rules which are discussed in the next section. To take an example, if, when A dies, he is the life tenant under a settlement, he is not "competent to dispose" of the settled property. One can speak of property of which a deceased person was competent to dispose as being his "free estate".

Uplift effect
15–47   The effect of s.62(1) is that so far as concerns the deceased's free estate, the death does not give rise to a charge to CGT, but it does give rise to an "uplift" in the base cost of his assets. This, of course, is advantageous for the future. If A bought an asset for £50,000 and later died when its market value was £60,000, the base cost becomes £60,000. On a future disposal of the asset for £65,000, the gain is £5,000 and not £15,000 so that £10,000 gains have been written off. It must be borne in mind, however, that IHT will (or may) be payable on the death of A on the full value of £60,000. Indeed the idea behind the exemption from CGT on death is that death should not be an occasion of charge to both taxes. But it goes a bit further than that, because there is no charge to CGT on death even if there is no charge to IHT either, as for instance where assets are left to a surviving spouse. (See para.20–02 below).

Disposal to legatee

The next question which arises is this: when the personal rep- **15–48**
resentatives come to dispose of the assets in the course of the
administration of the deceased's estate, is that disposal a chargeable event? The answer is that if the disposal is to a legatee that
is not a chargeable event, but if the disposal is to anyone else it is
a chargeable event.

Where a legatee receives an asset from the deceased's estate,
his base cost will be the market value of the asset at the time
of the deceased's death; s.62(4). "Legatee" is given an extended
meaning by s.64(2) and (3). It includes any person taking under
a testamentary disposition (a will) or under an intestacy or
partial intestacy, whether he takes beneficially or as trustee.
And where the personal representatives appropriate assets to
satisfy a legacy, the person taking under the appropriation is
deemed to be a legatee. Also, by s.62(6)–(9), if the deceased's
dispositions are varied by an instrument in writing made
expressly for the purpose of invoking the subsections by the
persons entitled within two years of the death, the variations
do not count as the disposals of the persons entering into the
variation, except such variations as are made for a consideration (other than a consideration consisting of some other variation).

Disposal other than to legatee

A disposal by personal representatives otherwise than to **15–49**
a legatee *does* involve a potential chargeable gain or allowable loss for the personal representatives, who are collectively
treated as a "person" for the purposes of CGT. This is so, for
example, if they sell an asset in order to pay IHT, or if they
simply re-arrange the investment portfolio. There is no provision for personal representatives to offset their losses against
gains of the deceased. As noted earlier, personal representatives
have an annual exemption available for the year of death and
the following two tax years (see para.15–08).

If the deceased had, in the year of assessment in which he died,
an excess of his own losses over gains these may be "rolled back-
wards" as deductions from gains by the deceased for the preceding three years: s.62(2).

Settled property

Definition

15–50 "Settled property" is defined in s.68 as "any property held in trust[11] other than property to which s.60 . . . applies." So the first thing to note is that there must be an actual trust of some sort–contrast the very broad definition of settlement for income tax, for which see para.12–11.

The next task is to find out what s.60 is all about. It deals with the situation where one person is nominee for another person or is a bare trustee for another person. Neither a nominee nor a bare trustee counts as a trustee, and the property they hold is not settled property. The property is treated as though it were vested in the person for whom the nominee or bare trustee is holding it, i.e. the beneficiary. Unfortunately (from the point of view of clarity) s.60 itself does not use the phrase "bare trustee," but there is an illuminating translation of the phrase used in the section, namely

> "trustee for another person absolutely entitled as against the trustee, or for any person who would be so entitled but for being an infant or other person under disability (or for two or more persons who are or would be jointly so entitled) . . .".

The phrase "bare trustee" does occur in the marginal note to s.60. Section 60(2) says this:

> "It is hereby declared that references in this Act to any asset held by a person as trustee for another person absolutely entitled as against the trustee are references to a case where that other person has the exclusive right, subject only to satisfying any outstanding charge, lien or other right of the trustee[12] to resort to the asset for payment of duty, taxes, costs or other outgoings, to direct how that asset shall be dealt with."

Jointly so entitled

15–51 The words "jointly so entitled" in s.60 do not refer only to persons who are technically joint tenants; they cover also persons who are tenants in common. In Scotland, this refers to person who own common property. So *concurrent interests* can exist

---

[11] A unit trust scheme does not count as a trust (nor does an investment trust company). Both count as companies, though with some special rules of their own.

[12] This does not include payment of an annuity under the trust. Thus the presence of an annuity prevents the beneficiaries being absolutely entitled: *Stephenson v Barclays Bank Trust Co Ltd* (1975).

(whether in the form of a joint tenancy or a tenancy in common or in common property) without the property in which the interests subsist being settled property, provided the "tenants" can direct the trustee how the asset shall be dealt with: see *Kidson v MacDonald* (1974). This point is not confined to real property; the word "jointly" refers to "persons who are, as it were, in the same interest", whatever the subject matter of the trust (per Walton J in *Stephenson v Barclays Bank Trust Co Ltd* (1975)). On the other hand it was held in both those cases that where there are *interests in succession* (e.g. where there is a trust for A for life with remainder to B) the trustees can never be bare trustees and the property must be settled property. This is because, although A and B are *together* entitled absolutely as against the trustee, they are not entitled "jointly" and so s.60 can never be satisfied.[13]

Absolutely entitled

If the beneficiaries' interests are contingent (i.e. conditional upon something happening, for example attaining a certain age) they are clearly not absolutely entitled as against the trustees, even if the only contingency is on their obtaining the age of majority. They are not absolutely entitled "but for their infancy" but because they only have contingent interests as they have to survive to that age to acquire an interest in the trust: see *Tomlinson v Glyns Executor Co* (1970). On the other hand, a direction that the property shall be payable to the beneficiary *when* (rather than *if*) he or she attains the age of majority will mean that the beneficiary is absolutely entitled to the property but for their age.

15–52

The essential criteria for a bare trust is that the beneficiary (or beneficiaries) must be able to direct the trustees as to how to deal with the trust property and to give a valid receipt for it. Actual transfer is not required, just the right to do so: *Stephenson v Barclays Bank Trust Co Ltd* (1975). This has been applied to what are known as "putting arrangements." Thus where all the members of a private company transferred their shares to trustees and subjected themselves to restrictions on transfer they were held to be absolutely entitled since they could collectively end the trust and so destroy or override any discretions or powers vested in the trustees.[14] Similarly where a family entitled to farming property set up a trust in which each member's interest was equivalent to their previous entitlements there was held to be no

---

[13] In *Booth v Ellard* (1980) it was accepted that the interests of the beneficiaries must be concurrent and all must be the same. See also *Harthan v Mason* (1980).

[14] *Booth v Ellard* (1980).

settlement for CGT purposes.[15] The importance of this is that there is no exit charge if one member takes his interest out of the trust: there can be no disposal if the same person owns the property before and after the event (see para.15–58 below).

Class and individual gifts

15–53 On the other hand, in the case of class gifts, e.g. "to such of my grandchildren born within 21 years of my death", the beneficiaries cannot be absolutely entitled until the class has closed, i.e. there can be no more potential beneficiaries. Until then the size of each grandchild's share is unknown.[16] Different considerations apply where each potential beneficiary has a defined share, irrespective of how many satisfy the contingency, e.g. "one quarter to each of my grandchildren who attains 21". In this case when each beneficiary attains a vested interest (i.e. attains 21) the question of whether he becomes absolutely entitled to that part of the settled property depends upon whether he can require the trustee to appropriate that part of it to him. In the case of land held on trust, for example, under English law no single beneficiary can require the trustees to sell the land and allocate a share of the proceeds. Only where all the beneficiaries have satisfied the contingency could such a sale be enforced by them. Thus in *Crowe v Appleby* (1975) where only one beneficiary had satisfied the contingency, it followed that he was not absolutely entitled against the trustees. The position would usually be different if the trust property consisted of money or quoted securities which are easily divisible.

If the trustees are not bare trustees then "any property held in trust" is settled property.

Trustees of the settlement

15–54 Section 69 provides that the trustees of a settlement are to be treated as a single and continuing body of persons. This is irrespective of any changes in the actual trustees themselves. Liability for the tax falls on those trustees in that capacity and not as individuals (s.65). Thus the trust through the trustees has a separate identity for CGT purposes. Therefore, the residence, etc. of the majority of the trustees fixes the residence of the trust for CGT purposes.

In that context, it was held in *Jasmine Trustees v Wells & Hind* (2007), that persons operating as trustees de son tort (those

---

[15] *Jenkins v Brown* (1989).

[16] For this purpose any individual is deemed to be capable of having children until he or she dies: *Figg v Clarke* (1997).

acting as trustees but not appointed as such) were not trustees of the settlement within s.69. Thus their residence did not count. As to their liability, they would be personally liable under s.1, but their acts would also be the acts of the proper trustees since they would be absolutely entitled to any trust property as against the trustees de son tort and s.60 could apply.

Disposals and settled property

We must now consider the events connected with settled prop-   **15–55**
erty (as defined above) which count as disposals.

Putting property into a settlement

A transfer of property into a settlement (but not a bare   **15–56**
trust under s.60) is a disposal of the entire property which thus becomes settled property (s.70). This is so even if the donor takes some interest as a beneficiary under the settlement or is a trustee or the sole trustee of the settlement. This is a pretty harsh rule. Suppose Mr Smith wishes to give his house to his nephew, but to retain for himself the right to occupy the house for the rest of his life, so that the nephew will only come into occupation when S dies (S for Smith and also for "settlor"). S can only carry out this transaction by putting the house into settlement. It is a transfer of property into a settlement and so it is treated as a disposal of the entire property. That means that the deemed consideration for the disposal is the whole capital value of the house. This does not accord with the reality, because in reality all that S has given away is the remainder interest. The same point can occur the other way round: S may want to allow his aged aunt to live in the house for her life. He makes a settlement under which the aunt gets a life interest and he retains the remainder interest. There is a charge to tax based on the value of "the entire property" when this transfer is made. In reality all that S has given away is a tiny fraction of the value of the entire property.

Actual disposals by the trustees

Trustees, as we have seen, though they are not "individu-   **15–57**
als," are "persons", and they are chargeable to CGT at the fixed rate of 20 per cent (or 28 per cent where the disposal is of residential property—see para.15–05) after the trust's annual exemption (see para.15–08). They are chargeable, for example, on gains made in the course of switching investments in the trust's portfolio. Where the settlor or the settlor's spouse or civil partner had an interest in the settlement the

gains were, up to 2007/08, taxable as if they had been realised by the settlor and not the trustees but this rule no longer
applies.

Deemed disposal on a person becoming absolutely liable as against the trustees

15–58   Under s.71(1) the trustees are deemed to have disposed of the
assets (or part of them) comprised in the settlement whenever a
beneficiary becomes absolutely entitled to the property (or part).
This is subject to a few exceptions where the reason for the absolute entitlement is the death of another beneficiary.

Suppose assets are held in trust for A contingently on his
attaining the age of 25. When A becomes 25 that is an occasion
of charge under s.71(1). The assets are deemed to have been disposed of by the trustees and immediately re-acquired by them, in
their capacity as bare trustees within s.60(1), for a consideration
equal to their market value. After that it makes no difference
whether the trustees hand over the property to A at once or keep
it as bare trustee for him. The actual handing over of the property to A is not a chargeable event because it is deemed to be A's
already by virtue of s.60(1). The upshot is that the trustees pay
tax on the gain represented by the increase in value of the assets
between the time when they were put into trust and the time when
A became 25, and A takes as his base cost the market value on the
day when he attained 25.

15–59   LOSSES   If an asset has fallen in value so as to create a loss
on the deemed disposal by the trustees, that loss is transferred
to A only if the trustees cannot either set it off against gains
arising in the same deemed disposal (e.g. A becomes absolutely
entitled to several assets, some showing a gain, some showing a
loss) or against trust gains earlier in the same tax year (ss.71(2)–
(2D)). For this purpose such a loss is deducted from trust gains
before any other losses. But A can only use that loss to offset
a subsequent gain by him (in that year or subsequently) on the
disposal of that asset, or if the asset is land, any asset which
is derived from it. Any such losses are a first deduction before
other losses.

Limited exceptions to the deemed disposal rule

15–60   In certain situations, since 2006 rather limited, IHT charges
the whole settled property where the holder of a life interest in
a settlement dies. To avoid a potential double charge therefore,
CGT does not apply where a beneficiary becomes absolutely
entitled as the result of a death of a prior beneficiary where

there would also be a potential charge to IHT. This is achieved by providing that there is an acquisition by the trustees at the value at the date of the death, but no corresponding disposal by them (s.73). In effect therefore, not only is there no charge but there is also an uplift in the base cost of the trust property, such as there is, as we have seen, on the death of an individual.

Until 2006, there was a universal charge to IHT on the death of the prior beneficiary in all such "fixed interest" trusts. But then the law was changed so that that type of IHT charge was limited to a few categories of prior interests (the remainder being subsumed into the more draconian discretionary trusts regime—see Ch.22). At the same time therefore the no-disposal/uplift exceptions for CGT were limited to those specific categories. As these categories are set out extensively in IHT law we will only refer to them by name here.

The exceptions in s.73 are therefore limited to where a person becomes absolutely entitled on the death of a person having one of the following interests:

1) an immediate post-death interest (see para.22–11 below);
2) a transitional serial interest (see para.22–13 below);
3) a disabled person's interest (see para.22–12 below);
4) an interest in a trust for a bereaved minor (see para.22–48 below); and
5) the death under 18 of a person entitled under an age 18-to-25 trust (see para.22–53 below).

Revertor to settlor

Even those limited exceptions to the deemed disposal rule are qualified if the person becoming absolutely entitled on the death is the settlor. This is known as revertor to settlor.   **15–61**

The background to this point is that no IHT is payable on the death of X in those limited situations where X has been given a life interest by S (settlor) in such terms that the property reverts, on X's death, to S. If in this situation S could also get, on the death of X, an uplift in the base cost for purposes of CGT that would be too favourable to S. So he cannot: see s.73(1)(b). If, on the life tenant's death, property reverts to the disponer (settlor), the disposal and re-acquisition shall be deemed to be for such consideration as to secure that neither a gain nor a loss accrues to the trustee. Thus, suppose S grants a life interest to X in property which at the time of the grant is worth £10,000. X dies at a time when the market value of the property is £14,000. The property reverts to S. The trustee is treated as re-acquiring the asset for

£10,000 (not £14,000) and that figure (£10,000) becomes S's base cost.

Termination of a prior life interest in possession—no-one becoming absolutely entitled

15–62   This situation is dealt with by s.72(1). Naturally, the termination of an interest in possession by the death of the person entitled to it and the absolute entitlement of some person often happen on the same event. If property is held in trust for A for life with remainder to B, the event of A's death brings about the termination of a life interest (A's) *and* the absolute entitlement of some person (B). In this situation it is ss.71(1) and 73 which apply. Section 72(1) applies only where there is a termination of an interest in possession by the death of the person entitled to it but still no one becomes absolutely entitled. This would be so, for example, where property is settled on A for life, remainder to B for life, remainder to C absolutely, and A dies. On A's death there is the termination of his interest by his death but no one becomes absolutely entitled; B becomes entitled for life and so s.72(1) applies. On B's subsequent death (or surrender) s.71(1) applies, because C does then become absolutely entitled. If B died before A, however, s.72(1) would not apply since B's interest is not in possession. Nor would s.71(1) apply because no one would become absolutely entitled.

Section 72(1) provides that there is a deemed acquisition (but no disposal) by the trustees at the then base price if there is a death of the person entitled to the interest in possession. As in s.73, there is no corresponding disposal by the trustees so that there will be an uplift in the base price. But also like s.73, after 2006 this only applies if that interest was one of the five types set out in para.15–60 above.

Person entitled to the interest

15–63   It is important to note that the limited exemption from charge and base uplift given by s.73(1)(a) and the limited base uplift given by s.72 (which we have just been speaking about) only apply where the event causing a person to become absolutely entitled or causing the termination of an interest in possession is the death of the person *entitled* to the interest. If A is life tenant with a relevant interest (with remainder to B) and A dies still holding the life tenancy, there is no charge to capital gains tax, only an uplift. But if A assigns his interest to X, there is a charge when A dies, even though X's interest comes to an end on A's death. B becomes absolutely entitled, and s.71(1) imposes a charge to tax. The charge is not relieved by s.73(1)(a) for the reason that B's becoming absolutely entitled is not caused by the death of the person *entitled* to the interest because A was not (at death) *entitled* to it.

Similarly, if A is life tenant with a relevant interest under a settlement for A for life, then for B for life, then for C absolutely. If A is still holding the life tenancy when he dies there is the termination of a life interest and an uplift of the base price, because the termination arises on the death of the person entitled. But if A had assigned his interest to X there is a charge on A's death; s.72(1) does not apply and there is no uplift of the base price.

The charge to tax under s.71(1) which arises on the death of a former life tenant who has assigned his interest will be in addition to a charge to IHT.

Transfers between trusts

Creation of separate settlement

Trustees are liable for CGT in respect of their own settlement. **15–64** As we have seen, by virtue of s.69 the trustees for the time being are regarded as one body for this purpose, so that there is no charge on a change of trustees. The position is more complex, however, where under a power in the settlement the trustees transfer assets to another trust, of which they may or may not be the trustees. The crucial question is whether that second settlement can be regarded as a separate settlement or as merely a subsidiary part of the first. If they are separate settlements then it appears that the trustees of the second trust will become absolutely entitled as against the trustees of the first, and an charge can be made under s.71(1), discussed above. In *Hoare Trustees v Gardner* (1978) the judge decided that the second trustees need not be *beneficially* entitled as against the original trustees, nor did the section require them to be *absolutely* entitled as against the whole world (clearly they were not so as against the second beneficiaries). This was so even though the trustees of both trusts were identical.

Subsidiary settlement

If the second settlement is, however, merely a subsidiary of **15–65** the first trust then the trustees of either trust will be liable for the gains of both but there will be no exit charge. This has been a particularly useful device for HMRC where one set of trustees is non-resident and so not chargeable to the tax. In *Roome v Edwards* (1982) Lord Wilberforce laid down the test to determine whether there are one or two settlements as follows:

"The question whether a particular set of facts amounts to a settlement should be approached by asking what a person, with knowledge of the legal content of the word under established doctrine and applying this knowledge in a practical and common-sense manner to the facts under examination would conclude."

In that case, since the original settlement was still in existence and the second settlement was treated as being held on the trusts of the first as added to and varied by the first, the two settlements could be treated as one.

Making the distinction

15–66   Each case depends upon its facts and there are no golden rules. Separate administration and separate trust accounts may be relevant.[17] In *Bond v Pickford* (1983) the Court of Appeal drew a distinction between trustees transferring property under a power which altered the operative trusts of a settlement, thus allowing removal of the assets from the original settlement altogether (referred to as powers in the wider form) where there would be a charge under s.71, and powers in a narrower form which do not confer such authority. In that case a power to allocate funds for discretionary beneficiaries which were subject to the rules of the trust was held to be a narrower form power. The trustees of the original settlement continued to be responsible in that capacity for the allocated funds.

HMRC have indicated in a Statement of Practice (SP 7/84) that there will be no charge under s.71(1) (and so no separate settlement) if there is an exercise of a power in the wider form if either it is revocable or where the trusts declared are not exhaustive so that they may at some time come back into the trusts or reference still has to be made to the trustees' original powers of administration or disposition. There will equally be no deemed disposal if the duties of the trustees of the second settlement fall to the trustees as trustees of the first. Separate identity of the trustees is irrelevant, as is the location of the mechanical powers of the trustees. However, in *Swires v Renton* (1991), Hoffmann J suggested that even if the funds were transferred under a wider form power the question remained as to whether there was a new settlement or whether it was being "grafted onto" the existing settlement. If any reference back to the original settlement was required then this would indicate that no new settlement had been created.

---

[17] Vinelott J in *Ewart v Taylor* (1983) regarded this as an important factor, together with the fact that the transfer to the second settlement was part of a scheme to wind up the first, in finding that the two settlements were separate.

Tax position of the beneficiaries

The general rule

The legislation is not notably generous to trustees or benefi- **15–67** ciaries, but beneficiaries do have one crumb of comfort. It is to be found in s.76(1). If a person, other than the settlor or settlor's spouse or civil partner, is holding an interest under a settlement and that interest was created for his benefit, then, unless the trustees are non-resident, in general no chargeable gain arises if he disposes of his interest. Thus, suppose property is held in trust for A for life with remainder to B absolutely. If A assigns (e.g. sells or gifts) his life interest that is not a chargeable event. The same is true if B sells or gifts his remainder interest. And if it happens that B dies while A is still alive, B's personal representatives can sell B's remainder interest without tax arising. But a person who acquired an interest for consideration in money or money's worth (other than consideration consisting of another interest under the settlement) and then sells the interest is liable to tax on any gain involved. So if X bought A's life interest (or B's remainder interest) and then sold it at a gain he would be liable to tax. And if X, having bought B's remainder interest and still holding it when A died, would be treated as disposing of the remainder interest in consideration of obtaining the settled property itself and so a charge to tax would arise: s.76(2).

Settlor, spouse or civil partner

There is an exception to the general rule that the disposal of **15–68** a non-purchased interest is not a chargeable event where the relevant interest is held in a settlement in which the settlor or his spouse or civil partner has an interest. Where such an interest, whether owned by the settlor or not, is disposed of for actual consideration (other than another interest in the settlement) the trustees will be deemed to have made a disposal of the assets to which that interest relates to themselves at market value: s.76A and Sch.4A. Unless the interest is in a specific fund or in a specific fraction of the income or capital, this means a deemed disposal of all the trust assets. This is intended to prevent, e.g. a settlor transferring an asset into a settlement (using one of the roll over reliefs) and then selling his interest in the settlement, thus effectively transferring the asset tax free. Liability for the tax falls on the trustees, but they have a right of recovery from the person disposing of the interest.

Adjustments

15–69   The legislation also permits adjustments of the interest of several beneficiaries amongst themselves without a charge to tax arising. "Partition" of settled property is quite a common occurrence. A, a life tenant, may surrender his life interest in part of the trust property in return for an interest in the capital. A is not treated as acquiring his interest in capital for money or money's worth because he has acquired it in exchange for "another interest" (i.e. his life interest) "under the settlement" and that does not count as money or money's worth. Consequently, if A were to carry out the above transaction and then sell his interest in capital (a remainder interest) at a gain, he would not be liable to tax.

Payment of the tax

15–70   A beneficiary may become liable to pay tax which has been assessed on the trustees. This will be so where the tax is not paid within six months of its due date and the asset concerned or a part of it or the proceeds of it are transferred by the trustees to the beneficiary. He can be assessed at any time within two years from the due date on the chargeable gain or, in the case of a transfer of a part, on a proportionate part of the chargeable gain; s.69(4).

CHAPTER 16

GAINS AND LOSSES

Introduction

Essentially the amount of a chargeable gain or of an allow- **16–01**
able loss is arrived at by comparing the consideration received
on the disposal of an asset with the cost of its acquisition. What
we must now do is to look in more detail at the way in which the
computation is done. If the asset is a foreign asset the consideration received and the costs of acquisition must first be converted
into sterling at the rate of exchange applicable at each event so
that the gain or loss may be affected by fluctuations in exchange
rates.[1] Further, by s.16(1) of TCGA 1992 a loss is to be computed
in the same way as a gain.

We will look first at the general rules of computation laid down
in Pt II, Ch.I (ss.15–20) and Ch.III (ss.37–52). Following the abolition of the reliefs for inflation (indexation relief) and length of
ownership (taper relief) as from 2008, those rules alone will now
produce the chargeable gain. That will then be subject to a charge
to tax once the total exceeds an individual's exempt amount for
the year.[2] The rate depends on whether the individual has any
unused income tax base-rate band (see para.15–05), whether the
gains relate to residential property (see para.15–09) or are subject
to entrepreneurs' relief or investors' relief (see para.17–16). Next
we shall look at the special rules where the asset disposed of was
owned by the taxpayer on 31 March 1982. These are necessary
because it should be remembered that no gains accruing before
then are taxable. Finally we look at the position where the computation produces a loss rather than a gain.

---

[1] *Bentley v Pike* (1981); *Capcount Trading v Evans* (1993) CA. This is not the
    position with regard to income taxation.
[2] Companies pay corporation tax on their chargeable gains and have no exempt
    amount. Trustees and personal representatives are charged at 20 or 28 per cent.
    The rate for certain business disposals is 10 per cent under entrepreneurs' or
    investors' relief. See para.17–16 below.

General rules—computing the chargeable gain

Income receipts and expenditure

16–02   First, there is to be excluded from the consideration for a disposal any sum which is charged to or taken into account for income tax (s.37). The purpose is of course to avoid a double-charge to both taxes. An example would be the whole of the consideration for the sale of an asset by a dealer in such assets. The section also applies to exclude those gains which are specifically charged to income tax, such as certain insurance policies and lease premiums, even though the amount is arrived at by a statutory computation (*Drummond v HMRC* (2009)). Special rules apply to assets which have enjoyed capital allowances.

Similarly expenditure which would be allowable in an income tax computation is not allowable for CGT (s.39). It does not matter that there was insufficient taxable income against which the expenditure could have been set.[3] In making this decision the section requires that the asset is presumed to be a fixed asset of a trade and the question asked whether the expenditure would have been allowable in an income tax computation of that, hypothetical, trade (the statutory hypothesis).[4] Since under income tax law extensive repairs may be carried out to an asset and still be allowable for that tax (*Odeon Cinemas Ltd v Jones* (1972)) this, in practice, restricts many claims.

Consideration

16–03   This is basically the value received for the asset. Usually the value received will be in the form of money but it could be in the form of goods, as the exchange of assets is a disposal. Remember also that in a number of cases, the market value of the asset disposed of displaces the actual consideration (ss.17 and 18): where the transaction is otherwise than at arm's length (e.g. gifts and sales at an undervalue), where it is between connected persons, and where consideration cannot be valued. See para.16–12 on the determination of market value). Apart from this, genuinely bad bargains will not be overridden.Sometimes the relevant consideration may depend upon the terms and form of the transaction adopted by the parties. In *HMRC v Collins* (2009), on a true construction of an agreement, the sum received was part of the consideration for the sale of some shares. The fact that the money was payable to a company at the taxpayer's direction and

---

[3]   See, e.g. *Raha v HMRC* (2010).
[4]   See, e.g. *Emmerson v Computer Time International* (1977) CA.

the agreement specified what the company was to do with the payment was irrelevant.

The courts will apply the agreed terms of the parties unless they are a sham or a fraud. It is not open to the taxpayer or the commissioners to argue that some other construction should be put upon the agreement simply because it would have achieved the same economic effect and be more advantageous or disadvantageous for tax purposes.[5]

Disposals for a deferred or contingent consideration: s.48

Suppose that A sells an asset to B for £100,000 payable immediately and £10,000 per month payable for the next 10 months. Alternatively, in addition, suppose that A and B contract that B will pay another £40,000 should planning permission be granted. In the first example, part of the payment is postponed (i.e. deferred) and in the second, it is not only postponed, part of it may never be paid (i.e. it is contingent). **16–04**

Section 48 anticipates these problems and makes it clear that no allowance is to be made for the fact that any part of the payment is deferred or is contingent. In the first example above, A will be treated as having disposed of the asset for £100,000 + 10 x £10,000, or £200,000. In the second, the deemed consideration is £240,000. In both cases, he is deemed to have received this amount at the date of sale, i.e. in accordance with s.28, just discussed. If it turns out that A never receives the full amount accounted for, s.48 again provides that the original tax computation is adjusted, with a repayment of tax where appropriate.

The position is more complex in relation to disposals where part of the consideration cannot be precisely identified at the date of sale. This has caused problems which had to be resolved by the House of Lords in *Marren v Ingles* (1980). In that case the taxpayer agreed to sell 60 shares in an unquoted company for £700 each, payable immediately, and further sum if the company was subsequently floated on the stock exchange, calculated by reference to the share price when floated. It was not possible to work out what that further sum would be until it was known what the share price on flotation was. When the company was floated the purchaser became liable to pay the taxpayer £2,825 for each share. Clearly there was a disposal of assets for at least £700 each but how to deal with the additional amount?

---

[5] Per Lightman J in *Spectros International Plc v Madden* (1997). See also *Fielder v Vedlynn Ltd* (1992); *Collins v HMRC* (2007) SpC.

Section 48, which provides that deferred or contingent consideration be added back onto the proceeds of the disposal as if paid at the time, can only apply if the deferred or contingent consideration is ascertained or ascertainable at the date of disposal. The solution in *Marren v Ingles* was to assume TWO assets and TWO disposals. The first disposal is that of the actual asset, as, for example in that case, shares. The consideration for the shares is the sum of the immediate consideration PLUS the value of the second asset—this is the right to the unascertained future sum. The second asset is valued on an actuarial basis at the date of the first disposal. The second, deemed, disposal is of the second asset, and is made when it becomes clear that a future payment will be made (or not) and at what amount. For example, assume A disposes of shares for £100,000 payable immediately and a percentage of company profits in three years' time. The actuarial value of the right to the future payment is £10,000. A is treated as disposing of the shares for the sum of the cash immediately paid and the right acquired—£110,000. In three years' time, she receives further consideration, based on the company profits, of £25,000. She is treated as disposing of the right to receive a future payment (the second asset) for £25,000. This asset has an acquisition cost of £10,000, and thus A has a gain of £15,000. Had she received nothing for the right (for example the shares did not reach the predetermined price), she would have a loss of £10,000 on the basis that her asset had become worthless. It this latter event, she could elect under s 279A for the loss on the second disposal to reduce the gain on the original disposal—one of the few situations where a loss can be set against gains generated earlier years of assessment).

16–05   An example of these rules of interpretation by the courts and the operation of s.48 is the case of *Garner v Pounds Shipowners and Shipbreakers Ltd* (2000) HL. The taxpayers sold an option to purchase land to M for £399,750. That money was paid to independent stakeholders who were to pay over the money only when the taxpayers obtained the release of some restrictive covenants over the land or as directed by M. If the taxpayers failed to obtain those releases then the money was to be repaid to M unless M decided in any event to exercise the option. The releases were achieved by the taxpayers at a price of £90,000. The stakeholders then paid £309,750 to the taxpayers and £90,000 to the holders of the restrictive covenants. In the event the option was never exercised. The question therefore arose as to what was the consideration for the grant of the option (and not the land).

The taxpayers had argued that they should be treated as having disposed of the option for the sum they received, or

£309,750. The House of Lords held that the consideration for the grant of the option was the full £399,750. In doing so they distinguished the earlier case of *Randall v Plumb* (1975). In that case consideration for an option to purchase land was paid directly to the grantors of the option on terms that they would have to repay part of it if planning permission was not subsequently obtained. Walton J. allowed a discount from the consideration paid for the option by taking into account the contingent possibility of repayment, which is permitted as an adjustment (subject to s.49).

The House of Lords expressly approved that decision but said that it had no application to the present case since the whole amount was paid to the taxpayers and no part of it was ever repaid to M. A payment to a third party did not alter the consideration received by the taxpayers for the grant of the option since it was clear that the parties had agreed that the payment of £399,750 was for the grant of the option only and not for both the option and the taxpayer to obtain the release of the covenants. The parties were bound by their clear agreement. If the contingency was directly related to the value of the consideration (as in *Randall v Plumb*) it could be taken into account in computing its value but if it was related to matters which did not directly bear upon that value it did not follow that it should be taken into account. As we shall see in a moment they were also unable to deduct that £90,000 as allowable expenditure.

The principle in *Garner* was applied by Park J, in *Burca v Parkinson* (2001) where A sold his shares to B having agreed to pay 60 per cent of the proceeds to C. The whole consideration had been received by A for tax purposes. The judge also said that the position would have been the same even if, which was not the case, A had received that amount as trustee for C; A had still disposed of 100 per cent of the shares himself and the total amount paid by B was the consideration for that disposal.

Contingent liabilities: s.49

16–06 Any obligation which might arise after the disposal of property in relation to that property can be regarded as a contingent liability. Warranties and representations given by the seller of shares might be regarded as one example, the facts in *Randall v Plumb*, discussed above, is another. Whilst in *Randall v Plumb*, a contingent liability was taken into account in determining the consideration for disposal, s.49 does not permit such liabilities to be taken into account in three situations, which will on the whole cover many contingent liabilities. The three categories are— liabilities of a person assigning a lease for defaults on a lease prior to the assignment, liabilities on the disposal of land arising out of a covenant for quiet enjoyment either as sellor or lessor and any contingent liability in respect of a warranty or representation made on the disposal by of sale or lease of property other than land. Where s.49 applies, there is no immediate deduction given but should the liability crystallise, the original computation is reopened, and account taken of the sum now due by the person making the disposal. So the difference is between an estimate of the value of a liability at the date of disposal (taking into account the likelihood of it occurring, etc.) but no adjustment whether it actually occurs or it doesn't and, under s.49, a "tax in full now, adjust later" process—ultimately accurate but slower.

Section 49 was considered by the Court of Session in the case of *Morrison v HMRC* (2014). In that case the taxpayer sold his major shareholding in a company, making a considerable gain. During negotiations, statements were made about profit forecasts by the taxpayer—but in his capacity as a director of the company and not in his personal capacity. These forecasts turned out to be overly optimistic and an action against him by the purchasers for misrepresentations made in his capacity as a director was settled by him on payment of £12 million. He argued, successfully in the end, that the contingent liability he incurred in his capacity as a director should be retrospectively taken into account under s.49. The court took the view that it did not matter, under the terms of s.49, that the liability was undertaken with his director's hat on, whilst the disposal was made wearing his owner's hat and permitted the deduction.

Allowable expenditure

16–07   The gain (or loss) is computed by deducting the allowable expenditure from the consideration. As we shall see the expenditure may in some cases be increased by way of a relief to counter the effects of inflation up to 1998. Section 38(1) provides the following heads:

1) expenditure wholly and exclusively incurred in the acquisition of the asset (together with the incidental costs) or, if the asset was not acquired, the expenditure incurred wholly and exclusively in producing it (e.g. the expenditure incurred in writing a book and thereby creating a copyright). Where the taxpayer acquired the asset on a market value disposal to him, e.g. a gift, that will form his acquisition cost;

2) expenditure incurred wholly and exclusively for the purpose of enhancing the value of the asset being

expenditure reflected in the "state or nature" of the asset at the date of disposal (e.g. extensions to a building).[6] In *HMRC v Blackwell* (2015) the Upper Tribunal took the view that the expenditure must be reflected not just in the asset as held by the seller, but in the bundle of rights and obligations acquired by a purchaser. So expenditure to get out of a prior contract which placed restrictions on the owner's disposal of shares was not relievable as there was no consequential alteration of the shares which were acquired by the purchaser. Expenditure incurred wholly and exclusively in establishing, preserving or defending one's title to, or right over, the asset (e.g. the costs involved in taking out probate) is also deductible;

3) the incidental costs of making the disposal.[7] In *Administrators of the Estate of Caton v Couch* (1997), it was held that whilst the cost of employing a valuer to value shares in a private company was allowable as an incidental cost of their disposal, subsequent costs in negotiating that value with HMRC and in (successfully) appealing against an assessment were not so allowable.

WHOLLY AND EXCLUSIVELY The expenditure under (a) and **16–08** (b) must be "wholly and exclusively" for the acquisition of the asset or for establishing, preserving or defending title to the asset. This has enabled the court to disallow an acquisition cost where acquiring the asset was part of an avoidance scheme.[8] In *IRC v Richard's Executors* (1971) the House of Lords, by a narrow majority, held that those words must be given a reasonable interpretation. They allowed the costs of obtaining a valuation for estate duty purposes as an expense establishing title since such a valuation was a necessary prerequisite for obtaining their title to the estate.

In *Garner v Pounds Shipowners and Shipbreakers Ltd* (2000)[9] the taxpayers also failed to have the £90,000 paid to the owners of the restrictive covenants deducted from the consideration

---

[6] There must be an identifiable change in the state or nature of the property: *Aberdeen Construction Group Ltd v IRC* (1978); *FD Fenton Will Trusts v HMRC* (2007); *Raha v HMRC* (2010) (52TC281) at 290: ". . . what [Section 38(1)(b)] is looking for is, as the result of relevant expenditure, an identifiable change for the better in the state or nature of the asset, and this must be a change distinct from the enhancement of value".

[7] IHT payable on a gift may also be allowable if a claim is made for roll-over relief on a gift of business assets; see para.17–25.

[8] *Eilbeck v Rawling* (1982).

[9] See para.16–05 above.

for the grant of the option under either paras 1) or 2). Since the option could have been exercised by M whether or not the restrictive covenants were removed, payment to achieve that could not be said to be wholly and exclusively incurred by the taxpayers in providing the option for the purposes of para.1). Further, for para.2) neither the obligation nor the payment of £90,000 was reflected in the value of the option (as opposed to the land itself) at the date of the agreement. The option was to purchase specified land at a specified price. In effect the expenditure was extraneous to the option and it was even arguable that the obligation to remove the covenants was part of the asset (option) being disposed of so that it could not also be expenditure relating to it. As the House of Lords pointed out, the position might have been different if M had exercised the option, since the £90,000 may then have been deductible from the purchase price for the land itself as distinct from the option.

16–09 APPORTIONMENT   Expenditure or consideration received on two or more assets may be apportioned between those assets if it is just and reasonable, so that where a company sold the shares of a subsidiary company and agreed to waive a debt owed to it by that subsidiary, the consideration received for the sale of the shares was held to be divisible between the two disposals—the sale of the shares and the waiver of the debt: *Aberdeen Construction Group Ltd v IRC* (1978). If, however, the consideration for the shares and the waiver are expressed as separate sums no further adjustment can be made: *Booth (EV) (Holdings) Ltd v Buckwell* (1980).

16–10 CONTRACT PRICE   In the absence of fraud or collusion, the acquisition cost (base price) is the value placed on the amount provided by the parties in the contract at the date of the acquisition. Thus if an asset is acquired by a company issuing new shares, credited as fully paid up, to the vendor, it is the value placed on those shares by the parties which forms the acquisition cost of the asset to the company for any subsequent disposal: *Stanton v Drayton Commercial Investment Co Ltd* (1982). HMRC's argument that market value should apply was rejected. Expenditure, to be allowable, however, must be in money or money's worth. In *Oram v Johnson* (1980) personal work by the taxpayer on renovating an old cottage was not allowed as an expense as enhancing the value of the asset; nothing had passed out from the taxpayer. If he had used a builder the expenditure would have been allowable. Certain kinds of expenditure are not deductible, notably expenditure on insuring an asset in respect of damage, injury, loss or depreciation. Another notable non-allowable expenditure is the payment of interest (except as provided by s.40 in relation to loans for construction work taken out by companies where the resulting building, etc. is being disposed of).

DEEMED DISPOSALS It will be recalled that there are many **16–11** instances where there is deemed to be a disposal (and re-acquisition). Can there be incidental costs of such a notional disposal? Section 38(4) says (rather laconically):

"Any provision . . . introducing the assumption that assets are sold and immediately re-acquired shall not imply that any expenditure is incurred as incidental to the sale or re-acquisition."

It has been held in the courts that real expenditure on a notional disposal is allowable (e.g. legal costs), but that notional expenditure is not. Real lawyers' fees could arise, for example, in respect of a deemed disposal and re-acquisition by trustees on the death of a life tenant. Such real fees are deductible. But where the deemed disposal and re-acquisition arises because the asset in question was held by the taxpayer on 31 March 1982 (see para.16–18 below) the taxpayer cannot say:

"If I had really sold and re-bought the shares on the stock exchange on that day I would have incurred brokers' fees and stamp duty, and I claim to deduct those notional expenses."

MARKET VALUE Deemed disposals and rebasing assets **16–12** owned prior to 31 March 1982 (see para.16–18 below) assume a disposal and reacquisition of the asset at market value. The statutory test for market value is the same as that for IHT (see para.21–32 below). Thus s.272 provides that market value means "the price which those assets might reasonably be expected to fetch on a sale in the open market" with no reduction for the fact that all the assets are being placed on the market at the same time. For the interpretation of s.272 see the cases on IHT (para.21–32 below).

A common problem with that test is that certain assets, especially shares in private companies, have restrictions on their sale so that in the real world there is no open market to provide a value. The answer is that, as for IHT, one has to imagine a hypothetical market (see para.21–34 below) in which any prospective purchaser of the shares has all the information which a prudent prospective purchaser might reasonably require on a private sale at arm's length (s.273). This hypothetical market can, however, take account of an actual prospective purchaser (see, e.g. *Marks v HMRC* (2011)). One unresolved problem is the value of such shares where value enhancing rights attaching to them are not available to any purchaser, hypothetical or real (see *Grays Timber Products Ltd v HMRC* (2010)).

16–13   VAT   A word must be said about VAT. If VAT has been suffered on the purchase of an asset but that VAT is available as input tax for set-off in the purchaser's VAT account, the cost of the asset for the purposes of CGT will be the cost exclusive of VAT. Where no VAT set-off is available, the cost will be inclusive of the VAT which has been borne. Where an asset is disposed of any VAT chargeable as output tax will be disregarded in computing the capital gain (because the disponer will have to pay over the VAT to HMRC). If the disponer is not selling in the course of a business VAT is not chargeable.

Part disposals

16–14   Where there is a part disposal the amounts of acquisition or production expenditure (see 1) above) and subsequent expenditure (see 2) above) have to be apportioned between the part disposed of and the part retained (s.42). The apportionment is done by applying to the total of expenditure the fraction:

$$\frac{A}{A + B}$$

where A is the consideration for the part disposal and B is the market value of the property retained. To take an example, suppose Mr Smith owns an asset which has a base cost of £10,000 and he sells part of that asset for £7,000 and the market value of the part he retains is £21,000. The "attributable" expenditure from the £10,000 is:

$$£10,000 \times \frac{£7,000}{£7,000 + £21,000} = £2,500$$

So the gain on this part disposal is £4,500 (i.e. the difference between the sale consideration (£7,000) and the attributable expenditure (£2,500)). The balance of expenditure (£7,500) which was not allowed on this part disposal is carried forward for use on any future disposal of the part of the asset which was retained.

Wasting assets

There is a restriction on the amount of expenditure that may **16–15** be deducted in respect of what are called "wasting assets". A wasting asset means (per s.44(1)) an asset which has a predictable life not exceeding 50 years. Plant and machinery are expressly regarded as having a life not exceeding 50 years. The residual or scrap value of the asset is deducted from the acquisition cost and the resulting sum is written-off on a straight line basis over the life of the asset. Let us take an example. Suppose Mr Jones bought an asset which had a predictable life of 30 years. He paid £10,000 for it. Ten years later Mr Jones sold the asset for £8,000. It has a scrap value of £1,000. The computation for calculating the gain on the occasion of the sale goes like this:

Proceeds of sale		£8,000
Less: cost	£10,000	
Deduct scrap value	£1,000	
	9,000	
Deduct written-off amount		
$\dfrac{10}{30} \times £9,000^{10}$	£3,000	
	£6,000	
Add on scrap value	£1,000	
	£7,000	£7,000
Chargeable gross gain		£1,000

Notice that this procedure, on the above facts, converts what at first sight looked like a loss (cost price £10,000; sale price £8,000) into a gain. The idea behind this is that if you buy a wasting asset and use it for a number of years and then sell it you have had the enjoyment of part of its useful life and you have sold it when its prospective useful life is diminished. So the Act deals with this situation by providing that the buying price must be notionally reduced to take account of the enjoyment of the asset which you have used up.

LEASES   A lease is a wasting asset when its future duration is **16–16** 50 years or less. But for leases the straight line basis of writing-off is not used. What is used is a fixed Table set out in Sch.8. On this Table the line of wastage is curved and it accelerates as the lease approaches its end since leases depreciate more rapidly towards the end of their life.

---

[10]   This is the writing-off. 10 is the length of ownership; 30 is the life of the asset.

Charging the gain to tax

16–17   Having calculated the total gains (i.e. the consideration for each disposal less the relevant allowable expenditure) of an individual in a tax year then, from 2016, insofar as they exceed the exempt amount for that year, they are charged at either 10 or 20 per cent (18 or 28 per cent if the disposal is of residential property) (s.4), or carried interest. The appropriate rate depends upon the individual's marginal rate of income tax. (It assumes that the gains are added on to the individual's total income for that year. Then insofar as they would still fall within the basic rate band for income tax they are charged at 10 or 18 per cent. Other gains are charged at 20 or 28 per cent.) By way of exception, gains eligible for entrepreneurs' relief or investors' relief are charged at 10 per cent.

From 1982–2008, figures used were the actual rates for income tax as appropriate. The actual amount payable, however, was lowered by a two stage reduction in the amount of the chargeable gain. This was first to allow for the effects of inflation from 1982 until 1998 (indexation relief), and then according to the length of ownership from 1998–2008 (taper relief). The result was the need for quite a complex calculation.

When those reliefs were abolished in 2008, a single flat rate of 18 per cent was imposed. There was an outcry, however, with regard to business assets. Until 1998 these had been given favourable treatment under the inappropriately named retirement relief, and from 1998–2008, taper relief had been much more generous to business than to other assets. Now they were to be shorn of any relief. The answer was the rapid introduction of entrepreneurs' relief in 2008 and the effect was to reduce the effective rate on the disposal of certain business assets to 10 per cent, but only on such gains up to £1 million over an individual's lifetime. That relief still applies today (see para.17–16 below). The rate is still 10 per cent, but the cumulative lifetime total is now £10 million

Rebasing—assets owned before 1 April 1982

16–18   All assets acquired before 31 March 1982 are treated as if they had been acquired at market value at 31 March 1982 (s.35). This takes all gains accrued before 31 March 1982 out of the charge to tax and is referred to as "rebasing". Where the taxpayer has acquired the asset after 31 March 1982 on a no gain/no loss transfer, e.g. as between spouses, from a transferor who owned the asset on 31 March 1982, the transferee is also deemed to have owned it then and rebasing will apply.

Special rules for shares—pooling arrangements

Until indexation relief was introduced in 1982, shares of the **16–19** same class in the same company held by a taxpayer were treated as a single asset, i.e. a pool of shares. Every time some were bought they were added to the pool (and the acquisition cost added to the acquisition costs of the pool) and when some were sold they were deducted from the pool and charged as a part disposal of the single pooled asset. Thus, if half the shares were sold, half the allowable expenditure of the pool was available.

This simple rule doesn't work when the computation of the gain depends on knowing when the shares were acquired—necessary for both indexation relief and taper relief and complex identification arrangements were in place until 2008 to accommodate these reliefs. Today, the length of ownership since 1998 and the effects of inflation between 1982 and 1998 are no longer of any relevance in computing the gain, but as anti-avoidance devices, two identification rules (the same day rules and the "bed and breakfasting" rules) are maintained.

THE CURRENT POSITION Subject to two exceptions, all shares **16–20** of the same class in the same company are treated as forming a single asset (a share pool (s.104). It is irrelevant when they were acquired.

SAME DAY RULE The first exception to the single pool **16–21** concept is that any shares disposed of must first be identified with any such shares acquired on the same day (s.105).

BED AND BREAKFASTING RULES The same day rule would not **16–22** on its own prevent what was known as "bed and breakfasting". That was a simple tax planning device whereby the taxpayer could utilise his annual exemption by selling a number of shares at a gain at the close of business on one day and buy them back again at the start of trading on the next day. The number of shares sold could be calculated so that the gain thus incurred would be equivalent to the exempt amount for the year. Thus there would be no actual charge to the tax, the annual exempt amount would have been utilised and the base price of the shares raised to the repurchase cost. Given the short time between the disposal and acquisition, there was limited risk to the owner of a significant share differential between sale and repurchase. Accordingly any shares sold must first be identified with any such shares acquired in the next 30 days after the disposal (s.106A). Thus there will be no gain and so no uplift in the base price. This will not, however, prevent a spouse or civil partner selling shares, giving the proceeds to the other spouse or partner who then buys the shares back with those proceeds.

Losses

16-23   We want to collect together under this heading certain leading points about losses. Some of the points have been mentioned before; some are new.

Losses are, in general, computed in the same way as gains: s.16(1).[11] If a transaction is such that a gain (if there had been one) would not be a chargeable gain, then if a loss occurs (instead of a gain) that loss is not an allowable loss; s.16(2). This provision has some very important consequences. A good example arises in connection with the disposal of private residences, gilt-edged securities or qualifying corporate bonds.

Loss relief
16-24   CGT is charged on the total amount of chargeable gains in a year of assessment after deducting any allowable losses (s.2). To the extent that there are insufficient gains in the year in which the loss was incurred, they can be carried forward indefinitely to reduce future gains.

16-25   EXEMPT AMOUNT   In relation to losses which are incurred in the same year of assessment as any chargeable gains, the losses must first reduce these gains, even if to do so wastes the annual exemption for that year. However, somewhat curiously, if the losses are not used in the year in which they occurred but are rolled forward against future gains, they only reduce gains which are not covered by the annual exemption (s.3(5A)). For example if, in year 1, Ben has incurred losses of £10,000 and gains of £7,000, the gains are reduced to nil, leaving only £3,000 of losses to be carried forward. £7,000 of loss relief has been wasted, as the gains would not have been taxed as a result of the annual exemption. If Ben decides to delay the disposal which gives rise to a gain until year 2, he will not waste any of the loss relief. If he again makes gains in year 2 of £7,000, no loss relief is used, as the gain is covered by the annual exemption, and he still has £10,000 of relief to roll forward to year 3 and so on.

Losses incurred in a disposal to a "connected person" are only

---

[11] In general, losses must be realised but remember the deemed disposal provisions where an asset has been destroyed, extinguished or become of negligible value, where an allowable loss may be claimed.

allowable against gains made on subsequent disposals to the same connected person: s.18(3).

CARRY BACK Losses may only be carried *back* against **16–26** gains of previous years on three occasions. First, under s.62(2), where the loss is incurred in the year of the taxpayer's death, the loss may be carried back for three years. Secondly, where the loss accrues in respect of a mineral lease it may be carried back for 15 years. The third is where the disposal of the asset was partly for contingent consideration, or what HMRC calls unascertainable deferred consideration, i.e. in the *Marren v Ingles* type of case which we dealt with in para.16–04. Remember in such a case where, e.g., shares are sold say for £100,000 and a percentage of the price of those shares if the company is floated on the stock exchange, there is an immediate disposal both of the shares and of the right to the as yet unknown additional payment. The consideration for that right is deemed to be an actuarial value which takes into account the possibilities of actually getting the money.

Sections 279A–279D are concerned with the situation where the taxpayer subsequently sells that right to the contingent payment, say three years later, for less than that actuarial value, thus incurring a loss in that later year. The taxpayer may have no gains against which to set off that loss, so he is now entitled to elect so that that loss is deemed to have accrued in the original year of the contract. That will reduce the gain on the original disposal. Any other gains available in that year must be used first. If necessary the carried back loss can be used against gains of the intermediate years. As with other losses, no carried back loss need be used to cancel gains up to the exempt amount.

CHAPTER 17

EXEMPTIONS AND RELIEFS

Introduction

17–01   This chapter discusses three different types of reliefs. The first is the exemption. An exemption arises where either some asset is expressed not to be a chargeable asset or some gain is expressed not to be a chargeable gain. More commonly, given the types of assets in this category, exemption prevents the taxpayer from claiming a capital loss, so is not necessarily a good thing for the taxpayer. The second type of relief gives a reduction in the rate of tax paid. Under this head we shall discuss the important relief, entrepreneur's relief, which applies to certain business disposals, including the disposal of shares. Where it applies, the rate of CGT is reduced from 18 per cent or 28 per cent to 10 per cent. The third type of relief is hold-over or roll-over relief. This type of relief has the effect of *deferring* the charge to tax on a disposal, but generally catches the gain on some subsequent event. A common characteristic of this third category is that it generally applies when it would be unduly harsh or inconvenient to charge tax *at this precise point*. Often in the disposals to which this relief applies, cash is not received for the asset, or, if cash is paid for the asset, it is spent on purchasing a replacement asset.

Remember that there is an annual exemption for all gains accruing to an individual up to the exempt amount for the year in question (see para.15–06).

Private Residences

17–02   This important exemption is dealt with in TCGA ss.222–226B. A gain on the disposal by an individual of a dwelling-house or part of a dwelling house, together with a certain amount of land attached, is not a chargeable gain if the house was the individual's only or main residence. This exemption takes most people's main asset out of the charge to CGT and is extremely important in a country where most families now own their own homes, which are generally of ever-increasing value. But that benevolence does not extend (as we shall see) to IHT; for that tax a private residence is no different from other property. The CGT exemption does not apply if the house was acquired wholly or partly for the purpose of realising a gain from its disposal: s.224(3).

Sole or main residence

To get the full CGT exemption the house must have been the **17–03** individual's only or main residence throughout his period of ownership, ignoring any period of ownership prior to 31 March 1982, except that it does not matter if it has not been such for all or any part of the last 18 months of his ownership (reduced from three years in 2015/16 except in relation to individuals who are disabled or who have moved into a care home: s.225E). The point of this exception is (we take it) to meet the case where an individual has moved to a new house before he has been able to sell his old one. If the house has not been the taxpayer's only or main residence throughout his period of ownership a fraction of the gain is exempted corresponding to the period of occupation.[1] In certain circumstances a period of absence can be disregarded. These include periods where the taxpayer was employed abroad and any period not exceeding three years. Where the taxpayer has to live in job-related accommodation the exemption will apply to a house bought as a future main residence even if he never lives in it.

TEMPORARY OCCUPATION The relief applies to a **17–04** dwelling-house or part of a dwelling-house which is or has been at any point the taxpayer's sole or main residence. The First-tier Tribunal docket is littered with claims by owners that temporary periods of occupation amount to occupation of a main residence. As noted above, the last period of ownership is treated as occupation provided the property is established to have been a main residence for even a short period which is likely to explain some of these attempts. The reduction of this final period from three years to 18 months may reduce some of this litigation.

In *Goodwin v Curtis* (1998), the Court of Appeal upheld a decision of the General Commissioners that mere temporary occupation of premises by a taxpayer may not be sufficient to make it his residence for the purposes of the relief. There must be some degree of permanence and continuity or expectation of continuity. In that case the taxpayer had already advertised

---

[1] As in *Henke v HMRC* (2006) Sp Comm. The land was bought in 1982 but the house was not occupied until 1993.

a farmhouse as being for sale before he moved into it. He lived in it for just over a month until the sale was completed. In the view of the Court of Appeal the facts indicated that there was an insufficient degree of permanence for it to be his residence. Each case will depend on its facts, but the important criterion will be the intention of the taxpayer when he occupies the house and not the length of occupation. The text is qualitative rather than one which looks at the length of occupation. A clear intention to occupy the house permanently will be sufficient, even if he has to move out after a short time, e.g. because he has changed jobs, whereas a longer period of occupation which is always temporary may not be so. On the other hand, occasional occupation over a longer period, but purely to renovate and sell the property, will not suffice.[2]

Dwelling-house or part of a dwelling-house

17–05   What amounts to a dwelling-house or part of a dwelling-house for this relief has been the subject of several cases. It has been held to include a caravan (admittedly connected to mains services),[3] but that is always a question of fact.[4]

More difficulties have arisen as to what amounts to part of a dwelling-house where there are other buildings close to the main house in the same ownership. Earlier cases tended towards the application of a functional test so, for example, the disposal of a bungalow built in the grounds of a house for the gardener and housekeeper[5] was given relief. Similarly, in *Williams v Merrylees* (1987) Vinelott J held that a lodge built some 200 yards from the main house could form an entity with the main house, the dwelling-house being split up into different buildings fulfilling different functions. The scale and layout of the buildings was important. Other cases have applied an additional test—the "closely adjacent test". Again in 1987, Walton J applied a much more precise (and restrictive) test in *Markey v Sanders* (1987). To succeed in a claim for relief the taxpayer would have to show that the second building: (1) increased the taxpayer's enjoyment of the first dwelling; and (2) was very closely adjacent to it. Since the employee's bungalow in that case was a long way from the main house and was screened from it, the judge was able to decide that it did not form part of the taxpayer's dwelling-house.

---

[2] See, e.g. *Springthorpe v HMRC* (2010).
[3] *Makins v Elson* (1977).
[4] *Moore v Thompson* (1986), where the caravan was not connected to main services and only occupied sporadically it was held not to come within the exemption.
[5] *Batey v Wakefield* (1981).

Subsequently, the Court of Appeal in *Lewis v Lady Rook* (1992) **17–06** seem to have adopted the narrower geographical (or proximity) approach as opposed to the entity approach. The test set out in that case was to ask whether the building being sold was within the curtilage of, and appurtenant to, the main building so as to constitute an entity which could be described as a dwelling-house, and a cottage 175 metres away was determined to be too far away. The Court of Appeal were cheerfully of the opinion that everyone would know what the curtilage of a house was, but it is nowhere defined in the tax legislation.[6] It is clear that HMRC regard *Lewis v Lady Rook* as reflecting the correct position in this area (CG 64245).

In *Honour v Norris* (1992) the above test was said to be applicable to the "country house" situation but not to the facts of that case. The taxpayer had acquired four separate flats in a block of flats and the fourth, acquired to accommodate their grown up children and their guests, was sold separately. The judge refused to lay down any general test for such urban cases. On the facts the fourth flat had never formed part of a single entity—it had been acquired as a separate unit conveniently close to the others. It was like a country house owner acquiring a bungalow in the nearby village.

The "additional buildings" problem only applies to buildings on land outside the "permitted area" (discussed next) attached to the main house, unless the buildings are used for non-residential purposes, so garages within the "permitted area" will qualify for relief but workshops may not.

Land occupied and enjoyed with the residence—"permitted area"

The exemption also applies to land occupied and enjoyed with **17–07** the residence, up to half a hectare in area. (To help in the visualisation of a hectare, it might help to know that an international football pitch must be between 0.62 and 0.82 hectares.) If this land is disposed of separately from the house it must be disposed of first, otherwise it will no longer be occupied and enjoyed with the

---

[6] There are many cases in other areas as to what amounts to the curtilage of a building. One example, for the purposes of the Housing Act 1980, is the definition laid down in *Dyer v Dorset CC* (1988) that the curtilage is a small area of land which is part and parcel of the building it contains or is attached to it. But in *Skerritts of Nottingham Ltd v Secretary of State* (2000), the Court of Appeal said that it was wrong to include smallness as a criterion. It was a question of fact and degree, so that a manor house might well include stables and other outbuildings. The Court also said that "curtilage" was an expression which not even lawyers could define precisely! Sometimes it depends on the facts and context—e.g. in relation to listed buildings for planning permission purposes: see, e.g. *Sumption v Greenwich LBC* (2007).

house at the time of its disposal, and no proportionate relief will be available.[7] A larger area than half an hectare may be allowed if it is required for the reasonable enjoyment of the house, given the size and character of the house: s.222. In *Longson v Baker* (2001) it was stressed that, to qualify, the additional area of land must be objectively assessed by relation to the house and not for a particular use of the land by the owners, in that case the land needed to keep horses. Evans Lombe J noted drily:

> "In my judgment it is not objectively required, i.e. necessary, to keep horses at a house in order to enjoy it as a residence. An individual tax-payer may subjectively wish to do so but that is not the same thing."

Where the land is greater than the permitted area, the gain will be apportioned according to the respective areas of the exempt and non-exempt land.[8]

There is no requirement that the land is actually physically attached to the house as long as it is the natural garden of the house, so a garden across a public road can qualify. On the other hand land owned apart from the house will not count just because it is used as a garden.[9]

Partial business use or private letting

17–08   If the gain accrues from a disposal of a dwelling-house part of which is used exclusively for the purposes of a trade, business, profession or vocation the exemption applies only to that part of the gain which falls to be apportioned to the "private" part of the house (s.224). (This is a point to be weighed against the income tax advantage of claiming that a part of one's house is being used exclusively for business, etc. purposes.) Similar provisions apply to any reconstruction, conversion or change of use of the property, but it seems that such events will only justify an apportionment if they amount to a change in the taxpayer's occupation.[10]

If the owner lets his house during his period of ownership the part of the gain attributable to that period is chargeable on a straight line basis (e.g. owned 10 years during which it was let for two, one-fifth of the total gain is chargeable). Similar apportionment would apply where part of the property was let on a self-contained basis for all or part of the period of ownership.

Further relief is available under s.223(4) where the house is

---

[7]   *Varty v Lynes* (1976).
[8]   *Henke v HMRC* (2006) Sp Comm.
[9]   *Wakeling v Pearce* (1995).
[10] *IRC v Green* (1982).

let as residential accommodation.[11] The chargeable gain is then reduced by the lower of the exempt gain (i.e. four-fifths of the gain in the example above) or £40,000. In practice lodgers are not treated as affecting the relief in contrast to tenants who rent part of the property on a self-contained basis.

There are a number of specific situations in which the exemption is extended:

- occupation of a dwelling-house held under a settlement by a person entitled to occupy it under the settlement: s.225. Usually this will be the life tenant but it can include a beneficiary under a discretionary trust where the trustees have a power to allow this;[12]
- occupation after the death of the owner by a beneficiary under the will or intestacy. Under s.225A, the relief may be claimed by personal representatives if the house has been occupied by persons entitled to at least 75 per cent of the proceeds of the house, or a 75 per cent interest in it, under a will or intestacy. This is calculated on the basis that the house is not needed to pay any IHT or other debt of the estate;
- the provision of accommodation to a vulnerable adult under an adult placement carers scheme does not affect the relief as the periods of such occupation are disregarded as a period of non-residence: s.225D; and
- where a couple separates and one person leaves the matrimonial home, any period after this is treated as a period of residence provided that person disposes of his interest to the spouse of civil partner who was previously living in the home with him, and that the disposal is part of the arrangements made on separation or divorce, etc.: s.225B.

Spouses and civil partners can only have one residence or main residence. If they are not separated it is no good claiming that Mon Repos is one's main residence and Dunromin is the other's main residence: s.222(6). Where a taxpayer, spouses or civil partners, have two or more residences, they may choose which is to be the "main" residence. This choice must be made within two years of the acquisition of a second or subsequent residence in which case it will be backdated for that period. In *Griffin v Craig-Harvey* (1993) the court held that the taxpayer had no right to make an election after two years from the second acquisition,

[11] This includes short-term holiday lets: *Owen v Elliott* (1990).
[12] *Sansom v Peay* (1976).

a decision which leaves many taxpayers out of time to make an election. If there is no election, HMRC can decide which is the taxpayer's main residence on the facts.

Restriction if exemption is combined with gifts relief

17–09   A number of avoidance schemes were used to extend the private residence exemption to a second house where it was combined with gifts relief under s.260 (see para.17–23). For example, suppose Harriet has a second home (with in-built gains) which she wishes to sell and give the proceeds to her children Mike and Emma. She gives the house to trustees of a settlement of which the beneficiaries are Mike and Emma (if Harriet had been a beneficiary then no gifts relief would have been available as it would be a transfer to settlor-interested settlement—see para.17–24). Harriet claims hold-over gifts relief so that no tax is payable at that stage. The trustees allow Mike to occupy the house as his sole residence. When the trustees sell the house—that sale will be exempt since the private residence exemption will apply to it (relevant occupation by a beneficiary under the settlement). Thus the held-over gain will disappear and the full proceeds of sale will have effectively passed from Harriet to the children without any tax being paid. To prevent this, s.226A, introduced in 2004, provides that, in such circumstances, if Harriet claims the gifts relief the trustees cannot claim the private residence exemption. Thus the tax is payable either on the transfer of the house to the settlement or on the sale by the trustees.

Chattels disposed of for £6,000 or less

17–10   Section 262 provides that "a gain accruing on a disposal of an asset which is tangible movable property [i.e. a chattel] shall not be a chargeable gain if the amount or value *of the consideration* for the disposal does not exceed £6,000". Section 262 does not apply to a disposal of currency of any description, nor to a disposal of commodities by a person dealing on a terminal market. A terminal market is not defined but it means a market in which you can buy or sell, e.g. cocoa, for a price fixed now but for delivery at some future date (e.g. three months hence). It is sometimes called a futures market. Notice that the figure of £6,000 refers to the amount of the consideration, not to the amount of the gain. The figure of £6,000 has not been raised since 1989. If it had been index-linked since 1989, the figure would now be nearer £15,000.

17–11   MARGINAL RELIEF   Where the amount of the consideration exceeds £6,000 there shall be excluded from any chargeable gain so much of it as exceeds five-thirds of the difference between the consideration and £6,000 (s.262(2)). Thus if X buys a chattel for £1,000 and sells it for £6,400, the chargeable gain is not £5,400 but $5/_3 \times £400$ (£6,400–£6,000), i.e. £667.

But the section is far from generous as regards losses. If there is a disposal at a loss, and the consideration for the disposal is less than £6,000, the consideration is deemed to be £6,000. Thus if a chattel was bought for £6,200 and sold for £5,800 the actual loss (£400) is not allowable; the loss relief is limited to £200 (s.262(3)).

SETS If two or more assets forming part of a set of articles **17–12** (say a set of Chippendale chairs) are disposed of by the same seller to the same buyer (or to different buyers who are acting in concert or who are connected persons) whether on the same or different occasions, the two or more transactions are treated as a single transaction (s.262(4)). The effect of this is to prevent a person disposing of a valuable set by a series of individual disposals which are worth less in aggregate than the set as a whole.

The disposals of two (or more) quite separate articles qualify separately for the relief. It is no bar to getting the relief that you have (in the same year) sold a table for £6,000 and a stamp for £6,000, or even for that matter two unconnected stamps for £6,000 each.

Where there is a disposal of a right or interest in a chattel, the consideration is deemed (for the purposes of the exemption only) to be the aggregate of the sum received and the market value of the remainder—that avoids selling successive part-interests in a chattel to obtain the relief.

Tangible movables which are wasting assets

No chargeable gain (or, more likely, an allowable loss) shall **17–13** accrue on the disposal of an asset which is tangible movable property (i.e. a chattel) and which is a wasting asset: s.45. It will be recalled that a wasting asset is an asset which has a predictable life not exceeding 50 years, and that plant and machinery are always treated as wasting assets. This exemption applies (unlike the exemption mentioned above, since it is not really an exemption from any charge) irrespective of the amount of the disposal consideration. In *HMRC v The Executors of Lord Howard of Henderskelfe* (2015) a valuable painting owned by an individual was eligible for this relief even though it was used as plant in the business of a company. This aspect of the decision was reversed in 2015: now the plant must be owned by the actual trader to qualify for relief.

Gilt-edged securities and qualifying corporate bonds

17–14   A gain is not a chargeable gain if it accrues on the disposal of certain specified gilt-edged securities and qualifying corporate bonds: see ss.115, 117 and Sch.9. The list of specified gilt-edged securities has been added to from time to time by statutory instrument and now comprises virtually all government stocks. At first sight this seems a generous gesture on the part of the Treasury, but losses occur in dealings on the gilt-edged market, and the rule that where no chargeable gain (if there had been a gain) would have arisen there can be no allowable loss has meant that this exemption has frequently operated to prohibit losses rather than to exempt gains. Qualifying corporate bonds, which similarly cannot give rise to a loss for an individual are defined to include normal[13] non-convertible corporate debentures.

For companies, most qualifying corporate bonds have been subsumed into their trading profits for corporation tax purposes within the loan relationship rules and taken out of the chargeable gain regime.

Miscellaneous gains

17–15   The following are not chargeable assets:

- betting or lottery winnings (s.51);
- sums obtained by way of compensation or damages for any wrong or injury suffered by an individual in his person or in his profession (e.g. personal injury and defamation) (s.51). (Were it not for this provision, the law might otherwise produce the slightly macabre result that someone who received compensation, for example, for an injury at work, would be regarded as part-disposing of himself for CGT purposes.);
- savings certificates and premium bonds, (s.121);
- receipts under a policy of life assurance or on its surrender where the money is paid to the original holder of the policy or his personal representatives or trustees (s.210). If the policy is assigned for money or money's worth (e.g. sold) and the assignee receives money under the policy, or surrenders it, that is a chargeable event;
- private cars (s.263);

---

[13] See e.g. *Weston v Garnett* (2005).

- foreign currency held in a bank account held by individuals, personal representatives or trustees (s.252) or acquired for personal expenditure abroad (s.269);
- assets held in individual savings account;
- disposals by charities (s.256) and gifts to charities (s.257); and
- decorations for valour (original owner only) (s.268).

Entrepreneurs' relief and investors' relief

Introduction and amount of entrepreneurs' relief

As a result of the abolition of taper and indexation reliefs, **17–16** as from 2008/09 (see para.16–17 above), a new relief, known as entrepreneurs' relief was introduced to assist owners of small businesses. The relevant provisions are to be found in ss.169H–169S.

The relief, which must be claimed, applies to the first £10 million of lifetime gains (after deducting the annual exempt amount, if available) which arise from a qualifying or associated disposal. The amount of the relief has been increased from £1 million in 2008 to £2 million in 2009, £5 million in 2010 and £10 million in 2011. The various disposals which together constitute a qualifying disposal, e.g. on the sale of a business and its assets, are treated as a single composite disposal for this purpose. Thus any losses so incurred, e.g. on the sale of a particular business asset, must be deducted from the gains arising on, e.g. the sale of other business assets. It is the resulting composite net gain (if any) which qualifies for the relief. If there are more losses than gains, then the relief does not apply to that disposal.

The net gains are charged at a flat rate of 10 per cent rather than the 18 per cent and 28 per cent rates which apply to other gains. Additional gains in excess of the £10 million limit do not qualify for the relief. Further, once the £10 million figure has been used by a taxpayer, the relief is exhausted for all future disposals. This is not a serial entrepreneur's relief.

Qualifying disposals

There are three principal categories of qualifying dispos- **17–17** als by individuals. These are based on those for retirement relief which was abolished in favour of taper relief in 1988, so earlier case law may be relevant. In categories 1) and 2) the assets in question must have been owned by the taxpayer for at least the whole of the year prior to the disposal. The categories are:

1) gains on the disposal of the whole or part of a trading business (this includes sole traders and partners who may use this relief when they dispose of their interest in the partnership). A trading business, which is any business carried on commercially with a view of profit, includes professions and vocations but does not include a property letting business other than furnished holiday lettings.

    The relief only applies to relevant business assets, i.e. those used in the business. Further, there is no relief for excluded assets which are held by the business such as shares or other investments. Goodwill is not an excluded asset for this purpose;

2) gains on the disposal of assets or an interest in assets within three years of the cessation of (the whole of) such a business. The assets must be relevant business assets and not excluded assets (see above); and

3) gains on a disposal of shares in a trading company (or the holding company of a trading company) provided:

    (a) the taxpayer has been an officer or employee (not necessarily full time) of the company (or its holding company or other member company of its trading group);[14]

    (b) it is his personal company, i.e. he owns at least 5 per cent of the ordinary share capital of the company which carry 5 per cent of the voting rights in the company; and

    (c) conditions (a) and (b) have applied either throughout the year prior to the disposal, or throughout the year prior to the company ceasing to be a trading company, if that cessation was itself within three years prior to the disposal. That does not apply, however, if the company ceases to be a trading company but becomes a member of a trading group.

A trading company and a trading group is one which is trading commercially and for profit and which does not carry on other activities to a substantial extent.

17–18   ASSOCIATED DISPOSALS If a partner or a shareholder/officer/ employee of the company makes a qualifying disposal under either 1) or 3) above, the relief will also be available on an

---

[14] Two First-tier Tribunal cases on whether a person was an officer or employee *Hirst* (2014) and *Corbett* (2014) gave a generous interpretation of these terms.

associated disposal of an asset (e.g. the premises on which the business is carried on) owned by the taxpayer.

Such disposals are associated if they take place at the same time as the qualifying disposal and are part of the individual's withdrawal from the business or company. Unlike a sole trader, there is no requirement that the business itself ceases. Further, the assets must have been used in the firm's or company's business for the year prior to the disposal or, if earlier, the year prior to the withdrawal from the business.

There are reductions where: (i) the asset was not wholly in business use throughout the period of ownership; (ii) only part of the asset was used in the business; (iii) the taxpayer was not involved in the business or company throughout the period of the business use of the asset; and (iv) rent was charged for the use of the asset (it is seen as an investment then). In each case only a "just and reasonable amount" of relief will be allowed.

TRUSTEES The relief applies to gains by trustees on disposals **17–19** of shares in a company or assets used in a business. There must be a beneficiary with an interest in possession relating to those assets who is a qualifying beneficiary. That person must satisfy the same criteria as would have applied if he had had been making the claim in his own name as an individual under 1), 2) or 3) above.

If there is another beneficiary, other than the qualifying beneficiary, with an interest in possession under the trust in the relevant assets, the amount of the relief is reduced to the proportion held by the qualifying beneficiary. That proportion is calculated by reference to the respective entitlements of the beneficiaries to the trust income.

The £10 million limit on the relief is calculated by reference to the qualifying beneficiary, so that a qualifying disposal by the trustees counts towards the beneficiary's lifetime allowance. For that purpose, where there is such a disposal by the trustees on the same day as one by the qualifying beneficiary in his own right, the disposal by the trustees is deemed to have occurred after that by the beneficiary. Thus the personal disposal will have first bite at the relief.

Potential difficulties
Since the categories of qualifying gains are derived from those **17–20** for retirement relief, they have inherited the problems of that relief relating to the interface between categories 1) and 2) where some but not all of the assets of a business are disposed of. Case law has established the following propositions in relation to both reliefs:

1) because roll-over relief for replacement of business assets is available (see para.17–27 below), category 2) is only available if the *whole of the business* has permanently ceased: *Marriot v Lane* (1996); if there is no such total cessation then category 1) requires a disposal of the whole *or part of* a business;

2) similarly is a question of fact as to whether a person has ceased carrying on one business and started up another, or where it is the same business with certain changes: *Rice v HMRC* (2014);

3) the disposal of some of the assets of the business does not amount to the disposal of a part of that business for that purpose if the business is in fact substantially still continuing: *McGregor v Adcock* (1977), *Russell v HMRC* (2013);

4) but if a disposal of business assets has the effect of creating a de facto disposal of part of a business that will suffice: *Pepper v Daffurn* (1993); *Wase v Bourke* (1996);

5) in deciding whether there has been such a disposal of part of a business, the courts will look at the position before and after the disposal of the assets and ask whether the changes caused by the disposal amount to a cessation of part of the business by the taxpayer. That is a question of fact: *Jarmin v Rawlings* (1994); *Barrett v Powell* (1998); *Purves v Harrison* (2001).

In the first case decided on entrepreneurs' relief, *Gilbert v HMRC* (2011), the question as to whether the disposal of business assets amounted to a disposal of part of the business (under 3) and 4) above), was answered by the First-tier Tribunal by applying the test laid down by Lord Walker in the House of Lords in *Maco Door and Window Hardware (UK) Ltd v HMRC* (2008) in relation to capital allowances:

> "[A] part of a trade must not simply be one of the activities carried out in the course of trade but a viable section of a composite trade which would still be recognisable as a trade if separated from the composite whole."

After noting that a sale as a going concern was a sufficient but not a necessary condition for the relief to be available, the Tribunal applied the test by assuming that the transferee was an empty shell before the transfer. On that basis the question was whether the activities of the transferee using only the assets and liabilities transferred would be capable of constituting a trade or a business.

In the case the transfer of a specific customer database, existing contracts and goodwill was a viable section when separated from the rest of the transferor's business.

Investors' relief

Investors' relief is an extenuation of entrepreneurs' relief introduced to encourage external investment by individuals in smaller commercial companies. It applies in relation to shares in unlisted trading companies or holding companies of a trading group. The shares must have been acquired on or after 17 March 2016 and, by disposal, must have been held continuously for at least three years, starting from 6 April 2016. The shares must be acquired by subscription rather than transfer. There is a lifetime cap of £10 million, in addition to the entrepreneurs' relief cap. The main difference between investors' relief and entrepreneurs' relief, apart from the three-year holding period, is the relaxation of the requirement that the shareholder must be an employee or a director of the company in which the shares are held.

17–21

Hold-over and roll-over reliefs

How hold-over and roll-over reliefs work

There are two main types of relief which have the effect of deferring a charge on the gain on the present disposal, catching it on a future disposal. They operate in similar fashion. The first type, hold-over relief, results in the gain staying attached to the asset presently being disposed of, to be taxed in the hands of another person on some future disposal. This works by allowing the amount of the chargeable gain which would otherwise be payable on a disposal from A to B to be deducted from the acquisition cost of B rather than chargeable on A. Effectively, this transfers the gain (or loss) during A's period of ownership to B. Suppose A buys an asset for £10,000. He disposes of it to B for £13,000. A therefore makes a gain of £3,000. If hold-over relief is available then, instead of charging that gain on the disposal, it will be deducted from B's acquisition cost. Thus B will be deemed to have acquired the asset for £10,000 (i.e. £13,000–£3,000). If B subsequently disposes of the asset to C for £20,000 he will therefore be treated as having made a gain of £10,000 (£20,000 – £10,000). Thus A's original gain of £3,000 and B's actual gain of £7,000 both become chargeable on B's disposal to C. In other words hold-over relief postpones or holds over the first gain, it does not exclude it. If B's disposal to C had also been eligible for hold-over relief then B's gain of £10,000 would not be chargeable

17–22

but C's acquisition cost would be reduced by that amount, and so on.

The second type of relief, roll-over, applies to two kinds of disposals of business assets—where the asset is replaced by another asset, and where a business is incorporated and assets of the business are transferred to a company in exchange for shares. The gain on the disposal of the asset is rolled over into its replacement or into the shares. The effect is that this gain will be charged on the disposal of the replacement asset or on the disposal of the shares. So, under roll-over relief, the gain sticks with the original owner, unlike holdover, where the gain sticks with the asset.

Gifts immediately chargeable to IHT

17–23 Between 1980 and 1989 all gifts between individuals were eligible for hold-over relief because gifts were also subject to IHT and it was thought inequitable to apply both taxes. This general relief was, however, abolished in 1989 on the (slightly flawed) basis that IHT now rarely applies to lifetime gifts (although see below in relation to gifts of business assets—para.17–25). However, s.260 applies hold-over relief on a lifetime disposal which counts as a chargeable transfer for the purposes of IHT, extended to some specific types of gift which are exempt from IHT.

The relief only applies to transfers which are chargeable when made, not potentially exempt transfers which are only chargeable to IHT if the donor dies within seven years of making the gift. These concepts are discussed at para.19–12 below, but the effect broadly is that the relief only applies in relation to transfers into and out of most trusts[15] or to a chargeable transfer which is not made to an individual, for example to a club or a company (see para.19–12).

Provided there is a chargeable transfer for the purposes of IHT, however, it does not matter that the amount of tax actually payable is negligible—see *Melville v IRC* (2000), para.19–06 below. Neither does it matter if there is no actual IHT because the transfer is within the transferor's nil-rate band (see para.21–02) or is covered by the IHT annual exemption (see para.20–04).

The relief is not available to companies or on the transfer of shares or securities to companies, or where the donee is not resident in the UK. Where it applies, the relief for gifts of business assets (para.17–25 below) does not apply. A claim for

---

[15] Those trusts which are outside this relief are those set out in para.22–09.

hold-over relief must be made jointly by the donor and donee and, if made, entitles the parties to postpone the gain in the way set out above.

The relief also applies to bad bargains taxable on full market value under s.17. In that case the amount which can be held-over is the difference between the price paid and the market value, i.e. the gift element. Finally we should note that the relief is available to certain gifts which are exempt from IHT altogether thus taking them outside the tax net. These include gifts to political parties and to maintenance funds for historic houses. The relief will also apply where a trust for a bereaved minor or an 18–25 trust[16] ends and no charge to IHT arises.

Restriction of gifts general relief

To prevent a number of avoidance schemes, often combining gifts relief, either under s.165 (gifts of business assets—see para.17–25 below) or s.260 (transfers chargeable to IHT—see para.17–23 above) with the private residence exemption (para.17–02 above), ss.169B–169G (introduced in 2004) provide that hold-over relief is not available on a transfer to trustees of a settlement in which the donor either has an interest at the time of transfer or acquires an interest in it within six years of the transfer (referred to as settlor-interested settlements). Thus the initial gift will be chargeable under the usual rules rather than being held over. In the latter case the relief is "clawed back" when the donor acquires such an interest. The schemes worked by the trustees being able to dissipate the held-over gain before selling the property on.

For example, David owns a house which is not his principal residence (and so not exempt from tax). It has, say, a market value of £450,000 with a potential gain of £150,000 if it is sold. David transfers the house to trustees of a settlement in which he has an interest, claiming hold-over relief. Erica, his daughter, is entitled to occupy the house under the terms of the trust and does so as her sole main residence. Erica then moves out and the trustees sell the house for £450,000. The held-over gain of £150,000 which would normally be chargeable at that stage is lost because the disposal by the trustees is, as we shall see, exempt under the private residence exemption rules. David therefore has de facto access to the full proceeds of the house without paying any CGT. Under the 2004 rules, David could not claim hold-over relief so that the gain would be chargeable in full on the transfer to the trust. The trustees, selling the house for what they are deemed to have acquired it for, would make no gain.

17–24

---

[16] These concepts are considered in Ch.22 below.

Gifts of business assets

17–25   Hold-over relief also applies to gifts of business assets (s.165). The relief arises where an individual makes a disposal otherwise than under a bargain at arm's length to a person resident in the UK of any asset[17] used for the purposes of a trade, profession or vocation carried on by the transferor or by his personal company or by a trading company which is a subsidiary of his personal company.[18] The relief also applies to a similar transfer of shares of an unquoted company or of the transferor's personal company but not if the gift of those shares is to a company.

Since this relief is a hold-over relief, the gain moves to the donee. The amount of the gain is deducted from the deemed acquisition cost of the donee (market value under s.17). Because the donee will therefore become liable to a potentially higher CGT bill on a subsequent disposal, any claim for this relief must be made by both the donor and donee (except where the transfer is to a trust, in which case the donor alone decides). There can be a difficult decision to make as to whether to elect for the gain to be held over if the initial disposal would qualify for entrepreneurs' relief. If the person acquiring the asset will not qualify for this relief on the subsequent disposal, the gain is likely to be charged eventually at a higher rate. This involves a decision as to whether to defer the gain or whether to pay reduced tax now. As with the relief for gifts subject to IHT (para.17–23), this relief is not available on transfers to a settlement in which the donor has an interest or in which he acquires an interest within six years of the transfer.

Where the relief is available on sales at an undervalue only the amount of that undervalue is available for the relief. If the gift was the subject of a charge to IHT the donor can add that tax paid to his acquisition cost.

Transfer of business to a company

17–26   Roll-over relief is available, unless the transferor elects to the contrary, where an unincorporated business (and not just its assets) are transferred to a company in return for shares in the company, i.e. where the business is incorporated: ss.162, 162A. The gain on the assets is rolled over against the acquisition cost of the shares. For example, assume Joe incorporates his business,

---

[17]   There are no restrictions similar to those applicable on business asset replacement relief—para.17–27.

[18]   This is a company in which the taxpayer can exercise at least 5 per cent of the votes.

acquiring shares which are valued at £100,000. The business has some capital assets showing a gain of £40,000. Unless Joe elects to the contrary, the £40,000 gain is deducted from the acquisition cost of the shares, which are deemed to have been acquired for £60,000. The company is deemed to acquire the assets at market value (s.17 will apply).[19]

Replacement of business assets

Sections 152–159 are the operative sections here. They provide relief in the roll-over form. The relief arises when a trader disposes of business assets (of certain types) at a gain, and uses the disposal consideration to acquire replacement assets for use in the trade.

17–27

The relief is given by allowing the trader to defer payment of tax on the disposal gain and (instead) to deduct the gain which he makes on the disposal of the old assets from the acquisition cost of the new assets. This will have the effect of increasing the tax payable when he comes (if he does) to dispose of the new assets in the future.

This causes a particular problem with respect to LLPs which go into winding up before the new asset has been disposed of. A similar problem arises with respect to the relief on gifts of business assets and the two are dealt with in that section (see para.17–25 above).

CONDITIONS FOR THE RELIEF   To get the relief the trader must acquire the new assets within three years after the disposal[20] (or within 12 months before the disposal). Once the replacement asset is acquired it must be used in the taxpayer's trade "on the acquisition." A gap will prevent the relief applying.[21] Both the old and new assets must have been so used for the purposes of the taxpayer's trade.

17–28

It is possible to acquire the "new" asset one year before the disposal of the old asset, provided of course that the old asset was part of the trader's assets when the new asset was acquired. But in *Watton v Tippett* (1997) no relief was allowed where a trader, having bought a single asset, disposed of part of it within a year

---

[19] See, e.g. *Gordon v IRC* (1991).
[20] This period can be extended by HMRC, but there is no appeal against their refusal to do so: *Steibelt v Paling* (1999).
[21] See *Campbell Connelly & Co Ltd v Barnett* (1993). There are special rules for groups of companies in this respect. In practice, if an asset requires capital expenditure on it before it can be used in the taxpayer's trade, the relief will apply if the work is completed within a reasonable time and it is then used in the trade. See *Steibelt v Paling* (1999).

and claimed to deduct the gain from the cost of the part retained. The original cost for the whole asset could not be severed since the part retained had never been acquired as such, it was never a "new asset."

Despite the fact that s.152(1) appears to require that the proceeds on the first disposal are "applied by [the taxpayer] in acquiring" the new asset, the courts have not strictly applied this. It would, for example, be difficult to apply where a replacement asset was acquired before the disposal of the original asset! Despite some reservations expressed by the courts it is sufficient for the relief to apply if the consideration on the disposal of the old assets is at least matched by the cost of the new assets. There is no need to demonstrate any form of tracing of the proceeds into the new asset. This enabled the judge in *Wardhaugh v Penrith Rugby Union Football Club* (2002) to ignore the effect of a Sports Council grant which partly funded the building of a new clubhouse. The whole of the gain arising from that sale could be held-over.

The relief only applies to assets set out in classes in s.155 (which can be added to but not limited by a Treasury Order). These are currently: (i) land and buildings; (ii) fixed plant and machinery[22]; (iii) ships; (iv) aircraft; (v) hovercraft; (vi) satellites, space stations and spacecraft; (vii) goodwill; (viii) certain farming quotas; (ix) fish quotas; (x) payment entitlements under the single payments scheme and (xi) rights of members of a Lloyd's syndicate. The old and new assets need not be of the same type, however.

17–29   LIMITS   Non-residents are usually only charged to CGT on assets situated in the UK which are used for the purposes of a business carried on in the UK. There is no relief for a non-resident where the replacement asset is outside the charge to tax because it is outside the UK: s.159. In addition there is no relief if the new assets were acquired wholly or partly for the purpose of realising a gain from their disposal.[23] There are further restrictions if the replacement asset is a wasting asset.

Where the whole of the proceeds of sale are not reinvested in acquiring a new asset, i.e. where the cost of the new asset is less than the proceeds of the sale of the old asset,[24] the amount

---

[22] Thus excluding movable machinery: *Williams v Evans* (1982).
[23] See, e.g. *Re Loquitur Ltd* (2003).
[24] Section 153. In *Wardhaugh v Penrith Rugby Union FC* (2002), above, HMRC's argument was that the grant should be deducted from the cost of the new asset so as to apply this restriction.

not reinvested will be treated as a chargeable gain and only the balance will be held over. For example, assume X sells an asset for £100,000 (with a gain of £40,000) and reinvests in an asset costing £90,000. The amount of the proceeds not reinvested, here £10,000, is subject to tax. The balance of the gain, £30,000, is deducted from the acquisition cost of the new asset, which now is deemed to be £60,000.

Similarly where the new asset is only partially used for the purposes of the business the relief will be restricted to the proportion used in the business.[25]

Hold-over/roll-over reliefs and LLPs

The reliefs for gifts of business assets and replacement of busi- **17–30**
ness assets (see paras 17–25 and 17–27 above) both operate by postponing the held-over gain until the asset, or new asset, is disposed of on a chargeable transaction. Because members of an LLP are taxed as if they and not the LLP own the assets they may well have postponed a gain by using one of those two reliefs. But when an LLP is wound up that tax transparency ceases, so that the LLP is deemed always to have owned the business assets as a body corporate.[26] Accordingly, when it makes a disposal of those assets it will be able to claim the full acquisition cost as an expense and no account will be taken of the reduction resulting from the hold-over relief already claimed by the individual members. Accordingly, ss.156A and 169A provide a charge on the members who claimed the hold-over relief, for replacement or gifts of business assets respectively, equivalent to the amount of the postponed gain.

---

[25] For an unfortunate example of this restriction see *Todd v Mudd* (1987).
[26] Section 59A(5).

PART FOUR

INHERITANCE TAX

CHAPTER 18

EVOLUTION OF INHERITANCE TAX

Inheritance Tax

Ever since 1894 there has been a tax aimed at non-commercial   **18–01**
transfers of capital, charging tax on the whole of the value so
transferred. The current version of this tax is known as IHT,
although as we shall see it is neither calculated by reference to
what a person inherits nor limited to inheritance on a death. It is
different from CGT since that taxes only the gain on a transfer,
does not apply on a death and applies in the main to commercial
transfers of capital. The relationship between the two taxes is
usually complementary, although there are overlaps in the area
of lifetime gifts, where paradoxically CGT is more likely to apply
than IHT.

Estate duty

The evolution of IHT can be traced back to estate duty intro-   **18–02**
duced in 1894. That tax charged all the property of an individual
which passed on his death, unless specifically exempted. In its
final form this included not only property which the deceased
owned at his death and which passed under his will or intestacy but also property which was deemed to pass on his death.
Such property included the full value of any settled property
in which the deceased had an interest (including certain discretionary trusts) and the value of any gift made by the deceased
either within seven years prior to his death or at any time if the
deceased had retained any interest in the property given. The
whole amount of the property so passing on the death was then
aggregated and tax charged on that amount. Thus estate duty
was a mutation duty (i.e. one charged on the property passing
from the deceased) and not an acquisition duty (i.e. one charged
according to the amount each person acquired on the death). But
only a death triggered a charge.

Capital transfer tax

In 1974 the incoming Labour government announced its   **18–03**
intention to repeal estate duty, which it finally did in 1975. The
replacement was known as capital transfer tax. The central idea

of this tax (introduced as the precursor of a wealth tax which never materialised) was to charge all non-commercial transfers of capital (known as chargeable transfers) made by an individual throughout his lifetime, with death being regarded as the final transfer. The important concept was that all such transfers were taxed on a cumulative basis. Thus the rate of tax for each successive transfer was calculated on the basis of the transferor's cumulative total at that time. Thus if X, having already made transfers of £100,000, made another transfer of £50,000, the rate of tax for that transfer would be calculated at that applicable for transfers between £100,000 and £150,000, and so on, until on X's death the rates payable would depend upon his whole cumulative total of lifetime transfers. The value of each transfer was calculated not on the value of the transfer as such but on the loss to the transferor. There were special rules for settlements. The law on capital transfer tax was consolidated in 1984 into the Capital Transfer Tax Act.

IHT

18–04   But by then this principle of taxing all transfers made by an individual throughout his lifetime had been reduced by the rule that the cumulative principle should only apply to gifts made within the previous 10 years. Thus in our example above, if X had made the £100,000 transfers more than 10 years before the transfer of £50,000, the latter would be taxed only on the rates between £0 and £50,000. If only £60,000 of the earlier transfers had been made within the past 10 years, the rate of tax on the £50,000 transfer would be calculated according to the rates between £60,000 and £110,000. More importantly, on a death the deceased's cumulative total would only be those transfers made within 10 years of the death and not those throughout his lifetime. In 1986 even more fundamental changes were made to the structure of capital transfer tax and the resulting product was renamed as the IHT we have today. **Even the 1984 consolidation, as amended, was renamed the Inheritance Tax Act 1984 (IHTA)[1] and references to sections in the following chapters are to that Act unless otherwise stated.**

18–05   1986 CHANGES   What then were the 1986 changes? Apart from a simplification of the rates of the tax, the major change was to take some lifetime transfers out of the charge to the tax

---

[1] Technically the law provides that the 1984 Act *may* be referred to as the Inheritance Tax Act 1984 rather than the Capital Transfer Tax Act, but, in practice, everybody does so.

altogether.[2] With one or two fairly significant exceptions[3] lifetime transfers will only be chargeable if either they were made within seven years prior to the death of the transferor or the transferor has retained a benefit in the property transferred. Most non-settlement lifetime transfers are now regarded as potentially exempt transfers which will only become retrospectively chargeable in their own right if the transferor dies within seven years of making them. Since the cumulative principle for those transfers which are chargeable was reduced from 10 to seven years, on a death the deceased's cumulative total relates to those transfers charged (at the time or retrospectively) within the past seven years.

HYBRID TAX IHT has therefore resurrected the old estate **18–06** duty concepts that a death rather than a lifetime transfer is the major trigger for a charge to the tax and that gifts made within seven years and those with a reservation of benefit (gifts with reservation) become chargeable on that death. But many aspects of capital transfer tax also remain. Charges on a death and on discretionary trusts[4] remain much as before, the way in which the value of the transfer is calculated is still the loss to the transferor, there is still a limited form of cumulation and in certain cases there is a charge even though no death has occurred. Thus IHT is a hybrid between estate duty and capital transfer tax, which charges more than just an inheritance on a death and which does so by reference to the total of the transfers made by the transferor and not by reference to the amount inherited, i.e. it is still a mutation and not an acquisitions tax. One curious consequence of the changes to this tax is that non-settlement lifetime gifts will rarely be chargeable to IHT (the non-commercial tax) on the full value transferred but to CGT (the commercial tax) on the notional gain made by the donor. Where both taxes are chargeable there is, as we have seen in para.16–04, a deferral relief from CGT.

STRUCTURAL CHANGES POST-1986 After almost 20 years of **18–07** the status quo, another change to the structure of the tax came in 2006 when the regime for fixed interest trusts was radically altered

---

[2] Thus triggering the reintroduction of the charge on lifetime gifts under CGT.
[3] Notably those relating to the creation and continued existence of most trusts, which are immediately chargeable.
[4] Other trusts are now also taxed in the same way as discretionary trusts since 2006.

with almost immediate effect. There was no prior consultation or warning and a limited time given for damage limitation.

The next change came in 2008, in response to political pressure resulting from the rapid advance in domestic house prices, which, unlike CGT, are not exempt from IHT. The percentage of the nil-rate band (effectively the IHT threshold) unused by a spouse or civil partner on their death could be carried forward and added to that of the survivor. This could occur e.g. because all the property was left to their surviving spouse/partner and so, as we shall see, is exempt from the tax. In that case 100 per cent can be carried forward. Alternatively, if part of the estate was chargeable, e.g. as being left to the children, but that part is say only 60 per cent of the nil-band limit, then 40 per cent can be carried forward. This change effectively doubled the tax threshold for most couples (but not co-habitees). In 2010, following the banking crisis, the nil-rate band was frozen at £325,000 until, initially, 2015 and subsequently until 2021. The freezing of this threshold was tempered by the introduction in 2016 of an additional nil rate band where a home was left to the family. This comes into effect in 2017.

Scope of this part

18–08   In the following chapters we shall examine the scope and effects of this hybrid known as IHT. The first question which needs an answer is what amounts to a chargeable lifetime transfer so as to give rise either to an immediate lifetime charge or to a retrospective charge if the transferor dies within seven years, explaining as we go the way in which gifts with reservation fit into this. Then we need to examine the charge which arises on the death of the transferor. Having established what is chargeable or potentially chargeable we need to look at the various exemptions and reliefs which are available against this charge. Having thus established the net charge so to speak we then examine how the charge is actually calculated and who ultimately has to account for and pay the tax. Because settlements are the subject of many special rules these are dealt with in a separate chapter.

CHAPTER 19

CHARGEABLE TRANSFERS

Introduction

IHT is only chargeable if there is a *chargeable transfer*. These may be made either during the transferor's lifetime or on his death, although, as we have seen, many of the former do not attract an immediate charge to the tax. Instead they may become retrospectively chargeable if the transferor dies within seven years of making them. Until then they are known as *potentially exempt transfers(PETs)*. There are special rules for lifetime transfers in which the transferor retains some interest in the property transferred, known as *gifts with reservation*. This chapter deals with what is meant by a chargeable lifetime transfer, what is a potentially exempt transfer, the rules for gifts with reservation, transfers on death, and one or two special charges, e.g. involving close companies as defined for corporation tax purposes). Settled property, being inevitably the most complex area, is dealt with separately in Ch.22. Remember that there are many exemptions and reliefs which apply to these various charges—these are set out in Ch.20.

19–01

Lifetime transfers

Section 1 declares: "Inheritance tax shall be charged on the value transferred by a chargeable transfer." What, then, is a "chargeable transfer"? The answer is in s.2(1): "A chargeable transfer is a transfer of value which is made by an individual but is not an exempt transfer."

19–02

So we need to know what is a transfer of value, what is the value transferred, what is an individual and what is an exempt transfer.

A "*transfer of value*" is defined by s.3(1) as:

". . . a disposition made by a person (the transferor) as a result of which the value of his estate immediately after the disposition is less than it would be but for the disposition: and the amount by which it is less is the *value transferred* by the transfer."

The two essential criteria for a charge are therefore a disposition and a loss to the transferor's estate.

The word *"individual"* is not defined by the Act, but of course it is a word well-known in tax law; it does not include companies, nor trustees nor personal representatives. However, as we shall see later, certain dispositions made by trustees of settled property give rise to charges to tax as if they were chargeable transfers, and transfers of value made by companies which are close companies may also give rise to tax liability.

Transfers which are *"exempt transfers"*, and therefore not changeable transfers, are dealt with in Ch.20.

It is also as well to say here that some kinds of property are designated as *"excluded property"*, though these are mainly overseas assets and certain assets, such as unit trusts, held by non-UK domiciled investors (s.6). Reversionary interests under settlements are also in general excluded property—we shall deal with those in Ch.22. Transfers of excluded property are not taken into account: s.3(2).

Loss to the transferor's estate

19–03   It is very important to appreciate that the *value transferred* by a transfer is measured under s.3(1) by the diminution in value of the transferor's estate, and not by the increase in value of the transferee's estate, which in this legislation is not limited to the property of a dead person. Of course, in many circumstances the result would be the same whichever measure one took. If Albert gives a motor car to his son Ben, Albert's estate is diminished and Ben's estate is increased by the same amount, namely the value of the car. But there are circumstances in which this is not so, and some of them are very important. For example, if Albert owns 51 per cent of the shares in a company and Ben owns none, and then Albert transfers 2 per cent of the shares to Ben, the diminution in Albert's estate is much greater than is the increase in Ben's estate, because Albert has given up control of the company and Ben has not obtained control.

19–04   ESTATE The word *"estate"* is defined in s.5(1) as the aggregate[1] of all the property to which [a person] is beneficially entitled, except excluded property and most interests in settled property.[2] The only interests in settled property which now (since 2006) form part of a person's estate are *an immediate post-death interest, a disabled person's interest, a transitional serial interest* or an interest in a *bereaved minor's trust* or in an *18–25 trust*. Those various terms are explained in Ch.22 below.

---

[1] See *St Barbe Green v IRC* (2005).
[2] Because the settlement itself is regarded as the taxable entity.

POWERS OF APPOINTMENT The word *"property"* is stated **19–05**
in s.272 to include "rights and interests of any description." In
particular, s.5(2) includes any general power of appointment
as being part of a person's estate.[3] The definition of a general
power for this purpose seems to continue the estate duty
concept[4] of any power which a person can appoint in his own
favour, e.g. "to such person as X shall appoint", or "to such of
X, Y, and Z as X shall appoint". It follows that the exercise of
such a power will be a transfer of value (disposition plus loss
to the estate) and also in some cases the omission to exercise
it (loss to estate and gain to the estate of the person entitled in
default of appointment: s.3(3)). If not exercised it will also form
part of the deceased's estate on death. In *Sillars v IRC* (2004),
the Special Commissioner held that the wording of s.5(2) was
wide enough to include all of a building society account to
which the deceased had added the names of her two daughters
some years before her death. The deceased could dispose of the
entire balance at any time—the amount was never divided up.[5]

PROPERTY The meaning of property in the context of a loss **19–06**
to the transferor's estate was considered by Lightman J and
the Court of Appeal in *Melville v IRC* (2001). The taxpayer
had settled property on discretionary trusts (an immediately
chargeable transfer) but had included a provision in the trust
deed whereby he had the right to require the trustees to transfer
the whole of the trust fund back to him at his request at any time
90 days after the date of the settlement and also had a veto on
any exercise by the trustees of their powers of appointment under
the trust. The judge and the Court of Appeal held that those
rights were property under s.272 and therefore formed part of the
taxpayer's estate for the purposes of s.3(1).[6] There was nothing in
the legislation to prevent the full meaning of the word property
being applied. It followed that the loss to his estate consequent
on the transfer into the settlement was negligible. It did, however,
remain a chargeable transfer for the purposes of relief from
CGT, since there was some loss to the estate (see para.19–03)
which was the object of the exercise. That object was, however,
negatived by a change in the law in 2002 (see para.22–60), but the
general principle in the case remains valid.

---

[3] See *Marquess of Linlithgow v HMRC* (2010).
[4] See, e.g. *Re Parsons* (1943).
[5] See also *Matthews v HMRC* [2012] UK FTT 658 to the same effect.
[6] For the application of this to Scottish property law, see *Marquess of Linlithgow v HMRC* (2010).

19–07 GROSSING UP One very important aspect of this diminution principle is that if the transferor pays the IHT the tax is itself taxable, because his estate is diminished not only by what he transfers to the transferee but also by what he has to pay to HMRC. The payment of the tax forms part of the loss to the transferor's estate. So there is a grossing-up process. We will deal with this concept more fully later on.

Disposition

19–08 It will be noticed that the definition of transfer of value includes the word "disposition". There is no general definition of this but it probably includes not only obvious transfers such as sales and gifts but also disclaimers[7] and waivers of possible future rights.[8] There have been two attempts since 1975 to charge interest-free loans but both have been repealed and the position remains obscure. It is, however, provided by s.3(3) that a disposition can be merely the omission to exercise a right. This provision prevents many possible avoidance devices. For example, but for this provision Albert could make a tax-free transfer to Ben (his son) by engaging him, for a lump sum paid in advance, to work for a specified time in his (Albert's) business and then standing by and omitting to sue for damages when Ben does not turn up. Section 3(3) only applies, however, if, as the result of an omission by you, your estate is diminished and another's[9] is increased, and it can be avoided if you can show that the omission was not deliberate.[10]

Non-commercial transfers

19–09 It has been said above that IHT is (in part) a tax on non-commercial transfers, i.e. "gifts tax". That phrase is not used in the legislation, but it is made clear by the use of other words, *"gratuitous benefit"*, in s.10(1) that the tax only bites on transfers which contain an element of gift. Sales at market value are not taxable because they do not involve any diminution in the value of the seller's estate. If Albert owns a car which is worth £800 and he sells it to Charles for £800, Albert's estate has the same value after the sale as it had before the sale; he has merely exchanged one asset (the car) for an equivalent asset (cash). But suppose

---

[7] Some disclaimers are expressly excluded from the charge, (e.g. of a legacy within two years of death: s.142). So it presumably follows that other disclaimers are included.

[8] Again some waivers, (e.g. of future dividends not declared for at least one year afterwards: s.15) are expressly excluded from the charge.

[9] Including most settlements.

[10] Does this include for example failure to exercise a beneficial option owing to lack of funds?

Albert sells the car, not for £800, but for £500. That may occur either: (1) because Albert wished to confer a benefit on Charles; or (2) because he made a bad bargain. A gift (as in (1)), is taxable: a bad bargain (as in (2)), is not taxable. This point is dealt with in s.10(1) which declares:

> "A disposition is not a transfer of value if it is shown that it was not intended, and was not made in a transaction intended, to confer any gratuitous benefit on any person and either—
> (a) that it was made in a transaction at arm's length between persons not connected with each other, or
> (b) that it was such as might be expected to be made in a transaction at arm's length between persons not connected with each other ...".

The subsection requires two conditions to be met; a subjective non-donative intent *and* the objective fact stated in (a) or the apparently objective fact stated in (b). Where the parties are connected (i.e. they are relatives, linked in a trust, partners or involved with a close company) the criterion imposed by (b) of what would be expected to amount to an arm's length sale was discussed in *IRC v Spencer-Nairn* (1991).

CONNECTED PERSONS *Spencer-Nairn* was an unusual case in **19–10** that the vendor was unaware that he was selling to a connected person (a company) and had negotiated on the basis that they were unconnected. He sold the property for £94,000 below the market value because he mistakenly thought that he was liable for repairs to the property. HMRC agreed that he had no gratuitous intention but argued that the discrepancy between the market value and the actual value of the land meant that it was not one which could have been expected on an arm's length sale. The Court of Session in Scotland dismissed the argument that any such discrepancy would automatically invoke the section, stating that it was merely one factor which had to be taken into account. They decided that a hypothetical arm's length vendor should be taken to have had the actual vendor's (reasonable) belief that he was liable for repairs and so, since the price was not unreasonable given that belief, they found for the taxpayer. They were impressed by the fact that the price had been negotiated between persons who thought they were acting at arm's length. One consequence of this decision is therefore that in assessing what can be expected on an arm's length sale certain subjective factors, such as the reasonable belief in this case, are to be taken into account.

Intent to confer a gratuitous benefit

19–11   Where the parties are not connected, the central issue is whether the transferor can show the negative intent of not conferring any gratuitous benefit on the transferee. This was considered by the Special Commissioners in *Executors of Postlethwaite v HMRC* (2006). They pointed out that the fact that there was a gratuitous benefit actually conferred was not determinative but simply a factor as to intent, which was the key issue. They considered that a payment made under a binding legal obligation would not be so intended. They also thought that past consideration might well negative the intention. On the facts they found no such intention since the money paid was a sum to which the recipient already had an economic entitlement.

Potentially exempt transfers

Definition

19–12   There are three types of lifetime transfer for IHT purposes—transfers which are exempt[11] (see Ch.20), transfers which are potentially exempt and transfers which are immediately chargeable. Exempt transfers do not have any IHT consequences and can be ignored. Most other lifetime transfers are PETs. Potential exemption is a temporary status. If the donor survives the transfer for seven years, the transfer becomes completed exempt and can now be ignored. If the donor dies within seven years of the transfer, it becomes chargeable. The third category consists of transfers which are neither exempt nor potentially exempt, and these are immediately chargeable to tax.

A PET is defined under s.3A(1) as: (i) a transfer made by an individual; (ii) which would otherwise be a chargeable transfer; (iii) which is made to another individual or into a *disabled trust* or on the coming to an end, during the lifetime of the beneficial holder, of an *immediate post-death interest* in the settlement, which then continues as a *bereaved minor's trust*.[12] Thus transfers to companies, unincorporated associations, sports clubs without charitable status, and most of the various charges involving trusts are not potentially exempt transfers. They are therefore immediately chargeable transfers.

In the case of a transfer to an individual the transfer will only be a PET if the property becomes part of that individual's estate or his estate is increased. Thus if David decides to pay

---

[11] Including the equivalent of exemption, such as not being a transfer of value.
[12] All these terms are explained in Ch.22.

his grandson's school fees and does so by paying the school direct he has not made a PET—the grandson's estate has not been increased. It would be a PET if David gave the money to his son who then used the money to pay the school fees as the son's estate will have been increased. Gifts with a reservation, i.e. where the donor retains some interest in the property, are the subject of special rules, set out in the following part of this chapter.

Effect of being a PET

We will explain the somewhat tortuous rules for calculating the **19–13** charges to IHT in Ch.21. For the moment it is sufficient to note that a lifetime transfer which is not a PET attracts an immediate charge based on the cumulative total of such transfers within the previous seven years. The current (2016/17) rate for immediately chargeable lifetime transfers is 20 per cent on cumulative transfers above £325,000. Thus if Edward, having made no previous transfers, creates two discretionary trusts in 2015 and 2016, each with a value of £325,000—the first will be tax free but the second will be chargeable at 20 per cent.

If the transfer is a PET then it is assumed at the time of the transfer that the donor will survive for seven years. This means that there is no immediate charge to tax and if the transferor lives for more than seven years there will be no charge at all as the transfer achieves exempt status. If, however, the transferor dies within that period the PET becomes chargeable at the appropriate rate for deaths (which is currently double the rate for lifetime transfers, subject to some relief if he has survived at least three years). This is the rate at the date of death rather than the rate in force when the transfer was made, unless the former is higher. Another effect of a PET retrospectively becoming a chargeable transfer is that it will have to be taken into account in working out the transferor's cumulative total for subsequent lifetime transfers. This can retrospectively affect the liability for those other transfers. Thus if in our example above, Edward had made a PET of £325,000 in 2014, which subsequently becomes chargeable on his death in 2016, not only is that transfer itself charged to tax but the relevant cumulative total of previous transfers for, say, a discretionary trust transfer in 2015 will change from zero to £325,000 and the latter will become chargeable at 20 per cent.[13]

---

[13] In fact, as we shall see, because Edward has died within seven years of setting up the discretionary trusts, additional tax above the 20 per cent becomes payable, up to the full death-rate, depending on the length of time Edward survived.

Gifts with reservation of benefit

Purpose of the legislation

19–14   With the introduction of the PET regime in 1986 it was inevitable that measures would be taken to prevent a transferor making a gift, e.g. of his house to his son or daughter, whilst retaining a benefit in that property, e.g. by continuing to live in the house. If the transferor lived for more than seven years after making the gift he would avoid any IHT and would have passed on his house to his son or daughter tax free, whilst in practice having made no material change in his circumstances. To prevent taxpayers having their cake and eating it in this way the concept of a gift with reservation was re-introduced by s.102 of and Sch.20 to FA 1986. This concept could be said to have been re-introduced because it had been necessary under estate duty law to prevent exactly the same abuse. The basic legislation is similar to that for estate duty and some of the cases decided under those rules are relevant here. One issue which also arose under the 1986 rules was decided in such a way by the House of Lords under the new rules that additional legislation, ss.102A, 102B and 102C was introduced in 1999.

One problem with using the former estate duty concept of a gift is that it does not always square with the IHT concept of a transfer of value. Thus, whilst a bad bargain may be a transfer of value if it is between connected persons because there will be a loss to the transferor's estate and it will not fall within the gratuitous benefit exemption, it is hard to see that there is any element of bounty so as to classify it as a gift.[14]

19–15   Section 102 of FA 1986 applies when an individual disposes of any property by way of gift and either:

(a) possession and enjoyment is not bona fide assumed by the donee at, or before the beginning of the relevant period; or

(b) at any time in the relevant period the property is not enjoyed to the entire exclusion, or virtually the entire exclusion,[15] of the donor and of any benefit to him by contract or otherwise.

The *relevant period* in which both possession and enjoyment

---

[14] It is also arguable that a disposition which is deemed by IHTA not to be a transfer of value, e.g. one for the maintenance of the family (see para.20–13), will still be a gift for this purpose.

[15] The words "or virtually" were not present in the original estate duty provisions and are intended to allow, e.g. the donor of a house to return to it on visits or a short holiday.

must be assumed and the entire exclusion of the donor is assessed, is seven years prior to the death of the donor. Thus if at any time in the seven years prior to his death the donor was not so excluded or possession was not taken up by the donee, the gift will be regarded as one subject to a reservation. It follows that if any such benefit is given up and possession has been assumed more than seven years before the death then there is no gift with a reservation and in fact no charge to IHT.

Effect of a reservation

There are two possible consequences of a gift being regarded **19–16** as one subject to a reservation. First, whenever it was made, if the gift is still subject to a reservation at the date of the donor's death, the property given is deemed to be part of the donor's estate at death and so chargeable as if he had never given it away.

Thus in *Sillars v IRC* (2004), where the deceased and her two daughters were joint tenants of a building society account, the deceased was deemed to own the whole amount at death. When the daughters' names were added to the account, the deceased was still entitled to a share of the whole and the property had not been enjoyed to the entire exclusion of the deceased. In *Buzzoni v HMRC* (2013), the Court of Appeal, overturning both tribunal decisions in the case, held in that case there was no reservation of benefit. A was the lessee of property and granted a sublease to B. Under the sublease, B undertook to perform A's obligations to the owner of the property which, it was argued by HMRC, meant that A retained a benefit from the sublease. There was, however, a further important factor which had to be taken into account, according to the Court of Appeal: prior to the grant of the sublease, B had already entered into covenants with the owner which were identical to the obligations undertaken in the sublease. This meant that B was not further burdened by the obligations in the sublease, as he was *already* burdened by the prior agreement with the owner. The sublease imposed no extra burden on B. The Court of Appeal held that the reservation of benefit rules did not bite unless there was detriment suffered by the donee, which there was not in this case. The limitation of *Buzzoni* is demonstrated in *Hood's Executors* (2016), where, with facts which were similar but with no prior undertaking directly between the sublessees and the owner, the reservation of benefit rules applied.

Secondly, if the gift ceases to be subject to a reservation within seven years before the donor's death, the donor is treated as if he had made a PET at that date. Thus the property will be retrospectively charged under the PET rules as if the donor had made a chargeable transfer of the property at the date when the reservation ceased.

Interpreting the legislation

19–17　Using, in part, the old estate duty cases it is possible to shed some light on how the courts will interpret the various parts of s.102 of FA 1986. With regard to the concept of the donee assuming bona fide possession in para.(a) it is clear that to do so the gift must be a perfect transfer in equity.[16] This was the decision in *Letts v IRC* (1957). Looking at para.(b), it has been held that the donor will not be entirely excluded from possession of the property unless that is the position in fact as well as in law. Thus in *Oakes v Commissioner of Stamp Duties* (1954), a settlor who settled property in which he had no interest was caught when he was appointed as a trustee with a right to remuneration, and in *Stamp Duties Commissioner of New South Wales v Permanent Trustee Co* (1956), where the settlor borrowed the interest arising from the settlement on his daughter, with no legal entitlement to do so, a similar result applied.

The inclusion of a benefit "by contract or otherwise" is intended to catch collateral benefits to the donor. In *Attorney General v Seccombe* (1911) it was held that such benefits had to be the subject of a legal entitlement. It is doubted whether that would now be the law. Thus it has been held that a gift into a discretionary trust of which the donor is a potential beneficiary is a gift with reservation under ground (b), (donor not entirely excluded, etc.). Further, if the donor may exercise a significant control over the trust, it will also be a gift with reservation under ground (a), (possession by the trustees not assumed, etc.).[17] Under s.102ZA, in the few situations where the holder of a beneficial interest in settled property is treated for tax purposes as owning the whole settled property,[18] for the purpose of s.102 that holder is treated as enjoying the whole property prior to the gift or termination of the interest.

Schedule 20 expressly excludes two factual situations from being a reservation of a benefit. Paragraph 6 provides that actual occupation of land by the donor in return for full consideration in money or where the donor comes back into actual occupation

---

[16] Remember that in general, equity will not perfect an imperfect gift so that if any formalities required to effect a gift have not been undertaken by the donor, there is no perfect gift.

[17] *Lyon's Personal Representatives v HMRC* (2007) Sp Comm, following Lightman J in *IRC v Eversden* (2002). The latter case was decided by the CA on a different point (2003), but the CA accepted the position of the judge on this point.

[18] See Ch.22 below.

of land owing to his incapacity and it is for reasonable provision for his care and maintenance by the donee who is a relative of the donor, are not to be regarded as a reservation of a benefit by the donor.

Benefits reserved or retained

The most complex of the cases are those which draw a distinc- **19–18** tion between a benefit reserved out of the property given away and a benefit retained by the donor which was never given away in the first place. The importance of this is that in the second case the property actually given away has never been the subject of a reservation. This is easier to state than to apply in practice, however. The trick is to separate the part retained by the donor from the part given away. This is sometimes explained by reference to *vertical and horizontal separation.*

For example if Fred owns two adjoining houses and gives one to Gillian whilst retaining the other this is said to be vertical separation. The fact that Fred has retained one house does not mean that he has retained any benefit in the other which thus becomes a PET.

Suppose, instead, Fred creates an interest, such as a lease, in his property and then gives away the rest, he has horizontally separated the two and so has no benefit in the part given away. It would be different if he gave away the whole property and was then given back the interest in it—he would have reserved a benefit in the property.

TIMING With regard to such horizontal separation the **19–19** timing of the separation is crucial. The original authority for its effectiveness is *Munro v Commissioner of Stamp Duties* (1934), where the donor gave away land subject to his interest as a partner in its use which had been created prior to the gift. He was held to have given away only the land subject to the partnership interest. He had not reserved his interest as a partner, he had simply never given it away at all. This decision was distinguished in *Nichols v IRC* (1975) where the donor gave his land away subject to a condition that it was leased back to him by the donee. He was held to have given away the whole property and reserved the benefit of the lease. The lease had not been created by a prior transaction unlike the partnership interest in *Munro.*

In *Ingram v IRC* (1999), decided under the modern regime, the donor transferred property to trustees and, in an attempt to avoid the decision in *Nicholls*, at the same time created the right to a lease of the property to herself. The Court of Appeal agreed with the general principle as to the timing of the separation in *Nichols* but it was rejected by the House of Lords. In their opinion a gift of the freehold of land with a condition that a lease back to the donor be granted was not a gift with reservation. All that the donor had given away was the reversions, in which she had no benefit. The ban was against a reservation on the *interest* disposed of and not the *property*. *Nichols* was distinguished on the basis that in that case there was an additional reservation under a different head because the donee had covenanted to repair the land and so the donor, in occupation of it under the lease, was not entirely excluded from benefit by contract. This allowed the House of Lords to decide that the general reservation point in *Nichols* was obiter.

Special rules for land

19–20 The success of what was known as the "lease carve out scheme" in *Ingram* "disappointed" HMRC, who then, in time-honoured fashion, took the first opportunity to introduce legislation to reverse the decision. The main section is s.102A inserted into FA 1986. It applies only where the gift is of an interest in land and where it would not otherwise be a gift with reservation under the general rules.[19] In practice it is of course in relation to land that such schemes will mainly apply because of the possibilities of creating horizontal interests in land. The section provides that where X makes a gift of an interest in land there will be a gift with a reservation if within the relevant period[20] either: (1) X (the donor) or his spouse has a *significant right or interest* in relation to the land; or (2) X or his spouse is a party to a *significant arrangement* in relation to the land (s.102A(2)).

19–21 SIGNIFICANT INTEREST An interest, right or arrangement is significant for this purpose if it *entitles* or *enables* X to occupy all or part of the land or to enjoy some right in relation to all or part of the land[21] otherwise than for full consideration in money or money's worth (s.102A(3)). This means that for the section to apply it must be X who occupies the land or enjoys the right, even if it is his spouse who has the interest. Thus if X gives some land to Y on condition that it is leased back to X's spouse, but X occupies the land with his spouse's consent, it will be caught because X's spouse has an interest which is a

---

[19] Such as a reservation of benefit by a contract (the covenant to repair) as in *Nicholls*.
[20] Remember that this is the seven years before X's subsequent death.
[21] This will include rights such as shooting rights, etc.

significant one since it has enabled X to occupy the land. The use of the word *enables* may cause problems since it is far less precise than *entitles*. For example, suppose that X gives land to Y on condition that it is leased back to Z who is not X's spouse. Z then allows X to occupy the land. Is X a party to a significant arrangement, i.e. one which enables him to occupy the land?

SEVEN YEAR LIMIT An important limit on the scope of **19–22** s.102A is that subs.(5) exempts interests or rights which X or his spouse were granted more than seven years before the gift of land.[22] Thus, at first sight, if X grants his spouse a lease in year one and gives the reversion to Y in year nine, there will be no reservation even if X continues to occupy the land. But this seven-year period does not apply to arrangements, so that any arrangement made at any time before the gift will count if it is significant. Therefore, if the above example can be regarded as an arrangement, it will still be a gift with reservation since X's occupation will make it significant. Thus it can be seen that these provisions apply to interests, etc. created well before the gift and not just to lease carve out schemes of the *Ingram* type. Under the old rules HMRC used to ignore events prior to the gift if they were "prior independent transactions".[23]

EXCEPTIONS Section 102A does not apply in certain **19–23** circumstances where the general rule in s.102 would also not apply, e.g. occupation by X due to unforeseen circumstances. Nor does it apply where X gives Y a lease and retains the reversion (s.102A(4)(b)) which is the converse to a lease carve out.

UNDIVIDED SHARES More fundamentally s.102A does not **19–24** apply to gifts of an undivided share in land (i.e. in England the creation of a tenancy in common, in Scotland gift of a share in the property, thus creating common property). In fact in such a case even the general provisions in s.102 are not to apply (s.102C(6)). Instead s.102B applies. Under that section, where X gives Y an undivided share in his land so that X and Y become tenants in common, or common owners in Scotland, he will have made a gift with reservation unless: (1) X does not occupy the land[24]; (2) X occupies the land to the entire exclusion of Y

---

[22] Be careful not to confuse this with the period of seven years before X's death in which the significant right, interest or arrangement must still exist before there can be a charge, whenever the gift was made.

[23] Which of course they seldom were in practice.

[24] Since s.102 does not apply X can receive rent, etc. from the land provided he is not in occupation of it.

for full consideration in money or money's worth[25]; or (3) X and Y occupy the land and X does not receive any benefit, other than a negligible one, provided by Y or at his expense for some reason connected with the gift. This last situation will therefore protect X if Y pays only his fair share of the outgoings of the land. There will also be no charge where X occupies the land due to unforeseen circumstances.

Effect of exempt transfers

19–25   Section 102(5) provides that where the gift is one of a selected number of exempt transfer categories, including transfers to a spouse, then the gift with reservation principle will not apply. Following the success of scheme utilising the inter-spouse exemption for interests in possession in *IRC v Eversden* targeted anti-avoidance provisions were inserted into s.102 (subss.(5A), (5B), and (5C)) closing down the scheme.

Income tax alternative—the POAT

19–26   Despite the legislative attempts to counter avoidance, a further number of successful schemes were marketed which enabled taxpayers to obtain a benefit from assets which they had given away without being caught by the gift with reservation rules. HMRC therefore changed their point of attack and Sch.15 to FA 2004 introduced the pre-owned asset tax. This is a charge to **income tax** (from 2005/06) where a person enjoys a benefit (either free or at low cost) from an asset he formerly owned or provided the funds to purchase (known as a pre-owned asset) at any time since March 1986. There are detailed provisions as to how the benefit is to be quantified for land, chattels and intangible assets.

It is clear that this charge is intended as a residual charge where the IHT rules have been avoided. Thus it does not apply: (i) where the asset was disposed of at arm's length or on arm's length terms; (ii) where the disposal was into a trust in which the taxpayer or spouse has an interest in possession (potential IHT charge then anyway); (iii) where the disposal was to a spouse; (iv) where the IHT gifts with reservation rules apply or would apply but for existing IHT exemptions such as gifts to charity; (v) where the IHT rules do not apply because the taxpayer has given part of their interest to someone with whom the share occupation; and (vi) where the IHT rules would apply but for the exception for cases where the former owner needs to move back into the gifted property following a change in his circumstances (e.g. for reasons

---

[25] This is similar to the position under ss.102 and 102A.

of age). As an alternative to this charge, a former owner may elect to have the asset(s) treated as part of their estate for IHT purposes.

Property subject to the charge

The final question involving gifts subject to a reservation is that if they do become chargeable to IHT what property is actually subject to the charge? The answers to this are to be found in Sch.20 to FA 1986. If the property originally given is still held by the donee unchanged in form then of course it will be that property, valued now, which is chargeable. But if the donee has parted with the original gift an alternative is required. In outline, if the donee sells or exchanges the asset for full consideration then that sum or replacement asset becomes the subject of any charge. In other cases the property with which he parted (including any replacement asset taken in full exchange) becomes the subject of the charge. The same rules apply broadly to gifts into a settlement. It is important to note that it is the full value of the property original given away which is brought into the charge to tax, irrespective of the value of the benefit exercised over the property. So, for example, if someone made a transfer into trust for his family and several years later, finding himself in straitened times, borrows some money back from the trust, it is the whole of the value in the trust which is caught by the rules, not the value of the benefit to the donor.

19–27

Transfers on death

Transfer of value

Section 4(1) declares that:

19–28

"On the death of any person tax shall be charged as if, immediately before his death he had made a transfer of value and the value transferred by it had been equal to the value of his estate immediately before his death."

It is this enactment which brought in IHT as a replacement of estate duty.

The effect of s.4 is that the deceased is deemed to have made a disposition of all his assets the moment before death. The total of those assets must then be added to the cumulative total of his chargeable lifetime transfers made in the past seven years and charged at the appropriate rate. The rate of tax on a death is twice that on a lifetime transfer, although the former may also be liable to CGT.

Retrospective effect

19–29 We have already seen that the death of the transferor will also make all PETs made within the past seven years retrospectively chargeable (and part of the cumulative total for subsequent previous transfers) and that a gift still subject to a reservation at the death will also become chargeable at the rates for a death. The death will also increase the rate of tax already paid on an immediately chargeable lifetime transfer made by the deceased within seven years prior to the death. One minor blessing is that since the deceased has transferred all his assets on his death there can be no question of grossing up the transfer to include the tax payable—that must come out of the assets transferred. Questions as to who pays the tax and who ultimately bears the cost (e.g. as between the beneficiaries) are the subject of Ch.23.

Timing of transfer

19–30 What is the point of deeming the transfer of value to have been made "immediately before" the death, not "on" the death? Presumably it is to knock out any argument that at the moment of death certain interests of the person dying cease to exist and therefore do not form part of his estate. This argument could have been put forward, for example, in relation to the interest of a joint tenant which is extinguished "on" the death: s.171(2).

Similarly exercising a power of appointment by will does not affect the fact that such a power formed part of the estate immediately before the death. Estate has the same meaning as for lifetime transfers. Moving the deemed transfer from the moment of death to "immediately before" the death also makes it easier for the legislation to lay down its own code of rules, untrammelled by the general law, as to which assets are to be treated as forming part of the estate and which are not. Such a code is laid down in ss.171–177. For example, there is an allowance for reasonable funeral expenses under s.172.

Common calamities

19–31 It is important to know what is the tax position if two (or more) persons die (for example in a car accident) virtually at the same instant. In Scotland, where the order of deaths is uncertain, they are treated as if neither survived the other.[26] This means that any property left by one to the other is not treated as part of the estate of the other for IHT purposes—it is not part of the other's estate immediately before death as required by s.4(1). However, the law of succession to property in such a case in England and Wales is stated

---

[26] Succession (Scotland) Act 2016 s.9.

in s.184 of the Law of Property Act 1925, namely that the younger person is deemed to have survived the elder person. This does cause a potential problem of double taxation—once in the estate of the elder, and again in the estate of the deemed survivor. For tax purposes s.4(2) provides that "where it cannot be known which of two or more persons who have died survived the other or others they shall be assumed to have died at the same instant." Suppose that the two persons are Albert and his son Ben. The effect is that the estate left by Albert to Ben is charged to tax on Albert's death but not also on Ben's death. Similarly, if Ben has left anything to Albert, that estate is charged on Ben's death but not also on Albert's death. Where the order of death *is* known (e.g. Albert dies five minutes before Ben) s.4(2) does not apply, but there may be "Quick Succession Relief": see para.20–34. An alternative is to provide in a will that property will only pass to a beneficiary if he survives the testator by a specified period. Such survivorship clauses, if limited to six months, will also avoid a double charge: s.92.

Other charges

This rather curious chapter title is taken from FA 1975 where "Other Charges" was used as a cross-heading to describe four sections, 39–42, grouped together in that Act as being, broadly speaking, anti-avoidance measures. This section covers various matters, mostly concerned with anti-avoidance, not dealt with elsewhere in the book. **19–32**

Close companies

In general, IHT is not charged on companies because they are not "individuals". There is obvious scope for avoidance here. But, by s.94, where a company which is a close company makes a transfer of value a tax charge may arise—not on the company but on its "participators", broadly shareholders. Such transfers cannot be PETs and so attract an immediate charge to the tax. The intention is to prevent such companies from being used to avoid the tax. Tax is charged as if each participator, domiciled here, had made a transfer of value proportionate to his interest in the company.[27] But against this can be set the amount (if any) by which the value of his estate is increased. **19–33**

---

[27] Close companies are defined by reference to control for corporation tax purposes. But see s.96 which excludes the ownership of preference shares for this purpose. Broadly, a company is "close" if it is controlled by five or fewer participators or participator who are directors or if, on a winding up, five or fewer participators would be entitled to receive more than 50 per cent of any distribution (CTA 2010 s.439(2)).

So (for example) a return of capital would be a gratuitous transfer by the company, but no tax would be payable because each member's estate would be increased by the amount received. His estate (for this purpose) does not include any rights or interests in the company.

Section 98 provides that where there is an alteration of such a company's shares or debentures or rights attaching to them so that there is a loss to a transferor's estate there will be a chargeable transfer by the participators. This is to prevent value being passed in ways that it might be impossible to establish that the transferor shareholder has made a disposition, e.g. on a reduction of capital or a purchase by a company of its own shares. The sections are aimed at various avoidance devices, and consequently s.102 provides that a "close company" includes not only a company which is a close company for purposes of corporation tax but also a company which would be such a close company if it were resident in the UK.

Future payments

19–34   This matter is dealt with (in rather obscure language) by s.262. Where a transfer of value takes the form of a disposition for which payments are made (or assets are transferred) more than a year after the disposition, each payment is taxed separately when it is made, the tax being based on a proportionate part of the value transferred. For example, if A buys a property for more than its market value, that is, on the general principles of the tax, a transfer of value by A of the amount by which the price exceeds the market value—the gratuitous element. The effect of this present section is that if A agrees to pay by instalments, each instalment counts as a separate transfer of value. (The rule does not apply to a disposition for no consideration at all, such as an ordinary seven-year covenant.) The point of the section is (presumably) to spread the amount of value transferred. Thus some of the instalments may fall within seven years before A's death, thus attracting a charge, whereas the earlier ones may escape such a charge under the PET rules.

Interest-free loans

19–35   This matter was originally intended to be dealt with by s.41 (of FA 1975) but that was replaced by FA 1976 s.115 before it came into effect. That section was itself repealed and there are no specific provisions now to deal with interest-free loans. The position is therefore covered only by the general provisions of the Act. It follows that a fixed-term loan of money or assets may be a transfer of value. For example, if A lends B £1,000 interest-free for five years, gratuitously, A is making a transfer to B of the then value of using the money for that period. But if the loan was repayable on demand, there would be no value transferred, and no IHT charge.

Annuity purchased in conjunction with life policy

Section 263 imposes a charge to tax where the purchase of an **19–36** annuity is an associated operation with the issue of a life policy on the life of the annuitant and the policy is vested in someone other than the purchaser of the annuity. The purchaser is treated as making a transfer of value at the time the life policy becomes vested in that other person. The amount of the transfer of value is whichever is the less of the following: (a) the sum paid for the annuity plus premiums paid under the policy up to the time of the transfer; (b) the greatest benefit capable of being conferred at any time by the policy. Such transfers are PETs.

It seems that this special charge to tax is additional to the charge which may arise (if no exemption applies) from the transferor's keeping the policy on foot by paying the premiums, each premium payment being a transfer of value.

The reason why HMRC are so concerned about back-to-back policies is that a linked contract for life assurance and an annuity with the same company can be obtained on very favourable terms, because if the company loses on the assurance policy it will gain on the annuity contract. Because of this background, HMRC will be prepared to treat the arrangements as not being associated operations (and hence not taxable) if the life policy has been issued on full medical evidence[28] and on no different terms from those which would have been obtainable without the annuity link.

Associated operations

It is stated in s.272 (the definitions section) that a "disposition" **19–37** includes "a disposition effected by *associated operations*" and "associated operations" are defined by s.268. They are

"(a) operations which affect the same property . . . or
(b) any two operations of which one is effected with reference to the other, or with a view to enabling the other to be effected or facilitating its being effected, and any further operation having a like relation to any of those two, and so on: whether those operations are effected by the same person or different persons, and whether or not they are simultaneous; and 'operation' includes an omission."

---

[28] See *Smith v HMRC* (2008) on that point.

A simple example of how this provision might work arises from an attempt to manipulate the exempt transfer provisions. As we shall see transfers between spouses are, in general, exempt and each individual may make exempt transfers up to £3,000 in each tax year. Suppose Albert is a wealthy taxpayer who has already given £3,000 to his son, Ben in the current year. Albert could give £3,000 to his wife Zö, who could then give that money to Ben, using her exempt amount. None of the transfers is a chargeable transfer. Under the associated operations provisions the transfer of the second £3,000 to Ben could be treated as if it had been made by Albert and so chargeable if Albert were to die within seven years, even if Zö is still alive.

19–38   LIMITATIONS   The definition of associated operations is on the face of it very wide. The section has been before the courts on a number of occasions involving settlements. In *Macpherson v IRC* (1988) the trustees entered into two transactions which together had the effect of lowering the charge to tax on the second. The House of Lords had no difficulty in deciding that these were associated operations but the case is worth noting because their Lordships imposed a restriction on the width of the section by insisting that each operation must be relevant to the scheme which created the benefit for the transferee.

That restrictive theme was taken up and developed by Park J and the Court of Appeal in *Rysaffe Trustee Co (CI) Ltd v IRC* (2003). The taxpayer had made five separate but basically identical discretionary settlements. HMRC sought to treat them as being one settlement, i.e. that together they amounted to a single disposition, the creation of a settlement. The judge held that each settlement was a separate settlement, each of which had been effected by a single disposition and not by a series of dispositions. Whilst the definition of "associated operations" was quite wide, its practical operation was very limited. It was simply a definition and not a catch-all anti-avoidance provision which could be invoked to nullify the effectiveness of any scheme or structure which could be said to have involved more than one operation and which was intended to avoid or reduce tax (i.e. it was not a *Ramsay* type of provision). Where two or more transactions take place, they may be associated operations in the sense that they were effected by reference to each other, etc. but they will only be *relevant* associated operations if they contribute to the actual transfer of value.

The judge approved and followed a decision of the Special Commissioners in *Reynaud v IRC* (1999). In that case the taxpayers transferred shares in a private company to trustees.

The company then purchased those shares from the trustees for cash. HMRC sought to add these two events together to say that the gifts were therefore of cash and not shares and so not eligible for business relief. The Commissioners refused, saying that the transfer of value (the shares) was effected by a single disposition and not by a series of dispositions. The same was true of each of the settlements in the present case, the value transferred had been completed by each transfer—no other transaction was needed to effect that, unlike the example given earlier of two transactions being used to effect a transfer from Albert to Ben. The judge's reasoning was subsequently upheld by the Court of Appeal. The inclusion of associated operations in the description of a disposition was not intended for cases where there was clearly a disposition of property falling within the Act, but where there was a dispute as to whether there was such a disposition at all.

CONSEQUENCES If the associated operations provision **19–39** applies then the consequence is that the chargeable transfer is deemed to take place at the time of the last of them: s.268(3). There is one statutory exception in s.268(2). The grant of a lease for full consideration is not to be associated with any operation effected more than three years earlier, e.g. a gift of the landlord's reversion.

Settled property
The application of IHT to settled property is the subject of **19–40** Ch.22 below.

CHAPTER 20

EXEMPTIONS AND RELIEFS

Introduction

20–01 The legislation gives relief from tax in various ways. Some kinds of property are declared to be excluded property. Some transactions are declared not to be transfers of value. Some transfers of value are declared to be exempt transfers, thus attracting no tax. Some transfers of value, though they are taxable, attract a reduced amount of tax. Some apply to lifetime transfers only, some to transfers on a death and others to all types of transfer. On the whole, it does not matter a great deal whether a transfer is exempt, not a transfer of value or whether it is of excluded property—no tax is generally charged in each case. One or two points of difference are noted below.

EXEMPT TRANSFERS

Transfers between spouses and civil partners: s.18

20–02 Transfers between spouses and civil partners are exempt transfers. This is true both of lifetime transfers and of transfers on death. This exemption is obviously of immense importance in tax planning. As we shall see in the next chapter, spouses and civil partners also have transferable nil-rate bands on death. The fact that no such largesse applies, e.g. to siblings sharing a house, was held not to be a breach of the human rights legislation by the European Court of Human Rights in *Burden v United Kingdom* (2008).

The exemption is stated in s.18:

> "A transfer of value is an exempt transfer to the extent that the value transferred is attributable to property which becomes comprised in the estate of the transferor's spouse or civil partner, or, so far as the value transferred is not so attributable, to the extent that that estate is increased."

The first part of the section gives exemption to the straightforward case where one spouse or civil partner transfers some item of cash or property to the other. The second part of the section deals with less clear-cut cases. An example would be a case where one spouse or civil partner forgives a debt owed to him (or her) by the other. The forgiveness is a transfer of value, but it is an exempt transfer because, although no property becomes comprised in the estate of the forgiven spouse or civil partner, that estate is increased by the amount of the debt.

Exceptions and limitations

The exemption does not apply if the disposition takes effect on the termination *after the transfer of value* of any interest or period. So if H (husband) leaves or settles property to X (any third party) for life and then to W (H's wife) the exemption does not apply.[1] Similarly if H leaves property to X for 10 years and then to W. Also, the exemption does not apply if the disposition depends on a condition which is not satisfied within 12 months. An example would be if H left property to W provided she becomes a vegetarian within 18 months. 14 months after H's death, W becomes a vegetarian. The exemption is not available. But the exemption is not excluded by reason only that the gift is conditional on one spouse or civil partner surviving the other for a specified period. So a survivorship clause in a will does not knock out the exemption provided the survivorship period is not more than 12 months. In practice wills are commonly drawn with a survivorship period of less than 6 months in order to satisfy s.92 and thus avoid the inadvertent tax consequences of the creation of a contingent interest in favour of the beneficiary. Under s.92, the estate is taxed according to the actual outcome under the survivorship clause.

As an anti-avoidance measure, the exemption does not apply if the spouse or civil partner has purchased the reversionary interest in the property: see s.56(2).

There is no requirement that the spouses or civil partners must be living together. But if the transferor is domiciled in the UK and the transferee is domiciled abroad, the exemption is subject to a restricted lifetime cumulative limit of the prevailing nil-rate band. For example, A gives £350,000 to his non-UK domiciled spouse in 2016. £325,000 of this is exempt but £25,000 is a PET. Subsequently in 2022 the nil-rate band is increased to £400,000. A can then transfer another £75,000 to his spouse within the exemption.

20–03

---

[1] But if H is either still alive when X dies, or he died no more then two years before, there will be an exemption on X's death: s.53(4).

Annual exemption: s.19

20–04 Lifetime transfers of value made by a transferor in any one year are exempt to the extent that the values transferred do not exceed the now small amount of £3,000, a figure which has not been increased for many years, probably because of the PET regime. The exemption applies both to lifetime transfers which are chargeable immediately, and PETs which become chargeable. The values are to be calculated for this purpose as values on which no tax is payable; in other words, without grossing up. The year ends on 5 April. Unused relief may be carried forward into the next year to be used after the amount for that year but any shortfall cannot be carried forward any further. Thus if in year 1, X gives away £2,500 he can carry forward £500 to year 2. If in that year he gives away £3,200 he uses the £3,000 for that year and £200 from year 1. The remaining £300 is lost.

As husband and wife and civil partners are separate chargeable individuals for the purposes of IHT, each can make gifts up to £3,000 per year without either of them incurring any IHT.

Where the transferor makes more than one transfer of value in a tax year the relief is normally given against earlier rather than later transfers. Where, there are both PETs and lifetime chargeable transfers in the same year, the relief is first given against any transfers which are not PETs in that year. If the PET subsequently becomes chargeable it will be treated as having been made after any lifetime chargeable transfer for the purposes of the exemption for that year. So, if A makes a PET in year 1 followed by a chargeable transfer in the same year, the chargeable transfer gets first allocation of the annual exemption. Any left over can be set against the earliest PET should it become chargeable.

Small gifts to same person: s.20

20–05 Lifetime transfers of value made by a transferor in any one tax year to any one person are exempt to the extent that the values transferred by them (calculated as values on which no tax is chargeable) do not exceed £250. This exemption does not apply to transfers on death, and it only applies to lifetime transfers which are "outright gifts", as distinct from gifts in settlement. It does not apply to part of gifts in excess of £250. Again the figure has not been increased for many years.

Learned articles have been published arguing that the wording of the legislation is such that this "small gifts exemption" and "the £3,000 exemption" (and some other exemptions) are not wholly independent and that in some circumstances they are not cumulative.[2] The position is unclear, however, and there is a good argument that the two exemptions are cumulative. So we think one can say that a taxpayer (Albert perhaps) can give up to £250 to any number of different persons in a year and can also make £3,000 worth of gifts, all exempt from tax, e.g. £3,250 to B plus £250 to C plus £250 to D and so on through the alphabet (if his generosity runs so far). The small amounts involved, however, mean that a resolution of this problem is unlikely.

Normal expenditure out of income: s.21

A lifetime transfer of value is an exempt transfer if, or to the extent that, it is shown: (a) that it was made as part of normal expenditure of the transferor; and (b) that (taking one year with another) it was made out of his income; and (c) that, after allowing for all transfers of value forming part of his normal expenditure, the transferor was left with sufficient income to maintain his usual standard of living.

Some guidance as to what is meant by "normal expenditure" for this purpose was provided by Lightman J in *Bennett v IRC* (1995). Mrs Bennett had been given a life interest under her husband's will with her sons taking the whole amount after her death. Initially the income produced by the trust fund was sufficient to meet her needs, which were described by the judge as "modest". Subsequently the income produced by the fund increased substantially and she instructed the trustees that since she did not require any additional income, the surplus income should be paid out to the sons. Her needs did indeed continue to be modest. The trustees did as instructed, although on a conservative basis and, by the date of her death, had made two sets of payments to the sons. Mrs Bennett died unexpectedly two years after giving this instruction and HMRC sought to charge the payments to the sons as PETs by her, which were activated by her death. The sons argued that the normal expenditure out of income exception applied.

Lightman J put forward three propositions. First, that for expenditure to be normal, each payment had to be shown to conform to an established pattern of expenditure by the payer. Such a pattern could be established by proof of the existence of

20–06

[2] See particularly David Feldman in [1977] B.T.R. 164.

a prior commitment or resolve (e.g. a regular payment) or by reference to a sequence of payments, e.g. by paying the instalments on a life assurance policy.[3] Thus a death bed commitment would not satisfy either requirement. There was no need, however, either for a legal obligation or a minimum period. Secondly, the amount need not be fixed and the recipient need not be the same, so that, e.g. paying the costs of elderly relatives' nursing home expenses would suffice. Thirdly, the fact that the income was unreasonable or idiosyncratic did not mean that it was not normal for the particular individual. Applying all this to the facts, the judge held that the exception applied in this case. There was a pattern in respect of the surplus income, which she genuinely did not need, and the payments to the sons had been made in accordance with that pattern.

Gifts in consideration of marriage or civil partnership: s.22

20–07   A gift in consideration of marriage or a civil partnership is not defined in the legislation. It has been established by previous case law that a gift is a gift in consideration of marriage if it fulfils three requisites: it is made on the occasion of a marriage; it is conditional on the marriage taking place; and it is made for the purpose of, or with a view to encouraging or facilitating, the particular marriage: see the estate duty case of *IRC v Lord Rennell* (1964) HL.[4] We can assume that the same criteria will apply to a civil partnership.

Transfers of value made by gifts in consideration of marriage or civil partnership are exempt under s.22 (if they are lifetime transfers or certain transfers under a settlement, as distinct from transfers on death) to the extent that the values transferred by such transfers made by any one transferor in respect of any one marriage (calculated net) do not exceed:

(a) in the case of gifts satisfying the conditions set out below by a parent of a party to the marriage or civil partnership, £5,000;

(b) in the case of other gifts satisfying those conditions, £2,500; and

(c) in any other case, £1,000.[5]

---

[3]   For an example of a case where there was no pattern of expenditure, see *Nadin v IRC* (1997).

[4]   Provided these conditions are fulfilled the motive of the donor is irrelevant. See *Re Park Dec'd. (No.2)* (1972).

[5]   Again these amounts have not been raised to cover the effects of inflation.

The conditions which have to be met to obtain the £5,000 or £2,500 exemption are:

(i) it is an outright gift to a child or remoter descendant of the transferor (thus each parent can give £5,000, and each grandparent £2,500, to the couple); or

(ii) the transferor is a parent or remoter ancestor of either party to the marriage or civil partnership, and either the gift is an outright gift to the other party to the marriage or civil partnership or the property comprised in the gift is settled by the gift; or

(iii) the transferor is a party to the marriage or civil partnership, and either the gift is an outright gift to the other party to the marriage or civil partnership or the property comprised in the gift is settled by the gift.

There are limits on who can benefit. To qualify for exemption an outright gift must be to a party to the marriage or civil partnership; and a settled gift can only include certain persons (notably the parties to the marriage and their issue) as beneficiaries or potential beneficiaries.

Gifts to charities: s.23

Transfers of value to charities are exempt transfers. There is no limit as to the amount and the exemption applies to both lifetime and death transfers. There are provisions which prevent the relief applying if the transfer is not an immediate and outright transfer, or if it could be used for other purposes.

20–08

Gifts to political parties: s.24

There is a similar unlimited exemption for gifts to political parties defined as one with either two members of the House of Commons or one member and at least 150,000 votes at the last general election.

20–09

Gifts to housing associations: s.24A

There is also a similar unlimited exemption for gifts to various providers of social housing, including housing associations.[6]

20–10

---

[6] These are defined by reference to the Housing Associations Act 1985 and Part 1 of the Housing Act 1996.

Gifts for national purposes, etc.: s.25

20–11   A transfer of value is an exempt transfer if it is made to certain bodies (sometimes referred to as "heritage bodies") being certain galleries, museums, libraries, national collections and preservation bodies, universities, university colleges, local authorities, or any government department. The bodies given this benefit are listed in Sch.3. They include the British Museum, the National Gallery, local authority museums, the National Trust, and "any government department," which would therefore include other national museums such as the Victoria and Albert Museum. The exemption applies to lifetime and death transfers, and there is no limit in amount. The exemption also applies where a PET is followed by a transfer to a Sch.3 body or the property is accepted by HMRC in satisfaction of tax under s.230: (s.26A). The exemption also applies to "gifts to the nation"—gifts of art or objects of pre-eminent important to the nation under the Cultural Gifts Scheme.[7]

Conditional exemption for works of art, historic buildings, etc.: ss.30–35A (as amended)

20–12   The things to which this conditional exemption relates are chattels of pre-eminent interest, works of art, scientific collections, land and buildings which are of outstanding scenic, architectural, historic or scientific interest and chattels historically associated with them. The sections apply to all transfers including to discretionary trusts, but the relief can only be sought in relation to a PET if it subsequently becomes chargeable. It is provided (no doubt as an anti-avoidance measure) that for relief to apply to a lifetime transfer the property must have either been owned for six years or the transferor must have acquired the property on a death which was itself a "conditionally exempt transfer" (see below). The relief must be claimed within two years.

To gain the relief the property has to be "designated" by the Treasury, and "undertakings" have to be given concerning preservation, access, etc. The rules relating to these undertakings were tightened in 1998, so that, for example, it is no longer sufficient to allow public access only by prior appointment.

A transfer is then called a "conditionally exempt transfer" so that any tax payable will be postponed. It is conditional because if an undertaking is not observed tax becomes payable on the

---

[7] FA 2012 Sch.14.

current value of the asset by reference to the transferor's cumulative total, but at the lifetime rate if the conditionally exempt transfer was not made on a death. Also, tax becomes payable on a subsequent sale or disposal of the property (including disposal on death).

There are two cases where a subsequent disposal is not a chargeable event: (a) if the subsequent death or gift is itself a conditionally exempt transfer or the undertaking previously given is replaced by an undertaking given by such person as HMRC think appropriate; (b) if within three years of the death the deceased's personal representatives (or, in the case of settled property, the trustees or the person next entitled) give the property or sell it by private treaty to one of the "heritage bodies" listed in Sch.3 (see para.20–11 above) or transfer the property to HMRC in satisfaction of tax.

Where the conditionally exempt transfer loses its exemption on a subsequent gift which is a PET, any IHT triggered will be available as a tax credit against the tax payable if the PET becomes chargeable.

The point of the exemption which has been discussed under this head,[8] as distinct from the heritage bodies exemption discussed above is that an ancestral home (for example), or a Rembrandt in an ancestral home, can be kept in the family.

A maintenance fund for historic houses, etc. can be set up under s.27. It is possible for property to be settled on trusts to finance the maintenance, repair or preservation of, or public access to, historic buildings or adjoining land without liability to inheritance tax. This relief, again, takes the form of a conditional exemption which becomes chargeable on the fund failing to meet the criteria.

DISPOSITIONS WHICH ARE NOT TRANSFERS OF VALUE

Dispositions for maintenance of family: s.11

The official HMRC view is that s.11 only applies to lifetime   **20–13**
transfers, and not to transfers on death. The point has never been tested in the courts, but HMRC view is probably correct, for one or other (or both) of two reasons: (1) The section uses the word "disposition". It is noticeable that the section relating to death (s.4) nowhere uses the word "disposition". It would seem to be

---

[8] It is sometimes called the "national heritage exemption". So we have the "national heritage exemption" as well as "heritage bodies" and "heritage property".

a fair inference that wherever in the IHT legislation the word "disposition" occurs the enactment is referring only to lifetime transfers; (2) the section uses the phrase "not a transfer of value", and it may well be (as some commentators assume) that wherever the legislation gives an exemption by saying that such-and-such shall "not be a transfer of value" that exemption is confined to lifetime transfers and does not cover transfers on death.

Section 11(1) declares that a disposition is not a transfer of value if it is made by one party to a marriage or civil partnership in favour of the other party or of a child of either party and is:

(a) for the maintenance of the other party; or
(b) for the maintenance, education or training of the child for a period ending not later than the year in which he attains the age of 18 or, after attaining that age, ceases to undergo full-time education or training.[9]

20–14 CHILDREN "Child" includes a step-child and an adopted child. A similar disposition in favour of an illegitimate child is exempt, but in this case only if the child is the child of the disponer (not of the other party to the marriage). A similar disposition in favour of a child who is someone else's child is exempt if the child is not in the care of a parent of his. But in this case, if the disposition is made after the child attains 18 years of age, it is only exempt if the child has for substantial periods before attaining that age been in the care of the disponer.

20–15 DEPENDENT RELATIVES Also, a disposition is not a transfer of value if it is made in favour of a dependent relative of the disponer or his spouse or civil partner and is a reasonable provision for his or her care or maintenance. Here there is an explicit reference to reasonableness (of amount), whereas in the case of a disposition to a spouse, civil partner or child there is no explicit mention of reasonableness. However, such a limit seems to be implicit, because it is stated that, where a disposition satisfies the conditions to a limited extent only, so much of it as satisfies them and so much of it as does not satisfy them shall be treated as separate dispositions.

---

[9] Quaere the position where the "child" leaves school, takes a gap year and starts university aged 19? Technically he/she ceased full-time education on leaving school, but not permanently.

Uses of the relief

Since all transfers between spouses or civil partners are **20–16** exempt,[10] this exemption has very little effect whilst either the marriage or civil partnership is on-going. In *Phizackerley v HMRC* (2007) Sp C, it was argued, as part of a tax planning scheme, that s.11 applied where a husband put his house into the joint names of himself and his wife during their marriage. The Special Commissioner rejected that argument on the basis that such an act was not for the maintenance of the wife. It was to give her security. But so far as a child is concerned s.11 is very useful as it exempts a payment made by a parent to assist (for example) a child who is a student if the payment is outside the "normal expenditure out of income" exemption (see para.20–06 above).[11]

The section applies also, however, to a disposition on the occasion of the dissolution or annulment of a marriage or civil partnership (and to a disposition varying a disposition so made) by subs.(6) which provides that in relation to those events "marriage" and "civil partnership" (see subs.(1)) includes a former marriage or civil partnership. In *G v G* (1975) a High Court judge held that the court has power to defer a decree absolute in order to prevent IHT arising.[12]

Dispositions allowable for income tax or conferring retirement benefits: s.12

A disposition made by any person is not a transfer of value **20–17** if it is allowable in computing that person's profits or gains for the purposes of income tax or corporation tax. It is difficult to think of a disposition which is allowable for income tax (or corporation tax) and yet which would need this section to protect it from IHT; most commonly such a disposition would be a disposition for value and would consequently be excluded from IHT by s.10 (no gratuitous intent). Perhaps certain kinds of business gifts or payments to departing employees would "fit the bill".

Contributions to approved retirement benefit schemes and approved personal pension schemes for employees and also dispositions to provide in some other way comparable benefits

---

[10] Under s.18, see para.20–02 above.
[11] The section may not apply if the child leaves school, goes out to work and re-enters full-time education after the age of 18. Has he already ceased to undertake full-time education?
[12] Such orders will usually be exempt under s.10 (no gratuitous benefit).

on or after retirement for an employee not connected with the disponer, or, after the death of the employee, for a widow, widower, civil partner or dependants, are not transfers of value.

Dispositions by close company on trust for benefit of employees: ss.13 & 13A

20–18   A disposition of property made to trustees by a close company whereby the property is to be held on certain trusts for the employees is not a transfer of value. The conditions of exemption are very strict and in practice not much use is made of this provision.

Waiver of remuneration: s.14

20–19   Sometimes an employee or, more commonly a director, waives (or repays) his remuneration for a period to his employer (company). If nothing were done about it, such waiver or repayment would be a chargeable transfer by the employee or director. Section 14 declares that the waiver or repayment shall not be a transfer of value provided that it is brought into charge in computing the profits or gains of the employer for income tax or corporation tax.

Waiver of dividends: s.15

20–20   A person who waives any dividend on shares of a company within 12 months *before* any right to the dividend has accrued does not by reason of the waiver make a transfer of value.

Grant of an agricultural tenancy: s.16

20–21   A grant of an agricultural tenancy is not a transfer of value if it is made for full consideration in money or money's worth. Otherwise the almost inevitable reduction in the value of the property (such leases have controlled rents) would lead to a charge.

EXCLUDED PROPERTY

Property outside the UK owned by non-UK domiciled persons: s.6

20–22   The most important example of excluded property is property situated outside the UK to which a non-UK domiciled person is beneficially entitled (s.6). This means that IHT does not reach offshore property owned by individuals who are not domiciled in the UK. Also within the definition of excluded property are holdings in open-ended investment companies (OEICs) and authorised unit trusts, even if situated in the UK. Decorations or awards (if not purchased), certain savings by persons domiciled in the Channel Islands or the Isle of Man are also included.

The effect of property being excluded is that it is excluded from the estate on death (s.5(1)(b)) and, in relation to lifetime transfers, the value of excluded property is not a transfer of value. This is similar to exemption, but not identical. For example, assume A, non-UK domiciled, owns 30 per cent of the shares in a UK company. The other 70 per cent are owned by a non-UK company, entirely owned by A. If A gives away the shares in the non-UK parent, the loss of value of these shares is not a transfer of value as they are excluded property. However, there will be a reduction in the value of the UK shares as they are no longer part of a controlling interest. This reduction will be a transfer of value.

Visiting forces and staff of allied headquarters: s.155

This paragraph gives certain exemptions to pay and tangible movables of members of visiting forces of designated countries (not being citizens of the UK and colonies) and personnel attached to a designated allied headquarters.   **20–23**

Reversionary interests: s.48.1

Reversionary interest are excluded property. They are discussed further at para.22–19.   **20–24**

MISCELLANEOUS RELIEFS

Family provision orders: s.146

A court has power, under the Inheritance (Provision for Family and Dependants) Act 1975 to order that provision be made for the family and dependants of a deceased person out of his estate, and for this purpose to change the destination of property. When a court makes an order of this kind the property shall be treated for the purposes of IHT as if it had on the deceased's death devolved in accordance with the order.[13]   **20–25**

---

[13] In Scotland, the surviving spouse and descendants are protected by fixed interests under the Succession (Scotland) Act 1964 Pt II. These are known as

Deaths of emergency personnel, members of the armed forces on active service, etc.: ss.153A, 154, 155A

20–26   This exemption applies to deaths as a result of injuries or diseases, etc. sustained in a person's capacity as an emergency responder, and deaths on active service against an enemy (or on other service of a warlike nature) and to death arising out of such service.[14] It is also extended to deaths of constables and service personnel who are deliberately targeted because of their status. The exemptions operate by means of excluding s.4, the section which charges to tax a transfer on death.

Alteration of dispositions taking effect on death, etc.: ss.17, 29A, 93, 142–145

20–27   Certain re-arrangements of the deceased's estate after death shall not be treated as transfers of value by the persons making them and, instead, tax shall be charged on the estate on death as if the deceased had left the property in accordance with the re-arrangements. Variations and their close relatives, disclaimers, are regarded by the government with a certain amount of suspicion on the basis that they facilitate tax avoidance. However they have been given reprieve for the time being following a review in 2015. They can be very useful for several reasons, but in particular they are often used where the will is inefficient for IHT purposes, for example where a person leaves property subject to 100 per cent relief to a spouse (exempt under s.18) and her chargeable estate to the children. This wastes relief. Here, IHT savings might be achieved if a variation is used so that the relieved property goes to the children and the unrelieved property is redirected to the spouse. Variations under the legislation are treated as if they had been made by the deceased in the will. In the event of a disclaimer, the disclaimed legacy will normally fall into the residue, and be taxed on that basis.

Variation of deceased's dispositions on death

20–28   Section 142 permits the variation or disclaimer of any of the dispositions whether effected by will or under the law relating to intestacy or otherwise of the property comprised in the deceased's estate immediately before his death. A variation redirects property in the estate to someone else, a disclaimer simply means that the

legal rights, or specifically *jus relictae* or *jus relicti* in relation to the rights of a surviving spouse, and *legitim* in relation to descendants.

[14] This includes service in Northern Ireland.

property falls into the residue of the estate. The effect of a claim under s.142 claim is that, for IHT purposes, the variation or disclaimer is not treated as a transfer of value by the person making it, rather tax is charged as if the variation had been effected by the deceased or (as the case may be) the disclaimed benefit had never been conferred. There can be no variation of property treated as part of the deceased's estate by virtue of the reservation of benefit rules.

The technical requirements of a variation or disclaimer under s.142(1) are:

- it must be made by the beneficiary within two years after the person's death (or, if the beneficiary has subsequently died, by his personal representatives);
- it must be made in writing, which, if a variation, must include a statement that s.142(1) is to apply (although an action of rectification to add this statement where the solicitor forgot was successful in *Vaughan-Jones v Vaughan-Jones*;
- in relation to disclaimers, the beneficiary must not have received any benefit from the property being disclaimed; and
- where the variation results in additional tax being payable, the deceased's personal representatives join in the election. They may only decline to join the election if insufficient assets are held by them for discharging the additional tax. Additional tax could become payable, for example, if some item of property which had been left by the deceased to his widow is now, by family agreement, to go to his daughter. Alternatively, if the variation redirects property to a charity, the lower rate of tax[15] may apply, but only if the charity has been notified of the variation.

CONSIDERATION The section does not apply to a variation **20–29** or disclaimer which is made for any consideration in money or money's worth other than consideration consisting of the making of another variation or disclaimer relating to the same estate. This means that if A varies her legacy of a diamond ring in favour of B, who in turn varies her legacy of a pearl necklace in favour of A, s.142(1) can apply to both variations. However, if a payment is made at the same time by B to A (perhaps to reflect the value differential between the two legacies), the A to B variation will not qualify as A received extraneous consideration. In *Lau v HMRC* [2009] a disclaimer by a son increased the

---

[15] See para.21–04 below.

residue which went to the surviving spouse (and thus became exempt). This was followed shortly afterwards by a gift from the surviving spouse to the son, which was treated as consideration for the disclaimer, even though there was no evidence of any binding agreement for the gift.

For the purpose of this section the deceased's estate includes excluded property but not settled property in which he had an interest in possession. It does not matter whether or not the administration of the estate is complete, and it does not matter that a benefit has been received under the original dispositions, and there is no objection to the variations extending beyond the deceased's family or beyond the original beneficiaries. Where a variation results in property being held in trust for a person for a period which ends not more than two years after the death, the disposition at the end of the period is treated as though it had had effect from the beginning of the period.

20–30   SECOND DEED RECTIFICATION   In *Russell v IRC* (1988), Knox J upheld HMRC's argument that s.142 could not apply where the beneficiaries, having already executed one deed of variation, executed a variation of that deed. The section only allows the first one to count as being read back into the will. On the other hand in *Lake v Lake* (1989), Mervyn Davies J held that a deed of disclaimer could be rectified by the court if the wording had failed to give effect to the joint intention of the parties, even though the amended wording would substantially improve the parties' tax position. The deed was also rectified in *Wills v Gibbs* (2008) on the basis that it gave effect to the maker's intentions and resolved a dispute between the parties.

The "two year discretionary trust"

20–31   The "two year discretionary trust" gives the maximum flexibility after death. In fact the trust can be for as long as is wished, but s.144 deems transfers out of such trusts within two years of the death to have been made by the deceased on death. This does not apply if in the meantime any immediate post-death or disabled person's interest has arisen under the settlement. The variation can create an immediate post-death interest, a bereaved minor's trust (see s.71A)[16] or an 18–25 trust (see s.71D)[17] and this will be charged as though the event in question had been provided for in the will.

---

[16] See Ch.21 below.
[17] See Ch.21 below.

Request to legatee

Section 143 deals with the case where assets are left to a legatee   **20–32**
with a request (which is not legally binding) that the legatee
should distribute them in accordance with the testator's wishes. If
within two years after the death the legatee does so distribute the
assets, the transfers by the legatee are not transfers of value and
tax shall be charged in relation to the death as if the property had
been bequeathed by the will to the transferees. (Such a provision
in a will is called a precatory trust; it is quite common, particularly in respect of household effects, etc.)

Linked exempt transfer

Section 29A is rather different in that it is in reality an anti-   **20–33**
avoidance provision. It applies whenever there is an exempt
transfer on a death, e.g. to a charity,[18] and the exempt beneficiary subsequently makes a disposition of property, which does
not derive from that transferred on the death, in settlement of a
claim against the deceased's estate. In that case the exemption
on the death is reduced by the amount transferred by the exempt
beneficiary. Thus if Paul agrees with a charity to leave them
£100,000 in his will if the charity will then pay £50,000 to his mis-
tress (who may have a claim against his estate), the effect of s.29A
will be that only £50,000 of the gift to the charity will be exempt.

Relief for successive charges: s.141

This is generally called "quick succession" relief. This relief   **20–34**
may reduce a tax charge on a death where the deceased had
received property by way of a chargeable transfer within five
years of his death, and tax had been chargeable on that earlier
transfer. The most common situation in which this relief will
apply is where a person, A, receives property from B on B's
death, and IHT was payable on B's estate. Then if A dies within
five years of B, with estate which is also subject to IHT, there
will be some relief. There is no need for A still to own the actual
property on his death. Relief would also apply where A received
property from B by virtue of a PET which has become chargeable as a result of B's death within seven years, and on which tax
became due. Much less common is the situation where the earlier
tax charge was caused by the lifetime termination of an interest
in possession trust or an exit charge out of a discretionary trust,
but relief would also be available in this event.

---

[18] Other exempt transfers covered are those to spouses, political parties, housing
associations, maintenance funds and employee trusts.

The relief is extended to the situation where A is deemed to own property on his death because it is in an interest in possession trust (see paras 22–14 to 22–17).

For a death the previous charge may be of any type, but for a settlement it must have been a previous charge on that settlement, or the creation of the settlement itself.

The relief operates by way of a "tax credit" against tax payable on the second charge. The calculation of this can be complicated, but broadly one needs to calculate the tax referable to the *increase* in the donee's estate on the first transfer. Assume B left A his entire estate of £100,000, all chargeable at 40 per cent. A receives £60,000. The maximum tax credit on A's estate is not the £40,000 paid by B's estate (40 per cent of £100,000) but 40 per cent of £60,000 (the increase in A's estate), i.e. £24,000. This is because the increase in A's estate is only £60,000. If A dies within one year of B, his estate receives 100 per cent of this but it is reduced by 20 per cent for each subsequent year between the transfers, so that if the gap is between 4 and 5 years it will only be 20 per cent.

Where the death for which the relief is available is subject to the lower rate of tax,[19] s.141A provides that the relief due to the estate as a whole must be apportioned by reference to the ratio of the tax payable on the deceased's free estate, any settlements in which he has an interest in possession and any property which passes on his death by survivorship (unless any of those components have been merged in the claim for the lower rate to apply in which case the merged component is used).

Voidable transfers: s.150

20–35   This relief refers to transfers set aside by law. An example would be a gift made within five years before bankruptcy, because such a gift could be set aside (under the Insolvency Act 1986 s.339) by the transferor's trustee in bankruptcy. Similarly equity will set aside a transfer made under a relevant mistake, e.g. as to the life expectancy of the transferors *Re Griffiths* (2008). If a transfer is so set aside, tax is repaid (with tax-free interest) and also the transfer is wiped out from the transferor's cumulative total of values transferred.

---

[19]   This happens where at least 10 per cent of the estate has been left to charity. The rate on the remaining amount above the nil-rate band limit is then reduced from 40 per cent to 36 per cent. See para.21–04 below.

Relief for business property: ss.103–114

Nature and extent of the relief

This relief (BPR) was brought in in 1976 in response to claims   **20–36**
that without some such relief many small businesses would face
closure because of the tax on transfers, e.g. from parent to child.
The relief has been liberalised by subsequent amendments and,
in many cases, stands at 100 per cent. Transfers of value in this
context include not only lifetime transfers but also transfers on
death and chargeable events in relation to settled property.

Where the whole or part of the value transferred by a transfer
of value is attributable to the value of any relevant business
property, the whole of that part of the value transferred shall be
treated as reduced by either 100 or 50 per cent. The value transferred is to be calculated as a value on which no tax is chargeable,
i.e. without grossing up. Relevant business property means:

  (i) a business or an interest in a business. This includes sole
       traders and partners disposing of all or part of their
       interests in a business[20];
 (ii) a holding of shares in or securities of a listed company
       which, together with others held by the transferor, gave
       him control of the company on all questions affecting the
       company[21];
(iii) a holding of securities in an unquoted company which
       together with other such securities and unquoted shares
       held by the transferor, gave him control of the company
       (as defined above);
 (iv) a holding, of any size, of shares in an unquoted company;
  (v) any land or building, machinery or plant which was used
       wholly or mainly for the purpose of a business carried
       on by a company of which the transferor had control (as
       defined above) or of which he was a partner.

Where land is used in the business, e.g. a farming business,
the full value of that land (including any development value) is

---

[20] In *Fetherstonaugh v IRC* (1984) a sole trader who used land owned by a
 settlement of which he was the life tenant in his business was allowed the relief
 on that land under this head. In *Russell v IRC* (1988) the relief was allowed
 where a legatee was entitled to a cash sum payable only out of the proceeds of
 sale of a business.
[21] Control is to be assessed at the time of the transfer. In assessing whether the
 transferor has voting control of a company no account is to be taken of the
 fact that other shares are held by an individual who cannot in practice exercise
 his votes, e.g. a five-year-old child: *Walding v IRC* (1996).

eligible for the relief. BPR applies to the value of the business as a whole, as a form of property distinct from the assets of the business for the time being. Since the charge to IHT depends upon the loss to the transferor, then to be consistent that is also the amount which is relieved by BPR.[22]

Exceptions—land and investments

20–37   No business, interest in a business or shares or securities in a company are eligible for BPR if the business (or the company's business) consists wholly or mainly either in dealing in securities, shares, land or buildings or in making or holding investments. There have been many unsuccessful attempts to show that the sometimes quite extensive activities which are involved when letting out land take it outside the investment business category. An example is *Pawson* (2013) in which the Upper Tribunal overturned the FTT's decision that running a holiday let qualified for the relief. It is important to note that the activity can amount to a business and still not qualify for relief— the letting of property often is a "business" itself. In order to bring the let property outside the investment category, it is necessary that there are considerable "non-investment" activities. Activities which are "investment" for these purposes will include management and maintenance: in *Martin v IRC* (1995) the Special Commissioner held that letting industrial units on three-year lets remained an investment business even though the taxpayer managed and maintained the units; all that was simply referable to the obligations under the leases—there were no additional charges for other services.[23] In deciding whether the activity is predominantly business or investment, one must look at the business "in the round": *IRC v George* (2003). The relevant income and profitability of the various activities is relevant but not determinative. Additional services, over and above the services relating to finding tenants and performing maintenance, can help support the claim that the property is not simply an investment.

This issue has arisen in connection with the owners of caravan sites. In several cases, culminating in *Weston v IRC* (2000), it was held that receiving rent in respect of caravan lets was investment business. The judge then stated that in deciding whether such a business was therefore excluded from the relief,

---

[22] *Re the Nelson Dance Family Settlement* (2009).

[23] This approach, that actively managing land leased to tenants is still an investment business, was approved in *IRC v George* (2004) and in *Clark v HMRC* Sp C (2005). As to a company making loans see *Phillips v HMRC* Sp C (2006).

it was first necessary to identify and separate the investment and non-investment activities and then to determine whether the business did consist wholly or mainly of the investment activities. In *Farmer v IRC* (1999), however, another Special Commissioner held that a farm which let properties, the income from which exceeded that of the farming business, was still predominantly a farming business. The matter had to be looked at in the round.[24]

The matter came before the Court of Appeal in *IRC v George* (2003) where the question as to whether a caravan site business was wholly or mainly one of making investments was held to be largely a question of fact for the Commissioner. In that case in that case, which involved a very actively run caravan park, the holding of property was only one component of the business and the commissioner had found that it was not the main component. An active family business of this kind should not be excluded from the relief merely because a part of it involved the use of land.

Away from caravan parks, the test was stated by the Court of Appeal in Northern Ireland in *McCall v HMRC* (2009), as being whether an intelligent businessman would regard it as being a business of holding investments or not. That would involve looking at the use to which the asset was being put and the way it was being turned to account. A landowner who derived income from land or a building would be treated as having a business of holding investments even though in order to obtain income he carried out incidental management and maintenance work, found tenants, granted leases, etc.

The previous paragraphs considered whether or not a single business is an investment business or not. A different issue might arise where there are two interrelated business, one of which would qualify for BPR, the other would not. This issue arose in *Brander v HMRC* (2010) where part of the activities of the farmer had been letting farm cottages and part had been contract farming and woodland management. HMRC sought to argue that there were in fact two businesses, and that the let cottages business did not qualify for relief. (Alternatively they argued that if there was one business, it was an investment business.) The Upper Tribunal held that on the facts, there was only one business, despite separate accounts, and that looking at the business as a whole, it was not predominantly investment. From the taxpayer's perspective, the single business approach has both risks and rewards—there may be 100 per cent relief, or there may

---

[24] As to balancing investment activity (rents) with others (building, sales etc.) see *Clark v HMRC* Sp C (2005).

be none. A two-business approach is more likely to ensure relief on the non-investment business.

Excluded items

20–38　　Certain items are excluded from the definition of relevant business property, e.g. shares or securities of a company which is in the process of liquidation, or surplus cash not required for the future use of the business.[25]

And, putting it broadly, property is not relevant business property unless it has been owned by the transferor throughout the two years immediately preceding the transfer. But there are provisions adjusting this rule where there have been replacements of property, the incorporation of a business, and acquisitions of property on the death of a spouse.

Reduction in value of transfer

20–39　　The relief is given by reducing the value of the net business assets that have been transferred. This means the value of the assets used in the business less any liabilities incurred for the purposes of the business. In *Mallender v IRC* (2001), the taxpayer negotiated a bank guarantee for the purposes of his business as a member of a Lloyd's insurance syndicate. In order to do that he had to give the bank a charge over the freehold reversion of some land held by him. The court refused to allow the value of that reversion as a business asset for the purposes of the relief. The only asset used in the business was the guarantee. There was no sufficient nexus between the business and the charge. An asset used to secure a loan for the purpose of a business was not itself an asset used in that business.

The relief is given automatically. For transfers within categories (i), (iii) and (iv) this relief is 100 per cent, so that most family businesses will be outside the tax. For categories (ii) and (v) the relief is 50 per cent. It is generally better therefore for a taxpayer's company to own the plant and machinery, etc. used in its business, rather than the taxpayer.

Interface with PETs and gifts with reservation

20–40　　Where the transferor makes a PET of relevant business property and then dies within seven years so that it becomes a chargeable transfer, the relief will only be available if the transferee still owns the property (or has sold it and replaced it with similarly qualifying property) and it would have qualified for the relief in the hands of the transferee (apart from the

---

[25] *Barclays Bank Trust Co Ltd v IRC* (1998).

minimum holding period) immediately before the transferor's death. Similarly, if the transferee died before the transferor whilst still owning the property (or replacement property), relief is available on the transferor's death. Similar rules apply where additional tax is payable on a lifetime transfer on the death of the transferor within seven years (see Ch.21). There is no such clawback, however, where a beneficiary sells the business after inheriting it on a death.

In deciding whether the relief applies to a gift subject to a reservation (either one which is still in existence at the transferor's death or which ceased only within the last seven years and so is a deemed PET), the criteria in the various categories are applied to the donee and not the donor, although the ownership of the donor can be added to that of the donee to establish the two year minimum ownership requirement. Paradoxically, however, in assessing whether the shares give control of the company, the shares will be regarded as being owned by the donor.

Interface with agricultural relief

As in *Re Nelson Dance Family Settlement* (2009), BPR may **20–41** be available where agricultural relief is also available to cover, e.g. any development value in the agricultural land. In such cases, agricultural relief takes priority.

Relief for agricultural property: ss.115–124C

This relief applies to lifetime transfers and transfers on death, **20–42** and it applies to transfers involving certain settlements as well as to "outright" transfers.

Conditions for the relief—length of ownership

Short-term purchasers of farms are excluded from the relief; **20–43** for the relief to apply, both the transferor and the property must fulfil certain conditions. The transferor must have either occupied the land for agricultural purposes throughout the last two years or have owned the property for the last seven years, it having been occupied by someone for agricultural purposes during that time. Where a person inherits a farm from his or her spouse or civil partner, the occupation or ownership of the deceased will count towards the minimum period, provided the spouse or civil partner fulfilled the above conditions.[26] For the property to qualify it must be agricultural property in one of the UK, the Channel Islands, the Isle of Man, or the European Economic

---

[26] See e.g. *Rosser v IRC* (2003).

Area (EEA). If one farm has been replaced by another, it is sufficient if occupation of the farms viewed together lasted for at least two out of five years immediately preceding the transfer.

Conditions for the relief—agricultural property

20–44   The relief only applies to agricultural property. "Agricultural property"[27] means:

> "agricultural land or pasture and includes woodland and any building used in connection with the intensive rearing of livestock and fish if occupied with agricultural land or pasture and the occupation is ancillary to that of the agricultural land or pasture; and also includes such cottages, farm buildings and farm-houses, together with the land occupied with them, as are of a character appropriate to the property" (s.115(2)).

The criteria for establishing whether the various buildings are of an appropriate character, etc. were set out in *Lloyds TSB v IRC* (2002). If they do not fall within that test, e.g. because they are very valuable compared to the farmland involved, they cannot be included as agricultural land or pasture: *Starke v IRC* (1995). HMRC's view was that the connection between the buildings (e.g. a farmhouse) and the land is that the transferor must have occupied and owned both so that common occupation on its own will not suffice. This view was supported by the Special Commissioner in *Rosser v IRC* (2003), although *Rosser* was overruled by the Upper Tribunal in *Hanson v HMRC* (2013). In *Hanson*, simplifying slightly, the deceased owned the farmhouse at the date of his death but he did not occupy it. He also had a small interest in the farm. The farmhouse was in fact occupied by his son, who also had a significant interest in the farm. It was conceded by HMRC that if the son's acres were to be taken into account for the purposes of judging whether the farmhouse was "of a character appropriate to the property" for the purposes of that section, then the farmhouse was of such a character. On the other side, it was conceded by the taxpayer that if no account is to be taken of that land, then there was insufficient supporting land to bring it within s.115(2). The Upper Tribunal decided that common occupation was sufficient, so that ownership of a farmhouse by the deceased but occupation by his son who also occupied and owned the farm was sufficient for the relief

---

[27] This includes land used for "short rotation coppicing" by virtue of s.154 of FA 1995. In essence this is the planting and harvesting of permanent trees within 10 years. It also includes "habitat land" and genuine farm cottages.

to apply. The tenor of the legislation was to concentrate on occupation and not the estate of the deceased.

Conditions for the relief—occupied for the purposes of agriculture

The relief only applies if the relevant property has been occu-   **20–45**
pied for the appropriate period "for the purposes of agriculture" (s.117). The meaning of this phrase was discussed by the Upper Tribunal in *HMRC v Atkinson* (2011). Farm offices could be so occupied if used to carry out administrative tasks necessary for running a farm; so too could a farm cottage if occupied by a farm worker but not if by an unconnected tenant. In the latter case there would be no connection between occupation of the cottage and the agricultural activities of the farm. In the case itself the property in question was the main farm house which had been occupied by a farmer until two years before his death. He farmed the land in partnership with his children. At that time he had to go into a care home. His furniture etc. was left in the house until his death. The tribunal asked itself whether the deceased's use of the house in those last years had some objective connection with the agricultural activities on the farm. On the facts there was no such connection—the house was never used for any purpose other than the deceased's residence and that no longer related to the farm.[28]

Applying the relief

The relief, where available, takes the form of reducing the agri-   **20–46**
cultural value of the agricultural property.

"The agricultural value" is "the value which would be the value of the property if the property were subject to a perpetual covenant (or EEA equivalent) prohibiting its use otherwise than as agricultural property": s.115(3). Thus there is no relief for any development value, although business relief may be available for that.

REDUCTIONS   The reduction is either of 100 or 50 per cent. In broad terms owner occupiers are entitled to a 100 per cent reduction, whilst agricultural landlords are entitled to a 50 per cent reduction unless the tenancy began or a tenant succeeded to the tenancy after August 1995 when 100 per cent relief is available, although of course on the value of the reversion and not the whole farm. The reduction in value because of the agricultural

---

[28] The tribunal also doubted the decision of the Special Commissioner in *Rosser v IRC* (2003) that a house cannot be a farmhouse if it is not occupied by the farmer him or herself. See the paragraph above.

tenancy will, of course, reduce the IHT payable on the land. There are no limits as to size of the farm or as to amount of the relief. As with business relief, this relief is given automatically. It is given in priority to business relief but both may be available, for example BPR may be available on farm implements. The availability of the relief for PETs and gifts with reservation is governed by the same rules as those for business relief.

Transfers of shares or debentures in a farming company controlled by the transferor can qualify for agricultural property relief.

Relief for woodlands: ss.125–130

Nature and extent of the relief

20–47 Relief is available where any part of the value of a person's estate immediately before his death is attributable to the value of land in the UK or the EEA on which trees or underwood are growing but which is not agricultural property. Deathbed purchases of woodland as a tax avoidance ploy will not work. For the relief to apply the deceased must either have been beneficially entitled to the land throughout the five years immediately before his death or have become beneficially entitled to it otherwise than for a consideration in money or money's worth, i.e. by a gift or inheritance.

Retrospective charge

20–48 The relief takes the form of leaving out of account, in determining the value transferred on death, the value of the trees or underwood. Notice that the relief does not apply to a lifetime transfer and also that it is only the value of the timber which is relieved, not the value of the land on which it is growing.

The relief is not absolute; a subsequent lifetime transfer of the timber can give rise to a retrospective charge to tax at the full rate at the date of the transfer. Tax will be charged on the sale proceeds of the timber if the transfer is for full consideration; otherwise on the then net value of the timber. If the transfer following the death is itself a chargeable transfer, e.g. a gift, there may be a tax charge on that disposal as well as the retrospective tax charge relating to the death, but the value transferred by the subsequent disposal will be calculated as if the value of the trees or underwood had been reduced by the amount of tax charged in respect of the death. BPR (at 50 per cent) will be available if the growing timber formed a business asset of the deceased at the date of death. The lower tax rate will not apply to the deferred charge.

If another death occurs, and there has been no disposal between the first death and the second death, the second death wipes out any possibility of a tax charge arising in respect of the first death.

CHAPTER 21

COMPUTATION

Introduction

21–01   IHT is charged on any lifetime transfer of value which is a chargeable transfer, and also on the deemed transfer of value made by a deceased person immediately before his death. (The charges on settled property are discussed in the next chapter.) Remember that a PET becomes a chargeable transfer on the death of the transferor within seven years. As we shall see, the existence of PETs complicates the computation rules. Remember also that a gift subject to a reservation still in existence at death is part of the deceased's estate. If the reservation has ceased before then the gift becomes a PET at that time so that if the reservation ceases more than seven years before the death the gift is exempt.

In the case of a lifetime transfer the charge is on the value transferred, the loss to the transferor's estate. In the case of a deemed transfer on death the charge is on the value of the deceased's estate. Section 3 declares that:

> "... a transfer of value is a disposition made by a person (the transferor) as a result of which the value of his estate is less than it would be but for the disposition; and the amount by which it is less is the value transferred by the transfer."

So for a lifetime transfer, one has to compare the value of the transferor's estate (remember that "estate" can refer to a living person's wealth, as well as to a dead person's) before the transfer with its value after the transfer. For a discussion as to how that comparison is to be made see para.19–03 above. For a death transfer this comparison does not arise.

Rates of tax

Nil-rate and chargeable bands

21–02   As we have already seen, everyone has a "nil-rate band", currently, and until 2020/21, £325,000.[1] Chargeable transfers within

---

[1]   Schedule 1.

that band are taxed at 0 per cent. Note that a transfer taxed at 0 per cent is very different from an exempt transfer. Whilst in both cases there is no tax to pay on the transfer, an exempt transfer does not use up any nil-rate band for the future, in contrast to a transfer chargeable at 0 per cent. So a chargeable transfer within the nil-rate band means there is less available for later transfers, which can lead to a higher tax bill in the future.

Another thing to note at this stage, although examples are given later, is that the nil-rate band isn't a once and for all relief, which once it is used up, stays used up for ever. It is sometimes described as "rolling" because, once a transfer is seven years old, it drops out of account. Any nil-rate band which was used by that transfer is added back to the amount available in the future. So an individual could make a chargeable transfer of, say, £325,000 every seven years, and still not pay any tax. When calculating the tax on any transfer, one looks back over the seven years prior to the transfer and check to see the value of the chargeable transfers in that period. If these have been in excess of £325,000, there is no nil-rate band for that transfer. This principle is applied equally on a death so that the rate takes into account the chargeable transfers made seven years prior to the death. Only where the transferor lives for more than seven years after making a chargeable transfer will it be taken out of the calculation. The effect of the transferor dying within seven years of making a chargeable transfer or a PET is discussed below.

The positive rates of tax are 40 per cent on death (and on the recalculation of tax on transfers within seven years of death) and 20 per cent on lifetime chargeable transfers.[2] (This is very much simpler than the original scheme of capital transfer tax which had eight bands of tax on death and another seven for lifetime transfers!)

EXAMPLES Thus if Fred, having made immediately **21–03** chargeable transfers of £325,000 in the previous seven years, makes another one of £100,000, that transfer will be charged at 20 per cent, since he will have exceeded the nil-rate band. If his cumulative total prior to the transfer had been £300,000, the £100,000 transfer would then have been chargeable at £25,000 × nil per cent (i.e. covered by the remaining nil-rate band) and £75,000 × 20 per cent. The position would have been the same if Fred, with a cumulative total of £300,000, had died and left an estate of £100,000, except that that the part of the estate not

---

[2] This may be reduced to 36 per cent if the charitable giving threshold has been reached—see para.21–04.

covered by any nil-rate band would then have been taxed at 40 per cent. The fact that lifetime rates are half those on death is counterbalanced by the fact that CGT may well be payable on a lifetime transfer whereas it does not apply on a death.

The lower rate of tax—10 per cent of the estate left to charity

21–04   FA 2012 introduced Sch.1A to IHTA to encourage charitable giving. The general principle is that where 10 per cent or more of an estate on death, discounting any that is subject to the available nil-rate band, is left to charity (as defined in s.23), the remaining estate is to be taxed at the lower rate of 36 per cent rather than 40 per cent.

To establish whether the 10 per cent threshold has been reached, the estate must first be divided into three components: the deceased's free estate, any property which passes by survivorship to another on the death, and any settled property in which the deceased had an interest in possession immediately before his death. Each component is then taken separately. At least 10 per cent of the "baseline amount" for each component must be left to charity for the reduction in tax rate to apply. That baseline is the value transferred by property in that component less any to which the nil-rate band applies (the nil-rate band has to be apportioned across the components by value, if more than one component) and then adding on the amount left to charity from that component.

To take the simplest example: X dies leaving £1,325,000 free estate, having made no previous chargeable transfers. He leaves £100,000 to charity. The baseline amount is £1,225,000 (value transferred (as £100,000 to charity is exempt)) − £325,000 (nil-rate band) and + £100,000 (amount left to charity). That is £1,000,000. The £100,000 left to charity is 10 per cent of that so that the other £900,000 will be charged at 36 per cent.

If there is an excess of relief, there is provision for an election to be made (by all the personal representatives, trustees or survivors as appropriate) to merge one or more components for the purpose of applying the lower rate provided that at least one of the components meets the 10 per cent threshold. Alternatively, if there is such an excess of relief, it can be applied by election to gifts with reservation which have been treated as part of the deceased's estate.

The relief will be given automatically unless there is an election (by the above persons) that it shall not apply to the relevant component. This might happen if the benefit would be minimal and the cost of valuing items left to charity relatively too expensive. All elections must be made within two years of the death.

The nil-rate band: spouses and civil partners—
transferable nil-rate band

The nil-rate band in effect fixes the IHT threshold on death   **21–05**
for most taxpayers for the year in question. That became a very
political issue in 2007. There was significant evidence that past
increases in the threshold had not kept pace with the increase in
housing values, and more estates were falling within the scope of
the tax. Remember that there is no private residence exemption
as there is for CGT.

Although transfers between spouses and civil partners were
exempt, most couples did not take advantage of their two separate, individual nil-rate bands. Thus suppose a couple, A and
B, own a house worth say £500,000 and have modest savings,
say of £100,000. A dies leaving all his property to B. There is no
charge to tax as that is an exempt transfer. B then dies later that
year, leaving all her property (including her inherited share of the
house) to the children. B's estate is now worth £600,000 because
it now includes A's estate. This is the problem of aggregation.
But only £325,000 of that is within the nil-rate band. The children
would have had to pay 40 per cent tax on the other £275,000,
some £110,000. In effect, none of A's nil-rate band has been
utilised.

TRANSFER OF PROPORTION OF UNUSED BAND   Prudent couples   **21–06**
could take steps to avoid this "use it or lose it" characteristic by
using discretionary trusts in their wills,[3] but in his pre-budget
report on 9 October 2007, the Chancellor announced that as
from that date *the percentage* of any unused nil-rate band on
a person's death could be transferred to a surviving spouse or
civil partner. This mitigates the aggregation problem. This is in
ss.8A and 8B and the transfer must be claimed by the survivor's
personal representatives. Thus in the example above, on B's
death she would have a total nil-rate band available of £650,000
(£325,000 + 100 per cent of A's £325,000); her estate would thus
pass to her children tax free. The claim must be made within
two years of the second death (or, if later, three months after the
personal representatives start to act as such).

---

[3] This worked by leaving estate to a discretionary trust, the beneficiaries of
which were usually the surviving spouse and other family. This was a chargeable transfer but charged at 0 per cent because it was covered by the nil-rate
band. The balance of the estate could be left as an exempt transfer to the surviving spouse. On the survivor's death, the value in the trust is not treated as
part of her estate. The advantage of the trust is that it can be used to provide
support for the survivor, without the adverse tax consequences of aggregation.

As noted above, it is the percentage unused which can be transferred, not the actual amount. Had B survived for a few more years and died when the nil-rate band, say, had risen to £350,000, her nil-rate band at death would be £700,000. That is her own £350,000 plus 100 per cent of A's nil-rate band *calculated at the then current figure* of £350,000 (and not the figure of £325,000 as at A's death). If, say, 50 per cent of A's nil-rate band had been used on his death (because he had left some chargeable legacies) then B would have been entitled to add £175,000 to her nil-rate band (i.e. 50 per cent of £350,000).

21–07   CUMULATIVE SURVIVORS   Where a person has survived more than one spouse or civil partner, the maximum additional nil-rate band which can be accumulated on their death is 100 per cent of the nil-rate band for the year of the survivor's death. Thus if B has survived both A and C, her former spouses, and then dies in 2016, she can only add £325,000 onto her own nil-rate band, even if she was entitled to 100 per cent proportion in respect of both A and C. This maximum also applies where B dies having survived her spouse A, who in turn survived his former spouse, C, etc. In such consecutive cases, where the personal representatives of A did not claim any unused nil-rate band from C's death, B's personal representatives may do so in order to reach the 100 per cent limit.

None of this largesse, however, extends to co-habiting couples who are neither spouses nor civil partners, e.g. two sisters sharing a house. That anomaly was unsuccessfully challenged as being a breach of human rights in *Burden v UK* (2008).

The residential nil-rate band (RNRB): ss.8E–8M

21–08   It was noted earlier that house prices have been outstripping increases to the nil-rate band. However, instead of increasing the nil-rate band, in 2015 a complex additional nil-rate band was introduced, which is available, broadly, where an individual leaves a property which is or has been his home to his children. It comes into effect in relation to deaths from 6 April 2017.

In outline, if an individual's estate includes (or used to include) a **"qualifying residential interest"** which goes wholly or in part to descendants (i.e. is **"closely inherited"**), the nil-rate band is subject to the **"residential enhancement"**. The residential enhancement is reduced by the **"taper threshold"** for large estates. There are **"downsizing"** provisions which protect the RNRB when a larger house has been replaced by a lower value house or, indeed, where there is no house at all by the date of death. To the extent that it is unused, it may be transferable to the surviving spouse/civil partner. A claim must be made within two years of death. We shall look briefly at each of these aspects.

A qualifying residential interest is, subject to the downsizing rules discussed below, any interest in a dwelling house which has or has been at some point been the deceased's residence. If there is more than one, the personal representatives can choose which one, even if it is not his actual home at the time of death. The house must be closely inherited, which means that it must be passed to the lineal descendants of the deceased—these include children and grandchildren, etc. and also include step children, adopted and foster children and minors for whom the deceased is a guardian. Most spouses and civil partners of lineal descendants are also included. Note there is no requirement that the person inheriting should live in the house—he or she can sell it immediately if they so wish. The relief may be extended to a property which is treated as part of the deceased's estate by virtue of the reservation of benefit rules. So, for example, if Bill gives his house away to Kate (his daughter, so a lineal descendant) but continues to reserve a benefit and so it is treated as part of his estate on death, provided the house has been Bill's residence at some point, it is a qualifying residential interest.

The residential enhancement is the value of the interest in the property, subject to maximum limit. The maximum starts at £100,000 in 2017/18 and rises in stages to £175,000 in 2020/21,[4] after which it will be indexed by the CPI.

There is a catch however: the additional nil-rate band is reduced rapidly once the total estate on death exceeds £2 million – by £1 for each £2 of the excess. So, in 2017/18 for example, an estate of £2 million potentially receives the full £100,000 additional nil-rate band, whereas an estate of £2.2 million receives nothing.

If the RNRB is unused on the first death, it may be transferred to a surviving spouse or civil partner, but only after taking into account the taper on the first death. It does not matter why the RNRB was unused, so even if the first to die did not own property, there is still the potential for a transfer. The provisions for transfer are similar to those for the standard nil-rate band—it is the unused percentage which is transferred, not the unused amount (see example at para.21–06) and the maximum extra that any person can accrue is 100 per cent. Although the relief

---

[4] Any unused residential enhancement can be transferred to a surviving spouse or civil partner in similar fashion to the standard nil-rate band. It cannot be an accident that two nil-rate bands at £325,000 each, plus two maximum residential enhancements of £175,000 equal £1 million—thus fulfilling a Conservative policy aim of achieving a £1 million nil-rate band.

only applies in relation to deaths on or after 6 April 2017, it does not matter for the purposes of the *transferred* RNRB when the first death took place—this can be at any time. By definition, no part of the RNRB will have been used in relation to a first death before 6 April 2017—it was not available on such deaths! However, a taper check will still have to be made on the first death, and for this purposes, it is assumed that the available RNRB was £100,000. So, assume Jenny died in 2010, leaving all her estate of £2,150,000 to her civil partner Charlotte. Jenny's assumed RNRB would be £100,000 before the taper. The taper would reduce this £100,000 by £75,000 (because the estate was £150,000 over the taper-free estate). This means that 25 per cent was unused and so on Charlotte's death, there will be an extra 25 per cent of whatever the RNRB is at that date, before any tapering based on the size of Charlotte's estate.

So far, it has been assumed that for the RNRB to be available on a death there must be a home in the estate which is left to the family. This creates an obvious disincentive for people to downsize, or even sell and move into residential care. There are rather complex provisions which enable a RNRB to be claimed here even though there is no property in the estate on death. The property must have been occupied by the deceased as a residence during his ownership and it must have been disposed of on or after 8 July 2015. A further requirement for the downsizing addition to be available is that the deceased must leave other assets up to the residential enhancement claimed to his lineal descendants. To take a simple example, if Sal moved into residential care in 2016 at which time she sold her house for £250,000, and then died in 2017, she would be entitled to a RNRB of £100,000 provided she left assets of at least that value to her family.

The effect of a death on chargeable transfers and PETs made within the previous seven years—taper relief

21–09   CHARGEABLE TRANSFERS To avoid taxpayers making immediately chargeable transfers shortly before death so as to attract the lower rate of tax, s.7(4) provides that where the transferor dies within seven years of making a chargeable transfer the rates applicable on a death will be retrospectively imposed on that transfer. Since the transfer may have already borne tax at the lifetime rate (it may have been covered by the nil-rate band) there is in effect an additional charge to tax (on the transferee) based on the original value of the transfer. That additional charge is computed by working out what the amount of tax would be if the current death rate had applied and deducting from that the tax already paid on the original transfer. However, in making this calculation, if the transferor has survived more than three years after making the transfer, only a percentage of the death rate will be used. This is known as taper relief. Thus if the transferor survives for six years only 20 per cent of the recalculated tax will be payable, used; for five years, 40 per cent; for four years, 60 per cent; and for three years, 80 per cent.

To take an example:

Suppose that George having already made chargeable transfers of £325,000 in the previous seven years makes a gift of £20,000 (gross) to a company. Since that is an immediately chargeable transfer, tax at 20 per cent will be payable, i.e. £4,000. If George dies two years later HMRC will claim extra tax from the company. The full death rate will be applied to give a figure of £8,000 tax (at 40 per cent) and the company will have to pay the extra £4,000. If George had survived for four years only 60 per cent of the death rate tax would be used to give a figure of £4,800 tax so that the company would only be liable to find an extra £800 tax.

Sometimes the application of taper relief means that no extra tax is payable on the death (e.g. if George had lived for more than five years in the above example, the recalculation at 40 per cent of the death rate would give a total of £3,200, which is less than the £4,000 already paid). There is no refund of any of the original tax, however. Section 131 provides that if the gift has fallen in value between the gift and the subsequent death, the additional tax is calculated on that reduced value,[5] but the original value remains as part of the transferor's cumulative total for the purposes of calculating the rate applicable to the transfer of his death estate. It is important to remember that whilst the recalculation on lifetime gifts is only necessary for gifts within seven years of death, chargeable transfers more than seven years old at the time of death still may be relevant to the calculation. There is no extra tax to pay in relation to such transfers, but they do continue to use up nil rate band for seven years after they are made. Assume Don makes chargeable transfers in years 1, 5 and then dies in year 9. When calculating the tax on transfers within the seven years of death, there is no extra tax to pay on the one in year 1 because it is outside this period. In relation to the extra tax on the transfer is year 5, the transfer in year 1 is still relevant because it still uses some or all the nil-rate band in relation to the

---

[5] This does not apply to wasting assets, i.e. those which are inevitably going to decrease in value.

year 5 transfer. By the date of death, the transfer in year 1 has "dropped out" and no longer uses up nil rate band in relation to the estate on death.

21-10   PETs The position is slightly more complicated where the transferor dies within seven years of making a PET (including a gift with reservation where that reservation has ceased within seven years of the death). As we have seen the PET will then become chargeable (on the transferee) in accordance with the transferor's cumulative total at the time when the PET was made, on the value then transferred (unless it has since fallen in value, when that lower value can be used). The rate of tax will, however, be the death rate applicable at the date of death (unless the rates have increased in which case the rates at the time of the transfer are used). Once again taper relief, calculated as above, will be available to lower the amount payable but of course there is no deduction for tax already paid since none was payable at the time. Thus, in the example above, if the gift had been made to Harry instead of a company, no tax would have been payable at the time. On George's death, Harry would have become liable to tax at £8,000 in the first scenario and £4,800 in the second.

21-11   EFFECT ON CUMULATIVE TOTAL But this activating of the charge has another effect. Since the transfer is no longer a PET it will be treated as if the transferor had always made a chargeable transfer at that time. Thus although it was not originally included in the transferor's cumulative total it will have to be so included retrospectively. Accordingly the tax payable on previous chargeable transfers may have to be recalculated on that basis.

To take a simple example:

Ian, having made no previous chargeable transfers, makes a PET of £200,000 to John. The next year he makes an immediately chargeable transfer to trustees of £200,000. Ian's cumulative total prior to that (at that time) is nil so that the chargeable transfer is within the nil-rate band. If Ian dies within seven years the PET becomes chargeable so that Ian's cumulative total at the time of the transfer to the trustees is recalculated at £200,000 and that transfer will now fall as to £125,000 into the nil-rate band and £75,000 into the taxable band (the tapered death rate applies as it was within seven years of the death).

Where the transferor has made a combination of PETs and chargeable transfers within seven years of his death the recalculations are almost endless.

Transfers of more than one property

It is provided by s.265 that "where the value transferred by a **21–12**
chargeable transfer is determined by reference to the values of
more than one property the tax chargeable on the value transferred shall be attributed to the respective values in the propor-
tions which they bear to their aggregate". This means that, for
example, if A leaves property worth £60,000 to B and property
worth £40,000 to C, the tax is spread evenly over the whole value
transferred. The gift to B bears 60 per cent of the tax bill and the
gift to C bears 40 per cent. Section 265 is "subject to" any provision reducing the amount of tax attributable to the value of any
particular property. So, for example, if on death X leaves a farm
to Y and shares in a quoted company to Z, Z does not enjoy any
part of the agricultural property relief.

Transfers on the same day

Lifetime transfers on the same day by the same transferor **21–13**
present some difficulty. The basic principle is stated in s.266(1):
where the value transferred by more than one chargeable transfer made by the same person on the same day depends on the
order in which the transfers are made, they shall be treated as
made in the order which results in the lowest value chargeable.
For example, if on the same day A makes a chargeable transfer
to B (A paying the tax) and a separate chargeable transfer to C
(C paying the tax), the gift to B will have to be grossed up, (see
para.21–17 below), whereas the gift to C will not. So it may be
"cheaper" in tax terms to count the gift to B before the gift to
C, because any available nil-rate band will be allocated first to
B's gift. The legislation permits this. Then, the order of the gifts
having been established, s.266(2) declares that there shall be an
"effective rate," namely the tax which would have been charged if
the transfers had been a single transfer. So A pays tax on the gift
to B and C pays tax on the gift to himself, both at the same rate.

Transfers reported late

This is dealt with by s.264. Where an earlier transfer is not **21–14**
notified to HMRC until after the tax has been paid on a later
transfer, the position depends upon the gap between the transfers. If the gap is seven years or more there is no problem since
they would not be cumulated together anyway and so tax plus
interest is payable on the earlier transfer at the rates then applying. If the gap is less than seven years the earlier (unreported)
transfer is charged at the rate then applying and the extra tax
which should have been collected on the second transfer (because
of cumulation) is now charged on the first one (plus interest).

Liabilities

21–15   In considering this topic it is necessary to distinguish between liabilities resulting from a chargeable transfer and other liabilities.

Liabilities resulting from a chargeable transfer

21–16   One has to remember that the value transferred on a lifetime transfer is the amount by which the transferor's estate immediately after the disposition is less than it would be if the disposition had not been made.

A chargeable transfer may give rise to IHT and at the same time to two other taxes—CGT and sometimes stamp duty. Also there may be incidental costs of the transfer, such as conveyancing fees. All these items, if paid by the transferor, will diminish the value of his estate immediately after the transfer. So, in the absence of any provision to the contrary, they would all increase the amount of the "value transferred" and so increase the amount of tax payable.

To some extent, the Act does make provisions to the contrary. Section 5(4) provides that in determining the value of the transferor's estate immediately after the transfer, his liability to IHT on the value transferred shall be taken into account, i.e included in the loss to the estate, but not his liability for any other tax or duty. And by s.164 the incidental expenses, if borne by the transferor, shall be left out of account and, if borne by the transferee, shall reduce the value transferred.

The point to grasp is that when one is considering liabilities immediately *after* the transfer, the effect of taking a liability into account is to increase the diminution in value of the transferor's estate and so increase the value transferred and so increase the IHT. Conversely, the effect of leaving a liability out of account is that that liability (e.g. liability to CGT or liability to pay conveyancing fees to one's solicitor) does not increase the IHT.

And if the CGT is borne by the transferee, that is treated (for IHT) as actually reducing the value transferred: s.165.

There are special rules about debts due to foreign residents (s.162(5)).

Grossing up—lifetime transfers

21–17   LOSS TO THE ESTATE   The principle of grossing up a lifetime transfer is embedded in s.5. As we have just seen, if the transferor is to pay the IHT, his liability to the tax is to be taken into account in calculating the diminution in his estate caused by the transfer. Thus the loss to his estate is both the transferred amount and the tax on that amount, and tax is charged on that total amount, i.e. tax is charged on tax—that is grossing up. If A makes a chargeable transfer to B of £x in cash or of property worth £x (tax free), A's estate is diminished by £x plus the relevant IHT. So £x must be grossed up to find what sum must be paid by A to HMRC to put £x into the hands of B free from any liability to the tax. If one calls that additional sum £y, A must pay £x to B and £y to HMRC.

EXCEPTIONS   If A makes a transfer to B, stipulating that B **21–18** must pay the IHT on it, no grossing up arises. This is because A's estate is not diminished by IHT, since he is not going to pay any of it. Since most lifetime transfers are now PETs, any tax which becomes chargeable will only be due after the transferor's death on the transferee so that no grossing up occurs.

In a general sense there is no grossing up either in the case of a transfer on death. This is because grossing up is, in effect, built into the situation since it is only the sums net of tax which will reach the beneficiaries. However, where a specific gift is left by will "tax-free" a kind of grossing up has to take place to determine the entitlements of other beneficiaries: see Ch.23 below, under the heading "Incidence".

COMPUTATIONS   With regard to the actual process of **21–19** grossing up, in principle it is just like grossing up for income tax. If A wants to put into the hands of B £40,000, one has to work out what sum, after deduction of tax, will leave £40,000 clear. But in practice it is often very much more complicated than is the income tax process. This is because: (a) the tax on any particular transfer has to take account of the transferor's previous tax history under the principle of cumulation; and (b) the particular gift itself may cross the rate bands.

The problem is in identifying the loss to the estate where the loss includes the tax. Unless you know what the tax is, you don't know what the loss is and, unless you know what the loss is, you don't know what the tax is.

This is the problem which is solved by grossing up – it gives you the sum which, after tax, is the amount that the recipient ends up with. Grossing up a lifetime transfer involves multiplying the part of the transfer not covered by the nil-rate band by 5/4.

So, if A gives £100,000 to B Ltd (a chargeable transfer, not a PET) and undertakes to pay any tax on the transfer then, assuming A has no nil-rate band available, the £100,000 is multiplied by 5/4 to give £125,000. This gives you the loss to the estate. Tax on £125,000 at 20% is £25,000, payable by A.

It should be noted that exactly the same result would be achieved by A giving B Ltd £125,000 where B Ltd pays the tax. In both scenarios, A's loss is £125,000, B Ltd ends up with £100,000 and HMRC receives £25,000.

21–20   Effects of grossing up   The effects of grossing up are therefore to increase both the tax payable on the individual transfer and the cumulative total of the transferor. On the other hand the transferee will receive a set amount, in our example £100,000 and not an amount variable according to the tax payable. As we have seen, however, this concept has been reduced in importance by the introduction of PETs. It is limited to those lifetime transfers which are not PETs.

Other liabilities

21–21   What we are talking about here is liabilities other than those which result from a chargeable transfer. The importance of the topic is that it is clearly relevant to the comparison which has to be made in the case of lifetime transfers between the value of a person's estate before and after the transfer (its relevance is to the "before" part) and it is clearly relevant to reduce the valuation of a person's estate on death. Clearly, the starting point on death is that the deceased's debts reduce the estate for IHT purposes.

21–22   Relevant liabilities   A liability is not taken into account unless it is a liability imposed by law or it was incurred by the transferor for a consideration in money or money's worth: s.5(5). Thus an outstanding mortgage on a house would be deductible but not a voluntary covenant. In *Curnock v IRC* (2003), where the bank agreed to pay a cheque drawn on the deceased's account but not cleared until after his death, it could not be regarded as a liability against the deceased's estate, since the cheque was regarded as part of the administration of the estate and so was not incurred for a consideration in money or money's worth.

21–23   Artificial debts   In establishing the value of an estate on death, s.5(5) is supplemented by s.103 of FA 1986. This section disallows what are known as "artificial debts". These are defined as debts for which the consideration was either directly derived from the deceased[6] or provided by another person to whose resources the deceased contributed. In the latter case there must be a causal link between the contribution of the deceased and

---

[6]   Unless it was a transfer of value. See *Phizackerley v HMRC* (2007) Sp Comm.

the debt transaction. A simple example of this section applying is where Jane gives away a valuable asset to Kate and three years later she buys it back for full market value but leaves the debt outstanding until the date of her death five years later. The gift to Kate will not be taxable since it was a PET made more than seven years before her death and the debt owed to Kate, having been made for full consideration, would be deductible under s.5(5). But since the consideration for the debt, the asset, derived from Jane's estate it would not be allowable under s.103 of FA 1986.

Where an artificial debt is paid off during the deceased's lifetime, the repayment is treated as a PET: s.103(5) of FA 1986. Act. Thus if Jane repaid Kate a year before her death it would become a chargeable transfer on her death. This will probably not apply, however, if Jane pays Kate the full amount immediately on buying the asset back—no debt has been incurred.

Debts relating to property not subject to tax: FA 2013 s.176

In 2013 anti-avoidance provisions were introduced to restrict the deduction of debts from the estate in three situations. The normal rule about deducting debts which are secured over particular property is that they reduce the value of that property, rather than being a general deduction against the estate. This was regarded as opening up avoidance opportunities. The first rule relates to excluded property (property outside the UK owned by a person not domiciled in the UK). Any debt for the purposes of acquiring, enhancing or maintaining excluded property must be set first against that property. This means that it is no longer possible to secure a loan over UK property, which would otherwise be reduced for IHT purposes, and use the loan to buy property outside the UK tax net. The second rule is similar in operation, but applies to property which is subject to agricultural or business property relief. Any debt for the purposes of acquiring, enhancing or maintaining such property must be set first against that property. The third rule is slightly different. It provides that a liability will only be deductible from the estate of a deceased person if it is repaid on or after their death. If the liability remains outstanding, there must be a 'real commercial reason' for non-repayment and it must not give rise to a tax advantage.

21–24

SUMMARY Before we leave liabilities, notice this general point about them: if it is a question of valuing an estate *before* a transfer (or immediately before death) it is advantageous to the taxpayer if a liability can be taken into account: if it is a question of valuing an estate *after* a transfer it is disadvantageous if a liability is to be taken into account.

21–25

Relief against double charges

21–26   Section 104 of FA 1986 allows regulations to be made to prevent double charges to IHT applying in certain situations. The Inheritance Tax (Double Charges Relief) Regulations 1987 (SI 1987/1130) and 2005 (SI 2005/3441) apply such a relief in five situations.

PET and transfer back

21–27   Where A makes a PET of some property to B, B transfers the property back to A (e.g. in his will), and A then dies within seven years of the PET. The double charge arises because the property would be chargeable on the gift to B (the PET has become chargeable) and also on A's death (it forms part of his estate). The solution is to either charge the property as part of A's estate at his death and ignore the PET or to tax the PET and ignore the value of the property on A's death, whichever produces the lower amount of tax.

Chargeable transfer and gift with reservation

21–28   Where A makes a gift subject to a reservation which is also a chargeable transfer, e.g. a gift of his house to a company but he continues to live in it, and he dies still enjoying that reservation (or did so within seven years of his death). Since tax will have been paid on the chargeable transfer and the house will still form part of his estate on his death (or will be a chargeable PET) there is again the potential for a double charge. The solution again is to take the lower of charging the house as part of A's estate at death and to ignore the gift or to tax the gift and ignore the house as part of A's estate (or as a chargeable PET).

Transfer and loan back

21–29   Where A makes a chargeable transfer (or chargeable PET) of money to B and B lends an equivalent sum back to A. A then dies with the loan to B outstanding. The double charge here arises because the debt would not be allowed under s.103 of FA 1986 as an artificial debt (see above). Thus the money given is chargeable on the transfer and as part of A's estate on death. The regulations provide that the tax payable is to be the lower of taxing the transfer and allowing the debt against the estate or ignoring the transfer and disallowing the debt.

Transfer and transfer back

21–30   Where A makes a chargeable transfer (but not a PET) and the transferee returns the property to A, which is beneficially owned by A on his death within seven years of the original transfer. The double charge in this case is the additional tax which will be payable on the original transfer because of A's death within seven years and the tax payable on the property as part of A's estate at his death. Again either the original transfer or the value of the property on A's death is to be ignored, although there is no relief for the tax already paid on the transfer.

Transfer of property and debt

Suppose A enters into arrangements whereby he transfers both **21–31** property (relevant property) and a debt owed to A. The debt is then written off. If on A's death the relevant property and the death are chargeable to IHT, two separate amounts must be calculated. The first is the tax chargeable on A's death disregarding the value transferred by the relevant property. The second is the amount so chargeable disregarding the value transferred by the debt. The tax chargeable is then reduced to the greater of those two amounts.

Valuation

Open market value

The basic principle of valuation is stated in s.160. Except as **21–32** otherwise provided the value at any time of any property shall be the price which the property might reasonably be expected to fetch if sold in the open market at that time. This is generally called "open market value" and takes us into the realms of a hypothetical sale.

The subsection then goes on to say (perhaps rather inconsistently) that the price shall not be assumed to be reduced on the ground that the whole property is to be, hypothetically, placed on the market at one and the same time. So if A owns 100,000 shares in XYZ Ltd the shares are valued (in the absence of an actual sale) without any reduction for the fact that if such a parcel of shares were put on the market at one time the price would be depressed.

ESTATE DUTY PRINCIPLES The definition of open market **21–33** value continues the valuation rule which existed for estate duty purposes. The general judicial definition is that it is the best price available from a hypothetical purchaser in the market and not necessarily the highest price.[7] If there are a range of prices which competent valuers would consider as open market values

---

[7] *Re Hayes WT* (1971); cf. *Ellesmere v IRC* (1918).

then the highest is no more likely than the lower. Although the purchaser is hypothetical there is nothing hypothetical about the market, which is one where serious men of business would operate. In practice this means focussing on what a relatively small number of people would be likely to have paid.[8] Thus there is no reason to invent non-existent speculative purchasers, so that if in the real world the asset is worthless, it is worthless.[9] On the other hand if there is a real potential purchaser that may be taken into account.[10] It seems that some account may be taken of the existence of a special purchaser, e.g. the owner of adjoining land, who might pay "over the odds" to acquire the property.[11]

21–34   RESTRICTIONS ON SALE If there is no open market, e.g. there are restrictions on sale, the property is to be valued under what is known as the *Crossman* principle on the assumption that a hypothetical purchaser buys freely in a hypothetical market but, having bought it, becomes subject to the restrictions.[12] This is particularly the case with private company shares which usually have some form of restriction attached to them. Section 168 provides that in such a case the hypothetical purchaser buying in the hypothetical market must be assumed to know all the information which a prudent prospective purchaser might reasonably require to know if he were buying from a willing vendor at arm's length.[13] This is in itself an exception to the basic rule that it is the market value of the property and not its intrinsic value which counts, e.g. a painting will be valued at its then market value even if it later turns out to be a forgery.

21–35   OTHER LIABILITIES The *Crossman* principle has also been applied where the property is subject to some form of liability other than a restriction on sale. This was the decision of the Court of Appeal in *Alexander v IRC* (1991). The property was a flat in which the deceased had acquired a leasehold interest at a discount under a statutory scheme. Under the lease the tenant had to repay that discount to the landlord if the lease was sold within five years. The tenant died within the first year. What

[8]   *IRC v Gray* (1994).
[9]   *HMRC v Bower* (2009).
[10]   *Marks v HMRC* (2011).
[11]   *IRC v Clay* (1914); cf. *IRC v Crossman* (1937).
[12]   *IRC v Crossman* (1937); *Re Lynall* (1972).
[13]   For example, whether the company's profits are increasing. The whole concept has a touch of Lewis Carroll about it.

was the value of the lease? The Court of Appeal held first that the obligation to repay was an incumbrance on the property incurred for a consideration and so fell to be taken into account in valuing the property. They then held that the value of the flat for IHT purposes was what a hypothetical purchaser would pay to acquire the lease subject to the obligation to repay the discount if there was a sale within five years but disregarding the fact that his own (hypothetical) purchase would have given rise to such a liability.

In *Walton v IRC* (1996) the deceased owned an interest in a tenancy (as a partnership asset). The other interest was held by one of his sons and the landlords were the deceased and his two sons. The court upheld a valuation of that interest on the basis that since it could not be assigned without the landlord's consent and that might be withheld, it could not take into account the value of the land as if the lease and reversion were merged. The intentions of the actual landlords could be taken into account; there was no requirement to use a hypothetical landlord.

The position is different if the vendor had special rights which would be lost to any purchaser. The decision in the income tax case of *Grays Timber Products v HMRC* (2010) suggests that such rights would not form any part of the open market value.[14]

Restriction on freedom to dispose: s.163

21–36

The rule referred to above on restrictions on sale could lead to abuse. To avoid this there is a complex provision which is best understood if we take one particular kind of restriction on freedom to dispose, namely an option. Suppose A grants to B an option to purchase a house. If the option price is the same as the then market price, say £250,000, there is no transfer of value. If the option price, say £235,000, is less than the then market price there is a transfer of value unless B pays for the option a sum (£15,000) equal to the difference between the prices. If, later, B exercises his option and buys the house for £235,000 when it is worth £260,000, the amount of the "value transferred" depends on how much consideration B gave for the option. If B gave no consideration, the "value transferred" by the sale is £25,000 (the gratuitous element). If B gave £15,000 for the option, the "value transferred" by the sale (assuming B pays the tax) is £245,000 (£260,000 − £15,000) less £235,000 = £10,000.

---

[14] See Geoffrey Morse, "Grays Timber Products Ltd v Revenue and Customs Commissioners: valuing employee shares with non-assignable rights" [2010] B.T.R. 210.

Valuation of related property: s.161

21–37   The concept of "related property" is an important one. Property is related to the property comprised in a person's estate if: (a) it is in the estate of his spouse or civil partner; or (b) it is (or has been within the preceding five years) the property of a charity, political party, etc., and became so on an exempt transfer made by him or his spouse.

Where the value of any property would be less than the appropriate portion of the value of the aggregate of that and any related property, it shall be the appropriate portion of the value of that aggregate. That is the rather obscure wording of s.161(1). It needs an example. The background is that the enactment is intended to stop up a tax-avoidance device. Suppose A owns 70 of the 100 issued shares in XYZ Ltd. Mrs A owns none. A transfers 30 shares to his wife. Controlling shares are worth say £10 each; non-controlling shares are worth say £6 each. The transfer to Mrs A is exempt. The legislation ensures that after the transfer A's holding is valued (e.g. on his subsequent death) as being worth not merely 40 × £6 (i.e. £240), but 40/70ths of the value of the combined (controlling) holding. The combined value is £700, so A's holding is valued at £400, and Mrs A's holding is valued at £300.

A relief is provided (by s.176) where property was valued on death on the related property basis and is subsequently (within three years of the death) sold for a lesser amount to those who inherited the property on the death on an arm's length sale.

Value of lessor's interest: s.170

21–38   In a settlement, sometimes the life tenant is treated as owning the whole settled property and the holder of the reversionary interest is treated as owning nothing, because his interest is "excluded property" (see Ch.20). In addition a lease for life, if the lease was not granted for full consideration, is treated (see s.43) as a settlement, but with the modification that the lessor's interest is not excluded property. This present section (s.170) provides that the value of the lessor's interest in the property shall be taken to be such part of the value of the property as bears to it the same proportion as the value of the consideration, at the time the lease was granted, bore to what would then have been the value of a full consideration. So, if L grants a lease for life to T at 75 per cent of full consideration, L's interest in the property is taken to be 75 per cent of the value of the property. (And, as we shall see, T's interest is taken by s.50(6) to be 25 per cent of that value.)

Value of life policies, etc.: s.167

This section provides that the value of certain life policies and **21–39** contracts for deferred annuities shall be treated as not less than the total of premiums paid (minus any surrender value paid, e.g. on a partial surrender) where that would be higher that its market value at the time of a lifetime transfer. This does not apply on a death.

Value transferred on death

IHT is charged on the death of a person as if, immediately **21–40** before his death, he had made a transfer of value and the value transferred by it had been equal to the value of his estate immediately before his death: s.4.[15] His estate does not include "excluded property": s.5(1). It does include property over which he had a general power to appoint or dispose, settled property in which he had a life interest (except, in certain circumstances, where the property reverts on the death to the settlor or the settlor's spouse) and his share in a joint tenancy, or common property in Scotland.[16]

OPEN MARKET VALUE: LOTTING On a death, therefore, **21–41** the whole of the deceased's estate must be valued on the open market basis on the assumption of a hypothetical sale of all the estate immediately before the death. The methods of ascertaining such a value are the same as for lifetime transfers (see para.21–32 above). One rule which is peculiar to ascertaining the market value on a death, however, is that where by taking a number of items together a higher price could be obtained that must be done, e.g. by valuing a set of Hepplewhite dining chairs as a single unit rather than by reference to each chair. (The related property rules, above, prevent this being avoided by transfers of part of such a set to a spouse and part to another.) This is known as the process of "lotting".[17] In *Gray v IRC* (1994), this approach was applied by the Court of Appeal to aggregate the deceased's partnership interest in a farming business, including a lease of the land farmed, with the deceased's freehold reversionary interest in that land. The

---

[15] In *Curnock v IRC* (2003), the deceased's attorney wrote a cheque for X a day before the deceased died. The cheque, for £6,000 was intended to use up the available lifetime transfer exemption. The cheque was not cleared until after the deceased's death. Since, until then, there was no complete gift, the money was part of the deceased's estate under s.4.

[16] Which is still in existence the moment before death.

[17] That phrase had been used in the House of Lords case which established this principle: *Buccleuch v IRC* (1967).

fact that taking the two together did not form a natural unit of property was irrelevant. The only question was whether a prudent hypothetical vendor would have adopted this course of action in order to obtain the most favourable price without undue expenditure of time and effort.

21–42   OTHER RULES   The Act also lays down some detailed rules, as follows:

1) an allowance shall be made for reasonable funeral expenses (s.172);
2) certain changes (whether increases or decreases) in the value of the estate which occur *by reason of* the death are treated as having occurred before the death. An example of an increase would be the proceeds of a life insurance policy; these proceeds count as part of the estate. An example of a decrease would occur if a restaurant business lost value through the death of its successful proprietor; this fact is to be taken into account in valuing the business as part of the deceased's estate (s.171). An allowance is also made for the extra expense of administering or realising foreign property (s.173);
3) sections 178–189 provide some relief where "qualifying investments" (notably quoted shares and holdings in an authorised unit trust) are sold within the 12 months following the death for less than the value at the date of death. In that case the sale proceeds can be substituted for that value; and
4) sections 190–198 provide a similar relief where land (which may include buildings) is sold within three years of the death for less than the value at death. To claim this relief legal title to the land must have been conveyed. A mere exchange of contracts, although a sale in equity, is not sufficient.[18]

---

[18]   *Jones v IRC* (1997).

CHAPTER 22

SETTLED PROPERTY

Development of the charges on settled property

The original intention in taxing settled property was said to **22–01** be to ensure that property within settlements bore the same level of taxation in the longer term as unsettled property. To achieve this therefore required a charge amounting to the equivalent of at least a charge on the death of each generation (trusts as such don't die) and on any property exiting the settlement in the meantime. The solution until 2006 was to tax the two generic types of settled property in different ways and to implement a special regime for specially favoured trusts.

Fixed interest trusts
Fixed interest trusts (where there was someone entitled to a **22–02** beneficial interest in possession, i.e. to the income as it arose) were taxed as if the whole settled property belonged to the holder of that interest. Thus on his or her death it formed part of their estate and tax was calculated (and paid by the trust) accordingly. Any lifetime charges (such as the ending of the interest otherwise than on a death), including creating the settlement, were PETs.

Discretionary and other non-fixed interest trusts
Other trusts without such a beneficial interest in possession, **22–03** usually discretionary trusts, were taxed as separate entities with their own cumulative total, etc. (They could not, by definition, be linked to a specific beneficiary so as to link into the tax in that way.) Charges were made on the whole settled property every 10 years and on property exiting from the trust. None of the charges, including setting up the trust, were PETs.

Specially favoured trusts
A group of trusts were treated separately for social and **22–04** political reasons. These included charitable trusts, trusts for a disabled person and an accumulation and maintenance trust (for a beneficiary under 25). They were generally exempt from all charges unless the criteria for exemption were lost, in which case a charge arose based on how long the trust had been so exempt.

Excluded settled property

22–05 Under s.48, settled property is excluded property if it is situated outside the UK and held on a trust which was set up by a person who was domiciled abroad when the settlement was made. As an anti-avoidance measure, introduced in 2012, where a UK domiciled person acquires an interest in settled excluded property in such a way that his estate is reduced, the property ceases to be excluded property. A charge will arise in the same way as if the property had not been excluded.

The 2006 revolution

22–06 With no prior consultation or warning, FA 2006 instituted a major change in the way that settled property became subject to IHT. In effect, most fixed interest trusts ceased to be taxed by reference to the beneficiary with an interest in possession. They were subsumed into the independent tax regime formerly applied only to discretionary trusts. Only a few exceptions were made and only two and a half years was allowed for taxpayers to amend their affairs. In addition the favourable regime for accumulation and maintenance trusts was substantially reduced.

The result is that, since 22 March 2006, most trusts have become subject to the ten year and exit charges and neither transfers out nor the creation of such trusts are PETs. Before, creating a fixed interest trust and other charges on such trusts, except on a death, were PETs.

Settlement

22–07 "Settled property" is not separately defined; it is simply property comprised in a settlement. What, then, is a settlement, for the purposes of the Act? Section 43 states that it is a disposition or dispositions whereby property is for the time being:

(1) held in trust for persons in succession; or
(2) held in trust for any person subject to a contingency; or
(3) held on discretionary trusts; or
(4) held on trust to accumulate the income; or
(5) charged (otherwise than for full consideration)[1] to pay an annuity; or

---

[1] An annuity not charged on property (e.g. an annuity purchased from an insurance company) is not a settlement. Even an annuity which is charged on property is not a settlement if it is granted for full consideration. Hence (probably) an annuity granted by continuing (commercial) partners for a former partner or his dependants is not a settlement.

(6) subject to a lease for life if the lease was not granted for full consideration.[2]

Property subject to provisions equivalent to heads (1)–(5) above under the law of a foreign country can constitute a "settlement." Foreign settled property is, however, excluded property unless the settlor was domiciled in the UK at the time the settlement was made.[3]

Neither a tenancy in common nor a joint tenancy or common property in Scotland therefore is as such a settlement, but either of them will be a settlement if it also falls under any of the heads enumerated above.

One or more settlements

Just as in CGT (see para.15–64 above) it is sometimes neces-   **22–08**
sary to decide whether a settlor has made one single settlement or more than one. This can arise (as in CGT) where a power is exercised so as to transfer assets out of a settlement. The question for IHT in such a case is whether the exercise of that power amounts to a disposition within s.43. In *Minden Trust (Cayman) Ltd v IRC* (1985), it was held that where the exercise of the power amounted to a transfer of the entire trust property into a sub-trust, that was a settlement within s.43. The question can also arise when the settlor creates a number of trusts around the same time, often in identical form—are they separate settlements or a single settlement?

This was the question in *Rysaffe Trustee Co (CI) Ltd v IRC* (2003). The settlor set up five identical discretionary trusts, different only in the date of creation. HMRC argued that these constituted a single settlement under s.43 since that section allowed for a settlement to be created by a disposition or *dispositions*. The Court of Appeal and the judge rejected that argument. Whether there was one or more settlements was basically a matter for the law of trusts and s.43 did not alter that. Whether a settlor chose, say, to set up a single trust of £1 million for five beneficiaries or five trusts of £200,000, one for each of the beneficiaries, was a matter for the settlor. The use of the plural *dispositions* in s.43 was there to cover the situation, e.g. where a settlor added property to an existing trust. On the facts these were five separate settlements.

---

[2] Presumably the point of this is to prevent a person from seeking to avoid the rules relating to settled property by granting a lease for life instead of a life tenancy.

[3] But not reversionary interests—see the end of this chapter. Domicile here has its extended meaning for IHT purposes.

Putting property into a settlement

22–09 Creating or adding to a settlement on a death is taxed as any other transfer on death under s.4. In the case of a lifetime transfer, it will be an immediately chargeable transfer and not a PET, unless it is either: (i) a gift into a trust with a disabled person's interest (see s.89B); or (ii) it occurs on the ending, inter vivos,[4] of *an immediate post-death interest*[5] where the property continues under the settlement to be held for a *bereaved minor*.[6] Schemes which sought to avoid the post-2006 immediate inter vivos charge on putting funds into a fixed interest trust by purchasing an interest in the settlement (including a reversionary interest—see para.22–19 below) which had not been subject to IHT were ended by FA 2010 ss.52 and 53. In such cases the purchased interest is deemed to form part of the purchaser's estate, so that there will be a charge on its ending or transfer, as well as it remaining part of the settled property for the 10-year and exit charges.

Settlements still subject to the beneficiary-link principle—categorisation

Three types of beneficial interest in possession

22–10 After 2006, only trusts with one of three specific types of beneficial interest in possession (one transitional) are still subject to the former fixed-interest trust IHT regime. That, as we shall see, in effect treats the whole settled property as part of the estate of the holder of that interest so as to impose the tax charges. These three are: an immediate post-death interest (an IPDI); a disabled person's interest; and a transitional serial interest (TSI).

Immediate post-death interest

22–11 An IPDI is defined in s.49A. This is a beneficial interest in possession in a settlement which: (i) was created on a death (by will or on intestacy); and (ii) whereby the owner of the interest became entitled to it on the death of the testator or intestate. An interest in a bereaved minor's trust and a disabled person's interest cannot be IPDIs. Thus a typical IPDI will be where A dies and leaves property to B for life and then to C for life and then to D. B will then have an IPDI. After B dies, C will not have an IPDI—condition (ii) will not be satisfied.

---

[4] Such as the ending of a determinable interest or a surrender of the interest.
[5] This is as defined in s.49A and para.22–11 below.
[6] See s.71A and para.22–48 below.

Disabled person's interest

Under s.89B a disabled person's interest is one held under the **22–12** terms of s.89 (trust set up for a disabled person) or s.89A (self-settlement by a person with a condition expected to lead to a disability). The conditions required for such a trust are: (i) that no interest in possession exists during the lifetime of the disabled person; and (ii) that at least half of the settled property must be applied for that person's benefit during his life. In *Barclays Bank Trust Company Ltd v HMRC* (2010), the Court of Appeal stated that a common sense (and so wider) interpretation should be given to the word "benefit" in that context.

Transitional serial interest

There are two categories of TSI, both of which are narrowly **22–13** defined. The first, under s.49C, is one which commenced on or after 22 March 2006 and before 6 October 2008 and which itself followed the termination of a prior interest in possession which commenced before 22 March 2006. The second is defined in s.49D.[7] It is a beneficial interest in possession in a settlement which followed a prior interest in possession established before 22 March 2006. Further conditions are that the prior interest ended on the death of the holder of that interest, the prior interest was in the beneficial ownership of the spouse or civil partner of the successor interest; and the holder of the successor interest became entitled to it at that time. This is therefore a very limited category of interest. It would apply, e.g. where a pre-March 2006 settlement left property to A for life, then to A's spouse, B, for life, remainder to C. If A dies, B will have a TSI.

Bereaved minor's trusts (see para.22–48 below) are excluded from TSIs, as are disabled person's interests (whether as the prior or successor interest).

Beneficial interest in possession

Each of the above only apply if they are beneficial interests in **22–14** possession in the settled property. It is still necessary therefore to decide what that means in this context. HMRC published a statement on 12 February 1976[8] setting out their understanding of the term "interest in possession." In particular they dealt with the position where a person is entitled to the income of the

---

[7] Section 49C applied a wider definition to those arising before that date. Trustees were given a transitional period, originally to 5 April 2008, but extended until 5 October 2008, to rearrange pre-March 2006 trusts so that they contained a TSI, either for an existing or other (younger) beneficiary and so retain the beneficiary-link principle for some time.

[8] See now HMRC IHTM 16062.

property subject to a power of revocation or appointment of the capital in the trust or a power of accumulation of income. It is accepted that, in general, it is entitlement to the income as it arises which indicates a beneficial interest in possession (e.g. s.50 defines the size of the interest by reference to the proportion of income received). HMRC's point was that if there is a power to accumulate income (which then gets added to the capital of the trust), there is no interest in possession, the trustees can withhold current income as it arises. In contrast, where the trustees have a power of revocation (i.e. they can terminate the interest) or appointment over the capital in which the interest subsists, the trustees can only deprive the beneficiary of future income, thus leaving him with a beneficial interest in possession in the meantime.

22–15   PEARSON V IRC   This view was tested all the way up to the House of Lords in *Pearson v IRC* (1980). By a majority of three to two, overruling both a unanimous Court of Appeal and the judge below, the House of Lords upheld HMRC's argument that a power to accumulate does prevent the person taking in default of accumulation from having a beneficial interest in possession. Lord Keith, in the majority, concluded that the daughter only had the right to a later payment if the trustees either by inaction or decision did not accumulate the income— she had no absolute right to the income as it accrued.

That majority decision, as Lord Russell (in the minority) implied, is based on two basic misconceptions: (1) as to the nature of a vested interest subject to defeasance; and (2) as to the difference between trusts and powers. The interest was an interest vested subject to defeasance, a perfectly acceptable form of beneficial interest in English law which gives the owner the right to the income until it is taken away. The obsession with it being an "absolute" interest is irrelevant. Powers of accumulation, like powers of revocation or appointment, are only powers, i.e. they must be exercised unanimously to take effect. If one trustee disagrees then the power will not apply and the income be paid under the underlying trust, in this case to the daughter. The reader is referred to the speech of Lord Russell for a perfect example of what the law ought to be.

It may be noted, however, that the decision was not all bad for taxpayers. It may be desirable to ensure that X receives all the income of a trust but does not have a beneficial interest in possession (to avoid the trust property being regarded as part of X's estate).[9] That should be possible by giving X a right to the

---

[9]   See *Moore & Osbourne v IRC* (1985) and *Stenhouse's Trustees v Lord Advocate* (1984).

income subject to a power of accumulation which is not intended to be exercised.

No income trusts An interest in possession can also exist where the settled property does not produce an income, provided that the beneficiary has a present right to present possession of the settled property, e.g. sole occupation of a house.[10]   **22–16**

Effect of powers The effect of powers generally in relation to the use of income or the right to possession arising under the trust depends upon whether they are classified as administrative (thus not affecting the beneficiary's right to the income (or possession) as it arises) or dispositive (with the opposite effect). In *Miller v IRC* (1987) the Court of Session held that a power to use income to maintain the capital value of the fund was an administrative power so that there remained an interest in possession. The criterion was said to be that administrative powers are those relating to the prudent management in discharge of the trustees' duty to maintain the trust estate. A dispositive power is one which diverts income away from one beneficiary for the benefit of others.   **22–17**

Settlements still subject to the beneficiary-link principle—charging provisions

Deemed holder entitled to all property

The basic point to grasp here is that the person holding the IPDI[11] is treated "as beneficially entitled to the property in which the interest subsists": s.49(1). So if A is entitled to an IPDI in Blackacre he is treated for the purposes of the tax as though he were the owner of Blackacre itself. And if B is entitled to an IPDI in a settled fund worth £500,000 he is treated as though he were the owner of £500,000. But if the holder is entitled to part only of the income of settled property his interest is taken to subsist in only a proportionate part of the capital. So, if B were entitled to, say, half the income of the settled fund he would be treated as the owner of £250,000 (s.50).   **22–18**

---

[10] *IRC v Lloyds Private Banking Ltd* (1998).
[11] References to IPDIs from here on will also apply to a disabled person's interest and a TSI.

Reversionary interests

22–19   It follows that a reversionary interest is not an interest in possession. A reversionary interest is defined in s.47 as "a future interest under a settlement, whether it is vested or contingent . . .". A future interest cannot be an interest in possession because it is not "*in possession*". An interest in possession means an immediate entitlement: a present right of present enjoyment. There is a distinction in the general law between a reversionary interest and a remainder interest, but the definition quoted above makes no distinction of this kind—both are reversionary interests. So, if property is held on trust for A for life with remainder to B absolutely, A has an interest in possession and B has a reversionary interest.

22–20   EXCLUDED PROPERTY   It was pointed out above that in this situation A is treated as though he were the owner of the settled property itself. If B were also to be treated as owning something there would be some degree of double taxation. So the legislation treats B as owning nothing. This is achieved by declaring a reversionary interest to be "excluded property": s.48(1). The effect of this is most clearly seen in relation to a death. Section 5 provides that "the estate of a person immediately before his death does not include excluded property". So, if property is settled on trust for A for life with remainder to B, and B dies while A is still alive. B's reversionary interest is not taxed on B's death.

There are three (perfectly reasonable) exceptions to this principle. A reversionary interest is not excluded property if: (1) it has at any time been acquired for consideration; or (2) it is one to which either the settlor or his spouse or civil partner is beneficially entitled; or (3) it is the interest expectant on the determination of a lease for life which is treated as a settlement. The problem of purchased reversions is dealt with at para.22–58, towards the end of this chapter.

Charge on the death of the beneficial owner

22–21   Let us again take the simple case of a settlement by which property is settled on the death of the settlor on A for life with remainder to B. A, the holder of an IPDI, dies. A's life interest is part of his estate immediately before his death (s.5) and so is taxed under s.4, just as is his unsettled property. The only special point that arises (and it is one that has already been made) is that (under s.49) A is treated as owning the settled property itself. So, if the subject-matter of the trust is Blackacre, what falls to be valued on A's death is Blackacre itself, and not merely A's life interest in Blackacre. Apart from this (very important) valuation point, there is no difference on the occasion of death between an IPDI and any other kind of property (except that the tax is normally payable by the trustees out of the settled property).

We now turn to look at the two circumstances in which a PET may be made during the lifetime of the holder of an IPDI.

Termination of a relevant interest in possession

This circumstance is dealt with in s.52(1) as follows: **22–22**

> "Where at any time during the life of a person beneficially entitled to an [IPDI, disabled person's interest or TSI] his interest comes to an end, tax shall be charged . . . as if at that time he had made a transfer of value and the value transferred had been equal to the value of the property in which his interest subsisted."

Notice the valuation point cropping up again in the last few words: what has to be valued is the property itself, not the value of the interest merely. There is no grossing up. The deemed transfer of value will be a PET, an exempt transfer or a chargeable transfer, depending on who is entitled to the reveision after termination. An example of an IPDI coming to an end during the lifetime of the holder would be a determinable interest such as where property is held on trust for X until she shall remarry and she does remarry. Another example would be where property is held on trust for Y for life with remainder to Z, and Y surrenders his life interest to Z. Y's interest has been extinguished by the surrender.

Disposal of a relevant interest in possession

This depends on s.51. Where a person beneficially entitled to   **22–23**
an IPDI, disabled person's interest or TSI disposes of his interest, the disposal is not a transfer of value but is treated as the coming to an end of his interest. So if a s.51 situation arises, it is equated with a s.52 situation: that is to say, disposing of the interest is treated as a coming to an end of the interest. So, if A gives away to X his IPDI in Blackacre, a tax charge arises just as if his interest had come to an end. Consequently there is a PET by A (without grossing up) on the whole value of Blackacre.

Extension of the termination and disposal rules

If the point were not dealt with in the legislation it would   **22–24**
be very easy to minimise the tax by depreciating the value of settled property by various transactions between the trustees and persons connected with the settlement.[12] The point is dealt with

---

[12] See, e.g. *Macpherson v IRC* (1988).

by s.52(3). If such a transaction takes place there is a deemed partial termination of the interest and so a PET arises. Thus, for example, if the trustees let a house rent-free to the holder of an IPDI on a lease a tax charge will arise. A depreciatory transaction by an individual is taxable on the ordinary principle that it diminishes his estate. But trustees do not have an estate. That is why it is necessary to have this express rule.

Qualifications to the termination and disposal rules

22–25   We now have to look at a number of qualifications to the disposal and termination rules.

22–26   NEW ENTITLEMENT   If A's IPDI terminates but he becomes on the same occasion entitled to the property or to another interest in possession in the property, there is no PET unless the later interest is of less value than the former, in which case there is a deemed transfer of value equal to the difference: ss.53(2) and 52(4). This exception is a logical consequence of the principle that the holder of an interest in possession is treated as the owner of the property.

22–27   DISPOSAL FOR A CONSIDERATION   If the holder of an IPDI disposes of his interest for a consideration (that is, sells it as distinct from giving it away) the value transferred is reduced by the amount of the consideration: s.52(2). So if A, the holder of an IPDI in settled property worth £700,000, sells his interest for £200,000, a PET arises not on the whole £700,000 but on £500,000. One might think that this provision would mean that no PET at all would arise if the holder of an IPDI were to sell his interest for its full market value. This is not really so because in practice a life interest (except in very rare circumstances) is always worth less than the property itself in which the interest subsists. The full market price of a life interest in Blackacre is almost certain to be less than the value of Blackacre itself. So if the life tenant sells his interest in Blackacre even for the full market price of the interest there may still be a PET of the difference on the disposal.

Relief for successive charges

22–28   There is "quick succession" relief for successive charges on relevant interests in possession under s.141 in the same way as on a death transfer. Thus if there is a charge on a settlement, by the activating of a PET, or the death of the holder of an IPDI, within five years of a previous chargeable transfer of the settled property (including the creation of the settlement), the tax payable on the second transfer is reduced by an amount equal to a percentage of the tax paid on the first, i.e. as a tax credit. If the period since the last chargeable transfer is one year or less that percentage is 100 per cent; if the period is not more than two years the reduction is 80 per cent; if the period is not more than three years the reduction is 60 per cent; if the period is not more than four years the reduction is 40 per cent; if the period is not more than five years the reduction is 20 per cent.

Close companies

We have seen (see para.19–36 above) that by ss.94–98 a **22–29** transfer of value of unsettled property by a close company can be apportioned to the participators.

In addition, where a close company is itself entitled to an IPDI or TSI the participators are treated as being the persons beneficially entitled to that interest according to their respective rights and interests in the company: s.101. Again these transfers will not be PETs.

Other settlements—the independent tax regime

Relevant property

We turn now to look at the IHT treatment of settlements other **22–30** than those which have an IPDI, a disabled person's interest or TSI in them. We must also exclude those specially favoured settlements such as charitable trusts, which we deal with below. For the majority of settlements after 22 March 2006, however, the charging provisions are in ss.58–85 of the Act. None of these charges are PETs.

The sections apply to "relevant property". Section 58 states that that means any settled property (which we have already defined) in which no *qualifying interest in possession* exists. Under s.59, a qualifying interest in possession is limited to IPDIs, disabled persons' interests and TSIs. Section 58 also excludes the specially favoured settlements from being relevant property.

The independent tax regime

The application of IHT to relevant property is to divorce the **22–31** settlement from any of its actual or potential beneficiaries and instead to treat it as a taxable entity in its own right. (This was necessary for discretionary trusts since there was no obvious beneficiary to link the trust to—it is of course not necessary for fixed interest trusts, that is therefore a matter of fiscal choice.) This independent tax system poses three questions. First, when will there be a charge to IHT? The issue there is that each generation of beneficiary in the nature of things dies (and so would attract a charge) every 33 years or so. Trusts, on the other hand, do not die. Secondly, what property and at what value will actually be charged, and third, at what rate? There is after all no beneficiary into whose estate the property is deemed to fall and so whose cumulative total can be utilised for that purpose.

22–32 PRINCIPAL AND EXIT CHARGES The answer provided is, roughly, to charge the trust to tax every 10 years in such a way as to provide a charge on the whole settled property every 30 years or so, and to charge any property leaving the settlement in the meantime. The 10-year charge is known as the *principal charge*, the exit charges as *interim charges*. In relation to both types of charge the three questions above must be answered, but it is important to keep them separate in your mind. The rules, particularly as to the calculation of rates involved, are complex, and further difficulties arise because of the more generous treatment of discretionary trusts in existence before 27 March 1974, i.e. the date when the tax was introduced. This is because the tax regime for discretionary trusts was altered dramatically from that under estate duty law and it was thought unfair to apply the full rigour to such trusts. In general the basic difference is that a post-26 March 1974 settlement carries with it the cumulative total of the settlor at the date of the settlement whereas an earlier one does not.

The principal or 10-year charge

When will there be a charge?

22–33 Section 64 provides that on the tenth anniversary of the date on which the settlement commenced and on every subsequent 10-year anniversary, a principal charge to IHT is to be levied. However, s.61 provides that no date prior to 1 April 1983 could be such an anniversary. It follows that settlements created prior to 1 April 1973 could not have a chargeable 10-year anniversary until after 1 April 1983. It therefore became something of a lottery as to how soon such a settlement (created before this tax was thought up) would be taxed. For example, a settlement created on 1 April 1973 will have been taxed on 1 April 1983 but a settlement created on 31 March 1973 would not have been taxed until 31 March 1993. What price tax planning?

It is obviously important therefore to decide when a settlement was created. Section 60 provides that this is when the property first becomes comprised in it, but for post-22 March 2006 settlements where a settlor, or his spouse or civil partner, has an IPDI or a disabled person's interest when the settlement is first created, the property is only treated as having become comprised in the

settlement when neither the settlor nor his spouse or civil partner
have such an interest (s.80).

What is subject to the charge?

A 10-year charge is levied on the value of the relevant property
comprised in the settlement, valued at the date of the charge.
Since the whole amount is being charged no question of grossing
up can arise. It is important to remember that this is all that is
being charged when grappling with the rules as to the calculation
of the applicable rates.

22–34

What rate is to be charged?

Here one has to distinguish between pre-27 March 1974 settlements and others.

22–35

SETTLEMENTS CREATED AFTER 26 MARCH 1974 The rate
of tax is calculated according to s.66. It is three-tenths of the
effective rate of tax payable on a *notional chargeable transfer*
made by a *notional transferor* with a *notional cumulative total*
charged at the lifetime rates.

The *notional chargeable transfer* consists of:

1) the relevant property in the settlement which is the subject
   of the anniversary charge, valued now;
2) the value of any relevant property comprised in any related
   settlement immediately after it commenced (s.62 defines
   that as one made by the settlor on the same day as the settlement except a charitable trust). (These should be avoided.);
3) the value of any "same day additions"—these are
   increases[13] in value on the same day as a result of a transfer or transfers by the settlor to two or more trusts created
   by the same settlor, referred to more fully below. (These
   should also be avoided.); and
4) where there has been a same day addition, the value
   immediately after that other settlement commenced of the
   relevant property then comprised in that other settlement.

In relation to a protected settlement, the calculation is as above
except that same day additions are left out of account (s.62B).

The *"transferor's" notional cumulative* total is:

---

[13] There is a de minimis exception as increases of up to £5,000 are ignored.

1) the settlor's seven-year cumulative total of chargeable transfers at the date of the creation of the settlement; and
2) the full amount charged to interim charges (see below) in the 10 years prior to the anniversary.

22–36   The method of calculation of the anniversary charge was altered in 2015 to restrict the use of what are known as pilot trusts—the setting up of small trusts on different days, to which are later added more substantial funds on the same day, usually on the settlor's death.[14] Such trusts, created as they were on different days were not "related" to each other, and generated certain tax advantages. The new method of calculation takes into account "same day additions", i.e. value added on the same day to more than one trust created by the same settlor (s.63A). The new rules apply to charges which arise on or after 18 November 2015, subject to transitional arrangements for "protected settlements". As the new rules apply to same day additions whether made before or after the changes in 2015, it was thought necessary to protect certain arrangements which had already been made. Section 63C preserves the position for existing settlements subject to conditions. There are two categories of protected settlements. The first is a settlement in existence on 10 December 2014 to which there has been no transfer of value by the settlor after that date. The second is a transitional rule, which permits a transfer of value to the settlement after 10 December 2014 on the death of the settlor, by a pre-existing will, provided the transfer is made before 6 April 2017. This gives settlors time to redraft their will if they see fit.

22–37   ADDITIONS There is an additional sting in the tail. If the settlor has added property during the 10-year period his cumulative total at that time will be used if it is higher than his total at the time of the creation of the settlement. Conversely, however, if property is comprised in the settlement but has ceased during the 10-year period to be relevant property the amount upon which an exit charge has been made can be deducted from the cumulative ladder (s.67).

22–38   In an attempt to display these rules in a different way it may be helpful to give an example.

X, with a cumulative total of previous chargeable transfers of £325,000, created a settlement on 1 December 2006, of £100,000. Subsequently he created another settlement worth £40,000. On

---

[14] *Rysaffe Trustee Co (CI) Ltd v IRC* (2003), referred to above, was an example of pilot trusts.

1 January 2015 he transferred £10,000 to each settlement (a "same day addition").

The 10-year charge on the first settlement will arise on 1 December 2016. Let us suppose that the settlement is then worth £200,000.

The notional transfer will be:

£200,000	(chargeable relevant property)
£50,000	(value of the same day addition, plus the value of the other settlement immediately after creation)
<u>£250,000</u>	

The notional cumulative total, since there have been no exit charges, is that of the settlor at the date of creation of the settlement, viz. £325,000 plus, potentially, the £10,000 added property. However, the added property makes no difference in this example as there is no nil-rate band left in any event.

> Calculate the notional tax at lifetime rates on such a transfer of £250,000
>
> As there is no nil-rate band left, i.e. tax on £250,000 at 40% = £100,000
>
> Next, express £100,000 as a percentage of £250,000 to give the effective rate of tax on the notional transfer, i.e. 40%.
>
> The rate chargeable is then $\frac{3}{10}$ of 40%, or 12%.
>
> *Remember* that rate is then only charged on £200,000, i.e. the value of the relevant property at the anniversary.

REDUCTIONS Under s.66(2) in applying this rate to the relevant property, if part of that property has not been subject to the trust for the whole 10-year period (e.g. additions to the property) the tax payable on that part of the relevant property is to be reduced by one-fortieth for each completed quarter of a year prior to its becoming comprised in the settlement. **22–39**

Thus if a settlement of £500,000 is subject to a 10-year charge of £30,000 under the rules above, but £100,000 was only added two years (or eight quarters) prior to that charge, the tax payable on that £100,000 is reduced as follows:

> the tax payable on that part is $\dfrac{£100,000 \times £30,000}{£500,000}$
>
> = £6,000; and
>
> that figure (£6,000) is reduced by $\frac{32}{40}$, i.e. reduced to £1,200.

SETTLEMENTS CREATED PRIOR TO 27 MARCH 1974 Section 66(6) amends the above rules for settlements in existence at the introduction of what is now IHT. The basic concept is, however, **22–40**

the same, i.e. three-tenths of the effective rate on a notional chargeable transfer made by a "transferor" with a notional cumulative total.

In this case, however, the notional transfer consists only of the chargeable relevant property and no account is taken of either other property in the settlement or related settlements, and no account is taken of same day additions.

Further, the notional cumulative total consists only of the amount subject to exit charges during the 10-year period. The settlor's prior total is ignored unless he has made an addition to the property after the March 1982, in which case his cumulative total then will be included.

In the first example given above therefore the notional transfer would be £200,000 and the notional cumulative total nil. The nil-rate band would therefore apply.

The interim or exit charges

When will there be a charge?

22–41 Section 65(1) provides that there will be a charge to IHT if either: (a) any part of the property ceases to be relevant property (e.g. on an advance of capital to a beneficiary); or (b) the trustees carry out a depreciatory value-shifting transaction which has the effect of reducing the value of the settled property, e.g. a loan to a beneficiary at a low rate of interest, etc.

The donative intent exception in s.10 applies to the second of these charges, as in effect does s.3(3), omission to exercise a right being regarded as equivalent to a transaction.[15]

There is no charge for trustees' costs and expenses, or for income distributions (i.e. income in the hands of the recipient). Nor is there a charge if the property ceases to be relevant property because it becomes comprised in a charitable trust (s.76).

What is subject to the charge?

22–42 Section 65(2) provides that the interim charges are to be levied on the amount by which the relevant property after the event is less than it would be but for the event. This is the standard measure for IHT, in effect the loss to the settlement's estate. It follows that unless the tax is paid by the beneficiary (i.e. it is a gross transfer) the transfer will have to be grossed up for tax purposes.

---

[15] The associated operations provisions also apply. See *MacPherson v IRC* (1988).

What rate is charged?

In this case it is necessary to distinguish between whether there **22–43** has been a 10-year principal charge or not.

ALL SETTLEMENTS PRIOR TO THE FIRST 10-YEAR CHARGE   Section   **22–44** 68 requires us to apply the *appropriate fraction* of the effective rate of tax on a *notional chargeable transfer* made by a "transferor" with a *notional cumulative total.*

The appropriate fraction is:

$$\frac{\text{number of quarters since the settlement commenced}}{40}$$

except for property which has not been in the settlement for the whole of that time, in which case for that property one uses only the number of quarters since it became relevant property.

The *notional transfer* consists of:

1) the value of the relevant property at the commencement of the settlement;
2) the value of any relevant property in a related settlement;
3) the value of any addition to the relevant property, valued at the date of entry;
4) the value of any property in the settlement which has subsequently become relevant property;
5) the value of any same day addition to another settlement of the same settlor; and
6) where there has been a same day addition, the value of relevant property in the other settlement immediately after its creation.

The *notional cumulative total* is the settlor's cumulative total at the date of the settlement, ignoring any transfers made on that day.
To take an example:

A set up a £200,000 discretionary trust on 4 January 2006. He had previously made chargeable transfers of £500,000. Also on 4 January 2006 he set up another £70,000 discretionary trust. On 10 February 2012 the trustees advanced £30,000 to F absolutely.
There is an interim charge on the £30,000 (ceases to be relevant property). There has been no previous 10-year charge.
To find the rate:
notional transfer

$$= £200,000 \text{ (value of settled property in 2006)}$$
$$+ \underline{£70,000} \text{ (related settlement)}$$
$$\underline{£270,000}$$

notional cumulative total = £500,000 (settlor's total in 2006)
So no nil-rate band left
£270,000 at 40% = £108,000
express £108,000 as a percentage of £270,000 (effective rate) = 40%.
The appropriate fraction is
$^{3}/_{10} \times {}^{24}/_{40}$ (no. of quarters since 2006) = $^{9}/_{50}$

so the rate chargeable on £30,000 is $^{9}/_{50}$ of 40%.

22–45 ALL SETTLEMENTS AFTER THE FIRST 10-YEAR CHARGES In such cases s.69 provides a, simpler way in certain circumstances of calculating the rates on an interim charge. It is simply the appropriate fraction of the rate charged on the last 10-year charge (ignoring any deduction for added property).

The appropriate fraction is:

$$\frac{\text{number of quarters completed since the last 10-year charge}}{40}$$

There are two complications however. First, where at the time of the interim charge the settlement includes relevant property which was not there at the 10-year charge, the 10-year charge has to be re-calculated to include the added property, valued at the time it becomes relevant property. Secondly, if there are same-day additions after the 10-year charge, again a re-calculation must be made of the last 10-year charge to take in to account same-day additions, as if they had been made before the last 10-year anniversary.

Special kinds of settlement

22–46 As we have said before, some special types of settlement are not relevant property and as such are not liable to the interim and principal charges even though there is no beneficial interest in possession. However, if the property ceases to be held on the specified trusts there is a flat rate charge which increases according to the length of time the property has been exempt and so avoided the 10-year charge (see s.70). This is subject to a maximum of 30 per cent and no period prior to 13 March 1975 will be counted.

The list of these trusts can be found in s.58(1). These include trusts for the benefit of employees, superannuation schemes, charitable trusts, and protective trusts, as well as the following trusts.

Pre-2006 accumulation and maintenance trusts

Until 22 March 2006 a similar favourable regime applied to accumulation and maintenance trusts. Under s.71 these only required (in general terms) that a beneficiary would, on or before the age of 25, acquire an interest in possession, the income in the meantime to be either applied for his or her maintenance or accumulated, and that the beneficiaries are or were the grandchildren of a common grandparent. Section 71 no longer applies to trusts created after 22 March 2006. Existing trusts could either simply lapse into the relevant property regime (although that in itself was not a chargeable event) or convert, by April 2008, into one of the two replacement categories: trusts for bereaved minors and age 18–25 trusts.

22–47

Trusts for bereaved minors

Under ss.71A and 71B, favourable treatment is given to a trust created either by the will, or on the intestacy, of a *parent* for the benefit of a *bereaved minor*. This also applies to any such trust established under the Criminal Injuries Compensation Scheme. A *bereaved minor* under s.71C means anyone under 18 who has lost at least one parent. Under s.71H, a *parent* in this context means anyone with parental responsibility as defined in the Children Act 1989.[16]

22–48

THE CONDITIONS. To receive the favourable treatment, the trust must satisfy three conditions (s.71A(3)):

22–49

(i) that the minor will on or before the age of 18 become absolutely entitled to the settled property, the income then arising and any accumulated income;

(ii) that until then, any income arising must be applied, if at all, for the minor's benefit; and

(iii) that until then, the minor is beneficially entitled to all the income arising, which may not be used for the benefit of any other person.

TAX ADVANTAGES There will be no charge on such a trust where the bereaved minor becomes absolutely entitled to the property on or before the age of 18. Nor where he or she dies

22–50

---

[16] Or the Children (Scotland) Act 1995, or the Children (Northern Ireland) Act 1995, as appropriate.

under that age, or where property is advanced to him or her (thus avoiding a partial exit charge).

22–51 TAX CHARGES Where the trust ceases to continue to comply with any of the conditions in para.22–48 above or the trustees involve themselves in a depreciatory value-shifting transaction there will be a charge to inheritance tax either on the whole of, or the reduction in the value of, the settled property, respectively.

22–52 The charge, which applies to all specially favoured trusts in similar circumstances, is a tapering charge based on the number of quarters of a year from the time when the conditions were first fulfilled to the date of charge. It is a flat rate charge on the scale set out in s.70:

0.25 per cent for each of the first 40 quarters (10 years—10 per cent).

0.20 per cent for each of the next 40 quarters (11–20 years— further 8 per cent).

0.15 per cent for each of the next 40 quarters (21–30 years— further 6 per cent).

0.10 per cent for each of the next 40 quarters (31–40 years— further 4 per cent).

0.05 per cent for each of the next 40 quarters (41–50 years— further 2 per cent).

Thus if the time lapse is 15 years the rate is 14 per cent.

Age 18–25 trusts

22–53 Under s.71D an age 18–25 trust is any settlement established by the will of a *parent*[17] or under the Criminal Injuries Compensation Scheme, whereby the property is held on trust for the benefit of a person under the age of 25, one of whose parents has died. It does not apply where the trust is one for a bereaved minor (above) or where there is a pre-22 March 2006 interest in possession, an IPDI, TSI or a disabled person's interest in the settled property.

22–54 CONDITIONS To receive favourable treatment, the trust must comply with the same three conditions as apply to a trust for a bereaved minor with the substitution of age 25 for age 18.

22–55 TAX ADVANTAGES UP TO AGE 18 Under s.71E, there is no charge to IHT if the beneficiary becomes absolutely entitled to

---

[17] As defined in s.71H. See para.22–48 above.

the property on or before the age of 18 (not 25 as under s.70). Nor is there a charge if he or she dies under that age, or if part of the property is advanced before that age, or if it becomes a trust for a bereaved minor.

TAX CHARGE AGE 18–25   Under s.71F, there is a charge to IHT,   **22–56**
similar to an interim charge on relevant property, if the beneficiary dies, becomes absolutely entitled to the trust property or receives an advancement of trust property after he or she has reached 18. In effect therefore the tax shelter only applies up to the age of 18.

The charge is calculated as: the *chargeable amount* × the *relevant fraction* × the *settlement rate*. The *chargeable amount* is the loss to the settled property. The *relevant fraction* is 3/10 of the number of complete quarters since the beneficiary attained 18 (or, if later, when the settlement was created) over 40. The *settlement rate* is that which would have been paid on a transfer of the whole settled property (valued at creation) + any related settlements + any subsequent additions to the property (valued then), by a transferor with the settlor's cumulative total as at the date of the settlement.

OTHER TAX CHARGES   Under s.71G, if the settlement ceases   **22–57**
to comply with the conditions required for it to be an 18–25 trust, or there is a depreciatory transaction by the trustees, the usual flat rate charges will apply as set out in para.22–52 above.

The purchase of a reversionary interest

We have noted that except in certain circumstances a reversion-   **22–58**
ary interest in settled property in the UK is excluded property. This was originally based on the now much reduced principle that for IHT purposes the life tenant owned the whole settled fund and the reversioner owned nothing. Now, since most trusts are now relevant property trusts, it is the trust (and trustees) and not individual interests of any kind which form the taxable unit for IHT purposes.

There are a number of special provisions in the legislation, however, some of which are designed to prevent over-charging in respect of reversionary interests and some of which are designed to prevent tax avoidance. We have already encountered one of those in para.22–21 above.

Purchased reversions

The most important provision is that a purchased reversion is   **22–59**
not excluded property: s.48(1)(a). This is to prevent an obvious form of avoidance. Suppose that £400,000 is settled on A for life, remainder to B. C purchases B's remainder for £90,000, which is

its market value. This is not a chargeable transfer since there will be no loss to C's estate and in any event no donative intent by B (protected by s.10). C has depleted his free estate by £90,000 and gained the reversion. If he could thus give the reversion to D as excluded property he would in effect have given D £90,000 free of IHT. Thus there is a charge on the gift to D since a reversion, once purchased is not excluded property.

Settlement powers

22–60   In order to avoid the continued success of avoidance schemes such as that upheld by the Court of Appeal in *Melville v IRC* (2001), what are called settlement powers[18] are no longer regarded as being property for IHT purposes (s.272, as amended). A settlement power is defined in s.47A as any power over, or exercisable (whether directly or indirectly) in relation to, settled property or a settlement. These would include both a power to direct the trustees to distribute trust assets and those in issue in *Melville*.

Purchased powers
22–61   Since such powers are not property they could be purchased for market value (which would not be a transfer of value not least as a result of the donative intent rule) and then transferred on by the purchaser free of any charge to the tax, who will thereby have disposed of the purchase price free of any IHT consequences. Accordingly, s.55A provides that where a settlement power is purchased for money or money's worth, the purchaser is to be treated as having made a transfer of value of the amount paid for the power. The donative intent provision in s.10 is disapplied as are the spouse, charities and public benefit exemptions.

Thus if X buys such a power from Y for £200,000 he will make a transfer of value of that amount. Conversely if X then gives the power to Z there can be no charge since the power is not property so there can be no loss to his estate. The position is the same therefore as with a purchased reversion by someone with a prior interest in the trust (charge on acquisition but not subsequent disposition) rather than the simple purchased reversion (no charge on acquisition but charge on subsequent disposition).

---

[18] In essence, a settlor creates a settlement but gives himself a power to recall the property after a certain time and a veto over any dispositive powers of the trustees. The case decided that those powers were property and so part of the settlor's estate after the transfer, thus drastically reducing the loss to his estate on the transfer.

CHAPTER 23

LIABILITY AND INCIDENCE

Introduction

In this chapter we deal with two matters which are separate but related, namely liability and incidence.

Liability is concerned with who is to pay the tax to HMRC. Incidence is concerned with who is ultimately to bear the burden of the tax. So, for example, an executor may be under a duty to pay the tax to HMRC. He then looks to the rules of incidence to see which beneficiary gets less because of the tax.

23–01

Liability

The following persons may, in various circumstances, be liable to pay the tax: transferor, transferee, trustee, beneficiary, settlor, personal representative. Does anyone feel left out?

The details are set out Pt VII ss.199–214 of IHTA.

23–02

Chargeable lifetime transfers: s.199

For *chargeable*[1] *lifetime transfers of unsettled property* the person primarily liable is the transferor. If the transferor does not pay, then the following persons are liable: anyone whose estate had been increased by the transfer—obviously this is usually the transferee; so far as the tax is attributable to the value of any particular property, any person in whom the property is vested (whether beneficially or otherwise) at any time after the transfer or who at any such time is beneficially entitled to an interest in possession in the property; and where by the chargeable transfer any property becomes comprised in a settlement, any person for whose benefit any of the property or income from it is applied.

23–03

Settled property: s.201

For *chargeable transfers of settled property* the persons liable are: (a) primarily the trustees of the settlement; and (b) any

23–04

---

[1] There rules are modified for PETs which become chargeable transfers on the transferor's death within seven years and for any additional "death rate" payable on such a death. See below.

person entitled (whether beneficially or not) to an interest in possession in the settled property; and (c) any person for whose benefit any of the settled property or income from it is applied; and (d) where the chargeable transfer is made during the life of the settlor and the trustees are not for the time being resident in the UK, the settlor.

Death: s.200

23–05   For *transfers on death* the persons liable are: (a) in respect of unsettled property and in respect of settled property being land in the UK which devolves upon them, the deceased's personal representatives[2]; (b) in respect of settled property, the trustees; (c) so far as the tax is attributable to the value of any particular property, any person in whom the property is vested (whether beneficially or otherwise) at any time after the death or who at any such time is beneficially entitled to an interest in possession in the property; and (d) so far as the tax is attributable to the value of any property which, immediately before the death, was comprised in a settlement, any person for whose benefit any of the property or income from it is applied after the death.[3]

Death within seven years of transfer

23–06   *Where the transferor dies within seven years* of making a chargeable transfer the additional tax which becomes payable (i.e. the difference between the lifetime rates and the death rates) is principally the liability of the transferee (s.204(7) and (8)). Similar rules apply where the transferor dies within seven years of making a PET and the transfer becomes chargeable. But if, for example, the transferee does not pay within 12 months the personal representatives are liable. All concerned are advised to take out insurance against such a contingent liability.

In any circumstances where two or more persons are liable for the same tax, each is liable to HMRC for the whole of it. But, of course, HMRC cannot get more tax than is due.

Property

23–07   References in the above contexts to any property include references to any property directly or indirectly representing

---

[2]   This liability is a personal liability of the personal representatives and not a liability of the deceased which they assume. See *IRC v Stannard* (1984).

[3]   Liability also extends to anyone who interferes or "intermeddles" in the estate to become an *executor de son tort*. See *IRC v Stype Investments (Jersey) Ltd* (1982).

it. So one does not escape the tax charge merely by selling the original property and investing the proceeds in some other property. (For the tax position of the purchaser, see para.23–09 below.)

Transfers between spouses and civil partners: s.203

Where a transferor is liable for any tax and by another transfer **23–08** of value made by him any property becomes the property of a person who at the time of both transfers was his spouse or civil partner, that spouse or civil partner is liable for so much of the tax as does not exceed the value of the property at the time of the transfer to him or her. See s.203, which is designed to stop up a rather crude avoidance device—namely, make a transfer of value to someone overseas and make also an exempt transfer of the rest of one's estate to one's spouse or civil partner, and leave HMRC to whistle for their money.

Exception of purchaser from liability

A purchaser of property is not liable for tax attributable **23–09** to the value of the property purchased, unless the property is subject to an HMRC charge (on which see para.23–14 below): s.199(3).

Limitations of liability

There are limitations on the extent to which a person is liable **23–10** for the tax. For instance, a personal representative is liable only to the extent of the assets he has received or might have received but for his own neglect or default. Somewhat similar limitations apply to trustees, beneficiaries and transferees: see s.204.

Incidence

We now come to the question of who is to bear the ultimate **23–11** burden of the tax, bearing in mind that the person, from the list above, who pays the tax may not be the person on whom the burden should ultimately fall.

Problems of incidence are most acute in relation to tax arising on death. In the case of lifetime transfers it is a matter between the parties as to who bears the tax. The main effect, as we have seen, will be as to whether "grossing up" is necessary in relation to lifetime transfers.

Testamentary expenses—charge on residue

Whilst prima facie each item of property comprised in a **23–12** person's estate at death carries its own burden of tax, this general principle is largely reversed by s.211. Section 211 provides that tax attributable to the value of property in the UK which vests in the deceased's personal representatives and which was not, immediately before the death, comprised in a settlement, is to be treated as part of the general testamentary and administration expenses of the deceased, unless the will provides to the contrary. As such expenses come first out of the residue rather than gifts of specific property or amounts of money, it is the residue which generally bears the tax. The tax comes out of specific gifts where the will directs that it should do so. So, if X is left £30,000 to bear its own tax, X does not receive £30,000, but £30,000 less the proportionate share of the tax on the whole estate. Other property not governed by s.211 is jointly-owned property passing by survivorship which will not vest in the personal representatives, and overseas property. In this case the position is not governed by IHTA but by general law. The position is not entirely clear but it seems likely that this is that such property bears its own tax unless, in the case of foreign property, the will makes it clear that it is not to do so. So, in nearly all cases, the residuary legatees will bear the tax burden.

Legacies, etc. free of tax

23–13   In general, as we have seen, it is possible for the testator to determine whether a legacy should bear its own tax or not. There is one exception to this power contained in s.41. Suppose a testator gives his residue equally to his wife and his mother, with a direction that the mother's share is to be free of IHT. The gift to the spouse is exempt, whilst that to the mother is chargeable. Section 41 provides that such a chargeable residuary gift must bear its own tax so that the direction that such tax shall be borne by the exempt gift of residue to the spouse is void.

This means that the net share actually received by the mother will be less than that received by the spouse since the former will be reduced by the tax payable on it. If the testator actually wishes the spouse and mother to receive equal net shares (i.e. after tax has been paid) this can be achieved if the will makes it clear that the mother's share of the residue, before tax, is to be enlarged by an amount which will ensure that when the tax is deducted from it her net share is equal to that of the spouse.[4] But this must be very clearly expressed and the courts will not infer it simply because the more likely explanation that the executors were intended to pay the tax due as a testamentary expense out of the gross residue before the shares were divided is prohibited by s.41.[5]

---

[4]   *Re Benham's Will Trusts* (1995).
[5]   *Re Ratcliffe* (1999).

Estate rate

It is important on a death to calculate the estate rate, i.e. the **23–14** rate of tax which applies to the whole estate, taking into account the nil-rate band. Thus if A dies, having made no previous chargeable transfers, leaving a chargeable estate (ignoring exempt transfers) of £425,000, tax will currently be chargeable at nil on £325,000 and at 40 per cent on £100,000. Thus the tax bill will be £40,000. Applied across all the assets this gives an average rate of 10.3 per cent. That rate will then be deducted from any legacies which have to bear their own tax before the money is paid over to the legatee. Tax-free legacies will be paid in full with the tax coming out of residue. This apparently simple calculation is, however, as in many areas of tax law, not always quite so simple.

Partially exempt transfers on death

In many cases the rule that IHT is a testamentary expense to **23–15** be paid out of residue causes no problems. Thus where all the legacies are both chargeable and tax free and the residue is also chargeable, the whole tax bill (at the estate rate) is charged on the residue. Similarly, if the legacies are either all exempt, or are to bear their own tax under the terms of the will, the residue and the tax-bearing legacies will simply bear their own tax at the estate rate. But problems arise in three not uncommon cases. These problems are the subject of ss.36–42. The following is an outline of the effect of these sections, which in practice involve many complex calculations:

1) Where the testator leaves a legacy free of tax[6] and an **23–16** exempt gift of residue, e.g. "£200,000 to my daughter, free of tax, residue to my wife". In this case, in order to work out how much tax should be charged on the legacy (i.e. the estate rate since the residue is exempt) it must be grossed up (in the same way as a net lifetime transfer). The tax then payable on that grossed up legacy is deducted from the residuary gift and the daughter will receive the net £200,000.

2) Where the testator makes both tax-free legacies and those **23–17** which must bear their own tax, together with an exempt gift of residue. Grossing up only the tax-free legacies would not be enough (since there are other legacies involved in assessing the tax liability) but grossing up all the legacies would be too much (since those bearing their

---

[6] Remember this will be the case unless the will provides to the contrary.

own tax are not required to be grossed up, just as with a gross lifetime transfer). The solution is to gross up the tax-free legacies at a rate of tax applicable to a hypothetical transfer of the total of the grossed-up tax-free legacies and those bearing their own tax. This is known as "double grossing up". In essence, the tax-free legacies are first grossed-up in the normal way, then the rate for grossing up a second time is calculated on a transfer of the total of that grossed-up figure plus the tax-bearing legacies (say 20 per cent). The tax-free legacies are then grossed-up again at that rate. The estate rate of tax is then calculated on the total of those doubly grossed up legacies and the tax bearing legacies (say 25 per cent). That rate will then be deducted from the residue in respect of the tax-free legacies and from the tax-bearing legacies in respect of their own tax.

23–18   3) Where the testator leaves both tax-free and tax-bearing legacies, as above, but the residue is partly chargeable and partly exempt. In this case, the tax-free gifts are again subject to a double grossing-up, but the second grossing up must be at a rate calculated on a hypothetical transfer of the total of the grossed up tax-free legacies, the tax-bearing legacies and the chargeable part of the residue (divided after deducting the single grossed up tax-free legacies and the tax-bearing legacies). After the tax-free legacies have been so doubly grossed-up, the estate rate is calculated on the total of the doubly grossed-up legacies, the tax-bearing legacies and the chargeable part of the residue (now divided after deducting the doubly grossed-up legacies and the tax-bearing legacies). That rate is then charged on the residue as a whole in respect of the tax-free legacies. Only after that will the residue be divided and the estate rate applied to the chargeable part. That rate will also be deducted from those legacies bearing their own tax.

CHAPTER 24

ADMINISTRATION AND COLLECTION

Introduction

Section 215 of IHTA announces that inheritance tax "shall be under the care and management of the Board" (i.e. Her Majesty's Commissioners of Revenue and Customs). Part VIII of IHTA (ss.215–261) provides detailed rules concerning the administration and collection of the tax. **24–01**

Delivery of an account: s.216

Subject to certain exceptions, the personal representatives of a deceased person are under a duty to deliver an account to HMRC specifying to the best of their knowledge and belief all appropriate property[1] and its value. And a similar duty rests on a transferor and a trustee[2] of a settlement concerning any lifetime transfer which is not a PET, which since 2006, now include creating settlements inter vivos. The transferee must also deliver an account in respect of a PET if the transferor dies within seven years and the personal representatives must also deliver an account of any PETs made by the deceased in the seven years prior to the death, again to the best of their knowledge and belief. **24–02**

If there are no personal representatives appointed within 12 months of the death the duty to account falls on those beneficially entitled to the property or an interest in the property (including certain discretionary beneficiaries). The phrase "best of their knowledge and belief" means the personal knowledge of the individual. This includes documents in his possession or custody but he is not required to be an information gatherer.[3] If, after making the fullest, practical enquiries, the personal representatives are unable to ascertain the exact value of any property, a provisional value can be given, pending a later exact valuation.

---

[1] Including any interests in possession or general powers of appointment held by the deceased.

[2] This includes a foreign trustee of a foreign trust made by a UK settlor: *Re Clore (dec'd) (No.3)* (1985).

[3] *Re Clore (dec'd) (No.3)* (1985).

24–03 TIME LIMITS AND PENALTIES Personal representatives must deliver their account within 12 months from the end of the month in which the death occurs or within three months of the time when they first acted (if this period expires later).

Any other person must deliver his account within 12 months from the end of the month in which the transfer took place, or (if it expires later) the period of three months from the date on which he first became liable for tax. (There are special rules about conditionally exempt works of art, etc. and about timber.) There are penalties in default both initially and for continuing default, and for providing incorrect information unless there is a reasonable excuse (s.245). There are also penalties for carelessly or deliberately providing inaccurate information (these are common with the other taxes (FA 2007 Sch.24). A technical failure should receive a sensible response from HMRC—see, e.g. *Cairns v HMRC* (2009).

Exceptions
24–04 There are a number of automatic types of exception to the obligation to deliver a formal IHT account.

EXCEPTED ESTATES ON DEATH There are currently three types of excepted estate where the personal representatives do not have to file an account. The first is where the total of the gross estate (before debts or any business or agricultural relief) and certain "specified" lifetime transfers by the deceased, is less than the relevant nil-rate band. In addition, of that property, not more than £150,000 must be settled property, the value of any property outside the UK must be less than £100,000, any chargeable transfers in the past seven years must be of cash, shares or land and less than £150,000 in total.

The second category is where the gross value of the estate and specified lifetime transfers by the deceased does not exceed £1 million and after the deduction of any spouse, civil partner or charity transfers (all exempt), the net figure is less than the relevant nil-rate band.

The third category is where the deceased was never domiciled in the UK and the estate in the UK consists only of cash or listed shares or securities with a gross value of less than £150,000.[4]

24–05 EXCEPTIONS FOR TRANSFERORS AND TRUSTEES With regard to immediately chargeable transfers (including creating a

---

[4] See the Inheritance Tax (Delivery of Accounts) (Excepted Estates) Regulations 2004 (SI 2004/2543) as amended.

settlement), if the property transferred is quoted securities or cash no account need be filed if the total, including the chargeable transfers made by the transferor in the last seven years, does not exceed the current nil-rate band. For transfers of other property, the threshold is 80 per cent of the nil-rate band. Similar rules apply in the few cases where a life tenant is still regarded as owning the settled property for IHT purposes and his interest comes to an end inter vivos.[5]

Where there is a chargeable transfer of relevant property in a settlement (the ten year and exit charges under most settlements), if certain conditions are met, there is no obligation on the trustees to file an account if the notional aggregated transfer does not exceed 80 per cent of the nil-rate band. The conditions are: (i) the settlor is and has at all material times been domiciled in the UK; (ii) the trustees are resident in the UK; and (iii) there are no related settlements.[6]

Probate

Personal representatives cannot get probate (or confirmation in Scotland) until they have paid the tax, and they cannot sell any of the estate assets (so as to get cash with which to pay the tax) until they have got probate. That looks like a vicious circle. But the problem can be overcome. The personal representatives can submit a provisional account and pay tax on that, then get probate, then sell off some of the estate assets, then submit a corrective or supplementary account and pay tax on that. **24–06**

Returns by certain persons acting for settlors: s.218

There is a special provision concerning overseas settlements. Where any person, in the course of a trade or profession (other than the profession of a barrister) has been concerned with the making of a settlement and knows or has reason to believe that the settlor was domiciled in the UK and that the trustees of the settlement are not or will not be resident in the UK, he must within three months of the making of the settlement make a return to HMRC stating the names and addresses of the settlor and of the trustees of the settlement. This requirement does not apply to a settlement made by will nor to any other settlement if such a return has already been made by another person or if an **24–07**

---

[5] See the Inheritance Tax (Delivery of Accounts) (Excepted Transfers and Excepted Terminations) Regulations 2008 (SI 2008/605).
[6] See the Inheritance Tax (Delivery of Accounts) (Excepted Settlements) Regulations 2008 (SI 2008/606).

account has been delivered in relation to it. The provision applies to (amongst others) solicitors and accountants and there are penalties in default (s.245A).

Returns following a variation of a disposition taking effect on death causing extra tax to be payable

24–08   Where there is an effective instrument varying a disposition taking effect on death made under s.142 and, as a consequence, additional tax has become payable, the parties to the instrument and the personal representatives (if they hold sufficient assets to discharge that liability) must deliver a copy of the instrument and notify HMRC of the additional tax. Notification by one discharges the others. If no additional tax becomes payable there is no need to inform HMRC.

Power to require information and inspect property: ss.219, 219A, 219B, 220, 220A

24–09   The powers of HMRC in relation to requiring information and getting access to property are now common across the taxes, and can be found in FA 2008.

Determination and appeals: ss.221–225

24–10   Instead of the word "assessment" which is the technical term applying to income tax, CGT and corporation tax, the term used in relation to IHT is "determination". The Commissioners make a determination and then serve a notice of determination.

Appeals (which must be made within 30 days of service of notice of determination) go to the tribunal except in two cases as follows: (1) where it is so agreed between the appellant and the tribunal, or where the High Court (on an application made by the appellant) is satisfied that the matters to be decided are likely to be substantially confined to questions of law and gives leave, the appeal goes to the High Court direct, thus cutting out the tribunal stage; (2) any question as to the value of land in the UK must be determined by the appropriate Lands Tribunal.

Payment of tax: ss.226–236

24–11   In general, IHT becomes due six months after the end of the month in which the chargeable transfer was made or, in the case of a transfer made after 5 April and before 1 October in any year otherwise than on death, at the end of April in the next year.

So in many instances tax is due before the account is due. Tax on PETs is due six months after the death which activates the charge. So is the additional tax payable on the death of the transfers of a chargeable transfer within seven years.

Tax which is due and unpaid attracts interest at prescribed rates and there is no income tax relief for the interest payments. Where there has been an overpayment of tax the repayment by HMRC carries interest (at the same rates as above) from the date on which the overpayment was made, and this interest is not subject to income tax.

Payment by instalments

In certain circumstances the tax can be paid by instalments. This facility applies only where the tax is attributable to certain kinds of property: land, controlling shares or securities; other shares or securities which are unquoted and in respect of which certain detailed conditions are satisfied; and a business or an interest in a business to the extent of its net value (as defined).[7]   **24–12**

The instalment provisions apply to transfers on death. They also apply, with certain modifications, to lifetime transfers but only if either: (a) the tax is borne by the person benefiting from the transfer; or (b) the property is settled property and remains in the settlement after the transfer.

Interest on land is payable in instalments from the date on which the first instalment fell due, but in other cases interest only runs if an instalment is in arrears so that there can be interest-free instalments.

Repayments

Where dispositions by the deceased are subsequently set aside, the liability to IHT may be reduced and a repayment of tax paid fall due. If the dispositions were void then interest is payable from the date of payment of the tax (s.235). If, however, they were voidable, interest only accrues from the date of the claim for repayment (s.236(3)). Dispositions set aside by equity for mistake fall into the latter category.[8]   **24–13**

HMRC charge for unpaid tax: ss.237 and 238

The word "charge" in this context is being used in the same sense in which a mortgage is a charge. Section 237 automatically imposes an HMRC charge on all property included in a   **24–14**

---

[7] Rather special instalment provisions apply to timber in certain circumstances.
[8] *Re Griffiths.*

chargeable transfer[9] and, in the case of settled property, on any property included in the settlement. The holder of the property can thus be liable for the tax. On a transfer on death, however, the charge does not apply to personal[10] or movable property in the UK comprised in the free estate of the deceased. A purchaser of land where the charge is not registered and a bona fide purchaser of personal property without notice is not subject to the charge; where this is the case the charge attaches to the proceeds of sale.

[9] It also applies to the various chargeable events connected with conditionally exempt heritage property.
[10] Until 1999 leaseholds counted as personal property for this purpose.

PART FIVE

VALUE ADDED TAX

CHAPTER 25

THE CHARGE TO VAT

Introduction

Value added tax is almost always known as VAT. Even the **25–01** VAT Act calls it that. So shall we. Not only does it save time, it also avoids awkward questions about whether we have the name right! We call it "value added tax", but the Irish call it "value-added tax", and are probably correct. Why? Because the name is a direct translation from the French *taxe sur la valeur ajoutée*—tax on added value. Somewhere we turned the noun "value" into an adjective.

VAT has turned from a foreign idea into Britain's second biggest tax in one generation. Why? There are two main reasons: a legal reason and a practical reason. The legal reason is that VAT is the only permissible general sales tax in the EU. When we joined the EC in 1973, we were obliged to adopt the tax. As we see below, virtually all of the basic legal concepts of the tax are a matter of the construction of European rather than UK law. That remains the position for the immediate future.

The practical reason is that the EU is, in fiscal terms, a customs union. For many centuries much English, then British, government revenue was earned from customs duties. Now the UK government gets precisely nothing from customs duties—they are a European tax, and cannot be imposed between the member states of the EU. We can only tax goods from other European countries to the same extent as we tax domestic production. So we tax both equally—and that is the heart of VAT.

VAT is a charge on:

- domestic supplies of goods and services;
- cross-border acquisitions from other states in the EU; and
- imports from states outside the EU.

Each of these three charges is a distinct but related part of the tax. However, in this and the following chapters, we shall deal with the tax on the assumption that all relevant aspects of taxable transactions take place in the UK.

The importance of the EU

The Directives

25-02   The UK adopted VAT as part of its Treaty obligations on joining the EC. Article 113 of the current, 2009, EU Treaty provides for the harmonisation of "turnover" taxes in the EU to protect the internal market and avoid distortion of competition. This has been effected by the successive introduction of a number of Directives on VAT.

The principles of EC VAT were laid down in 1967 in the First VAT Directive (Directive 27/227). Four further directives followed over the next ten years and EC VAT law was consolidated into the Sixth VAT Directive in 1977 (Directive 77/388). That Directive was itself subsequently amended and added to by a succession of directives until the relevant EC law was again consolidated in 2006 into what is called the Recast VAT Directive (Directive 2006/112). That Directive has been operative throughout the 27 Member States of the EU[1] as from 1 January 2007. From now on we shall refer to this latest directive as "the Directive" in the text.

Since 2007, there have been a number of further directives amending that Directive. These relate to the place of supply of services (Directive 2008/8), refunds (Directive 2008/9), reduced rates of VAT (Directive 2010/47), minimum standard rate of VAT (Directive 2010/88), invoicing (Directive 2010/45), fraud (Directive 2013/42), reverse charge (Directive 2013/43) and French regions (Directive 2013/42). Whilst some of these are concerned purely with supplies between different member states, others are central to the UK's freedom of action in charging VAT across the board.

25-03   IMPORTANCE OF EU LAW   For the time being, the importance of the Directive and EU law in general in VAT cannot be over-emphasised. Not only does it trump national law when there is a difference, but principles of EU law have to be applied in interpreting and applying the Directive. EU law also governs the vexed questions of VAT abuse and avoidance. We must look at each of these issues in turn.

25-04   CONSEQUENCE OF DIRECT EFFECT   The primary reason for the Directive's pre-eminence in VAT law is that it has long been held by the European Court of Justice (originally ECJ, now CJEU) to have direct effect.[2] In extreme cases, this means that a provision of national law which is incompatible

---

[1]   This includes the Isle of Man but not the Channel Islands for this purpose.
[2]   See, e.g. *Finanzamt Munchen III* v *Mosche* (1997) ECJ.

with the Directive is disapplied as against certain individuals affected by it. In *Fleming* v *HMRC* (2008), the House of Lords accepted that the failure by the UK law to provide a transitional period for the introduction of a three-year time limit for certain repayment claims was simply contrary to the Directive. Accordingly the time limit was disapplied as against the claimants whose claim predated the introduction of the three-year limit in 1997. There was some disagreement as to how long that disapplication should last. FA 2008 duly introduced a transitional period of a year to March 2009 for claims which accrued before 1997.

But in most cases, the idiosyncratic UK concept of zero-rating apart (see below), direct effect means that the relevant national provision must be construed so as to give effect to the Directive for all purposes. In practical terms it is therefore very common now for a dispute before a UK court as to the effect of a provision in a UK statute on VAT to be argued in terms of whether it complies with the relevant article of the Directive, or even simply to construe the Directive, ignoring the UK statute, and we shall come across many such examples as we look at the tax. The CJEU has in fact ruled that in certain cases national courts should refer the issue to it, even if the parties have not asked for a reference.[3] It follows that the basic framework of VAT is also derived from the Directive, e.g. as to what exemptions are permitted[4] or in what circumstances illegal transactions are taxable.[5]

IMPLEMENTING THE DIRECTIVE As with all directives, **25–05** transposing the Directive into national law requires member states to comply with the general principles of Community Law, including that of equality of treatment.[6] Failure by the UK authorities to implement the Directive properly can lead to the EC Commission asking the CJEU to order the UK to correct its error and, if it has charged less VAT than it should have done, it may have to account to the EU (in its budget contribution) as if it had properly implemented the Directive.[7]

POLITICAL CHALLENGE TO IMPLEMENTATION An interesting **25–06** development in relation to this requirement arose during the fevered political climate in the UK prior to the 2016

---

[3] *Fazenda Publica v Camara Municipal do Porto* (2001)
[4] See, e.g. *Norbury Developments Ltd v CEC* (1999).
[5] *Fischer v Finanzamt Donaueschingen* (1998).
[6] *Idéal Tourisme SA v Belgian State* (2001).
[7] *Fazenda Publica v Camara Municipal do Porto* (2001).

referendum on its membership of the EU in June 2016. In the case of *Commission v United Kingdom* (2015) the CJEU ruled that the UK was not entitled to apply a reduced rate of VAT to the provision of solar panels as it was in fact doing. It did not fit within the categories of reduced rate allowed for in the Directive. During the Budget debate the UK parliament rejected any attempt to change UK VAT law to accommodate that ruling. It also voted to zero-rate women's sanitary products although the Directive requires at least a reduced rate to be applied to them and a clause was added to the Finance Bill to that effect. This was on the basis that following Conclusions of the European Council in March 2016, the Commission will issue proposals to give member states more flexibility on VAT rates. Given the UK's current intention to leave the EU, these problems will presumably disappear in time.

25–07   OTHER AREAS   The Directive is not exhaustive, however. In particular, it does not lay down any procedural rules relating to the operation of VAT. Thus it is for member states to provide safeguards for rights (e.g. as to payment and repayment of the tax) conferred by Community Law. But, in *Marks and Spencer Plc v CEC* (2002),[8] the ECJ ruled that: (i) the fact that a directive has been properly implemented does not affect an individual's right to ensure full application of the rights conferred under it, provided they are sufficiently precise and unconditional, e.g. as in that case, the right to recover wrongly-paid tax based on a misinterpretation by the HMRC of the Directive; and (ii) whilst the rules for collection and repayment of overpaid tax were a matter for domestic law, the general principles of Community law would be applied to them.

Thus national rules could not distinguish between repayment claims based on community rights and purely domestic rights (*principle of equality of treatment*). Further, they could not make it impossible nor excessively difficult to exercise those rights (*principle of effectiveness*) nor must they go further than is necessary to achieve their object (*principle of proportionality*). Thus, whilst a time limit for making repayment claims was not as such incompatible with Community law, the scheme in the case was.

---

[8]   This decision was applied to the facts by the CA (2004). See also the decision in *Local Authorities Mutual Investment Trust v CEC* (2004) on the validity of time limits on the claiming of input tax. These principles do not apply if there is no Community right involved, e.g. a claim by CEC for repayment of money wrongly repaid to the taxable person: *R. v CEC Ex p. Building Societies Ombudsman Co Ltd* (2000).

The period allowed for claims had to be both reasonable and allow for transitional arrangements for pre-existing claims—the UK, by imposing limitation periods for claims retrospectively, was in clear breach of the principle of effectiveness. Finally, the ECJ held (iii) that retrospective withdrawal of a Community right such as the right in this case was also a breach of the *principle of legitimate expectation.*

In a second reference, in *Marks & Spencer Plc v HMRC* (2008), it was held by the ECJ that whilst there was no enforceable Community right with regard to zero-rating, the principles of Community law applied to the consequences of the national court misinterpreting the national legislation. Fiscal neutrality and equal treatment had to be applied. In *Sub One Ltd v HMRC* (2014), the Court of Appeal further held that whilst the UK could (within limits) set out the criteria for zero-rating, those must be interpreted and applied in accordance with EU law principles. We will return to zero-rating in Ch.26. In *JD Wetherspoon v HMRC* (2009), the ECJ also had to consider the application of Community principles to the question of rounding up or rounding down fractions of a penny as the VAT charged on a supply, even though EU law made no specific reference to the issue.

Application of principles of community law

It is therefore not just in the wording of the Directive itself that   **25–08**
the influence of Community law is felt. In applying the terms of the Directive[9] the UK courts are currently obliged to apply those broader Community law principles of construction. This was recognised very early by Nolan J in *Yoga for Health Foundation v CEC* (1984). Thus many decisions are based upon EC principles such as equal treatment, legitimate expectation, legal certainty, proportionality, non-discrimination, equivalence and effectiveness.

FISCAL NEUTRALITY There is a particular stress on the   **25–09**
principle of fiscal neutrality. The current application of this principle was set out by the ECJ in *Rank Group Plc v HMRC* (2012). It precludes treating similar goods and supplies of services differently for VAT purposes as that would distort competition. It will be applied if the supplies in question are identical or similar from the point of view of, and meet the

---

[9] Including any decision to implement one of the derogations allowed by the directive: *Finanzamt Bergisch Gladbach v Skripalle* (1997). But see *Belgocodex SA v Belgium* (2000) on the rights of member states to revoke such derogations. See also the comments of Lindsay J in *HMRC v Weald Leasing Ltd* (2008) at [31].

needs of, a typical customer. To this end, their use must be comparable and any differences between them must not have a significant influence on the decision of the consumer whether to use one supply or the other. Thus two forms of slot machines were to be taxed the same, even though UK domestic law distinguished between them for gaming duty purposes. Another example, the ECJ decision in *Gregg v CEC* (1999), is that there could be no distinction between a nursing home run by a company and one by a partnership.

The principle also requires that there be no distinction between lawful and unlawful activities unless there is no possibility of competition between the lawful and unlawful sectors.[10] Thus in *CEC v Polak*,[11] VAT was applied to the activities of an escort agency. It was not clear that the activities of the agency were unlawful throughout the Community. Unlike narcotics or forgery, prostitution was not itself illegal. The Court also applied the principle of *proximity* so that the time spent by the escorts which was a separate and legitimate activity of the agency could be separated from the activities of the escorts and their clients.

In *Sub One Ltd v HMRC* (2014), the Court of Appeal, by reference to Community law, substituted an objective for a subjective test which had previously been applied by the UK courts to decide on the scope of the non-zero-rated supplies of hot food. As a result of the previous (erroneous) test several tribunal cases had been decided in favour of the trader, whereas the application of the new test would have produced a different result, as in this case. The trader argued that to do so was contrary to the principle of fiscal neutrality. That was rejected by the Court of Appeal. First the UK courts had not deliberately ignored Community law[12]. Second the previous cases were effective only for the year in question and third there was no Community right for a trader to be treated in the same way as other traders who had secured a windfall due to a misapplication of the law.

In *Marks & Spencer Plc v HMRC* (2008), the ECJ considered that on a claim for repayment of wrongly charged VAT, the defence of unjust enrichment was not an automatic breach of the fiscal neutrality principle. The defence of unjust enrichment arose from the fact that the tax which Marks and Spencer were claiming back had in fact been paid to them by their customers when buying chocolate teacakes (which should have been zero-rated) so that the company would in effect be receiving a windfall. In

---

[10] *Staatsesecretaris van Financïn v Coffeeshop Siberïvof* (1999).
[11] *CEC v Polak* (2002).
[12] See *Commission of the European Communities v Italy* (1988).

this case, however, the ECJ held that the principle of fiscal neutrality would prevail. Marks and Spencer were what is known as payment traders, i.e. they had to account for VAT to HMRC since they collected more than they paid, whereas another supplier of chocolate teacakes, Tesco Supermarkets, were repayment traders, i.e. they received VAT back from HMRC since they paid more than they collected. The unjust enrichment principle would only apply to the former and so that would infringe fiscal neutrality.[13]

The CJEU has also ruled in a series of cases[14] that the right to refuse payment on the grounds of unjust enrichment is to be interpreted restrictively and that it is contrary to Community law for Member States to impose requirements which make it excessively difficult to secure the repayment whether by way of presumption or by rules of evidence.

CORE OF THE PRINCIPLE   In *Lex Services Plc v CEC* (2004),   **25–10**
Lord Walker, without referring the matter to the ECJ, considered that the principle of fiscal neutrality had a core, which he described as:

> "whether goods purchased by the final consumer have been through the hands of a dozen different traders at successive stages of their manufacture, distribution and marketing or are the product of a single manufacturer who is also the retailer the VAT system should . . . produce the same end result" (and similar for services).[15]

But he also considered that the principle was qualified by that of legal certainty and does not require that transactions, which have the same economic or business effect, should for that reason be treated alike for VAT purposes,[16] thus, in that case distinguishing between a car dealer who gives a discount on the list price of a new car and one who gives a generous part exchange

---

[13] For an overview of the whole Marks and Spencer VAT litigation, see *Marks and Spencer Plc v HMRC* (2009).

[14] Derived from the decision in *Amministratzione delle Finanze delo Stato v San Giorgio SpA* (1983). See especially *Weber's Wine World Handels-GmbH v Abgabenberufungskommission Wein* (2005).

[15] *Lex Services Plc v CEC* (2004) at [26].

[16] "The principle of the neutrality of VAT does not mean that a taxable person with a choice between two transactions may choose one of them and avail himself of the effects of the other." *CEC v Cantor Fitzgerald International* (2001) at [33]. See Geoffrey Morse, "Lex Services Plc v Customs and Excise Commissioners; Customs and Excise Commissioners v Euphony Communications Ltd; Principle of Fiscal Neutrality Constrained" [2004] B.T.R. 99.

allowance on the customer's old car, even though the net price paid by the customer is the same in both cases.

25–11   EFFECTIVENESS   The principle of effectiveness has been used mainly in respect of repayment claims for overpaid or wrongly paid VAT. We have already seen in the case of *Marks and Spencer Plc v CEC* (2002) that it is available to ensure that such claims by a taxable person are neither impossible nor excessively difficult. Recent litigation has been concerned instead with the question as to whether and, if so, how it also applies to such claims by the non-registered final consumer against HMRC. Thus in *Investment Trust Companies v HMRC* (2012), the companies had paid VAT on the supplies to them of certain services. Those supplies should have been exempt from the tax. The suppliers recovered the tax they had accounted for from HMRC and passed it on to the companies. But because of a three-year limitation period and the method of accounting for VAT that was less than the VAT paid by the companies. They therefore brought an action for restitution of the additional amount on the grounds of mistake. The judge held that although the claim was well founded under English law, it failed because of s.80(7) of the VAT Act which removed any such obligation to repay from HMRC.

The question then arose as to whether the companies had any rights under Community law. Following three decisions of the ECJ,[17] the judge held that the principle of effectiveness required national law to provide an effective remedy in these circumstances for the ultimate consumer where reimbursement by the supplier was impossible or excessively difficult. In *Banca Antoniana Popolare Veneta SpA v Ministero dell'Economia e delle Finaze, Agenze delle Entrate* (2012), the ECJ held that a system whereby the supplier could reclaim overpaid VAT within a two year period and the customer had a 10-year right to recover the tax from the supplier was not contrary to the principle of effectiveness.

After a prolonged sequence of litigation between *Littlewoods Retail Ltd* and *HMRC*, including a reference to the CJEU, The Court of Appeal held (in 2015) that the provisions of the VAT Act which disapplied restitutionary claims in relation to overpaid VAT did not comply with Community law in the circumstances of that case. Those provisions had therefore to be set aside and

---

[17] *Reetsma Cigarettenfabriken GmbH v Ministerio delle Finanze* (2008) ECJ; *JP Morgan Fleming Claverhouse Investment Trust Plc v HMRC* (2008) ECJ; *Danfoss A/S v Skatteministeriet* (2011) ECJ.

compound interest was awarded rather than the simple interest paid by HMRC. HMRC had been enriched by the time involved before repayment. We shall return to repayments in Ch.26.

Fraud, evasion, abusive practices and avoidance

As we shall see, VAT basically has two financial components. **25–12** A makes a taxable supply to B. A must account to the HMRC for VAT on that supply (output tax). B may then (unless he is the final consumer) claim that back from HMRC as input tax (but of course will himself have to account for ouput tax on supplies from him, say to C, and so on). It is in the order of things that suppliers will seek both to minimise their accountability for output tax and maximise their claims for input tax. Apart from using actually fraudulent figures, which of course can be rectified (and prosecuted on), these may take the form of a fully-disclosed tax planning scheme, be part of a complex series of transactions designed to achieve an evasion of the tax (e.g. the so-called carousel fraud) or somewhere in between.

It is also in the nature of things that the HMRC will seek to counter these activities. But unlike other UK taxes, if it uses the statutory scheme for recovery it can currently only do this within an EU framework and the ECJ has laid down some pretty clear guidance as to the parameters within which the UK authorities must work.

OBJECTIVE NATURE OF THE TAX In the case of fraud or **25–13** evasion, the ECJ held in *Teleos Plc v CEC* (2008) that although the HMRC are entitled under EU law to take measures to counter the actual fraud or evasion, they must not offend the principle of proportionality, i.e. they must not render the obtaining of a Community right impossible or excessively difficult. In *JP Commodities Ltd v HMRC* (2008) it was held that a simple requirement to include the VAT registration number of the recipient of an intra EC supply by an exporter seeking to claim that it was a zero-rated export supply, was proportionate. It was a small thing to ask (unless of course the recipient did not have one, which was the whole purpose of the exercise).

It has been held, however, by the House of Lords in *HMRC v Total Network SL* (2008), that in default of using that statutory recovery scheme, HMRC does have the ability to bring a civil claim for damages for the tort of conspiracy based on harm intentionally inflicted by persons combining for that purpose, whether or not it would be actionable against any one individually.

25–14 TRANSACTIONS CONNECTED WITH EVASION OF VAT Various schemes have been devised for the fraudulent evasion of VAT. These all involve a failure by one trader to account for VAT and after a number of transactions involving those goods (typically mobile phones or computer chips) a claim for repayment of that VAT by another trader. Variously know as missing trader inter-Community VAT fraud, or its more complicated contra trading variation, questions arise as to whether those involved in the chain, other than the fraudsters themselves, can claim input tax relief in respect of their transaction.[18] Any such claim cannot be rejected simply on the basis that the transaction was part of a fraudulent scheme. The ECJ in *Optigen Ltd v CEC* (2006) said that the right to deduct input tax was an integral part of VAT and that what constitutes a taxable supply is to be determined by wholly objective criteria. Motive is irrelevant. In *Kittel v Belgium* (2006), the ECJ therefore said that such an intermediary would be entitled to a repayment of input tax provided he did not and could not have known that it was linked to a fraud. Only therefore if he knew or should have known of the fraudulent evasion of tax, i.e. that there was no other reasonable explanation, will he lose the right of repayment of input tax.

A significant number of cases have since had to decide how to apply the *Kittel* test. In *Livewire Telecom Ltd v HMRC* (2009), it was said that there was no need to prove a conspiracy but that the trader knew or should have known of the connection between his own transaction and the fraud (either the failure to pay or the dishonest cover up). An example is where the trader knew it could make a great deal of money in a short time, without any risk, and it knew it would be repaid for all its transactions out of VAT repayments. It was offered loans to purchase mobile phones which made no commercial sense and sold those phones to three buyers who each bought exactly the number supplied to the trader.[19]

Guidance was given by the Court of Appeal in *Mobilix Ltd v HMRC* (2010). Claims would only fail if the trader knew or should have known of the fraudulent connection. If the trader should have known that the only reasonable explanation for the transaction was that it was connected with fraud then he would be caught. This is to be judged on the totality of the facts.[19a] It was not enough, however, if it was simply more likely than not so

---

[18] For a detailed explanation of these schemes, see *HMRC v Livewire Telecom Ltd* (2009).

[19] *Tarlo Worldwide Ltd v HMRC* (2012).

[19a] A good example is *Davis & Dann Ltd v HMRC* (2016), where the CA overruled the Upper Tribunal. It concerned dealings on the "grey market".

connected. The fraud by others could precede or follow the trader's purchase and the input tax denied need not equate with the tax lost by the fraud. Further, courts should not unduly focus on whether the trader acted with due diligence. The test in *Mobilix* has since been followed by subsequent Upper Tribunal decisions, despite a challenge based on the (original) French text of the judgement in *Kittel*, which it was argued required an involvement in, rather than a connection with, the fraud by the trader.[20]

There continue to be many cases involving missing trader fraud but the test in *Mobilix* has been consistently applied and most disputes have been as to the facts. The Court of Appeal reaffirmed the *Mobilix* test in *Fonecomp Ltd v HMRC* (2015) and refused to accept a limitation that the default and the purchase had to occur in the same chain of supply (which would have excluded contra trading). The connection had to be determined on the objective evidence and not the trader's knowledge as to how the fraud had been perpetrated. A gloss was added in *E Buyer Ltd v HMRC* (2016), where the Upper Tribunal ruled that where actual knowledge was alleged, then if that in fact amounted to an allegation of dishonesty, sufficient particulars must be disclosed.

Where the trader is a company, the knowledge of an individual who played the major role in the fraud can be attributed to the company for this purpose.[21]

AVOIDANCE—OTHER ABUSIVE PRACTICES Those decisions **25–15** on the objective nature of non-fraudulent supplies are subject to one major limitation, laid down by the ECJ in *Halifax Plc v CEC* (2006) and confirmed by them in *Kittel v Belgium* (2008). It is subject to the principle that Community Law cannot be relied on for abusive or fraudulent ends. But the ECJ also stressed that there is a need for legal certainty in the system of VAT and there is certainly no requirement that a supplier should structure its business so as to attract the highest possible tax. As a result it set out two requirements for a practice to be regarded as an abusive practice for VAT:

1) after applying the relevant national and EC rules, a tax advantage (e.g. a repayment claim)[22] accrues which would be contrary to the purpose of the Directive; and

---

[20] *POWA (Jersey) Ltd v HMRC* (2012); *HMRC v S & I Electronics Plc* (2012).
[21] *HMRC v Greener Solutions Ltd* (2012).
[22] Most of the cases have involved these, but the CA in *Debenhams Retail Ltd v CEC* (2005) [52] considered that it would equally apply to a claim to lower output tax.

2) the essential[23] aim of the transaction concerned is to obtain that advantage.

If there are other commercial explanations then the doctrine will not apply. If applied, it is a rule of construction which requires the relevant provision to be construed so as to prevent artificial deductions.[24]

The ECJ added that any such finding of an abusive practice would not lead to any criminal sanctions. Instead the transaction would have to be *redefined*. This would entail establishing the situation which would have obtained in the absence of the transaction constituting such a practice. This could involve the payment or repayment of the tax and any third party rights.

25–16 APPLYING THE TESTS   In the *Halifax* case, the ECJ stated that in applying these difficult tests as to advantage and essential aim, national courts must work on objective factors and determine the real substance and significance of the relevant transaction(s). They could, however, have regard to the purely artificial nature of a transaction and any links of a legal, economic and/or personal nature between the operators involved in a tax reduction scheme.

In *HMRC v Weald Leasing Ltd* (2008), Lindsay J rejected the Commissioners' argument that it would be sufficient to show that in a case where the essential aim of a series of transactions was to obtain a tax advantage, with no commercial motive, the transactions were not part of normal commercial operations. There had, in addition, to be something which was contrary to the purposes of the directive. In that case, simply being able to deduct a greater amount of input tax than would have been available without it, could not be so described.

In *University of Huddersfield Education Corp v HMRC* (2014) the Upper Tribunal found that there was no commercial purpose to the scheme and so there was no need to identify whether there had been a commercial purpose to part of it. Further the essential aim of the transaction was to obtain a tax advantage. They distinguished *Weald Leasing*. That case was not authority for the proposition that where a scheme was devised to create an absolute right to deduct input tax but also created a liability to account for output tax, it was necessary to see how much output tax was first accounted for.

---

[23] They also used the word "sole" aim, which has caused some disagreements.
[24] Per Norris J in *HMRC v Moorbury Ltd* (2010).

Sometimes a scheme will fail without recourse to the abuse principles. In *WHA Ltd v HMRC* (2013), the Supreme Court considered the abusive practices tests in relation to an avoidance scheme, the effect of which was that an insurer seemed to be able to claim repayment of input tax in relation to non-taxable supplies (where no corresponding output tax had been paid). The scheme failed on its merits, however, as it was contrary to the principles: (i) that the deduction of input tax was meant to relieve the trader entirely of the burden of the VAT it paid in the course of its business; and (ii) that tax was only chargeable on the value added at each stage of the process. In this case, however, on the facts the trader had not actually born the burden of paying the VAT nor had it added any value. As such the abuse principle did not need not be applied.

The Supreme Court upheld the application of the *Halifax* tests in *Pendragon Plc v HMRC* (2015). This was a scheme which used the special provisions designed to tax second hand car sales only on the dealer's mark-up rather than the total cost to its demonstrator models. The scheme was contrary to the EU policy underlying the margin scheme. The trader's intention was to apply that scheme to prevent any charge arising on the consideration at all. And the *essential* aim of the scheme was to obtain a tax advantage; the use of a chain of contracts and the use of a foreign bank in that chain were both unnecessary and artificial.

By way of contrast, the Upper Tribunal refused to apply the abuse principle in *HMRC v Newey* (2015). Mr Newey was a loan broker who made only exempt supplies and so could not set off any of his inputs (you have to make taxable supplies for that). He therefore moved his operation to a company registered in Jersey (A Ltd) which used UK-based lenders. All the work was carried on in the UK by Newey as its sub-contractor. A Ltd now claimed to be making the supplies and if that was so then the inputs could be recovered. The CJEU, on a reference in 2013, simply restated the question—did the contractual terms between A Ltd and the clients genuinely reflect the economic reality or was Newey in reality still making the supplies in the UK? The Tribunal thought that the former was the correct analysis. None of the transactions could be regarded as abusive and the contractual arrangements could only be set aside if they were wholly artificial and set up with the *sole* aim of obtaining a tax advantage. Thus there was no abuse. The question was whether the structure gave rise to abuse in the context of the overall factual matrix; not whether the change in structure resulted in a tax advantage as compared with the previous arrangements.

The "scheme" in Newey was of course much simpler than in

the other cases and the conclusion that A Ltd was the supplier was not contrary to the common concept of supplier and client with an intermediary. It was on the face of it a normal commercial operation, albeit with a heavy UK involvement. On the other hand, as the Supreme Court pointed out in *Pendragon*, tax avoidance schemes are rarely designed exclusively to give rise to tax avoidance. Further the Supreme Court in that case was concerned with the "essential" rather than the "sole" purpose of the scheme as applied in *Newey*. Whatever the merits, it does seem as if the decision in *Newey* to date is going back to the pre-1980s idea of form over substance. HMRC, however, have been given leave to appeal to the Court of Appeal.

VAT in the UK

25–17   In the UK, VAT is imposed by the Value Added Tax Act 1994 (the VAT Act), a consolidation measure, together with significant provisions in delegated legislation. Partly as a result of a series of cases brought against the UK Government by taxpayers and by the European Commission, many of the original differences that used to exist between the EC VAT and its UK version have been removed.

VAT law is a curious mix of broad principles and considerable amounts of detail. This is because of the nature of the tax. In principle it is a very broad-based tax, much broader than income tax or corporation tax. Potentially it applies to any economic transaction under which anyone adds value to any business activity; that is, under which anyone recovers not only the cost of materials used in a transaction, but also the cost of his or her own labour (or that of employees) or a profit. Of course, both are usually the aim. VAT therefore can apply to any economic activity. Further, it applies directly to those activities, not at one remove in the way corporation tax or income tax do. We must in every case establish who is making a supply, to whom, and of what. Easy? No, because what appear to be even straight forward everyday transactions need careful analysis to establish the VAT consequences often involving a number of supplies.

Sources of VAT law

25–18   At the same time, therefore, UK VAT law has to follow a European paradigm and deal with considerable detail. Both make the traditional pattern of imposition by means only of primary legislation inappropriate. In practice, there are four tiers of operative legislation. The top tier, as we have seen, is formed by the Directive. The next tier is the VAT Act and amending Finance Acts. Below that are a considerable number of orders in Council and other delegated legislation. Then comes the fourth layer: official Notices. These Notices are issued by HMRC and, unusually, have, at least in part, legislative status. Taxpayers to whom the Notices are issued are obliged to follow their contents. By this multiple means, the law is imposed. Supported both by considerable use of the appeals process, and also by agreements with trade organisations, extra-statutory concessions, parliamentary questions, press releases, and information sheets and notes, those who need to do so can find out at least what the local VAT offices think they should be doing. Of this wealth of material, you may find it useful to obtain one Notice in particular. Notice No.700, *The VAT Guide*, is an excellent summary, with worked examples, of the tax for those who have to operate it. The latest version (April 2015) is available free online or from your local VAT office.

Administration and appeals

VAT administration is the task of HMRC. Before its fusion with the Inland Revenue, VAT was under the control of HM Customs and Excise, the oldest British government department. Day to day administration is still undertaken by a local VAT office responsible for overseeing registration and collection of the tax which usually works on an invoice basis.[25] There are both civil and criminal penalties for, e.g., failing to register[26] or making returns.

APPEALS Appeals are now heard, like other tax appeals, by the First-instance Tribunal (Tax Chamber), which has replaced the VAT and duties tribunal. Appeals from that tribunal on a point of law are heard by the Upper Tribunal (Tax and Chancery Chamber) which has replaced the High Court on such appeals. Further appeals lie with leave to the Court of Appeal (or the Inner House of the Court of Session in Scotland) and the Supreme Court. There is also always, currently, the chance of a reference to the ECJ in Luxembourg.[27]

25–19

25–20

---

[25] See *Elliniko Dimosio v Karageorgou* (2006) ECJ.

[26] See *Khan v CEC* (2006).

[27] See para.25–02 above. There will be no reference to the ECJ, however, if the matter has been resolved or is clear. In other cases a reference will usually be made. See, e.g. *Town and Country Factors Ltd v CEC* (1998).

How VAT works

25-21   As we shall see, VAT is charged on a supply of goods and services by the supplier. It is an indirect tax in the sense that it is charged as part of the purchase price for those goods and services and accounted for by the recipient of that consideration. The tax operates as a *value-added* tax. This requires an examination of the way VAT works from the viewpoint of a trader rather than on a transaction-by-transaction basis.

25-22   EXAMPLE Alan owns a forest. He sells planks of wood cut from the trees. Beech buys the planks and turns them into chair frames. Caitlin buys the chair frames from Beech, upholsters them, and turns them into chairs. Den buys the chairs from Caitlin, and sells them to customers in his shop. Six of the chairs are bought by Eka for £200 each. How does VAT apply to this series of transactions? Let us assume that A, B, C, and D, but not E, are all registered for VAT.

A sells the planks from which the parts are made for £10 to B. To this must be added VAT at 20 per cent (the standard rate). B therefore pays A £12. A keeps the £10 but pays the £2 to HMRC. B sells the chair frames to C for £30, again plus VAT. B therefore charges C £30 plus £6 VAT. Of that £6 he receives, B sets off the £2 he paid to A and hands the £4 balance to HMRC. B's profit is £20. Similarly D pays C £100 plus VAT (£20). C sets off the £6 VAT he paid to B and accounts for the balance of £14 to HMRC. D's profit is £70.

The sale by D to E at £200 since it is not stated to be plus VAT must include the VAT. (It could have been at £200 plus VAT (£40) so that D would set off the £20 VAT paid to C and account for the balance of £20 to HMRC—his profit would be £100.) Instead the sale to E is at £166.33 with VAT of £33.67. (Inclusive VAT is one-sixth of the whole—£33.67 is 20 per cent of £166.33.) D will therefore deduct the £20 paid to C from £33.67 and account for the balance. D's profit is £66.33. E cannot set off the VAT as he is the final consumer.

In essence therefore E has paid VAT at the standard rate on the full purchase price of £166.33 (£33.67). But this has been collected in stages from each supplier in the chain: £2 from A, £4 from B, £14 from C and £13.67 from D. Each of them, by setting off what they paid from what they collected have paid VAT on the value added at that stage of production. So A, B, C and D are in effect tax collectors and are known as taxable persons. They are not taxpayers; they do not bear the tax. That is E's prerogative.

INPUTS AND OUTPUTS   As this example shows, the tax is **25-23**
turned into a value-added tax by allowing each taxable person
to collect VAT on the full sale price, but deduct from it any
VAT paid out in making the sales. In VAT terms, the VAT
collected by a trader is known as the *output tax* (or tax on
outputs). The VAT incurred by the trader is *input tax* (or tax
on inputs to the business). The VAT payable to HMRC is the
balance of output tax less input tax.

This position is complicated by the fact that, in addition to
standard-rated supplies, there are exempt, reduced-rate and,
peculiar to the UK, zero-rated supplies. We shall deal with those
in the next chapter. The detailed rules as to the collection and
computation of the tax are dealt with in Ch.26. We must now
turn to when the tax will be charged.

When VAT applies

The three key questions to be answered in determining the **25-24**
structure of VAT are: who are the taxable persons? on what are
they taxed? when, and how much, tax is paid?

Taxpayers and taxable persons

In a practical sense, the taxpayers of VAT are the final con- **25-25**
sumers who buy the goods and services subject to the tax. The
legal obligation to account for the tax, however, is not placed
on them, but on those that supply them. These are called not
taxpayers but *taxable persons* in the VAT legislation. This helps
us keep in mind that the tax is imposed on transactions rather
than persons, although the taxable persons are those required to
collect the tax. Who are taxable persons? Section 3(1) of the VAT
Act tells us that "a person is a taxable person for the purposes
of this Act while he is, or is required to be, registered under this
Act". We will explore later who is in these two categories.

Scope of the tax

What is subject to VAT? Section 4(1) of the Act says that **25-26**
"VAT shall be charged on any supply of goods or services made
in the UK, where it is a taxable supply made by a taxable person
in the course or furtherance of any business carried on by him";
while s.4(2) adds that a "taxable supply is a supply of goods or
services made in the UK other than an exempt supply". We must
add to this helpful definition the further guidance that *supply*
includes all forms of supply, but not anything done otherwise
than for a consideration, and that anything which is not a supply
of goods but is done for a consideration (including, if so done,

the granting, assignment or surrender of any right) is a supply of services (s.5(2)).

25–27   THE DIRECTIVE   But wait a minute. VAT is a European tax. Has the British legislation carried out the requirements of European law? The key provision is art.2 of the VAT Directive. This provides that "The following transactions shall be subject to value added tax: 1. the supply of goods [or services] effected for consideration within the territory of the Member State by a taxable person acting as such . . .".

To this we must add art.9 of the Directive: "Taxable person" shall mean any person who independently carries out in any place any economic activity including those specified, whatever the purpose or results of that activity.

Despite the differences in wording, the structure of the British VAT is that required in EU law. We should therefore read the British charging provisions in the light of the European provisions—with two cautions. The same words may appear in the two texts, but with different meanings. For example, we shall see that *taxable person* in the European text does not have the same meaning as *taxable person* in the British text. The second warning is that words in the European text may appear to be ordinary English words when they are not. *Consideration* is an example of this, as again we see below. One reason for this is that the European text exists in several equally authoritative language versions.

Subject to those warnings that—as in any tax law—we must always remember precisely what each word means, we can use the two sets of provisions to state the key structure of the VAT as it applies to supplies internal to the UK.

The charge to VAT

25–28   VAT on domestic supplies applies to:

- supplies;
- of goods and services;
- for consideration;
- other than exempt supplies;
- in the UK;
- by a taxable person;
- as part of the economic activities of that person.

Each of these elements must be present, or be deemed to be present, before the tax operates on a supply. A supply made when one or more of the elements of the tax are missing is said to be outside the scope of the tax. It is a criminal offence deliberately to charge VAT on a supply that is outside the scope of the tax. These seven elements are therefore the necessary criteria for the operation of the tax. They are not sufficient to determine tax liability in full, but we shall examine these key issues first, then deal with the other provisions.

Supplies

The phrase *supplies of goods and services for consideration* **25–29** should seem familiar to a student of commercial law, and who should therefore have heard of the Supply of Goods and Services Acts of 1982 and 1994. Unfortunately, the analogy is not valid. None of the words in that phrase bear the same meaning as in English contract and commercial law, although there is a large area of overlap between the two sets of rules in practice. This is both because VAT is a European tax, and cannot be confined by the commercial rules of any one country, and also because the aim of VAT is different. It is to ensure that the tax is collected regardless of the legal niceties of a particular transaction. See, for example, the early case of *CEC v Oliver* (1980). The High Court had to decide whether a sale through a car auction that was later established to be a void contract was a "supply". Under commercial law principles it was not, but the judge rejected the analogy and found it was a supply.

Similarly the CJEU held that a sale effected by the fraudulent use of a credit card was nevertheless a supply for VAT purposes: *Dixons Retail Plc v HMRC* (2013).

UNLAWFUL TRANSACTIONS On that basis, the ECJ has **25–30** made it clear that the principle of fiscal neutrality requires that there be no general distinction between lawful and unlawful transactions. If VAT were not levied on the latter then the unlawful trader would in effect receive a tax subsidy as against the lawful trader making a similar supply. Only trades which are per se illegal and so cannot be performed lawfully such as illegal drugs, are outside the neutrality principle.[28] A straightforward theft is not however a supply by the victim to the thief.[29]

SELF-SUPPLIES VAT is a tax on trading transactions, and **25–31** the main base of the tax is commercial sales. More broadly, the tax operates when someone does something that realises

---

[28] *Staastssecretaris van Financiën v Coffeeshop Siberië vof* (1999) ECJ.
[29] *British American Tobacco International Ltd v Belgian State* (2006) ECJ.

value to that person from some other person. The word used for this is *supply*. I supply you with, say, buttered toast or a musical performance, and you pay me. But I cannot, in the ordinary sense, supply myself with the buttered toast. Nor do I supply myself with the butter or the loaf that I use to make the meal. In other words, self-supply is not a supply. Where, for example, a manufacturer makes bolts that are then used by that manufacturer in making windows to sell to others, the manufacturer supplies windows, not bolts. There must be a customer for there to be a supply.

Exceptions to this general rule exist to avoid distortion of competition in certain market sectors. The exceptions are limited, and in the UK they are confined to: self-supplies of motor vehicles by vehicle manufacturers, self- supplies of commercial buildings by building developers in certain circumstances, and self-supplies of printed stationery.

25–32   DEFINING A SUPPLY   Neither British nor EU VAT laws define *supply*, beyond the vague guidance in the VAT Act that "supply ... includes all forms of supply". Nor is a general definition possible. This is because the English term *supply*, useful and concise though it is, is a term untranslatable into many western European languages. There is therefore no equivalent of it in the French original EC text, or the German, Spanish or other official texts. Any attempt at defining supply must therefore be made in the context of the kind of supply, of goods or of services.

25–33   PASSING OF TITLE   Despite the warning set out above, lawyers looking at the concept of a supply of goods will be tempted to turn to the commercial law of their own systems to establish when the goods transfer from supplier to customer. Under commercial law rules, that usually occurs when ownership, title, or risk transfers. Of course, if there is title reservation, then ownership does not transfer, although risk may. Is there a supply when goods are handed over, but the ownership is not, and is it relevant that risk passes? For VAT purposes, there are two issues here. First, a supply of the use of goods (for example, equipment leasing) is not a supply of goods at all—it is a supply of services. Secondly, a supply of goods does not always take place if and when the local commercial laws determine that title has transferred. This is because supply is a European concept. The Directive, having refrained from defining supply, defines instead *supply of goods* as *the transfer of the right to dispose of tangible property as owner* (art.14). Following this, the ECJ has ruled that in the case of a supply of goods it is not relevant whether title to the goods has passed under the national law: *Staatssecretaris van Financiën v SAFE BV* (1991).

IDENTITY OF SUPPLIER Similarly, although the identity of **25–34** the supplier is usually simply a matter of contract law, where VAT is concerned the position must be looked at from an EU perspective—has there been a transfer of tangible property by X so as to empower Y to dispose of it as if he were the owner. If so, then the fact that there is no contract between X and Y, because X is simply carrying out Z's contractual obligations to Y, will not affect the issue. There is still a supply by Z to Y. But if the contract between Z and Y is partially novated so as to create a contract between X and Y, then there will be a supply to Y by X and not by Z.[30]

TAX ON CONSUMPTION VAT is in essence a tax on **25–35** consumption. In *Parker Hale Ltd v CEC* (2000) this was held to include the voluntary handing-in of handguns in return for compensation from the government. A supply of goods would give rise to consumption wherever a right was acquired to dispose of those goods as owner. In that context the fact that the government intended to destroy the handguns was irrelevant. That case was followed by the Court of Appeal in *Stewart v CEC* (2002)—a supply included the transfer of the whole property in the goods and consumption could be presumed irrespective of the motives or intentions of the recipient.

SERVICES The definition of *supply* in the context of a supply **25–36** of services is even more difficult to establish. It is intertwined with two other definitions, that of services, and that of consideration. This is clear from UK law itself: "anything which is not a supply of goods but is done for a consideration (including, if so done, the granting, assignment or surrender of any right) is a supply of services" (s.5(2)). In *Trinity Mirror Plc v CEC* (2002), it was accepted by the Court of Appeal, upholding the decision of the judge below, that there were six characteristics of a supply of services. In addition to it not being a supply of goods (see the next paragraph) and being done for consideration, the characteristics are: that it must have constituted a transaction; that something must have been done by the supplier; that which was done must have been capable

---

[30] See the analysis in *Telewest Communications Plc v CEC* (2005) CA.

of being used by and for the benefit of an identified recipient; and that benefit must be regarded as a cost component of the activity of another person in the commercial chain.

There was no requirement that the activity had to be part of the company's turnover, as in income or corporation tax. Thus issuing shares to raise funds was a supply of services by the company.[31]

Goods and services

25–37   There is no general definition in the UK VAT legislation of *goods*. Instead, we must turn to Sch.4 to the VAT Act. There we are told (in para.1) that a transfer of the whole property in goods is a supply of goods, but anything less is a supply of services. Likewise, the transfer of possession as part of an agreement for sale is a supply of goods, as is transfer of possession where a sale expressly contemplated. A credit sale or hire-purchase is therefore a supply of goods. Equipment leasing, where a sale might occur, is not.

The main point to grasp is that "goods and services" for VAT purposes can mean whatever the Treasury want them to mean. They can by order treat any transaction as a supply of goods, or of services, or as neither (s.5).

25–38   LAND, ETC. Land is an example of this. Land cannot be moved, so it cannot be goods. But neither is it a service. What, then, do we make of the provision that the supply of a major interest in land is a supply of goods (para.3). For VAT purposes, land has to be deemed to be goods or services. This is because, as we have seen, anything which is not goods is a service. In the binary world of VAT, a sale of land, or of a lease of more than 21 years (a major interest: s.96) is a supply of goods. All else to do with land is a supply of services.

The same is true of other forms of property that do not naturally fit into the deliberately simplified framework of VAT. Supplies of intellectual property, and of the right to use that property are alike treated as supplies of services, even when title is transferred. (This is implied by para.1 of Sch.5.) Supplies of electricity and similar intangibles are supplies of goods (Sch.4 para.3).

25–39   GOODS AND SERVICES Tricky problems also occur where a supply is both goods and services. For example, the supply of buttered toast is a supply of the butter, the bread, and the effort

---

[31] But not raising money by borrowing—in that case the supply was made to the company. Remember it is always essential to identify the exact nature of the supply.

of toasting and buttering the bread. Is that goods or services or both? The practical answer may be that it does not matter. The difference between goods and services is only of importance if it changes the amount of tax due, or when the tax is due. The only general difference between goods and service lies in the timing rules about when supplies occur. Otherwise, the problem is the more detailed one of whether a particular supply is charged at one rate of VAT or another. In our example, the tax rate on buttered toast is different to the tax rate on a loaf of bread, so the detail is important. We return to it when we deal with tax rates.

Consideration

A supply is only subject to VAT if it is made *for consideration*, **25–40** or is deemed to be made for consideration. The idea behind this requirement is an economic one. To be taxable, a transaction must be one that adds value. Consequently, unless in some way value is realised from a supply, there is nothing to tax. In practice, value is realised if the supplier gets paid for the supply. If nobody pays, there is no added value. It is in this way that the rule has been interpreted by the ECJ in a case which nicely illustrates the clash between traditional English thinking and the more general approach required for VAT.

EUROPEAN MEANING   In *Apple and Pear Development Council* **25–41** *v CEC* (1988), the Council carried out two groups of activities. The first group was of ordinary trading activities. The second group comprised activities financed by a statutory levy, and required by the law establishing the Council. The Council claimed that all its activities were for consideration. Much of the argument about this was framed in terms of the English law of contract. Was the statutory levy consideration for the supplies made to those who paid the levy of the statutory services? The case was argued in this way until it came to the House of Lords. The House noted that the point was one of European law, not English law, and found that a reference to the ECJ was necessary.

The ECJ noted that the question was a general one. Based on a linguistic analysis of the multilingual forms of the texts of the directives, the court laid down the test that there must be a payment for a supply, and that the payment and supply must be directly linked. In accordance with practice, the ECJ left it for the national court to determine whether there was a direct link on the facts of the particular case.

25–42   DIRECT LINK   The direct link test means that not all supplies for which payments are made are supplies for consideration (or against payment). There must be a legal relationship between the parties,[32] reciprocal performance and the remuneration received must constitute the value actually given by the provider.[32a] The ECJ itself has ruled in several cases that there was no such direct link, e.g. donations to a street musician,[33] payments to a farmer in return for not using land,[34] and the provision of free transport by an employer for its employees.[35] That Court also ruled that payments towards the cost of legal aid in Finland which depended purely on the circumstances of the payee and not the cost of the supply did not satisfy the direct link test—the disparity between the two was too great.[36] That was distinguished by the Upper Tribunal where the payee paid a fixed amount irrespective of personal circumstances even though that was not the full cost of the service—there was no rule that the payment must be the full cost of the supply.[37]

But there is no need for the supplier to be legally bound to provide all the services, e.g. in a "spot the ball" competition where payment of the prize money was not legally enforceable. There was reciprocity and the amount paid related directly to the services.[38]

Further, the CJEU in *Dixons Retail Plc v HMRC* (2014), held that there is no requirement in the Directive for the consideration to be paid directly by the person to whom the goods or services were provided. In that case the use of a credit card to pay for goods was a supply for a consideration even though the actual payment to the supplier was made by the card company. It was therefore irrelevant that the card had been used fraudulently so that the recipient of the goods never reimbursed the card company. On the other hand, an ongoing but never implemented intention to pay for services which are thus actually provided free is not enough to establish a link.[39]

---

[32] This was established in *Stewart v CEC* (2002), because once the scheme (handing in of handguns) had been promulgated and acted upon, the owner could insist on its being carried out.

[32a] *Lebara Ltd v HMRC* (2012).

[33] *Tolsma v Inspecteur der Omzetbelasting Leeuwarden* (1994).

[34] *Landboden-Agrardienste GmbH & Co KG v Finanzamt Calau* (1998).

[35] *Julius Fillibeck Söhne GmbH & Co KG v Finanzamt Neustadt* (1998).

[36] *Commission of the EC v Finland* (2009) ECJ.

[37] *Wakefield College v HMRC* (2016).

[38] *Town and Country Factors Ltd v CEC* (2002).

[39] *Norseman Gold Plc v HMRC* (2016).

USING NON-TAXABLE AGENTS   In the UK the issue has arisen **25–43** originally mainly in connection with supplies by clothing and other companies through "hostesses" holding parties in their own homes. Thus in *Rosgill Group Ltd v CEC* (1997)[40] at such a party sufficient goods were sold to entitle the hostess either to take a cash commission of £2.89 or to obtain a discount on a blouse of £7.23. She chose the latter, thus paying some £20 for a blouse priced at £28. The Court of Appeal held that the consideration for the supply of the blouse by the company to the hostess was not only the cash she paid but also the holding of the party. There was a direct link between the latter and the supply of the blouse, both contractually (she was entitled to the discount) and causatively (without the party there would have been no supply of the blouse at the reduced price).

DISCOUNT OR CONSIDERATION   The question in such cases is **25–44** whether the price reduction or cash commission received by the agents is simply a discount on the single transaction (e.g. of the sale of the blouse to her) or whether the agents have provided some form of consideration, usually in the form of services, for that reduction, so that there is in effect additional consideration provided by the agent for the supply (e.g. of the blouse) to her by the main supplier. In that latter case, as we shall see (in Ch.27), there is no discount for VAT purposes at all. In *CEC v Littlewoods Organisation Plc* (2001), the Court of Appeal held on the facts that there was no direct link between the agent's right to take commission on sales made by him or her in the form of a reduction in the price of goods supplied to the agent and any services provided by the agent to Littlewoods. This was in the main because it was impossible to tell whether that commission had been earned in respect of purchases by the agent on his or her own account or on purchases negotiated by the agent by third parties—the right to the commission was simply triggered by a payment of money by the agent to Littlewoods.

NON-CASH CONSIDERATION   But if it is clear that the right to **25–45** the commission is linked to the supply of goods or services to a third party, negotiated by the agent, then it seems that there will be a direct link between the supply of those services by the agent to the main supplier and the commission. It follows that if that is taken in the form of discounted goods[41] it will amount

---

[40] See also *Naturally Yours Cosmetics Ltd v CEC* (1988).
[41] If taken purely in the form of a cash payment then there is no supply of goods or services to the agent for which it can form consideration.

to the provision of non-cash consideration by the agent for those goods as in *Rosgill*.[42] This distinction can produce some strange results which seem difficult at times to reconcile with the principle of fiscal neutrality.[43] We shall return to it again in Ch.27 when we consider the actual value of a supply—at this stage we are merely identifying what the supply is made in return for. In *CEC v Euphony Communications Ltd* (2004), Hart J took a different route by regarding the supply of services by the agent (in introducing a new customer) as a separate supply by the agent so that the consideration for that supply (the commission in the form of a price reduction on goods) could not be a discount.

25–46   PART EXCHANGE DEALS The same Court of Appeal in *Littlewoods* also heard the cases of *Lex Services Plc v CEC* and *CEC v Bugeja* which involved part exchange deals. They upheld the principle that the goods tendered in part exchange must form part of the consideration for the supply. The *Lex Services* case has since been upheld by the House of Lords (2004). The question which then arises is what value is to be attributed to those goods. Again we will come back to that in Ch.27.

Specific problems concerning supplies of goods or services
25–47   The basic requirement of a supply of goods or services for a consideration has led to a number of specific problems for the courts to deal with. Three of these are sufficiently fundamental to VAT as to require some consideration at this point.

25–48   IDENTIFYING WHAT IS SUPPLIED AND TO WHOM VAT depends upon a supply to fix upon for there to be a charge. Sometimes identifying exactly who is supplying what and to whom is far from straightforward, but by doing so the VAT position is thereby clarified. In *CEC v Diners Club Ltd* (1989) an everyday cash card transaction whereby the card holder used his card to buy goods from a retailer so that there was an assignment of the debt by the retailer to the card company and the payment of that debt by the company less commission, was held to constitute a supply of financial services by the card company to the retailer, in addition to the supply by the retailer to the card company.

---

[42] See, e.g. *Bertelsmann AG v Finanzamt Wiedenbruck* (2001).
[43] See Geoffrey Morse, "Identifying the Taxable Amount for Value Added Tax of a Supply of Goods at a Reduced Cash Price: A Question of Analysis or Principle" [2002] B.T.R. 179.

In *Vehicle Control Services Ltd v HMRC* (2013), the company provided car park management services to landowners. Under that contract the company could tow away illegally parked cars or impose penalties. HMRC argued that the company was acting as the landowner's agent when collecting those penalties and so they were part of the consideration for the supply of car parking services to the landowners. The Court of Appeal disagreed. There was no agency and the monies collected could be classified as damages for trespass—it was not part of the supply to the landowners. There was no payment by the landowner to the company.

THIRD PARTY SUPPLIES In *Trustees of Nell Gwyn House Maintenance Fund v CEC* (1999) the trustees of a maintenance fund for a block of flats were required and did employ staff to provide maintenance, etc. of the building. The House of Lords held that they were supplying the whole services of the staff to the tenants (i.e. the total cost of the operation) and not just the act of arranging for the staff to work (i.e. the organisation costs only). There is a clear distinction between A paying B for services to be provided by B, and A putting B in funds so that B could arrange for C to provide the services. This was clearly the former.   **25–49**

Similarly, if A supplies goods to B for a sum, out of which A will have to pay C for services rendered to A, A will have to account for VAT on the whole amount received from B.[44] Only if the services were provided by C to B will the amount paid to C be deductible from the supply by A. This distinction was applied in *Debenhams Retail Plc v CEC* (2005).[45] Debenhams sold say a coat for £100 but purported to say, in their till receipt, that if this was a store card purchase, that £97.50 was paid to Debenhams for the coat and £2.50 to DRS, an independent Debenhams company, for the provision of financial services (an exempt supply). The CA held that on the facts there was only one contract and one supply, by Debenhams for £100. Thus output tax had to be accounted for on the full amount. But, even on the assumption that there had been two contracts, the consideration for the supply by Debenhams would still have been £100.   **25–50**

---

[44] The result is the same if A donates part of the sum to a charity designated by B: *Findel Plc v HMRC* (2011).

[45] See Geoffrey Morse, "Identifying Supplies. Further Reflections on Third Party and Multiple Supplies: Debenhams Retail plc v CEC and College of Estate Management v CEC" [2006] B.T.R. 54.

25–51 THE PLANTIFLOR CASE This distinction was central to the decision in *CEC v Plantiflor Ltd* (2002). The company supplied plants to customers partly by mail order. Delivery, if requested, was by Parcelforce and £2.50 was charged for postage and packing of which £1.63 related to the charge by Parcelforce. The Court of Appeal held that there were three supplies. The first was of the goods by Plantiflor to the customer; the second was of the service of arranging delivery of the goods and packaging the goods, also by Plantiflor to the customer; and the third was of the actual delivery which was supplied by Parcelforce to the customer. There was no fourth supply of services by Parcelforce to Plantiflor. On that analysis the consideration for the supply by Plantiflor to the customer could not include the £1.63 since it was the consideration for the supply by Parcelforce to the customer and to hold otherwise would be to impose VAT twice on the same consideration (although in that case the supply by Parcelforce was in fact an exempt supply).

The House of Lords came to a different conclusion, however, which had also been favoured by the judge but not the Tribunal. By a majority (4:1) they considered that the delivery to the customer by Parcelforce was made solely under a contract with Plantiflor acting as principal and not as an agent for the customer. It followed that the only supply of the delivery of the goods for a consideration was made by Parcelforce to Plantiflor (i.e. there *was* a fourth supply). The £1.63 was paid by the customer to Plantiflor not for delivery of the goods but for the supply of the benefit of its arrangement with Parcelforce to deliver goods to them free of any charge to the customer (who was never under any obligation to pay Parcelforce anything). It was therefore part of the consideration paid for that supply by Plantiflor. In effect, Plantiflor were supplying the delivery services of Parcelforce as part of their overall supply to the customer in the same way as the trustees in the *Nell Gwyn* case were supplying the maintenance services.

25–52 PARALLEL OR SIMULTANEOUS SUPPLIES The case of *Loyalty Management UK Ltd v HMRC* (2007) raised the complex issue as to whether A could in a single transaction make two supplies, one of goods to B (the final consumer of the goods) and one of services to C (a trader). C had made a payment to A as a service charge and was claiming an input tax credit on that payment. The company (C) operated the Nectar rewards card scheme. The collector (B) using the scheme, accumulated points by shopping at certain stores and garages (the sponsors), which could then be used to redeem goods from one of a list of specified suppliers (A). The sponsors paid C an agreed sum per point issued and charged VAT on those sums. C paid A a service charge and paid VAT on it. It now claimed to deduct those payments as input tax. The judge refused to allow the claim, regarding the payment by C as simply providing third party consideration for the (sole) supply of the goods to B.

The Court of Appeal disagreed. Whilst it was true that there could be no parallel supply of goods to C in those circumstances, since C was never entitled to the goods (e.g. the television, above) at all,[46] it was clear law that there could be a parallel supply of services to C.[47]

The House of Lords referred the case to the ECJ. That Court, in *HMRC v Loyalty Management UK Ltd* (2010), ruled that HMRC were correct in their analysis. The payments by C to the redeemers (A) were third-party consideration for the original supply of the loyalty awards. They were of a fixed amount for each point redeemed against all or part of the loyalty reward.

When the case then arrived back at the Supreme Court (2013), that Court by a 3:2 majority declined to follow the decision of the CJEU. That Court, it said, had concentrated only on the contract between A and B, which since B made no actual payment to A might suggest third party consideration by C. But if the total contractual nexus was taken into account, C's payments to A were in return for fulfilling its obligation to ensure that A provided goods and services in return for points. It was therefore a cost of C's business and C should be entitled to deduct the VAT paid on them.[48]

Single transaction—multiple or separate supplies

What is the position when in return for a single consideration **25–53** a person receives several benefits? Are these separate supplies, (so that some might be exempt or taxed at different rates) or can they be taken together to form a single supply? If the answer is the latter then a second question is whether that supply is one of goods or one of services or exempt, or zero-rated, etc.

PRINCIPAL/ANCILLARY TEST The situation was initially **25–54** clarified by the ECJ in *Card Protection Plan Ltd v CEC* (1999). It is necessary to identify the essential features of the

---

[46] Following the ECJ's decision in *Auto Lease Holland BV v Bundesamt für Finanzen* (2005).

[47] Applying the analysis in *CEC v Redrow Group Plc* (1999) HL. See Geoffrey Morse, "HMRC v Total UK Ltd and Loyalty Management UK Ltd v HMRC: The Price of Customer Loyalty – Voucher Schemes and Fiscal Neutrality Revisited" [2008] B.T.R. 17 and Ch.27 below.

[48] See [2013] B.T.R. 387.

transaction. In particular there will be a single supply if one or more elements can be regarded as the principal supply and others can be regarded as ancillary. "Ancillary" in the context of services means that it does not constitute an aim in itself but only a means for customers of better enjoying the principal service supplied. Itemising the different services in price terms might be significant, but is not conclusive.

That principal/ancillary test, i.e.: (a) is one part of a supply of services really ancillary to another part; and (b) ancillary for that purpose meaning that it does not constitute an aim in itself but is only a means of better enjoying the principal service supplied, was adopted in relation to supplies of services by the courts on several subsequent occasions. The House of Lords itself, having originally referred the matter to the ECJ, had to apply that court's test to the facts of *Card Protection* itself. That company insured credit card holders against loss but also kept a register of the cards and notified the credit companies if they were lost or stolen. The House of Lords ruled that it was important to determine the essential element of the supply, which in that case was the insurance. The other elements were mainly administrative and so ancillary to that element. Their Lordships stressed that the question should be answered from an economic point of view and courts should refrain from making overzealous or artificial divisions.[49]

25–55   THE ARTIFICIAL TO SPLIT TEST In two subsequent cases, however, the House of Lords extended the test from that originally derived from the *Card Protection* case. The principal/ancillary test was said to be only appropriate to certain cases.[50] There were many cases where although one aspect of the supply was in no way ancillary to the other, there would still a single supply. Referring back to the ECJ *Card Protection* decision, their Lordships applied a second, now predominant test, which might be called the "artificial to split test". The ECJ in *Card Protection* had emphasised that the normal rule was that every supply was to be regarded as a separate and distinct supply but that supplies which objectively from the view-point of a typical customer constituted a single service from an economic point

---

[49] See also *CEC v BT Plc* (1999) in relation to a delivery charge on the purchase of a new car; *Pilgrims Language Course Ltd v CEC* (1999), accommodation on residential educational courses; *Peugeot Motor Co Plc v CEC* (2003), free car insurance on a new car.

[50] See also *Kimberley-Clark Ltd v CEC* (2004) as to the application of the test to a composite supply of goods rather than goods and services and the need to distinguish between the supply to the retailer and then to the customer.

of view should not be artificially split, as that would distort the system of VAT. It follows that predominance plays no part in such a test—see *American Express Services Europe Ltd v HMRC* (2010).

Applying that test, their Lordships held in *Dr Beynon and Partners v CEC* (2005) that although diagnosing and then prescribing medicines were in no way ancillary to their administration, the whole was from an economic point of view a single supply of medical services. Similarly it was held in *College of Estate Management v CEC* (2005) that although course materials provided in a distance-learning package (amounting to 94 per cent of the costs) could not be said to be ancillary to the teaching element, there was, from an economic point of view, a single supply of educational services and not a separate supply of the materials. To achieve these results, their Lordships said that the analysis should seek to achieve "a level of generality, consistent with economic and social reality." In both cases they overruled the Court of Appeal who had instead asked whether from the purchaser's point of view each supply was capable of being a separate independent supply.[51]

Applying this test is a matter of law. In *Weight Watchers (UK) Ltd v HMRC* (2008), the judge upheld the decision of the VAT Tribunal that at the initial meeting of Weight Watchers a client was given separate supplies of literature and weight reducing services, but reversed their decision that the same applied to subsequent meetings attended by the client. On the artificial to split test that was a single supply of weight reducing services. The Court of Appeal agreed with him on subsequent meetings, but reversed him on the initial meeting point.[52] Whether or not the supplies are invoiced separately or jointly is not conclusive, but it is a factor to be considered.[53]

EFFECT OF FISCAL NEUTRALITY What is the position if **25–56** by treating two supplies as part of a complex single supply one of those supplies thereby loses its exempt, reduced-rate

---

[51] See Geoffrey Morse, "Separate or Composite Supplies for VAT – Assessing the Level of Generality: Dr Beynon and Partners v Customs & Excise Commissioners" [2005] B.T.R. 190; Morse, "Identifying supplies. Further Reflections on Third Party and Multiple Supplies: Debenhams Retail plc v CEC and College of Estate Management v CEC" [2006] B.T.R. 54.

[52] The Court of Appeal applied a similar analysis to a scheme which provided food packs and advice for those wishing to lose weight—it was a single economic supply of weight reducing services: *HMRC v David Baxendale Ltd* (2009).

[53] See, e.g. *Purple Parking Ltd v HMRC* (2012) CJEU and *Honourable Society of Middle Temple v HMRC* (2013).

or zero-rated status and becomes part of a single standard-rated supply? Does this offend the principle of fiscal neutrality on the basis that if they were supplied separately different tax consequences would apply? The issue was raised before the CJEU in *Purple Parking Ltd v HMRC* (2012). The Court decided that the provision of airport parking and a shuttle bus to the terminal was a single supply of which the parking was the predominant element (and so standard rated) so that the transport element lost its zero-rated status. It then considered that whether this infringed the principle of fiscal neutrality, given the difference if the two were supplied separately, was a matter for the national court. But a complex supply of services consisting of several elements was not automatically similar for that purpose to the supply of those elements separately. In *The Honourable Society of Middle Temple v HMRC* (2013), the Upper Tribunal stated that the neutrality principle did not require a service to have the same VAT liability when it was supplied separately and when it was part of a complex single supply.

25–57   PROVISION OF A RANGE OF SERVICES   The test has also been applied where the customer pays for the right to a number of services, e.g. to the use of various leisure facilities provided by the supplier. Where there is no specific allocation of each service, it is not possible to itemise the supply by reference to subsequent use by the customer. There is a single supply at the time of the contract of the right to use the various services. This was the decision of the Court of Session in *Highland Council v HMRC* (2008). It is different if the supply is of the right to a single service (at say a reduction), as in *British Railways Board v CEC* (1977).

25–58   CATEGORISING THE SINGLE SUPPLY   If the decision is that there is a single composite supply, it is of course necessary to categorise that supply for the purposes of applying VAT to it (e.g. is it an exempt or zero-rated supply). This will be done by identifying, in the economic and reality context set out above, the predominant elements of the supply.[54]

25–59   TWO SUPPLIERS   The Court of Appeal, in *Telewest Communications Plc v CEC* (2005) held that there can be no single supply if the two supplies are actually made by separate

---

[54] *Levob Verzekeringen BV v Staatssecrataris van Financiën* (2006) ECJ; *Byrom v HMRC* (2006).

suppliers—fiscal neutrality should not be confused with economic reality.

LIMITATIONS ON EFFECT OF FINDING A SINGLE COMPOSITE **25–60** SUPPLY In *Talacre Beach Caravan Sales Ltd v CEC* (2006), a question arose as to what the position would be if a composite supply consisting of elements A (caravan) and B (certain fittings) was found to be a single supply, with supply A being the predominant supply, if that supply was within a zero-rated category, but B was expressly excluded from that category by the legislation. Could the single supply categorisation take B into the zero-rated category and so in effect override the legislation. The ECJ was clear that it could not and that the same would also apply to the categories of exempt supply.[55] That result was then confused following the decision of the CJEU in *European Commission v France* (2010) that a Member State, in choosing to exercise its right under the Directive to apply (or carve out) a reduced rate to a particular category of supply which was part of a composite supply, had complied with its Treaty obligations and the *Card Protection* principle could not be used to compel differently. In that case the reduced rate had been applied to the transportation of bodies by vehicle whist all other funeral services were standard rated.

It was then argued in two subsequent UK cases that, following that decision, HMRC could not use the *Card Protection* principle to deny a reduced rate on part of a single complex supply which would have been subject to that rate if taxed separately. In *Wm Morrison Supermarkets Ltd v HMRC* (2013), the issue concerned the supply of charcoal as part of a disposable barbecue. In *Colaingrove Ltd v HMRC* (2015) it was the supply of electricity as part of serviced holiday accommodation. In both cases there was a single composite standard-rated supply (of a barbecue or holiday accommodation) by applying the *Card Protection* test. In neither case had the UK legislation on reduced-rate supplies sought to "carve out" the charcoal or electricity from a composite supply as in the French case. The intention was that if the composite supply had been predominantly one of charcoal or electricity, the reduced rate would have been applied. In other words the categories of reduced-rate supplies were subject to the *Card Protection* principle, not the other way around.

---

[55] See [2007] B.T.R.17 as to the possible consequences of this decision, and *Hartwell v CEC* (2003).

Where there are two supplies to different customers but only one payment of consideration by one customer

25–61   This problem arises because just as in income tax, and for similar reasons, VAT has a rule that where a business makes a supply of business assets otherwise than for a consideration then there is a deemed supply at the cost to the supplier (Sch.4 para.5).[56] In *CEC v Telemed Ltd* (1992), Telemed produced medical videos which it distributed free to doctors. The videos contained advertisements for drug companies for which it charged a fee. It was argued that the company was therefore making two supplies, one of the services to the drug companies for a fee and one of the videos to the doctors which were caught by para.5. This was rejected by the judge on the basis that the company only supplied the videos as part of its contractual obligation to the advertisers. This approach was followed by the House of Lords in *CEC v Professional Footballers Association* (1993) in deciding that trophies presented at an annual dinner and met out of the cost of tickets for the dinner were not separate supplies under para.5. There was a direct link between the consideration paid for the tickets and the awards.

Taxable supplies and exempt supplies

25–62   All supplies (even zero-rated ones) within the scope of the tax are taxable supplies unless they are exempt supplies (VAT Act s.4(2)). A supply is exempt if, and only if, it is one of the kinds of supply listed in Sch.9 to the VAT Act. This copies into the UK law directly operative provisions of EU law. Exemption covers some major kinds of economic activity such as financial supplies and many kinds of health, education and welfare activity. We will examine some of these in the next chapter.

In the UK

25–63   The Directive contains a number of provisions to establish where a supply of goods (arts 31–42) and services (arts 43–61) takes place. These raise many complex issues which are outside the scope of this book. The basic rules are that a supply of goods takes place where the goods are located at the time of the supply or where they are located prior to dispatch to the customer.

---

[56] Such as gifts given by petrol companies to customers who have collected vouchers: *Kuwait Petroleum GB Ltd v CEC* (1999). Whether there has been a supply for no consideration requires an analysis of what the parties thought they were agreeing to. See *Kuwait Petroleum GB Ltd v CEC* (2001) and *Peugeot Motor Company Ltd v CEC* (2003). If there is such a supply, output tax is payable on it irrespective of the trader's other supplies: *Scottish Football League v HMRC* (2013).

For services it is the place where the supplier has his business or establishment or, failing that, his usual residential address. There are many special rules, however.

Taxable persons

The structure of European VAT is such that anyone **25–64** independently (i.e. not as an employee) making a taxable supply for consideration can be regarded as a taxable person. UK VAT does not work this way. Instead, it sets a threshold of activity before the imposition is necessary. Any person, including a company[57] and an LLP, whose level of activities is at or above the level of the threshold is required to register with the VAT office for the locality, and to impose VAT on all taxable supplies made. If there is a failure to register, VAT will be deemed to have been charged by the taxpayer. Those not required to register may, however do so on a voluntary basis. A person who has the intention, confirmed by objective evidence, to commence independently an economic activity and who has incurred the first investment expenditure for that purpose is a taxable person and so able to claim input tax even without a formal registration.[58]

CHARITIES, PUBLIC BODIES For VAT purposes, a *person* **25–65** is any individual or any body of persons with separate legal personality (such as a company or limited liability partnership) that is engaged in economic activities. This includes non-profit organisations that do not pay income tax or corporation tax such as charities and clubs as well as companies. Article 13 of the Directive provides that national and local government bodies, and others "governed by public law" are taxable persons for a limited number of purposes and where their treatment as non-taxable persons would lead to a significant distortion of competition.[59] But otherwise they are not to be taxable persons "in respect of the activities in which they engage as public authorities" and, even better, in respect of certain exempt supplies they are better off if they are so regarded. There are often difficult questions as to whether a body is so operating as a public authority and the courts are wary of laying down binding rules.[60] In some cases, the exemptions apply to

---

[57] Where a company is a taxable person, the individual who is the sole shareholder, employee and manager is not a taxable person under the Directive: *Van der Steen v Inspecteur van de Belastingdienst* (2008).

[58] *Finanzamt Goslar v Breitsohl* (2001).

[59] See, e.g. *Isle of Wight Council v HMRC* (2015).

[60] See, e.g. *Edinburgh Telford College v HMRC* (2006) CS (IH) and cases discussed there.

organisations with similar objects to a public authority. In *HMRC v Open University* (2016), an exemption for educational services was held by the Court of Appeal to apply to the BBC on that basis, even though it was not as such a public body for VAT purposes. Thus its supplies to the Open University were exempt.

25–66   PARTNERSHIPS A partnership despite its lack of legal personality in England, Wales and Northern Ireland, is also treated as a separate person (unlike the income tax approach). A partnership is therefore separate from the individual partners and is registered as the taxable person. The liability for VAT remains a partnership debt, however, so that all partners remain liable, even if they have ceased to be partners, until HMRC has either been informed of the change or the partnership has been de-registered.[61] But that does not apply to someone who has never been a partner, even if held out as such.[62] An individual partner may have a separate registration for other business activities, including making supplies to the firm.[63]

25–67   GROUPS, ETC. Companies and other large organisations can register divisions or separate parts of the organisation separately. For example, if only part of an organisation is making supplies to which VAT applies, that part can register separately from any other part. This excludes those other parts from the requirements of VAT, but it also means that any supplies made by that part of the organisation to the other parts are subject to VAT.

By contrast, a group of companies can make a common registration for VAT in the name of one of the companies. Where this happens, supplies between companies within the group are outside the scope of the tax. It is only supplies by the group to others that are caught. For this purpose, two companies are in a group if both are based in the UK and one controls the other or both are controlled by the same third person (VAT Act s.43A).[64] Each of the companies must be involved in an economic activity, so that a company that is purely a holding company has to be left out (*Polysar Investments* (1993)).

---

[61] *CEC v Jamieson* (2002).
[62] *HMRC v Pal* (2008).
[63] *Staatssecretaris van Financiën v Heerma* (2001).
[64] Group registration, once obtained, is only lost where either the company or HMRC takes formal steps: *CEC v Barclays Bank Plc* (2001).

REGISTRATION THRESHOLDS A person (in the sense just **25–68** described) is required to register for VAT if the total turnover from taxable supplies in any period of 12 months is currently £83,000 or more or if there are reasonable grounds to believe that the rates of taxable supplies in the next 30 days will exceed £83,000. (These are the 2016 figures—they are adjusted every year.) Any exempt supplies or supplies outside the scope of VAT are excluded from the total. The total is calculated on the assumption that no VAT is charged on the supplies. Note that the amount is for turnover, not profit. It is irrelevant that the person is making a loss, or is not in business to make a profit. It also applies to persons, not to businesses. If I run two businesses, one as a farmer, and one as a sports journalist, I must account for total turnover from both my activities even though they may be treated separately for income tax purposes. The test is applied each month on a rolling basis. However, if the person can show that supplies for the current year are below £81,000 (in 2015), then the requirement to register does not apply. There is some scope for abuse of this provision by dividing turnover between different legal persons to ensure each is below the limit. Where that happens, the VAT office has the right to impose a group registration to bring all the associated avoiders into the tax net.

VOLUNTARY REGISTRATION A person not required to register **25–69** under any of these provisions has the right to register on a voluntary basis. Why should anyone want to become a taxpayer voluntarily? In the case of a tax like income tax, there are few, if any, good reasons. VAT is not a tax like income tax. As we shall see later, a VAT payer may actually receive money from the government, rather than pay it. Few businesses can resist a government handout.

A further reason is that those who are registered for VAT usually prefer to buy from others who are registered—it is cheaper. Someone who expects to have to register a business in any event may find it advantageous to register before being compelled to do so. Not all traders that could ask for voluntary registration do so. Some refrain from registering in order to avoid VAT. The irony is that they end up paying more VAT by doing so. We see why in the next chapters.

Economic activities

The final element in the structure of VAT is that activities **25–70** are only relevant if they are economic activities of the taxable person (in art.9 of the Directive) or, in the UK text, *in the course* *or furtherance of a business carried on by him.* In this phrase, business is defined as including any trade profession or vocation (s.94). In practice, although the UK legislation has continued to use the reference to business, it is more accurate to think of the more general, and broader, European phrase. In part, this is because it is clear that VAT is wider than the implicit reference in s.94 to the income taxation of trading etc. income might imply.

25–71   BUSINESS   The early cases, using the UK text, concentrated on the meaning of a "business". Thus in *CEC v Royal Exchange Theatre Trust* (1979) the raising of money by a charitable trust to convert the Manchester Corn Exchange into a theatre and the subsequent gift of the theatre was held not to be a business. Similarly a charity that supplied goods to beneficiaries without payment, or for a token fee, was not acting as a business: *Whitechapel Art Gallery v CEC* (1986), where the running of an art gallery to which free admission was granted was accepted as outside the scope of VAT. An interesting example of a marginal case is the decision in *Lord Fisher v CEC* (1981), which established that shooting (and equally hunting and fishing) one's own land with one's own friends contributing to one's costs is not always a business.

25–72   ECONOMIC ACTIVITY   Modern cases are now argued on the basis of the "economic activities" test in the Directive. The House of Lords in *ICAEW v CEC* (1999) had to decide whether the regulatory services provide by the Institute of Chartered Accountants on behalf of the government in respect of insolvency practitioners, licensed auditors, etc. fell within VAT. After reviewing the decisions of the ECJ, they held that the Institute was not carrying on an economic activity. It was not enough that it was making supplies for a consideration, there was no element of commercial activity. What was needed were activities of an economic nature.[65]

25–73   EXPLOITATION OF PROPERTY   The Directive includes the exploitation of property within the definition of an economic activity. The ECJ has stated that exploitation in that context refers to all transactions by which it is sought to obtain income from the property on a continuing basis. On the other hand it held that the activity by governments of allocating frequencies and then licences for mobile phone operators was not such an

---

[65] See also *University of Southampton v HMRC* (2006), as to publicly funded research undertaken by the university.

activity. It was a precondition to the carrying on of an economic activity by the telephone companies.[66]

OBJECTIVE CONCEPT   The ECJ in *Optigen Ltd v CEC* (2006)   **25–74** made it clear that whether an activity is an economic activity has to be decided on purely objective grounds. The motive of the person making it is irrelevant. Thus a transaction which is not itself in any way fraudulent and fulfils the objective criteria of commerciality, is an economic activity even though it forms part of an overall fraudulent or tax avoidance scheme. Further, if the trade is lawful, there is an economic activity irrespective of whether any trader is acting fraudulently or not: see *R. v Hashash* (2008), applying decisions of the ECJ.

This objective approach was confirmed in *Rēdlihs v Valsts ieņēmumu dienests* (2013). Mr Redlihs purchased a forest in Latvia and then supplied the timber on many occasions in order to repair storm damage. The CJEU held that the question as to whether he was carrying on an economic activity was objective and was not affected by the purpose or results of that activity. The sale of timber was exploitation of that property. He had taken steps similar to those deployed by a trader in forest management.

SERVICES   Article 9 of the Directive states that an economic   **25–75** activity includes all activities of producers, traders or persons supplying services, and in particular the exploitation of tangible or intangible property for the purpose of obtaining income therefrom on a continuing basis. This has been widely defined but it does not include the mere acquisition, holding and transfer of shares in a company. A private shareholder as such is not a taxable person. This also applies to any purely financial holding in any undertaking.[67] More recently it has been held to exclude the entry of a partner into a partnership in return for a payment of capital.[68]

ACTING AS SUCH   The tax applies to economic activities of   **25–76** taxable persons *acting as such*. An individual buying a house to live in, or buying a car for private use, is not engaging in an

---

[66] *T-Mobile Austria GmbH v Republic of Austria* (2008); *Hutchinson 3G UK Ltd v HMRC* (2008). In both cases the Advocate General came to the opposite, and it would seem more logical, conclusion that this was the exploitation of intangible property.

[67] See *Harnas & Helm CV v Staatssecretaris van Financiën* (1997) ECJ; *Wellcome Trust Ltd v CEC* (1996) ECJ.

[68] *KapHagRenditefonds 35 Spreecenter Berlin-Hellersdorf 3. Tranche GbR v Finanzamt Charlottenburg* (2005) ECJ.

economic activity but a private activity. This is true also when the house or car is sold. There is a complication here to which we must return. If a private person sells a car, there is no VAT on the sale. If a car dealer sells it, there is VAT. The same thing applies to antiques, and to horses and ponies. Whether VAT applies therefore partly depends on the identity of the seller, not the kind of goods. This can cause problems, and special rules apply to these occasional or second-hand goods.

Agents and employees

Employees

25–77   VAT only applies to a person carrying on an economic activity or business. The most important group of people excluded from VAT by this rule are employees. An employee is carrying on the employer's business as agent, and is not in business by himself or herself. VAT therefore does not apply to the payment of earnings by employer to employee. If the employee's services are supplied to some third party, any VAT is applied to the charge made by the employer to the third party for those services. The effect of this important exclusion is that the added value on which someone is charged includes the total of all payments to employees.

The rule applies to office holders such as company directors as well, unless the office holder is holding that office as part of a separate business. For example, a partner in a firm of solicitors may act as a director of a client's business in order to advise the client. Fees paid to the director, or the partnership, should be subject to VAT (s.94(4)).

Commercial agents

25–78   The position is more complex for other agents. By definition, an agent is someone making supplies on behalf of someone else. If the person is an agent rather than an independent contractor, the supply is not made by the agent but by the agent's principal. It is therefore important to decide whether a person is making a supply on their own behalf or on behalf of a principal. This is mainly because of the registration threshold. If the supplies are made as agents then they will be counted towards the principal's total (who may well be registered for VAT anyway)—so VAT would be chargeable and accounted for by the principal. But taken individually, the suppliers, if acting as independent contractors, may well not reach the registration threshold and so no VAT would be chargeable. The latest, colourful, case on this involved dancers in a lap-dance club. They were held to be independent contractors and not agents for the club, which was

472

not therefore liable to account for VAT in respect of their charges to the clients.[69]

UNDISCLOSED AGENCY There is a complication where the **25–79** identity of the principal is unknown to the buyer. Take the case of an auctioneer. The auctioned goods are not owned by the auctioneer, but the buyer usually does not know the identity of the seller. The buyer of, say, antique furniture has therefore no way of knowing if the seller is a registered person for VAT purposes, or whether the sale is an economic activity within the scope of VAT. At the same time, the only activity on which an auctioneer is liable for VAT as an agent is the service as an agent. To avoid complications, auctioneers and other agents where the agency is not disclosed are treated as making the supplies themselves. If the agency is disclosed, the VAT is imposed by the principal.

---

[69] *Spearmint Rhino Ventures (UK) Ltd v CRC* (2007).

CHAPTER 26

VAT RATES AND EXEMPTIONS

Introduction

26–01   If the British VAT were a simple form of value-added tax with a single rate, the previous chapter would have covered most of the problems. It is not, and it does not. In this chapter therefore we discuss the rate structure of the tax and the extensive way in which exemptions apply to the tax. In the next chapter we discuss the surprisingly complex problem as to how the value of a taxable supply is found and the rules as to the payment of the tax, including how input tax is deducted.

The VAT rate structure

26–02   The simplest form of VAT would have one rate of VAT applying equally to all supplies of goods and services. But the UK structure is far more complex.

The structure under the Directive

26–03   The Directive, in art.97, requires every member state to have a standard rate of VAT of not less than 15 per cent. In addition, arts 98 and 99 allow for the use of reduced rate bands of VAT, of not less than 5 per cent, on certain specified supplies (listed in Annex III to the Directive). There are also special provisions (e.g. for supplies of gas and electricity) and a considerable number of "temporary" variations, often specific to a particular member state. One of these allows the UK to maintain its anomalous zero-rated list of supplies.[1] The Directive (in Title IX) also lists those supplies which are exempt from the tax altogether and so cannot amount to taxable supplies. That list is currently mandatory.

The structure in the UK

26–04   The UK rate structure for taxable supplies is as follows:

    1) a standard rate of 20 per cent;

---

[1] These are described in the Directive (art.110) as supplies with deductibility of the VAT paid at the preceding stage.

2) a reduced rate of 5 per cent on certain specified types of supply;
3) zero-rate (0 per cent) on another group of specified supplies;
4) special rates for special regimes such as the 4 per cent flat rate scheme for farmers;
5) a general flat rate scheme for small businesses.

There are also the categories of exempt supply as required by the Directive. By definition, they are not taxable supplies.

ZERO-RATING AS A SUBSIDY As a result, the UK has one of **26–05** the most complex rate structures for VAT in the developed world. The structure, gives scope for many disputes and distortions to competition. The UK is the only major system to use its VAT through the use of zero rating, as a subsidy for certain kinds of domestic activity. Why? The zero-rates reflect the exemptions that used to apply to taxes before VAT. However, the zero-rate in VAT is not the same thing as a zero sales tax. It is in reality a subsidy resulting in regular repayments of tax to those who sell zero-rated goods because since they are still making taxable supplies, they will have no output tax (zero-rated) but will be able to reclaim their input tax. They are known as repayment traders.

Add to that the predictable consumers' resistance to a rate increase, the pressure to retain the regular tax rebate paid to those who are zero-rated, and we see why the lobby for the status quo is a strong one. This was manifested most recently in the reaction to the proposals in Budget 2012 to take all takeaway hot pies and pasties out of the zero-rating umbrella (see para.26–13 below). This all makes the British VAT one of the most inefficient around. We saw a similar situation in the reduced rate of VAT on domestic fuel supplies. The debate over the attempt to increase the VAT on domestic fuel to the standard rate from a zero-rate resulted in a government defeat in the Commons and the original compromise of 8 per cent has since been reduced to 5 per cent. Further the opposition to applying any payable rate of VAT to women's sanitary products in Budget 2016 debate lead to a relaxation by the EU as to rigid application of the rate structure. It is precisely because of all this that we must spend some time looking at the rate structure.

APPLYING THE RATES There is a strict order for determining **26–06** at what rate, if any, VAT applies to a supply:

1) Exclude any supply that is outside the scope of the tax, or deemed not to be a supply of goods or services. If it is not excluded:
2) See if the supply is exempt. If it is not exempt:
3) See if the supply is one of those listed as zero-rated. If it is not listed:
4) See if any special tax regime or reduced rate applies. If it does not:
5) Apply the standard rate.

The order is important because it means that anything to which a special category does not apply is to be taxed at the standard rate, without exception. The flat rate scheme for small business does not effect the actual rate applied to the supply, it relates, rather to the accountability of the supplier to HMRC. We must therefore now explore zero-rating, the reduced rate categories, exempt supplies, the special regimes and the flat rate scheme.

Zero-rated supplies

26–07 A supply is zero-rated if it is listed in Sch.8 to the VAT Act. The Schedule is divided into (currently) 18 groups,[2] several of which are of considerable complexity.

The policy of zero-rating

26–08 Two themes run through the Schedule. The first is of international supplies: see Group 7 (international services), Group 8 (transport), Group 10 (gold) and Group 13 (imports, exports, etc.), Group 17 (emissions trading) and Group 18 (European research) for the main relevant groups. The policy here is to ensure that no British VAT gets hidden in the cost of any goods or services offered on the international market. Any VAT imposed on a supply or its inputs in the UK before export is therefore rebated in full, and no VAT is applied on export. The purpose is to keep British goods and services as competitive as possible.

A second theme is that of supplies of a social or community nature. These include: Group 1 (food), Group 2 (domestic sewerage and water supplies), Group 3 (books), Group 4 (talking books for the blind), Group 5 (construction of homes and some other buildings), Group 6 (listed buildings), Group 8 (transport), Group 9 (houseboats and caravans used as homes), Group 11 (bank notes) is somewhat anomalous, Group 12 (medicines), Group 15 (charities), Group 16 (children's clothes and protective clothing) and Group 19 (women's sanitary products).

---

[2] Confusingly numbered 1–19. Group 14 was repealed in 1999.

THE UK'S FREEDOM OF ACTION The European Commission **26–09** has always been opposed to this concept on the basis that it distorts the application of the tax. But the concept was sanctioned by the ECJ in *EC Commission v United Kingdom* (1988) and is allowed as a "temporary measure" in art.110 of the Directive. It is referred to there (not entirely accurately) as supplies with refund of tax paid at the preceding stage. An attack based on the concept of direct effect failed before the Court of Appeal in *Marks and Spencer Plc v CEC* (2000).

The current status at that time of zero-rating was initially discussed by the ECJ in *Talacre Beach Caravan Sales Ltd v CEC* (2006). The ECJ pointed out that it was a derogation from the obligation to charge the standard rate and that, as such, must not only be strictly construed (as are the categories of exempt supply) but is also subject to a number of conditions. These are principally that the categories must have been in force on 1 January 1991, and that they can only be allowed for clearly defined social reasons, for the benefit of the final consumer[3] and in accordance with Community Law. Thus the current list of zero-rated supplies was thought to be finite and could only be reduced by the UK parliament. It follows that any "anomalies" could only be rectified by taking some supplies out of zero-rating rather than by adding new ones. In the *Talacre* case itself, the ECJ held that the composite supply principle could not be used to zero-rate a supply which was expressly excluded by the Act.[4] This rigidity was, however, relaxed by a Conclusion of the European Council in March 2016, following a clear political impetus in the UK to change women's sanitary products from a reduced rate to a zero-rated supply. That change was included in the Finance Bill 2016.

In *Marks & Spencer Plc v HMRC* (2008), the ECJ held that although zero-rating conferred no Community rights, the consequences of the misinterpretation of the national law were subject to the principle of equal treatment. Initially it was held in *HMRC v EB Central Services Ltd* (2008) that the wording of Sch.8 was to be interpreted using national law provisions rather than in line with the Directive, since it was a derogation from the Directive. But the Court of Appeal in *Sub One Ltd v HMRC* (2014), reversing an earlier decision of that Court, applied Community law in opting for an objective rather than a subjective meaning

---

[3] This means a non-business consumer. Thus, e.g. water supplies to industry (Group 2) are not zero-rated.
[4] See para.26–59 above.

to a particular provision. They did this by referring to the EU Treaty itself which required member states to respect the primacy of EU law.

One result of the attractiveness to suppliers of zero-rating is that Sch.8 is now of considerable complexity. Each group contains a detailed list of what exactly amounts to a zero-rated supply. In Budget 2012, HMRC announced that they were intending to end some of the anomalies that have resulted from this complexity. These proposed changes, which are intended to reduce the number of zero-rated supplies were subjected to a consultation,[5] and in two cases (takeaway hot pies and pasties and caravans) provoked a public outcry. As a result, the proposals were modified. The original proposal, to tax static holiday caravans at the standard rate, was modified to a proposal to tax them at the reduced rate (5 per cent) as from April 2013. For takeaway hot pies, see para.26–13 below.

Food

26–10   Group 1, which is headed "Food", is very complex. This applies to any supply within four categories of which the most important is food of a kind used for human consumption. But that general class is subject to no less than seven lists of excepted items, which are therefore standard rated, unless they fall within a further seven lists of items overriding those excepted items, in which case they become zero-rated again.

The detailed nature of this structure throws up many unusual cases. Thus, for example, animal foodstuffs are generally zero-rated as one of the four categories but pet foods are an excepted, and so standard rated, item. Apparently rabbit food is zero-rated but ferret food is not, ferrets but not rabbits being generally kept as pets.[6] Beverages such as syrups and concentrates are excepted items but teas are items which override that exception. Iced tea concentrate is regarded as a tea for this purpose even though a large amount of sugar is added—it is not a "soft drink".[7] There are very many other cases of this nature, which occupy the First-tier Tribunal.

Most of these seemingly endless cases which will still arise are very fact specific and require a value judgement as to whether a particular item is or is not within: (a) a general category; (b) an

---

[5]   VAT: *Addressing Borderline Anomalies*: HMRC Consultation Document (21 March 2012).
[6]   See *Supreme Petfoods Ltd v HMRC* (2011) FTT.
[7]   See *Thorncroft Ltd v HMRC* (2011) FTT.

excepted item; or (c) an item overriding an exception. Sometimes this involves questions as to whether something is similar to something. In *Proctor & Gamble UK v HMRC* (2009), the Court of Appeal was clear that all such questions should be resolved at the First-tier Tribunal level and that appeals should only be allowed if there was an obvious error by the tribunal. It seems that is not always difficult, however, to allege such an error and to reach the Upper Tribunal.[8]

BISCUITS, CRISPS AND CAKES, ETC. The intention is, we **26-11** assume, to charge non-basic foodstuffs but to zero-rate the essentials of life. Thus zero-rating does not apply for example to confectionery but it does apply to cakes and biscuits "other than biscuits wholly or partly covered with chocolate or some product similar in taste and appearance". This means that, for reasons which are not entirely clear, chocolate cakes are zero-rated but chocolate biscuits are standard-rated. That in turn leads to disputes as to whether a particular product is a cake or a biscuit or neither.[9]

Crisps are equally regarded as not being worthy of zero rating. This embargo also includes "similar products made from the potato". In *Proctor & Gamble UK v HMRC* (2009), the issue was as to whether basic Pringles were such. The issue reached the Court of Appeal (the amount at stake was estimated at over £100million) who said that the two issues of "made from potato" and "similarity" were to be taken together. Since such Pringles contained 42 per cent potato, that was sufficient for a finding that they were made from potato and similar to crisps, even though crisps have some 80 per cent potato content.[10]

CATERING There is also a general exception to zero-rating **26-12** for a supply "in the course of catering". That in turn is defined as including a supply of food for consumption on the premises on which it is supplied (i.e. food eaten in a restaurant or café)

---

[8] As the *GlaxoSmithKline Services Unlimited v HMRC* (2010) case indicates. The Upper Tribunal duly upheld that decision of the First-Tier Tribunal.

[9] See, e.g. *CEC v Ferrero UK Ltd* (1997) as to the position of wafer products. Other disputes have centred around bagels, dips and jelly products, and even as to the nature of "sweetness" in confectionery. The issue of chocolate tea cakes sparked off the Marks & Spencer Plc litigation.

[10] See [2009] B.T.R. 401. Since then a tribunal, applying a mixed quantative/function test, has held that products containing under 30 per cent potato with considerably more wheat were not made from potato, wheat being the defining ingredient: *United Biscuits (UK) Ltd v HMRC* [2011] UKFTT 673 (TC).

and any supply of *hot* food for consumption off the premises.[11] Because that definition is inclusive only, it follows that even cold food supplied in the course of catering will be standard rated. In *CEC v Safeway Stores Plc* (1997), Keane J regarded the test as to what is in the course of catering as being an objective one. Would an ordinary person regard it as being such a supply. It could include the delivery of food to a house if there was more, such as table service etc. But he stressed that no one factor was conclusive. He held that where customers bought "party trays", which had been pre-ordered, from the delicatessen counter of a supermarket, that was not such a supply since most people would regard the host/hostess and not the supermarket as doing the catering.

That approach was approved by a majority of the Court of Appeal in *HMRC v Compass Contract Services UK Ltd* (2006). In that case, the BBC Television Centre had outsourced the provision of food to its employees and visitors to the taxpayers who sold sandwiches and salads. That was held not to be a supply in the course of catering; nor was it on the premises, even though there were chairs etc. provided by the BBC close by. Apart from the contract with the employer, there was no difference between this and a high street sandwich shop.[12] Why should a contract with an employer affect the liability of the customer to pay VAT?

26–13   RECTIFYING ANOMALIES RE SUPPLIES IN THE COURSE OF CATERING   In March 2012, HMRC announced two significant proposed changes to the definition of when food will be supplied in the course of catering.[13] First new Note 3A provides that premises for this purpose includes "any area set aside for the consumption of food by the supplier's customers, whether or not the area may also be used by the customers of other suppliers". This is intended to cover such things as motorway service and food court areas as well as tables and chairs outside cafes. It may well also reverse the decision in *Compass* as there is now no longer any need for common ownership of the outlet and place of consumption.

Secondly, the draft of Note 3B originally provided that hot food in this context, means food or any part of which, is "above the ambient air temperature at the time it is *provided* to the

---

[11] Whether it is on or off the premises is a question of fact: *HMRC v Compass Contract Services UK Ltd* (2006).

[12] See, e.g. *R v CEC Ex p. Sims* (1988).

[13] See VAT (Zero-rating and Exemptions) Order 2012 and the Treasury letter of 28 May 2012 to the Chair of the Treasury Select Committee.

customer, other than freshly baked bread". Until then, the test was whether the items were to be *consumed* at above the ambient air temperature. The change would have nullified a number of decisions, notably in *John Pimblett and Sons Ltd v CEC* (1988), to the effect that the issue as to whether it was intended to provide fresh food or hot food was to be decided subjectively. Additionally, supermarket-roasted chickens, for example were thus now standard rated.

In response to a public outcry over this so-called "pasty tax", the government changed its mind. Instead, standard-rate VAT is now applied to food that is kept hot (supermarket chickens), heated to order or marketed as hot, but not to food (pasties etc.) left to cool naturally.

So the basic test remained as to whether the food has been heated for the purposes of enabling it to be *consumed* hot rather than whether it has been *provided* hot. But the sting was taken out of that retreat, when the Court of Appeal, in *Sub One Ltd v HMRC* (2014), reversing the earlier decision of that Court in *Pimblett*, decided that that test should be applied objectively. It was not a question as to the subjective intention of the trader but what the assumed common intention of the supplier and customer was. Was it a term of the bargain between them that the product be supplied in order to be eaten hot? The subjective approach had led to a substantial number of First-tier tribunal cases which seemed to be similar in outcome to the toss of a coin.

RELEVANT FACTORS—SUPPLIES OF COLD FOOD OFF THE **26–14** PREMISES There may still be supplies of cold food off the premises which may nevertheless be supplies in the course of catering. The CJEU has heard a number of combined cases[14] on a reference from Germany, which applies a reduced rate to some supplies of food. The issue, interpreting the German code, was whether certain composite supplies of take away food from street kiosks were predominantly supplies of *catering* (i.e. of services) or predominantly supplies of *food* (i.e. of goods). Since UK law applies a different test of a supply *of food in the course of catering* the First-tier Tribunal in *Value Catering Ltd v HMRC* (2011) considered that those cases were of little relevance to us. A supply in the course of catering is not a supply of catering as such. The significance for Germany was that certain supplies of hot food would be subject to the reduced rate. In the UK, all supplies of hot food are deemed to be in the course of catering. HMRC accordingly indicated that

---

[14] *Finanzampt Burgdorf v Manfred Bog* (2011) ECJ.

the decisions had no impact on such supplies in the UK. The question was therefore whether the decisions had any impact on supplies of cold food in the UK. The answer was a qualified no, since the tribunal in *Value Catering* applied some of the tests used by the ECJ as indicia of catering to the UK issue of a supply in the course of catering.

The tribunal in *Value Catering* then came up with a list of nine factors from *Safeway*, *Compass* and *Bog* to be considered when deciding this issue, although none were said to be decisive and the list was not definitive. These were: (i) whether the food was supplied in connection with an occasion or event and the supplier knew of this; (ii) whether the food was made to order or prepared in anticipation of demand; (iii) whether the customer could suggest a menu; (iv) the degree of preparation which remained to be carried out by the customer; (v) whether the food was well presented and could be put on the table with no further steps being taken; (vi) whether crockery and cutlery were provided along with the food itself or available as an optional extra; (vii) whether and how and at what time the food was delivered by the supplier; (viii) whether a waiting service was provided; and (ix) whether the food was a complete meal. The caterers in that case supplied food at shows and events to customers with a stand or pitch at such events. They also sold and hired out equipment. It set up temporary kitchens at the events. After detailed analysis, the tribunal concluded that all were supplies in the course of catering. It was a supply of ready-prepared, ready to serve, ready-to-eat, well-presented food delivered to the stands.

Other groups

26–15   Other groups have also led to litigation. Thus in Group 3 (books, etc.), we have legal definitions as to what amounts to books,[15] booklets and newspapers[16] and in Group 8 (transport) detailed reasons as to why a roller coaster could not be included as being the transport of twelve or more passengers.[17] In general zero-rating for transport only applies to vehicles, ship or aircraft designed or adapted to carry ten or more passengers. In *Cirdan Sailing Trust v CEC* (2006), a boat with nine berths but which could carry 14 passengers was held not to fall within that category. The design, layout and use of the boat all pointed to

---

[15] *Odhams Leisure Group Ltd v CEC* (1992); *CEC v Colour Offset Ltd* (1995). Recent issues have revolved around "photo-books" generated from the internet and digital photography. See *Harrier LLC v HMRC* (2011).

[16] *Geoffrey E Snushall Ltd v CEC* (1982).

[17] *CEC v Blackpool Pleasure Beach Co* (1974).

nine being the correct number to apply in this context. In *Davies v HMRC* (2012), the trader supplied limousines to customers which had originally been designed to carry ten persons but which had been adapted to carry only nine. The Upper Tribunal held that it was the configuration at the time of the supply of services which counted and so the services were standard-rated.

Group 16 (children's clothing) raises difficult questions as to size and style since it excludes those suitable for older persons (over 13). In *H & M Hennes Ltd v CEC* (2005) the distinction was held to be one of age rather than of physical development and then adjudicated on questions of height.

Reduced rate supplies

There are a number of specified supplies which attract a **26–16** reduced rate of VAT, currently 5 per cent which is the minimum allowed by art.98 of the Directive. These can be found in Sch.7A to the VAT Act. Originally designed to avoid the political fall-out from taxing domestic fuel consumption, the current selection can be seen as an eclectic and subjective list, chosen from the list of permitted such supplies in Annex III to the Directive.[18] Unlike zero-rating, reduced rate supplies are common throughout the EU. Member states have the option to apply a reduced rate to all, some, or none of the permitted categories of supply. But as the CJEU pointed out in *European Commission v Luxembourg* (2015) and *European Commission v France* (2015) the wording of each permitted group in the Directive has to be restrictively construed since these categories are exceptions to the general rule of standard-rating taxable supplies. As we saw in Ch.25, in the case of a multiple single supply the *Card Protection* principle overrides a reduced rate supply which is subsumed into the overall supply and is not the main element of it, although a member state may expressly carve out one element of such a supply as a reduced-rated supply if that category is allowed for in the Directive.

As a result of the political climate in the UK prior to the 2016 referendum on UK membership of the EU, the European Council agreed to provide for more flexibility on VAT rates. As a result, the tax on women's sanitary products was changed from a reduced rate to a zero-rate in the Finance Bill 2016. The Government also decided not to amend UK law to comply with a CJEU ruling that solar panels should be taxed at the full rate and not the reduced rate since they did not fit into the categories allowed for in the Directive (see para.25–04 above).

---

[18] There are 18 categories in that list.

The current groups

26–17   There are currently 12 groups of reduced rate supplies.[19] These are: supplies of domestic fuel or power (Group 1), installation of energy-saving materials (Group 2), grant-funded installation of heating equipment or security goods or connection of gas safety (Group 3), women's sanitary products (Group 4), children's car seats (Group 5), residential conversions (Group 6), residential renovations and alterations (Group 7), certain contraceptive products (Group 8), welfare advice or information given by a charity or a state-regulated welfare institution or agency (Group 9), supplying and servicing mobility aids in private dwellings (Group 10), smoking cessation products (Group 11), static caravans (Group 12), and cable suspended passenger transport systems (Group 13). Looking at the Schedule will show you not only how detailed some of these groups are but may also extend your knowledge—see, for example, the concept of a "booster seat" in relation to children's car seats.

Exempt supplies

26–18   A supply is exempt if it is within the terms of one of the groups in Sch.9. The Schedule presents a similar but not identical exercise to Sch.8, and again contains several themes. The chief difference is that behind Sch.9 are detailed provisions in arts 131–166 of the Directive. The details of this Schedule are therefore, like reduced rate supplies decided by direct reference to terms of the Directive as interpreted by the CJEU. Where the UK provision is wider than the Directive it is not open to HMRC to rely on that wider wording than the Directive although, of course, the UK wording will have to be changed.[20] Unlike zero-rating which is limited only by EU law, exemption is entirely a matter of EU law and is mandatory.[21] Therefore, if the UK wording is narrower than the Directive, the wider meaning of the latter will be applied.

One example of this is the decision of the CJEU in *HMRC v Bridport and West Dorset Golf Club* (2014). Under UK law the exemption for supplies concerning taking part in sporting activities (required by the Directive) was limited in the case of golf clubs to members of at least three months' standing, thus excluding green fees paid by non-members. The club duly charged and accounted for VAT on those fees. It now challenged

---

[19] Groups are often added by SI almost annually it seems. See e.g. the VAT (Reduced Rate) Orders 2006 and 2007, SIs 2006/1472 and 2007/1601. Static holiday caravans were added to the list as from April 2013.

[20] See *CEC v Civil Service Motoring Association Ltd* (1998), per Mummery LJ.

[21] See *EC Commission v UK* (1988).

that provision on the basis that there was no justification for it in the Directive. HMRC argued that it was justified by a provision in the Directive which allowed an exception for additional income by carrying out transactions which were in direct competition with those of commercial enterprises. The Upper Tribunal (2012) referred the matter to the CJEU. That court held that the exemption in the Directive was wide enough to cover the supply of a sporting activity by a non-profit making body (the club) whether it was provided to a member or a visitor. Member States could not exclude a group of recipients from the exemption. The derogation in the Directive did not apply to override that.

As a result, HMRC repaid the VAT to the club, but this sparked a series of repayment claims by other golf clubs which we will return to in the next chapter.

STRICT INTERPRETATION Given this need for the UK **26–19** Schedule to comply with the Directive, the UK courts have struggled to decide how they should construe the relevant legislation. It has often been said that, since these are exemptions, the words must be construed strictly. But Chadwick LJ in *Expert Witness Institute v CEC* (2002) said that that did not mean the most restricted or most narrow meaning—strict should not be equated with restricted. The task of the court was to give the exempting words a meaning which they could fairly and properly bear in the context in which they were used. In *CEC v Electronic Data Systems Ltd* (2003), Jonathan Parker LJ, pointed out the inherent tension between this need for a strict construction and the need to adopt the purposive approach to EC legislation in the Directive. His solution was to interpret the exemption in a way which did not have the effect of extending its scope beyond its fair meaning, as ascertained by adopting a purposive approach. The principle of fiscal neutrality between suppliers will not apply if the exemption requires the identity or form of the supplier as a pre-requisite to exemption.[22]

Types of supply

One group of exemptions deals with supplies where it has **26–20** proved extremely difficult to apply VAT. The main group of this kind is Group 5 (financial services), and linked with it is Group 2 (insurance). The chief problem is isolating the value added in a financial supply such as a loan, or under insurance against a risk. There are also complexities in some kinds of supplies of land (Group 1), and in betting (Group 4). In practice, it can prove

---

[22] *HMRC v Empowerment Enterprises Ltd* (2008).

easier to put excise taxes on these kinds of supply, and leave them excluded from VAT. This happens in most European countries (including the UK) with insurance and betting and with many land transactions. The question of VAT on financial supplies also causes a direct overlap with income tax.

A second group of supplies are those made to individuals rather than for commercial purposes, and left out for social reasons. These include education (Group 6), health and welfare (Group 7), burials (Group 8), cultural services (Group 13), sports events (Group 10) and charity fund-raising (Group 12). The oddments include postal services (Group 3). Why add VAT to stamps at least while the state runs the postal service? Another is works of art (if there is an IHT or CGT exemption applying).

EXEMPTIONS AND MULTIPLE SUPPLIES   An exempt supply can be subsumed into a composite supply under the *Card Protection* principle (see Ch.24). That single supply may then be exempt if that is the predominant element from the point of view of the consumer determined objectively. That was the decision of the CJEU in *Mesto Zamberk v Financni Reditelstvi Hradci Kralove* (2014). The Czech court had referred the matter to the CJEU. It concerned admission to an aquatic park which contained a swimming pool, paddling pool, a natural river, water slides, a massage pool, a beach volleyball court, areas for table tennis and sports equipment for hire. The CJEU held that non-organised and unsystematic sporting activities such as these which were not aimed at sporting competitions were nevertheless well within the sports exemption in the Directive. It then laid down the above test as to whether the sporting activities were the predominant element in the single complex supply which involved the other amusements.

26–21   QUESTIONS OF INTERPRETATION—EDUCATION   As with zero-rating, the individual groups have given rise to a substantial body of interpretative litigation. To take an example,[23] Group 6 on education sets out six different items, of which item 1 is the provision by an *eligible body* of education, research (where supplied to an eligible body) or vocational training and item 4 covers the supply of any goods or services which are closely related to a supply within item 1, by or to the body making

---

[23] Group 13 (cultural services) has also led to some detailed litigation in the ECJ on the purpose of the Directive and the UK implementation: see *CEC v Zoological Society of London* (2002). See also on Group 9 (subscriptions) *Expert Witness Institute v CEC* (2002).

that item 1 supply. An eligible body is carefully defined but includes schools, universities and colleges. Thus, neither fees for universities nor school fees,[24] attract VAT.

The exemption does not, however, apply to a private body providing courses which lead to a degree from a university. UK law only covers actual universities and any college, institution, school or hall of such a university. Having failed to comply with those UK requirements, the provider sought to rely on Community law. But in *Finance and Business Training Ltd v HMRC* (2016), the Court of Appeal rejected that claim. UK law had laid down the criteria required by Community law[25] to decide which bodies were entitled to the exemption within the parameters of the Directive. The further criteria to be applied when deciding what constituted a hall, etc. of a university had been set out in *HMRC v School of Finance and Management (London) Ltd* (2001). It was also not a breach of fiscal neutrality since although the supplies were the same as those by a university, etc. the supplier was not.

In *CEC v University of Leicester Students' Union* (2001), it was held that since the students' union was not itself an eligible body nor under its constitution was it part of the university which was such a body, it was not making exempt supplies. In *EC Commission v Germany* (2002) the ECJ declared that a provision of German law which exempted research done by universities for a consideration was contrary to the Directive. The purpose of the exemption was not to hinder education by making the cost of it subject to VAT, but if a university charged VAT on its commercial research that would not increase the cost of university education. Further, contrary to current UK government thinking, the ECJ held that although such projects might be of assistance to university education, they were not essential to the objectives of teaching students to enable them to carry out a profession. Such projects were therefore not closely related to university education.

The "loan" of teaching staff from one educational institution to another will fall within the exemption if it is a supply for the better enjoyment of educational services. It will be a supply closely related to education.[26]

The question as to when a supply is closely related (under item 4) to a supply of education in item 1 arose in *HMRC*

---

[24] However these are paid. See *Birkdale School Sheffield v HMRC* (2008).

[25] See *Minister Finansow v MDDPsp z oo Akademia Biznesu, sp komandytowa* (2014).

[26] *Horizon College v Staatssecretarit van Financiën* (2008) ECJ; cf. *HMRC v Robert Gordon University* (2008) CSIH.

v Brockenhurst College (2015). The college, as part of its courses on catering and hospitality, ran a restaurant in which all aspects were undertaken by the students so that they could learn skills in a practical context. Members of the public paid to eat in the restaurant, so could the supplies to them be regarded as closely related to the supply of education to the students? The issue was whether for the supply to be closely related the students must have actually benefited from the subject matter of the supply (food, etc.) or did they simply have to participate in the making of the supply. The Upper Tribunal thought that the second was enough, but the Court of Appeal regarded the matter as open and decided that the CJEU should rule on this since the wording of item 4 came from the Directive itself. There were also a substantial number of similar institutions in the UK (including public theatre performances by the performing arts students at the college). That reference to the CJEU is currently pending.

Item 2 of Group 6 applies the exemption to a person providing private tuition independently of an employer. It is a question of fact as to whether the person is making the supply under a contract with the customer or as part of a contract between his employer and the customer.[27]

26–21A APPLYING DISCRETIONS The Directive sometimes allows Member States some discretion in applying the exempt groups. For example, betting, lotteries and other forms of gambling are to be exempt "subject to conditions and limitations laid down by each member state". Group 4 of the Schedule sets out the UK conditions, etc. It originally differentiated between two similar types of slot machine. One was exempt from VAT but subject instead to gaming duty, whilst the other was not exempt but was not subject to gaming duty. In *Rank Group Ltd v HMRC* (2012), the ECJ, applying the principle of fiscal neutrality, rejected the different VAT treatment of the two types of slot machine. From the point of view of the typical consumer they were sufficiently similar to invoke the principle. Domestic UK tax law was irrelevant.

Zero-rating and exemption compared

26–22 The reason for zero-rating rather than exempting certain favoured supplies is the need to impose no tax on supplies that cannot be exempted under EC law. Ironically, however, zero-rating is more advantageous than exemption, so the effect in the UK of the European rule is the reverse of that intended.

---

[27] See, e.g. *Marcus Webb Golf Professional v HMRC* (2012)

Advantages of zero-rating

26–23

The advantages of zero-rating and the disadvantages of exemption were the reasons for the dispute in *Royal Bank of Scotland Group Plc v CEC* (2002). The bank issued its own bank notes (zero-rated), but it also issued them through its cash machines to customers of other banks on a reciprocal basis in return for a fee. In respect of that fee the bank was held to be providing financial services to the other banks (an exempt supply) and not issuing its own bank notes.

Zero-rating, as we have seen, is known in Community circles as exemption with credit. They intend this to emphasise the fact that those making zero-rated supplies can claim refunds for input tax incurred for the purpose of those supplies. This is because they are technically taxable supplies, although no new tax will be paid. By contrast, an exempt supply is one for which no input tax credit is possible. The comparative effect of these categories depends on the identities both of suppliers and those being supplied.

Input tax

26–24

It is largely a matter of indifference to taxable persons receiving inputs whether the inputs are taxed at the standard rate or at a zero-rate. The only difference is one of cash-flow. They must pay the input tax on the standard-rated supply before reclaiming it. By contrast, an exempt supply to a taxable person is more expensive. This is because the supplier will probably pass on any input tax as part of the non-taxable price for the supply. The recipient therefore pays for that VAT, but cannot reclaim it. In other words, a taxable person would rather buy supplies taxed at the standard rate than exempt supplies. This also explains why taxable persons may prefer to deal with a registered supplier rather than a supplier that chooses to remain unregistered when under the compulsory limit for registration.

An ordinary consumer cannot claim back any VAT. Nor can a claim be made by someone who makes only exempt supplies, or who is not registered for VAT. In each case, they have to bear the cost of VAT whether it is express or hidden. For them, therefore, zero-rated supplies are better than exempt supplies, because there is less total VAT. For them exempt supplies *are* in effect taxed supplies, while zero-rate taxable supplies are not.

PARTIAL EXEMPTION   A problem arises for those who make both taxable supplies and exempt supplies, whether or not they are mixed. The supplier, if registered, is entitled to an input tax credit for input tax incurred for the purpose of taxable supplies. It is not entitled to a tax credit in respect of input tax for exempt

26–25

supplies. Anyone in this position must therefore take steps to identify which inputs relate to the taxable supplies, and which relate to the exempt supplies. The ECJ has ruled in *Midland Bank Plc v CEC* (2000) that there must be an immediate and direct link between a particular input transaction and a taxable rather than an exempt output transaction for the input tax to be deductible. It must also be a cost component of it. Some of the complexities of this are discussed below. In practice many input supplies are linked to both exempt and taxable output supplies, e.g. electricity used by a shop which sells both taxable and exempt goods. Many such traders agree a percentage with their local VAT offices so that, for example, they can claim 60 per cent of the input tax as a fair share of total inputs. The flat rate scheme for small businesses may also simplify the position.

Special regimes

26–26   VAT also lends itself to the development of a multiplicity of special schemes. As with the schedules on zero-rating and exemption, we derive little benefit from a detailed study of these schemes, but they do solve some tricky practical problems.

One series of special schemes (provided for in official Notices in the 727 series) is that for retailers. These are designed to deal with the problems of those selling a mixture of goods that are taxed at different rates, or are exempt. Examples are the supermarket, high-street retailers and even the corner shop. They can agree with the local VAT office to avoid having to make separate calculations of VAT on every sale, or having to separate zero-rated goods from standard-rated goods.

Another set of special schemes are those dealing with goods sold by dealers but bought by them from private customers. For example, if I sell my private car to a dealer, I add no VAT to it. But I bought my car from a garage and paid VAT when I did so. If the dealer charges VAT on the whole price of the car when selling it to another customer, it is being double taxed. To avoid this, a *margin scheme* operates. In effect, the dealer has to account for VAT only on the difference between the price paid to me and the price for which the car is sold. Similar regimes apply to antiques.

A further group who get special attention are farmers. The problem here is the assumed aversion of small farmers from keeping accounts and so registering for VAT. Yet someone buying from a farmer wants an input tax credit for any supply, on which the farmer would charge VAT. The compromise, made at European level, for those farmers who did not register, is a deemed input tax equal to 4 per cent of the output.

The flat rate scheme for small businesses

Under s.26B of the VAT Act small businesses may use a flat **26–27** rate scheme in calculating their VAT. This does not strictly vary the rate of VAT charged by the supplier, it relates to the accountability of the supplier to the CEC, but it is more convenient to deal with it here than in the next chapter. The scheme is currently available to businesses where estimated turnover next year will be no more than £150,000 (which includes zero-rated supplies) and which has no more than £230,000 tax exclusive annual business income (which would include exempt supplies). Such businesses may choose to operate the flat rate scheme rather than become involved in keeping detailed records of its outputs and inputs. Instead the VAT payable will be calculated by applying a flat rate percentage to the supplier's total tax inclusive business turnover (i.e. all its business income). The relevant percentage depends upon which trade sector the business, or main business, falls under. The current (2016) percentages vary from 4 per cent (retailing food, confectionery, tobacco, newspapers or children's clothing) to 14.5 per cent (accountants, architects and civil engineers, computer consultants, labour-only building services and lawyer or legal services). Such businesses will therefore lose the right to claim any input tax credits but will still be able to issue tax invoices (and so collect output tax) at the appropriate (normal) rate, be it standard, reduced or zero-rated. There is also a concession which gives a limited right to recover input tax on capital assets acquired with a VAT inclusive value of £2,000 or more.

CHAPTER 27

VAT COMPUTATION AND ACCOUNTABILITY

Introduction

27–01 Having established that there is a charge to VAT and what the appropriate rate is, the final questions for domestic supplies are: what is the value of the supply so that the amount can be calculated? When is that tax charged? And how is it actually accounted for to HMRC?

Valuation

Everything which constitutes the consideration

27–02 On how much do we impose the VAT? Section 19 of the VAT Act provides that where the consideration for a supply is in monetary form, the value is the amount that, when the VAT is added, equals the consideration. For example, if the price I pay for a supply is £120.00, the VAT rate being 20 per cent, then the value of the supply for VAT purposes is £100. Similarly, if the price I pay is £100, then the value of the supply is £83.33, with VAT of £16.67, i.e. 20 per cent of £83.33 payable. This suggests that if we offer you a price for a product, the price is VAT-inclusive, rather than VAT-exclusive.

Section 19 is the UK's implementation of arts 73–80 of the Directive, which have direct effect. As originally enacted the section was found to be inconsistent with some of the provisions of the Directive and it was amended in 1992 to provide only the general rule set out above. The Directive is in fact far more detailed and so all the recent disputes as to valuation of a supply have in fact been decided by reference to that rather than the VAT Act.

Article 73 provides that the taxable amount of a supply is "everything which constitutes the consideration which has been or is to be obtained by the purchaser, the customer or a third party for the supply, including subsidies directly linked to the price of such supplies".

Article 73 was considered by the CJEU in *International Bingo Technology SA v Tribunal Economico-Administrativo Regional de Cataluna* (2013). The company operated bingo games by selling bingo cards for a set price. Under Spanish law a fixed percentage of that price had to be paid out as winnings. The CJEU held that the consideration received by the company for the purposes of VAT was the net price after the fixed deduction, since the latter was mandatory. The company could not make full use of the total amount received since it had to return that fixed percentage by law. That will not of course be the case in relation to normal operating costs as VAT is a tax on turnover and the costs are covered by the input tax rules.

SUPPLIES FREE OF CHARGE   In the case of goods supplied   **27–03**
free of charge but caught by para.5 of Sch.4 (see Ch.25), art.74 provides that the consideration is their purchase or cost price. In *Kuwait Petroleum (GB) Ltd v CEC* (2001), this was applied to "free" gifts purchased and provided by Kuwait in return for coupons given by the company on the sale of petrol. It was not there decided whether such gifts could then amount to a post-supply discount in relation to the petrol (see para.27–15 below).

INCIDENTAL EXPENSES AND TAXES   Article 78 provides that   **27–04**
the consideration is to include any incidental expenses and taxes other than VAT itself. What is an incidental expense depends upon first deciding exactly what the supply amounts to. If the supply, properly ascertained, consists of two elements, X and Y, it is not then permissible to use art.78 to argue that X is an incidental expense of Y for the purpose of whether there is a single supply in which X is subsumed into Y. Article 73 applies only therefore to determine the value of the consideration so ascertained (i.e. X and Y). Thus in *CEC v BT Plc* (1999) where the House of Lords held that the supply was a composite supply both of a new car and its delivery direct to the customer, it could not be said that the delivery costs were incidental expenses of the supply of the car under art.78.

The consideration for the supply therefore includes all taxes, duties, levies and charges excluding the VAT itself. But, as we shall see (para.27–15), this does not include taxes paid by the supplier on behalf of the customer, i.e. where the tax is imposed on the customer rather than the supplier. An example would be stamp duty payable on the purchase of a house, paid by the solicitor on the client's behalf. But tax charged on the supplier (e.g. on the import of a car) and passed on to the customer (on the sale of the car) is part of the consideration for the supply provided there is a direct link between the tax paid and the supply.[1]

27–05   SUBSIDIES   Since art.73 includes subsidies directly linked to the price of the supply as part of the consideration, such subsidies will only include those which constitute the whole or part of the consideration.[2] But in *Keeping Newcastle Warm v CEC* (2002), on the other hand, there was no dispute that a flat rate £10 subsidy, paid under a Government scheme for assisting energy savings, formed part of the consideration for the supply of energy saving advice by the suppliers. It was argued that since this subsidy was not linked to the price of the supplies it did not fall to be included in the value of the supply since it was not within the specific wording of art.73. The CJEU ruled that since it formed part of the consideration for the supply, the subsidy fell within the general wording of art.73 and formed part of the taxable amount.

27–06   IDENTIFYING THE CONSIDERATION   The value of a supply is therefore inextricably linked to the consideration for the supply, which as we have seen means what is received as a direct link for the supply; e.g. the fact of the hostess holding a party in return for a discounted blouse in *Rosgill Group v CEC* (1997), which we discussed in Ch.24. It is important to stress again that it is necessary first to decide precisely what the supply is, and what the consideration for it is, before applying any part of the valuation provisions. Those provisions (including the permitted deductions set out below) cannot be used in that identification process; they are concerned only with the value of the consideration of that supply once ascertained. Thus in the *Trustees of Nell Gwyn House Maintenance Fund v CEC* (1999) where, as we have seen, it was held that the trustees were supplying to the tenants of a block of flats not only the maintenance staff but also the whole costs of the maintenance of the block, it was not permissible to then argue that the payments for the staff were received from the tenants as repayment for expenses paid out on their behalf under art.79, discussed below.

Non-cash consideration

27–07   Where there is an element of non-cash consideration involved in the supply, the question is of course what monetary value to give it. There have been many European and UK cases on which formula is to be used.

---

[1] *Lidl & Companhia v Fazenda Publica* (2011) ECJ.
[2] *Office des Produits Wallons ASBL v Belgium* (2003).

MONETARY EQUIVALENT The generally accepted analysis of **27–08** these cases was set out by Chadwick LJ in *CEC v Littlewoods Organisation Plc* (2001). The consideration must be capable of being expressed in money or a monetary equivalent and the basis of the assessment is the subjective value of the consideration. By subjective, is meant not the traditional UK meaning of the word "subjective", but the consideration actually received for the goods or services actually supplied. That is distinct from some "objective" value which is independent of the actual transaction—it is therefore the value which the parties must be taken to have adopted for themselves for the purposes of the transaction which applies.[3] Only if it is impossible to ascertain such a value will the amount be the cost to the supplier.

"SUBJECTIVE VALUE" In many cases this subjective value **27–09** is relatively easy to ascertain, especially where the supply is of an item at a reduced price from its catalogue or retail price. Thus, in the *Rosgill* case the value of the consideration was the £8 reduction in the catalogue price paid by the hostess for the blouse. That was the value the parties had implicitly attributed to her holding the party, etc.[4] This cannot happen, however, if the goods have no catalogue or retail price as was the case in *Empire Stores Ltd v CEC* (1994) where "free" goods provided to an agent as commission for sales from their catalogue to third parties had no market value which could have been attributed by the parties to them. The cost to the supplier was therefore used.

ATTRIBUTION It follows that the key question is whether the **27–10** parties must be taken to have attributed a value to the non-cash consideration.

In *CEC v Westmorland Motorway Services Ltd* (1998) a coach driver was provided by the motorway service station with a free meal if he took a coach party of 20 or more people there and remained there for at least half an hour. Clearly there was a supply of a meal to the driver for a consideration but what was its monetary value? There were two possible cash valuations: what it cost the service station to provide the meal (cost price) or some other (higher) value attributed to it by the parties (i.e. in this case what it would have cost the driver to buy the meal—the retail

---

[3] As opposed to what they think they adopted as the value—that would be the UK meaning of subjective.

[4] See also *e.g. CEC v Euphony Communications Ltd* (2004).

price). The Court of Appeal held that on the facts the parties had impliedly attributed the latter value.

27–11 NOT EXTRINSIC VALUE   A variation on this accepted approach was taken by Carnwath J in *CEC v Bugeja* (2000). The case concerned the supply of videos which were sold for £20 each or £10 plus the return of a previously bought video. The judge held that since it was shown that the actual replacement cost of a video to the supplier was £3 that was the subjective value of a returned video, making the consideration for the supply of the second video £13. Goods, unlike services in cases such as *Westmorland*, could have a value established by extrinsic evidence. That decision was, however, reversed by the same Court of Appeal as in the *Littlewoods* case (2001), applying Chadwick LJ's principles. There could be no valid distinction drawn between goods and services and there was no difficulty in discovering the "subjective" value of the returned video, i.e. the £10 reduction in the purchase price of the second video. That was the value placed on it by the parties in respect of the second purchase transaction and not simply the value placed on it by one party for the purposes of a different transaction (buying a replacement).

27–12 PART-EXCHANGE VALUE   That same Court of Appeal (2001) also approved the decision of Arden J in *Lex Services Plc v CEC* (2000). That case demonstrates very clearly the difference between the subjective and objective value as described by Chadwick LJ. It was the everyday situation where a customer trades in his used car in part exchange for a new car. Rather than give the customer a reduction on the list price of the new car (which was frowned on by the manufacturers), to expedite a sale the salesman would give the customer a part exchange price in excess of the used car's trade value. The latter was used, however, as quantifying the repayment to the buyer if the deal fell through. The value to be attributed to the used car as part consideration for the new car was the inflated value as agreed between the parties. Thus VAT was in effect chargeable on the full list price of the new car even though in practice the garage received less than that amount (i.e. reduced by the inflated part of the part exchange allowance). The logic of this approach when compared with the VAT treatment of a simple discount off the list price is discussed below at para.27–23. Nevertheless, the Court of Appeal's decision was upheld in identical terms by the House of Lords (2004).

27–13 ZERO VALUE   In one case the subjective value of the part exchanged goods was held to be zero. In *CEC v Ping (Europe)*

Ltd (2002) the company sold a new golf club to a customer for £22 plus the return of an old club which had been declared illegal under the rules of golf. In those unusual circumstances the value attributed by the parties to the returned club was nil—it was worthless. There were no normal rules of trade relevant to this transaction.

Allowable deductions

Article 73 is subject to art.79 which allows certain items to be deducted from the consideration. These are: (a) price reductions for early payment; (b) price discounts and rebates allowed at the time of the supply; and (c) amounts received by the supplier from a customer as repayment for expenses paid out on behalf of the customer to a third party.

27-14

With regard to such expenses under para.(c), there is a clear distinction between expenses paid to a third party C which have been incurred by A in the course of making his own supply of services to B and as part of the whole of the services rendered to him by B, which would not be deductible by A under para.(c); and where specific services have been supplied by C to B (not A) and A has merely acted as B's known and authorised representative in paying C, which would be so deductible. In *CEC v Plantiflor Ltd* (2002) the company (A) sent plants by mail order to customers (B) and charged B the costs required by Parcelforce (C) to deliver the plants. The House of Lords, having found that the delivery was part of the services provided by A to B (there being a separate supply by C to B) refused to allow that amount as an expense with regard to the consideration for the supply by A to B.[5]

Discounts

Price rebates and discounts at the point of sale are thus allowed under art.79.

27-15

These will reduce the value of the supply accordingly. Price reductions made *after* the time of the supply are allowable under art.90 at the time of the reduction by way of a repayment of VAT already paid by the supplier. The interaction of these two articles on contemporary and post-supply discounts, was considered by the ECJ in *Freemans Plc v CEC* (2001). The company sold goods through agents selling either to themselves or others from a catalogue. Every time an agent made a payment to the company, 10 per cent of that amount was credited to a separate account in the name of the agent. The agent could either take that amount in

---

[5] See also *Debenhams Retail Plc v CEC* (2005), where the services were actually supplied by C to A.

cash or reduce the balance owed for goods already purchased, but it could not be used to reduce the catalogue price of goods at the time of purchase. The ECJ held that art.79 could not apply since no reduction was given against the actual purchase—the 10 per cent credit in effect gave the agent a right to a future discount against the purchase. That fell within art.90 which would apply when the credit was actually used to reduce the balance owed. In effect it was a post-supply discount on the original order and not a pre-sale discount on a subsequent order.

27–16   CASH COMMISSION   A similar decision was made by the Court of Appeal in *Littlewoods Organisation Plc v CEC* (2001). In this case the agents selling through a catalogue and who either bought goods for themselves or for others (referred to as the primary goods) were entitled to take either a 10 per cent cash commission or a 12.5 per cent discount on a future purchase (of secondary goods). The Court of Appeal was only concerned with the VAT situation arising in the context of goods purchased by the agents for themselves. They held that the cash commission operated as a post-supply discount on the primary goods under art.90—it was only payable after the sale; the non-cash commission was, however, allowable as a discount under art.79 against the value of the secondary goods as a discount at the point of supply of those goods. The non-cash commission which arose from goods ordered by the agents for third parties would have raised another question— was that not a discount but a recognition of the consideration provided by the agents to the company in selling goods on their behalf, as in the *Rossgill* case? We will return to that issue at para.27–23.

Vouchers

27–17   SAME SUPPLIER   The issue of consideration/discount was also at the centre of the initial dispute when a supplier provides a coupon or voucher on a first supply which can be used to obtain a reduction on the price of a second supply from the *same* supplier. The issue was resolved by the ECJ in *Boots Co Ltd v CEC* (1990) when it held that the customer had not provided any consideration for the voucher, which in any event had no monetary value as such. It was instead merely an undertaking by Boots to give a discount on the second purchase to which art.79 would apply. This approach was followed by the Court of Appeal in *Tesco Plc v CEC* (2003) in relation to its "clubcard" scheme. Under that scheme when a person purchased goods at

Tesco and presented a clubcard at the checkout, he or she was awarded points based on the amount spent. Those points could then be used to reduce the purchase price of subsequent goods purchased in the supermarket. Again there was no consideration provided by the customer for the award of those points which operated as a simple discount on the second purchase. The major factor was that on the first purchase a customer paid the same amount whether or not a card was presented.

VOUCHERS REDEEMABLE DOWN THE SUPPLY CHAIN The **27–18** position is more complex if the person providing the voucher and the person making the supply at which it can be used to effect a reduction are not the same. The usual situation is where the reduction is made further down the supply chain of the same goods. Two issues commonly arise. The first is what is the value of a retail supply where, e.g. the money off coupon is provided by the manufacturer (A) to the customer (C), say in a magazine. (A) supplies the relevant goods directly to the retailer (B), who then takes the coupon as part of the price of the supply to (C). (A) then reimburses (B) the amount of the coupon. In *Yorkshire Co-operatives Ltd v CEC* (2003), the ECJ held that insofar as the supply from (B) to (C) was concerned the consideration provided by (C) was the cash and the coupon, the face value of which was the value of that consideration. (B) got full value for the supply since it was reimbursed by (A).

VOUCHERS IN SAME SUPPLY CHAIN AS A POST SUPPLY **27–19** DISCOUNT The second issue, in that situation, is what is the knock-on effect if any on the supply by (A) to (B)—is (A)'s reimbursement of (B) in effect a post supply discount under art.90? That question came before the ECJ in *EC Commission v Germany* (2003). The situation was more complex in that the voucher was issued by the manufacturer (A) who supplied the goods to a wholesaler (B). (B) in turn supplied the goods to the retailer (C), who then supplied the goods to the customer (D), taking the coupon as part consideration. (A) then reimbursed (C) direct. It was argued that to allow this reimbursement from (A) to (C) to operate as a post-supply discount on the supply from (A) to (B) (there was no supply from (A) to (C)) would distort the system of VAT since it would be rewriting a supply which had not been affected by the reimbursement. The ECJ held that art.90 did apply to the supply from (A) to (B) since there was the overriding principle of fiscal neutrality. (A) should not have to account for VAT on more than it actually received by way of consideration. The position would be even clearer if there had been a direct supply from (A) to (C) (i.e. cutting out the wholesaler) as in the *Yorkshire* case above.

27–20   VOUCHERS OUTSIDE THE CHAIN OF SUPPLY (THIRD PARTY VOUCHERS) AS A POST-SUPPLY DISCOUNT   The position is different if the supplier provides vouchers which are exchangeable not for the supplier's goods either directly (as in *Boots*) or further down the supply chain (as in *EC Commission v Germany*), but for goods from other retail outlets. We have already seen in *Kuwait Petroleum (GB) Ltd v CEC* (1999), that if the supplier obtains the goods from the third parties and then provides them to the customer, those goods are deemed to have been supplied at market value under para.4 of Sch.5. But that case did not decide whether the cost to the supplier of redeeming those vouchers could be deducted from the value of the primary supply as a post-supply discount under art.90. The position is even more acute where the vouchers are exchangeable with the third parties for goods. Those third parties then being reimbursed by the supplier. After all, just as in the cases above, the supplier in these cases ultimately receives less consideration for the primary supply because of having to fund the voucher scheme (i.e. by buying the goods or reimbursing the retailers who redeem the vouchers).

The issue was, however, directly in point in *HMRC v Total UK Ltd* (2008). The Court of Appeal held that there was no such art.90 discount. They adopted the wording of the Advocate General in *EC Commission v Germany* that it was not like a normal discount or rebate scheme. This scheme involved the supplier supplying more goods (petrol and vouchers for the redemption goods) at the same price, rather than supplying the same goods (petrol) at a lower price. In the supply chain cases only one set of goods was involved and the reduction was given on those goods, albeit down the line.

The Court of Appeal also dismissed an argument based on fiscal neutrality. That point is dealt with next below. There is a related point as to the VAT implications when such (third party) vouchers are redeemed by the customer and the goods are supplied by the retailer, who is then reimbursed by the issuer of the vouchers. That was dealt with in the case of *HMRC v Loyalty Management UK Ltd* (2013) as described in Ch.26, above and [2008] B.T.R. 17.

Limited to amount paid

27–21   Underlying the test that in valuing non-cash consideration it is the amount received by the supplier which matters, is the principle that it would be unjust to tax a supplier on a figure which is in excess of what the customer actually pays, however many steps there are in the supply chain. This limited principle was set out by the ECJ in *Elida Gibbs Ltd v CEC* (1996). A good example is *Argos Distributors Ltd v CEC* (1996). Argos sold vouchers redeemable at its shops, only for goods to the value shown on the vouchers, to employers, who then gave them to their employees as incentives. Argos sold the vouchers to the employers at 95 per cent of their face value. Thus, for example, suppose Argos sold a voucher with a face value of £100 to Fred for £95. Fred gave that voucher to his employee Sid, who bought goods worth £100 from Argos with it. What was the value of the supply by Argos to Sid? The ECJ held that it was the amount actually received by Argos for those goods, i.e. £95. That was the amount which Argos actually received for the goods and fiscal neutrality required that VAT be charged on no higher figure.[6]

TRI-PARTITE AGREEMENTS This principle has its limits, **27–22** however, and has not been applied where there is a tri-partite situation. In *Kingfisher Plc v CEC* (2000), P supplied vouchers to its customers (usually on credit) which could then be used to buy goods from W using the face value of the vouchers for the shelf price of the goods. W then invoiced P for the vouchers redeemed by it and P paid W 90 per cent of that value. The judge held that the supply by W to the customer was the full shelf price and not the 90 per cent eventually received from P. There were separate supplies by W to the customer, by P to the customer and by P to W (of financial services). W was getting the benefit of those services provided by P—in *Argos* there was no such agreement, the company gave its own discount. This approach was upheld by the ECJ in *CEC v Primback Ltd* (2001). X sold furniture on interest free terms to its customers. They borrowed the full list price from Y, the finance company. The customer over time repaid that full amount to Y but Y paid X less than the full price up front. Again the value of the supply by X to its customers was held to be at the full list price and not the amount received from Y. Here the price agreed between X and a customer and the price paid by the customer were the same—that was not true of the arrangement between Argos and the purchasers of its vouchers.

Discounts or consideration—limited value of fiscal neutrality

In *Elida Gibbs Ltd v CEC* (1996), the ECJ put forward the **27–23** following explanation of their application of fiscal neutrality:

---

[6] The Advocate General in that case thought that the 5 per cent could not be a discount under art.79 since it was not given to the customer (Sid) at the point of sale. The Court did not express any views on that point.

"The basic principle of the VAT system is that it is intended to tax only the final consumer. Consequently the taxable amount serving as a basis for the VAT to be collected by the tax authorities cannot exceed the consideration actually paid by the final consumer which is the basis for calculating the VAT ultimately borne by him."

An examination of the various cases just discussed in relation to the various aspects of valuation reveals that in fact the VAT position is very different depending upon the analysis by the Courts as to what the transaction involves, even though in wider economic terms, especially from the point of view of the consumer, the consequences are identical.[7]

To reiterate two examples. A buys a car from B with a list price of £10,000 and B takes in part exchange A's old car which has a trade value of £2,000. If B allows A £2,000 on the traded-in car but gives A a £500 discount on the list price, the value of the supply of the new car to A will be £9,500 (the £500 being a discount under art.79). But if instead B allows A £2,500 on the part-exchanged car and then charges the full list price on the new car, the value of the supply by B to A is £10,000 (*Lex Services* case). Again, if B allows only £2,000 on the part exchange and charges A the full list price, but gives A a purchase plus voucher worth £500 which B will accept as part consideration for the new car, the value of the supply of the new car is only £9,500 (*Hartwell Plc v CEC* (2003)). Yet in all three cases A has handed over his old car and £7,500.

27–24   NEUTRALITY OR CERTAINTY   The reason for the disparity is that in situations (i) and (iii) the £500 is treated as being either a discount or as part of the consideration with no monetary value, and the value of the non-cash consideration (the old car) is agreed at £2,000, whereas in (ii) the agreed subjective value of that car is £2,500 and that must form part of the consideration. When this issue was put to the House of Lords in the *Lex Services* case, Lord Walker rejected any argument based on a wider application of the principal of fiscal neutrality on the basis of applying the principle of legal certainty. The principle, he said, does not require that transactions which have the same economic or business effect should for that reason be treated alike for VAT purposes. If a taxable person has a choice between two transactions he may not choose one of them and avail himself of the VAT effects of the other. There is no doctrine of commercial reality.

---

[7] See [2002] B.T.R.179; [2003] B.T.R.153 and [2004] B.T.R.99 for detailed analyses of this problem.

POST-SUPPLY DISCOUNTS AND FISCAL NEUTRALITY This **27–25** restrictive approach to the principle of fiscal neutrality was also applied by the CA in *Total UK Ltd v HMRC* (2008). In that case, Total offered vouchers to customers buying petrol. These vouchers could then be redeemed for goods at third party retailers such as Marks & Spencer. Total were not allowed to deduct the costs of reimbursing the retailers for the goods supplied in return for the vouchers as a post-supply discount on the price of the petrol. In analytical terms, more goods were supplied at the same cost and not the same goods at a lower cost. Total then argued that this result in fact infringed the principle in *Elida Gibbs* of fiscal neutrality. They were having to account for output tax (on the petrol) on an amount which was in fact greater than the net amount they actually received. Had they simply allowed the vouchers to be redeemed against future purchases of petrol or given cash-back the deduction would have been allowed. That could not be correct. Although the judge had agreed with this, the Court of Appeal was very dismissive of the neutrality argument on the basis that the *Elida Gibbs* case was no authority for such a general proposition[8] and specifically only applied to same vouchers applicable to goods in the same supply chain. Nothing in that case altered the fact that this was not a price discount scheme and so could not reduce the amount of the supply.

SEPARATE SUPPLIES A different method of avoiding the **27–26** principle of fiscal neutrality was used by Hart J in *CEC v Euphony Communications Ltd* (2004). There the judge drew a distinction between cash commission earned by agents in respect of their becoming a customer and using the supplier's services (regarded as a post-supply discount under art.90 on the services supplied to them) and that earned by introducing new customers to the supplier. That was the subjective value of the consideration for the supply of services by the agent to the supplier. The judge decided that the principle of fiscal neutrality could not apply where there was a separate supply by the agent to the supplier in addition to the supply by the supplier to the agent—even though the amount received by the supplier was in reality the same in both cases. It is clear that so far as the UK is concerned, the principle of fiscal neutrality in this area has a rather limited role.

---

[8] Citing *Primback* and *Kingfisher* as authority (see para.27–22 above). The value of the supply is based on the tax paid by the consumer and not on that collected by the supplier. See [2008] B.T.R.17.

Accounting for VAT

27–27   As we have seen the VAT payable to the VAT office is the balance (if positive) of output tax less input tax. If the balance is negative then a claim for repayment can be made. This balance requires accounting rules to determine when VAT is to be collected and returned to the VAT office, and what input tax can be deducted from the output tax. VAT laws have a special language for this as well:

- **Tax periods** are the periods for which the taxable person must make returns to the VAT office.
- **A tax invoice** is the formal document required when a supply is made.
- **The tax point** is the time when VAT has to be charged on a supply, and therefore determines the tax period in which output tax on a supply must be returned.
- The **tax credit** is the amount of input tax that can be set against output tax for each tax period.

Tax periods
27–28   All registered persons must make regular returns to the VAT office and there are provisions for assessments in default. In the case of larger traders, this is done on a quarterly basis so that it is received by the VAT office within a month of the end of the quarter. For smaller traders, annual accounting is possible. Under this scheme returns are only made once a year and arrangements are made for instalments payments of VAT, monthly or quarterly, depending on the size of turnover, throughout the year on an estimated basis. Some traders are allowed to make monthly returns. These include exporters because, as we shall see, their returns amount to requests for refunds of tax, and so involve a payment by the VAT office to them. Very large traders, on the other hand, are required to make monthly payments on account.

Each return requires that the trader total up the output tax on all outputs made in the period covered by the return. A tax credit can then be claimed for all input tax incurred during the period, provided that the input tax is claimable as part of the credit.

In each case, the trader must have documentary evidence to substantiate the amounts returned which must be kept for six years. These are open to inspection by the VAT office who may make retrospective assessments. In the case of most transactions, the required evidence is a *tax invoice*. The actual amount payable is based on these invoices, although small traders may pay on a cash basis, i.e. the difference between output tax collected and input tax paid in any particular period.

Tax invoices

Each taxable supply must be documented in the required way.   **27–29**
In most cases, this is by the issue of a special invoice recording the transaction, called a tax invoice. A taxable person supplying goods or services to another taxable person must issue the latter with an invoice recording the key details of the supply. These include the VAT registration details of the supplier (including the VAT number that all registered persons are given on registration), names and addresses, the amount payable for the supply, and the amount of VAT on the supply. In this way, documentary evidence is recorded of the precise details of the transaction, including both the person who should be paying the VAT to the local VAT office, and the person who will be reclaiming that amount as input tax. This is one of the secret efficiencies of VAT: if the purchaser does not have a tax invoice, no input tax can be claimed. If the purchaser produces the tax invoice, the VAT office has the information to check that the supplier has paid in the VAT. Electronic invoicing is allowed, see Directive 1058/10.

Tax points

Tax point is the VAT term for the time of supply. Article 63   **27–30**
of the Directive states that VAT becomes chargeable when the goods or services are supplied. When then does a supply occur? The answer cannot be defined in terms of passing of title. Instead, the rule must be completely practical—it has to be applied by the sales assistant or bookkeeper recording the transaction. In addition, revenue protection requires that the tax point is something that cannot be postponed or avoided.

The solution, as allowed by the Directive and adopted by s.6, is a two-tier one. The formal time of supply of goods is either when the goods are delivered (or made available) to the customer, or when payment is made for the supply, whichever is earlier.[9] In the case of services the alternative to earlier payment is when the supplies are rendered. In practice, however, the tax point is usually the time when the tax invoice is issued. To tie the two together, the law requires that the tax invoice be issued not later than 14 days after the formal time of supply, in which case the date of the invoice will become the tax point. Normal practice with sales of goods is to issue the tax invoice at the same time as the sale and payment, but the rules give a little flexibility. Goods

---

[9]   See, e.g. *CEC v Richmond Theatre Management Ltd* (1995).

sold on "sale or return" are taxed when there is known to be a sale or after 12 months, if earlier.

27-31 PAYMENTS ON ACCOUNT   Article 65 of the Directive provides that where a payment is made on account (e.g. a deposit) before the goods and services are supplied (the tax point), VAT becomes chargeable on the amount of such a payment on receipt. In *BUPA Hospitals Ltd v CEC* (2006), the ECJ held that could not apply unless all the relevant information about the future chargeable supply (e.g. as to future delivery or future performance) was already known. Payments on account of supplies which had not been clearly identified could not be subject to VAT.

27-32 INTERNET SALES   *HMRC v Robertson's Electrical Ltd* (2006) involved a common form of selling goods over the internet. Goods ordered online were paid for by the customers recording their credit or debit card details on the website. The invoice was prepared either at the date of dispatch or within seven days of the date of delivery. As required by the then consumer law[10] all goods not faulty or misdescribed could be returned within seven days of receipt. The taxpayers argued that as a result the goods were sold on a sale or return basis and the tax point was therefore the date when the customer no longer had the right to return perfect goods. The Inner House of the Court of Session disagreed. There was an outright sale at the date when the goods were ordered and paid for and that was the tax point. It was in effect a sale subject to a condition subsequent.

27-33 TAX RETURNS   All taxable persons must include in their tax returns all supplies where the tax point is within the period covered by the tax return, whether or not the payment has actually been made. They will also want to claim a tax credit for all input tax where the tax point is in that period.

Tax credits—input tax

Right to reclaim input tax
27-34 A taxable person[11] can claim a tax credit for all input tax incurred in a tax period in making taxable outputs. The UK system is contained in ss.24–26B of the VAT Act which mirror,

---

[10] The Consumer Protection (Distant Selling) Regulations 2000; see now the Consumer Contracts (Information, Cancellation and Additional Charges) Regulations 2013.
[11] See *Finanzamt Goslar v Breitsohl* (2001).

but which have largely been ignored in legal disputes in favour of the wording of the Directive. The two key conditions are that the claimant holds tax invoices for the sum of input tax claimed (art.178),[12] and that there was an immediate and direct link between the input tax transaction and a particular taxable output transaction the input tax was incurred *for the purposes of* the taxed transaction (art.168).

FOR THE PURPOSES OF THE TAXED TRANSACTION There is 27–35 therefore no right to deduct input tax if the relevant supply was made not to the taxable person but, e.g. directly to one of its employees, albeit in a business context, e.g. legal defence costs of an employee, paid by the employer, charged with dangerous driving in a company car in the course of business.[13] On the other hand, where the input transaction was incurred in the course of the business, e.g. a lease of premises for a restaurant, input tax may still be claimed even after the business has ceased but only so far as is necessary to wind up the business.[14] Where the taxable person uses the inputs for the purpose of a business but the outputs are to be disregarded, there must be an apportionment: *HMRC v Gracechurch Management Services Ltd* (2008). We shall return to the other test of an immediate and direct link shortly.

DISALLOWED INPUTS The Treasury has power to disallow 27–36 some kinds of input tax regardless of the reason for it is incurred (s.26). This power is allowed by European law under art.176. The British rules disallow expenditure on a number of inputs, in particular on private cars (with exceptions such as the purchase of cars for resale),[15] most forms of business entertainment,[16] and expenditure on accommodation provided for staff. Further, under s.26A, any taxable person who has made a claim for a tax credit but has not actually paid the supplier within six months of the supply, will be required to repay the credit claimed.

---

[12] This includes any document regarded by a member state as an invoice and allows member states to require additional evidence under national rules for the prevention of fraud: *Reisdorf v Finanzampt Köln-West* (1997).

[13] *HMRC v Jeancharm Ltd* (2005) CA.

[14] *I/S Fini H v Skatteministeriet* (2005) ECJ.

[15] This exclusion is valid even though cars are essential tools in the business concerned or could not be used for private purposes: *Royscot Leasing Ltd v CEC* (1999).

[16] As to what this amounts to see, e.g. *BMW (GB) Ltd v CEC* (1997) and *CEC v Kilroy Television Co Ltd* (1997).

27–37   POLICY CONSIDERATIONS   There is an inherent policy conflict in these rules. The tax authorities are concerned to maximise tax revenues. From their viewpoint, input tax is lost tax, and is therefore to be discouraged. But VAT is a tax on value-added, that is, a tax on the differences between inputs and outputs. Any attempt to reduce the entitlement to input tax so as to tax more than the value added is wrong in principle. The dilemma is heightened by the natural temptation of taxpayers to claim as much input tax as possible. The CJEU in *Mahageben kit v Nemzeti Ado-es Vamhivatal Del-dunantuli Regioanalis Ado Foigazgatosaga* (2012) reaffirmed that the right to deduct input tax paid by taxable persons which has an immediate and direct link to an ouput transaction of theirs is a fundamental principle of VAT. Accordingly, it can only be refused if it can be established objectively that the claimant knew or ought to have known that by his purchase he was taking part in a transaction connected with the fraudulent evasion of VAT (see Ch.25 above). On the other hand, in *EMS Bulgaria Transport OOD v Direcktor na Direktsia 'Obxhalvane I upravlenie na izppalnenieto' Plovdiv* (2012), the CJEU held that the imposition of time limits on claims is allowed by Community law so long as they are equivalent to similar rights under national and Community law and do not make claims impossible or excessively difficult to make.

Of course, if the input tax invoices are shams then they will be discounted. In *HMRC v Dempster* (2008), it was said that a sham for this purpose was whether the rights and obligations for VAT purposes expressed in the invoice were different from those which the parties intended to create.

Direct and immediate link
27–38   There is an early decision, entirely on the wording of the UK statute and not the Directive, that the test is essentially a subjective one. In *Ian Flockton Developments Ltd v CEC* (1987), an engineering company successfully claimed input tax credit arising from the costs of maintain and running a racehorse. The court said that where there was no obvious connection between the expenditure and the business it was for the trader to show a link, but its subjective intention was paramount. The issue was however, one of mixed law and fact.

But since then the matter has been taken up by the CJEU. In *Midland Bank v CEC* (2000), that Court said that the diversity of commercial and professional transactions makes it impossible to set out a single method of determining the necessary relationship between input and output transactions in order for input tax to become deductible. It is for the national courts to decide how to apply the direct and immediate link test of the facts of each case, taking into account all the surrounding circumstances.

THE BASIC TEST—TAXABLE SUPPLIES ONLY If a trader is **27–39** making taxable supplies only then the issue is whether the input supplies are used for the purpose of those taxable supplies. Or to put in another way, is there an immediate and direct link between the input transactions and the trader's business? Guidance on applying this test in such a context was given by the House of Lords in *CEC v Redrow Group Plc* (1999). The company built and sold new houses. As part of a marketing scheme they paid prospective purchasers' estate agents' fees on selling their own houses. The company instructed the estate agents and monitored their activities. These expenses were not payable if the sale of the new house fell through. The House of Lords held that the input tax attributable to those fees was deductible. It was not necessary to show that there was a direct link between the payment of the input tax and the specific supply of houses by the taxpayers to the purchasers (output tax). The test was whether the input supply was received in connection with the business for the purpose of being incorporated within its economic activities. The fact that a third party benefited was irrelevant. On the facts, once it was found that there was a supply of services by the estate agents to Redrow input tax could be deducted.[17]

TAXABLE AND EXEMPT SUPPLIES There is, however, a clear **27–40** need to make such direct links if the trader is making both taxable and exempt supplies since there is no input tax credit in relation to supplies to the trader which are used for the purposes of exempt supplies. The solution in the VAT (General) Regulations 1995 is to identify input supplies which are used exclusively for the business of making taxable or exempt supplies as appropriate[18] and then to apportion those supplies which are not exclusively used for one such set of supplies (e.g. the cost of office equipment) according to the ratio of taxable to exempt supplies (the turnover method).[19] Further if an input is initially related to a taxable supply but is actually used in relation to an exempt supply, no deduction is allowed.[20]

---

[17] That "input reasoning" was also applied in *WHA Ltd v CEC* (2003) where a garage charged an insurance company in respect of repairs to cars owned by those insured by the company.

[18] See, e.g. *CEC v Harpcombe Ltd* (1996).

[19] But see para.27–45 below.

[20] *Tremerton Ltd v CEC* (1999). This may not be so if the reason for the change is

27–41   IDENTIFYING THE LINK   In deciding in such cases whether there is an immediate and direct link between the whole or part of an input supply and a taxable activity for the purposes of attribution, the basic test was set out by the ECJ in *BLP Group Plc v CEC* (1995) and is known as the *BLP* test. Sometimes this test has been formulated as to whether the input supply is part of the cost component of the taxable activity or essential to it. It is not enough that it is a consequence of that activity. Nor is it permissible to look beyond that purpose to some ultimate aim, or to apply a "but for" test. That is not enough. Thus the costs of legal services given to a bank after it had advised on a takeover were not so directly attributable to that advice (a taxable activity as opposed to general banking which is exempt)—it was a consequence of it; nor was it enough that it would not have been incurred but for the taxable activity.[21]

27–42   CONSEQUENCES OF TOTAL ATTRIBUTION   Under reg.101 of the 1995 General Regulations, if the whole of the input supply can be so attributed to a taxable activity, it is reclaimable in full. If none of it so relates, then none can be reclaimed. But if only part of it can be so attributed, then the question of apportionment arises.

27–43   CONSEQUENCES OF PARTIAL ATTRIBUTION   The effect of reg.101, where part of an input transaction can be identified with a taxable activity, is that the proportion of input tax which is allowed as a credit is generally equal to the ratio of the trader's exempt supplies to taxable supplies and not the part identified as applicable to a taxable activity.[22] This, however, may produce a surprising result. In *Mayflower Theatre Trust Ltd v HMRC* (2007), the trust paid production companies to put on plays, etc. at the theatre. Those were taxable supplies and the Trust incurred substantial input tax on them. Its problem was that 80 per cent of its output supplies were the sales of tickets which were exempt supplies. The other 20 per cent, however, were taxable supplies of theatre programmes, catering, etc. Applying the *BLP* test, the CA held that there was an immediate and direct link between the payments to the production companies and the sale of the programmes. The subject matter

---

beyond the trader's control or the taxable supplies never materialised: *Midland Bank v CEC* (2000).

[21] *Midland Bank Plc v CEC* (2000) ECJ. See also *Dial-a-Phone Ltd v CEC* (2004) CA.

[22] For an alternative ratio, see para.27–45 below.

of the productions formed part of the raw material used in the programmes and that objective link was sufficient to satisfy the test. Further, although there was no such link with the other taxable supplies, the effect of the 1995 General Regulations was that a full 20 per cent of the input tax was recoverable and not just the percentage attributable to the programmes.

OVERHEADS AND RESIDUAL COSTS   A business making both 27–44 taxable and exempt supplies may have overheads or residual costs (such as rent, fuel, etc.) which cannot be specifically attributed to any supply. In such a case, the supplier may deduct the relevant percentage of any input tax which is attributable to such costs of the business.[23] All that is needed is a direct and immediate link with the whole economic activity of the taxpayer. Thus, although the legal fees could not be attributed to any taxable supply in the *Midland Bank* case, they were attributed to overheads and so partly allowable.

Although this is a different methodology from that of attributing inputs to both specific exempt and taxable supplies as in the *Mayflower* case above, the appropriate proportion in the case of overheads is also generally based on the ratio of the taxpayer's taxable and exempt supplies and so the result would have been the same in that case even if the overheads approach had been used.

It was said in *Abbey National Plc v CEC* (2001) ECJ, that if the input supplies could be attributed to the overheads of the taxable economic activities they would be fully deducible even though they might not attach to any specific supply.[24] That accords with the *BLP* test that it is the taxable activity with which the connection must be made and not necessarily with any specific supply. That approach was adopted by the CJEU in *Kreztechnic AG v Finanzampt Linz* (2005). It has since been confirmed by the Court of Appeal in *Volkswagen Financial Services (UK) Ltd v HMRC* (2015).[25] The company made taxable supplies of cars and exempt supplies of financial services. In addition to specific inputs, it had inputs on general overheads which it had apportioned between the two types of supply, which HMRC had challenged. The Court of Appeal allowed the company's claim. It did not matter that those costs had not been specifically built into the cost of

---

[23] *Abbey National Plc v CEC* (2001) ECJ; *Kretztechnik AG v Finanzampt Linz* (2005) ECJ. This is based on the need for fiscal neutrality and the ability to deduct relevant inputs to preserve the sanctity of the system.

[24] And so not at all, if fully attributable to the overheads of the exempt supplies only, or to a separate activity which does not form part of the VAT business.

[25] See also *HMRC v Smart* (2016),

the taxable supply of the cars; that was not a pre-condition. It depended instead on their use being for the purpose of the company's business as a whole.

27–45   ALTERNATIVE PARTIAL ATTRIBUTION METHOD As an alternative to the turnover method of attribution of input tax not directly attributable to either taxable or exempt supplies, reg.102 allows for an alternative method. This is known as a Partial Exemption Special Method (PESM). Such a method must more fairly and reasonably represent the amount used in making the taxable supplies. The onus is on the supplier to show that.[26] That is decided by reference to the real economic use (and not necessarily physical use) of the asset, i.e. having regard to economic reality.[27] Each case will therefore depend heavily on its facts. A recent example is the case of *HMRC v London Clubs Management Ltd* (2011). That concerned a number of casinos who made taxable supplies of catering and slot machines and exempt supplies of other gambling forms. The Court of Appeal upheld the supplier's contention that a method based on floor space would be more fair and reasonable.

Bad debt relief

27–46   Since liability to account for VAT arises at the tax point there would be a problem for a trader who has issued a tax invoice in one quarter, and so accounted for the output tax on that invoice, if the customer subsequently defaults on payment so that the trader never actually receives that tax. From 1990 onwards therefore there has been an allowance for such bad debts. Section 36 currently provides that any supply on which a taxpayer has accounted for VAT to HMRC, and on which there is a debt (whether in cash or in kind) which is more than six months old and which has been written off in the trader's books is eligible for such relief (i.e. the output tax paid can be reclaimed). Where the trader has accepted a lower sum in settlement of the debt, the amount foregone will be eligible for bad-debt relief.[28] Repayment of the relief is required if the debt is subsequently repaid or if the debt has been assigned to a person connected with the trader and payment is made to that person.

---

[26] *Royal Bank of Scotland v HMRC* (2007).
[27] *St Helen's School (Northern) Ltd v HMRC* (2006); see also *Volkswagen Financial Services (UK) Ltd v HMRC* (2015).
[28] *CPG Logistics Ltd v HMRC* (2010).

Recovery of overpaid tax

27–47 EU law requires in principle that any tax levied in breach of EU law must be repaid.[29] UK law accordingly in s.80 of the Act requires such repayment to anyone who has paid VAT to them which was not in fact due to HMRC. Usually this arises where a trader has accounted for VAT in the usual way on the basis that it was making standard-rated taxable supplies. There is then a decision of the CJEU that such supplies were not in fact standard-rated supplies and so the tax has been wrongly accounted for. Any claim for repayment is limited to amounts for the three years prior to the claim.[30]

In making such a repayment of overpaid output tax HMRC may set off any previously wrongly repaid input tax (paid by HMRC under the mistaken impression that the trader's supplies were not exempt) irrespective of any time limits for recovery of that repayment under s.81 of the Act.[31]

Section 80 is the only remedy available to the taxable person to claim recovery of the tax (s.80(7)), the common law remedy of restitution cannot apply. But it must still be an adequate remedy under EU law (the *San Giorgio* test) and this enabled the Court of Appeal in *Littlewoods Retail Ltd v HMRC* (2015) to disapply the UK Act which allows only for simple interest to be paid and order that compound interest be paid on such repayments. This is unlikely to be the last word on that issue, however.

27–48 UNJUST ENRICHMENT There is a potentially inherent problem, however, in the cases where VAT has been wrongly charged and accounted for by a supplier. The taxable person, remember, is not the ultimate bearer of the tax. That VAT will therefore actually have been charged and paid by the consumer to the supplier before being then handed over to HMRC. So if the supplier then receives a repayment of that VAT from HMRC, it will receive a windfall if it is unlikely or impracticable for the supplier to then pass that repayment on to its customers. Thus s.80(3) provides that HMRC is not liable to repay overpaid VAT if to do so would unjustly enrich the supplier. In Ch.25 we noted the decision in the *Bridport and West Dorset Golf Club* case that VAT had been wrongly charged on green fees. In that case HMRC reimbursed the club but as a result a number of other golf clubs now sought repayment. At that

---

[29] *Amministratrazione delle Finanze dello Stato v San Giorgio SpA* (1983).

[30] A challenge to this limitation period based on EU principles failed in *Leeds City Council v HMRC* (2015).

[31] *Birmingham Hippodrome Theatre Trust Ltd v HMRC* (2013).

point HMRC refused on the basis of unjust enrichment. The clubs were not in practice going to reimburse the golfers who had actually paid the VAT on those fees to them.[32]

In such cases EU law allows a defence of unjust enrichment to repayment claims,[33] but it cannot apply in full where either the whole charge was not passed on entirely to the consumer, in which case the amount not passed on must be repaid, or where the supplier suffered damage as a result, in which case that amount must be repaid. In all cases EU law also requires that national law does not make it virtually impossible or excessively difficult to secure a repayment. It is for the UK courts to determine in each case the factual situation.

27–49 REPAYMENTS TO THE FINAL CONSUMER Section 80 only applies to repayment claims by the supplier. EU and UK law also allow a claim in restitution against HMRC by a consumer who has wrongly paid VAT on a supply.[34] Section 80(7) of the Act which limits HMRC's liability to repay to actions under s.80 has no application to common law claims for restitution.[35]

There is of course a problem as to how the two claims for recovery sit with one another. This was the subject of an application for judicial review *in R. (on the application of Premier Foods (Holdings) Ltd) v HMRC* (2015). Premier Foods had paid VAT to one of its suppliers. That VAT should not have been paid. Ordinarily that VAT would be repaid to the supplier who would then pass it on to Premier Foods (unlike the green fees type of situations this was a single supplier/recipient transaction), but the supplier was now insolvent. Any repayment to the supplier would thus fall into its general assets available to all its creditors and Premier Foods would not recover all or possibly any of the VAT. Since this was not a matter on which an appeal to the Tribunal lay, Premier Foods sought judicial review of HMRC's decision to repay the money to the supplier. The judge held that any repayment to the supplier would amount to unjust enrichment under s.80(3) and thus the mechanism to pay the money directly to the applicants could be utilised.

---

[32] The first of these claims came before the first instance tribunal in *The Berkshire Golf Club v HMRC* (2015).
[33] *Webers Wine World Handels-GmbH v Abgabenberufungskommission Wein* (2005) CJEU. See also *Reed Employment Ltd v HMRC* (2014).
[34] *Reetsma Cigaretttenfabriken GmbH v Ministerio delle Finanze* (2008).
[35] *Investment Trust Companies (in Liquidation) v HMRC* (2015).

INDEX

LEGAL TAXONOMY
FROM SWEET & MAXWELL

This index has been prepared using Sweet and Maxwell's Legal Taxonomy. Main index entries conform to keywords provided by the Legal Taxonomy except where references to specific documents or non-standard terms (denoted by quotation marks) have been included. These keywords provide a means of identifying similar concepts in other Sweet & Maxwell publications and online services to which keywords from the Legal Taxonomy have been applied. Readers may find some minor differences between terms used in the text and those which appear in the index. Suggestions to *sweet&maxwell.taxonomy@thomson.com*

18–25 trusts
inheritance tax
conditions, 22–54
generally, 22–53
other tax charges, 22–58
tax advantages up to aged 18, 22–55
tax charges aged 18–25, 22–56
Abuse of rights
tax compliance, 3–48
Accounts
capital expenditure
adjustment, 8–13
trading income
generally accepted accounting practice, 5–16
importance, 5–15
taxable profits, 5–16
Accumulation and maintenance trusts
inheritance tax, 22–47
Administration of estates
see also **Inheritance tax**
estate income
administrators, 12–24
beneficiaries, 12–25
beneficiaries with entitlements, 12–27
introduction, 12–01, 12–23
residuary beneficiaries, 12–26
Agents
see **Commercial agents**

Agricultural holdings
inheritance tax, 20–21
Agricultural property relief
agricultural property defined, 20–44
application, 20–42, 20–46
business property relief and, 20–41
conditions, 20–43—20–45
length of ownership, 20–43
occupation, 20–45
reduction, 20–46
Agricultural tenancies
see **Agricultural holdings**
Alterations
residential property
reduced rate VAT, 26–17
Annual allowances
pension contributions, 10–12
Annual exemption
inheritance tax, 20–04
Annual investment allowances
plant and machinery allowances, 8–15
Annual payments
charge to tax, 7–17—7–22
deductions, 7–29—7–31
exempt payments, 7–19, 7–21
history, 7–15—7–16
importance, 7–28
meaning, 7–19, 7–23—7–27, 7–30
mortgage interest, 7–20
nature of
binding legal obligation, 7–23

ejusdem generis, 7–23
frequency, 7–19, 7–24
income not capital, 7–26—7–27
pure profit income, 7–25
Annual tax on enveloped dwellings
property income, 6–14
Annuities
income tax, 11–17
inheritance tax, 19–36
taxable income, 3–16
Anti-avoidance
see **Tax avoidance**
Appeals
generally, 2–17—2–18
inheritance tax, 24–10
right of appeal, 4–22—4–25
Scotland, 2–23, 2–24
tribunals, 2–19—2–21
VAT, 25–20
Wales, 2–23, 2–25
Arm's length transactions
capital gains tax, 15–17—15–18,
15–42
Armed forces
inheritance tax
death on active service, 20–26
visiting forces, 20–23
Artificial transactions in land
property income, 6–11
Artistic works
inheritance tax, 20–12
Assessment
trading income, 5–47
Assets
see also **Capital gains tax**
capital gains tax
capital sum derived from,
15–21—15–22
generally, 15–14
options, 15–42
personal and other rights, 15–15
wasting assets, 16–15
wasting assets
capital gains tax, 16–15, 17–13
Associated operations
inheritance tax
chargeable transfers,
19–37—19–39
Attendance allowance
taxation of social security benefits,
10–17
Badges of trade
see **Trading income**

Balancing adjustments
plant and machinery allowances,
8–19—8–20
Beneficiaries
see also **Administration of estates;
Settled property; Trusts**
capital gains tax
adjustments, 15–69
general rule, 15–67
liability to tax, 15–70
souses or civil partners, 15–68
protection of trust, 12–10
trust income
accumulated income, 12–09
computation of, 12–07
entitlement to, 12–08
vested and contingent interests
distinguished, 12–09
vulnerable beneficiaries' trusts,
12–10
Benefits
see **Social security income**
Benefits in kind
employment income
credit tokens, 9–22
exempted benefits, 9–29
expense payments, 9–18
fair bargain, 9–30
generally, 9–17
living accommodation, 9–23
loans, 9–27
lower paid employment, 9–31
mileage allowances, 9–26
ministers of religion, 9–31
residual liability to charge, 9–28
vehicles, 9–24—9–25
vouchers, 9–19—9–21
Bereaved minors trusts
inheritance tax
conditions, 22–49–50
generally, 22–48
tax advantages, 22
tax charges, 22–51—22–52
Books
VAT, 26–15
Border Force
tax authorities, 2–13
Burials and cremation
see also **Funeral expenses**
VAT, 26–20
Business property relief
agricultural property relief and,
20–41

excluded items, 20–38
extent of relief, 20–36
gifts with reservation of benefit and,
  20–40
investments, 20–37
nature of relief, 20–36
potentially exempt transfers and,
  20–40
real property, 20–37
reduction in value of transfer, 20–39
Capital allowances
changes to system, 8–04—8–06
depreciation, 8–12—8–13
history, 8–04—8–05
introduction, 8–01—8–03
other allowances, 8–03, 8–21
plant and machinery allowances
  annual investment allowances,
    8–15
  balancing adjustments,
    8–19—8–20
  books, 8–10
  claiming allowances, 8–11
  enhanced allowances, 8–16
  generally, 8–03
  first-year allowances, 8–16
  improvements, 8–09
  meaning, 8–07—8–10
  operation of scheme, 8–14
  part of premises, 8–08—8–09
  pooling, 8–18
  professions, 8–10
  types, 8–14
  use of allowances, 8–12—8–14
  wholly and exclusively rule, 8–11
  writing-down allowances, 8–17
object of tax, 8–04—8–06
Capital expenditure
see also **Capital allowances**
adjustment to accounts, 8–13
generally, 8–21
Capital gains
see also **Capital gains tax**
charge to tax, 16–17
computation
  apportionment, 16–09
  consideration, 16–03
  contract price, 16–10
  deemed disposals, 16–11
  income receipts and expenditure,
    16–02
  leases, 16–16
  market value, 16–12

part disposals, 16–14
wasting assets, 16–15
wholly and exclusively rule, 16–08
VAT, 16–13
consideration
  contingent consideration,
    16–04—16–05
  deferred consideration,
    16–04—16–05
  generally, 16–03
contingent liabilities
  allowable expenditure, 16–07
  generally, 16–06
deemed disposals, 15–58—15–61,
  16–11
definition, 15–10
entrepreneurs' relief, 16–17
exemptions
  charities' disposals, 17–15
  chattels disposed for less than
    £6000, 17–10—17–12
  compensation, 17–15
  damages, 17–15
  foreign currencies, 17–15
  gambling, 17–15
  gilts, 17–14
  introduction, 17–01
  life insurance, 17–15
  lotteries, 17–15
  premium savings bonds, 17–15
  private cars, 17–15
  private residence relief,
    17–02—17–09
  qualifying corporate bonds,
    17–14
  savings, 17–15
  share incentive plans, 17–15
  tangible moveables, 17–13
  wasting assets, 17–13
indexation relief, 16–17
introduction, 16–01
rebasing, 16–18
reliefs
  entrepreneurs' relief, 16–17
  indexation relief, 16–17
  rebasing, 16–18
  taper relief, 16–17
shares
  bed and breakfasting rules, 16–22
  pooling, 16–19—16–20
  same day rule, 16–21
taper relief, 16–17
taxable income, 3–16

Capital gains tax
see also **Capital gains; Capital losses; Reliefs**
assets
  capital sum derived from, 15–21—15–22
  generally, 15–14
  options, 15–42
  personal and other rights, 15–15
beneficiaries
  adjustments, 15–69
  general rule, 15–67
  liability to tax, 15–70
  souses or civil partners, 15–68
capital distributions, 15–33
capital gains, 15–10
capital sum derived from assets, 15–21—15–22
charge to tax, 15–09
charities, 15–45
chattels disposed for less than £6000
  generally, 17–10
  marginal relief, 17–11
  sets, 17–12
civil partners
  beneficiaries' liability to tax, 15–68
  disposals between, 15–44
  tax rates, 15–07
companies
  company adjustments, 15–34—15–35
  generally, 15–04
contractual disposals
  conditional contracts, 15–28
  timing, 15–27—15–28
death
  assets of deceased, 15–46
  chargeable event, 15–46
  disposal to legatee, 15–48
  disposal to other than legatee, 15–49
  uplift effect, 15–47
debts
  allowable losses, 15–37
  assignees, 15–39
  debt on security, 15–38
  loans to traders, 15–37
  nature of, 15–36
  property in satisfaction of, 15–40
deemed disposals, 15–58—15–61, 16–11
disposals

arm's length, 15–18
capital sum derived from assets, 15–21—15–22
charities' disposals, 17–15
civil partners, 15–44
conditional contracts, 15–28
connected persons, 15–18
date of disposal, 15–27—15–28
deemed disposals, 15–58—15–61, 16–11
entrepreneurs' relief and, 17–18
generally, 15–16
gifts, 15–17
loss, destruction and negligible value, 15–23—15–26
market value rule, 15–18—15–19
meaning, 15–16
not at arm's length, 15–17—15–18
part disposals, 15–20
spouses, 15–44
timing by contract, 15–27—15–28
entrepreneurs' relief
  amount, 17–16
  associated disposals, 17–18
  difficulties, 17–20
  generally, 17–16
  investors' relief, 17–21
  qualifying disposals, 17–17
  trustees, 17–19
history, 3–09, 15–03
holdover relief
  gifts immediately chargeable to inheritance tax, 17–23—17–24
  gifts of business assets, 17–25
  limited liability partnerships, 17–30
  operation of, 17–22
individuals, 15–04
inflation and, 15–02
introduction, 15–01
investors' relief, 17–21
land transactions, 6–12
marginal relief, 17–11
options
  meaning, 15–41
  not at arm's length, 15–42
persons
  connected persons, 15–18
  meaning, 15–12
  residence, 15–13
private residence relief
  additional buildings, 17–06

dwelling-house, 17–05—17–06
generally, 17–02
gifts relief and, 17–09
part of dwelling, 17–05—17–06
partial business use, 17–08
permitted area, 17–07
private letting, 17–08
sole or main residence, 17–03
temporary occupation, 17–04
reliefs
  entrepreneurs' relief,
    17–16—17–21
  hold-over relief, 17–22—17–25,
    17–30
  investors' relief, 17–21
  marginal relief, 17–11
  private residence relief,
    17–02—17–09
  roll-over relief, 17–26—17–30
  taper relief, 15–03
roll-over relief
  limited liability partnerships,
    17–30
  replacement of business assets,
    17–27—17–29
  transfer of business of company,
    17–26
share capital
  reorganisation of capital,
    15–34—15–35
settled property
  absolute entitlement, 15–52
  beneficiaries' tax liability,
    15–67—15–70
  class gifts, 15–53
  concurrent interests, 15–51
  deemed disposals, 15–58—15–61
  definition, 15–50
  disposals and, 15–55—15–63
  disposals by trustees,
    15–57—15–59
  individual gifts, 15–53
  "jointly so entitled", 15–51
  person entitled to interest,
    15–63
  putting property into settlement,
    15–56
  termination of interest in
    possession, 15–62
  transfers between trusts,
    15–64—15–66
  trustees, 15–54
spouses

beneficiaries' liability to tax,
  15–68
disposals between, 15–44
tax rates, 15–07
taper relief, 15–03
tax avoidance
  company adjustments, 15–35
tax rates
  exempt amount, 15–06
  flat rate, 15–05
  residential property, 15–09
  spouses and civil partners, 15–07
  trustees, 15–08
trading stock
  generally, 15–29
  groups of companies, 15–32
  transfers from, 15–31
  transfers to, 15–30
transfers between trusts
  creation of separate settlement,
    15–64
  distinguishing settlements,
    15–66
  subsidiary settlement, 15–65
value shifting, 15–43
Capital losses
generally, 16–23
loss relief
  carry back, 16–26
  exempt amount, 16–25
  generally, 16–24
Caravans
VAT, 26–17
Carry-forward reliefs
corporation tax, 14–36
trading income, 5–42—5–44
Cars
capital gains, 17–15
employment income, 9–24—9–25
mileage allowances, 9–26
Catering industry
VAT, 26–12—26–13
Charge to tax
annual payments, 7–17—7–22
capital gains, 16–17
capital gains tax, 15–09
charging provisions
  generally, 3–16
  mutual exclusivity, 3–18
  relationship between taxes and,
    3–17—3–18
  taxable income, 3–16
companies, 14–03

Chargeable transfers
inheritance tax
annuities purchased with life
policies, 19–36
associated operations,
19–37—19–39
close companies, 19–33
future payments, 19–34
generally, 21–09
gifts with reservation of benefit,
19–14—19–27
interest-free loans, 19–35
introduction, 19–01
liabilities arising from, 21–16
lifetime transfers, 19–02—19–08
meaning, 19–02
non-commercial transfers,
19–09—19–11
other charges, 19–32—19–40
potentially exempt
transfers, 19–12—19–13,
21–10—21–11
same-day transfers, 21–13
settled property, 19–40
transfer of several properties,
21–12
transfers on death,
19–28—19–31
transfers reported late, 21–14
Charities
capital gains tax
generally, 15–45
exempt disposals, 17–15
covenants, 12–29
exemptions
income tax, 12–28
inheritance tax, 20–08
gift aid
annual payments, 12–29
one-off payments, 12–30
operation, 12–30—12–31
qualifying donations,
12–32—12–33
inheritance tax
exemptions, 20–08
VAT, 25–65
Chattels
capital gains
generally, 17–10
marginal relief, 17–11
sets, 17–12
inheritance tax
pre-eminent interest, 20–12

Child benefit
income tax, 13–31
tax charge, 10–17—10–18
Child restraints
VAT, 26–17
Child tax credit
see also **Tax credits**
operation of system, 13–32
tax charge, 10–17
taxable income, 13–16
threshold, 13–32
Children
child benefit, 10–17—10–18
child tax credit
generally, 10–17
operation of system, 13–32
taxable income, 13–16
threshold, 13–32
inheritance tax
bereaved minors trusts,
22–48—22–52
dispositions for maintenance of
family, 20–14
VAT
child restraints, 26–17
children's clothing, 26–15
Civil partners
capital gains tax
beneficiaries' liability to tax,
15–68
disposals between, 15–44
tax rates, 15–07
inheritance tax
generally, 20–02—20–03
gifts in consideration of civil
partnership, 20–07
liability, 23–08
nil-rate band, 21–05—21–07
Close companies
see also **Companies**
corporation tax, 14–18
inheritance tax
chargeable transfers, 19–33
dispositions for benefit of
employees, 20–18
Commercial agents
VAT
generally, 25–78
undisclosed agency, 25–79
settled property, 22–29
Companies
see also **Corporation tax; Groups of
companies**

capital gains tax
  company adjustments,
    15–34—15–35
  generally, 15–04
charge to tax, 14–03
charging provisions, 14–04
close companies
  corporation tax, 14–18
  inheritance tax, 19–33, 20–18,
    22–29
incorporation
  tax advantages and
    disadvantages, 14–07—14–09
introduction, 14–01
legislation, 14–02
meaning, 14–05
permanent establishment, 14–05
residence, 14–05
Compensation
  capital gains, 17–15
Compliance
  tax laws, 3–48—3–49
Consideration
  capital gains
    contingent consideration,
      16–04—16–05
    deferred consideration,
      16–04—16–05
    generally, 16–03
  inheritance tax
    dispositions taking effect on
      death, 20–29
  VAT
    direct link, 25–42
    discounts, 25–44
    free supplies, 27–03
    identifying, 27–06
    incidental expenses, 27–04
    items constituting, 27–02
    meaning, 25–40—25–41
    non-cash consideration, 25–45,
      27–07—27–13
    part-exchange deals, 25–46
    requirement for, 25–40
    subsidies, 27–05
    use of non-taxable agents,
      25–43
Consolidation
  tax laws, 3–27
Consultation
  HMRC guidance, 3–32
Contraception
  VAT, 26–17

Copyright
  taxation of intellectual property
    rights, 7–10
Corporation tax
  see also **Companies**
  close companies, 14–18
  computation of profits
    meaning of "profits",
      14–13—14–15
    tax avoidance, 14–14
  deductions from total profits
    carry-forward reliefs, 14–36
    change of ownership, 14–38
    charges on income, 14–31—14–32
    company reconstructions, 14–37
    generally, 14–30
    group relief, 14–39
    investment management
      expenses, 14–33
    losses, 14–34
    restrictions on loss relief, 14–40
    set-off against profits, 14–35
  definition, 14–03
  distributions
    close companies, 14–18
    demergers, 14–20
    excluded items, 14–19
    generally, 14–16
    meaning, 14–17
  history of tax law, 3–08
  incorporation and, 14–07—14–09
  intangible assets
    capital expenditure,
      14–27—14–28
    computation of gains, 14–27
    generally, 14–24
    intellectual property, 14–26
    meaning, 14–25
    tax avoidance, 14–29
  intellectual property, 14–26
  introduction, 14–01
  legislative framework, 14–02
  loan relationships, 14–21—14–23
  loss relief
    carry-forward reliefs, 14–36
    change of ownership, 14–38
    company reconstructions, 14–37
    generally, 14–34
    group relief, 14–39
    restrictions on, 14–40
    set-off against profits, 14–35
  object of tax, 14–06
  self-assessment, 14–11

tax codes, 14–10
tax rates, 14–12
tax reform, 14–10
tax year, 14–11
Council tax
local taxation, 2–33
property income, 6–15
Credit tokens
employment income, 9–22
Cultural services
VAT, 26–20
Damages
capital gains, 17–15
Death
capital gains tax
assets of deceased, 15–46
chargeable event, 15–46
disposal to legatee, 15–48
disposal to other than legatee, 15–49
uplift effect, 15–47
inheritance tax
changes in value by reason of death, 21–42
death of emergency personnel, 20–26
death on active service, 20–26
transfers on death, 19–28—19–31, 20–27—20–33, 21–40—21–41
Debts
capital gains tax
allowable losses, 15–37
assignees, 15–39
debt on security, 15–38
loans to traders, 15–37
nature of, 15–36
property in satisfaction of, 15–40
inheritance tax
artificial debts, 21–23
debts relating to property not subject to tax, 21–24
Deductions
corporation tax
carry-forward reliefs, 14–36
change of ownership, 14–38
charges on income, 14–31—14–32
company reconstructions, 14–37
generally, 14–30
group relief, 14–39
investment management expenses, 14–33
losses, 14–34

restrictions on loss relief, 14–40
set-off against profits, 14–35
employment income
non-domiciled employees, 9–43
professional fees, 9–43
rules, 9–36—9–37
salary sacrifice, 9–12
seafarers, 9–43
travelling expenses, 9–40—9–42
wholly and exclusively rule, 9–38—9–39
trading income, 5–39
Dependants
inheritance tax
dispositions for maintenance of family, 20–15
Depreciation
capital gains tax, 8–12—8–13
Devolved legislation
tax laws, 3–21
Disabled persons
beneficial interest in possession inheritance tax, 22–12
Discounts
VAT
cash commission, 27–16
price rebates, 27–15
Discretionary trusts
inheritance tax, 22–03
Disposals
capital gains tax
arm's length, 15–18
capital sum derived from assets, 15–21—15–22
charities' disposals, 17–15
civil partners, 15–44
conditional contracts, 15–28
connected persons, 15–18
date of disposal, 15–27—15–28
deemed disposals, 15–58—15–61, 16–11
entrepreneurs' relief and, 17–18
generally, 15–16
gifts, 15–17
loss, destruction and negligible value, 15–23—15–26
market value rule, 15–18—15–19
meaning, 15–16
not at arm's length, 15–17—15–18
part disposals, 15–20
spouses, 15–44
timing by contract, 15–27—15–28

Distributions
corporation tax
close companies, 14–18
demergers, 14–20
excluded items, 14–19
generally, 14–16
meaning, 14–17
taxable income, 3–16
Dividends
double taxation, 11–14
exemptions, 11–15
foreign companies, 11–16
income tax, 11–12—11–13
inheritance tax
waiver of dividends, 20–20
tax rates
dividend rate, 13–21
dividend trust rate, 12–05
taxable income, 3–16
Double charges relief
inheritance tax
chargeable transfers, 21–28
gifts with reservation of benefit,
21–28
potentially exempt transfers and
transfer back, 21–27
statutory provisions, 21–26
transfer and loan back, 21–29
transfer and transfer back, 21–30
transfer of property and debt,
21–31
Double taxation
dividends, 11–14
Drawdown
occupational pensions, 10–13
E-tax
see **Tax administration**
Earned income
taxable income, 3–16
Economic activities
see also **Trading income**
VAT
"business", 25–71
exploitation of property, 25–73
meaning, 25–70—25–72
objective concept, 25–74
private activity distinguished,
25–76
services, 25–75
Education
VAT, 26–20, 26–22
Electricity supply
VAT, 26–17

Emergency services
inheritance tax
death of emergency personnel,
20–26
Emoluments
see **Employment income**
Employees
see also **Employment income;
Trading income**
VAT, 25–77
Employment income
benefits in kind
credit tokens, 9–22
exempted benefits, 9–29
expense payments, 9–18
fair bargain, 9–30
generally, 9–17
living accommodation, 9–23
loans, 9–27
lower paid employment, 9–31
mileage allowances, 9–26
ministers of religion, 9–31
residual liability to charge, 9–28
vehicles, 9–24—9–25
vouchers, 9–19—9–21
deductions
non-domiciled employees, 9–43
professional fees, 9–43
rules, 9–36—9–37
salary sacrifice, 9–12
seafarers, 9–43
travelling expenses, 9–40—9–42
wholly and exclusively rule,
9–38—9–39
earnings
amounts treated as, 9–32—9–33
deductions from, 9–12
emoluments, 9–10
meaning, 9–09
negative earnings, 9–13
"reward for services" test, 9–11
"specific employment income",
9–11
employees
entitlement rules, 9–04
meaning, 9–03—9–06
professionals, 9–05—9–06
self-employment, 9–04
employment, 9–03—9–06
exempt income, 9–34—9–35
gifts
assessable payments, 9–14—9–15
sports testimonials, 9–15

grossing-up, 13–05
introduction, 9–01—9–02
IR 35 companies, 9–07—9–08
marginal rate, 9–01
non-cash payments, 9–16
PAYE
  advantages, 9–53
  personal service companies,
    9–07—9–08
  tax codes, 9–54
personal service companies,
  9–07—9–08
Schedule E, 9–02
securities
  incentives, 9–47
  Part 7 rules, 9–48
  sharesave schemes, 9–50—9–52
  SIPs, 9–49
tax codes, 9–54
tax credits, 9–01, 9–03
taxable income, 3–16
termination payments, 9–44—9–46
vouchers
  cash vouchers, 9–20
  generally, 9–19
  non-cash vouchers, 9–21
Employment status
  see also **Employment income**
  trading income
    agency workers, 5–04
    divers and diving supervisors,
      5–04
    employees and self-employed,
      5–03—5–04
Energy efficiency
  VAT, 26–17
Enforcement
  civil enforcement
    correcting returns, 4–15—4–16
    freedom of information,
      4–20—4–21
    generally, 4–14
    HMRCs information powers,
      4–17
    making enquiries, 4–15—4–16
    penalties, 4–18
    time limits, 4–19
  criminal enforcement, 4–26
  generally, 2–01, 2–04
Enhanced allowances
  see **Capital allowances**
Entrepreneurs' relief
  amount, 17–16

associated disposals, 17–18
difficulties, 17–20
generally, 16–17, 17–16
investors' relief, 17–21
qualifying disposals, 17–17
trustees, 17–19
Estate duty
  inheritance tax
    valuation of property, 21–33
Estate income
  taxable income, 3–16
Estates
  see **Administration of estates**
EU law
  generally, 3–24
  impact of, 2–27—2–29
  VAT
    abusive practices, 25–12—25–16
    application of principles,
      25–08—25–11
    directives, 25–02—25–07
    effectiveness, 25–11
    exempt supplies, 26–18
    fiscal neutrality, 25–09—25–10
    fraud, 25–12
    objective nature of tax, 25–13
    recovery of overpaid tax, 27–47
    tax avoidance, 25–12, 25–15
    tax evasion, 25–12, 25–14
    tax rates, 26–03
Exempt income
  see **Employment income; Pensions**
Exempt supplies
  see also **VAT**
  discretion, 26–23
  education, 26–22
  EU law, 26–18
  financial services, 26–20
  gambling, 26–20
  insurance, 26–20
  interpretation, 26–19, 26–22
  land, 26–20
  multiple supplies, 26–21
  partial exemption, 26–27
  socially exempt supplies, 26–20
  zero rating compared, 26–24
Exemptions
  see also **Reliefs**
  capital gains
    charities' disposals, 17–15
    chattels disposed for less than
      £6000, 17–10—17–12
    compensation, 17–15

damages, 17–15
employee share-ownership plans,
  17–15
foreign currency, 17–15
gambling, 17–15
gilts, 17–14
introduction, 17–01
life assurance, 17–15
lottery winnings, 17–15
premium bonds, 17–15
private cars, 17–15
private residence relief,
  17–02—17–09
qualifying corporate bonds,
  17–14
savings, 17–15
tangible moveables, 17–13
wasting assets, 17–13
charities, 12–28
inheritance tax
agricultural tenancies, 20–21
annual exemption, 20–04
chattels of pre-eminent interest,
  20–12
civil partners, 20–02—20–03
death of emergency personnel,
  20–26
death on active service, 20–26
dispositions allowable for income
  tax, 20–17
dispositions by close company for
  benefit of employees, 20–18
dispositions for maintenance of
  family, 20–13—20–16
dispositions taking effect on
  death, 20–27—20–33
family provision orders, 20–25
gifts for national purposes, 20–11
gifts in consideration of marriage
  or civil partnership, 20–07
gifts to charities, 20–08
gifts to housing associations,
  20–10
gifts to political parties, 20–09
grant of agricultural tenancy,
  20–21
historic buildings, 20–12
introduction, 20–01
normal expenditure out of
  income, 20–06
scientific collections, 20–12
small gifts to same person, 20–05
spouses, 20–02—20–03

waiver of dividends, 20–20
waiver of remuneration, 20–19
works of art, 20–12
occupational pensions,
  10–08—10–09
Exit charges
settled property
circumstances giving rise to, 22–41
notional cumulative total, 22–44
notional transfer, 22–44
rate of charge, 22–43—22–45
settlements after first 10-year
  charge, 22–45
settlements prior to first 10-year
  charge, 22–44
subject of charge, 22–42
Expenses
inheritance tax
funeral expenses, 21–42
trading income
apportionment, 5–31
basic rules, 5–27
deductions, 5–39
interest, 5–37
legal and accountancy charges,
  5–36
object test, 5–32—5–34
repairs and improvements, 5–38
revenue expenditure, 5–28—5–29
specific expenses, 5–35—5–38
travel, 5–35
wholly and exclusively rule,
  5–30
Explanatory notes
statutory interpretation, 3–34
Extra-statutory concessions
tax laws, 3–25
Family provision orders
inheritance tax, 20–25
Financial services
VAT, 26–20
First-year allowances
plant and machinery allowances,
  8–16
Fiscal neutrality
VAT
certainty, 27–24
consideration, 27–23
discounts, 27–23, 27–25
EU law, 25–09—25–10
separate supplies, 27–26
Fixed interest trusts
see **Settled property**

Food
VAT
  biscuits, 26–11
  cakes, 26–11
  catering, 26–12—26–13
  cold food, 26–14
  crisps, 26–11
  generally, 26–10
  hot food, 26–12
Foreign companies
dividends, 11–16
Foreign currencies
capital gains, 17–15
Foreign property
inheritance tax, 20–22
Fraud
tax compliance, 3–48
VAT fraud, 25–12
Fund raising
VAT, 26–20
Funeral expenses
see also **Burials and cremation**
inheritance tax, 21–42
Gambling
capital gains, 17–15
VAT, 26–20
Gas safety
VAT, 26–17
Gas supply
VAT, 26–17
General anti-abuse rule
DOTAS, 3–51
GAAR Study, 3–52
generally, 3–50
Gift aid
see **Charities**
Gifts
capital gains tax
  business assets, 17–25
  class gifts, 15–53
  disposals, 15–17
  gifts chargeable to inheritance
    tax, 17–23—17–24
  individual gifts, 15–53
employment income
  assessable payments, 9–14—9–15
  sports testimonials, 9–15
gift aid
  annual payments, 12–29
  one-off payments, 12–30
  operation, 12–30—12–31
  qualifying donations,
    12–32—12–33

hold-over relief
  gifts immediately chargeable to
    inheritance tax, 17–23—17–24
  gifts of business assets, 17–25
inheritance tax
  benefits reserved or retained,
    19–18
  business property relief and,
    20–40
  effect of reservation, 19–16
  exempt transfers, 19–25
  gifts for national purposes, 20–11
  gifts in consideration of marriage
    or civil partnership, 20–07
  gifts to charities, 20–08
  gifts to housing associations,
    20–10
  gifts to political parties, 20–09
  income tax alternative, 19–26
  land, 19–20—19–24
  pre-owned asset tax, 19–26
  property subject to charge, 19–27
  purpose of legislation,
    19–14—19–15
  small gifts to same person, 20–05
  statutory interpretation, 19–17
  timing, 19–19
Gilts
capital gains, 17–14
Goodwill
taxation of intellectual property
  rights, 7–12
Grossing-up
income tax, 13–05
inheritance tax
  computation, 21–19
  effect of, 21–20
  exceptions, 21–18
  generally, 19–07
  loss to estate, 21–17
Group relief
corporation tax, 14–39
Groups of companies
VAT, 25–67
Health
VAT, 26–20
Historic buildings
inheritance tax, 20–12
HMRC
constitution, 2–12
reviews of decisions, 2–16
scope of responsibilities, 2–13
self assessment, 2–14

HMRC guidance
  booklets, 3–39
  briefs, 3–38
  consultations, 3–32
  explanatory notes, 3–34
  generally, 3–29—3–30
  indirect guidance, 3–40
  instruction manuals, 3–37
  leaflets, 3–39
  notices, 3–38
  Parliamentary Ombudsman, 3–35
  Parliamentary proceedings, 3–35
  press releases, 3–39
  primary legislation, 3–31
  secondary legislation, 3–31
  statements of practice, 3–36
  tax information and impact notes,
    3–33
Hold-over relief
  capital gains tax
    gifts immediately chargeable to
      inheritance tax, 17–23—17–24
    gifts of business assets, 17–25
    limited liability partnerships,
      17–30
    operation of, 17–22
Housing associations
  gifts to
    inheritance tax, 20–10
Human rights
  impact of, 2–30—2–31
Income
  see also **Corporation tax;
    Employment income; Income
    tax**
  charges on, 13–10
  classifications of, 13–08
  grossing-up, 13–05
  partnership income, 13–07
  scope of, 7–35
  taxable income, 13–16—13–18
  total income, 13–09—13–15
  trust income, 13–06
  types of income
    fallback provisions for "other
      income", 7–13, 7–32—7–35
    generally, 13–04
    non-earned income, 11–18
Income tax
  see also **Employment income;
    Investment income; Pensions;
    Savings income**
  deductions

  expenses, 13–15
  interest payments, 13–11—13–14
  generally, 13–02
  grossing-up, 13–05
history of tax law, 3–04—3–07
income
  charges on income, 13–10
  classifications of income, 13–08
  fallback provisions for "other
    income", 7–13, 7–32—7–35
  grossing-up, 13–05
  partnership income, 13–07
  scope of, 7–35
  trust income, 13–06
  types of income, 13–04
income tax lock, 13–21
interest
  ISAs, 11–09
  Islamic finance, 11–06
  meaning, 11–05
  National Savings and
    Investments, 11–08
  non-taxed interest, 11–07—11–10
  paying tax on, 11–11
  sharesave schemes, 11–10
loans, 13–12—13–14
non-earned income, 11–18
personal allowances, 13–17—13–18
tax rates
  additional rate, 13–21
  basic rate, 13–21
  dividend rate, 13–21
  higher rate, 13–21
  income tax lock, 13–21
  nil rate, 13–21
  Scotland, 13–22
  Wales, 13–22
  zero rate, 13–21
trading income, 5–01—5–48
Individual savings accounts
  taxation of interest, 11–09
Individuals
  income tax
    additional rate, 13–21
    basic rate, 13–21
    charges on income, 13–10
    classifications of income, 13–08
    deductible expenses, 13–15
    deductible interest payments,
      13–11—13–14
    dividend rate, 13–21
    generally, 13–02
    grossing-up, 13–05

higher rate, 13–21
income sources, 13–03—13–08
income tax lock, 13–21
loans, 13–12—13–14
nil rate, 13–21
partnership income, 13–07
personal allowances,
   13–17—13–18
Scotland, 13–22
tax rates, 13–19—13–22
taxable income, 13–16—13–18
total income, 13–09—13–15
trust income, 13–06
types of income, 13–04
Wales, 13–22
zero rate, 13–21
introduction, 13–01
national insurance contributions
  Class 1, 13–25
  Class 2, 13–26
  Class 3, 13–27—13–28
  Class 4, 13–26
  generally, 13–23—13–24
  pensioners, 13–24
tax credits, 13–29—13–32
tax rates, 13–33
welfare benefits, 13–29—13–32

Inheritance tax
administration and collection
  appeals, 24–10
  charge for unpaid tax, 24–14
  delivery of an account,
    24–02—24–06
  determination, 24–10
  introduction, 24–01
  overseas settlements, 24–07
  payment by instalments, 24–12
  payment of tax due,
    24–11—24–13
  power to inspect property, 24–09
  power to require information,
    24–09
  repayments, 24–13
  returns by persons acting for
    settlor, 24–07
  returns following variation of
    disposition, 24–08
agricultural property relief
  agricultural property defined,
    20–44
  application, 20–42, 20–46
  business property relief and,
    20–41

conditions, 20–43—20–45
  length of ownership, 20–43
  occupation, 20–45
  reduction, 20–46
agricultural tenancies, 20–21
annual exemption, 20–04
annuities purchased with life
  policies, 19–36
armed forces
  death on active service, 20–26
associated operations,
  19–37—19–39
business property relief
  agricultural property relief and,
    20–41
  excluded items, 20–38
  extent of relief, 20–36
  gifts with reservation of benefit
    and, 20–40
  investments, 20–37
  nature of relief, 20–36
  potentially exempt transfers and,
    20–40
  real property, 20–37
  reduction in value of transfer,
    20–39
chargeable transfers
  annuities purchased with life
    policies, 19–36
  associated operations,
    19–37—19–39
  close companies, 19–33
  future payments, 19–34
  generally, 21–09
  gifts with reservation of benefit,
    19–14—19–27
  interest-free loans, 19–35
  introduction, 19–01
  liabilities arising from, 21–16
  lifetime transfers,
    19–02—19–08
  meaning, 19–02
  non-commercial transfers,
    19–09—19–11
  other charges, 19–32—19–40
  potentially exempt transfers,
    19–12—19–13, 21–10—21–11
  same-day transfers, 21–13
  settled property, 19–40
  transfer of several properties,
    21–12
  transfers on death, 19–28—19–31
  transfers reported late, 21–14

chattels of pre-eminent interest,
  20–12
civil partners, 20–02—20–03, 20–07,
  21–05—21–07
close companies
  chargeable transfers, 19–33
  dispositions for benefit of
    employees, 20–18
computation
  chargeable transfers,
    21–09—21–14
  double charges relief,
    21–26—21–31
  introduction, 21–01
  liabilities, 21–15—21–25
  potentially exempt transfers,
    21–10—21–11
  tax rates, 21–02—21–08
  valuation, 21–32—
delivery of an account
  duty of personal representatives,
    24–02
  excepted estates on death, 24–04
  exceptions for transferors and
    trustees, 24–05
  penalties, 24–03
  probate, 24–06
  time limits, 24–03
dispositions for maintenance of
  family
  children, 20–14
  dependent relatives, 20–15
  scope of exemption, 20–13
  uses of relief, 20–16
dispositions taking effect on death
  alterations of, 20–27—20–28
  consideration, 20–29
  linked exempt transfer, 20–33
  request to legatee, 20–32
  second deed rectification, 20–30
  two year discretionary trust,
    20–31
double charges relief
  chargeable transfers, 21–28
  gifts with reservation of benefit,
    21–28
  potentially exempt transfers and
    transfer back, 21–27
  statutory provisions, 21–26
  transfer and loan back, 21–29
  transfer and transfer back, 21–30
  transfer of property and debt,
    21–31

emergency services
  death of emergency personnel,
    20–26
excluded property
  foreign property owned by
    non-UK domiciled persons,
    20–22
  reversionary interests, 20–24
  visiting forces, 20–23
exemptions
  agricultural tenancies, 20–21
  annual exemption, 20–04
  chattels of pre-eminent interest,
    20–12
  civil partners, 20–02—20–03
  death of emergency personnel,
    20–26
  death on active service, 20–26
  dispositions allowable for income
    tax, 20–17
  dispositions by close company for
    benefit of employees, 20–18
  dispositions for maintenance of
    family, 20–13—20–16
  dispositions taking effect on
    death, 20–27—20–33
  family provision orders, 20–25
  gifts for national purposes, 20–11
  gifts in consideration of marriage
    or civil partnership, 20–07
  gifts to charities, 20–08
  gifts to housing associations,
    20–10
  gifts to political parties, 20–09
  grant of agricultural tenancy,
    20–21
  historic buildings, 20–12
  introduction, 20–01
  normal expenditure out of
    income, 20–06
  scientific collections, 20–12
  small gifts to same person, 20–05
  spouses, 20–02—20–03
  waiver of dividends, 20–20
  waiver of remuneration, 20–19
  works of art, 20–12
family provision orders, 20–25
future payments, 19–34
gifts
  for national purposes, 20–11
  in consideration of marriage or
    civil partnership, 20–07
  small gifts to same person, 20–05

to charities, 20–08
to housing associations, 20–10
to political parties, 20–09
gifts with reservation of benefit
benefits reserved or retained,
19–18
effect of reservation, 19–16
exempt transfers, 19–25
income tax alternative, 19–26
pre-owned asset tax, 19–26
property subject to charge, 19–27
purpose of legislation,
19–14—19–15
land, 19–20—19–24
statutory interpretation, 19–17
timing, 19–19
grossing-up
computation, 21–19
effect of, 21–20
exceptions, 21–18
loss to estate, 21–17
historic buildings, 20–12
history
1986 changes, 18–05
capital transfer tax, 18–03
estate duty, 18–02
generally, 3–12
hybrid tax, as, 18–06
Inheritance Tax Act 1984, 18–04
introduction, 18–01
post-1986 changes, 18–07
scope and effects, 18–08
incidence
estate rate, 23–14
introduction, 23–01, 23–11
partially exempt transfers on
death, 23–15—23–18
tax free gifts, 23–13
testamentary expenses, 23–12
interest-free loans, 19–35
land
exceptions, 19–23
gifts with reservation of benefit,
19–20—19–24
lease carve out schemes, 19–20
seven-year limit, 19–22
significant interest, 19–21
undivided shares, 19–24
liabilities
artificial debts, 21–23
debts relating to property not
subject to tax, 21–24
generally, 21–16

grossing-up lifetime transfers,
21–17—21–20
not resulting from chargeable
transfer, 21–21—21–23
relevant liabilities, 21–22
resulting from chargeable
transfer, 21–16
summary, 21–25
liability
chargeable lifetime transfers,
23–03
death, transfer on, 23–05
death within seven years of
transfer, 23–06
introduction, 23–01
limitations, 23–10
persons liable to tax, 23–02
property, 23–07
purchaser exception, 23–09
settled property, 23–04
transfers between spouses and
civil partners, 23–08
lifetime transfers
dispositions, 19–08
exempt transfers, 19–02
grossing-up, 19–07,
21–17—21–20
loss to transferor's estate, 19–03
meaning of estate, 19–04
powers of appointment, 19–05
property, 19–06
transfers of value, 19–02
loans to pay, 13–14
nil-rate band
civil partners, 21–05—21–07
cumulative survivors, 21–07
generally, 21–02—21–03
residential nil-rate band, 21–08
spouses, 21–05—21–07
transferable nil-rate band,
21–05—21–07
non-commercial transfers
connected persons, 19–10
intent to confer gratuitous
benefit, 19–11
market value, 19–09
normal expenditure out of income,
20–06
other charges
annuities purchased with life
policies, 19–36
associated operations,
19–37—19–39

close companies, 19–33
future payments, 19–34
generally, 19–32
interest-free loans, 19–35
settled property, 19–40
potentially exempt transfers
chargeable transfers,
21–10—21–11
definition, 19–12
double charges relief, 21–27
effect of, 19–13
reliefs
agricultural property,
20–42—20–46
business property, 20–36—20–41
successive charges, 20–34
voidable transfers, 20–35
woodlands, 20–47—20–48
reversionary interests, 20–24
scientific collections, 20–12
settled property
18-25 trusts, 22–53—22–58
accumulation and maintenance
trusts, 22–47
bereaved minors trusts,
22–48—22–52
categorisation, 22–10—22–17
charging provisions,
22–18—22–29
definition, 22–07
development of charges,
22–01—22–08
discretionary trusts, 22–03
excluded settled property,
22–05
exit charges, 22–41—22–45
fixed interest trusts, 22–02
generally, 19–40
independent tax regime,
22–30—22–32
interim charges, 22–41—22–45
multiple settlements, 22–08
non-fixed interest trusts, 22–03
putting property into settlement,
22–09
relevant property, 22–30
reversionary interests,
22–58—22–59
settlement powers, 22–60—22–61
special kinds, 22–46—22–57
specially favoured trusts, 22–04
ten year charge, 22–33—22–40
small gifts to same person, 20–05

spouses, 20–02—20–03, 20–07,
21–05—21–07
tax rates
chargeable bands, 21–02—20–13
lower rate where legacy to
charity, 21–04
nil-rate band, 21–02—21–03,
21–05—21–08
residential nil-rate band, 21–08
transferable nil-rate band,
21–05—21–07
transfers on death
common calamities, 19–31
retrospective effect, 19–29
timing, 19–30
transfer of value, 19–28
variation of deceased's
dispositions, 20–27—20–33
valuation
changes in value by reason of
death, 21–42
estate duty principles, 21–33
funeral expenses, 21–42
land sold for less than value at
death, 21–42
lessor's interest, 21–38
lotting, 21–41
life policies, 21–39
open market value, 21–32—21–35
qualifying investments, 21–42
related property, 21–37
restrictions on freedom to
dispose, 21–36
restrictions on sale, 21–34
value transferred on death,
21–40—21–41
waivers
of dividends, 20–20
of remuneration, 20–19
woodlands relief
nature of relief, 20–47
retrospective charges, 20–48
works of art, 20–12
Input tax
see also **VAT**
generally, 26–26
right to reclaim, 27–34—27–37
Insurance
VAT, 26–20
Intangible assets
corporation tax
capital expenditure,
14–27—14–28

computation of gains, 14–27
generally, 14–24
intellectual property, 14–26
meaning, 14–25
tax avoidance, 14–29
taxable income, 3–16
Intellectual property
corporation tax, 14–26
introduction, 7–01—7–03
receipts
copyright, 7–10
generally, 7–04
goodwill, 7–12
know-how, 7–09
licensing agreements, 7–14
other income, 7–13
patents, 7–08
reform, 7–05—7–07
scope of income, 7–34
trade marks, 7–11
Interest
income tax
ISAs, 11–09
Islamic finance, 11–06
meaning, 11–05
National Savings and
Investments, 11–08
non-taxed interest, 11–07—11–10
paying tax, 11–11
sharesave schemes, 11–10
taxable income, 3–16
International taxation
see also **EU law**
generally, 1–14—1–15, 2–26, 2–32
human rights, 2–30—2–31
Interpretation
legislation
approach to, 3–42—3–44
case law, 3–53—3–57
generally, 3–28, 3–41
Investment income
annuities, 11–17
dividends
double taxation, 11–14
exemptions, 11–15
foreign companies, 11–16
income tax, 11–12—11–13
interest
ISAs, 11–09
Islamic finance, 11–06
meaning, 11–05
National Savings and
Investments, 11–08

non-taxed interest, 11–07—11–10
paying tax on, 11–11
sharesave schemes, 11–10
introduction, 11–01—11–03
non-earned income, 11–18
Part 4 rules, 11–03
Part 6 rules, 11–04
UK resident companies, 11–02
Investments
inheritance tax
business property relief, 20–37
valuation of property, 21–42
Islamic finance
taxation of interest, 11–06
Judicial review
tribunal decisions, 2–22
Know-how
taxation of intellectual property
rights, 7–09
Land
see **Real property**
Land and building transaction tax
sale of land, 6–13
Legislation
application of, 3–45—3–47
Bill of Rights, 3–19
charging provisions
generally, 3–16
mutual exclusivity, 3–18
relationship between taxes and,
3–17—3–18
taxable income, 3–16
compliance, 3–48—3–49
consolidation, 3–27
delegated legislation, 3–22—3–23
devolved legislation, 3–21
EU law, 3–24
extra-statutory concessions, 3–25
finance acts, 3–20
form of tax
annual tax, 3–14
generally, 3–13
schedular tax, 3–15
generally, 3–01—3–02
history
capital gains tax, 3–09
corporation tax, 3–08
generally, 3–03
income tax, 3–04—3–07
inheritance tax, 3–12
national insurance, 3–10
stamp duty, 3–03
VAT, 3–11

international tax agreements, 3–26
interpretation
  approach to, 3–42—3–44
  case law, 3–53—3–57
  generally, 3–28, 3–41
  subordinate legislation, 3–22—3–23
Liabilities
inheritance tax
  artificial debts, 21–23
  debts relating to property not
    subject to tax, 21–24
  generally, 21–16
  grossing-up lifetime transfers,
    21–17—21–20
  not resulting from chargeable
    transfer, 21–21—21–23
  relevant liabilities, 21–22
  resulting from chargeable
    transfer, 21–16
  summary, 21–25
nil-rate band
  civil partners, 21–05—21–07
  cumulative survivors, 21–07
  generally, 21–02—21–03
  residential nil-rate band, 21–08
  spouses, 21–05—21–07
  transferable nil-rate band,
    21–05—21–07
Licensing agreements
taxation of intellectual property
  rights, 7–14
Life insurance
capital gains, 17–15
inheritance tax
  annuities purchased with life
    policies, 19–36
  valuation of property, 21–39
Lifetime allowances
pension contributions, 10–12
Lifetime transfers
see **Inheritance tax**
Limited liability partnerships
capital gains tax
  hold-over and roll-over reliefs,
    17–30
Loan relationships
taxable income, 3–16
Loans
capital gains tax
  loans to traders, 15–37
income tax
  benefits in kind, 9–27
  generally, 13–12—13–14

inheritance tax
  interest-free loans, 19–35
  transfer and loan back, 21–29
Loss relief
see also **Reliefs; Trading income**
capital gains tax
  carry back, 16–26
  exempt amount, 16–25
  generally, 16–24
corporation tax
  carry-forward reliefs, 14–36
  change of ownership, 14–38
  company reconstructions, 14–37
  generally, 14–34
  group relief, 14–39
  restrictions on, 14–40
  set-off against profits, 14–35
trading income
  carry-back of terminal losses,
    5–45
  carry-forward against subsequent
    profits, 5–42—5–44
  early years, 5–46
  introduction, 5–40
  set-off against general income
    and capital gains, 5–41
Lotteries
capital gains, 17–15
Marginal relief
capital gains tax, 17–11
Market value
inheritance tax
  valuation of property,
    21–32—21–35
Mobility aids
VAT, 26–17
National Crime Agency
tax authorities, 2–13
National insurance
history of tax law, 3–10
national insurance contributions
  Class 1, 13–25
  Class 2, 13–26
  Class 3, 13–27—13–28
  Class 4, 13–26
  generally, 13–23—13–24
  pensioners, 13–24
National Savings
taxation of interest, 11–08
Newspapers
VAT, 26–15
Non-commercial transfers
see **Inheritance tax**

Non-domestic rates
local taxation, 2–33
Non-earned income
see also **Investment income; Savings income**
annuities, 11–17
forms, 11–18
Normal expenditure out of income
inheritance tax, 20–06
Notices
HMRC guidance, 3–38
Occupational pensions
annual allowances, 10–12
drawdowns, 10–13
exemptions, 10–08—10–09
generally, 10–08
lifetime allowances, 10–12
Part 9 rules, 10–10
protecting pensioners, 10–14—10–15
scheme rules, 10–11
tax benefits, 10–16
Office for National Statistics
annual report, 13–33
Options
capital gains tax
meaning, 15–41
not at arm's length, 15–42
connected persons, 15–18
residence, 15–13
Parliamentary and Health Service Ombudsman
guidance on tax laws, 3–35
Parliamentary proceedings
guidance on tax laws, 3–35
Partial exemption
VAT, 26–27
Partnerships
income tax, 13–07
VAT, 25–66
Patents
taxation of intellectual property rights, 7–08
PAYE
advantages, 9–53
personal service companies, 9–07—9–08
tax codes, 9–54
Pension income
taxable income, 3–16
Pensions
introduction, 10–01
occupational pensions
annual limits, 10–12

drawdowns, 10–13
exemptions, 10–08—10–09
generally, 10–08
lifetime limits, 10–12
Part 9 rules, 10–10
protecting pensioners, 10–14—10–15
scheme rules, 10–11
tax benefits, 10–16
pension income
meaning, 10–02
tax legislation, 10–06
three pillars, 10–03—10–05
state pension, 10–07
Permanent establishment
corporation tax, 14–05
PETs
see **Potentially exempt transfers**
Plant and machinery
capital allowances
annual investment allowances, 8–15
balancing adjustments, 8–19—8–20
books, 8–10
claiming allowances, 8–11
enhanced allowances, 8–16
generally, 8–03
first-year allowances, 8–16
improvements, 8–09
meaning, 8–07—8–10
operation of scheme, 8–14
part of premises, 8–08—8–09
pooling, 8–18
professions, 8–10
types, 8–14
use of allowances, 8–12—8–14
wholly and exclusively rule, 8–11
writing-down allowances, 8–17
loans to buy, 13–13
wasting assets, 16–15
Political parties
gifts to
inheritance tax, 20–09
Pooling
assets
plant and machinery allowances, 8–18
shares
capital gains tax, 16–19—16–20
Postal services
VAT, 26–20

Potentially exempt transfers
inheritance tax
business property relief, 20–40
chargeable transfers,
21–10—21–11
definition, 19–12
double charges relief, 21–27
effect of, 19–13
Premium savings bonds
capital gains, 17–15
Press releases
HMRC guidance, 3–39
Primary legislation
national archives, 3–31
Private residence relief
capital gains tax
additional buildings, 17–06
dwelling-house, 17–05—17–06
generally, 17–02
gifts relief and, 17–09
part of dwelling, 17–05—17–06
partial business use, 17–08
permitted area, 17–07
private letting, 17–08
sole or main residence, 17–03
temporary occupation, 17–04
Professions
tax expertise, 1–20—1–24
taxable income, 3–16
Profits
property income
computation, 6–13
taxable income, 3–16
trading income
assessment basis, 5–47
computation, 5–15
Property income
annual tax on enveloped dwellings,
6–14
artificial transactions in land,
6–11
business rate, 6–15
capital gains tax, 6–12
council tax, 6–15
history, 6–02
introduction, 6–01
land transfer taxes, 6–13
property business income
calculating profits, 6–07
generally, 6–03—6–06
qualifying care relief, 6–10
rent-a-room, 6–09
taxing land, 6–08

stamp duty, 6–13
taxable income, 3–16
Public authorities
VAT, 25–65
Quick succession relief
inheritance tax, 22–28
Real property
see also **Land and buildings
transaction tax; Stamp duty**
inheritance tax
business property relief, 20–37
exceptions, 19–23
gifts with reservation of benefit,
19–20—19–24
lease carve out schemes, 19–20
liability, 23–07
seven-year limit, 19–22
significant interest, 19–21
undivided shares, 19–24
VAT
exempt supplies, 26–20
reduced rates, 26–17
Rebasing
capital gains tax, 16–18
Records
tax administration, 4–13
Recovery of overpayments
VAT
EU law, 27–47
repayment to final consumer,
27–49
unjust enrichment, 27–48
Reduced rates
VAT, 26–16—26–17
Reliefs
see also **Capital gains; Exemptions;
Loss relief**
agricultural property relief
agricultural property defined,
20–44
application, 20–42, 20–46
business property relief and,
20–41
conditions, 20–43—20–45
length of ownership, 20–43
occupation, 20–45
reduction, 20–46
bad debt relief, 27–46
business property relief
agricultural property relief and,
20–41
excluded items, 20–38
extent of relief, 20–36

gifts with reservation of benefit
and, 20–40
investments, 20–37
nature of relief, 20–36
potentially exempt transfers and,
20–40
real property, 20–37
reduction in value of transfer,
20–39
entrepreneurs' relief
amount, 17–16
associated disposals, 17–18
difficulties, 17–20
generally, 16–17, 17–16
investors' relief, 17–21
qualifying disposals, 17–17
trustees, 17–19
holdover relief
gifts immediately chargeable to
inheritance tax, 17–23—17–24
gifts of business assets, 17–25
limited liability partnerships,
17–30
operation of, 17–22
indexation relief, 16–17
investors' relief, 17–21
marginal relief, 17–11
private residence relief
additional buildings, 17–06
dwelling-house, 17–05—17–06
generally, 17–02
gifts relief and, 17–09
part of dwelling, 17–05—17–06
partial business use, 17–08
permitted area, 17–07
private letting, 17–08
sole or main residence, 17–03
temporary occupation, 17–04
qualifying care relief, 6–10
quick succession relief, 20–34,
22–28
rebasing, 16–18
rent-a-room relief, 6–09
roll-over relief
limited liability partnerships,
17–30
replacement of business assets,
17-27—17–29
transfer of business of company,
17–26
successive charges relief, 20–34,
22–28
taper relief, 16–17

voidable transfers, 20–35
woodlands relief
nature of relief, 20–47
retrospective charges, 20–48
Residence
corporation tax, 14–05
Reversionary interests
inheritance tax, 20–24,
22–58—22–59
Roll-over relief
capital gains tax
limited liability partnerships,
17–30
replacement of business assets,
17-27—17–29
transfer of business of company,
17–26
Savings
capital gains, 17–15
Savings income
see also **Dividends; Investment
income**
interest
ISAs, 11–09
Islamic finance, 11–06
meaning, 11–05
National Savings and
Investments, 11–08
non-taxed interest, 11–07—11–10
paying tax on, 11–11
sharesave schemes, 11–10
introduction, 11–01—11–03
Part 4 rules, 11–03
Part 6 rules, 11–04
Scotland
appeals, 2–24
generally, 2–23
income tax rates, 13–22
tax administration, 2–24
VAT appeals, 25–20
Self-assessment
corporation tax, 14–11
income tax, 13–02
Self-employment
employment income, 9–04
trading income, 5–03—5–04
Set-off
capital gains, 5–41
corporation tax, 14–35
trading income, 5–41
Settled property
see also **Trusts**
18-25 trusts

conditions, 22–54
generally, 22–53
other tax charges, 22–58
tax advantages up to aged 18,
22–55
tax charges aged 18–25, 22–56
accumulation and maintenance
trusts, 22–47
bereaved minors trusts
conditions, 22–49–50
generally, 22–48
tax advantages, 22
tax charges, 22–51—22–52
capital gains tax
absolute entitlement, 15–52
beneficiaries' tax liability,
15–67—15–70
class gifts, 15–53
concurrent interests, 15–51
deemed disposals, 15–58—15–61
definition, 15–50
disposals and, 15–55—15–63
disposals by trustees,
15–57—15–59
individual gifts, 15–53
"jointly so entitled", 15–51
person entitled to interest, 15–63
putting property into settlement,
15–56
termination of interest in
possession, 15–62
transfers between trusts,
15–64—15–66
trustees, 15–54
categorisation
disabled person's interest, 22–12
effect of powers, 22–17
immediate post-death interest,
22–11
"interest in possession", 22–14
no income trusts, 22–16
Pearson v IRC, 22–15
transitional serial interest, 22–13
types of beneficial interest in
possession, 22–10
charging provisions
close companies, 22–29
death of beneficial owner, 22–21
deemed holder, 22–18
disposal for a consideration,
22–27
disposal of relevant interest,
22–23—22–27

excluded property, 22–20
new entitlement, 22–26
reversionary interests, 22–19
successive charges relief, 22–28
termination of relevant interest,
22–22, 22–24
definition, 22–07
development of charges
2006 changes, 22–06
definition, 22–07
discretionary trusts, 22–03
excluded settled property, 22–05
fixed interest trusts, 22–02
generally, 22–01
more than one settlement, 22–08
non-fixed interest trusts, 22–03
specially favoured trusts, 22–04
discretionary trusts, 22–03
excluded settled property, 22–05
exit charges
circumstances giving rise to,
22–41
notional cumulative total, 22–44
notional transfer, 22–44
rate of charge, 22–43—22–45
settlements after first 10-year
charge, 22–45
settlements prior to first 10-year
charge, 22–44
subject of charge, 22–42
fixed interest trusts, 22–02
independent tax regime
exit charges, 22–32
generally, 22–31
principal charges, 22–32
relevant property, 22–30
inheritance tax
18-25 trusts, 22–53—22–58
accumulation and maintenance
trusts, 22–47
bereaved minors trusts,
22–48—22–52
categorisation, 22–10—22–17
charging provisions,
22–18—22–29
definition, 22–07
development of charges,
22–01—22–08
discretionary trusts, 22–03
excluded settled property, 22–05
exit charges, 22–41—22–45
fixed interest trusts, 22–02
generally, 19–40

independent tax regime,
22–30—22–32
interim charges, 22–41—22–45
liability, 23–04
multiple settlements, 22–08
non-fixed interest trusts, 22–03
putting property into settlement,
22–09
relevant property, 22–30
reversionary interests,
22–58—22–59
settlement powers, 22–60—22–61
special kinds, 22–46—22–57
specially favoured trusts, 22–04
ten year charge, 22–33—22–40
interim charges, 22–41—22–45
multiple settlements, 22–08
non-fixed interest trusts, 22–03
putting property into settlement,
22–09
relevant property, 22–30
reversionary interests,
22–58—22–59
settlement powers, 22–60—22–61
special kinds
18–25 trusts, 22–53—22–57
accumulation and maintenance
trusts, 22–47
bereaved minors trusts,
22–48—22–52
generally, 22–46
specially favoured trusts, 22–04
ten year charge
additions, 22–37—22–38
circumstances giving rise to,
22–33
notional chargeable transfer,
22–36
notional cumulative total, 22–36
rate of charge, 22–35—22–36
reductions, 22–39
settlements prior to 27 March
1974, 22–40
subject of charge, 22–34
Settlements
see also Capital gains tax;
Inheritance tax; Settled property;
Trusts
capital settlements
benefits received by unmarried
minors, 12–18—12–20
capital sums paid to settler,
12–21—12–22

settlor retaining an interest,
12–15—12–17
income settlements, 12–11, 12–14
Share capital
capital gains tax
reorganisation of capital,
15–34—15–35
Share incentive plans
capital gains, 17–15
employment income, 9–49
Shares
capital gains tax
bed and breakfasting rules,
16–22
pooling, 16–19—16–20
same day rule, 16–21
Sharesave schemes
employment income, 9–50—9–52
savings income, 11–10
SIPs
see Share investment plans
Small businesses
flat rate scheme, 26–29
Social security income
attendance allowance, 10–17
child benefit, 10–17—10–18
child tax credit, 10–17
exempt benefits, 10–17
meaning, 10–17
taxable income, 3–16
Social welfare
VAT, 26–20
Specially favoured trusts
see Settled property
Sporting events
VAT, 26–20
Spouses
capital gains tax
beneficiaries' liability to tax,
15–68
disposals between, 15–44
tax rates, 15–07
inheritance tax
generally, 20–02—20–03
gifts in consideration of marriage,
20–07
liability, 23–08
nil-rate band, 21–05—21–07
Stamp duty
history of tax law, 3–03
sale of land, 6–13
State pension
income tax, 10–07

Statements of practice
HMRC guidance, 3–36
Subordinate legislation
national archives, 3–31
tax laws, 3–22—3–23
Successive charges relief
see **Quick succession relief**
Supplies
VAT
definition, 25–29, 25–32
identity of supplier, 25–34
identity of supply, 25–48
parallel supplies, 25–52
passing of title, 25–33
Plantifor case, 25–51
self-supply, 25–31
services, 25–36
simultaneous supplies, 25–52
tax on consumption, 25–35
third party supplies,
25–49—25–51
unlawful transactions, 25–30
Taper relief
capital gains tax, 15–03
Tax
collection, 1–17, 2–01, 2–04
constitutional basis, 2–02—2–03
efficiency, 1–12
elements of, 1–18
enforcement, 2–01, 2–04
fairness, 1–08—1–11
introduction, 1–16
meaning, 1–01—1–02
principles, 1–07
purpose of, 1–03—1–06
tax base, 1–18
UK taxes
generally, 2–05—2–07
imposing, 2–08—2–11
Tax administration
appeal rights, 4–22—4–25
civil enforcement
correcting returns, 4–15—4–16
freedom of information,
4–20—4–21
generally, 4–14
HMRCs information powers,
4–17
making enquiries, 4–15—4–16
penalties, 4–18
time limits, 4–19
criminal enforcement, 4–26
e-tax, 4–05—4–07

imposing UK taxes, 2–08—2–11
inheritance tax
appeals, 24–10
charge for unpaid tax, 24–14
delivery of an account,
24–02—24–06
determination, 24–10
introduction, 24–01
overseas settlements, 24–07
payment by instalments, 24–12
payment of tax due, 24–11—24–13
power to inspect property, 24–09
power to require information,
24–09
repayments, 24–13
returns by persons acting for
settlor, 24–07
returns following variation of
disposition, 24–08
introduction, 4–01—4–04
keeping records, 4–13
Scotland, 2–24
tax authorities, 2–06, 2–12—2–15
tax returns
generally, 4–08—4–12
inheritance tax, 24–07—24–08
VAT, 27–33
Wales, 2–25
Tax authorities
Border Force, 2–13
controlling, 2–15
HMRC, 2–12—2–14
National Crime Agency, 2–13
Tax avoidance
capital gains tax
company adjustments, 15–35
meaning, 1–13
non-earned income, 11–18
tax compliance, 3–48
"tax mitigation", 1–13
trusts, 12–12
VAT
EU law, 25–12, 25–15
"Tax base"
meaning, 1–18
Tax codes
PAYE, 9–54
Tax credits
child tax credit
generally, 10–17
operation of system, 13–32
taxable income, 13–16
threshold, 13–32

employment income, 9–01, 9–03
exemption from income tax, 13–30
tax rates, 13–20
thresholds, 13–32
working tax credit, 13–32
Tax evasion
meaning, 1–13
tax compliance, 3–48
VAT
EU law, 25–12, 25–14
"Tax gap"
tax compliance, 3–49
Tax law rewrite
see **Tax reform**
Tax mitigation
see **Tax avoidance**
Tax point
VAT
internet sales, 27–32
meaning, 27–30
payments on account, 27–31
tax returns, 27–33
Tax rates
capital gains tax
exempt amount, 15–06
flat rate, 15–05
residential property, 15–09
spouses and civil partners, 15–07
trustees, 15–08
corporation tax, 14–12
generally, 13–33
income tax
additional rate, 13–21
basic rate, 13–21
dividend rate, 13–21
higher rate, 13–21
income tax lock, 13–21
nil rate, 13–21
Scotland, 13–22
Wales, 13–22
zero rate, 13–21
inheritance tax
chargeable bands, 21–02—20–13
lower rate where legacy to
charity, 21–04
nil-rate band, 21–02—21–03,
21–05—21–08
residential nil-rate band, 21–08
settled property, 22–35—22–36,
22–43—22–45, 22–51—22–52,
22–56
transferable nil-rate band,
21–05—21–07

settled property
18–25 trusts, 22–56
bereaved minors trusts,
22–51—22–52
exit charges, 22–43—22–45
ten year charge, 22–35—22–36
VAT
application of rate, 26–06
EU law, 26–03
flat rate scheme, 26–29
introduction, 26–01
reduced rates, 26–16—26–17
structure, 26–02—25–06
UK structure, 26–04
zero rated supplies, 26–05,
26–07—26–15
Tax reform
capital allowances, 8–02
corporation tax, 14–02, 14–10
employment income, 9–09
generally, 3–07
intellectual property, 7–01, 7–06,
7–17, 7–33, 7–34
pensions, 10–09
property income, 6–02, 6–07
tax simplification, 1–12
trading income, 5–01
Tax returns
inheritance tax
persons acting for settlor,
24–07
variation of disposition, 24–08
VAT, 27–33
Tax year
corporation tax, 14–11
Taxable persons
VAT
charities, 25–65
generally, 25–64
groups of companies, 25–67
partnerships, 25–66
public bodies, 25–65
registration thresholds, 25–68
voluntary registration, 25–69
Taxable supplies
see **Supplies; VAT**
Taxation of individuals
see **Individuals**
Ten year charge
settled property
additions, 22–37—22–38
circumstances giving rise to,
22–33

notional chargeable transfer, 22–36
notional cumulative total, 22–36
rate of charge, 22–35—22–36
reductions, 22–39
settlements prior to 27 March 1974, 22–40
subject of charge, 22–34

Trade marks
taxation of intellectual property rights, 7–11

Trading income
see also **Employment income**
accounts
generally accepted accounting practice, 5–16
importance, 5–15
taxable profits, 5–16
assessment, 5–47
badges of trade
length of ownership, 5–09
meaning, 5–07
motive, 5–13
reason for sale, 5–12
repetition, 5–10
subject of sale, 5–08
supplementary work, 5–11
computation of profits
accounts, importance of, 5–15
cash basis for small businesses, 5–17
compensation, 5–20
fixed deductions, 5–18
generally accepted accounting practice, 5–16
trading receipts, 5–19
voluntary payments, 5–21
employment status
agency workers, 5–04
divers and diving supervisors, 5–04
employees and self-employed, 5–03—5–04
expenses
apportionment, 5–31
basic rules, 5–27
deductions, 5–39
interest, 5–37
legal and accountancy charges, 5–36
object test, 5–32—5–34
repairs and improvements, 5–38
revenue expenditure, 5–28—5–29

specific expenses, 5–35—5–38
travel, 5–35
wholly and exclusively rule, 5–30
introduction, 5–01—5–02
losses
carry-back of terminal losses, 5–45
carry-forward against subsequent profits, 5–42—5–44
early years, 5–46
introduction, 5–40
set-off against general income and capital gains, 5–41
post-cessation receipts, 5–48
profession
definition, 5–02, 5–14
profits
assessment basis, 5–47
computation, 5–15
trading
badges of trade, 5–07—5–13
definition, 5–02, 5–05
statutory trades, 5–13
taxable income, 3–16
trading stock
accounting, 5–22
stock transfers, 5–25
transfer pricing, 5–26
valuation, 5–23
work in progress, 5–24
vocation
definition, 5–02, 5–14
whether person trading, 5–06

Trading losses
see **Losses**

Trading stock
capital gains tax
generally, 15–29
groups of companies, 15–32
transfers from, 15–31
transfers to, 15–30
trading income
accounting, 5–22
stock transfers, 5–25
transfer pricing, 5–26
valuation, 5–23
work in progress, 5–24

Transport
VAT, 26–15

Travelling expenses
deductions
employment income, 9–40—9–42
trading income, 5–35

Tribunals
appeals, 2–19—2–21
devolved taxes, 2–23
judicial review, 2–22
Trust income
see **Trusts**
Trustees
entrepreneurs' relief, 17–19
tax payable by
dividend trust rate, 12–05
exemption of first slice of income,
12–04
generally, 12–03
trust expenses, 12–06
trust rate, 12–05
Trusts
see also **Administration of estates;**
Settled property
beneficiaries
computation of income, 12–07
entitlement to income, 12–08
income accumulated by trust,
12–09
protection of trust, 12–10
vested and contingent interests
distinguished, 12–09
vulnerable beneficiaries' trusts,
12–10
capital gains tax
creation of separate settlement,
15–64
distinguishing settlements, 15–66
subsidiary settlement, 15–65
introduction, 12–01
settlements
capital settlements, 12–11,
12–15—12–22
civil partners, 12–13
income settlements, 12–11, 12–14
parental settlements, 12–13,
12–18—12–20
spouses, 12–13
tax avoidance, 12–12
tax rules, 12–13
trust income
beneficiaries, 12–07—12–09
exemption of first slice, 12–04
generally, 12–02
taxable income, 3–16
trustees
dividend trust rate, 12–05
exemption of first slice of income,
12–04

generally, 12–03
trust expenses, 12–06
trust rate, 12–05
Unjust enrichment
recovery of overpaid VAT, 27–48
Valuation
inheritance tax
changes in value by reason of
death, 21–42
estate duty principles, 21–33
funeral expenses, 21–42
land sold for less than value at
death, 21–42
lessor's interest, 21–38
lotting, 21–41
life policies, 21–39
open market value, 21–32—21–35
qualifying investments, 21–42
related property, 21–37
restrictions on freedom to
dispose, 21–36
restrictions on sale, 21–34
value transferred on death,
21–40—21–41
VAT
allowable deductions, 27–14
consideration, 27–02—27–06
discounts, 27–15—27–16
fiscal neutrality, 27–23—27–26
non-cash consideration,
27–07—27–22
Value shifting
capital gains tax, 15–43
VAT
accounting
generally, 27–27
tax invoices, 27–29
tax periods, 27–28
tax points, 27–30—27–33
appeals, 25–20
application
key questions, 25–24
scope of tax, 25–26
taxpayers and taxable persons,
25–25
VAT directive, 25–27
bad debt relief, 27–46
charge
consideration, 25–40—25–46
economic activities,
25–70—25–76
elements, 25–28
exempt supplies, 25–62

goods and services,
  25–37—25–39, 25–47—25–52
location of supply, 25–63
multiple supplies in single
  transaction, 25–53—25–61
supplies, 25–29—25–36
taxable persons, 25–64—25–69
taxable supplies, 25–62
commercial agents
generally, 25–78
undisclosed agency, 25–79
computation
generally, 27–01
valuation, 27–02—27–26
consideration
direct link, 25–42
discounts, 25–44
free supplies, 27–03
identifying, 27–06
incidental expenses, 27–04
items constituting, 27–02
meaning, 25–40—25–41
non-cash consideration, 25–45,
  27–07—27–13
part-exchange deals, 25–46
requirement for, 25–40
subsidies, 27–05
use of non-taxable agents, 25–43
direct and immediate link
basic test, 27–39
generally, 27–38
identifying link, 27–41
overheads, 27–44
partial attribution, 27–43,
  27–45
residual costs, 27–44
taxable and exempt supplies,
  27–40
taxable supplies only, 27–39
total attribution, 27–42
Directives
direct effect, 25–04
generally, 25–02
implementation, 25–05—25–06
importance of, 25–03
discounts
cash commission, 27–16
price rebates, 27–15
economic activities
"business", 25–71
exploitation of property, 25–73
meaning, 25–70—25–72
objective concept, 25–74

private activity distinguished,
  25–76
services, 25–75
employees, 25–77
EU law
abusive practices, 25–12—25–16
application of principles,
  25–08—25–11
directives, 25–02—25–07
effectiveness, 25–11
evasion, 25–12, 25–14
exempt supplies, 26–18
fiscal neutrality, 25–09—25–10
fraud, 25–12
objective nature of tax, 25–13
tax avoidance, 25–12, 25–15
tax rates, 26–03
exempt supplies
discretion, 26–23
education, 26–22
EU law, 26–18
financial services, 26–20
gambling, 26–20
insurance, 26–20
interpretation, 26–19, 26–22
land, 26–20
multiple supplies, 26–21
partial exemption, 26–27
socially exempt supplies, 26–20
zero rating compared, 26–24
fiscal neutrality
certainty, 27–24
consideration, 27–23
discounts, 27–23, 27–25
EU law, 25–09—25–10
separate supplies, 27–26
flat rate scheme, 26–29
goods and services
generally, 25–37
land, 25–38
meaning, 25–39
history of tax law, 3–11
input tax
generally, 26–26
right to reclaim, 27–34—27–37
introduction, 25–01
multiple supplies in single
  transaction
artificial to split test, 25–55
categorising single supply, 25–58
different customers, 25–61
fiscal neutrality, 25–56
generally, 25–53

limit on single composite supply, 25–60
principal/ancillary test, 25–54
provision of range of services, 25–57
two suppliers, 25–59
non-cash consideration
attribution, 27–10
extrinsic value, 27–11
generally, 27–07
limited to amount paid, 27–21—27–22
monetary equivalent, 27–08
part exchange, 27–12
subjective value, 27–09
tri-partite agreements, 27–22
vouchers, 27–17—27–20
zero value, 27–13
operation
example, 25–22
generally, 25–21
inputs and outputs, 25–23
partial exemption, 26–27
recovery of overpayments
EU law, 27–47
repayment to final consumer, 27–49
unjust enrichment, 27–48
reduced rates, 26–16—26–17
registration
registration thresholds, 25–68
voluntary registration, 25–69
small businesses, 26–29
special regimes, 26–28
supplies
definition, 25–29, 25–32
identity of supplier, 25–34
identity of supply, 25–48
parallel supplies, 25–52
passing of title, 25–33
Plantifor case, 25–51
self-supply, 25–31
services, 25–36
simultaneous supplies, 25–52
tax on consumption, 25–35
third party supplies, 25–49—25–51
unlawful transactions, 25–30
tax administration, 25–19
tax invoices, 27–29
tax periods, 27–28
tax point
internet sales, 27–32

meaning, 27–30
payments on account, 27–31
tax returns, 27–33
tax rates
application of, 26–06
EU law, 26–03
flat rate scheme, 26–29
introduction, 26–01
reduced rate supplies, 26–16—26–17
structure, 26–02—25–06
UK structure, 26–04
zero rated supplies, 26–05, 26–07—26–15
tax returns, 27–33
taxable persons
charities, 25–65
generally, 25–64
groups of companies, 25–67
partnerships, 25–66
public bodies, 25–65
registration thresholds, 25–68
voluntary registration, 25–69
UK legislation
application, 25–17
sources of law, 25–18
valuation
allowable deductions, 27–14
consideration, 27–02—27–06
discounts, 27–15—27–16
fiscal neutrality, 27–23—27–26
non-cash consideration, 27–07—27–22
vouchers
redeemable down supply chain, 27–18
same supplier, 27–17
same supply chain as post supply discount, 27–19
third party vouchers, 27–20
zero rating
advantages of, 26–25
as subsidy, 26–05
books, 26–15
children's clothing, 26–15
exempt supplies compared, 26–24
food, 26–10—26–14
introduction, 26–07
motorway services, 26–13
newspapers, 26–15
policy, 26–08—26–09
transport, 26–15

VAT registration
registration thresholds, 25–68
voluntary registration, 25–69
Visiting forces
inheritance tax, 20–23
Vouchers
employment income
cash vouchers, 9–20
generally, 9–19
non-cash vouchers, 9–21
VAT
redeemable down supply chain,
27–18
same supplier, 27–17
same supply chain as post
supply discount,
27–19
third party vouchers, 27–20
Waivers
inheritance tax
dividends, 20–20
remuneration, 20–19
Wales
appeals, 2–25
generally, 2–23
income tax rates, 13–22
tax administration, 2–25
Wasting assets
capital gains, 16–15, 17–13
Wholly and exclusively rule
capital allowances, 8–11, 16–08

employment income, 9–38—9–39
trading income, 5–30
Woodlands relief
inheritance tax
nature of relief, 20–47
retrospective charges, 20–48
Works of art
see **Artistic works**
Writing-down allowances
plant and machinery allowances,
8–17
Zero rating
see also **VAT**
advantages of, 26–25
as subsidy, 26–05
books, 26–15
children's clothing, 26–15
exempt supplies compared, 26–24
food
biscuits, 26–11
cakes, 26–11
catering, 26–12—26–13
cold food, 26–14
crisps, 26–11
generally, 26–10
hot food, 26–12
introduction, 26–07
motorway services, 26–13
newspapers, 26–15
policy, 26–08—26–09
transport, 26–15